English Lexicogenesis

English Lexicogenesis

D. GARY MILLER

OXFORD
UNIVERSITY PRESS

Great Clarendon Street, Oxford OX2 6DP,
United Kingdom

Oxford University Press is a department of the University of Oxford.
It furthers the University's objective of excellence in research, scholarship,
and education by publishing worldwide. Oxford is a registered trade mark of
Oxford University Press in the UK and in certain other countries

© D. Gary Miller 2014

The moral rights of the author have been asserted

First Edition published in 2014

Impression: 3

All rights reserved. No part of this publication may be reproduced, stored in
a retrieval system, or transmitted, in any form or by any means, without the
prior permission in writing of Oxford University Press, or as expressly permitted
by law, by licence, or under terms agreed with the appropriate reprographics
rights organization. Enquiries concerning reproduction outside the scope of the
above should be sent to the Rights Department, Oxford University Press, at the
address above

You must not circulate this work in any other form
and you must impose this same condition on any acquirer

Published in the United States of America by Oxford University Press
198 Madison Avenue, New York, NY 10016, United States of America

British Library Cataloguing in Publication Data

Data available

Library of Congress Control Number: 2013945602

ISBN 978–0–19–968988–0

As printed and bound by
CPI Group (UK) Ltd, Croydon CR0 4YY

Contents

Preface	x
Dating and other conventions	xiii
Bibliographical abbreviations	xv
General abbreviations	xviii

1 Theoretical assumptions	1
1.1 Basic phrase structure	1
1.2 Word structure	3
1.3 Inflection	5
1.4 Deradical, denominal, and deverbal derivation	7
1.5 Overt formatives	8
1.6 Conversion	10
1.7 Backformation	14
1.8 Productivity	15
1.9 Features and feature change	19
1.10 Lexicalization	21
1.11 Summary	26
2 Productivity and constraints	27
2.1 Blocking	27
2.2 Phonological constraints	30
2.3 Affixal restrictions	33
2.4 Syntactic constraints	35
2.5 Semantic constraints	36
2.6 Processing constraints	39
2.7 Processing and recursion: What do speakers count?	39
2.8 Turkish causatives	42
2.9 Summary	44
3 Compounding	45
3.1 Core properties of compounds	46
3.2 Synthetic compounds	48
3.3 Endocentric compounds	51
3.4 Exocentric compounds	53
3.5 Dvandva (or copulative) compounds	55
3.6 Appositional or identificational compounds	59

	3.7 Retronym formation	60
	3.8 Summary	61
4	New patterns of derivation	63
	4.1 Particles	63
	4.2 Syntactic morphology	65
	4.3 Scalar/evaluative particles and P–V verbs	69
	4.4 V–P nouns	71
	4.5 The suffix *-ee*	74
	4.6 Double *-er*	75
	4.7 Deverbal *-able* and the *laugh-at-able* type	79
	4.8 Summary	81
5	Novel word crafting	83
	5.1 Lexicogenesis	83
	5.2 Need is the mother of all invention—or is it?	85
	5.3 Analogical creations	88
	5.4 Puns	89
	5.5 Language play	90
	5.6 Figures of speech and rhetorical devices	93
	5.7 Verbal art	95
	5.8 Art from the ordinary: P-stacking	96
	5.9 Summary	99
6	Metaphor and metonymy	101
	6.1 Metaphor	101
	6.2 Metaphorical change	103
	6.3 Concrete > abstract	104
	6.4 Metonymy	107
	6.5 Transferred epithet	108
	6.6 Pure metonymy	109
	6.7 Part-whole transfer (synecdoche)	110
	6.8 Transfer of characteristic (antonomasia, eponymy)	112
	6.9 English-specific eponymy	114
	6.10 Summary	116
7	Folk etymology and tabu	117
	7.1 Folk etymology	117
	7.2 Religious tabu	120
	7.3 Secular tabu	121
	7.4 Summary	124

8　The cycle of expressivity　125
　8.1　Loss and renewal of expressivity　125
　8.2　Extralinguistic input　127
　8.3　The cognitive dimension　128
　8.4　Polysemic extension, limitation, and semantic features　129
　8.5　Semantic shifts　132
　8.6　Melioration and pejoration　133
　8.7　Borrowing and semantic transfer　135
　8.8　Calquing, or loan translation　137
　8.9　On the phonological form of loanwords　138
　8.10　Dating borrowings and neologisms　139
　8.11　Summary　140

9　Phonological form and abridgments　141
　9.1　Syllable structure and the sonority hierarchy　141
　9.2　Prosodic structures　144
　9.3　Abbreviations and alphabetisms　147
　9.4　Acronyms　148
　9.5　Suffixes as full words　150
　9.6　Summary　152

10　Sound symbolism　154
　10.1　Types of sound-symbolic motivation　154
　10.2　Onomatopoeia　156
　10.3　Synesthesia　157
　10.4　Stretch　161
　10.5　Movable *s-*/*s*-mobile　162
　10.6　Prefixation of *ka-*/*ker-*　163
　10.7　Phonesthesia　164
　10.8　Initial *gl-* in Germanic and English　167
　10.9　Sound and meaning in poetry　169
　10.10　Summary　171

11　Clipping　173
　11.1　Clipping as a process　173
　11.2　Right-edge English clips　174
　11.3　Left-edge clips　175
　11.4　Clips of compounds and fixed phrases　176
　11.5　Truncated names　177
　11.6　Special formations　179
　11.7　Suffixed formations　181

11.8	Essential properties of English clips	182
11.9	Clips in other languages	184
11.10	Summary	185

12 Blending — 187

12.1	Blending as a process	187
12.2	Typical lexical blends	189
12.3	Special formations	192
12.4	Attempts at classification	193
12.5	Analysis of blends	195
12.6	Selection and sequencing of input constituents	199
12.7	Sound-symbolic motivation	201
12.8	Summary	203
	Appendix: Alphabetical list of blends	204

13 Formative extraction, combining forms, and neoclassical compounding — 207

13.1	Formative extraction/secretion	207
13.2	Extractions from Ancient Greek words	208
13.3	Modern extractions	208
13.4	Combining forms	210
13.5	Combining forms of Ancient Greek origin	213
13.6	Neoclassical compounds	215
13.7	Derivation from neoclassical compounds	217
13.8	Summary	219

14 Reduplicative and conjunctive formations — 220

14.1	Total reduplication	220
14.2	Rhyming pairs	221
14.3	Yiddish-English echoic dismissive *shm-*	223
14.4	Gradation	224
14.5	Conjunctive binomials	226
14.6	Pāṇini's rule	229
14.7	Linking prepositions	233
14.8	Linking *-cum-*	234
14.9	Infixing reduplicatives	235
14.10	Summary	235

15 Core and expressive morphology: Conclusion — 237

15.1	General properties	237
15.2	Specific properties	240
15.3	Summary and conclusions	243

Appendix I. Special phonetic symbols	247
Appendix II. The Indo-European phonological system	251
References	254
Index of affixes and affixed forms	299
Index of selected names	301
Index of subjects	302

Preface

Conception and scope

Lexicogenesis is a highfalutin Greek term for 'word origin' or 'word creation'. To date it is not recognized by the *OED* although widely employed in English (e.g. Hagège 1993; Picone 1994; 1996; Geeraerts 2002). I have elected to use the word *lexicogenesis* rather than *word formation*, *morphology*, etc., because the target is both more general and less inclusive than what the latter generally imply. Deviations from ordinary word formation are treated here as legitimate forms of word formation. Expressive morphology is also examined for the sake of contrast with core morphology, and for several construct types the motivation is metrical or phonological and semantic-pragmatic, not morphological. This monograph, then, is about the interaction between various lexicogenic operations, expressive or playful morphology (clips, blends, and the like), and language play (word games: Pig Latin etc.). In sharp contrast to the standard literature on word formation, in the current work language play, creative language, and expressive morphology are treated as evidence for productivity—but productivity of what? Clearly not standard word formation, hence the choice of the term *lexicogenesis*.

The idea for this work and its title I owe to Jean Tournier's *Introduction descriptive à la lexicogénétique de l'anglais contemporain* (1985). Peter Farb's *Word Play* (1973) has also provided inspiration, as has the pleasantly popular *The Life of Language* by Steinmetz and Kipfer (2006). My main impetus has been the line *Up from out of in under there* in a poem by Morris Bishop (§5.8), which got me interested in linguistics nearly fifty years ago. In that sense, this work has been in progress throughout my entire career.

This book is about the mechanisms for the coining or invention of novel words. It is customary to distinguish between NONCE formations, or spontaneous, utilitarian coinages (Bacchielli 2010), and NEOLOGISMS, which have lost their status as nonce formations but are still considered new by most members of a speech community (Fischer 1998; Cook 2010). In practical terms, most nonce formations will never be known (Munat 2007a: xiii). Mikhail Epstein's PROTOLOGISM (2005) for a word waiting for acceptance is inadequate because its composition suggests a very different meaning. Since this book is about the processes by which new words are coined rather than the new words themselves, *neologism* will include nonce formations. Following the message of the papers in Munat (2007a), the formation of all words, no matter how ephemeral, must be investigated because of the light they shed on the status of the word formation processes themselves (cf. Bacchielli 2010).

Traditionally, studies of these topics focused either on affixation, compounding, and semantic change or on more playful formations like clipping and blending. All of these are crucial in novel word crafting.

This work is a semi-technical monograph with reference-type collections of data. It is not a textbook for beginners. Nor is it a study of English morphology, although that topic cannot be avoided, especially for the more recent types of word formation which have received insufficient analysis in the literature. The traditional affixes and morphological operations inherited from Germanic and transferred from French are well known and thoroughly treated in all works on English morphology and word formation. In the interest of space and consistent with our focus on contemporary English lexicogenesis, this work ignores the traditional prefixes and suffixes, which are discussed in all of the handbooks. In other words, a certain amount of core English morphology is taken for granted. An excellent overview is Bauer, Lieber, and Plag (2013). Additionally, my diachronic databases provide perspective on the length of time the less standard processes have been in the language, and how they have developed.

While this work is taxonomic in its historical collections of data, it is not devoid of theoretical interest. Since the objective is to *analyze* recent trends in English lexicogenesis, linguistic theory plays an important role in the new morphological types, for which a certain amount of contemporary generative theory is presupposed. For the more technical discussions, references are provided as aids to the reader.

Brief plan of the current work

The first four chapters deal with morphology as it relates to English. Chapter 1 defines the terms as they will be used throughout this work. Chapter 2 discusses some of the constraints on derivations as an aspect of productivity. Chapter 3 introduces a typology of English compounds. Chapter 4 is about particles in word formation and some recent construct types specific to English.

Chapter 5 focuses on the analogical and imaginative aspects of neologistic creation.

Chapter 6 is the first of several chapters that deal with semantics, particularly metaphor and metonymy; Chapter 7 treats folk etymology and tabu; and Chapter 8 describes the cycle of expressivity, its loss and renewal.

Chapter 9 outlines the essentials of the phonological structure of words, in terms of segments, syllables, and the metrical foot, that are necessary for understanding the remainder of the monograph. The second part begins a discussion of word abridgments.

Chapters 10–14 explore expressive formations and language play. Chapter 10 is about the acoustic and perceptual motivation of word forms. Chapters 11–13 treat various aspects and functions of truncation: Chapter 11 is about clipping *per se*, and Chapter 12 deals with clipping plus compounding, specifically the form and sequencing of input constituents and the prosodic constraints on the outputs of blends.

Chapter 13 treats the extraction of new formatives, combining forms, and neoclassical compounding.

Chapter 14 discusses the principles that underlie the formation and ordering of the constituents in reduplicative and conjunctive formations.

Chapter 15 summarizes the conclusions about the relationship(s) between core morphology and expressive morphology or language play.

Acknowledgments

Parts of this work have been presented at conferences and colloquia, and other parts read by friends and colleagues. For discussion of particular words, topics, or sections, I am indebted to Gülşat Aygen, Kenny Baclawski, David Basilico, Alan Bell, Dinah Belyayeva, Geert Booij, Denis Bouchard, Janice Bragdon, Charles Brasart, Bert Cappelle, Michael Crema, Veneeta Dayal, Marcel den Dikken, Lynn Dirk, Stig Eliasson, Tom Ernst, Sadek Fodil, Zygmunt Frajzyngier, Jules Gliesche, Youssef Haddad, Alice Harris, Brent Henderson, Gunlög Josefsson, Edith Kaan, Jonathan Keane, Alan Libert, Andrew McIntyre, Craig Melchert, Irene Moyna, Russell Nekorchuk, David Pharies, Eric Potsdam, Susan Shear, Halldór Sigurðsson, Chris Smith, Peter Svenonius, Leslie Jo Tyler, Nelleke van Deusen, Elly van Gelderen, Ratree Wayland, Ann Wehmeyer, and Sean Witty.

For making their forthcoming work available to me, I am grateful to Kenny Baclawski, Sadek Fodil, Boris Lefilliâtre, Andrew McIntyre, David Pharies, and Chris Smith.

Special thanks are due to David Pharies, who read and commented on the entire manuscript. Andrew McIntyre offered sound advice on countless points and commented extensively on nearly all of the major theoretical points. And, of course, the usual anonymous readers for Oxford University Press have been responsible for changes in the focus and content. To one in particular I am grateful for references to the Rzeszów school of diachronic semantics (Kiełtyka, Kleparski, and others).

As always, I am indebted to my friend John Davey for convincing me that Oxford University Press has the perfect series for this monograph, as well as for his special role in finding expertly competent readers and seeing the work through the reviewing process.

For easy access to *OED* 2/3 online, I am indebted to John Davey and Ralph Watson.

Finally, this work never could have been completed without the enduring patience and support of my wife, Judith.

D. Gary Miller
dgm@ufl.edu
May 2013

Dating and other conventions

To avoid the problem of BC/AD vs. BCE/CE ('Common Era') and obviate lengthy references ('second half of the 1st century BC(E)'), a modified/simplified version of the conventions of Miller (1994) will be adopted to simplify dating. Dates are given in brackets, e.g. [750], which will be roughly equivalent to [mid c8], more simply, [c8^m]. A date in brackets following a word indicates the first date of occurrence. For instance, *prōfānitās* PROFANITY [1607] means that the English reflex of this Latin word is first attested in a text from 1607. All dates will be understood to be CE unless specified BCE. Most dates are approximate signalled by [*c.*] (= *circa* 'about') or equivalent. Following are the dating conventions standardly used in this work:

[c10]	10th century; as date of first occurrence = begins in the 10th century
[c10$^{1/2}$]	first half of c10
[c10$^{2/2}$]	second half of c10
[c12^b]	beginning of the 12th century
[c12^e]	end of c12
[c12^m]	middle of c12
[c13/14]	c13 or c14 (uncertain)
[c13^e/14^b]	same but with narrower range
[110–240]	110 CE to 240 CE
[240–110 BCE]	240 BC/BCE to 110 BC/BCE
[*c.*1150]	around 1150 (corroborated by independent evidence)
[?*c.*1150]	the approximate date is not independently verifiable
[*a.*1150]	before 1150
[*p.*1150]	after 1150
[n.d.]	no date available

For some dating, the century in which a word is first attested, e.g. [c15], is adequate, and for antiquity, approximate dating is frequently all that is available. Given that a word is almost invariably in the language for some time before it first occurs in print, loose dating is in a non-trivial sense more accurate than narrow dating. That being said, whenever possible, entries in this work employ the most current dating available. The main problem is that dates are subject to change as additional evidence is accumulated.

OED 3 (in progress) gives the most complete and carefully dated entries, but the main revisions were originally in the middle of the alphabet (*m–o*) and sporadic elsewhere. As of March, 2012, revised entries pervade the alphabet, and around 2,000 new and revised entries are published each quarter, but many dates are still from *OED* 2 (1989).

For medieval texts the problems are different. The date of first occurrence in the *MED* (*Middle English Dictionary*, ed. Kurath et al.) is usually followed, given that for early works it is more complete than the *OED*; but only the estimated date of composition is cited, not also the approximate date of the manuscript. Exceptions include: (1) words first attested in Chaucer are always indicated as such by means of [Ch.] rather than a date; (2) for many texts, a looser date must suffice. One reason is that the dates of many texts are not known for certain, and all that can be said is that a given text had to antedate its author's death, e.g. [*a*.1349] for Richard Rolle (instead of *OED*'s "*c*.1340"), or [*a*.1382] for Wyclif and the Early Version of the Wyclifite Bible translation.

In sum, all words provided with a date are conveniently available in the *OED* online unless another source is specifically indicated for an earlier verifiable date. Like dates, glosses are also provided from the *OED*. To minimize unwieldiness, glosses are provided only where semantic contrasts are crucial, or where meanings other than the modern ones are at issue.

As to other conventions, the following (mostly standard) are also employed:

*	reconstructed (of proto-forms); illformed (of sentences/words)
	after a word (e.g. Goth. *hāhan**) = attested but not in the citation form
?*	possibly ungrammatical or illformed (marginal at best)
?	questionable form; marginally acceptable sentence
%	accepted by some speakers but not others
#	pragmatically difficult, like *#dream-freeze*, not necessarily ungrammatical
|	(poetic texts) line division
>	'is realized as', 'becomes' (in historical changes or direction of borrowing)
<	'is derived from' (in historical changes or direction of borrowing)
→	'leads to; results in'
	x → y = 'x is replaced by y'
⇒	x ⇒ y 'x is transformed into y'
~>	'tends to become'
~	'varies with'
≈	'strongly covaries with'
=	'is equivalent or identical to'
≠	'is not the same as'
†	with a year, e.g. [†1900] = died (of people)
	with a word, e.g. †*meritory* = obsolete (also used of glosses)
[ ]	phonetic representations; dates; Indo-European roots
/ /	phonologically contrastive representation
{ }	morpholexical representation
< >	graphic representation (more usually, forms in a given script are just italicized)
√	(radical sign) root

Bibliographical abbreviations

AHD	*The American Heritage Dictionary of the English Language*, ed. William Morris. Boston: Houghton Mifflin (1969).
AHDR	*The American Heritage Dictionary of Indo-European Roots*, ed. Calvert Watkins. 2nd edn. Boston: Houghton Mifflin (2000).
AND	*Anglo-Norman Dictionary*, ed. Louise W. Stone, T. B. W. Reid, and William Rothwell. London: Modern Humanities Research Associations (1977–92). Online, ed. D. A Trotter et al.: www.anglo-norman.net/gate/ (Ongoing).
Cath(olicon) Angl(icum)	*Catholicon Anglicum: An English–Latin Wordbook, dated 1483*, ed. Sidney J. H. Herrtage. London: N. Trübner (1881).
CDEE	*The Concise Oxford Dictionary of English Etymology*, ed. Terry F. Hoad. Oxford: Oxford University Press (1996 [1986]).
Ch.	*The Riverside Chaucer*, ed. Larry D. Benson. 3rd edn. Boston: Houghton Mifflin (1987).
CHEL	*The Cambridge History of the English Language*, gen. ed. Richard M. Hogg. 5 vols. Cambridge: Cambridge University Press (1992–9).
Vol. 1	*The Beginnings to 1066*, ed. Richard M. Hogg (1992).
Vol. 2	*1066–1476*, ed. Norman Blake (1992).
Vol. 3	*1476–1776*, ed. Roger Lass (1999).
Vol. 4	*1776–1997*, ed. Suzanne Romaine (1999).
Vol. 5	*English in Britain and Overseas: Origins and Development*, ed. Robert Burchfield (1994).
COED	*Concise Oxford English Dictionary*. Available online at: www.oup.com/uk/pressreleases/30544650/
DELG	*Dictionnaire étymologique de la langue grecque*. 4 vols. By Pierre Chantraine. Paris: Klincksieck (1968–80).
DELL	*Dictionnaire étymologique de la langue latine*. By Alfred Ernout and Antoine Meillet. 3rd edn. 2 vols. Paris: Klincksieck (1951).
DLG	*Dictionnaire de la langue gauloise: une approche linguistique du vieux-celtique continental*. By Xavier Delamarre. Paris: Éditions Errance (2001).
EDG	*Etymological Dictionary of Greek*. By Robert Beekes. 2 vols. Leiden: Brill (2009).

EDHIL	*Etymological Dictionary of the Hittite Inherited Lexicon*. By Alwin Kloekhorst, Leiden: Brill (2008).
EDL	*Etymological Dictionary of Latin and the Other Italic Languages*. By Michiel de Vaan. Leiden: Brill (2008).
EDPC	*Etymological Dictionary of Proto-Celtic*. By Ranko Matasović. Leiden: Brill (2009).
EIE	*Early Influences on English: From its Beginnings to the Renaissance*. By D. Gary Miller. Oxford: Oxford University Press (2012).
HED	*Hittite Etymological Dictionary*. By Jaan Puhvel. Berlin: Mouton de Gruyter (1984–).
HFW	*A History of Foreign Words in English*. By Mary Sidney Serjeantson. New York: Barnes & Noble (1961 [1935]).
HGE	*A Handbook of Germanic Etymology*. By Vladimir E. Orel. Leiden: Brill (2003).
IEL	*Indo-European Linguistics*. By Michael Meier-Brügger, with Matthias Fritz and Manfred Mayrhofer. Translated by Charles Gertmenian. Berlin: Walter de Gruyter (2003).
LIV	*Lexikon der indogermanischen Verben: Die Wurzeln und ihre Primärstamm-bildungen*, ed. Helmut Rix et al. 2nd edn. Wiesbaden: Ludwig Reichert (2001).
LL	*De lingua latina* [On the Latin Language]. By Marcus Terentius Varro, ed. and trans. Roland G. Kent, Loeb Classical Library. Cambridge, Mass.: Harvard University Press (1938, 1977).
LSDE	*Latin Suffixal Derivatives in English and their Indo-European Ancestry*. By D. Gary Miller. Oxford: Oxford University Press (2006; repr. with corrections, 2012).
MED	*Middle English Dictionary*, ed. Hans Kurath, Sherman M. Kuhn, J. Reidy, Robert E. Lewis, et al. Ann Arbor: University of Michigan Press (1952–2001). The online *MED* is available at: ets.umdl.umich.edu/m/med/
MITWPL	*MIT Working Papers in Linguistics*. Dept. of Linguistics and Philosophy, MIT, Cambridge, Mass.
NDE	*A New Dictionary of Eponyms*. By Morton S. Freeman. Oxford: Oxford University Press (1997).
NOWELE	*North-Western European Language Evolution*. Odense: Odense University Press.
ODFW	*The Oxford Dictionary of Foreign Words and Phrases*, ed. Jennifer Speake. Oxford: Oxford University Press (1997).
ODNW	*The Oxford Dictionary of New Words*, ed. Elizabeth Knowles with Julia Elliott. Oxford: Oxford University Press (1997).

OED	*The Oxford English Dictionary* online, 2nd edn (1989) and 3rd edn (in progress), ed. John A. Simpson. Oxford: Oxford University Press (2000–): oed.com/
ODS	*The Oxford Dictionary of Slang*, ed. John Ayto. Oxford: Oxford University Press (1998).
PParv/Prompt. Parv.	*Promptorium Parvulorum* (ed. Mayhew 1908; Way 1843–65).
RR	*De re rustica* [On Agriculture]. By Marcus Terentius Varro. *M. Terenti Varronis Rerum Rusticarum libri tres*, ed. Henricius Keil and Georgius Goetz. Leipzig: Teubner (1929).
SPE	*The Sound Pattern of English*. By Noam Chomsky and Morris Halle. New York: Harper & Row (1968).
WALS	*The World Atlas of Language Structures*, ed. Martin Haspelmath et al. Oxford: Oxford University Press (2005). Also online at: wals.info/index
WALS CD	The interactive CD of WALS.

General abbreviations

A	adjective (in category labels)	CAUS/caus	causative
		CE	Common Era
a.	*ante* 'before' (in dates)	Celt.	Celtic
ABL	ablative	cent.	central (in phonetics and as a feature)
ABS	absolutive		
ACC	accusative	cent.	century
ADJ/adj	adjective	cf.	compare
ad loc.	at the place (in the text)	Ch.	Chaucer
Adv/adv.	adverb	ch.	chapter
AF	Anglo-French	Chron	Chronicle
aff.	affix	CIRCUM	circumlative
AG	Ancient Greek	Cl	Classical (ME, etc.)
AG	agent(ive) (in glosses)	CL	Classical Latin
Agr	agreement	CNJ	conjunction
AL	Anglo-Latin	Compl	complement
ALL/all.	allative	CONJ	conjunction
AN	Anglo-Norman	cont.	continuant (in phonetic descriptions)
AOR	aorist		
AP	adjective phrase	cont.	continued
Appl	applicative	CP	Complementizer Phrase
Arab.	Arabic	cpd.	compound
Asp	aspect	D	determiner
asp.	aspirated	Dan.	Danish
Att.	Attic (Greek)	DAT/dat.	dative
AUX	auxiliary	DBY	Derbyshire
Av(est).	Avestan	desid	desiderative
BCE	Before Common Era	Det	determiner
Brit. Lat.	Latin in British sources	dial.	dialect, dialectal
		diph.	diphthong, diphthongization
C	Complementizer		
c	century	dist.	distal
c.	*circa*, about (of dates)	Dor.	Doric (Greek)

DP	Determiner Phrase	Fin.	finite
Du.	Dutch	FP	functional phrase
E	English	fr.	fragment
E-language	external language	freq.	frequent
eccl.	ecclesiastical	ft	foot/feet
EccL	Ecclesiastical Latin	ftn.	footnote
ed.	(with name) editor/ edited by	FUT/fut.	future
		G	Greek (Ancient Greek)
edn	edition	Gallorom.	Gallo-Romance
eds	editors	Gaul.	Gaulish
e.g.	*exempli gratia*, for example	GEN/gen.	genitive
		gen. ed.	general editor
EG	Ecclesiastical Greek	Germ.	German
EL	Early Latin	GL/Gl	glide
EME	Early Middle English	Gmc.	Germanic
EMnE	Early Modern English	Gosp	Gospel
Eng.	English	Goth.	Gothic
EOE	Early Old English	Grd	gerund
epigr.	epigraphic	HAB	habitual
Epist.	Epistle	Hitt.	Hittite
esp.	especially	Hom.	Homer
et al.	et alii; and other people	Hz.	Hertz
etc.	etcetera; and other things	I-language	internalized language
etym.	etymology	ibid.	in the same work
EWS	Early West Saxon	Ice.	Icelandic
excl.	excluding	id.	the same (meaning)
F	feminine (in glosses)	i.e.	*id est*, that is
F	foot (in metrical schemata)	IE	Indo-European
		Il.	*Iliad*
F	French	IMPF	imperfect
f.	folio (in ms. references)	impf.	imperfect
f.	following (one page)	IMPV	imperative
Far.	Faroese	INCH	inchoative
fem.	feminine	IND	indicative
ff.	following (two pages)	indef.	indefinite
FIENT	fientive ('become')	INF/inf.	infinitive

Infl	inflectional element/(head of) S	MF	Middle French
		MG	Medieval Greek
inscr(s).	inscription(s)	MHG	Middle High German
INST	instrumental	MID	middle
Intro	introduction	Mid. Iran.	Middle Iranian
Ir.	Irish	Mk	Mark (Gospel)
Ital.	Italian	ML	Medieval Latin
J	John (Gospel)	MLG	Middle Low German
Kn	Knossos	Mn	Modern (French, etc.)
L	Latin	MnE	Modern English
labvel	labiovelar	MnG	Modern Greek
Lat.	Latin	mod.	modern
LG	Late Greek	MP	Mood Phrase
Li	Lindisfarne	MS/ms.	manuscript
LIQ/Liq	liquid	MSS/mss.	manuscripts
lit.	literally	MSw.	Middle Swedish
Lith.	Lithuanian	Mt	Matthew (Gospel)
Lk	Luke (Gospel)	Myc.	Mycenaean (Greek)
LL	Late Latin	N	neuter (in glosses)
LME	Late Middle English	N	noun
LML	Late Medieval Latin	n.	note
LOC/loc.	locative	NAS/Nas	nasal
LOE	Late Old English	n.d.	no date available
LP	lexical phrase	NE	New (= Modern) English (in quotes)
LV	Late Version		
LWS	Late West Saxon	NEG/Neg/neg.	negative; negator
M	mood	neut.	neuter
m	masculine	NL	Neolatin
m.	meter	NOM/nom.	nominative
μ	mora	NOMZ	nominalizer
masc.	masculine	NONFIN	nonfinite
MDu.	Middle Dutch	Norw.	Norwegian
ME	Middle English	NP	Noun Phrase
med.	medical, medicine	N.T.	New Testament
Med.	Median	nt.	neuter
MEDP	mediopassive	Num	number

O	old (with language names)	PLUPF	pluperfect
		POSS	possessive
Obj./obj.	object	PP	prepositional phrase
OBL	oblique (case)	pp.	pages
OBST/Obst	obstruent	PPP	past passive participle
Od.	*Odyssey*	PR	Pāṇini's rule
OE	Old English	prep.	preparation
OF	Old French	PRES	present
OHG	Old High German	prn.	pronoun
OIce	Old Icelandic	prob.	probably
OIr	Old Irish	PROG	progressive
OL	Old Latin	prox.	proximal
ON	Old Norse	PrP	present participle
ONF	Old North/Norman French	Prt	participle
		PST/pst	past (tense)
OPT/opt.	optative	PTC/ptc.	particle
orig.	original(ly)	P–V	particle-verb (noun)
OS	Old Saxon	q.v.	quod vide ('which see')
OV	object-verb	REFL	reflexive
P	phrase (after N, V, etc.)	reiterat.	reiterative
P	pre/postposition	rel.	relative
p.	*post* 'after' (in dates)	retrfl	retroflex
p.	page	rev.	revised
pal.	palatal, palatalization	rhet.	rhetorical
PAP	past active participle	Ru	Rushworth
PART	participle; participial (mood)	Russ.	Russian
		RV	Rig Veda (in Sanskrit glosses)
PASS/pass.	passive		
p.c.	personal correspondence	S	strong (syllable)
Pers	person	σ	syllable
Pers.	Persian	SBJ	subjunctive
PF	perfect (in glosses)	Sc	Scandinavian
PHON	phonological component	Schol.	Scholastic
phps.	perhaps	SEM	semantic component
PIE	Proto-Indo-European	SG/sg.	singular
Pl/pl.	plural	SH	Sonority Hierarchy

Skt	Sanskrit	vcd	voiced
sme.	someone	Ved.	Vedic
SOV	subject-object-verb	vel.	velar
Sp.	Spanish	viz.	*videlicet* 'namely'
Spec	specifier	VL	Vulgar Latin
SUB	subessive	v.l.	varia lectio ('variant reading')
Subj./subj.	subject		
SUPER	superessive	v.ll.	variant readings
superl.	superlative	VO	verb-object
SV	subject-verb	VOC/voc.	vocative
s.v.	*sub vide* 'see under'	vol., vols	volume(s)
SVO	subject-verb-object	VP	Verb Phrase
Sw(ed).	Swedish	V–P	verb-particle (noun)
T	Tense	vs.	versus
Tns	Tense	vs.	verse (in text references)
TOP	topic	VSO	verb-subject-object
tr.	translated by (with name)	W	weak (syllable)
trans	transitive (in glosses)	WGmc.	West Germanic
transl.	translation	w. lit	with literature (references)
V	vowel (phonological contexts)	WS	West Saxon
V	verb	X	any lexical or functional category
V2	verb-second (order)	XP	any lexical or functional phrase
v	small V		
v.	*vide* 'see'		

Some terms in the list are represented by more than one symbol (e.g. 'N', 'nt.', 'neut.'; or 'L', 'Lat.'). This reflects the usage of different authors cited.

1

Theoretical assumptions

Much of linguistic terminology is used differently by different linguists. Portions of this work are in the generative framework and the terminology is used accordingly. This chapter introduces the core terms used throughout this book, in particular those connected with the properties of words and their constituent parts. Derivation will be featured throughout. Inflection is introduced solely to illustrate how it will be applied in this work. Also introduced is the role of features in the projection of aspect, voice, tense, mood, cause, change of state, etc. It is argued that Chomsky's I-language plays an important role in lexicalization and productivity, and that institutionalization and backformation are relevant only in the history of the E-language.

1.1 Basic phrase structure

This section presents a traditional and very similar modern conception of phrase structure that will be applied to word structure in §1.2. The essence is that both phrases and words consist of a head and satellites.

A word plus its satellites constitutes a PHRASE, and all phrases have a HEAD. In the noun phrase (NP) *undrinkable water*, the noun *water* is head of the phrase because it projects, i.e. determines that the phrase is a noun phrase. An adjective (A) also heads its own phrase and can have its own satellites, as in *very undrinkable water*. The head of the adjective phrase (AP) *very undrinkable* is *undrinkable*.

Traditional grammar (e.g. Bloomfield 1933: 194f.) maintained that the sentence is exocentric (headless) but that phrases are endocentric (headed). Bloomfield is explicit that every phrase has a head of its own kind: a noun phrase (NP) has a noun (N) head, a verb phrase (VP) has a verb (V) head, and so on. Each phrase, according to Bloomfield, can have satellites, namely a specifier (Spec) and a complement (Compl).

In the generative model, the traditional observation was formalized as X-bar theory. See (1), where XP is a phrase of any kind (VP, NP, etc.) and X (or X°/X-zero) its head (V, N, etc.). X' (X-bar) represents an intermediate level.

(1) X-bar theory

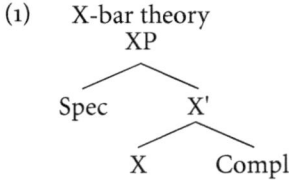

The Spec is said to asymmetrically (or antisymmetrically) C-COMMAND the complement. That is, while X and the complement c-command each other, the complement does not c-command the specifier, hence the asymmetry/antisymmetry (cf. §3.2).

"An X° (zero-level) category is a head or a category formed by adjunction to the head X, which projects" (Chomsky 1995: 245).

In a bare phrase structure model, the difference between a head X and the XP it projects is of no theoretical significance (Chomsky 1995: 241–9; 2005: 14), and there are no bar levels. A complement is a word or phrase that merges with a head. A specifier is any other phrase that merges with the unit formed by first merger (Chomsky 1995: 245). COMPLEMENT and SPECIFIER "are just notations for first-Merge and later-Merge" (Chomsky 2005: 14). There is "no distinction between lexical items and 'heads' projected from them.... [A]n item can be both an X° and an XP" (Chomsky 1995: 249).

Chomsky (1986b) made S endocentric with the asymmetrical structure of (1). Its head is Tense (T) or, better, Mood (M) (Aygen 2002), which has scope over the entire sentence:

(2) Sentential scope of Tense/Mood (Ross 1967)
   (a) *I must see you yesterday
   (b) *I saw you tomorrow

Moreover, the only part of the sentence that is universally obligatory is the Mood (or Force) element. For Chomsky (1995: 69, w. lit), the FORCE INDICATOR determined the type of clause/sentence, i.e. declarative, interrogative, imperative, etc., called MOOD by other linguists, e.g. Aygen (2002), for whom Mood and epistemic modality license nominative case. Rizzi (1997) developed an elaborated CP as a place for mood (force), topics, focus, and finiteness: ForceP–TopicP*–FocusP–TopicP*–Fin[ite] (the asterisk * indicates that topics can iterate). Force is subdivided according to the illocutionary force of the sentence, e.g. interrogative, declarative, exclamative (Rizzi 2001; 2004), similar to Mood speech act, etc., of Cinque (1999). It is therefore reasonable to think of Mood as the basic head of S, with more detailed subdivisions made as needed.

(3) M(ood) = head of S(entence)

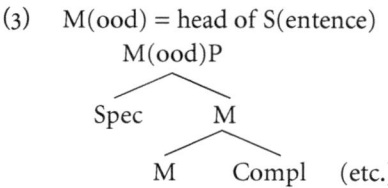

1.2 Word structure

This section applies the endocentric structure of §1.1 (phrases) to words. The objective is not to identify the different types of word or even define what a word is, but only to illustrate the structural properties of words that are relevant to this monograph.[1]

As a morphological entity, a word consists of a string of elements that make up the form and meaning of the whole. In *un-drink-able*, hyphens separate the formal morphological units, distinguished here as follows: *un-* and *-able* are MORPHEMES or FORMATIVES, *drink* is a ROOT which can be categorized as a verb or a noun (Chapter 4). The term *morpheme* generally refers to a unit with meaning but in the generative model can also be applied to non-meaning-bearing elements (like linking vowels in compounds) and to roots, especially by linguists who use *morpheme* as little more than a convenient label with no theoretical significance (e.g. Halle 1973; Aronoff 1976). In some models (e.g. Carstairs-McCarthy 2005), MORPHEMES are functional and differ from LEXEMES, which are open-class items. This work will use *morpheme* more generically, although it will generally imply a unity of form and meaning/function, and lexical morphemes will be distinguished from functional.

Returning to *un-drink-able*, *un-* negates the meaning of *drink-able* 'able to be drunk' and *-able* states the capacity of a passive event to be fulfilled (§4.7). The morphological shape cannot be permuted; there is no **drink-un-able*, etc. (Halle 1973).

A syntactic head can consist of more than one morphological word (as in *a New York attorney, a Mickey Mouse course*), a compound (*road rage is a serious problem*), a frozen phrase (*jack-in-the-box*), or even a sentence (*a how-they-do-it book*) (cf. Sproat 1985; Di Sciullo and Williams 1987).

Morphological constructs also have a head which projects and therefore bears the syntactic category feature and other essential features, such as countability, animacy, concreteness, number, etc. (Miller 1993; Padrosa-Trias 2010: 83–96—both w. lit).[2] The

---

[1] Overviews of morphology and word structure: Štekauer and Lieber (2005), Aronoff and Fuderman (2005), Lieber and Štekauer (2009), Aronoff (2011), Fábregas and Scalise (2012), Štekauer et al. (2012). On the notion *word* and crosslinguistic differences, see Anderson (1985b: 150–58), Di Sciullo and Williams (1987), Miller (1993), Bauer (2000), Baker (2003), Dixon and Aikhenvald (2003), Štekauer et al. (2012, esp. ch. 2).

[2] The head is defined differently in different frameworks, but most frameworks admit headedness. For instance, for Štekauer (2005: 225), "the onomasiological base is the head because it is this constituent that stands for the most general class of all constituents...." On this conception the head is also defined by its content, not by its position. One of its main functions is that "the head determines the word-class and is the

head can appear in any position (*pace* Williams 1981) but is generally parametrized. In English, it is usually on the right. In a few rare word types like *en-able* the head (category determiner) is *en-*, and in this case it is not also the MORPHOSYNTACTIC LOCUS, or place of inflections (Zwicky 1985): *en-able-s*, not **en-s-able*. In strong verbs, like *sing, sang*, the tense head in this model is identified syntactically and not by position in the word.

In *-ish* nouns, *-ish* is the head and assigns to the noun whatever theta-role (§2.5) *like* would assign: *like a child ~ childlike ~ childish* (NEG *un-childish*); cf. *how childish/unchildish were they?* In adjectives, *-ish* has a [+DEGREE] feature that delimits the adjectival head. Like comparatives, *-ish* adjectives are not (further) gradable, comparable, or *un-* negatable: **how older/greenish are they?*, **so older/whitish*, **very longer/oldish*, **un-later/*un-greenish* (Walinska de Hackbeil 1983; 1986).

Coordinate compounds, or dvanvas (e.g. *dog-cat* (fight), §3.5), in which all major constituents are concatenated heads, argue strongly against any positional definition of head and require a way of recognizing heads independently of their position. In morphology, as in syntax, the head is the structural constituent that projects its category and other essential features. This will be elaborated in Chapters 3 and 4.

Paradigmatic suppletion, e.g. *go/went, be/is/was*, permits an analysis of these as lexical words that differ phonologically, extending the notion of possible word (Corbett 2007). In the model under discussion, these are analyzed as contextual exponents of the same roots, i.e. √GO, √BE.

Word has also been used in the sense of a phonological unit (Greek *phōnḗ* 'sound'), defined by stress, restrictions on sound sequences, etc. For instance, *I'll* and *should've* are phonological (p-)words. They are not morphological units because (i) they are not formed by morphology (*I'll* is not *I + ll*, as *seedy* is *seed + y*), and (ii) contractions like *I'll* are produced by phonological welding of *I will*. Finally, such p-words are not syntactic words because they do not undergo movement as a syntactic unit, as shown in (4).

(4) (a) Dana thinks (that) who will win
    (b) Dana thinks (that) who'll win
    (c) who does Dana think ~~who~~ will win
    (d) *who'll does Dana think ~~who(wi)ll~~ win   (Miller 1993: 86)

The *who will* of (4a) appears contracted in (4b) and with movement of *who* in (4c), where the crossed out ~~who~~ marks the position from which *who* moved. What is important is that the contracted form *who'll* cannot move as a single syntactic unit, as shown by (4d).

---

distributional equivalent of the whole naming unit" (ibid., p. 225); cf. Selkirk (1982: 9). Scalise et al. (2009) separate categorial, semantic, and morphological heads.

A word can also be a LISTEME (coined by Di Sciullo and Williams 1987), one of the listed units of language, but this is not the same as a word by any definition (cf. §1.10).

Throughout this work, *word* (as distinct from *p-word*, PROSODIC WORD, and other types of word §9.2) will refer to the composite of roots and formatives (constituent parts) that make up a real or potential syntactic head.

1.3 Inflection

Since inflection does not figure prominently in the lexicogenic processes examined in this work, it is introduced here solely to illustrate how it gets attached to a derived word in the model under discussion.

Inflections are the heads of functional or relational categories. More traditionally, inflection involves the part of a word that interacts with syntax. One type of interaction involves AGREEMENT with a syntactic subject.[3] The verb *be*, for instance, assumes the form *am* when *I* is the subject, *is* with *he*, *she*, *it*, or a singular noun for a subject, etc.

In contrast to derivation, inflection is generally claimed to be obligatory (Miller 2010: vol. 2, ch. 4; cf. Corbett 2010: 147), but what does this mean? Even a default has exceptions (Yang 2005: 273). In English, the *-s* plural is the default, by definition productive (Bauer 2001: 60ff.), but lexical exceptions like *oxen* exist. Default implies that, for instance, a new count noun is automatically inflected for (singular/plural) number (*quark/quark-s*), and a new verb automatically takes agreement (*s/he lase-s, they lase*). Counterexamples (e.g. Štekauer, to appear) are theory-internal. Tense is not an obligatory category in Eskimo-Aleut. In a syntactic model of morphology, if a tense feature is present in the computation, an exponent is obligatorily inserted. The optionality is in the fact that a tense feature may not be present in the computation.

Agreement is an interface phenomenon because feature indices contrary to the lexical index can be imposed (Bouchard 1984: 40, 70, etc.). In French, *Jean est petit* 'John is small' is the norm, but to insult John as effeminate, feminine gender is imposed on *Jean*, which licenses *Jean est petite* with the feminine index of the adjective (Denis Bouchard, p.c.). The problem for non-syntactic theories of morphology is that the grammar cannot in principle 'know' what extralinguistic forms of agreement someone's worldview will find acceptable and would automatically reject lexically or grammatically unspecified mismatches.

One formulation of agreement is via an Agree relation.

---

[3] On agreement generalities, see Brown et al. (2003), Baerman et al. (2005), Corbett (2009), and for theoretical discussion, Baker (2008). The exchange between Alsina and Arsenijević (2012a; 2012b) and Wechsler and Zlatić (2012) is grounded in a different framework and, oddly, pays no attention to Baker's work.

(5) Agree (Chomsky, simplified)
α Agrees with β where:
(a) α and β have non-distinct features;
(b) α asymetrically c-commands β.

Agree standardly requires the probe to asymmetrically c-command the goal, but Baker (2008) argues that it must be able to work in either direction.

Agree yields valuation of a probe's features. Features are either INTERPRETABLE (necessary for semantic interpretation, e.g. ±human) or UNINTERPRETABLE, which trigger some operation but have no semantic interpretation. In the case of standard subject agreement (Agr), T has interpretable tense and uninterpretable/unvalued phi (person, number) and case features (see §1.9). T probes for a goal with matching interpretable features in its c-command domain, i.e. the phi-features of the DP in SpecνP[CAUS/AG] (§4.4.1) or a phi-bearing [D-] agreement morpheme on the verbal head. Matching creates Agree which in turn eliminates the uninterpretable features.

On the order of Agr elements (Person, Number) with respect to the Verb, the most natural pattern seems to be Pers–V–Num, which would explain why Pers and Num are so frequently conflated, to avoid separation of the Agr constituents. If statistics mean anything, Pers–V–Num is by far the most frequent and should be accorded privileged status. The second most common, V–Pers–Num, follows from suffixing both Agr constituents to the verb in their most natural order. The third most frequent, Pers–Num–V, amounts to the same constituents prefixed in the same order (Miller 2010: ii. 31f.).

For nouns in highly inflected languages, Booij's (1996) INHERENT INFLECTION, e.g. gender (a property of roots), is frequently conflated with CONTEXTUAL INFLECTION, like structural case, assigned syntactically. Also conflated is number, a semantic property that is neither inherent nor syntactically assigned.[4] In a syntactic model, all of these originate in different places and are spelled out with a vocabulary item that conflates them. For instance, L *porca* 'pig' is feminine and singular and nominative (subject) case. In 'I saw the (male) pig', the form is *porcum*, which is accusative (object) case but also conflates masculine gender and singular number.

In a language like West Greenlandic, semantic elements like number typically precede case; cf. /iγλu/ 'temporary shelter' IGLOO [1856] (Schultz-Lorentzen 1945: 34):[5]

---

[4] For Booij, plural inflection is inherent, as are comparative and superlative, and tense and aspect on verbs. Person and number on verbs is contextual, as is concord on adjectives and structural case for nouns. This is of course stipulative in that it follows from no principles. Moreover, number frequently has derivational properties (Štekauer et al. 2012: 30–35).

[5] West Greenlandic forms are in older orthography: *g* = voiced velar continuant /γ/, *dl* = lateral fricative /λ/, but distinctive /u/ is substituted for allophonic [o] in orthographic *igdlo*, and /i/ for [e] in *igdlum/ne*.

(6) Case and number in West Greenlandic (Eskimo-Aleut family)

	SG	PL
absolutive	igdlu	igdlu-t
locative 'in'	igdlu-m-i	igdlu-n-i
allative 'to'	igdlu-m-ut	igdlu-n-ut

No theoretical significance is ascribed to the terms *inflection* and *derivation*. This traditional dichotomy is too simplistic even for the ancient Indo-European languages for which it was devised (Miller 1993; 2006; 2010). For instance, affixes with category features (noun, verb, etc.) have different properties from functional markers (aspect, voice, tense, mood, etc.), and those differ from formatives of (syntactico-)semantic content (causative, change of state), or purely cultural/semantic affixes (evaluatives, evidentials, degree indicators, etc.). The fuzzy boundaries between traditional inflection and derivation, including the fact that in many languages one and the same category can be both or neither, are illustrated in Fortin (2011) and Štekauer et al. (2012: 19–35). The latter, rather than discard the labels, settle on 'prototypical' inflection or derivation with a continuum between the extremes. But 'both' or 'neither' is not a continuum, and the terminology is vacuous. All that is relevant on a language-specific basis is the projection of the features.

In this work, the term *inflection* is reserved for agreement and concord, i.e. material that is adjoined at spellout as a result of the Agree relations in the syntactic computation. Many non-inflectional affixes will count non-technically as derivational for our purposes simply because of the lack of non-dichotomized terminology.

1.4 Deradical, denominal, and deverbal derivation

Derivation is the operation by which one form is created from another. The created form, or DERIVATIVE, differs from the original ROOT or BASE form in category (noun, verb, etc.) or category content (*farm* and its derivative *farmer* are both nouns, but differ in meaning).

English introduced a verb *(to) flan* [c.1987] 'assault with a custard pie' (Ayto 1989: 149). The verb *flan* is derived from the noun *flan* [1846] and, as is typical, the derivative embodies the meaning of the base. Earlier, a verb *to author* [1598] was derived from the noun *author* [c.1300]. The derivational layers are illustrated in (7). In (7a) derivation is effected by conversion (cf. Sproat 1985: 377), and in (7b) by affixation (the noun) and conversion (the verb).

(7) The deverbal and denominal derivational cycle
   (a) base (root) verb → derived (deverbal) noun → denominal verb (etc.)
       shine (past *shone*)   shine   shine (past *shined*)
       ring (past *rang*)   ring   ring (past *ringed*)
   (b) $stick_V$ → $sticker_N$ → *(to)* $sticker_V$

A more recent example is: $feed_V \rightarrow feeder_N$ [1855] 'transportation serving outlying areas' $\rightarrow feeder_V$ [1988] 'to convey by means of a subsidiary transport system linking with a main transport centre' (Ayto 1989: 146). In *Newsweek* (April 27, 1992) there appeared an editorial by Robert J. Samuelson containing the phrase *the rise in lawyering*, and since then the verb *to lawyer* has gained in frequency, as has the phrase *to lawyer up*. An earlier verb *lawyer* [1797] meant 'to subject to lawyer's review'.

The cycle in (7) is the traditional view. The different stages in (7) belong to different historical layers. Synchronically, in the model under discussion, the base verb *shine* would itself be categorized from a root √SHINE, and a derivation would consist at most of two stages. For instance, in (7b) the noun *sticker* would be derived from a root √STICK, not a fully categorized verb, and the verb *sticker* would be derived from the categorized noun *sticker*. The first stage is deradical derivation rather than deverbal.

In more theory-neutral terms, lexical entries can be underspecified or neutral to word class (Farrell 2001; cf. Štekauer et al. 2012: 214). Additional examples of differences between deradical and deverbal or denominal derivation can be found in §1.6.1.

1.5 Overt formatives

Nearly any formal device can signal derivation, and most of the following are also found in inflection.

1.5.1 Affixation

The crosslinguistically most frequent overt formative (Štekauer et al. 2012: 212) is the SUFFIX (NL *suffixum*, neuter of L *suffixus* 'fastened behind': L *sub* 'under; behind' + *fixus* 'fastened'). Suffixes constitute one of the most productive means of derivation in English, as in $fool_N$-ish_A-$ness_N$.

Next in frequency is the PREFIX (L *prae* 'in front'), e.g. *en-* 'put in(to)' (Konkol 1960: 113ff.; Kastovsky 2002: 106): *endanger* [1477] 'put in danger', *enlist* [1665] 'put on a list'; $trance_N \rightarrow en$-$trance_V$ [1593].

The sequence $chant_N \rightarrow en$-$chant_V \rightarrow en$-$chant_V$-$ment_N$ exhibits both a prefix and a suffix, generically referred to in all theories as AFFIXES (L *ad* 'to; at; by').

INFIXATION is the least frequent type of affixation crosslinguistically (Štekauer et al. (2012: 198–203). Infixes are not productive in English morphology, where they are residual and meaningless root alternants; cf. *con-ting-ent* beside *con-tig-uous*. In several types of language play, however, they figure prominently, e.g. *guaran-damn-tee* (§5.5).

Combined prefixation and suffixation, as in en-$vigor_N$-ate_V (no *en-$vigor$ or *$vigor$-ate), is not the same as a CIRCUMFIX, which is a crosslinguistically rare type of split morpheme whose constituent parts possess no independent meaning (Štekauer et al. 2012: 204–12).[6] In *envigorate*, both *en-* and *-ate* exist independently and each contributes its own meaning. Similarly, in German past participles like *gesprochen* 'spoken' (*sprechen* 'to speak'), both *-en* and *ge-* exist independently of one another, e.g. *Berg* 'mountain' : *Gebirge* 'mountain range'. Even in past participles *ge-* in the weak verb class is accompanied by *-t* instead of *-en*, e.g. *gehandelt* 'handled' (*handeln* 'to handle').

The word's (positive or negative) polarity can be reversed by an affix, such as *dis-*. Compare *en-franchise* 'endow with the rights of citizenship, especially voting' : *disenfranchise* 'deprive of citizenship, especially the right to vote'. *Dis-* has several different meanings: negative *disallow* [1377], *disavow* [1393]; reversative *dishonor* [1393], *disarm* [Ch.]; ablatival *dislodge* [a.1450], *displace* [1552], etc. (cf. Kastovsky 2002: 106f.).

1.5.2 Stem change

Consonantal changes, except in a few Latinate derivations (e.g. *elide* : *elision*), are residual and unproductive in English. Examples: *excu*[s]$_N$: *excu*[z]$_V$, *advi*[s]$_N$: *advi*[z]$_V$, *relie*[f]$_N$: *relie*[v]$_V$, *inten*[t]$_N$: *inten*[d]$_V$, *offen*[s]$_N$: *offen*[d]$_V$, etc. CONSONANT GRADATION is rare in English expressive language, e.g. *snicker/snigger*, but more frequent crosslinguistically (§10.3.2).

1.5.3 Apophony/Ablaut

APOPHONY/ABLAUT (vowel change) occurs in English strong verbs, e.g. *sing* : *sang* : *sung*. This is an inflectional contrast, but note the derived noun *song*. Apophony in both inflection and derivation has been shrinking through the history of English, but continues to be available in synesthesia (e.g. *bing, bang, bong*, §10.3.2) and, less productively, in reduplicative and conjunctive formations (e.g. *mishmash*, §14.4). Crosslinguistically, apophony occurs both in expressive morphology (§§10.3, 14.4.3, 15.2) and in core morphology (Štekauer et al. 2012: 229–33).

1.5.4 Accent

Several noun–verb pairs are distinguished on the surface by the position of the accent; e.g. *súbject* : *subjéct; présent* : *presént; cónvict* : *convíct; prógress* : *progréss; ímplement* : *impleménnt* (~ *ímplemènt*). This pattern started with a few examples and expanded to over a hundred. The earliest examples are *cónflict*$_N$ [1440] / *conflíct*$_V$ [1432], *cónduct*$_N$ [1290] / *condúct*$_V$ [1400], *ábstract*$_N$ [1387] / *abstráct*$_V$ [1542] (Miller

---

[6] At least one of their examples should be incorrect by their own criteria: Sp. *en-jaul-ar* [in-cage-inf] 'to encage' (p. 210) should not contain a circumfix because *en-* is 'in' and *-ar* is the standard infinitival suffix for the *-a-* verb class. Both exist independently and each contributes separately to the construct.

2010: 1.218, w. lit). By way of analysis, of course, the accentual distinction is a secondary reflex of conversion (cf. SPE 77–84; Kiparsky 1982a: 13; Štekauer 1996: 55–95; Štekauer et al. 2012: 225–9; Bermúdez-Otero 2012: §4.2).

1.6 Conversion

Conversion is the usual term for change of category (N, V, etc.) without a phonologically overt formative.[7] It is accomplished in many different ways in different frameworks (see Martsa 2012), some with a bidirectional lexical rule (e.g. Haspelmath 2002), others with a zero affix (Marchand 1960: 293–308; 1963; 1964; Kastovsky 1969; 2005), still others by functional or semantic shift, and recently by movement into an empty category. The confusion is not just terminological. For some it is not derivational, and different things are subsumed. Constructions like *the poor* are variously treated. Since they have no plural inflection (**the poors*), they do not behave like nouns. In line with one traditional account of these as 'elliptical' (e.g. Kastovsky 2005a: 35; Balteiro 2007a: 41ff.), they are analyzed here as a noun phrase with empty (e) head, viz. [$_{DP}$...*the* [$_{AP}$...*good* [$_{NP}$...e]]].

This section introduces the terminology as it will be used in this work. For expositional simplicity, only denominal derivation is treated here. Conversion to an adjective is discussed in Chapter 4.

Older examples include the denominal verbs *(to) belt* [a.1325], *ransom* [c.1350], *mirror* [?1410], *mother* [a.1425], *marshal* [c.1450] (modern sense [1464]), *garden* [1577], *pocket* [1588], *lecture* [a.1592], *fuel* [a.1593], *parrot* [1596], *channel* [1598], *gossip* [1611], *champion* [a.1616], *bottle* [1622], *position* [1647], *deluge* [1649], *parody* [1733], *background* [1768], *impact* [1935] ([1601] 'pack in'), *decision* [a.1945], *input* [1946] 'feed in data' ([a.1382 Wyclif] 'impose'), *flatline* [1975], etc. (cf. Konkol 1960).

Prevailing accounts, as mentioned above, differ markedly from one another. Part of the problem is theory-internal and another part is that there are different kinds of conversion. One is deradical/denominal, like *parrot* → *(to) parrot*, as in this section. Another is more complicated, involving conversion of a categorized verb (originating as a root) to a noun (§§3.2, 4.4). Since a syntactic account is unavoidable in those instances, by extrapolation the same kind of unified account is assumed here.[8]

---

[7] For discussion, see Konkol (1960: 90ff.), Marchand (1963; 1964), Kastovsky (1969), Pennanen (1971), Karius (1985), Štekauer (1996), Kiparsky (1997), Tyler (1999), Don et al. (2000), Farrell (2001), Hale and Keyser (1993b; 1997; 1998; 1999a; 2002), Plag (2003: 107–16), Arad (2003), Bauer and Valera (2005), Don (2004; 2005a; 2005b), Lieber (2004: 89–95; 2005: 418–22), Harley (2005), Levinson (2007), Balteiro (2007a; 2007b), García Velasco (2009), and Martsa (2012), with a complete overview of the literature excluding the most recent generative work. Smith (2005) is a detailed study of noun–adjective conversion. Semantic accounts, like that of Balteiro or Martsa, can handle the type *parrot$_N$* > *parrot$_V$*, but not the more difficult types in chapter 4, where conversion is part of a complex derivation.

[8] Especially useless for the more complicated cases are accounts like that of Balteiro, for whom conversion is "a conceptual syntactic-semantic process, consisting in the use of an already existing lexical

Terminology should reflect analysis. If a unified account of the diverse types can be accomplished, nothing precludes application of the term *conversion* to all of them. I will use conversion to mean movement into an empty head (§§3.2, 4.4). This kind of syntactic model accounts for the semantics by formalizing a representation such as that of Rappaport Hovav and Levin (1998), e.g. for a location verb: [x CAUSE [BECOME [y <PLACE>]]]. Even if the relationships among these can be accounted for by polysemy (Martsa 2012), the specific forms must still be derived, especially in more complex cases.

In their seminal study of zero verbs, Clark and Clark (1979) classified over 1,300 verbs into five main categories, based on the thematic role of the base noun:

(8) Zero verbs (Clark and Clark)
    (a) location: *bottle the wine*   160
    (b) locatum:[9]   *saddle the horse*   336
    (c) instrument: *hammer the nail*   313
    (d) goal: *coil the rope*   112
    (e) agent: *umpire the game*   85

The semantic relations of the core zero verb types in English are outlined in (9).

(9) (a) ACTOR [be an actor; do what an actor does; perform X]: *umpire* (the game) 'perform the task of an umpire'; cf. *marshal, parrot, mother*, etc.

    (b) GOAL [turn X into noun]: *cripple* 'cause to become a cripple'; *coil* (the rope) 'put the rope into a coil'

    (c) INSTRUMENT [utilize X to affect object]: *hammer* 'hit with a hammer'; cf. *ransom, glue*, etc.

    (d) LOCATION [put object in X]: *bottle* 'put in a bottle'; cf. *bag, corral, garage, pocket, position*, etc.

    (e) LOCATUM [put X in/on object]: *saddle* 'provide (a horse) with a saddle'; cf. *fuel, cork, belt, channel, paint, water, seed, blindfold*, etc.

    (f) PRIVATIVE [remove X from object]: *skin* 'deprive of skin' (cf. Plag 1999: 219ff.; Tyler 1999)

---

item . . . in a different syntactic context, which leads to a change of category or word-class" (Balteiro 2007a: 65). However, Balteiro's view of directionality is on the right track: "whenever conversion is assumed, a directional relation between a base word and the output of the process is also necessarily assumed since, as the word conversion itself indicates, there is a turn/change/transformation or reorganisation of something into something else which also (and inevitably) implies a direction" (2007b: 84). As will be argued in chapter 4, directionality is a product of head movement and attraction by an appropriate category feature.

[9] *Locatum* requires explanation. It is sometimes also called *ornative* (e.g. Plag 2003: 112) 'provide with x', e.g. *staff*. The best paraphrase of *saddle* is 'provide/fit (a horse) with a saddle' (Hale and Keyser 1999a: 460; Harley 2005), but a have-on interpretation, viz. 'the horse has a saddle on', has also been suggested (Kiparsky 1997: 484f.). A variant of this is the *put on* interpretation (Fábregas and Scalise 2012: 93).

Causative, resultative, inchoative, etc., are sometimes included (e.g. Martsa 2012: 88, w. lit), but these are treated here as semantic primitives underlying all of the types, e.g. *bottle* is underlyingly 'cause to get-to-be in a bottle' (cf. above).

Some derivatives allow more than one interpretation, e.g. *stone* 'pelt with stones' and 'remove stones from' (fruit); *dust* 'remove dust from' and 'cover with powder'; *glue* and *cork* can be instrument or locatum verbs. Kiparsky (1997) observes that when the item is a plausible location or locatum, both readings are generally possible. The polysemy of agents, instruments, etc. (§8.3) accounts for the semantic overlap (Martsa 2012: 149–68).

The account of denominal verbs by Tyler (1999) is unique and will be followed here. By means of a slightly different grouping, she reduces four of the main classes to two:

(10) Core denominal verb types (Tyler 1999: 119)[10]
    (a) Goal verbs: Base Noun$_{GOAL}$, Affected Argument$_{THEME}$
        (1) location: *bottle*$_{GOAL}$ *the wine*$_{THEME}$
        (2) goal: *coil*$_{GOAL}$ *the rope*$_{THEME}$
    (b) Theme verbs: Base Noun$_{THEME}$, Affected Argument$_{GOAL}$
        (1) locatum: *saddle*$_{THEME}$ *the horse*$_{GOAL}$
        (2) instrument: *hammer*$_{THEME}$ *the nail*$_{GOAL}$

These two classes, Tyler observes, represent over 90% of the transitive zero verbs in Clark and Clark (1979). On all other accounts, location and locatum verbs pattern together as opposed to instrument verbs, and goal verbs are seldom mentioned. However, as in Hale and Keyser (2002: 161, 185ff.), the instrumental preposition *with* is associated with a theme role (§§2.4, 2.5.1).

Kiparsky (1997:486) maintains that PSEUDO-DENOMINAL verbs are lexically related derivations from the same root and contrast with true denominals whose underlying nominal meaning is quite specific (e.g. *pocket, oil, bottle*). True denominals, like (11a), do not admit non-cognate PP copies. Contrast the alleged pseudo-denominal in (11b).

(11)   (a) #*she taped the picture on the wall with pushpins*
      (b) *he hammered the desk with his shoe*   (Kiparsky 1997: 488f.)

Arad (2003) structurally distinguishes denominal (11a) from deradical (11b) (cf. Don 2005a; 2005b; Levinson 2007: 103–7). However, according to the *OED*, the noun *tape* has almost no figurative meanings (the main exception is a (British?) military term) but refers to a narrow strip or ribbon of some material. By contrast, since the noun

---

[10] GOAL is defined as the target of movement/motion or change. THEME is the object undergoing motion/change in the expression of an event.

hammer has some ten different figurative meanings involving items of distinct shapes, UNDERSPECIFICATION accounts better for the facts: *hammer* does not require the use of a hammer but implies only 'to pound something with a hammering motion' (Tyler 1999: 156). Taking *hammer* as underspecified for shape is consistent with its PP copies. *Tape*, by sharp contrast, is not underspecified for shape, which explains why its copies must involve something tapelike. Indeed, Tyler points out that most of Kiparsky's 'true denominals' involve nouns that evoke a very specific mental schema, e.g. *snowplow, bicycle, charcoal, chain*. I conclude that all zero-derived verbs are the same, differing only in the (under)specification of the shape of the underlying object, and are derived by syntactic head movement like all other examples of conversion (Ch. 4).

1.6.1 Conversion in (poly)synthetic languages

The term *zero*-derivation must not be taken too literally. From English noun/verb pairs, one can get the misleading idea that 'zero' implies the complete absence of any affix. Crosslinguistically, however, conversion entails only the absence of a derivational marker in the technical sense. In most languages, either the noun or the verb or both require separate formatives to render them employable in syntax. Many such examples can be found in Štekauer et al. (2012: 213–24); cf. Martsa (2012: 69–78). Consider the examples in (12) from West Greenlandic (data from Schultz-Lorentzen 1927).[11]

(12) Zero verbs in West Greenlandic (Eskimo-Aleut family)
    (a) *ulik* 'cover'   :   *ulig-pa-a* 'covers it'
    (b) *uqaq* 'tongue'   :   *uqar-pu-q* [uses the tongue] 'speaks'
    (c) *qalak* 'bubble'   :   *qalag-pu-q* 'bubbles, boils'
    (d) *qapuk* 'foam'   :   *qapug-pu-q* 'foams'
    (e) *igdlaq* 'laughter' :   *igdlar-pu-q* 'laughs'

The verbs in (12) qualify as zero derivatives because all that is present is a mood marker (indicative intransitive *-pu-*/transitive *-pa-*) and a person suffix (*-q* 3SG subject, *-a-a* 3SG subject/3SG object). Any mood marker can be present, e.g. interrogative *-vi-*, conditional *-gu-*, etc. Without one of these, no verb can appear in syntax. The crucial fact about the forms in (12) is absence of any derivational affix that is not already on the categorized or derived noun (*qa-lak, qa-puk*), which makes the verbs true denominals, not deradicals. Beyond the syntactic wellformedness affixes, the verbs *ulig-paa* and *qapug-puq* contain nothing more than the noun bases *ulik, qa-puk*.

---

[11] West Greenlandic data are cited in (older) orthography: *q* = voiceless uvular stop, *r* = voiced uvular continuant /ʁ/, *g* = voiced velar continuant /ɣ/; *dl* = lateral fricative [λ]. Phonemic /u/ is substituted for allophonic [o] before /q/ (orthographic *oqaq, -poq*).

1.7 Backformation

This section begins with the premise that backformation is meaningful only historically (Marchand 1960; Štekauer et al. 2012: 234ff.). Synchronically, a previously nonexisting verb, for instance, is lexically stipulated to underlie a nominal that intrinsically contains it. A putative base is thus assumed by a speaker to exist in order to underlie a derived form. Historically, then, a backformation is an ad hoc creation that ensures the correct application of a derivation (Miller 2010: 1.101). Since children do not know if a given form is backformed or not (cf. McIntyre 2009), that form must be synchronically available as input to a given derivation.

Heuristically (not derivationally), the process is often accomplished by de-affixation. Thus, *donate* [1845] was backformed from *donation* [c.1425] to serve as a putative base from which the latter could be derived. Backformation is clearest when a form is created to underlie a borrowing. For instance, Old French *begar(d)* entered English as *beggar*, and already in Early Middle English a verb *beg* [a.1225] was created to underlie it. German *Schwindler* entered English as *swindler* [1774], and a verb *swindle* [1782] was backformed. For other examples, see Pennanen (1966; 1975), Shimamura (1983), Plag (1999: 206–13), Miller (1993: 110–15; 2006: 6f.), and especially Biłynsky (2013).

The usual way to recognize a backformation is by the first-attestation dates of related forms. Since existing forms can accidentally remain unattested in written records, this is not infallible, but the longer the intervening time, the more secure is the probability of backformation. *Peddle* [1650], *edit* [1791], and *sculpt* [1864] are backformations. The forms *peddl-er* [1307], *edit-or* [1649] (< L *ēditor*), *sculpt-or* [1634] are readily analyzed as agentives in -E/OR, which are derived from verbs, cf. *act-or*, *sing-er*. Since the nouns *editor* (etc.) originally had no verb base in English, one was created to underlie the agent noun. More simply, if an *act-or* ACTS, an *edit-or* EDITS, and a new verb is born. Recent formations in this class are the technical *lase (off)* [1962] 'cut (off) with a laser', backformed from *laser* [1960], the popular *auth* (from *author*), and *voy* (from *voyeur*), the last in the *Urban Dictionary*.[12]

Backformation in English is rare before 1500, but early examples include *backbite* [a.1300] from gerundial *backbiting* [c.1175], or *blaspheme* [1340] from *blasphemy* [a.1225]. More recent examples: *atone* [1555] from *atonement* [1513], *grovel* [1605] (*groveling* [c.1400]), *star-gaze* [1639] (*star-gazer* [1560]), *scavenge* [a.1644] (*scavenger* [1530]), *effervesce* [1747] (*effervescence* [1651]), *resurrect* [1773] (*resurrection* [c.1290]), *enthuse* [1827] (*enthusiasm* [1603]), *televise* [1927] (*television* [1907]).

Some of the models for backformations were themselves backformations. Given L *cre-ā-re* 'to create' : *cre-ā-tiō* 'creation', *create* was backformed (Chaucer's *creat* is

---

[12] http://www.urbandictionary.com/define.php?term=voy

only a past participle). L *ping-e-re* 'to paint' should have given **pinge* in English, not *paint*, which was backformed from *painter* (< *pi(n)ct-or*). From *or-i-* 'arise' : *or-i-ent-* 'rising; east; ORIENT' came an English noun *orient* which, by conversion, yielded a verb *(to) orient* 'locate to face east', then 'locate to face any point on the compass'. From that was derived a noun *orientation* 'act of orienting', whence backformed *orientate* [1848]. Many English verbs in *-ate* were backformed from nouns in *-ator*, *-ation* (*LSDE* 7, 253ff.).

Backformed nouns can underlie an adjective, e.g. *greed* [1609] from *greedy* [OE], *haze* [1706] from *hazy* [1625]. More recent are *sleaze* [1967] (cf. *sleazy* [1644]; modern sense [1941]), *glitz* [1977] (cf. *glitzy* [1966]), *ditz* [1984] (cf. *ditzy* [1976]).

An example of inflectional backformation is the reanalysis of *pease* [OE] as plural (*peas*), resulting in the creation of a new singular *pea* [1666] (Miller 2012: 73, w. lit). Many other examples can be found in Koziol (1972: 316).

1.8 Productivity

"Productivity is all about potential. A process is productive if it has the potential to lead to new coinages, or to the extent to which it does lead to new coinages" (Bauer 2001: 41). Not all potential words are equally probable, of course. Several factors may keep a potential construct from occurring (Bauer 2001: 42f., 143; 2005: 328–32). For instance, there may simply be no use for a word, e.g. *twenty-five-some*. Therefore, PROFITABILITY (pragmatic utility) is a relevant consideration distinct from AVAILABILITY.[13] The latter is determined by the language system; the former, extralinguistic (Bauer 2001: 211). It is argued below that the latter is also a product of individual grammars.

Productivity has been typically measured by the number of high- and low-frequency words. For instance, Plag (2003: 55ff.) cites a corpus of *-able* derivatives ranging from hapaxes (attested once), like *abusable*, *accruable*, to *acceptable* (3,416 times). A higher number of hapaxes attests to the availability of the formation, hence greater productivity, while a large number of high-frequency items indicates lower productivity. The main formulas proposed to measure productivity are discussed by Bauer (2005). The fallacy is that statistics do not constitute an independently motivated theory of morphological computation. An algorithmic model has been developed by Yang (2005), who finds that for a rule to be productive, it must apply to the majority of words to which it *can* apply. In brief, gaps arise when productivity fails (Halle 1973), and productivity fails when the exceptions are too numerous (Yang 2005; Yang et al. 2013).

---

[13] These terms were first introduced by Corbin (1987) as *rentabilité* 'profitability' and *disponibilité* 'availability'. The English translations are due to Carstairs-McCarthy (1992); cf. Bauer (2005: 324).

On most accounts, productivity is reduced to one of the two kinds of frequency:

(i) *Type frequency* involves the number of constructs of a given formation, each counted one time, e.g. agentives in *-tor* (*administrator, tutor*, etc.).
(ii) *Token frequency* involves the number of occurrences of a particular construct. The three occurrences of *frequency* in this paragraph count as one construct, not three.

The reason productivity cannot be reduced to frequency is illustrated neatly by Bauer (2001: 48). On the one hand, *a-* can productively form new words (*aglaze, aclutter*, etc.) even if the total number is small. On the other hand, English has over 700 *-ment* derivatives, but it is not productive. "Type frequency is the result of past productivity rather than an indication of present productivity" (Bauer, p. 48f.); cf. Cowie and Dalton-Puffer (2002: 416ff.), who emphasize that the boundary between synchrony (the contemporary language) and diachrony (history of the language) is often blurred or difficult to determine. Nevertheless, as emphasized by Corbett (2010: 145), "synchronic derivability is a key part of productivity".

Given that dictionaries often include only established words and ignore neologisms and rare words, and that absolute dates of coinages can rarely be established, Bauer (2001: 157ff., 205) concludes that a less ambiguous criterion is AVAILABILITY: A morphological process is available if it can be used to produce new words on a given base at a given time by virtually anyone in a given speech community (Bauer 2001: 205). This allows for purely stylistic creativity (Cowie 2000), but is incomplete to the extent that many other factors determine availability to an individual. For example, Körtvélyessy (2009) discusses the sociolinguistic variables of gender, age, education, occupation, and language background.

Availability itself can be relative. Štekauer (2005) distinguishes four different levels at which productivity can be determined: (i) Onomasiological Types, (ii) Word Formation Types, (iii) Morphological Types, (iv) Word Formation Rules. In principle, a new form should be maximally motivated by all of these factors together. Other frameworks also examine productivity on different levels, including extralinguistic. For instance, if a category is not very stable, like the dual in Ancient Greek, the productivity of any formal markers (exponents) must be considered relative to that.

In the model of Yang (2005), productivity is a function of rules that are "predictable" and "generalizable". A non-default rule can be productive. Essentially, then, productivity is categorial (cf. Yang et al. 2013). More traditionally, productivity was defined with reference to a DOMAIN of application (Aronoff 1976; Anderson 1985a: 19f.; Miller 1993; Plag 1999). "A pattern of word formation can never apply to just any word of a language, but only to some subset of words. This subset of possible bases is called the pattern's *domain*" (Rainer 2005a: 335). Domain includes potential form classes as well as the constraints discussed in Chapter 2, without which productivity cannot be evaluated. For the former, Latin had many transfers to the recent thematic neuter, e.g. *caelus* → *caelum* 'sky' (Rovai 2012). As to constraints, one cannot argue, for instance, that *-ish* is not productive because of the absence of **fishish* (§2.2.1), or that *-ize* is not productive because there is no **politize* (§2.2.2).

Locale is another factor in frequency increases, leading to or denying the productivity that can lead to institutionalization (§1.10), given that different regions deal with different issues (cf. Fischer 1998: 174, 181). Institutionalization may or may not affect productivity, but an increase in productivity can positively effect institutionalization (Fischer 1998: 180).

Traditional studies of productivity used dictionaries and corpora. The limitations of these sources are discussed by Schröder and Mühleisen (2010), who get entirely different results with online elicitation tests, which measure coinage potential and wellformedness judgments. In one test, 189 informants produced 425 new verbs with the prefix *over-* and 502 with *under-*, with no preference for native bases (*overspit*), Latinate (*overacquire*), converted bases (*underbrown*), etc. In another experiment, 1,000 not-previously-recorded *-ee* words were tested, of which 748 turned out to have been used by the respondents. These new handles on productivity yield different results from the traditional methods.

A given affix or category may be more productive in some registers than others, showing that productivity can be contingent on social context, genre, and stylistic factors, as emphasized by Baayen (2006: 20). Different kinds of texts in Middle English, for instance, exhibit differences in affix productivity:

> Derivatives with *-cion* [*-tion*] are consistently the most frequent in each genre, though medical texts and letters use them far more than the end-rhymed poetry selected for the corpus. Medical texts led in uses of *-cion* in part because of the sheer variety of medical procedures described. Lexemes with *-age* have minimal use in medical texts, but they are much more frequent in poetry, which tends to discuss a wider range of thematic issues (*marriage, dotage, servage, pilgrimage*, etc.). The suffix *-ity* has similar frequencies in poetry and letters, but like *-ness*, it is used far more frequently in medical texts than in letters or poetry. These higher frequencies appear because medical writers relied often on particular deadjectival nominalizations to represent descriptive states that can be observed within the human body (e.g., *whiteness, carnosity*). Thus, the particular semantic needs of writers and audiences in different genres affect the distributions of borrowed derivatives within vernacular texts. This point is not surprising in and of itself, but previous scholarship has not made clear how particular genres affect the use of particular suffixes in M[iddle]E[nglish]. (Palmer 2009: 330)

In other words, evaluating productivity historically is not a simple question of counting types or tokens: genre and other factors must be considered.

In one experiment by Körtvélyessy (2009), respondents were asked to select a word for a person who produces yogurts, choosing from *yogurter, yogurtist, yogurtnik, yogurtman, yogurt producer*, etc. (14 choices), or make up a word of their own. Sex played no role but age and desire for originality did. In particular, the types chosen by

18–24-year-olds were not productive in other age groups. Respondents with higher levels of education preferred a more transparent structure of their coinages. Hardly surprisingly, students were the most creative. Language background also played a role. Many examples of playful language, including bilingual puns, among second language learners have been reported (e.g. Kramsch 2009; Bell 2012).

Bauer (2001: 57f.; 2005: 330) denies that idiosyncratic formations are an indication of productivity, which contradicts the fact that a formation can remain available for a small number of individuals. Bauer excludes as indicators of productivity poetic and highly literary creations, words in newspaper (and other) headlines, playful formations that ignore the meaning of a morpheme, constructs limited to a single individual, new technical terms, and a single new word with a given morpheme. Again, for the purposes of the present monograph, where productivity can be evaluated for individuals, there is no reason to exclude poetic art, clever advertisers, and idiosyncratic constructs. This is one of the crucial differences between our conception of lexicogenesis and standard accounts of word formation.

The sociolinguistic variables above prove that individuals play a crucial role in productivity which must therefore be defined with reference to Chomsky's (1986a) I(nternalized)-language (individual grammars) or E(xternal)-language (a language in the broad sense, like "English").[14]

Bauer's anti-productivity examples involve single occurrences, for which there is no question of productivity in the E-language, but they are at least suggestive of I-language productivity. What is crucial is the interaction between I-language(s) and the E-language. In a discussion of the origin and spread of the English suffix -*en* (*whiten*, *darken*, etc.), Miller (2010: 2.119) concludes:

> -*en* is past its period of productivity from the E-language point of view. The nineteenth-century examples and occasional modern coinages indicate that -*en* affixation remains AVAILABLE (able to be used at any time...), but only for some speakers, for novel I-language creations. Most striking is how few of the recent constructs make it to standard E-language usage. This suggests that productivity, which is all about POTENTIAL..., can be relevant to only a small number of individual grammars (I-language).

This succinctly captures differences between diachronic, synchronic, and idiosyncratic productivity. Many speakers, myself included, have difficulty accepting novel -*en* constructs (e.g. *braven*, *coarsen*, *crispen*, *embiggen*, *harshen*, *neaten*, *smarten*, *steepen*, *tarten*, *tauten*) for the simple reason that the suffix has ceased to be available for those individuals for whom the institutionalized types are lexically calcified. This does not mean, of course, that native speakers cannot process these

---

[14] E-language is a difficult concept. As in Miller (2010), it will be understood here as a collectivity of I-language utterances within one or more speech communities of varying size (to be identified in each case) and circumscribed in time. This formulation is advantageous in historical perspective where only attestations and no grammaticality judgments are available.

forms. Because the derivation of similar forms is well known to every native speaker, novel -*en* formations are readily understood even by those of us who would never use them.

I-language brings in the aspect of individual background and creativity. A typical view is that there is no contradiction between productivity and creativity: "productivity is a matter of time. Creative patterns may develop into productive ones" (Fischer 1998: 1). This defines productivity in terms of the E-language and creativity in terms of I-language. Indeed, creativity—the ability to break formulaicity and re-form patterns (Carter 2004; Bell 2012)—is individual-specific, but productivity is also relevant on an individual basis. What must ultimately be investigated is (i) the extent to which I-language productivity can spread to other individuals and eventually lead to E-language productivity, and (ii) the means by which E-language productivity is ignored by some individuals and as a consequence diminishes. These issues will not be examined in this work.

1.9 Features and feature change

In recent years there has been a shift from syntactic parameters to lexical features which determine the parameters and their values. It was unclear how the species-specific rules, constraints, principles, parameters, etc., which had been attributed to UG (Universal Grammar), could have evolved (Chomsky 2007). Chomsky (2005) proposes special design features of language that include genetic endowment (a universal inventory of formal features), experience, and principles not specific to the faculty of language. Under this conception, the variety of attested I-languages must be accounted for without UG or traditional parameters (Chomsky 2007: 4). Rather, innate lexical features have been proposed. Some of these features appear to go back to *Homo erectus* (van Gelderen 2012, w. lit).[15]

The lexicon contains feature information that is relevant to phonology, syntax, and semantics (Chomsky 1995: 230ff., 270–79). Formal features can be intrinsic (e.g. gender) or optional (case, number). More importantly, formal features divide into INTERPRETABLE features—those necessary for semantic interpretation (e.g. ±human)—and UNINTERPRETABLE features, which are valued and trigger some operation but have no semantic interpretation and are deleted in the phonological component.

Uninterpretable features include (structural) case and phi features such as person and number, which are copies of information already present in the syntactic computation and therefore require no semantic interpretation (Chomsky 2001; cf. 2004: 106ff.; 2005: 17ff.; 2007). Phonological features are accessed in the phonological component.

---

[15] Thanks to Elly van Gelderen for discussion of this section. For further details see van Gelderen (2012).

To illustrate loss of semantic features, consider the change of *will*, which in Old English had the features [volition, expectation, future] and today for most speakers has only [future] (van Gelderen, e.g. 2012). Van Gelderen (2011) posits a series of feature changes: semantic > interpretable > uninterpretable, parallel to Argument/Adjunct > Spec > Head. One of her examples is the agreement cycle: demonstrative/noun > emphatic subject > pronoun > agreement (Agr).

The last two stages can be exemplified by the Mongolian languages Khalkha and Buryat (cf. Miller 2010: 1.202ff., w. lit):

(13) Subject (> clitic) > agreement (Mongolian)
    (a) Khalkha
        med – ne   bi
        know-PRES   I
        'I know'
    (b) Buryat
        (bi)   *jaba-na-b*
        (I)   go-PRES-1SG
        'I am going'

The clitic pronoun in (13a) becomes the agreement marker in (13b). The emphatic pronoun remains optional/emphatic in (13b).

The feature changes in the complete cycle would be as follows: the noun has semantic features and an interpretable phi (person, number) feature. The change to an emphatic subject involves a renewal (even if the form remains the same) which contributes new (optional) semantic features (Elly van Gelderen, p.c.). In the change to a pronoun, an uninterpretable phi feature is acquired. In the final change to an agreement marker, the interpretable phi feature is reanalyzed as uninterpretable.

Just as children first acquire all features as (semantic or) interpretable and later (re)analyze some of them as uninterpretable (Radford 2000), so in language change semantic features are reanalyzed as interpretable and then as uninterpretable (van Gelderen 2011; 2012). One of van Gelderen's examples (2011: 7) is *I have a garden*, in which *have* has semantic features that are lost in *I have seen the garden*, where *have* is a probe for a lexical verb and as such has uninterpretable features.

Functional categories are not part of ordinary lexicogenesis. All the creativity in the world does not permit a speaker to invent a new article (determiner), complementizer, aspect marker, or preposition. The major exception seems to be that degree words are subject to constant renewal (§8.1), but these also have lexical meaning. Functional elements, as noted above, evolve by reanalysis and are not invented in language play—unless an entire language is being invented. In the realm of aspect, even such regionalisms as *fixing to* [1854] evolve by reanalysis from *fix* in the sense of 'decide, determine' [1788]. In practical terms, then, lexicogenesis is limited to lexical (non-functional) categories, and those have semantic features.

In the renewal of degree words, the first stage involves loss of semantic features. Consider *dead right* and *filthy rich*.[16] The "meaning" of the degree qualifiers is '(high) degree'; *dead* has lost its core semantic features of 'not alive', and *filthy* has lost semantic features pertaining to 'dirt', although the element of disdain remains present, and it is likely the lexical meaning that permits lexicogenic creation. To act as probe for an adjective, these degree words have acquired an uninterpretable degree feature.

Since lexical items are created with a meaning in mind, neologisms are necessarily equipped with appropriate semantic features. As to other features, if a noun, for instance, is created, it will bear such interpretable features as [±human] and uninterpretable phi features (person, number) for agreement (§1.3).

In summary, all morphological operations are determined by features. Functional markers (aspect, voice, tense, mood, etc.) have uninterpretable features to probe for the lexical items in their domain. Cause and Change of State project as verbalizers (§4.3f.) which, like Tense, have interpretable tense and aspect features but uninterpretable phi features (van Gelderen 2011: 10). Cultural/semantic affixes (evaluatives, evidentials, degree indicators, etc.) have features to project a head in syntax. And so on.

1.10 Lexicalization

For lexicographers, the lexicon includes all known words, but this is irrelevant to individuals, whose lexicon is far smaller and simultaneously much larger in terms of idiosyncratic words and uses, and continues to change through adulthood (Aitchison 2003). Among theoretical linguists there is no agreement on what the lexicon is or does. Lexicalization is equally enigmatic. Whether a derived word is registered in the lexicon or not is entirely theory-dependent and differs from one formal theory to another.

Lexicalization must also be considered in the context of the related issues of arbitrariness (which entails automatic lexical registration), conventionalization, and institutionalization, which are discussed in more detail in Chapter 5. Our focus in this section is on the generative framework and what little empirical evidence there is for the content of the lexicon.

Everyone acknowledges that basic words like *cat* must be registered in the lexicon for the simple reason that they are arbitrary (de Saussure 1916). The question is to what extent motivated words are also listed in the lexicon. Motivated can include anything from onomatopoeic, like *cuckoo* (which however remains arbitrary: §10.2), to morphologically complex words with compositional meaning, like *foolishnesslessness* (§2.7).

---

[16] As an extreme example, 'shit' means 'good' in many Germanic languages (Hamans 2013: 309).

On some accounts, frequency plays a major role. One standard doctrine is stated by Plag (2003: 53f.): "high-frequency words (e.g. *acceptable*) are more likely to be stored as whole words in the mental lexicon than are low-frequency words (e.g. *actualizable*)." Stated otherwise, a word like *actualizable* is readily composable/interpretable and therefore does not need to be stored. But does this entail that it not be stored? The storage hypothesis is extrapolated from psycholinguistic experiments which show that (i) the more frequently a lexical item is used the more quickly it is recognized (Whitney 1998, w. lit); (ii) unusual language takes longer to process (e.g. Millar 2011), suggesting storage of formulaic language (Conklin and Schmitt 2012); and (iii) high-frequency words are more easily activated, hence the assumption that they must be stored. However, it is also a fact that exceptions are processed more quickly than regular forms (Yang 2005; Yang et al. 2013).

The most easily activated words and phrases may be holistically stored for rapid retrieval, perhaps by means of a new neurological access pathway that bypasses the original componential route (Wray 2002; 2008; 2012: 234, w. lit). Whatever the means, there are differences between the processing of formulaic and non-formulaic language, even if there is no unique definition of formulaic language (Wray 2012, w. lit). Wray also mentions processing differences between unanalyzable strings (*hocus pocus, by and large*, etc.), transparent lexical bundles (*have a nice day*), metaphorical collocations (*spill the beans*), and so on. Crucially, frequency cannot be the only factor, since infrequent idioms and frequent lexical bundles have an equivalent processing advantage and, as noted above, irregular forms ('exceptions') are processed faster than regular forms. It turns out that SALIENCE is more important than frequency for both words and phrases. Wray (2012: 242ff.) discusses recent experiments which show that low-frequency words with a greater salience (those that attract more attention) are more easily recalled than high-frequency words. The flipside is that function words of even the highest frequency can be very low in salience.

It must be emphasized that lexical storage of whole words is not incompatible with morphological processing (Pinker and Prince 1988) or morphological derivation (Halle 1973; Yang 2005; Yang et al. 2013). Even though established words may have idiosyncrasies in meaning, speakers still recognize their structure—even if they regard e.g. *settlement* "as 'more affixed' than *government*" (Hay and Baayen 2005: 343)—and this must be captured, along with the relationship between the formal mechanisms that create new words and the analysis of existing words (Aronoff 1976; Anshen and Aronoff 1988; Selkirk 1982: 11f.; Yang 2005; Yang et al. 2013, etc.). It is generally assumed, then, that new/possible words are created by the same principles and rules that govern the form (constituency and constituent order) of existing words. Aronoff (1983) reports on experiments showing that the more productive the morphology, the less likely speakers are to be able to distinguish actual (by assumption listed) from potential words. He concludes that actual/potential is not a useful criterion. See, however, §1.8 for the importance of potential word formation as an ingredient of productivity.

Many discussions assume that lexicalization is

a gradual, historical process, involving phonological and semantic changes and the loss of motivation. These changes may be combined in a single word.... The process of lexicalization in general, as well as its result, namely the irregularity of the lexicon, can only be explained historically. (Lipka 2002: 113)

One problem with that statement is that historical changes do not occur in a vacuum. "Since they occur in real time in some synchronic system, they necessarily interact with and are constrained in the same manner as other properties in the same grammar" (Miller 2010: 1.36). A second problem is that not everyone agrees that the lexicon is the repository of the irregular. It is true that any form or phrase that does not conform to rules of form or interpretation must be memorized by the native speaker and therefore listed in the lexicon (in all theories). For Di Sciullo and Williams (1987: 14ff.) the lexicon is indeed about the lawless, and listedness is claimed to be irrelevant to word formation because some syntactic objects must also be listed, along with many derived words and a number of compounds.

Aronoff (1988: 787) reiterates his view that lexical listing is necessary to capture blocking, e.g. of *stealer* by *thief*, and account for the inheritance by derivatives of idiosyncrasies in form and meaning. However, blocking itself may be nothing more than an optimality consideration regarding synonyms, given that *stealer* is becoming very popular (§2.1). In this instance, however, since *thief* is an arbitrary lexical item it must be registered in the lexicon regardless of whether it blocks *stealer* or not. The blocking argument would be compelling only if there are examples in the other direction, where a derived formation blocks an underived one. The obscure *cooper* is usually replaced by *barrel-maker* in American English, but this is not blocking so much as a compositional alternative for a little-used word. More common historically is a semantic split between a transparent form like *goodest* and the less transparent *best* (§8.1). This relates to compositionality rather than lexicalization *per se*.

As emphasized by Hohenhaus (2005: 357), conjectures about the lexicon range from maximally rich (including all existing words) to the minimal lexicon in which only the idiosyncratic/unpredictable is listed. The latter has been generally assumed as an economy measure in the generative framework (Aronoff 1976; Kiparsky 1982a; 1982b; etc.), but (i) there is no unequivocal evidence for any of these positions, and (ii) it remains nothing more than an assumption that economy is relevant to natural languages or should play a role in evaluating grammars.

Hohenhaus (2005) discusses lexicalization in the context of institutionalization. Institutionalized words are those which belong to the norm of the community and are generally known to most members of that community (cf. Fischer 1998: 172; Hohenhaus 2005). He concludes that the lexicon has to be more than a simple list of 'words'. Rote-learning, memorized building blocks of various sizes and associations between them, form a large and integral part of 'lexical knowledge' alongside (competence-)knowledge of morphemes plus the productive morphological rule-system for on-line (de-)composition of complex words. In short, lexicalization/listing is of great relevance even beyond word-formation! (Hohenhaus 2005: 371)

Some models of phonology require more than just listing of the unpredictable. One hypothesis of speakers' knowledge is the principle of LEXICAL RESTRUCTURING: a form is (re)lexicalized in its (new) output shape unless there is good reason for it not to be.[17] The question is, what constitutes good evidence? This issue is taken up in Miller (2010: 1.146–50), who concludes:

phonetic details are more perceptually salient, probably for semantic reasons bound to particular lexical items, than previously realized. These phonetic details have important implications for derivation and for change, especially in the realm of derivatives becoming dissociated from their bases and evolving into separate lexical items. (Miller 2010: 1.150)

In other words, there is suggestive evidence for the potential lexicalization of all output forms, consistent with "the more general view in memory research that any experience leaves a memory trace" (Hay and Baayen 2005: 343, w. lit). This is supported by the numerous formations produced by analogy with existing constructs, no matter how derivationally complex or easily derived, which in turn presupposes a mental lexicon of those constructs. In Dutch, for example, stem alternants of adjectives like *goed* 'good', inflected *goede* [ɣudə] ~ [ɣuyə], must be lexically listed to predict derivatives: *goed-ig* [ɣudəχ] ~ [ɣuyəχ] 'good-natured' but *goeierd* [ɣuyərt] (*[ɣudərt]) 'good-natured person' (Booij 2009: 500f.).

The lexicon in Distributed Morphology[18] is directly relevant to chapter 4, and is therefore introduced here. It also contributes another dimension on the uses of the lexicon(s) and ties up some loose ends from other sections of this chapter. In Distributed Morphology there is no morphological component and no word formation in the lexicon. The lexicon is a "list of atomic elements for syntactic composition" (Marantz 1997: 201). There are three non-computational lists:

(a) The *narrow lexicon* (also called *syntactic terminals*) contains the list of roots and abstract morphemes (mentioned in several places in this chapter) that feed the computational operation of Merge. The abstract/functional morphemes consist entirely of non-phonetic features, like [pl] (plural) or the

---

[17] Compare Gess (2003: 77): "As a change spreads, some speakers will begin to store some of the output forms (i.e., the most frequent ones) as lexical representations, through lexical optimization (according to which underlying representations directly reflect output forms, unless alternations dictate otherwise...)." In Optimality Theory, one suggested generalization is FAITH-lex, "which requires faithfulness to an input lexeme" (Cho 2009: 463).

[18] http://www.ling.upenn.edu/~rnoyer/dm/

features that comprise the determiner D. Roots include √CAT, √OX, √SIT, which are sequences of phonological features, plus, in some cases, non-phonological diacritics (Embick and Noyer 2007). These bundles of features have no phonetic realization.

(b) The *encyclopedia* registers meanings and relates vocabulary items to meanings. Marantz (1995; 1997) argues that the word is no different from a phrasal idiom with respect to idiosyncratic meaning, although there are differences in complexity (Wulff 2013). This list contains phrasal idioms, such as *kick the bucket*, idiosyncratic word meanings, such as the entity rather than process meaning of *transmission* (Aronoff 1976), and also captures the inherent semantic arbitrariness of the open-class roots (*cat, dog,...*). L-morphemes (similar to traditional lexical morphemes), then, consist of phonological representations with encyclopedic (not featural) meanings, and are always idioms. This list is consulted subsequent to the output of interpretation in the phonological component (PHON) and the semantic component (SEM).

(c) The *vocabulary* is the list of exponents that provides phonological content (which may be null) to the abstract morphemes in the terminal nodes together with rules of insertion. One vocabulary item (root or functional head) is inserted into one terminal node. Since this is post-syntactic, it is referred to as *Late Insertion*. This list is consulted at PHON and contains the rules that supply the phonological exponents to the abstract morphemes (Embick and Noyer 2007).

The explicit claim of the Distributed Morphology model is that phonological, structural, and semantic representations are separate.[19] One reason for this is that people can think of a concept but not its phonological form, or a word's form but cannot access its meaning, or they may recall the syllable structure but not the target word, and so on. In short, words are stored in many forms, e.g. by morphological composition (a speaker cannot think of a word but knows it has an *-ity* suffix), meaning or semantic class (a speaker cannot think of *zucchini* but knows it is a kind of squash), phonological structure (a speaker cannot think of *Minelli* but knows it has three syllables, or substitutes *Monty E. Python* for *Milton E. Proby*), etc. (Miller 2010: 1.98–102).

To this can be added the hypothesis in §1.9 that the lexicon contains feature information which is relevant to phonology, syntax, and semantics. Despite the redundancy, then, the lexicon(s) must contain a large amount of information relevant to all words or potential words.

To conclude this section, lexicalization, or the listing of a form in the lexicon (or combination of lexicons), is theory-dependent. What little empirical evidence exists

---

[19] This general idea is not new. For example, Szymanek (1988) separates cognitive categories (concepts), derivational categories (functions/meanings), and derivational exponents (formatives).

suggests that, despite redundancy, all words, regardless of how produced or compositional, are subject to registration in the mental lexicon (cf. Anshen and Aronoff 1988). This does not mean they will be. It remains a matter of selection as to which output forms get lexicalized on an I-language basis, and which of those in turn get institutionalized on an E-language basis. The less compositional a form is, the more subject it is to lexicalization, which also correlates with changes in meaning along non-compositional lines.

1.11 Summary

Of the many uses and definitions of *word*, this work will be concerned with phonological, prosodic, and morphological properties. When unspecified, *word* denotes the composite of roots and formatives (constituent parts) that make up a (real or potential) syntactic head. Headedness is an important property of words and phrases. Core word formation is hierarchical, like syntactic structures, and for that reason is considered syntactic in some frameworks. It will be argued in subsequent chapters that lexicogenesis by prosodic templates and certain other means may yield a syntactic head that is not hierarchical.

Inflection in this work is restricted to agreement and concord material that is adjoined at spellout as a result of the Agree features from the syntactic computation.

Derivation of lexical items (nouns, verbs, etc.) is effected by various means, including affixation, stem change, apophony (vowel gradation), accent, and conversion, all effected by features. Conversion will be particularly important in this work because many new words are productively formed by attraction of a root or a categorized item into an empty head bearing category and other (e.g. event) features.

Backformation is meaningful only in the perspective of the history of the E-language. In terms of I-languages (individual grammars), all forms are synchronically derivable which entails that inputs to a given computation are lexically listed, or assumed by the speaker to be lexically listed.

Productivity is necessarily defined with reference to a domain of application, including the constraints to be discussed in Chapter 2. It has also been formulated in terms of I-language rather than E-language for the simple reason that a given affix or process is never available to every individual to coin novel words. In historical perspective, of course, only E-language is accessible, requiring decisions on whether a cluster of new formations in a given period indicates productivity for a large segment of the population or not. At any time in history, however, it is the creativity of individuals (I-languages) that yields neologisms. Creative neologisms provide a lot of information about productive word formation processes (Schröder and Mühleisen 2010: 55).

Lexicalization is here defined with reference to I-language and institutionalization with respect to E-language.

2

Productivity and constraints

This chapter illustrates some of the potential, ephemeral, categorical, and processing constraints on derivations that appear to inhibit productivity. A morpheme can be productive if the constraints are reckoned as part of its domain of application. Most constraints are violable in varying degrees in different contexts. At least syntactic and semantic constraints cannot be broken without a change in the lexical features. Affix recursivity is subject to the constraint that the iterations must be processable. Three scalar degrees are approaching the upper limits of processing. More repetitions become difficult and are apt to be given a simple emphatic interpretation.

2.1 Blocking

This section argues that blocking has been overused in the literature. Apart from a few technical uses that are theory-specific, the main type is token or synonymy blocking, which amounts to a preference for contrast or avoiding synonyms (cf. Kiparsky 1983; Sproat 1985; Plag 1999; Giegerich 2001; Rainer 2005a). It is readily overridden by individual creativity.

The idea of blocking is "the nonoccurrence of one form due to the simple existence of another" (Aronoff 1976: 43). Aronoff's assumptions are summarized by Embick and Marantz (2008: 19): (i) each lexical item is associated with a set of meaning cells to be occupied by one phonological form each; (ii) the competition that results in blocking is between words that share the same root; (iii) since only elements that are irregular in some way must be listed, blocking can obtain only between irregular or unproductive formations; (iv) the objects in competition by virtue of blocking are words.

In a series of papers over the past few decades Paul Kiparsky has presented a number of different views of how blocking works. In his early model of lexical phonology and morphology (Kiparsky 1982a; 1982b), blocking is accounted for by level ordering coupled with the Elsewhere Condition, which gives applicational precedence to listed/irregular forms: "blocking is pre-emption by prior application" (Kiparsky 1982b: 136). English denominal and deverbal derivation figure prominently. Level 1 suffixes, e.g. *-tion*, *-ce*, can make verbs (cf. *to commission, reverence*), but productive (level 2) suffixes like -*er* make (zero-derived) deverbal nouns (cf. *a sticker*) but not denominal verbs.[1] Exceptions involving level 1 are often lexical gaps, but exceptions involving level 2 suffixes are problematic. The non-existence of **to singer* is accounted for but verbs like *to scavenger* [1843], *waiter* [1862], etc., are not.

Sproat (1985: 566ff.) argues that blocking is a more general phenomenon, independent of level ordering. With reference to denominal and deverbal derivation he suggests that, since level 1 -*ity* and level 2 -*ness* are semantically similar, whatever rules out **to scarcity* should rule out **to promptness*, **to scarceness*.

The nonexistence of **to singer* might be accounted for by token blocking by the existing verb *to sing*, which would not differ in meaning from a putative **to singer*. On this type of account, *fail* blocks **to failure*, but the absence of **to cult* allows *to culture*. *To mirror* has no base **mirr*. *Edit* normally blocks *to editor* [1961]. *Err* blocks *to error* [1× 1828], but the *Urban Dictionary* quotes "The computer program keeps erroring"[2] (with a more specialized meaning than *err* has?). Where a corresponding verb does not exist or does not have the same meaning, blocking cannot apply, allowing *to skewer* [1701], *lawyer* [1797], *router* [1890], and the more recent verbs *sticker* [1976], *feeder* [1988] (§1.4), *stockbroker* [n.d.]. I recently heard a person trying to rid the house of woodpeckers say, "I chased it from one spot and it started woodpeckering on the other side." This may be language play but illustrates the same productivity of denominal -*er* derivation.

For Giegerich (2001) synonymy blocking of lexically unrelated words with the same meaning, e.g. *bitch/*dogess, pork/*pig meat*, is no different from the blocking of lexically related forms: a root (level 1) formation like *warmth* blocks a level 2 productive derivative like **warmness*. An important part of his argument is that some examples of synonymy blocking are based on insufficient semantic analysis. In this case, *warmness* is attested in the *OED* since Ælfric (Old English), and Dirk (2006) found about 64,900 entries of *warmness* on Yahoo, where it is not clear if a difference from *warmth* is intended or not. She also found that creativity overrides synonymy blocking which at most constitutes a preference, e.g. *stealer* got about 430,000 hits on Yahoo, 5% of the number of entries for its supposed blocker *thief*. *Stealer* is attested since 1508 (*OED*), and in Shakespeare *stealers* means 'hands' (*Hamlet* III.ii.323). Additionally, *thief* usually implies professional or habitual stealing:

If *stealer* is used when *thief* exists, there might be strong motivation ('Contrast') for the hearer to assume that *stealer* does not mean what *thief* means.... while there is potentially some sort of interaction between *thief* and the hypothetical root nominalization *stealer*, it is not

---

[1] Examples of denominal verb formation (the third stage in (7) in §1.4) are rarer today than around the end of c16 (Konkol 1960): *(to) buckler* [a.1593], *exception, intelligence, intercession, remembrance, reprisal, supplication*—all [1593], *character* [1594], *commotion* [1599], *indulgence* [1599], *epistle* [1671]. Why the derivational cycle should be more constrained today than formerly is not clear.

[2] www.urbandictionary.com/define.php?term=erroring&defid=2432130

competition for grammaticality. Rather, the effect has to do with what a root nominalization *stealer* could be used for (in terms of semantic space) given that *thief* exists. Thus, there is no blocking effect that determines what is grammatical and what is not; any effect of *thief* on *stealer* has to do with how objects that are generated by the grammar might be employed, not with whether the object in question can be generated in the first place.

(Embick and Marantz 2008: 16)

Moreover, *stealer* is like *breaker* in normally requiring an object, e.g. *girlfriend-stealer*, *scene-stealer*, etc., like *rule-breaker*, *heart-breaker* (§2.4; Embick and Marantz 2008: 15). While *password-thief* makes as much sense as *password-stealer*, in baseball only a *base-stealer* is plausible. A *base-thief* could only be someone who habitually picks up the bases and absconds with them.

This view of blocking differs markedly from recent Optimality Theory approaches (e.g. Kiparsky 2010), where blocking is a filter that applies to the output of the generative system and resolves competition between all potentially competing expressions whose meaning is compatible with a given input or intended meaning. Faithfulness requires an exponent for each category and markedness requires that it be single. The correct outputs are produced by ranking markedness and faithfulness. Reranking allows for overt competition, but since reranking is always after the fact, nothing is actually predicted. And this type of account is inadequate to handle the *thief/stealer* problem.

According to Embick (2007) and Embick and Marantz (2008), (i) there is no blocking between words or between words and phrases (or larger objects), and (ii) blocking in the sense of competition for the expression of syntactic or semantic features is limited to the insertion of the phonological exponents (or vocabulary items) of those features. All morphology in the Distributed Morphology model is syntactic, which accounts for POSER BLOCKING (Poser 1992), the alleged blocking of larger structures (phrases) by single words. Comparatives like *smarter* appear to block (*)*more smart*, but in a syntactic model of morphology, the same structure underlies both. When the degree element *-er* and the adjective *smart* combine into a single complex head, the output is *smarter*. With longer words, like *intelligent*, there is no complex head formation, and the output is *more intelligent* rather than *intelligenter (Embick and Marantz 2008: 8f., 44–8).

In the example of *stealer/thief*, it is not a question of grammatical blocking but of function. Since several different functions have existed for *stealer*, the formation is acceptable. This does not preclude the possibility that some speakers may simply prefer a more transparent, compositional term. Examples exist like the replacement of *cooper* by *barrel-maker*, and the partial functional split between *goodest* and *best* (§1.10). *Cooper* shows that one factor is salience; cf. "the higher the frequency of the blocking word, the stronger the blocking effect" (Rainer 2005a: 337). Conversely, one can extrapolate that a rare word of limited salience has next to no blocking effect.

Goodest shows that another factor is function: token blocking is irrelevant if a derived form is semantically different.

Much putative synonymy blocking in the literature (see Giegerich 2001) does not hold. For instance, **dogess* is not blocked by *bitch* because (i) despite (borrowed) *lioness, tigress, -ess* is not a simple feminine suffix (Miller 1983), and (ii) as *bitch* becomes more of a human derogative, its canine function is frequently replaced by *female dog*. If there is any synonymy blocking, this is the output that should be blocked. *Pig meat* is not blocked by *pork* for the simple reason that (at least in some varieties of American English) *pork* is used of specific cuts or culinary preparations of pig meat. *Deer meat* is often substituted for *venison*, which is not generally applied to *reindeer (meat)* at all.

Then there is the matter of PARTIAL BLOCKING. For instance, from *furious* there is no **furiosity* (cf. *curious–curiosity*), which is supposedly blocked by *fury*, but that does not block *furiousness*. Likewise, *glory* supposedly blocks **gloriosity* but not *gloriousness*. Aronoff (1976) attributes *gloriousness* etc. to the productivity of *-ness* and suggests that blocking applies only to a listed form like *glory* which takes the place of **gloriosity*. For Embick and Marantz (2008: 21–5) there is no need to prevent **gloriosity*, which is not generated because *-ness* is stipulated as the phonological form of the abstract nominal to *glorious*. Paradoxically, they acknowledge that *gloriosity* does in fact exist, primarily in a religious sense, implying a structure *glori-osity* (an 'emphatic' to *glory*) rather than a derivative of *glorious*. *Gloriosity* as an emphatic for *glory* accounts for one of the uses, but the split between *gloriousness* and *gloriosity* is similar to that between *hyperactiveness* and *hyperactivity, audaciousness* and *audacity*, etc. (Giegerich 2001; Miller 2012: 178f.—both w. lit). The rarity of *gloriosity* in the latter sense is due to the fact that its usefulness is limited.

Meibauer (2014) accepts the view of Traugott (2004: 19) that "anti-synonymy, in so far as it operates, does so AFTER a form has come into existence; it does not block innovation but rather motivates realignment among forms competing over time."

Blocking has undergone many transformations. All attempts to make it a grammatical constraint have failed. What token blocking exists is a manifestation of the AVOID SYNONYMY principle (§2.5.4). As such, it is a matter of personal preference for contrast or the avoidance of perceived synonyms. This is evident from the fact that synonymy blocking is overridden by individual creativity, and appears to be irrelevant in clips (Meibauer 2014) and in slang (§5.2), but see §15.3.

2.2 Phonological constraints

Many kinds of phonological constraint have been discussed in the literature. A sampling is reviewed here. It must be emphasized that different formatives are sensitive to different phonological constraints, and some constraints can apply at one stage in a language's history but not another.

2.2.1 The haplological constraint

The haplological constraint involves an IDENTITY sequencing prohibition, also in some contexts called the OBLIGATORY CONTOUR PRINCIPLE (OCP), e.g. *sheepish, farmerish* but **fishish, *rubbishish; shortage* but **largeage; treasonous* but **menaceous, towelette* but **carpetette; novelly* but ([simple +ly] >) *simply, pro(ba)bly, Glou(ce)ster, humb(le)ly*, etc. (Dressler 1977: 41; Malkiel 1977; Yip 1998; Raffelsiefen 1999: 241–52; Miller 2010: 1.67, w. lit).

The progressive of the verb *lightning* [1903], as in *It's thundering and —*, should be *lightninging*, but is usually *lightning* (Stemberger 1981).

The suffix *-ify* excludes identical consecutive onsets, as in **stiffify, *toughify* (LSDE 247).

The suffix *-ity* obeys the constraint in never attaching to bases ending in *t* (**contentity, *ineptity, *abstractity, *covertity, *perfectity*), which is remarkable in light of borrowed *entity, identity, quantity, sanctity, vastity* (LSDE 27).

One nearly universal exception to the haplological constraint is reduplication, e.g. G *léloipa* 'I have left', perfect of *leípō* 'I leave'. This may imply that the domain of the haplological constraint prototypically does not involve the left edge of the word. More to the point, languages with the less frequent right-edge reduplication suggest that haplology is morpheme-specific.

2.2.2 Stress clash

STRESS CLASH prevents a number of otherwise wellformed combinations: *màrketéer* but **stòre-éer, càmeléer* but **giràffe-éer*, etc.; *rùralìze* but **políte-ìze, wómanìze* but **gírlìze*, etc. (Raffelsiefen 1999: 231–6; cf. Rainer 2005a: 344). On exceptions like *banálìze*, see Plag (1999: 166f., 183ff.).

The suffix *-ation* does not attach to iambic bases (**distùrbátion*) unless the stress can shift, as in *ìnspirátion* (LSDE 98); *-ify* allows up to two unstressed syllables. Contrast *solídify* with **beaútifulìfy*, but restressed *?beaùtifúlìfy* is not as bad (LSDE 247).

2.2.3 The homophony constraint

The HOMOPHONY CONSTRAINT makes phonological and morphological operations sensitive to the amount of homophony they create among distinct lexical items (Kaplan 2011). For instance, Latin ablatives like *fugā* do not undergo iambic shortening because they would merge with nominative *fuga* 'flight' (Miller 2010: 1.188ff.). Homophonic avoidance in paradigms is well established. For instance, in Icelandic the genitive plural *-na* continues to be replaced by the more regular *-a* except in neuters, where it would be identical to the nominative singular, e.g. *tunga* 'tongue', *auga* 'eye' (Baerman 2011: 23f.). For avoidance of pernicious homophony, see §7.3

(end). The reason is maintenance (or establishment) of contrasts important to communication:

> Phonological contrast exists in order to serve lexical contrasts. This paper adds to evidence in the literature that phonological rules are sensitive, either directly or indirectly, not just to high-level phonological contrasts but also to the lexical contrasts that are ultimately crucial for successful communication. (Kaplan 2011: 667)

2.2.4 Dissimilatory constraint

Early Latin had a constraint barring *l...l*, e.g. *nāvālis* NAVAL but **lūnālis* > *lūnāris* LUNAR (not **lunal*). Miller (2006/2012: 135-8) records 37 different examples of the Latin 'lunar' type. In post-Classical Latin the constraint was relaxed; cf. *lēgālis* [Quintilian] LEGAL, *locālis* [c2^b] LOCAL, etc.

2.2.5 Arbitrary constraints

A combination of arbitrary phonological constraints applied to *-en* affixation from its inception (Jespersen 1942: 355f.; Miller 2010: 2.114f., w. lit; cf. §5.3 below):

(1) Constraints on *-en* affixation

i	ii	iii	iv
tough-en	*earnest-en	*firm-en	*numb-en
weak-en	*modest-en	*shy-en	*blond-en
crisp-en	*basic-en	*full-en	*grand-en
brisk-en	*stubborn-en	*dear-en	*orang(e)-en
swift-en	*vivid-en	*clean-en	*round-en
length-en	*seductive-en	*slow-en	*strange-en

The wellformed group (i) consists of monosyllabic roots ending in an obstruent (*whiten*, *redden*) or cluster (*crispen*, *swiften*).³ The sonority (§9.1) of root-final consonants must be no higher than a fricative or stop. Group (ii) shows that non-trochaic feet (§9.2) are excluded. Constraint (iii) prohibits roots ending in a sonorant. Constructs like **easyen*, **yellowen* are predicted to be illformed because they violate both the non-trochaic foot constraint (ii) and the root-final sonorant constraint (iii). Group (iv) shows that *-en* does not attach to bases ending in a nasal plus voiced consonant.

In German, denominal verb conversion is impossible if the noun ends in a vowel, e.g. **kaffee-(e)n* 'drink coffee', **taxi-en* 'go by taxi', but Dutch does not have this

---

³ In the older formations, /t/ was deleted after a fricative and before *-(e)n*, e.g. *fasten* /fǽsən/, *listen* /lísən/. Deletion of /t/ remained productive until more recently, when words like *swiften* [1638] with [t] were introduced. That *t*-deletion had nothing to do with verbs in *-en per se* is clear from words like *often*.

constraint: *koffie-en* 'drink coffee', *taxi-en* 'go by taxi' (Don 2005a; 2005b; García Velasco 2009: 1182).

2.3 Affixal restrictions

Formatives can be restricted to particular bases, e.g. English *-ric* is limited to *bishop*, and *-ter* occurs only in *laughter* and *slaughter* (Bauer 2001: 135).

Coinages with *-ity* are restricted to certain Latinate affixes, most notably *-al* (*marginality*), *-able* (*drinkability*), *-id* (*pinguidity*). Raffelsiefen (1999: 259f.) also mentions *-ous* in this connection (*generous : generosity*), but that alternation obtains mostly in borrowings. English *-ous* coinages do not typically make *-osity* nouns (e.g. *glamorous : *glamorosity*) because *-ness* is more productive (Aronoff 1976: 37–45). However, (i) *-ness* and *-ity* are not synonymous but select different domains of their adjectival bases (Miller 2012: 177ff.; Baeskow 2012, both w. lit), and (ii) although not recognized by the *OED*, *glamorosity* gets many hits on Google, illustrating that people invent forms all the time whether or not they are recognized by lexicographers or predicted by linguists. As to *-osity* derivatives in general, Arnold Zwicky observes the following in his Language Log (3/1/2007):[4]

> The suffix *-ity* isn't really productive. Some abstract nouns in *-ity* (like *curiosity*) are established and reasonably frequent, but outside of this set, such nouns are conspicuous. They stand out as fresh creations, and are likely to be seen as special in meaning or use: choosing a noun in *-ity* instead of using an existing abstract noun (*furiosity* instead of *fury*) or forming a noun with *-ness*, the all-purpose suffix deriving abstract nouns from adjectives (*fabulosity* instead of *fabulousness*), will suggest that you intend to convey something other than mere abstraction. Maybe you're conveying something more than mere abstraction (fabulosity is especially fabulous), or something less (seriosity is hedged seriousness), or you're ostentatiously playing with the language.

Indeed, as noted by Baayen (2006: 20), "morphological categories might be more productive in some registers than in others".

Verbs in *-ify* preferentially derive nominalizations in *-ification* (Bauer 2001: 142, 182; cf. Plag 1999: esp. 192–204).

The only nominal that can affix to English *-ize* is *-ation* (Rainer 2005a: 342f., w. lit). Beyond that, *-(a)tion* is restricted to Latinate vocabulary, and not used on native bases: **break-(a)tion*, **kill-(a)tion*, including denominals like **cork(a)tion*, **hammer(a)tion*. *Flirtation* [1718], *starvation* [1778] are among the few exceptions (Marchand 1969: 260). Rare others like *backwardation* are not in general use or are jocular/exclamatory (*thunderation*), and the effect is due to violation of the Latinate

---

[4] itre.cis.upenn.edu/%7Emyl/languagelog/archives/004254.html

constraint (Plag 1999: 70f.; Bauer 2001: 182f.; Miller 2006: 97f.; 2012: 179f.).[5] This is in fact a pragmatic or sociolinguistic restriction: "Learnèd affixes... are often limited to learnèd bases, and when they are applied to ordinary words, jocular effects may arise" (Rainer 2005a: 349).

Violation of an affixal restriction explains the effect of such forms as *womanity* [1836] and *governator* [1× 1522], recently [c.2002] applied (after his role in the 'Terminator' series) as a blend (§12.1) to Arnold Schwarzenegger when campaigning for governor of California, and now he is 'The Governator' in an animated TV series.[6] Similar is *confessionator* [n.d.], cited by Munat (2007b: 171).

Lexical constraints can have phonological sensitivity, e.g. deverbal nominalizing -*al* attaches only to bases with main stress on the final syllable: *refúsal, arríval*, but *abólishal, *devélopal, etc. (Carstairs-McCarthy 1998). Giegerich (2001) adds that the verbs are usually resultative-transitive eventive verbs, e.g. *acquittal, perusal, referral, rehearsal, renewal, withdrawal*. This does not explain *arrival*. Another formulation is that -*al* attaches only to Latinate prefix-root verbs that happen to have final stress (Rainer 2005a: 344f., w. lit), but that does not predict that *derival, *reduceal, etc. are illformed. This motivates the formulation that final stress is a necessary but not a sufficient condition for -*al* affixation because of gaps like *derival beside *arrival* (Kaisse 2005: 32). In fact, there is a large number of gaps (Giegerich 2001): *appeasal, *enactal, *improval, *incital, *investal, *procural, etc. Giegerich takes this to mean that -*ment* is more productive than -*al*, and is favored by bases eligible for both.

The major domain of -*ment* is to verbs in -*ish*: *accomplishment, establishment*, etc. But even here, -*ment* occasionally yields to other suffixes, *diminishment* to *diminution*, *publishment* to *publication*, etc. (Bauer 2001: 138). The absence of *breakment, *killment, etc. shows that -*ment* never became totally productive in English (*LSDE* 78f.).

Lexical constraints seem able to be violated freely in popular speech, as reported by Arnold Zwicky (citing several blogs in the Language Log entry above) in connection with -*ness*:

(2) Extensions of -*ness*
 N + -*ness* = N: *mathness, schoolness, paperness*,...
 V + -*ness* = N: *studyness, typeness, swimness*,...
 V + -*ness* = V: *not much time to writeness*; *while i studyness all the time*
 Adj + -*ness* = Adj: *It's the wonderfulness poem*; *that is very coolness*

These appear to illustrate Bauer's point that productivity is not to be determined by playful formations that ignore the meaning of a morpheme (§1.8). However, since

---

[5] Since speakers are unaware of etymology, Latinate affixes can be reformulated as attaching to a stem, vs. native affixes which attach to a phonological word (Plag 1999: 58ff., 87ff.; cf. Selkirk 1982: 95ff.).

[6] Ironically, *governor* [a.1300] (from French) goes back to L *gubernātor* 'ship's pilot', a formation similar to *governator*, but *govern* [1297] has been assimilated (§8.7) to English, rendering *governator* comical.

some of the types in (2) go back nearly a century, one can inquire whether a morpheme's meaning is determined by theoretical linguists or by the people who use the language. Older examples include *we-ness* [1920], *on-the-make-ness* [1923], *moneyness* [1936], *middle-of-the-road-ness* [1994], etc. (cf. Baeskow 2012: 9, 28). *Wonderfulness* [1385] and *coolness* [OE] have long histories.

Zwicky adds that in his experience, nouns in *-ness* are the most productive of the types in (2), and in a follow-up blog (May 12) adds nouns in *-iness*.[7]

One is also reminded of such popular formations as *do-gooder* [1901] (for *gooddoer*) and *jump-roping* [n.d.] (for *rope-jumping*).

On a more general note, the ordinary principles of affixation can be suspended or expanded in language play. Bloomfield (1933: 180) cites *devil-may-care-ish*, and Spencer (2005: 83) mentions *a why-does-it-have-to-be-me-ish* expression. *Moreish* [1691] means 'causing one to want *more* (food or drink)'. In *all-overish* [1832], *-ish* has an indefinite distributed meaning. Finally, *-ish* can attract other suffixes, as in *an I-dont-know-howishness* [1815].

While *-ism* has special properties (§9.5), Colbert's *orthodox owning-a-sailboat-ism* ("The Colbert Report" (TV), 2/13/2012) is independent in the sense that one might refer to *orthodox owning-a-sailboat-ness*. A person could be described as *orthodox owning-a-sailboat-istic* and so on. An atheist friend described himself as an *I-don't-give-a-damn-ist*. Native speakers know immediately what these constructs are intended to mean, whether they would use them or not. All of this emphasizes the extent to which productivity and expressivity must be defined in terms of individual creativity (§1.8). The special effect derives from the stretch of ordinary morphology.

2.4 Syntactic constraints

A prototypical transitive verb has two arguments, an Actor and an Undergoer (patient/theme), which can be represented informally as 1<2>. The notation expresses the leading idea that the actor is *external* to the VP, not selected by the verb, while the patient/theme argument is a complement of the verb *internal* to the VP (§1.1). The numerical notation also has the advantage of avoiding arbitrary labels of the roles played by the arguments or so-called THEMATIC ROLES (θ-/THETA-ROLES, for short).[8]

One of the main syntactic constraints for our purposes is that in a compound like *rat-eating*, *rat* must be the complement, never the subject (§3.2). A verb must merge

---

[7] itre.cis.upenn.edu/%7Emyl/languagelog/archives/004254.html
[8] The θ-role of the external argument (1-role) varies with the predicate, and is compositionally assigned by the verb and its internal arguments, as illustrated in (i) (cf. Chomsky 1981: 103ff.; Miller 2010: 1.149).

(i)   (a) *The Gator threw the football*   (*Gator* = Agent)
    (b) *The Gator threw a party*   (*Gator* = Source)
    (c) *The Gator threw a knee*   (*Gator* = Experiencer)

first with an internal argument (object), not with the subject which is external to the core VP, as illustrated in (3).

(3) Transitive shell: light verb version (Chomsky 1995: 315, 352)

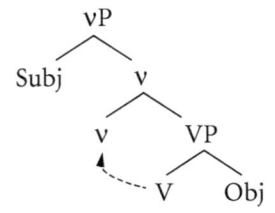

```
           vP
          /  \
       Subj   v
             / \
            v   VP
            ↑  / \
            ⋯ V   Obj
```

According to Chomsky, *v* is a light verb, V raises overtly to the light verb *v*, forming the complex Vb = [*v* V n]. For more discussion of *v*[caus], see §4.3f.

Some derivatives may occur more frequently in composition for the simple reason that the verb is obligatorily transitive. For instance, since *solve* requires a direct object (cf. **Leslie solves*), *solver* cannot exist except when a complement is present, e.g. *solver of problems*, or in a compound like *problem-solver*. This is typical, as shown in (4).

(4) Non-idiosyncratic gaps in agentive formation
    (a) **solver*   but   *problem-solver*   (Miller 1993: 71)
    (b) **Löser*   but   *Problem-löser* 'id.' [German]   (Fanselow 1988: 103ff.)
    (c) **ḥallāl*   but   *ḥallāl mašākil* 'id.' [Arabic]   (Youssef Haddad, p.c.)

This distribution is typical also of change of state verbs whose complement is obligatory, e.g. **Kelly broke*, **breaker* 'one who breaks', but *idol-breaker, breaker of idols*. As an instrument, of course, *breaker* is fine. Also, elliptically for *horse-breaker* etc.

Word schema rules (e.g. Haspelmath 2002: 50, example 3.16) can derive *-er* nouns but cannot explain any of the syntactic properties, e.g. the fact that *trainer of dogs* must have trained some dogs while a *dogtrainer* could be a novice who has never trained any dogs (van Hout and Roeper 1998; Spencer 2005: 90).

Finally, **the writer of a newspaper column by a journalist* (Rappaport and Levin 1989; Grimshaw 1990: 142) shows the incompatibility of equivalent active *-er* and passive *by*. Lieber's (2004; 2005) feature account of *-er* as [+material, dynamic] does not explain any of these syntactic facts. Indeed [dynamic] predicts that *knower* [Ch.] and *haver* [1400] should not exist, but cf. *the knower of such information* [2000] etc.

2.5 Semantic constraints

A semantic constraint involves an incompatibility in meaning between a morpheme and a base, or between two morphemes, or even between two words. Of the four examples in this section, the first brings in thematic roles, the second the overlap of manner and instrument verbs with respect to *dis*-prefixation, the third individual- and stage-level predicates, and the fourth involves synonyms.

2.5.1 Thematic roles

As noted in §2.4, a prototypical transitive verb has two arguments, or THEMATIC ROLES (θ-/THETA-ROLES), an Actor/agent and an Undergoer/theme, which can be represented informally as 1<2>. Intransitive verbs have only one argument. This allows for two types of intransitive verbs, those with only a 1-role (UNERGATIVES) and those with only a 2-role (UNACCUSATIVES).

Since *-ee* is the 2-role of a typical transitive verb (cf. Sproat 1985: 321), a verb must have a 2-role in order to take *-ee* affixation. This implies that unaccusatives but not unergatives can take *-ee*, which is entirely correct (Miller 2010: 2.151, w. lit):

(5) (a) unaccusative: *arrivee, fallee, swellee, returnee, escapee*
    (b) unergative: **runnee, *coughee, *swimmee, *cryee, *sleepee, *sneezee*

While one could build into a word-formation rule the fact that **be-er, *seem-er, (late bloomer* but) **late/good-seemer*, Dutch **schijn-er* 'seemer', **blijk-er* 'appearer', etc., are impossible, such notations would be arbitrary and miss the point—in this case, that raising verbs assign no thematic roles (Miller 1993: 70f., w. lit). In general, verbs without thematic roles cannot take *-er*: **snower, *rainer*.[9]

2.5.2 Manner/instrument verbs and dis- prefixation

Another semantic constraint involves the inability of manner and instrument verbs to take *dis*- prefixation (cf. Lieber 2004: 116):

(6) (a) Manner of motion verbs: **diswalk, *disjog, *dismeander*
    (b) Instrument verbs: **dishammer, *disbicycle, *dissnowplow, *dischain*

Overlap between instrument and manner verbs is problematic for Rappaport Hovav and Levin (1998) because their fixed event structure template [x ACT < >], where x is a variable and ACT is the English noun, permits only one constant (manner, instrument, place, state) to be inserted in the angle brackets: e.g. if instrument is inserted, manner cannot be. Thus, a verb can be either an instrument verb or a manner verb, but not both. Kiparsky's LEXICALIZATION CONSTRAINT (1997: 490) has the same effect: "A verb can inherently express at most one semantic role (theme,

---

[9] Exceptions occur in language play, e.g. "It's a real *snower* today" would involve 'a major snowstorm'. Crucially, in this case *snower* is not compositionally derived but is analogical to "a real *howler*" 'wind storm', "a real *looker*" 'good-looker', *scorcher, sizzler*, etc. Similarly, the examples in (5b) can be created by transitivizing the verb. Poets play with thematic roles. For instance, translating the opening line of Vergil's *Aeneid* as 'Arms and the man I sing' implies *sing* as an ordinary transitive verb (i.e. taking more than cognate objects as in *sing a song*), in which case the 'man' could be described as the *singee*.

instrument, direction, path...)." Nevertheless, it seems entirely natural that instrument verbs should also be able to express manner (of motion), as in (*dis)bicycle. It is well known that languages tend to syncretize manner and instrument. This is true of case systems, e.g. the Latin ablative, the Greek dative (see Croft 1991; 1998), and of adpositions, e.g. Eng. *with* expresses both manner (*I did it with ease*) and instrument (*Gary sliced the turkey with a blunt knife*).

2.5.3 *Stage- and individual-level predicates*

The suffix *-ship* can only attach to stage-level predicates (Aronoff 2001). Stage-level predicates apply to temporary stages and typically express transient properties. By contrast, individual-level predicates are timeless and express stable or enduring properties of individuals. More simply, states can be temporary, variable, or permanent (*LSDE* §1.11, w. lit). Words denoting a temporary state, like *friend, king, airman*, can take *-ship*: *friendship, kingship, airmanship*. Those generally conceptualized as permanent states, like *parent, woman, niece*, do not fit well with *-ship*: ??*parentship*, ??*womanship*, ??*nieceship*. The power of tradition is exemplified by the strangeness of words like ??*wifeship*, ??*husbandship*, despite modern social mores that make wives and husbands disposable. Beyond that, of course, *-ship* expresses a relation on relational bases (*friendship*), a skill on the base of a person with a skill (*penmanship, doctorship*), or an office or period of office on a base denoting a position or office (*priestship, ladyship*). In the absence of one of those, *-ship* cannot be applied, implying that *milkmanship, *postmanship require no skill. Finally, Aronoff compares *-hood* with reference to a word like *father*, which ought to denote a permanent state but adapts to the semantic constraints of *-ship*: "*Fatherhood* means 'the state or condition of being a father'; *fathership* means 'the state or condition of being the oldest member of a community'" (Aronoff 2001: 172). In other words, *father* can only be the base of *fathership* when it has its temporary meaning.

2.5.4 *Avoid Synonymy*

As the tradition realized (e.g. Bloomfield 1933: 145), true synonymy is very rare. Apparent exceptions include slang (§5.2, end) and clips (Chapter 11), but expressive meanings have their own importance. While AVOID SYNONYMY is relative and can be overridden by creativity (§2.1), the maintenance (or establishment) of semantic contrasts is important for successful communication. Specifically, it motivates distinctions among competing words or morphological derivatives such that *thief* and *stealer*, for instance, prefer different contexts (§2.1). The flipside involves avoidance of homophony (§§2.2.3, 7.3). Both exemplify the desire to avoid ambiguity, and this aversion pervades all sorts of formations, e.g. *hot hot* vs. *spicy hot* (§14.1).

2.6 Processing constraints

Of the processing constraints that have been adduced, one involves FREQUENCY and another COMPLEXITY. Frequency can apply to the base, the affix, and/or the derivative (cf. Hay 2001; 2002; Hay and Plag 2004). For the base, for instance, *taste* is more frequent than *tasteless*. Derived *exactly* is more frequent than the base *exact*.

Words of high productivity occur outside suffixes of low productivity, e.g. *dep-th-less* but not **dep-less-th*, **limit-less-th*.

Hay builds a lot on the idea that suffixes that violate word-internal phonotactics are more productive than those that do not. For instance, *inhuman* contains a word-internal violation /nh/, which makes the morpheme boundary perceptually salient. In many languages, however, affixes at morpheme boundaries behave exactly as word-internally (Miller 2010: 1.226–30), which renders this criterion of limited use outside of English.

Frequency and complexity can interact. Suffixes that are more easily parsed are preferentially on the outside of suffixes that are less easily parsed (Hay 2002). This can predict *home-less-ness* over **home-less-ity*, since *-less* is more easily parsed than *-ity*. Also in *improvement*, *-ment* is more easily parsable than in *government* because *improve* is more frequent than *improvement* but *government* is more frequent than *govern*. The readily decomposable *improvement* cannot take *-al* (**improvemental*), but the less easily decomposable *government* can, hence *governmental* (cf. Rainer 2005a: 339). In fact, *improvemental* gets many hits on Google, e.g. improvemental repair, media, services, gallery, design sponge. Ultimately, then, processing constraints must be distinguished from phonological and affixal constraints (§2.2f.), as in **homelessity*, where there is a stress problem as well as a derivational base problem.

The next two sections discuss issues of processing in greater detail.

2.7 Processing and recursion: What do speakers count?

It has sometimes been suggested that prefixes are recursive and suffixes are not (cf. Roeper 1999). It is true that prefixes readily iterate, as in *pro-pro-pro-choice*, *un-un-cola* (Tyler 1988; cf. Halle 1973). As to suffixes, all speakers reject Roeper's **follow-up-up* and **sleep-over-over* because they cannot assign them a meaning, but they are mixed on ?**oddness-ness* 'the oddness of too many odd situations', and many find acceptable his (starred) *coffee-maker-er* 'coffee-maker-maker'. Andrew McIntyre (p.c.) mentions ?*Chomsky-esque-esque* 'reminiscent of someone/something reminiscent of Chomsky' and ?*psychology-ology* 'study of the study of the mind' or 'study of the history of psychology'. Of these two examples, *Chomsky-esque-esque* is typically ranked higher than *psychology-ology*, which strikes some speakers as a put-down, on a par with *psychology-shmychology*. That would seem to throw at least some of these formations into the realm of speech play. It is also a fact that the identity constraint (§2.2.1) is being relaxed, especially among younger speakers (cf. §15.1).

There is also a reading on *coffee-maker-er* that features simple reduplication of *-er* and means nothing more than 'coffee-maker'. This kind of reduplication is becoming more common. Sean Witty (p.c.) finds on Google an example of a resort boasting of its refrigerators with an *icemakerer*, which clearly does not mean 'maker of icemakers'.

There are two kinds of recursion. Consider first the iterativity of prefixes in (7).

(7) Prefix iterativity
   (a) *I've reread the book*
   (b) *I've rereread the book*
   (c) *I've rerereread the book*

Most speakers do not count repetitions of *re-* beyond one or two. For some speakers (7a) can mean 'I've read the book a second time' or simply 'I've read the book n times'. Technically, (7b) means 'I've read the book three times', but most speakers simply take that as an emphatic for 'multiple times'. Certainly (7c) is never anything but an emphatic declaration of multiple times. This implies two different analyses for (7): one in which the first (or first and second) *re-* will get a precise semantic interpretation, and one in which the repetitions of *re-* are phonological copies iconic to some notion of multiplicity and *re-* gets a semantic interpretation as 'n times'. That is, *re-* has two interpretations in this context: 'another time' or 'n times'. In the first instance, the output contains one or two instances of *re-*. On the second interpretation, the output construct can have any number of optional copies of *re-*.

Consider next the recursion of the Latin diminutive suffix in (8), cited by Varro, *De lingua latina* 8.75–9, 9.74 (Miller 2006: 58).[10]

(8) Diminutive iterativity (Latin)
   (a) *canis* 'dog', *catus* 'cat'
      (1) *catulus* 'young animal; pup; whelp'
      (2) *catellus* 'small puppy'
      (3) *catellulus* 'tiny little pup'
   (b) *cista* 'box'
      (1) *cistula* 'little box'
      (2) *cistella* 'very small box'
      (3) *cistellula* 'tiny little box'

The interpretation of evaluative suffixes is similar to that of prefixes. Two or three repetitions of the suffix do not necessarily entail two or three different degrees of size (Prieto 2005; Fortin 2011). Unfortunately, Varro does not mention whether more

---

[10] The allomorphy *-ul-*, *-ell-*, *-ellul-* results from earlier syncope of **-(e)lo-(e)lo-*. and a metrical constraint that requires dactylic *-ellulu-* to the total exclusion of amphibrachic **-ulellu-* (Miller 2010: 1.258). All of these are the same affix semantactically, regardless of the phonological realization.

than three suffix repetitions are possible, and no examples occur in the extant literature. One can only speculate that if more were produced, they would not be counted, but would only mean 'extremely small'.

Similarly, Latin can distinguish up to three scalar degrees of iterativity on verbs, as in (9), from Varro, *De lingua latina* 8.60 (Miller 2006: 252f.).

(9) Verbal iteration (Latin)
 (a) *canō* 'I sing'
 (b) *cantō* 'I keep on singing'
 (c) *cantitō* 'I sing repeatedly'

Again, Varro does not mention whether the Romans could say anything like **cantititō* 'I keep on repeatedly singing a lot', and no such examples are attested. One can only speculate that speakers may have occasionally produced such superemphatic forms as part of creative language play. A repetition of three was within the realm of core Latin morphology. Anything beyond that would have been language play.

In short, both prefixes and suffixes, when iterated, may or may not be counted, entailing two different analyses. One features reapplication with the same affix in the computation, and the other involves only one application but with multiple phonological copies articulated.

Most suffixes are more constrained in their reiterability because of lexical/semantic restrictions. In general, affix iteration is constrained by interaction with other affixes.

Many prefixes admit of the same two types of derivation. Consider *over* in (10).

(10) (a) *I over-over-heated the beans*
 (b) *I over-over-over-heated the beans*

(10a) means 'I too often made the beans overhot' (Andrew McIntyre, p.c.) but (10b) can only mean 'heated the beans to some phenomenal temperature'. There is no way each *over* has its own specific meaning, and therefore no need for more than one *over* in the computation.

Consider next the more complex examples in (11).[11]

(11) (a) *they over-re-over-warmed the beans*
  'they too often again made the beans too warm'
 (b) *they re-over-re-over-warmed the beans*
  'when they warmed the beans on yet another occasion, they repeated the blunder of warming them too much'

---

[11] The interpretation of (11a) is supplied by Andrew McIntyre (p.c.). My own judgments are idiosyncratic. McIntyre emphasizes that *over* can measure the frequency of the event as well as the degree of the state.

What is important in (11) is that each *over* is structurally different and must therefore merge successively in the computation. This is no different from suffix recursion in *kindlinesslessly* or *foolishnesslessness* 'the degree of lacking foolishness'. Since the suffix *-ness* attracts a state that can be measured in degrees (Miller 2006: 27, w. lit), after *foolish* is constructed it can merge with *-ness* and after *foolishnessless* is constructed it can merge again with *-ness*. This is predicted on a syntactic account. There is no difference in the recursivity of productive prefixes and suffixes that cannot be accounted for independently of their position.

2.8 Turkish causatives

While this book is about English lexicogenesis, it is occasionally helpful to illustrate a point with a typological parallel. In this instance, Turkish causatives offer an extreme example of the ability of speakers to process highly complex data. A glance over the sentences in (12) will suffice to reveal the extent to which an interpretation can be assigned to multiple iterations.

At issue in (12) are morphological causatives. "A causative is an expression in which an event (the caused event) is depicted as taking place BECAUSE someone does something or because something happens" (Goddard 1998: 260). Causatives are formed in many ways crosslinguistically, e.g. affixation, stem change, incorporation (Štekauer et al. 2012: 275–80). Most basic are the MORPHOLOGICAL or SYNTHETIC causative and the ANALYTIC or SYNTACTIC causative. The latter consists of a separate causative word in syntax, like English *have someone do something*, *make someone do something*, etc. English also has LEXICAL causatives like *kill* 'cause to become dead', but no true morphological causative. The suffixes *-en* (*blacken* 'cause to become black') and *-ify* (*clarify* 'make clear') are sometimes included here, but both of these are INCHOATIVE as well: *the sauce thickened* = 'became thick'; *the fat liquified* = 'became liquid' (Walinska de Hackbeil 1985; Embick 2004b; Miller 2010: 2.108ff.).

Turkish has a morphological causative (12), as recursive as any productive syntactic causative, upper limits being imposed by constraints on processing (Gülşat Aygen, p.c.).[12]

(12) Causative recursivity (Turkish)
    (a) ben   tavuk   piş – ir – di -m
         I   chicken cook-TRANS-PST-1SG
         'I cooked chicken'

---

[12] Although the alternation *-t-/-tir-* is phonologically discontinuous (cf. Rubino 2005: 17), it counts as recursive because it is the same affix from the point of view of the projected semantic features.

(b) ben   tavuk   piş-   ir - t - ti - m
    I   chicken   cook-TRANS-CAUS-PST-1SG
    'I had someone cook chicken'

(c) ben   tavuk   piş - ir - t - tir - di - m
    I   chicken   cook-TRANS-CAUS-CAUS-PST-1SG
    'I had someone have someone else cook chicken'

(d) ben   tavuk   piş - ir - t - tir - t - ti - m
    I   chicken   cook-TRANS-CAUS-CAUS-CAUS-PST-1SG
    'I had someone have someone else have yet someone else cook chicken'

(e) ben   tavuk   piş - ir - t - tir - t - tir - di - m
    I   chicken   cook-TRANS-CAUS-CAUS-CAUS-CAUS-PST-1SG
    'I had the fourth person cook chicken'

(f) ben tavuk   piş - ir   - t - tir - t - tir - t - ti - m
    I   chicken   cook-TRANS-CAUS-CAUS-CAUS-CAUS-CAUS-PST-1SG
    'I avoided cooking chicken at any expense'

Speakers can process up to four causative suffixes. With the fifth occurrence, the meaning simply involves major avoidance of the chicken-cooking task.

In the final analysis, one must consider the reason for the apparent discrepancy in the number of affix repetitions that are subject to meaningful processing in different languages. Why, for instance, does Turkish allow four meaningful repetitions of the causative affix while Latin seems to allow a maximum of three suffix repetitions? By contrast, English *re-* can be processed technically or loosely on its first occurrence and the third repetition is emphatic pure and simple. Likewise, the third repetition of *over-* seems to entail the emphatic interpretation. As noted by Fortin (2011: 158), expressive repetitions yield "diminishing returns".

It seems to be the case that three scalar degrees are approaching the upper limits of processing. According to Gülşat Aygen (p.c.), the four Turkish causatives require a large amount of concentration to process, and are easier to process when written. The most common recurrence of the morpheme would be up to three; four is more rare, and subject to an emphatic (or dialectal) interpretation. Many languages allow up to three iterations. The phenomenon is so widespread that the term TRIPLICATION has been applied to it (Wiltshire and Marantz 2000; Rubino 2005). Štekauer et al. (2012: 118f.) distinguish this from affix recursion (pp. 144–55), but many of the examples in this chapter involve affixes which behave the same as words and reduplicating syllables. To conclude, then, many prefixes and suffixes allow recursion to the extent that they can be processed. Three and more repetitions become difficult and are apt to be given a simple emphatic interpretation.

2.9 Summary

The fact that a number of constraints may apply in connection with a given affix, for instance, does not entail that the affix is not productive. Productivity must be defined with reference to a domain. That domain includes the constraints that can apply.

Constraints are violable in varying degrees in different contexts. The dissimilatory constraint (§2.2.4) is generally the weakest, even though it can be highly ranked for specific phonological sequences at particular times in a language's history. The homophony constraint may be universal but is seldom deterministic, for the simple reason that a certain amount of homophony is inevitable. The question, then, on a language-particular basis is: how much homophony is tolerated and in what contexts? The haplological constraint is the most general crosslinguistically but inevitably trumped by reduplication, often in the same languages in which it is otherwise operative.

Processing constraints should be restricted to linguistic complexity and not generalized to cases like *homelessity*. Lexical constraints are all language-particular, and many languages have a lexicon stratified in such a way that certain affixes are sensitive to native or borrowed bases. In genres like popular speech, certain productive affixes can violate lexical constraints. Examples are *mathness*, *studyness*, and *writeness*. Humor is another effect of breaking lexical constraints, e.g. *womanity*, *confessionator*.

In the final analysis, creativity overrides lexical constraints. Restricted as -*th* was, *warmth* spawned *coolth* [1547] (§5.3), then Horace Walpole coined *gloomth* [1753] and in 1754 wrote "the height of its greenth, blueth, gloomth". Since 1856, *greenth* has slowly gained popularity, and now gets many hits on Google. This is one example of a spread from one individual to a collectivity of I-languages, i.e. the E-language.

Syntactic and semantic constraints are not readily broken except by a change in the lexical features, which can be done by a poet or in language play. The difference between unergative and unaccusative verbs, for instance, is set on a language-particular basis; once set, the distinction determines which affixes a given verb can take, except that thematic roles can be altered, as done frequently by poets. Generally speaking, lexical features are subject to alteration and/or language change.

Recursion may be the sole component of Universal Grammar (Hauser, Chomsky, and Fitch 2002), but it seems to be more restricted in syntax than in other aspects of cognition (Levinson 2013). Recursion is one core element of productivity; cf. Roeper (2011): "the child seeks recursion as the core of productivity." Recursivity is characteristic of prefixes, but certain suffixes iterate freely when a semantic interpretation is readily available and when iteration is not constrained by interaction with other affixes. All affix recursion is subject to the constraint that the iterations must be processable. Three scalar degrees are approaching the upper limits of processing. More repetitions become difficult and are apt to be given a simple emphatic interpretation. This is regularly the case with diminutives, augmentatives, and other affixes that have gradable interpretations.

3

Compounding

This chapter presents an overview of English compounds according to the criteria below. Subsequent chapters will build on this with additional types and other lexicogenic operations that resemble compounding but whose structure is different. It is thus important to identify the structure of compounds and related constructs here and in Chapter 4 in order to highlight the differences between these and superficially similar formations.

Compounds have been classified into subordinate, attributive, and coordinate, all of which can be endocentric or exocentric (Scalise and Bisetto 2009). Padrosa-Trias (2010) rigthly derives the first two from the head–non-head relation but wrongly rejects dvandva (coordinate: see §3.5) and appositional (identificational) compounds. Moreover, there is a long tradition, followed here, that exocentric compounds are in fact endocentric. SYNTHETIC or VERBAL compounds have a deverbal constituent with a satellite that bears a thematic role, as in *peace-making, truck-driver*, semantic role (e.g. locational *rope-walking*, instrumental *knife-fighting*), or adverbial (*quick-stepping*). ROOT or PRIMARY compounds are merged nominals (*tax-form, arms factory*). Similar-appearing constructs can be either synthetic [[*cement-mix*]*er*] or root [[*hand*][*mix-er*]] (one held in the hand). In the latter, *hand* is a semantic locational, not an argument of *mix*, which has no argument structure: **hand-mixer of eggs*. Contrast the synthetic compound *hand-weaver*, in which *hand* is a free instrumental ('by hand') and *weave* has an argument structure that can be satisfied outside the compound: *hand-weaver of rugs* (*rugs* satisfies the theme argument).[1]

---

[1] Fundamental literature on English compounding and its history includes Carr (1939), Marchand (1969: 11–127), Koziol (1972: 48–88), Roeper and Siegel (1978), Selkirk (1982), Botha (1984), Tournier (1985: 107–38), Roeper (1988a, etc.), Sauer (1992), Miller (1993: ch. 4), Olsen (2000a; 2000b), Adams (1973; 2001), Bauer (2004), Dressler (2005), Lieber (1992; 2005; 2008; 2009a; 2009b), Kastovsky (2009), Lieber and Štekauer (2009), Harley (2009), Carstairs-McCarthy (2010), Padrosa-Trias (2010) (with an up-to-date taxonomy), Bauer et al. (2013), and, with major comparisons to English, Moyna (2011).

3.1 Core properties of compounds

Compounds are formed by combining two or more words to make one syntactic head (§1.1). The basic problem in English is recognizing/identifying compounds. Spelling is not a reliable criterion because compounds may be written together, hyphenated, as separate words, or all three ways. Moreover, different conventions prevail in US and British spelling, and with the same word over time or just in different writers. All three spellings prevail in *road(-)kill* [1943] and *snail(-)mail* [1982]. Typical examples follow:

(1) Form of English compounds
   (a) Univerbated: *snowman* [1827], *cheapskate* [1896], *bullshit* [?1915], *gridlock* [1980], *sleazebag* [1981], *skuzzbucket* [1983], *crackhead* [1986]
   (b) Hyphenated: *Bible-thumper* [1889], *laid-back* [1908], *double-dipping* [1940], *feel-good* [1972], *body-piercing* [1977], *high-five* [1980]
   (c) Separated: *paper chase* [1856], *dream team* [1925], *shelf life* [1927], *reality check* [1935; 1960+], *feeding frenzy* [1960], *happy hour* [1961], *gas guzzler* [1973], *fuck buddy* [1973], *date rape* [1975], *control freak* [1985], *granny dumping* [1987], *road rage* [1988], *trophy wife* [1989]

Hundreds of modern slang compounds can be found in Mattiello (2008). Since the meaning of compounds is maximally underdetermined, interpretating them requires all kinds of extralinguistic, contextual, and pragmatic information (Meibauer 2014).

On the recursivity of compounds, *air bag malfunction safety recall follow-up notice* is reported by Arnold Zwicky (1/31/12).[2] Spencer (1991: 48) cites *student film society committee scandal inquiry*. Germanic is especially rich in recursive compounds. All languages with compounds feature recursivity (Štekauer et al. 2012: 93–8), but right-branching compounds are more restricted (Mukai 2008).

One traditional heuristic for determining compound status is stress, but this works best for synthetic compounds and most two-word endocentrics (Plag 2005; Giegerich 2009). The compound *blackbird* has one stress, on the first syllable; the phrase *black bird* has two stresses, a primary on *bird*, and a secondary on *black*. Most recent studies fail to separate out dvandvas and assume, for instance, that *steel bridge* is a compound (e.g. Arndt-Lappe 2011: 550), which is out of the question in varieties of English where the constituents are invariably separable, e.g. *steel and wrought iron bridge*.

A second traditional test involves meaning. A *wíse guy* [1896] may or may not be a *wìse gúy*. A *black bird* is by definition black, while a *blackbird* need not be black if, for instance, it fell into a can of red paint. Durkin (2011: 37) adds that female and young male blackbirds are generally brown.

[2] arnoldzwicky.wordpress.com

A third test involves INSEPARABILITY: *truck fast driver (Lieber 2005: 377).

Fourth, in a phrase, each constituent can be modified, as in *a (very) (black/red/ blue) (baby) bird*. In compounds, as emphasized by Bloomfield (1933: 232), the constituent parts cannot be modified: *a (*very) blackbird*, with *very* modifying *black*, is impossible, but the whole compound can be modified, as *a (baby) blackbird*.

Fifth, until recently, root (but not synthetic) compounds in English admitted plural first members only when they were (i) pluralia tantum (*clothes-brush*), (ii) irregular in form (*teeth-marks*), or (iii) collective or idiosyncratically interpreted (*materials center ≠ material center, numbers racket ≠ number racket*) (Kiparsky 1982b: 137f.). An increasing trend allows *-s* on a regular basis, as in *job(s) list, 50% sale(s) rack* (§3.3).

Finally, compounds in most languages restrict functional categories (Miller 1993: 89–94; 2010: 2.140; Moyna 2011: 24ff.):

(2) Absence of functional categories in English compounds

    (a) Det.:   (*the/a*) *the-Bronx-hater (cf. *the Bronx* but (*the/a*) *Bronx-hater*)
    (b) Aspect: *book-having-read (cf. *book-reading*)

Book-reading and *worm-eaten* show that only certain aspect and voice heads can occur. Tests for the absence of functional categories in compounds include the failure to license appropriate adverbs. The perfective aspect of *eaten* in *worm-eaten* can be contrasted with the ungrammaticality of a perfective adverb, e.g. *the worm-eaten (*completely) meat*. For the meaning, cf. *the meat was (completely) worm-eaten (completely)*. For the licensing of adverbs with compounds more generally, see Fu, Roeper, and Borer (2001).

Most Western languages observe the same restrictions on functional elements, e.g. Sp. *sacacorchos* [remove corks] 'corkscrew' but **sacaqué* 'remove what', **sacaeste* 'remove this one', **sacaloscorchos* 'remove the corks', etc. (Moyna 2011: 25, 207).

Compounds sometimes originate as separate lexical items in a phrase and may differ from the phrase in meaning: (phrase) *blàck bírd ≠* (cpd.) *bláckbird*. Currently variable (partly regional, partly idiosyncratic) phrase or compound structures include: *ice(d) créam ~ ícecream; ice(d) téa ~ ícetea; ice(d) cóffee ~ ícecoffee; apple píe ~ ápplepie* (cf. Bloomfield 1933: 180, 228). For Giegerich (2004; 2009), the variability is indicative of a compound in the process of lexicalization, where the stress may shift to the first syllable. But he has not shown that *ice(d) créam* is not a phrase; some speakers can coordinate it: *ice(d) and melted créam*, but not **íce-and-melted-cream*. One natural evolution seems to be from phrase to frozen collocation to compound (cf. Dressler 1987a: 115).

Conversely, compounds can be (re)analyzed as single words (§1.1): [[cup][board]] is reanalyzed as [cupboard], as indicated by the phonological adjustments: (American) /kʌ́pbɔ̀rd/ > /kʌ́bɚd/. The same is true of *necklace, breakfast*, etc. (cf. Raffelsiefen 1999: 249).

Many scholars include entire sentences as compound constituents (e.g. Lieber 2005: 377; Szymanek 2005: 433; Meibauer 2007; Padrosa-Trias 2010: 107ff.), but Miller (1993: 94) analyzes examples like "I have the *that-I-am-being-called-upon-every-five-minutes* headache" as sentential NP modifiers, analogous to relative clauses or adjectives (cf. Bauer and Renouf 2001; Moyna 2011: 36) in that they constitute a separate syntactic head (§1.2). If the entire construction is a compound, it is a drastic violation of the NO-PHRASE CONSTRAINT (Aronoff 1976: 21ff.; Botha 1984), which is ironically misnamed in exemplifying what it prohibits (cf. Rainer 2005a: 335). The following sentence from the Wikipedia article[3] about the film *Alfie* contains two good examples: "In addition to maintaining a casual relationship with a single mother named Julie (Marisa Tomei) that he refers to as his 'semi-regular-quasi-sort-of-girlfriend thing', he also sleeps with various girls on the side, such as the married-yet-neglected-by-her-husband blonde named Dorie (Jane Krakowski) whom he regularly meets for sex after work in the back of his limo."

Clausal modifiers are not limited to compounds (Spencer 2005: 83; see §2.3, end). By the inseparability criterion the structure may be a phrase for some, a compound for others. Lieber (2005: 377) does not accept **a who's the boss filthy wink* (for *a filthy who's the boss wink*); others (myself included) find her starred example perfectly good. The ad hoc and witty status of these imparts a playful aspect to them (Meibauer 2007).

Language play occurs in Latin, which did not favor complex compounds but could make mock-Greek names like *Quod-semel-arrip-ides Numquam-erip-ides* (Plautus, *Persa* 705) 'What-he-has-once-taken-never-again-will-he-give-back' (Fruyt 2002: 265) (§15.1).

3.2 Synthetic compounds

This section outlines the properties of synthetic compounds. Most of the properties in this section and §3.3 are from papers by Tom Roeper and can be found in Sproat (1985).

Synthetic compounds have a deverbal constituent whose verb takes a nominal complement (*peace-making, truckdriver*) that cannot be plural (**trucks-driver, *mice-eater, *worms-eaten*), in contrast to a typical root compound like *truck(s) factory* (§3.3).

Technically, *hand-painter* can be 'one who paints hands' in which *hand* is the theme argument, or a free instrumental as in *a hand-painter of signs*.

Because of a syntactic constraint (§2.4), the nominal sister of the deverbal element can never have a subject interpretation: *rat-eating* can never involve rats doing the eating. It can be a free semantic adjunct (agentive *mouse-eaten*, instrumental *handcarve*, locational *home-school*) or the theme argument of the verb (*type-setting*).

---

[3] en.wikipedia.org/wiki/Alfie_%282004_film%29

Since *truck* satisfies *drive*'s theme role in *truck-driver*, another theme in syntax is ungrammatical: **a truck-driver of Macks*, **a car-driver of Isuzus* (Sproat: 1985: 204ff.). Contrast *a charcoal-broiler of steaks* with *charcoal* as a free instrumental semantic adjunct ('with charcoal'), and *steaks* satisfies the theme argument of *broil* in syntax.

In general, no thematic role can be satisfied twice. Since -*er* in *(truck-)driver* satisfies the verb's external argument (agent role), it cannot be satisfied again in syntax: **a truck-driver by experts*; cf. *truck-driving by experts* (Sproat 1985: 168–78).

If the external argument is not saturated, it remains as an implicit argument for bound adjuncts (*tomato-growing by farmers*), control of an infinitival subject, and anaphor binding: *broadjumping to make oneself famous*. Root compounds by contrast have no implicit arguments: **tomato-growth by farmers*, **the broadjump to make oneself famous*.

Verbs with two obligatory arguments (*put the book on the shelf*, **put the book*, **put on the shelf*) cannot appear in a synthetic compound, e.g. **book-putting*, **shelf-putting*, **shelf-book-putting*, **book-putter on shelves* (Sproat 1985: 207ff.). This is parametric; cf. Germ. *kindern-spielzeug-gebend* [children-toy(s)-giving] 'giving toys to children'.

The best analysis of *truck-driver* remains merging *truck* and *drive*, followed by merger with -*er*. According to some analysts, this overgenerates and falsely predicts verbs like **to truck-drive*. They claim the constituent structure must be *truck+driver* rather than *truckdrive+er* (e.g. Lieber 1992: 85; 2004; 2005: 380f.), but that cannot work for *sound-sleeper* etc. (Jespersen 1942: vi. 293; Warren 1984: 233). Harley (2009) employs the feature [±affix] for modificational compounds like *quick-acting* and case theory for the *truckdriver* type, both of which are problematic (Padrosa-Trias 2010: 68ff.). Moreover, Spencer (2011: 489) notes that Harley's restriction "English...$v°$ cannot host internally complex heads containing more than one Root element" (p. 141) does not explain the difference between *Tom has been truck-driving* and **Tom truck-drove*. I will argue that antisymmetry (§1.1) rules out **to truck-drive*, **truck-drove*. Complements can be licensed by antisymmetry (Roeper 1999; Di Sciullo 2003; 2005; Miller 2010: 2.33–6). In the absence of an antisymmetrically c-commanding affix, the derivation crashes and overgeneration vanishes. This predicts that derivatives like *truck-driving* are wellformed but that verbs without an antisymmetric derivation are not.

In English, verbs with incorporated thematic object occur mostly as backformations and preferably in the -*ing* form. Constructs like (3a), despite recent proliferation (Miller 1993: 110–15), continue to have a questionable status (3b), except in derivation (3c).[4]

---

[4] Jonathan Keane has brought it to my attention that (3a, b) are accepted by many younger speakers, so a change is in progress. Especially interesting are the preferences that currently hold. *S/he meat-eats* is judged better than *I meat-eat*, and -*ed* past tenses are generally good for younger speakers: *I cattle-butchered* is rated higher than *I meat-ate*, almost to the point of preferring *I meat-eated* with a derived verb. This implies that the licensing properties of -*ing* are being generalized to -*s* and -*ed*. Eventually, antisymmetry may play no role in these formations.

(3) (a) ?*to meat-eat, ?*to building-make
    (b) *I meat-ate for years
    (c) meat-eating, meat-eater

In German, as in older contemporary English, a satellite to an infinitive can bear an oblique semantic role (4a), but cannot be the thematic object (4b) (Fanselow 1988: 110ff.), except in derivation (4c, d) (Jules Gliesche, p.c.).

(4) Incorporated nouns (German)
    (a) *hand-fegen* 'to hand-sweep' (i.e. 'with a hand')
    (b) **apfel-essen* 'to apple-eat'
    (c) *(das) Apfel-essen* '(the) apple-eating'
    (d) *apfel-essend* 'apple-eating', *Apfel-esser* 'apple-eater'

Additionally, German permits a number projection in such compounds, e.g. *das Äpfel-essen* 'apples-eating' (Barrie 2006: 167–72).

Dutch has the same distribution. The infinitive with incorporated object is illformed as an infinitive (5a), as shown also by (5b) with purposive adjuncts. Tensed forms are equally bad (5c). But if the infinitive is converted to a noun, the result is wellformed (5d). And forms with derivational suffix are wellformed (5e) (Edith Kaan, p.c.).

(5) Incorporated nouns (Dutch)
    (a) **appel(s)-eten* [apple(s)-eat.INF] 'to apple(s)-eat'
    (b) **(om te) appel(s)-eten* '(in order to) apple(s)-eat[5]
    (c) *(ik) *appel(s)-at* '(I) apple(s)-ate'
    (d) *(het) appel(s)-eten* '(the) apple(s)-eating'
    (e) *appel(s)-eter* 'apple(s)-eater'

As to why a converted noun licenses an incorporated object when the formally identical infinitive does not, as in German *(das) Apfelessen* 'apple-eating' (4c) vs. **apfelessen* 'to apple-eat' (4b), the difference lies in the abstract noun head outside of the verbal complex that c-commands the MoodP (MP) structure (§1.1). This is illustrated in (6), which is simplified for clarity.

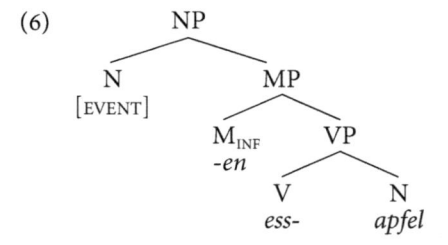

(6)
```
           NP
          /  \
         N    MP
      [EVENT] / \
           M_INF  VP
           -en   /  \
                V    N
              ess-  apfel
```

---

[5] *Appels om te eten* 'apples to eat' and *om appels te eten* 'to eat apples' are phrasal.

Read: the categorized verb *ess-* 'eat' merges with *apfel* (*apfeless-*), then that construct merges with the infinitive M head *-en* (*apfelessen*), which then undergoes conversion[6] to a noun by moving into the empty noun head bearing an event feature to attract the infinitive.[7] What the examples in (3–5) have in common is impossibility of an incorporated complement unless, as a parameter, it is licensed by an antisymmetrically c-commanding head with nominal features.

Some object-incorporating languages may require antisymmetry. Barrie (2006) argues that in a VO language, incorporated structures are always OV because the object moves to a higher position. In the Indo-European languages, where verbs do not generally bear a [+affix] feature, incorporation must be specially licensed. A potentially verbal root like Latin *-vor-* 'eating', however, bears a [+affix] feature, and thus requires an incorporated thematic object, as in *carni-vorus* [Pliny] 'meat-eating' CARNIVORE [1854].

3.3 Endocentric compounds

In an endocentric formation, one of two merged words is a satellite and the other the construct's head which determines its lexical-syntactic category (Bloomfield 1933: 235). Also projecting from the head are features of countability, gender, animacy, concreteness, number, etc. (e.g. Selkirk 1982: 21f.; Bauer 1983: 178; Sproat 1985; Di Sciullo and Williams 1987: 24; Padrosa-Trias 2010: 83–96).

Endocentric (but not synthetic) compounds can take *-s-*, as in *job(s) list, gift(s) report, truck(s) auction, antique(s) bazaar*, etc. (Gordon 1985; Sproat 1985: 412–27; Sneed 2002). Trips (2006: 315–26) traces the type to genitival *-s-*, as in OE *(wið...) cynnes mann(um)* '(with) kin's men' > OE *cinnesmen* KINSMEN. Under the influence of *londes men* 'land's men' the original compound *landman* became *landsman*. Another Old English *-s-* compound is *dōmesdæȝ* DOOMSDAY, originally a genitival calque on L *diēs īrae* 'day of wrath; judgment day'. Significantly, the modern *-s* forms are largely permutable only with genitivals: *division of parts ~ parts division*; contrast *pizza with anchovies ~ anchovy (*anchovies) pizza, famous for diamonds ~ diamond(*s) famous, rich in jewels ~ jewel(*s) rich*. Juncture *-s-* is limited to inanimates: a *cat's tail* is not the same as a *cattail* although the original form of the latter was *cattes tayle* [1548].[8]

---

[6] Most studies of conversion focus on alternations like *parrot*$_N$ → *parrot*$_V$ which are not as simple as they superficially appear (§1.6) but can be handled in any number of ways. It is only more complex derivations like (6) that provide decisive evidence for a syntactic account of conversion.

[7] For the conversion of an infinitive to an event nominal (signaled by a definite article) more generally, cf. Ital. *ricerc-are* 'to seek' : *il ricercare* 'seeking'; Ancient Greek *didásk-ein* 'to teach' : *tò didáskein* 'teaching'; etc. (Wackernagel 1926: 270ff.; Yoon 1996; Alexiadou 2001:158–62; Miller 2002: 286ff.).

[8] In German, the old genitival *-s* has spread as a compound linking element, as in *Universitätsbibliothek* 'university library', in which *Universität-s* is not the genitive of *Universität* (Kastovsky 2009: 331; Štekauer et al. 2012: 78, w. lit).

Any deverbal element of a root compound exists independently of the compound. With *consumer spending*, cf. *the spending was low this year* (implying the spending by consumers). Moreover, in contrast to synthetic compounds (§3.2), endocentrics permit a subject interpretation of the satellite: *consumer spending* involves consumers who spend (cf. *consumer purchase*). Similar are *dog barking, student swimming* (Sproat 1985: 278).

While synthetic compounds take prefixes like *re-* internally (*story-retelling/*restory-telling*), root compounds attach prefixes to the entire compound: *re-brainwashing* is not the same as synthetic *brain-rewashing* in which the brain is the literal washee.

Negative *non-* can never have phrasal scope in root/endocentric compounds; cf. *non-troop-deployment* 'the deployment of non-troops' and *troop-non-deployment* 'the non-deployment of troops'. Contrast the phrasal scope of synthetic *non-troop-deploying* 'not deploying troops'.

Multi-word compounds consist of a series of binary mergers; cf. *desk warehouse* (7).

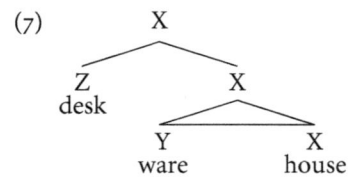

(7)
```
         X
        / \
       Z   X
      desk / \
          Y   X
         ware house
```

In English compounds, the head X is on the right: [blow]$_V$ + [pipe]$_N$ makes a compound [$_N$ [blow]$_V$ [pipe]$_N$]$_N$ of the category N (noun).[9] Semantically, the class of elements denoted by the compound tends to be a subset of the class denoted by the head, e.g. a *blowpipe* is a subclass of *pipes*. Even if a *greenhouse* is not a house (e.g. Aronoff and Fuderman 2005: 108), it is a structure resembling a house. In any event, endocentric compounds are not reversible. A *desk warehouse* and a *warehouse desk* are not the same, any more than are a *racehorse* and a *horserace* (Selkirk 1982: 22, 26; Zwicky 1985: 15f.). The constituents are not conjunctive: a *school teacher* is not 'a school and/or a teacher'.

Categories represented are the following (Grd = gerund, Prt = participle):

N–N	*fantasy football, power nap*	Grd–N	*drinking water*
N–A	*sky blue, stone cold, oil rich*	P–A	*overwide, underripe*
A–A	*red hot, wide awake*	A–Prt	*new-fallen, easy-going, ill-bred*
A–N	*fast food, software, wetsuit*	Ptc–N	*offprint, outgrowth, incrowd*
A–V	*sweet-talk, slow-bake, ill-treat*	Ptc–A	*overconfident, underripe*

---

[9] Spanish is left-headed in some types, e.g. *ducha (de) teléfono* [shower (of) telephone] 'hand shower', but right-headed in others, e.g. *maleducado* 'ill-bred' (Moyna 2011: 66). Many languages of course regularly feature left-headed compounds (Štekauer et al. 2012: 75f.).

N–V	spoonfeed, machine wash	N–Prt	poverty stricken, sun dried
V–N	crashpad, blowpipe	P–N	afterthought, overestimate (§4.3)
V–V	jump start, glide-walk	Ptc–V	outeat, undercook, offset, outsource

Lieber (2005: 378) claims that only the first four entries in the left column are productive, but N–V is also productive, and the A–A type is largely frozen (Huddleston and Pullum 2002: 528). Some derive the P and Ptc types by affixation rather than compounding, but if both are the result of merge and/or adjunction, the distinction is unnecessary.

The P–N type is tricky. An *afterlife*, for instance, is a life after the present one, i.e. the P gives an attribute to the noun (Padrosa-Trias 2010: 149). *In-house* etc. are exocentric.

The Ptc-N type has a long history, as shown by *outhouse* [1301] 'subsidiary building' (cf. OIce *úthús* 'id.'); [1819] 'outside lavatory'.

Bright-eyed is not A-Prt but rather [[A–N]ed], hence the meaning 'having bright eyes' (cf. Padrosa-Trias 2010: 169f., 173f.). That is also the type in *open-ended, broad-chested*. In the A-Prt type, as noted by Randall (1982), the adjective must represent a result state, as in *thin-sliced* 'sliced until thin', *fine-smashed, clean-shaven*. Similarly, *new-fallen* snow cannot be 'new' until it is fallen, hence also *still-born, foreign-built, ready-made*. That excludes **raw-eaten* 'eaten while raw' (not 'eaten until in a raw state'), **rusty-bought, *idiotic-said, *naked-seen*. Otherwise, the adjective must be adverbial: *slow-bake, ill-treat, cold-rinse, quick-brew, quick-fried, free-spirited, fine-tuned, widespread, well-wished* (cf. Padrosa-Trias 2010: 163).

3.4 Exocentric compounds

Exocentric compounds have no phonologically realized element to determine category, semantic class (agent, instrument), or other properties, such as gender or number (Scalise, Fábregas, and Forza 2009). That *sit-in* is a noun is not predictable from the immediate overt structure of $[sit]_V + [in]_P$. This and the productive verb–particle type *drive-by* [1951], *sing-along* [1959] are treated in §4.4. In this section and throughout Chapter 4 it is argued that there is a null head with appropriate semantic and category features to effect conversion, and that consequently no compounds are in fact exocentric (cf. Lieber 1980; 1981; 1983; Kiparsky 1982a; 1982b; Sproat 1985: 371–82; Štekauer et al. 2012: 80ff., w. lit).

The so-called Romance type of V–N compound (see e.g. Fradin 2009) is a relatively small class in English of limited productivity. Verb–object examples include *drawbridge* [a1300], *cutpurse* [1362], *pickpurse* [Ch.], *breakfast* [1463], *cutthroat* [1535$_N$, 1567$_A$], *telltale* [1548], *scarecrow* [1553], *breakneck* [1562], *do-nothing* [1579], *pickpocket* [1591], *skim milk* [1598], *spitfire* [1600], *lack-lustre* [a1616], *push-plow* [1670], *killjoy* [1776], *push-button* [?1874], *kickass* [1977], *kissass* [n.d.]; verb–subject *watch-dog* [a1616], *blowfish* [1893] (Marchand 1969: 380f.; Miller 1975: 51f.); verb–adjective: *drop-dead* [1962], *feelgood* [1972] (as a name [1962]).

The verbal stem was traditionally analyzed either as an imperative or as a 3SG form, both of which are impossible (Fradin 2009). In many cases there is no overt formal difference. In the Latin type *Vert-i-cordia* 'she [Venus] who changes the heart' (Bork 1990: §194), *vert-i-* is not unambiguously a verb stem. Occasional decisive forms occur. Ancient Greek used a verb stem consisting of the conjugation vowel, e.g. *ekh-é-pōlos* 'holding the foals', *tal-a-penthḗs* 'bearing grief' (Meissner and Tribulato 2002: 298f.; cf. Ralli and Karasimos 2009 for Modern Greek). Western languages like Spanish, where the V–N type is productive, exclude functional elements like tense and mood as well as internal inflections like person, number (§3.1; Moyna 2011: 24ff., 204).

The *drawbridge, pickpocket* type was introduced under French influence and never attained full productivity in English. The reason is that this type does not conform to the productive syntactic derivation of verbal compounds by means of left adjunction (see Chapter 4). That is, the productive derivation would yield *pocketpicker* [1622].

Sometimes considered a subclass of exocentric compounds is the *bahuvrihi* (Sanskrit *bahu-* 'much' + *vrīhi-* 'rice'), which is illustrated by the name itself. Like English *redhead* (except that the lexical-syntactic category in Sanskrit is adjective), it is not an 'abundance of rice' but 'having an abundance of rice'. Similarly, a *redhead* is not a 'red head' but rather '(someone) who has a red head' (i.e. red hair). With the structure of *redhead* in (8a) (cf. Moyna 2011: 54), note the abbreviated parallel of *redheaded* in (8b).

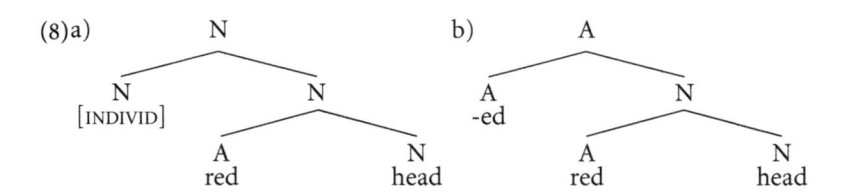

(8)a)
```
          N
        /   \
       N     N
  [INDIVID] / \
           A   N
          red head
```
b)
```
          A
        /   \
       A     N
      -ed   / \
           A   N
          red head
```

In (8b) *red* merges with *head* and that unit in turn merges with *-ed*. In the slightly more abstract (8a) the merged unit *redhead* is attracted by an abstract INDIVIDUAL noun which yields a person or thing interpretation.[10] Metonymy predicts several interpretations and therefore cannot explain the consistent INDIVIDUAL interpretation (*pace* Lieber 2009a). Crucially, INDIVIDUAL is not stipulated because a *redhead* cannot be an EVENT or STATE.

---

[10] For a person or thing choice, note the type *asswipe* [1953] 'contemptible person', [1958] 'toilet paper'. According to the classification of Levinson (2007: 22f.), things or entities are subsumed under predicates of INDIVIDUALS, encompassing individuals and entities, in contrast to events and states which are subclasses of EVENTUALITIES. *Redhead* and the like differ from clipped constructs like *sabertooth* [tiger], *whitewall* [tire], etc. (Zwicky 1985: 15f.; Sproat 1985: 379ff.), whose meaning requires specific knowledge.

In *egghead* [1907], the distance is more remote because no part is actually involved in the meaning. Rather, *head* is a metonym for 'person' and *egg* metaphorically specifies the type of person as an intellectual. Some older examples include *redneck* [1830], *featherbrain* [1839], *four-eyes* [1874] (1755 of a kind of bird), *peabrain* [1938].

The verbs *two-time* [1924], *hotwire* [1947] (Mattiello 2008: 84) would be derived as in (8) except that the compound would undergo verbalization (see Chapter 4).

3.5 Dvandva (or copulative) compounds

The essence of a DVANDVA is two or more conjoined heads, as in (9), where CNJ is an abstract conjunction and no individual constituent heads the construct (Miller 1987).[11]

(9)   X
    ┌──────┼──────┐
    X_1 CNJ X_2 CNJ X_3 ... X^n

One test for a dvandva (Sanskrit 'pair') is that all constituents must belong to the same lexical-syntactic category: N+N *cat-dog*, A+A *grey-blue* [1834]/*gray-blue* [1884], V+V *stop-go* [1918] (**red-go*). This is true of syntactic coordination (**I saw a cat and go*), but not of other compound types which admit mixed categories (Miller 1987).

Semantically, dvandvas are conjunctive 'X *and* Y' (e.g. *XY* (chromosome) [1911], *pale dry* [1843], *passive-aggressive* [1945]) or disjunctive 'X *or* Y' (e.g. *pass-fail* [1930]). There is also a type interpreted 'X *nor* Y' (cf. Renner 2008), e.g. Sp. *centro-derecha* 'center-right', "an ideology somewhere between the center and the right" (Moyna 2011: 50). Iconic sequencing (§14.6.2) represents yet another type, e.g. *dinner dance* [1901], *dive-bomb* [1935], *drink-drive* [1968], *cook-chill* [1982] (*ODNW* 74), *flash-bang* (grenade) [1987], *fly-drive* [1992]. Bauer's 'translative' type *Paris–Rome* (flight) is a subspecies of this class. *Add-drop* [n.d.] may belong here, but it is more often a simultaneous process of adding one course and dropping another. For instance, a UF undergrad missed class because she "was add-dropping".

---

[11] Dvandvas have been variously called (or distinguished from) *concatenative, copulative, coordinat(iv)e, binomial,* and *co-compounds*. Bauer (2008; 2009: 351f.) separates coordinate compounds on semantic grounds and has the most restrictive definition of *dvandva*. Our definition is more encompassing: dvandvas are distinguished only from those coordinate compounds that differ structurally. Dvandvas are discussed by Hatcher (1951), Sproat (1985), Miller (1987), Olsen (2001; 2004), Wälchli (2005), who includes only 'natural' coordinates (items expected to cooccur), Bauer (2008; 2009; 2010a), Renner (2008), Kiparsky (2010), Arcodia (2010), Arcodia et al. (2010), Moyna (2011: ch. 8), Štekauer et al. (2012: 88–93).

For the recent verb–verb type, see Wald and Besserman (2002), Ralli (2009), Nicholas and Joseph (2009), and Moyna (2011: 242f.). All of these support Hatcher (not mentioned by any of them) regarding the recentness of the V–V innovation.

Finally, there is the type in which the compounded elements cumulatively constitute a hyperonym, e.g. Mandarin Chinese *chē-mǎ* '[vehicle-horse] 'traffic', *jī-yā-yú-ròu* [chicken-duck-fish-pork] 'animal foodstuffs' (Anderson 1985a: 50f.). Words combined into a single compound must constitute some unitary concept or they could not be combined to begin with. Even with this interpretation, then, the essence is conjunction. This type is supposedly not structurally reversible (anonymous referee; cf. Štekauer et al. 2012: 55ff.), but that is determined in part language-specifically, and in part by productivity vs. lexical freezing. In Kannada some are reversible and some are not, e.g. *bassu karu* [bus-car] 'vehicles', *kurci mēju* [chair-desk] ~ *mēju kurci* [desk-chair] 'furniture', *kallu manu* [stone-dirt] ~ *manu kallu* [dirt-stone] 'construction debris' (Sridhar 1990: 283f.; Susan Shear, p.c.).

Some examples cited as dvandvas were reanalyzed from something else, e.g. *drop-kick* [1857] was a noun by origin. Reanalysis is a major source of V–V compounds (Wald and Besserman 2002). *Trickle-irrigate* [1971] was backformed from *trickle irrigation* [1969]. In this case, speakers who take *trickle-irrigate* as a basic verb generally interpret it N–V 'irrigate by means of a trickle' (cf. Padrosa-Trias 2010: 159f.). *Drip dry* first occurs in 1916 apparently in the meaning 'drip until dry'. Even in 1953 *rinse out, drip dry* admits the same interpretation, suggesting a V–A$_{\text{RESULTATIVE}}$ origin of the compound. The verb *drip-dries* first occurs in 1954. Reanalysis could make this a V–V compound for some speakers; cf. *blow-dry* [1966].

Bauer (2008: 4) considers *freeze-dry* [1949] and *stir-fry* [1959] headed, but which is the head? Is it 'freeze until dry' or 'dry by freezing', or is it simply V–V 'freeze and dry'? The OED considers *stir-fry* a V–V compound but *freeze-dry* a backformation (cf. *freeze-drying* [1944], *freeze-dried* [1946]), which is irrelevant to a language learner today (§1.7). Similarly, *crash-land* [1941] historically postdates *crash landing* [1928]. *Drink-drive* [n.d.] began as an adjective [1968].

Strip search originated as a V–V dvandva which underwent conversion to a noun [1947]. Today the verb is typically analyzed as 'perform a strip-search', i.e. the noun is taken as basic and endocentric, as is *shrink-wrap* [1961] (cf. Padrosa-Trias 2010: 151).

Many V–V types can be interpreted as endocentric, e.g. *fry-seal* [n.d.] can be 'seal by frying' as well as 'fry and seal'. Because of the bare monosyllabic stems, the category of the lefthand member is often ambiguous, e.g. *sleepwalk* [1923] (OED: a backformation), *kick-start* [1914$_{\text{N}}$, 1928$_{\text{V}}$].

V–V dvandvas originated in English by backformation and reanalysis, but their recent proliferation has produced a category for which new members can be freely created. The crucial point for V–V dvandvas is that a single object must be able to satisfy the argument structure of both. *Stir-fry* involves concoctions that are both stirred and fried. *Dunk-fry* would be equally imaginable, but not #*dream-freeze* or #*eat-kick*.

Deaf-mute [1837] is a dvandva with a 'simultaneous' relationship of the constituents (Lieber 2008); cf. Sp. *rojiverde* 'red [and] green' (Moyna 2011: 50). Of course *blue-green* can also have the 'X *nor* Y' interpretation and involve an intermediate hue, like Bauer's (2008: 10) COMPROMISE compounds, e.g. Sp. *sureste* 'southeast'; similarly, Sp. *aguanieve* is neither 'water' nor 'snow' but 'sleet' (Moyna, p. 53).

All members of the compound can retain full phonological word status, as evidenced by (among other things) the accent of each member: *séa-lánd*, *Héwlett-Páckard*, *thríller-chíller*, *mále-fémale* relationship, a *cát-dóg* fight (Sproat 1985: 382–411), Russ. *mát'-otéc* 'parents'. Stress clash (§2.2) is ignored in dvandvas in many languages, e.g. *cát-dóg*, Russ. *otcá-máteri* 'of parents'. In Ancient Greek, dvandvas had only one accent, e.g. *andró-gunos* [male-female] ANDROGYNE [1552], *gún-andros* [female-male] 'of doubtful sex' GYNANDROUS [1807], *zōó-phuton* [animal-plant] ZOOPHYTE [1621].

Germanic supposedly had no dvandvas (Carr 1939: 40ff., 161f.), but note OE *wīdbrād* 'wide and broad' (> 'widespread'), *grǣʒhǣwe* 'gray-blue', *hǣwengrēne* 'blue-green, cerulean'. Most taxonomies fail in missing the fact that speakers' judgments differ because there is a tendency to reanalyze dvandvas as endocentric (cf. Padrosa-Trias 2010: 141). For some speakers, especially those who grew up with crayons making the distinction, *blue-green* [1764] of an intermediate shade (*neither-nor* interpretation) is today a shade of green, while *green-blue* [1685] of a flame with both colors (conjunctive interpretation) is typically a shade of blue. This is classified as an "intermediate-denoting" compound by Wälchli (2005: 162), a "compromise" by Bauer (2008), and a "mixture" by Lieber (2008), but the relationship of the constituents has changed diachronically.

Wolf-dog is both endocentric, 'a dog for hunting wolves' [1652], and a dvandva as 'a cross between a wolf and a dog' [1736].

Pantyhose [1959] was originally 'a panty and a hose', as in the Underalls ad. Technically, *hose-panty* would have meant the same thing, but for most if not all speakers of contemporary English *pantyhose* is endocentric (a kind of hose). Significantly, all speakers consulted rejected **panty-and-hose*.

Bitter-sweet [1611] (a noun in Chaucer) for some speakers means 'bitter and sweet'; for them *sweet-bitter* would be the same thing except that *bitter-sweet* is formulaically packaged. Others interpret *bitter-sweet* as a dvandva when applied to life and emotions, but endocentric in the context of chocolate, where it denotes a subclass of sweet (the variety that is somewhat bitter). Still others get only the endocentric interpretation.

3.5.1 *The order of dvandva constituents*

Dvandvas are structurally reversible. A *cat-dog* fight or a *dog-cat* fight would both involve a fight between the same two animals. Various cultural and pragmatic factors determine linearization. A *red-green* [1878] (of color blindness) and a *green-red* [n.d.] personality would both indicate a slightly schizophrenic individual. If anything, the first member of a dvandva might be interpreted as the more dominant or important of the two, but other factors (male before female, shorter before longer, etc.) determine the linearization, as in *male-female* [1774] relationship. Earlier, *male-female* [1587] denoted a hermaphrodite, as did *female-male* [1621]. The latter could also be used as a dvandva adjective, e.g. *female-male* garments [1919], relationships [1951], interaction [1976], but more rarely than *male-female*.

In Kannada, dvandvas are generally reversible, e.g. *taayi-tande* [mother-father] ~ *tande-taayi* [father-mother] 'parents', and both can optionally insert *mattu* 'and'. Adjectival dvandvas can take *-u* 'and' or *-o* 'or' on both constituents, e.g. *kemp-u niliy-u* 'red and blue', *kemp-o niliy-o* 'red or blue' (Aronoff and Sridhar 1988: 187).

Russian generally follows Pāṇini's rule (§14.6) of shorter before longer (Dinah Belyayeva, p.c.): *mat'-otec* (**otec-mat'*) 'parents' but *oca-materi* (**materi-oca*) 'of parents' (*mat'* 'mother', *otec* 'father'). When equisyllabic, the constituents are reversible: *muža-ženi* ~ *ženi-muža* 'of a married couple' vs. *muž-žena* (**žena-muž*) 'married couple' (*muž* 'man, husband', *žena* 'woman, wife').

In Basque, culturally more important items (power and perceptual markedness §14.5.2) precede less important, or, if both are of equal importance, shorter precede longer, and equisyllabic constituents are reversible unless they are iconically sequenced. Examples in different categories include *aitâmak* 'father and mother' (**amâitak* 'mother and father'), *seme-alaba-k* 'sons and daughters' (**alaba-seme-ak*), *uŕe-ziłaŕa* 'gold and silver', *mendi-zelai-ak* 'mountains and plains' ~ *zelai-mendi-ak* 'plains and mountains' (Jacobsen 1982).

In Spanish, it appears from the appendix in Moyna (2011: 417–32) that with non-equisyllabic words, shorter precedes longer in the unmarked case, but it is not clear what determines the order of equisyllabic constituents.

3.5.2 *Summary of dvandva properties*

A true dvandva in English admits at least optional insertion of a conjunction; cf. *cat-and-dog* [1821] (fight), *milk-and-water* [1511] (color), *up-and-down* [1616] (motion), *bubble-and-squeak* [1767] (meat and cabbage), *cut-and-dry* [1883] (case), *surf and turf* [1990] (dinner), and *life-(or-)death* [1842] (situation) (Miller 1993: 83f.).

In some of the above, as in *black-and-white* ('print or photograph' [1830], 'police car' [1965]), *and* cannot be deleted in contrast with *black-(and-)white* issue, relationship, etc., first in 1895 of a mixed marriage. The conjunction is a convenient way to disambiguate superficially similar compound types, e.g. *government-binding* is at least four ways ambiguous: (i) 'binding (of) the government', i.e. gridlock, (ii) 'binding in (by...) the government', (iii) 'governmental binding' (endocentric root compound), and (iv) the dvandva *government-(and-)binding* is a theory advanced by Chomsky (1981).

Crucially, dvandvas behave like compounds in not allowing internal modification or functional elements, e.g. **a cat-and-big-dog fight*. *Very pale dry sherry* means 'very pale *and* very dry', not **'very pale but (less) dry'*.

Padrosa-Trias (2010) claims that dvandvas are not compounds but asyndetic syntactic coordinations. This is incorrect because dvandvas (i) disallow internal modification and functional elements, (ii) are single heads in syntax, (iii) differ in agreement and other inflectional properties from the same words coordinated syndetically or asyndetically in syntax, (iv) crosslinguistically enter into further morphological derivation (see below), and (v) even superficially are not necessarily asyndetic.

Dvandvas, like other compounds, can enter into further derivation, e.g. from *mother-(and-)father* (relationship) is made *mother-(and-)father-liness*. In Ancient Greek, *kalòs k' agathós* 'beautiful and good' makes a noun *kalo-k'-agath-íā* 'nobleness and goodness', out of which an unambiguous adjectival dvandva *kalo-k'-agath-ós* 'beautiful and good' was created.

3.6 Appositional or identificational compounds

The constituents in appositional compounds are theta-identified, i.e. referentially identical (Moyna 2011: 221, w. lit).[12] The test for an appositional compound involves the interpretation of the XY constituents as 'an X which is a Y and a Y which is an X'. An *actor-director* [1905] is an actor who is a director and a director who is an actor; cf. *actor-playwright* [1887], *actor-producer* [1927]. For Bloomfield (1933: 235) and Olsen (2001; 2004) this is a "copulative" relationship, for Lieber (2008) "simultaneous", and for Renner (2008: 607) "multifunctional".

Identificational compounds differ from true dvandvas in which the constituents are not coextensional. A *toy gun* [1880] is both a toy which is a type of gun and a gun which is a type of toy. Contrast a typical dvandva: *sea-land* is 'both sea and land'; it is precisely not 'sea which is land and land which is sea'. However, *fighter-bomber* [1936] is either a dvandva or an appositional compound, and that has been seen as a reason to reduce the taxonomy by allowing coordinate compounds another interpretation. Following Bauer (2008), Moyna (2011: 49) and others combine the two; cf. Sp. *verdiazul* 'green (and) blue' (non-identificational) and *actor-bailarín* 'actor-dancer' (identificational). But there are structural differences. Appositionals do not contain an abstract conjunction and do not admit an overt conjunction (**toy-and-gun*, **woman-and-doctor*). Conjunctive dvandvas do not have theta-identified constituents. In short, whatever one chooses to call these, they are structurally different. The only similarity is multiple-headedness. There is no single constituent as the unique head, and the internal structure is not hierarchical.

---

[12] 'Appositional' is a traditional term (Wälchli 2005: 161; Bauer 2008: 4) that has nothing to do with the 'appositive' compounds (the *swordfish* type) in Scalise and Bisetto (2009), which they group with attributive compounds (*high school, blue cheese, white collar*) into ATAP compounds. They combine the *prince-bishop* and *mother–child* types under COORDINATE compounds.

In one interpretation, a *woman doctor* [1854] is both a woman who is a doctor and a doctor who is a woman.

Jazz-rock is multivalent. As an appositional, it is 'jazz which is a type of rock and rock which is a type of jazz' [1969]. In *jazz-rock fusion* [1968], it is a dvandva denoting a combination of jazz and rock.

An *owner-occupier* [1900] can be interpreted as a subclass of occupiers, namely, the owner variety (endocentric), but what differentiates it from an unambiguous endocentric is that the occupier is also a subclass of owners.

Stress on these is apparently variable. In *owner-builder* [1969], *singer-guitarist* 1731], etc., both words are stressed in some varieties (my own included), in others only the second word is stressed (Olsen 2000a); cf. Arnold Zwicky in his blog about *cannibal shrimp*.[13] It is also of some interest that the morphosyntactic locus is invariably on the right: *owner-builders*, not **owners-builder*, **owners-builders*.

Older identificational compounds include OE *werewulf* [man-wolf] WER(E)WOLF, *āʒend-frēa* [owner-lord], *frēa-dryhten* [lord-master/ruler], *frēa-wine* [lord-friend], etc. (Carr 1939: 327–32). *Hōr-cwene* [adulterer-woman] is shared with OIce *hór-kona* 'id., adulteress' (HGE 182). This type increases in productivity in medieval times, e.g. ME *woman-friend* [1325], *merchant-adventurer* [1496–7]. More recent examples include *merchant-tailor* [1533], *turkey-hen* [1552], *woman poet* [1617], *lady-actor* [a1687], *shepherd girl* [1757], *lady-doctor* [1858], *girlfriend* [1859], *player-manager* [1895], *trophy wife* [1989], *boy toy* [1982] (British *toy boy* [1981] §14.2.1) 'male plaything for a woman'. The last word is also endocentric in the sense of '(a female who is) a toy for a boy' [1984] and 'a toy suitable for a boy' [1971], contrasted with a *girl toy* 'toy suitable for a girl'.

3.7 Retronym formation

The word *retronym* first appeared in print in 1980 in an article by William Safire, who attributes the term and early examples (like *hard-cover* [1949]) to Frank Mankiewicz, then president of National Public Radio. Essentially, a retronym is a clarificatory phrase/compound created out of a word by opposition to a popular collateral use of the base word. The oldest retronym may be *hard currency* [1851], by opposition to paper money. Examples adduced by Safire (1995) include: *time* (vs. *virtual time*) ⇒ *real time* [1946]; *guitar* (vs. *electric guitar*) ⇒ *acoustic guitar* [1953]; *journalism* (vs. *electronic journalism*) ⇒ *print journalism* [1961]; *ski* (vs. *water ski*) ⇒ *snow ski* [1975]; *mail* (vs. *voice mail*, *e-mail*) ⇒ *hard mail* [n.d.] (cf. *hard copy* [1964], *hard fax* [n.d.]), *snail mail* [1982]; *coffee* (vs. *decaf*) ⇒ *caffeinated coffee* (~ *caf*) [1995]. Then there is the ultimate in retronyms, *Christmas Eve day morning*!

[13] arnoldzwicky.wordpress.com/2011/12/03/cannibal-shrimp/#more-7972

In the realm of technology, *terrestrial television* [n.d.] was created to distinguish *television* from *satellite television* [1966]. *Terrestrial phone* [1976] or *land phone* [n.d.] came about in contrast to *satellite telephone* [1968]/*satellite phone* [1982] and *cell phone* [1983].

Retronyms are known in scientific circles as well. *Classical mechanics* [1933] was created by opposition to *quantum mechanics* [1922]; cf. *quantum theory* [1912]. *Nuclei* in physics were initially bound (by implication) but with the creation of *unbound nuclei* are now called *bound nuclei* [1937]. And so on (Ahmad 2000: 719).

3.8 Summary

Compounds are prototypically inseparable, constituents cannot be modified separately, and in English, as in most languages, functional categories are highly restricted.

The first problem treated involves the alleged overgeneration that results from deriving synthetic compounds like *truck-driver* from *truck-drive* plus *-er*. It has been wrongly claimed that this predicts verbs like **to truck-drive*. This chapter has shown precisely why that prediction is not made. Specifically, complements are licensed by antisymmetry. In the absence of an antisymmetrically c-commanding affix with a category feature, the derivation crashes. This predicts that derivatives like *truck-driving* are wellformed but that verbs without an antisymmetric derivation are not.

With endocentric compounds, the head (on the right in English) determines the lexical-syntactic category, deverbal elements exist independently, *re-* attaches to the entire compound (vs. synthetic compounds where *re-* attaches internally), and negating *non-* never has phrasal scope.

Retronym formation in most cases creates an endocentric compound, e.g. *snow ski*, by opposition to the productivity of a different manifestation of the concept, in this case, *water ski*.

In exocentric compounds there is no phonologically realized element that determines the lexical-syntactic category. Metonymy cannot explain the consistent INDIVIDUAL interpretation, which is not stipulated because a *redhead*, for instance, cannot be an EVENT or STATE. Nouns like *lookout* can have an INDIVIDUAL or an EVENT feature. In §4.4 it will be argued that a verbalized root is attracted to an empty noun with one of these features. Since there is no way that could be effected by metonymy, by extrapolation abstract noun heads with the same features must be available for the *redhead* type. In light of the abstract head, no compound is exocentric.

Dvandvas have two or more conjoined heads, and no single constituent heads the construct but a dvandva is a single head in syntax. All constituents must belong to the same lexical-syntactic category. Dvandvas are structurally reversible, but shorter constituents tend to precede longer ones (§14.6), and various cultural and pragmatic factors otherwise determine linearization. Dvandvas can be distinguished from other compounds by means of an overt conjunction.

While sometimes conflated with dvandvas, appositional / identificational compounds differ in structure. They also have multiple heads with no single constituent as head of the construct, but appositionals have theta-identified constituents, which conjunctive dvandvas do not, and never admit an overt conjunction or a cumulative interpretation.

4

New patterns of derivation

This chapter presents an analysis of the recent verb–particle construct types *knockout, get-at-able, march-through-ee, fixer-upper*. Although languages generally do not attach suffixes to particles, English is the major exception (cf. Roeper 1999). No one has advanced a satisfactory account (see Miller 2013) which explains both the form and the meaning of these formations. I will be using a model of morphology that is constrained by principles of syntax and independently derives the form and meaning of the constructs. To avoid the charge that my analyses are theory-internal, they are based on semantic representations from *non-generative* sources. A semantic representation by itself is insufficient as an analysis because it is compatible with more than one formal output. For instance, in noun formation *knockout* and **outknock* could both have the same meaning, and the form *knockout* has to be PREDICTED and **outknock* excluded. The independent semantic representation and the syntactic model together predict all and only the correct outputs by means of left adjunction and other independently motivated mechanisms. To explain *cookout* vs. *outcook* the different syntactic positions of particles are invoked.[1]

4.1 Particles

Since this chapter is about particles and what suffixes can attach to them, a discussion of particles is in order. Those in (1) are the most relevant for our purposes.

---

[1] Thanks to Andrew McIntyre for extensive discussion of this chapter. The syntactic model employed here is somewhat generic in combining elements of several models (e.g. Baker 1988; Julien 2002; 2007; Ramchand 2008; Bye and Svenonius 2010; 2012) with Distributed Morphology, on which see Halle and Marantz (1993, 1994), Embick and Noyer (2007), Levinson (2007), and Rolf Noyer's UPenn website: http://www.ling.upenn.edu/~rnoyer/dm/. The model used here has fewer idiosyncrasies. Unlike many analyses in the Distributed Morphology framework, my derivations regularly incorporate the modifications by Embick (2004a; 2004b). Beyond that, my analyses differ markedly from lexicalist accounts (against which see Williams 2007), like that of Berg (1998), but also from the syntax-based account by Roeper (1999) and Roeper, Snyder, and Hiramatsu (2003), for whom all particles originate in the same clitic position. Relevant aspects of Roeper's analyses and the model employed here will be explained in the appropriate sections.

(1) Brief particle typology (Dehé et al. 2002; McIntyre 2004a, 2007)
    (a) Spatial (*walk through, throw the ball down*)
    (b) Aspectual
        (1) Transitivizing (*think the problem through*)
        (2) Telic (*drink up*)
        (3) Non-transitivizing/non-perfective (durative, ingressive, punctualizing)
            (a) *fight (*battles/enemies) on*
            (b) *sing (*songs) along*
            (c) *type (*the essay) away*
            (d) *play (*the guitar) on/around/along*
    (c) Non-spatial and non-aspectual (*tell someone off, work off (a debt)*, etc.)
    (d) Scalar/Evaluative (*overeat, overestimate, undervalue*) (Rousseau 1995b; McIntyre 2003: 131ff.)
    (e) Comparative (*outcook, outeat*) (Miller 2013; cf. McIntyre 2003: 122f.)

Aspectual and other functional particles do not license a bare noun; cf. **a drink-up (of water)*, **a chew-up (of food)*, **a finish-up (of the work)*. Only those with lexical content license a noun: *a buildup* (#*of houses*), good only in the sense of 'accumulation' (Miller 2013).

Another fact to be explained is that there are differences on which suffixes can attach to words with even the same particles, as shown in (2), from Miller (1993: 132, w. lit).

(2)   (a) Particle precedes suffix
        (1) %*march-through-ee, explain-away-ee*
        (2) **march-ee through, *explain-ee away*
        (3) ?**march-ee through-ee* (only language play for comic effect?)
    (b) Suffix precedes particle
        (1) **march-through-ing, *explain-away-ing*
        (2) *(the) march-ing through (of the house)*
        (3) **marching throughing*
    (c) Suffix precedes or follows particle
        (1) *(the data are easily) wade-through-able, explain-away-able*
        (2) *(the data are easily) wade-able through, explain-able away*
        (3) ?*wadeable throughable* (%*pickable-upable*: Farrell 2005: 102)
    (d) Suffix precedes and follows particle
        (1) ?*breaker in*
        (2) ?**break-in-er*
        (3) *break-er-in-er*

None of the formations in (2) are easy to account for. Some speakers have an animacy restriction on *-ee* which blocks type (2a1). On (2d), in some instances the older forms are slightly questionable today.

The difference between *explaining away* and **explanation away* is explicable by the different type of derivation of *-tion* and *-ing* formations. The latter are productively derived from English verbs, including phrasal verbs, in sharp contrast to the former: apart from verbs in *-ify* and *-ize* (where *-ation* prevails), *-tion* can attach only to unsuffixed Latinate verbs (*LSDE* 97f., w. lit). **Explain-away-tion* is ruled out because the suffix *-tion* is severely restricted lexically (cf. §2.3) in requiring the Latinate stem *explan-* which disallows an English particle.

The goal of this chapter is to explain the distribution in (2). One factor will be the syntactic positions of the different kinds of particle. Another will be the syntactic derivation of the individual suffixes. These two factors, together with independent semantic representations, predict the forms in (2) with no additional stipulations.

4.2 Syntactic morphology

The main tenet of models of syntactic morphology is that there is a single computational component. The grammar constructs words by the same operation of Merge that creates phrases (Chomsky 1995+). If the categories merged are zero-level, the result is a word. Phrases are formed by merger of higher-level categories. All word formation is syntactic. Hierarchical tree structures of terminal nodes are present at all levels of representation. In other words, all syntactic and morphological elements (phrases, words) have the same kind of constituent structure, representable with binary branching tree diagrams.

Structure is neither stipulated nor a given. It is bottom-up and no longer top-down because it is entirely based on projection of lexical / semantic features (§1.9). An abstract lexical item consists of a set of semantic features. To take a simple example, the verb *hit* projects an obligatory causative feature, hence *I hit the ball* but not **the ball hit*. Contrast a verb like *break*: *I broke the vase / the vase broke*. This verb in English projects an optional causative feature. Semantic features go beyond the mental lexicon of individuals in the sense that verbs of the *break* class crosslinguistically exhibit a causative/anticausative alternation, but verbs of the *hit* class do not. If a speaker elects to say something equivalent to 'the ball hit', the obligatory causative feature of *hit* requires obligatory transitivity, e.g. *the ball hit itself*. To summarize, the structure is projected from semantic features in the lexicon, and without them, there would be no structure.

All words originate as roots (Levinson 2007) and must be categorized by a functional element, e.g. small v for verb, n for noun, etc. I will ignore most categorizers (except v) in the interest of simpler derivations and assume the conventional D (Determiner) as the licenser for a noun. This is the so-called FUNCTIONAL PHRASE (FP) hypothesis, according to which each lexical category is a complement of a corresponding functional head (Abney 1987), i.e. the F head is the probe. Just as CP is the FP to IP ([$_C$ *that* [$_{IP}$ *they went*]]), various Aux(iliary)P heads are probes for VPs (*may go, have gone*), DP heads for NPs (*the dog*), and Deg(ree)P heads for APs (*so good*).

4.2.1 *Basic clausal architecture*

The modified architecture that I will be using is laid out in the idealized schema in (3), which contains the core (non-fused) projections encountered crosslinguistically, some occurring in more than one projection (e.g. Asp[ect]). If CP (or its expansions) is present, it would be above MP (or its expansions).

(3) Idealized architecture

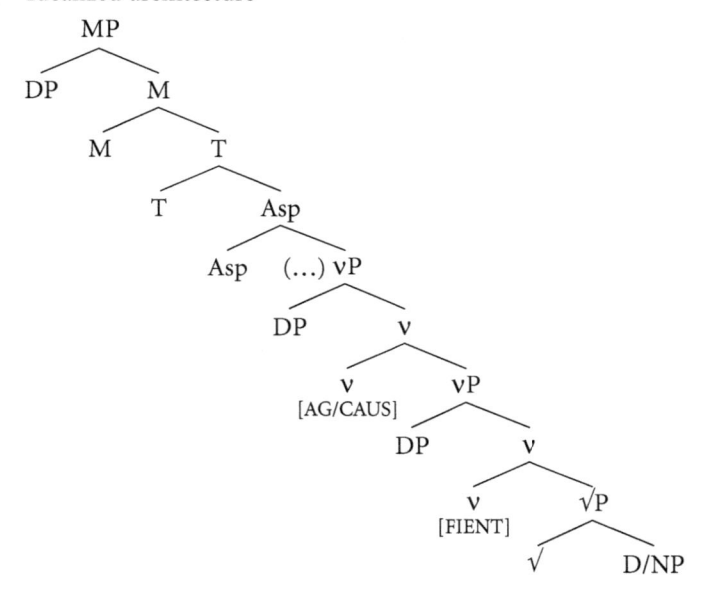

```
        MP
       /  \
      DP   M
          / \
         M   T
            / \
           T   Asp
              /  \
            Asp  (...) vP
                 /  \
                DP   v
                    / \
                   v   vP
               [AG/CAUS] / \
                        DP  v
                           / \
                          v   √P
                      [FIENT] / \
                             √  D/NP
```

Reading the structure in (3) bottom-up, an event-denoting root (√) can merge with a complement D/NP. RootP (√P) corresponds to a result state. It is selected by small *v*[FIENT], a verbalizing head with a FIENTIVE feature similar to the traditional BECOME operator.[2] That in turn can be selected by a *v*[CAUS/AG] (causative/agentive) head which introduces the causer of the event.[3]

If *v*[FIENT] bears a feature to force movement, e.g. an EPP (Extended Projection Principle) feature, the root's D/NP complement will be attracted to its specifier

---

[2] *v*[FIENT] is a functional head which denotes a transition event that moves toward a result state, i.e. turns the state into an event that has that state as a result (Embick 2004a; 2004b; Basilico 2008; forthcoming; Miller 2010: 2.108ff., 144, 152ff.).

[3] Although her assumptions about what can occupy the specifier of process position are very different, this is broadly consistent with Ramchand (2008: §3.1.2), for whom "initiation, process and result are claimed to be the abstract structuring principles behind all eventive predications."

position for high transitivity and, on some accounts, theta-role assignment. Also, structural object case is assigned (or valued) in that position by the Voice/CAUSE (AGENTIVE) head which projects an external argument.

In a bottom-up grammar, of course, selection can only be accomplished by feature matching. Chomsky (2004: 111f.) abandons s[emantic]-selection, which formerly blocked convergence, in favor of the idea that deviant mergers are discarded at the C–I (conceptual–intentional) interface.

4.2.2 Preposition incorporation and left-adjunction

One type of *over*-prefixation that must be separated from the particle constructs in this chapter involves residues of P-incorporation, as in *the river overflowed its bank*, from *the river flowed over its bank* (cf. Iwata 2004: 273). P-incorporation explains the observation (e.g. Lieber 2004: 131) that spatial *over* prefers intransitive verbs and adds an argument. In Old English the process could apply to nearly any preposition; cf. (4).

(4) P-incorporation (Old English)
  (a) þonne mōt   hē   feohtan   on   hine   (Laws of Ælfred 76 §42.4)
      then   can   he   fight.INF on   him
      'then he can fight against him'
  (b) gif hine mon on wōh   onfeohteð   (Laws of Ælfred 76 §42.6)
      if   him   man wrongly   on.fight.3SG
      'if a man fights against him wrongly'

In (4a) the full PP occurs, while in (4b) the P is incorporated into the verb; see (5).

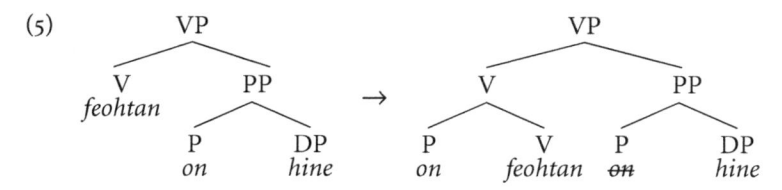

(5)
```
       VP                              VP
      /  \                            /  \
     V    PP          →              V    PP
  feohtan / \                       / \   / \
         P   DP                    P   V  P   DP
         on  hine                  on feohtan o̶n̶ hine
```

In general, with P-incorporation (Baker 1988), the object is stranded from the P by (left-)adjunction of the P to its c-commanding verb (represented by splitting the verb-node and crossing out *on* in its position of origin), as in most (especially older) Indo-European languages (Miller 1993, w. lit).

Following a long tradition, I assume that left adjunction is the norm in head movement, which involves raising from head to higher head.[4] The only exceptions to

---

[4] Despite some theoretical disputes and attempts to explain away head movement, it is accepted here without argument, and it does not reduce to an Agree relationship (*pace* Roberts 2010). For recent discussion, see Baker (2009), Matushansky (2011), Bye and Svenonius (2010; 2012).

left adjunction involve non-verbal functional heads and their complements, e.g. preposition plus object (*in prison* : *imprison*), Degree plus root (*over load* : *overload*), i.e. possible phase heads (§4.6). Apart from those, (left-)adjunction is entirely regular in word formation.

4.2.3 *Semantic representations and syntactic derivations*

This section illustrates the use of independent semantic representations coupled with a syntactic model. A syntactic formalization will be given for a non-generative semantic structure posited by van Kemenade and Los (2003: 90) for *he painted the door green* from [CAUSE [ACT(*he*), BECOME[GREEN(*door*)]], BY[PAINT (*he*)]].

The syntactic representation will be, in effect, 'he CAUSE (the) door BECOME green by paint':

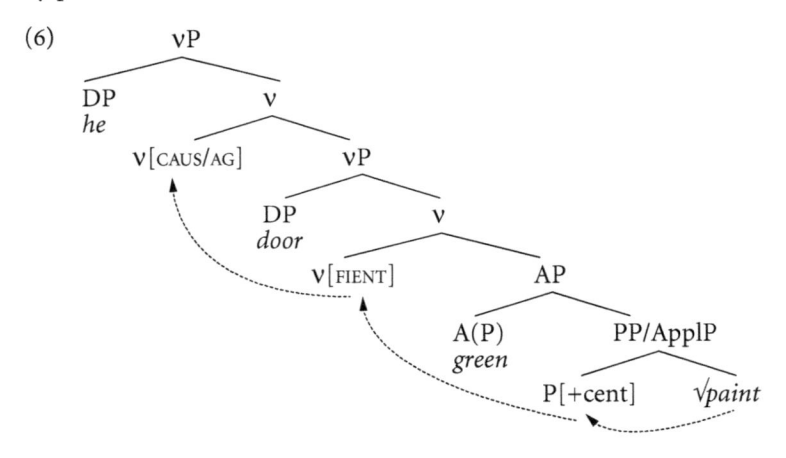

(6)
```
              vP
           /      \
         DP         v
         he      /    \
              v[CAUS/AG]  vP
                       /      \
                     DP         v
                     door    /     \
                         v[FIENT]    AP
                                   /    \
                                 A(P)    PP/ApplP
                                 green  /       \
                                     P[+cent]   √paint
```

Toward the bottom of the tree, the Adjective Phrase (AP) has merged with a prepositional phrase, more technically an applicative (McGinnis 2005), projected from a feature that introduces an oblique argument. The head of the Applicative Phrase is an abstract preposition with a [+cent(ral)] feature denoting a *with/by* relation necessary for semantic interpretation of the root (Tyler 1999: 129–36, 143; Hale and Keyser 2002: 161, 185ff.). Small *v* is, as above, a verbal categorizer. The higher one has a causative or agentive feature, the lower one (the FIENTIVE projection) corresponds roughly to the traditional BECOME operator. The radical (root) entry differs from a categorized item in leaving it open for surface nouns, verbs, and adjectives to undergo the same derivation.

The root *knock* moves into the abstract P for the 'by' interpretation, then incorporates the fientive and the causative/agentive projections, which make it a verb with the appropriate 'cause to become' semantics.

Head movement ignores *green* which is potentially phrasal; cf. *he painted the door very green*. However, in some varieties of English it is a simple head, which means *paint* can (left-)adjoin to it, yielding *%he green-painted the door*. Crucially, the proof that *green* is a simple head is that it cannot be modified: **he very-green-painted the door*, which all speakers agree is worse than *he green-painted the door*. Crucially also, the syntactic configuration in (6) predicts that **paint-greened* is not a possible output.

In the remainder of this chapter, the theoretical principles of this macrosection will be applied to English particle formations to show how the correct outputs are predicted by means of independent semantic representations formalized in a syntactic model with no extra stipulations.

4.3 Scalar/evaluative particles and P–V verbs

There have been many attempts at analyzing evaluative *over*-prefixation (see McIntyre 2003: 132ff.; Iwata 2004; Lieber 2004: 132; 2005: 399). This section argues that *over* originates as a Degree head equivalent to 'too much', and that all of the relevant facts are explained by this kind of syntactic derivation.

It is generally stated that eventive roots do not allow objects (**they overdrank the wine*), but permissive dialects and many exceptions have been noted.[5] The facts of scalar *over* are as follows: for (non-obligatorily transitive) eventive roots, the complement position is saturated by an abstract Degree head that gets spelled out as *over*, as in (7a), unless the complement is unbounded and atelic, compatible with the semantic properties of *over*. Deadjectivals (*they overtightened the bolts*) and denominals (*they oversnowplowed the street*) are invariably transitive.[6] This requires a structural account. Deadjectivals are transitive because Spec*v*P[FIENT] is available as an argument position. That is, *they overheated the engine* would derive on this analysis from something like 'they caused the engine to get-to-be too (overly) hot' (cf. McIntyre 2003: 137), the lower portion of which appears in (7b). For the denominals,

---

[5] Andrew McIntyre (p.c.) mentions *overdo the irony, overfeed the cow, overtreat/overpsychoanalyze the patients*, but some of these are denominal. Iwata (2004: 245, 271) cites *overbuild hotels*, but also "people who *overeat spicy foods*" plus six other examples like it. Most *over* verbs that allow objects are obligatorily transitive (**I did* (only good as an auxiliary), **I psychoanalyzed*, etc.) while the roots that generally disallow complements with *over* (*eat, drink*) are not obligatorily transitive. Moroeover, Iwata (p. 271) notes two different meanings of *over*, as in **overeat lunch* vs. *overeat sweets, fatty foods*. The former is 'excess', the latter quantifies a proportion. I take this to mean that generics like *lunch* are saturated while specifics like *spicy foods* are only quantified; cf. also contrastive *they overdrank the red wine* (vs. **they overdrank the wine*). Unbounded objects like *wine* are good in *I overdrank wine* (Jonathan Keane, p.c.). Bounded objects are good only if contrastive (*I overdrank the wine but barely touched the beer*) and not involving a specified measure (**I overdrank a/the glass of wine*) that would create telicity (Russ Nekorchuk, p.c.).

[6] Andrew McIntyre (p.c.) mentions one potential counterexample to the generalization about denominals: some speakers do not get *%oversmoke cigarettes*, but this is not denominal (it is built on the categorized verb *smoke*) and is therefore sensitive to the generic object constraint. Contrast the genuine denominal verb which is transitive: *I oversmoked the turkey*.

there is a locational constraint: *overload the truck/#overload the books*, good in the sense of 'pack them too full (of information)', not in the sense of 'load too many of them (on something)' (Iwata 2004, w. lit). This follows structurally from (7c) in which there is no place for a locational (e.g. *on*-phrase) to be realized. In other words, one can *load something in/on something* but not **overload something in/on something*, for the simple reason that the position for the locational *in/on*-phrase is occupied by the root LOAD.

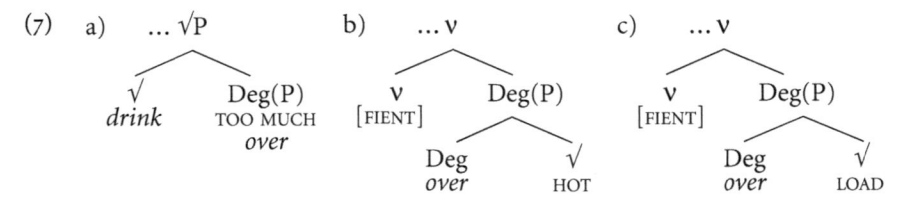

(7) a) ... √P
      √ drink   Deg(P) TOO MUCH
                 over

    b) ... v
       v [FIENT]   Deg(P)
                   Deg   √
                   over   HOT

    c) ... v
       v [FIENT]   Deg(P)
                   Deg   √
                   over   LOAD

In (7a) the abstract Degree head TOO MUCH is instantiated as *over*, which (left-)adjoins to the root *drink*, yielding *overdrink*. The radical (root) entry differs from a categorized item and leaves it open for other surface categories (nouns etc.) to undergo the derivation.

In (7b) the small *v* (verbalizing head) has a FIENTIVE feature analogous to the BECOME operator. That is, the meaning is 'get to be over-HOT'. Like prepositions (*in + prison → imprison*), degree heads linearize to the left of their complements (Miller 2010: 2.36), yielding a string *over*-HOT, which then moves into the fientive head creating an unaccusative verb *overheat*, as in *I overheated in the desert* ('I became too hot'). If this merges with a higher causative/agentive projection (*v*P[CAUS/AG]), the result is transitive/causative *overheat* something. The same structure with no NP in Spec,*v*P[FIENT] yields an antipassive *I overheated last winter*, i.e. 'I made [the house] too hot' (cf. Basilico 2008: 1726ff.; Miller 2010: 2.154f.).

In general, comparative and scalar/evaluative particles behave alike in permitting only prefixed verbs and no bare noun derivatives:

(8) (a) (an) *undercook/**cook-under, *overeat, *overthink, *únderestimate
    (b) (an) *undervalue/**value-under

Independent nouns can make similar-appearing formations, e.g. an *undervalue* [1611] or *underprice* is 'an amount/price below the real value' (*OED*) and derives from a PP; cf. *an overstock/understock, overkill, oversight, underéstimate*, some of which are endocentric (§3.3). An *overestimate* is a kind of estimate, etc. The deverbal nouns in (8) are impossible for the simple reason that purely functional particles do not license conversion to a noun (Miller 2013). Since for Roeper (1999) all particles originate in the same clitic position, there is no reason (8) should not exist. Also, the V–P type (***cook-under* etc.) in (8) is doubly bad because normal (left-)adjunction in (7a) could only yield a P–V form.

4.4 V–P nouns

Nouns like *lookout* [1699] 'watchman', [1700] 'station for a watchman' are proper to English.[7] Apart from two dubious examples, the earliest follow (Bragdon 2006):

> *runabout* [1378] (*Robert renne-aboute*, a descriptive surname in *Piers Plowman*), [1549] 'person who runs about from place to place' (pl. *Runabouts*)
> *lean-to* [1453–4]
> *sit-up* [1483] 'surprise', [1843] 'act of sitting up', [1955] 'physical exercise'
> *startup* [1517] 'rustic boot', [1557] 'upstart, parvenu'
> *Passover* [1530] (Tyndale, *Exodus* 12.11)
> *runaway* [1547]
> *put-off* [1548] 'dismissal', [1623] 'postponement'
> *wind-up* [1573] 'conclusion' (*the windupal(l) of that me(e)ting*)
> *pull-down* [1588] 'act of pulling down; something pulled down'
> *set-up* [1607]
> *set-out* adj. [1608]; noun [1806] 'display', [1809] 'a spread of food', [1821] 'beginning'
> *drawback* [1619] 'one who delays', [1720] 'hindrance', [1753] 'diminution'

The question is, to what extent does the structure projected from the semantic features predict the output forms of these constructs? Recall that English has many noun pairs with different meanings, e.g.

> startup : upstart   setup : upset
> lookout : outlook   layout : outlay
> layover : overlay   hangover : overhang
> breakout : outbreak

The question is why one semantic representation is associated with P–V and another with V–P. From the semantic point of view, either could have the same meaning. Recall that Old English had only the P–V type, which therefore had to be able to bear both sets of meanings. Meaning by itself is thus compatible with either V–P or P–V order. This is where the structure comes in, and again, it is not ad hoc, stipulated, or in any sense a given, but projected from the semantic features.

As noted above, purely functional particles do not license conversion to a noun. The various syntactic positions of particles with lexical content determine whether

---

[7] Thanks to Zygmunt Frajzyngier for valuable comments on this section. The history and derivation of bare nouns that consist of a verb plus particle (type *breakout*) or P–V nouns (like *outbreak*) are detailed in Miller (2013). Early examples in other Germanic languages, like Sw. *Kikut/kikut* 'lookout (place)', Dan. *Kigud*, Old Dutch *kijcuut*, etc., beside modern Sw. *utkik*, Du. *uitkijk* 'lookout', are also discussed in Miller (2013).

the converted noun has a P–V or V–P structure. With a rigorous application of (left-) adjunction, the structures projected by independently obtained semantic representations *predict* the proper V–P or P–V output with no stipulations.

4.4.1 V–P nouns with full argument structure

One well-known V–P noun that can have an external argument and a complement is *knockout* (adj. [1818], event noun [1854], person [1892]), illustrated by *(Ali's) knockout (of Frazier)* in (9).

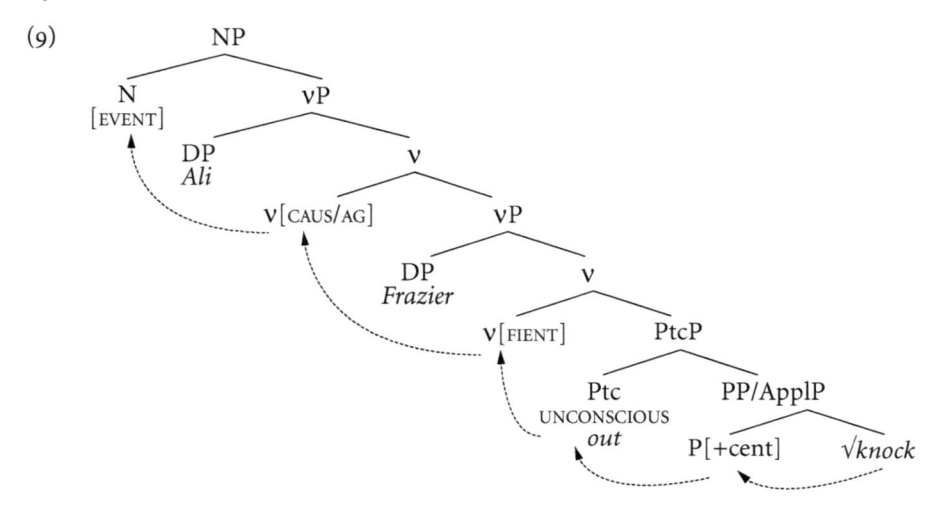

(9)
```
           NP
          /  \
         N    vP
      [EVENT]/  \
           DP    v
           Ali  / \
          v[CAUS/AG] vP
                    /  \
                  DP    v
                Frazier/ \
                   v[FIENT] PtcP
                           /    \
                         Ptc   PP/ApplP
                     UNCONSCIOUS /    \
                         out  P[+cent] √knock
```

The intent of (9) is to capture '(the/an) event (of) Ali caus(ing) Frazier (to) get-to-be [in the result state] UNCONSCIOUS/out by knock(ing)'. Toward the bottom of the tree, the Particle Phrase (PtcP) has a particle with the semantic content of UNCONSCIOUS as its head. It has merged with an applicative (McGinnis 2005), which introduces an oblique argument. The head of the Applicative Phrase is an abstract preposition with a [+cent(ral)] feature denoting a *with/by* relation necessary for semantic interpretation of the root (Tyler 1999: 129–36, 143; Hale and Keyser 2002: 161, 185ff.). The higher *v* has a causative or agentive feature, and the lower one is fientive (cf. BECOME). The radical (root) entry, as always, differs from a categorized item in leaving it open for surface nouns, verbs, and adjectives to undergo the same derivation.

The features in the verbalizing projection (§3.4) license the attracting event (or individual) noun which forces *knock* to move overtly and adjoin to *out*. Head movement, of course, bypasses the phrasal projections containing the names in (8). The root *knock* moves into the abstract P for the 'by' interpretation, then (left-) adjoins to *out*, yielding *knockout*, which then incorporates the fientive and the causative/agentive projections, which make it a verb with the appropriate 'cause to become' semantics. Finally, the verbalized *knockout* is nominalized by moving into the empty noun head.

Crucially, the syntactic configuration in (9) predicts that *knockout* is the only possible output and that **outknock* is completely impossible in the intended meaning.

Other words of the *knockout* class include *pull-down* [1588], *drawback* [1619], *knockdown* [1690], *castoff* [1740], *breakup* [1795], *breakout* [1820], *breakdown* [1832], *lay-out* [1852], *break-in* [1856], *layoff* [1889], *throw-down* [1896], *takeover* [1917], *breakthrough* [1918], *build-up* [1927], *turnaround* [1936], *knock-over* [1952].

4.4.2 *V–P nouns with simpler argument structure*

Particles whose function is arguably adverbial make only V–P nouns, e.g. *sit-up* [1484] 'surprise' (**upsit*), *run-away* [1547] (**away-run*), *come-down* [1563] 'ruined edifice', [1840] 'descent, downfall', *stand-by* [1796] (**bystand*), *walk-about* [1828] (**aboutwalk*), *walk-through* [1920] (**throughwalk*), *sleepover* [1935], *carryout* [1935$_A$, 1940$_N$].

Out is semantically an adverb in *cookout*, which means 'cook outside/outdoors', again having lexical content to license conversion. As an adverb, *out* is adjoined to the functional verbalizing projection. Crucially, there is no result state, hence no vP [FIENT] projection. The meaning of the verb portion of the derivation in (10) is 'do a cooking' (or the like). See Folli and Harley (2007) for v[AG] alone.

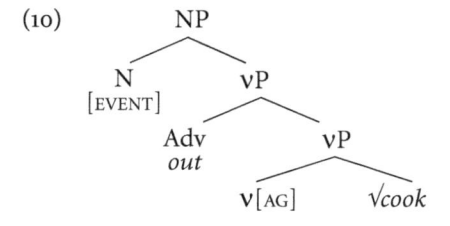

(10)
```
           NP
          /  \
         N    vP
      [EVENT] / \
           Adv   vP
           out   / \
              v[AG] √cook
```

In this configuration, *cook* can adjoin to *out*, but not vice versa, correctly yielding *cookout* as the only possible noun. The derivation also explains the noun's lack of a complex event structure. I assume that the noun *lookout* is derived similarly, except that the abstract noun in its unmarked interpretation bears a probing [AG/INDIVIDUAL] feature.

For *sleepover* and *carryout*, some speakers admit a complement (Lieber 2005: 399f.), suggesting a change in progress involving a switch to more argument structure, as in (9).

An unaccusative like *the car broke down* derives from 'the car got-to-be down/ DYSFUNCTIONAL by break(ing)' (11).

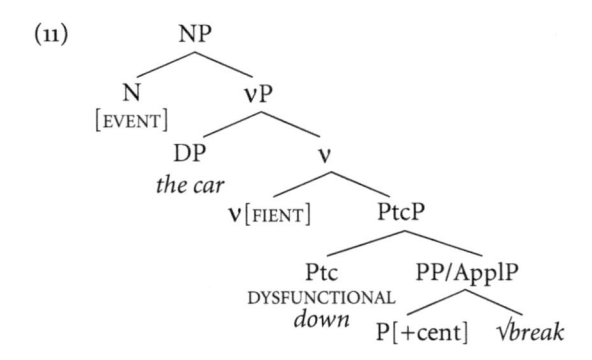

(11)
```
          NP
         /  \
        N    vP
     [EVENT] / \
           DP   v
        the car/ \
          v[FIENT] PtcP
                  /   \
                Ptc   PP/ApplP
           DYSFUNCTIONAL / \
               down  P[+cent] √break
```

There is no causative projection and the lexical content of the particle licenses conversion to the noun. *Break* is correctly predicted to (left-)adjoin to *down*, yielding *breakdown*. *Breakup* is similarly derived, but *up* would be the spellout of a different abstract feature. *The fire burned out* would have a similar derivation, viz. 'the fire got-to-be GONE/EXTINGUISHED/out by burning', hence the noun *burn-out*. The modern psychological sense of *burnout* [1975] derives from a verb *burn out* in the new sense, which would presumably derive from something like 'get-to-be EXHAUSTED by OVERWORK'.

4.5 The suffix *-ee*

The suffix *-ee* has a variety of functions (Barker 1998; Muñoz 2003). The concern here is its productive complement role and the constructs in (2a) above, i.e. %*march-through-ee*, *explain-away-ee*, but not *march-ee through, *explain-ee away, ?**march-ee through-ee* (which evokes humor in language play).

In *march-through-ee* 'that which is marched through', *through* is a preposition; *-ee* should be its complement, but that does not explain how it heads the construct. Like *-er*, it must originate in a c-commanding noun node. Also like *-er*, it saturates an argument position, this time the complement position. Unlike *-er*, *-ee* has no agent or causer, hence the impossibility of *(*an*) *employee by Mary* (van Hout and Roeper 1998: 177f.). It has an event that can be marginally modified, as in %*the march-through-ee for the past year* (*finally surrendered*). Since *-ee* nouns represent states, it is not surprising that the event is marginal. There is no syntactic evidence for external causation. Thus *march-through-ee* derives from (12), the basic idea of which is 'get-to-be through [x] by march(ing)', in which *through* differs from the particles in the other derivations in this chapter only in having a complement of its own.

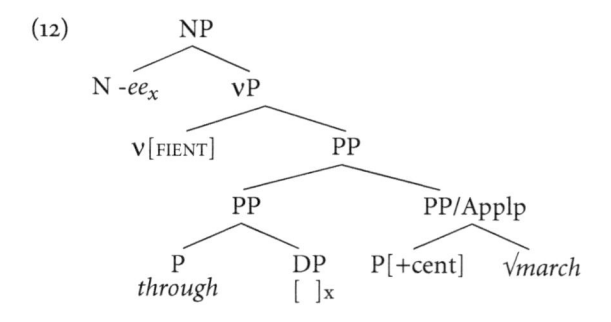

(12)
```
              NP
             /  \
         N -eeₓ   vP
                 /  \
            v[FIENT]  PP
                     /  \
                   PP    PP/Applp
                  /  \    /    \
                 P   DP  P[+cent] √march
              through [ ]x
```

In this configuration, the root *march* first incorporates the central P which imparts the means interpretation. Next *march* (left-)adjoins to *through*, yielding *march-through*, which then undergoes verbalization in *v*[FIENT], and finally adjoins to *-ee*. The suffix *-ee* is referentially coindexed with the null complement of *through*, which will be theta-identified with a noun in syntax. To concretize, in several wars Warsaw$_x$ was the march-through-ee$_x$. A similar derivation, but with an abstract event noun in place of *-ee*, would yield *march-through*.

Crucially, the syntactic configuration predicts that only *march-through(-ee)* is possible, and that **through-march(-ee)*, **through-ee-march*, etc., are completely impossible formations in the intended meaning.

4.6 Double -er

Barring residues, the oldest forms of (2d) in (13a) are deviant today, and the intermediate forms in (13b) have an archaic ring[8] compared to their replacements in (13c).

(13) (a) *onlooker* [1606], *outlooker* [1606], *outbreaker* [c.1650], *outspeaker* [1858]
     (b) *?%breaker out, ?%looker on, ?%speaker out* [all * for me]
     (c) *break-er-out-er, look-er-on-er, speak-er-out-er*

The *-er* type behaves differently from the others in (2) above in allowing the suffix both before and after the P-word. The productive double *-er* type is not mentioned by Jespersen (1942), but note *picker-upper* [1913], *builder-upper, dragger-downer* [1931], *fixer-upper* [1932], *finder-outer* [1934], *helper-outer, warmer-upper* [1935], *stepper-upper* [1936], *giver-upper, looker-oner, tearer-downer* [1937], etc. (Denison 2008:

---

[8] Historically (13b) was the most frequent type (Chapman 2008: 273). McIntyre (2001) cites *a washer up* (which to me is *), but mentions (p.c.) that *washer-up* and *wash-up-er* are ?? for him and that the norm in Australian English is also *washer-upper*. Generally speaking, double *-er* is preferred (Chapman 2008: 268), especially among younger speakers, when the formation is not avoided because of prescriptive uncertainty.

210). Many examples can be found in Farrell (2005: 102f.), McIntyre (2004b; 2009), Walker (2009), Cappelle (2003; 2010).

A few of the observations in McIntyre's contributions include: (i) *fixer-upper* as a building has a patient interpretation, but can also be agentive; (ii) final reduplication (*picker-upperer*) is fairly common, in obvious violation of the haplological constraint; (iii) double *-er* is now matched by double *-ed* (e.g. *fucked-upedness*). Cappelle (2003) mentions the following: *singer-alonger* (a song that makes you sing along), "a Harry Potter *knower all abouter*", "public toilet *hanger arounder*", "life *fritter-awayer*", "bandwagon *hopper-onner*", and occasional double plurals like *runners-awayers*. McIntyre (2009) discusses *site watcher-overer*, *maze-goer-througher*, *movie writer-abouter*, *photo looker-at-er*.

It has been argued that only one *-er* is productive and the other a phonological copy, but which is which? Based on the contrast between *picker-upper* and *picker-uppee*, to the total exclusion of **pickee-upper*, Miller (1993: 132f.) claims that the inner *-er* is redundant. Cappelle (2003; 2010) and McIntyre (2009) agree, citing *breaker-upper/breaker-uppee*, and *eye-putter-outee*.[9] This is confirmed by *the present giver-out-er-er* (McIntyre 2001; 2004b; 2009) with final *-er* reduplicated in violation of at least the haplological constraint (§2.2); cf. also *sorter-outerer*, *giver-upperer* (Elenbaas 2007: 18), but *knocker-overer* (Denison 2008: 211) has one *-er* on *over*. Cappelle also notes that the second *-er* should be the head because it takes number inflection, e.g. *picker-uppers*. The total absence of **pickers-upper* (but note *passers-byers, pickers-uppers*: Fortin 2011: 95) shows that this is not just a morphosyntactic locus (*mother-in-laws*) problem because *mothers-in-law* is not judged nearly as illformed, and some speakers continue to find it quite acceptable.

On the other hand, if the inner *-er* is redundant, why is the simple construct **break-out-er* such a monstrosity? The inner *-er* appears necessary as some sort of licenser for the outer *-er*. At first glance, this might look like an antisymmetric effect (something on the left licenses something on the right), but when **break-out-er* is confronted with *%break-out-ee, take-out-ee*, etc., the anomaly of *breaker-outer* re-emerges, except that *break-out-ee* is the only possibility, as noted above.

The double *-er* forms are genuine nominalizations. McIntyre (2001) cites the examples with complement in (14).

(14) (a) *a fucker-upper of people's lives*
    (b) *a filler-inner of forms* (some speakers: 'one who pours concrete in a frame')

The *-er* suffix obligatorily saturates the agent position (i.e. is the agent) and closes it generically or existentially. Thus a *knockout* as a person differs from a *knocker-outer*

---

[9] Andrew McIntyre (p.c.) mentions the sentence "The soldier didn't like shooting people, but he reasoned that it's better to be a *taker-outer* than a *take-(er)-out-ee*".

in that the latter is more compositionally literal as an agentive and gets the generic or characterizing interpretation of *-er*.[10]

When the verb and particle are not phase-fixed, *-er* is not blocked, hence the older type *breaker out* (13b).[11] That type is derivable like *explaining away*, i.e. by moving the verb and thereby stranding the P-word, prior to fixing of the phase complement.

In what follows, a solution for the *breaker-outer* type is sketched. Assuming the derivation of *knockout* in §4.4, we can posit (15) to underlie *breaker-outer*, from something like 'one who causes (someone) to get-to-be out by break(ing)'.

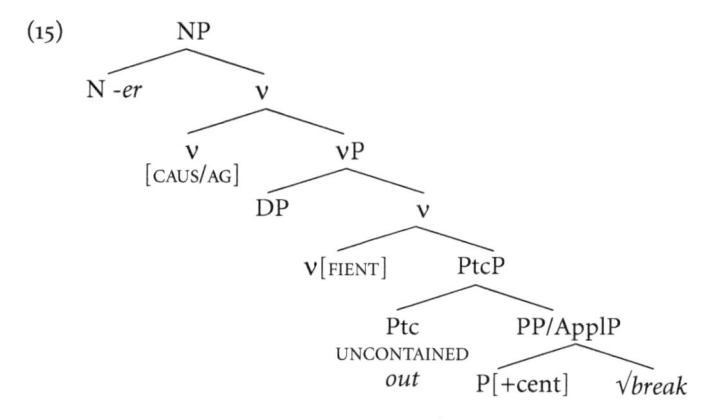

(15)
```
        NP
       /  \
    N -er   v
           / \
          v   vP
       [CAUS/AG]
              / \
             DP  v
                / \
           v[FIENT] PtcP
                    /  \
                  Ptc   PP/ApplP
              UNCONTAINED  /  \
                  out   P[+cent] √break
```

The root *break* first incorporates the central P which imparts the means interpretation. Next *break* (left-)adjoins to *out* but does not get phase-fixed because the higher structure forces something to move, thus ruling out **breakouter*. Two derivations are possible, depending on whether *out* or *break* moves to the edge of *v*P and escapes phase fixing. If *break* moves first, that would give *breaker*, to which *out* should adjoin, yielding ?*outbreaker* (type (13a) above). This is the less preferred derivation.

---

[10] Agentives crosslinguistically subdivide into two classes (Vendler 1967): (i) specific states of actors who perform habitual activities, e.g. *smokers, painters*; (ii) variable generic states, e.g. *rulers, servants*. Type (i) designates a permanent or habitual characteristic of an individual actor. In type (ii), the action is performed relative to a situation that can be ongoing, hypothetical, or interrupted (*LSDE* 91, w. lit). Since this cannot be a language-specific quirk of particular affixes, it must be structural, corresponding to the two kinds of closure, existential and generic.

[11] A PHASE is a self-contained unit of syntactic computation that is sent to spellout. At spellout, the complement of the phase-defining head is transferred to the phonological (PHON) and semantic (SEM) interfaces for interpretation and fixing (Chomsky, e.g. 2001; 2005: 17ff.; 2008).

Phases minimize computational load. At least *v*P and CP are phases, *v*P because it introduces full argument structure, CP because it constitutes full propositional structure. On the sound side, these units exhibit relative independence. Other possible phases and criteria for phasehood remain under discussion, e.g. Chomsky (2008). Marantz (2007) and Basilico (2008; forthcoming) argue that *v*P[FIENT] is a phase.

Once constructed, a phase becomes impenetrable by the Phase Impenetrability Condition (PIC). Consequently, anything in the complement of the phase that must move is forced to move to the edge ((outer) specifier or adjunct) of the complement of the phase prior to spellout, or it becomes trapped, and will be spelled out in its base position.

If *out* moves to the edge of the *v*P phase, it must eventually be joined by *break*, but [[break] [out]] will not be phase-fixed. This permits both to adjoin independently to a fissioned *-er*, giving *breaker-outer*, the rationale for fissioning being that two phonologically independent constituents can adjoin to it. The constituent order [[break] [out]] permits *out* to adjoin to *-er*, but *-er* most naturally attracts a verb, motivating fission, which splits a single morpheme (one bundle of features) into two or more positions of exponence (Halle 1997: 432ff.; Halle and Vaux 1998: 227ff.).

One potential problem with this analysis is the apparent lack of a similar derivation of other constructs, e.g. *-able*, giving things like *?explainable awayable*. Perhaps nothing rules these out, thus accounting for recent constructs like *pickable-upable* reported by Farrell (2005: 103). And some of these, like *?explainable awayable*, may be avoided because of their phonological heaviness (Andrew McIntyre, p.c.).

With fissioning of a single head, there is still only one head for semantic purposes (contrast suffix reapplications that count semantically §2.6), which happens to be split. What then predicts where inflection goes? Perhaps there is again a choice. Since the morphosyntactic locus in English is on the right in the unmarked case, that is the most natural place for it. However, if it is true that the constituents remain phonologically independent, this accounts for two additional facts. First, these constructs bear two stresses (*fíxer-úpper, breáker-oúter*), which is very unusual in word formation, being matched by dvandvas (*cát-dóg fight*) which have notoriously independent constituents, admitting an optional conjunction (*cát-and-dóg fight*) (§3.5.2). Second, phonological independence of the two constituents can predict the type *runners-awayers* with double inflection mentioned by Cappelle (2003). McIntyre (2009) relates this to the *%sisters-in-laws* type. Double inflection is most frequent on left-headed forms, like *passers-bys*. Phonological independence can also predict the participle *fixered-uppered* spontaneously uttered by the same individual who "*fixer-uppered* a house". McIntyre (2009) also reports *fixing-upping*. All of these seem to suggest some independence of the constituents even after undergoing denominal conversion.

Finally, fissioning of *-er* accounts for why the type *??breakouter* is so monstrous for so many current English speakers. In verbal configurations, *-er* attaches most naturally to the verb, which is not satisfied at all in the *??breakouter* type. Chapman (2008: 279) considers this another productive pattern and thinks that *picker-upper* is just an intermediate stage in the development from *picker-up* to *pick-upper*. But another problem with the *pick-upper* type is the stress-clash and the problem of which stress to suppress. *Picker-up* and *picker-upper* preserve the stress of both constituents (cf. McIntyre 2004b; Denison 2008: 212f., both w. lit).

Ackema and Neeleman (2004: 160f.) give an optimality account of double *-er*, but a phase theoretical account is more explanatory of all of the quirky properties of this English-unique construct. At the same time, some optimality may be at issue, but only as part of the motivation for the fissioning of *-er*. If attachment to a verb were the sole requirement, ?*outbreaker* or ?*breaker out* should be perfectly wellformed. The only way attachment to a verb and adjunction of [[break] [out]] to -*er* can be satisfied is by fissioning -*er*.

Much remains poorly understood about double -*er* agentives because the change is in progress and the full range of possible constructs has yet to be realized. As more examples emerge, the analysis will have to change commensurately.

4.7 Deverbal -*able* and the *laugh-at-able* type

Deverbal -*able* has many different functions and semantic values (*LSDE*² 223–32, 391; Miller 2012: 181f.). Only relevant here is passive -*able* which states the capacity of a passive event to be fulfilled (*LSDE*² 230ff., 391). This section argues that the option of *explainable-away* or *explain-away-able* is contingent on the head or non-head status of the particle.

The entries in (16) are cited by McIntyre (2001). Many more are listed in Farrell (2005: 102f.).

(16) *use-up-able, pick-up-able (?%pickable up), unmake-upable (?*unmakable up)*

Early examples include *come-at-able* [1687], *laugh-at-able* [1759], *get-at-able* [1799], *unrelyuponable* [1840], *unkeepoffable* [1843], *undowithoutable* [1844] (cf. Jespersen 1942: 40ff.), *untalkaboutable* [1862], *unwipeupable* [a.1864], *ungetonable* [1873], *undryupable* [1888], *unputdownable* [1947], *unwearoutable* [1968], *unswitchoffable* [1974]. These constructs have been sufficiently well entrenched in English that there are even early derivatives, like *comeatability* [1760], *getatability* [1863], *getatableness* [1890].

The major concern of this section are the types *think-through-able* and *explain-away-able*. In this case, the older *thinkable through* and *explainable away* remain viable options.

Baker (2003: 285) argues that -*able* is an adjectival head that takes a passive verb phrase as its complement. It is not quite that simple, because there are many active -*able* formations, which shows that passive is structural and not part of the meaning of -*able*. Even with passive -*able* there is considerable variation. While -*able* originates as an adjective in all cases, it is a probe for several different features. For most speakers in my sample (see below), -*able* attracts a passive *v*P or, for a smaller number, a middle. There are also speakers for whom -*able* attracts AspP (as evidenced by the allowance of aspectual adverbs) plus a passive *v*P. A slightly smaller number of speakers permit certain mood/modal adverbs, signalling that for them -*able* attracts MP along with the relevant features of a passive *v*P, as illustrated in (17), with my grammaticality judgments.[12]

---

[12] Of the 32 American English speakers I have interviewed on -*able*, 3 reject the agent *by*-phrase under all circumstances, and 3 others get it marginally but regularly have only the middle structure with *for*. This

(17) Adverbial evidence for higher sentential structure with -*able*
 (a) AspP: *Carthage was destroyable completely (by Rome)*[13]
 (b) MP: (1) *Carthage was destroyable eventually (by Rome)* [potential]
   (2) ?*Carthage was destroyable unfortunately (by Rome)* [evaluative]
   (3) **Carthage was destroyable certainly (by Rome)* [epistemic]
   (4) ***Carthage was destroyable frankly (by Rome)* [speech act]

In *explainable away*, *explain* does not adjoin to *away*. In *explainawayable (problem)* (18), *explain* adjoins to *away* in a derivation whose semantic content is 'able to be caused (the problem) [to] get-to-be GONE/*away* by explain(ing)'. For heuristic reasons, the potential mood and aspect projections are ignored here.

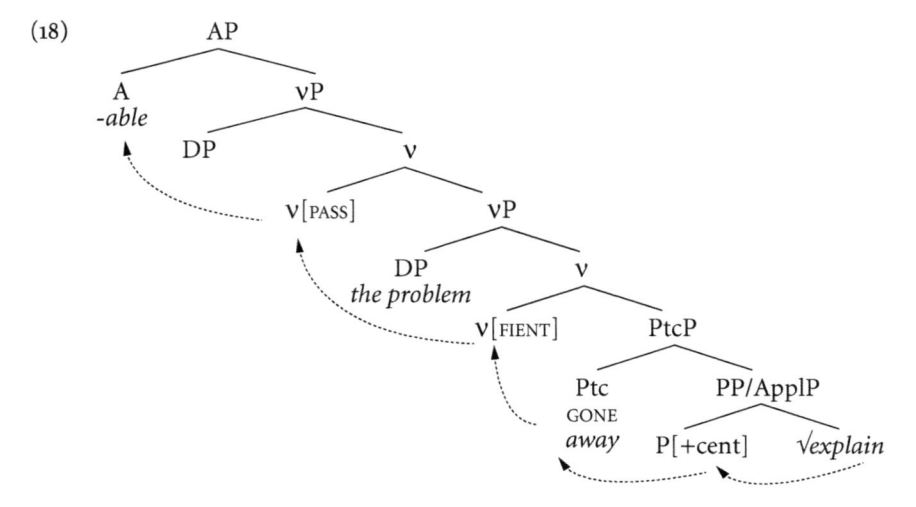

(18)
```
             AP
           /    \
          A      vP
        -able   /  \
              DP    v
                   / \
              v[PASS]  vP
                      /  \
                    DP    v
                the problem / \
                      v[FIENT] PtcP
                              /    \
                            Ptc    PP/ApplP
                           GONE    /     \
                           away  P[+cent] √explain
```

Explain (left-)adjoins to *away*, and that amalgam then undergoes verbalization and passivization and adjoins to -*able*. What predicts whether *explain* adjoins to *away* or not? In *explainable away*, *away* is phrasal on the evidence of potential modifiers, like *explainable right away*. In *explainawayable*, no modifiers of *away* are possible because *away* is a head pure and simple, enabling participation in head movement.

The prepositional types *march-through-able* and *marchable through* are similar except that in place of a particle, there is a preposition with null complement to be

---

seems generational, since they are from different parts of the country but all 6 are in their 20s. Most speakers accept more of the sentential structure in (17). Twenty-six get the *by*-phrase. Of those, an additional 5 get the *by*-phrase plus (17a). This leaves a total of 21 who get the *by*-phrase plus (17a) and (17b1). Most of those find (17b2) marginal in contrast to the ungrammatical (17b3, 4). The majority of speakers in my sample, then, get a structure higher than a passive *v*P.

[13] One reader mentions that since *Joe's face was red completely* is also good, *completely* proves nothing. But *completely* in the reader's example can only be emphatic. In (17) the adverbs (on which see Cinque 1999 etc.) must be construed in a non-emphatic manner, and with no pause before them.

theta-identified with a noun in syntax, as in §4.5. The derivation in (19) captures a semantic representation 'able [to] be caused [to] get-to-be through (something) by march(ing)'.

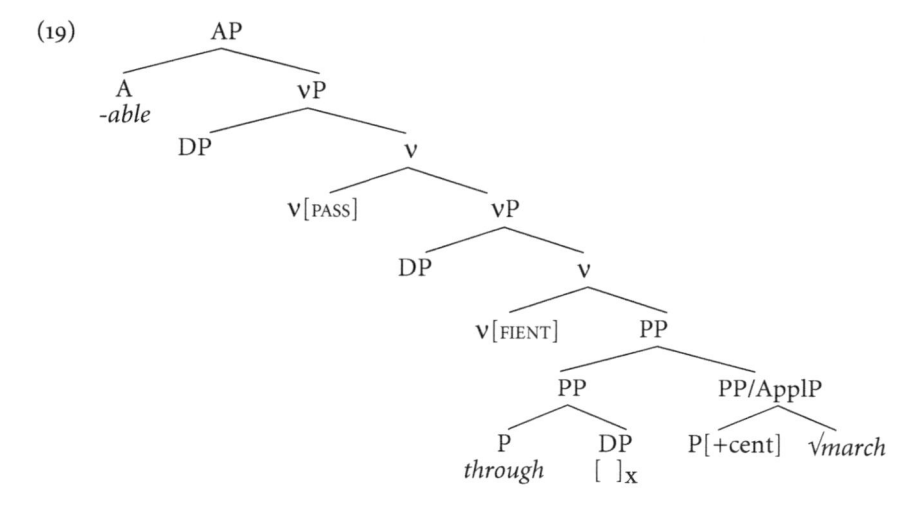

(19)

```
              AP
             /  \
            A    vP
          -able / \
               DP  v
                  / \
                 /   \
            v[PASS]   vP
                     /  \
                    DP   v
                        / \
                       /   \
                  v[FIENT]  PP
                           /  \
                          PP   PP/ApplP
                         /  \    /    \
                        P   DP  P[+cent] √march
                     through [ ]ₓ
```

What determines whether or not *march* adjoins to *through* is the head or phrasal status of *through*. If it is phrasal, as in *marchable right through*, adjunction cannot occur. If it is a simple head, *march* adjoins and the output is *march-through-able*. Crucially, those are the only possibilities. There is no way a **through-march-able* or anything else could be derived from the syntactic configuration in (19).

4.8 Summary

Derivationally, words with particles constitute one of the most difficult aspects of English word formation. The problem has been exacerbated by attempts to create a unified analysis of particles (e.g. Roeper 1999). While this is a reasonable goal, a unified account does not entail that all particles originate in a single place, such as Roeper's CLITIC POSITION. In fact, accounts of that type have complicated the issue by making it impossible to rule out certain noun formations resulting from conversion, or to adequately predict whether the converted noun will have a V–P or a P–V structure.

This chapter has argued that particles have several different functions and syntactic positions. Those that originate in functional projections do not license conversion to a noun. The various syntactic positions of particles determine whether the converted noun has a V–P or P–V structure. Since this is predictable from the hierarchical configuration in conjunction with independently motivated semantic representations, there is no need for stipulations.

Recent theoretical advances, such as phase theory, provide for more sophisticated analyses of one of the most difficult problems in English morphology. When coupled with the morphological device of fissioning, even the notoriously difficult English double -*er* agentives admit a straightforward account.

For several of the difficult types in this chapter, whether or not the particle (or preposition) participates in head movement and undergoes adjunction depends on its status as a head or phrasal category.

With the possible exception of the type ?*marchee-throughee*, which seems to occur only in language play (to this point in the history of English, at least), the rest of the formations in this chapter belong to the core morphology of English. This will become important in later chapters where the theme of language play is developed and distinguished from core morphology.

5

Novel word crafting

This chapter focuses on analogy (since all neologisms are modeled on prior knowledge), creativity, and imagination. Types of language play discussed range from puns to games like Pig Latin, spoonerisms, Homer Simpson's -*ma*- infixation, and expletive insertion. The domain for all of these is argued to involve the prosodic properties of output words. In figures of speech and rhetorical devices, motivated properties of words are extended to larger units of speech. Our final examples derive from verbal art. One is the playful creation of novel words, another includes innovations in the use of stacked prepositions.

5.1 Lexicogenesis

Lexicogenesis is defined with reference to the operations involved in creating words.

Cook (2010: 2) claims to distinguish two kinds of neologism but in reality recognizes three: (i) novel constructs (e.g. *webisode* for *web* × *episode*), (ii) existing words with new meanings, e.g. *circuit, digital, logic*—all dating to the Middle English period and recycled by computer scientists with new but readily derivable meanings (Ahmad 2000: 714), and (iii) new category functions like the verb *(to) google* from the noun *Google*.

Tournier (e.g. 1988; 1991) defines four macro mechanisms that yield four types of neologism. The first is morphosemantic for deriving novel forms and meanings via prefixation, suffixation, backformation, compounding, blending, and onomatopoeia. The second is semantic for applying old names to novel concepts via metaphor, metonymy, and conversion. The third is morphological in that only the form is altered via clipping and acronomy. The fourth is borrowing.

Some additional mechanisms are mentioned by Geeraerts (2002: 32):

Lexicogenesis involves the mechanisms for introducing new pairs of word forms and word meanings—all the traditional mechanisms, in other words, like word formation, word creation (the creation of entirely new roots), borrowing, blending, truncation, ellipsis, folk etymology and others, that introduce new items into the onomasiological inventory of a language. Crucially, the semasiological extension of the range of meanings of an existing word is itself one of the major mechanisms of onomasiological change—one of the mechanisms, that is, through which a concept to be expressed gets linked to a lexical expression.

Tournier's classification will be refined to distinguish grammatical knowledge from the more consciously motivated processes (see Chapter 15), to which will be added Geeraerts' more general onomasiological perspective. *Onomasiology* (G *ónoma* 'name'), coined in German by Zauner (1902), is the science of the means of expressing a given concept. The present book, like any work on neologisms, is concerned with onomasiological change and the various means by which it is accomplished. More generally, all of this can be subsumed under lexical change, an aspect of language change (Fischer 1998).

Motivations of core lexical change are summarized by Grzega and Schöner (2007: 36) as follows, together with my own illustrations:

Onomasiological fuzziness: color shade between red and yellow → *orange* (§8.5)
Dominance of the prototype: *xerox* for *photocopy*, *coke* for *cola*, etc. (§6.7)
Demographics: G *sullogismós* 'reasoning' in philosophy → SYLLOGISM (§8.4)
Pre- and proscriptivism: *mentally retarded* → *intellectually/cognitively disabled*
   Political correctness: *plagiarism* → *unauthorized copying of written materials*
Flattery/insult: *nag, lamb* (§6.1); *jock, prick*; *hammerhead* (§6.7); *dunce* (§6.8)
Disguising language: *accidental killing by one's own troops* → *friendly fire*
   Disinformation/propaganda: *death panels, liberal media, the real America*
Tabu deformation and euphemism: *gee(z)* for *Jesus* (§7.2), *shtup* for *fuck* (§7.3)
   Avoidance of pernicious homophony: loss of *pussy* in the sense of 'kitten' (§7.3)
Avoidance of ambiguity: *hot hot* to disambiguate from *spicy hot* (§14.1)
Formal split: *(to) stiff* 'make stiff; cheat' → *stiffen* 'make stiff'/*stiff* 'cheat' (Miller 2010: ii. 116); *flower* →*flower/flour* (§6.5)
Word play/punning: *ambisextrous* (*ambidextrous*), *outercourse* (*intercourse*) (§5.4)
Communicative economy: *facsimile telegraph(y)* → *telefax* → *fax* (§11.3)
   Wit + economy: *WASP* (§9.4); *local low cost phone call* → *Lo-Call* (§12.4)
Folk eymology: F *chaise longue* 'long chair' → *chaise-lounge* (§7.1)
Morphological regularization: *warmness* beside *warmth* (§2.1), *edit* after *editor* (§1.7)
Plasticity/salience: onomatopoeia (Chapter 10), hyperbole, tautology, etc. (§8.1)
Anthropological salience (prototypicality): underived property concepts (e.g. *wide, flat*) contrast with result states (*flattened*), but a subclass of property concepts have a result state antonym, e.g. *raw/cooked, solid/melted* (LSDE 4–17, w. lit)
Cultural salience: American football metaphors: *fumble, Monday morning quarterback, first down, punt*
   Cultural change: meal between breakfast and lunch → *brunch* (§12.1)
   Changes in scientific knowledge: *bacillus, bacterium* (§8.7); *pixel* (§12.3)
Change in real-world referent: *electricity* [1646] 'property of rubbed amber' (§6.2)
Change in world view: *homosexual/queer* → *gay* (§§7.3, 8.2)
Emulation of a prestige language/variety: *lingerie, liqueur, cuisine* (§8.7)

Additional motivations will be added in subsequent chapters, but these examples are typical and provide a succinct account of the varied purposes for lexicogenesis.

5.2 Need is the mother of all invention—or is it?

The lexicon is completely open. Words come and go. Recall the fate of *groovy*. As an extension from the literal meaning 'having or resembling a groove' [1853], in 1937 *groovy* was adapted as a term for capable jazz musicians playing 'in the groove', then in the end of the 1950s applied more generally in the sense of 'excellent; cool'. By the end of the 60s the word was moribund but it enjoyed a resurgence in the late 70s. By the 90s it was seldom heard, and it is now completely dead in most circles. The fate of a word is contingent entirely on its degree of acceptance by the public. In this case, the word was used mostly by young people and never attained acceptance in influential circles.

Even words that have become fully INSTITUTIONALIZED (§1.8) can fall into disuse and disappear. The standard Old English word *rōd* ROOD was displaced by borrowed *cross* (Miller 2012: 46f.). Although the *OED* records attestations of *rood* as recently as 2006, it occurs only in highly literary and theologically or historically oriented texts, and most native speakers of English would be entirely clueless as to its meaning.

It is interesting to speculate on why some words do not exist despite an obvious need. For instance, *overwhelm* [a.1338] had no opposite until recently when *underwhelm* [1956] made it to the *OED* (but is still labeled 'jocular'). Similarly, I have witnessed several attempts at creating an antonym for *exaggerate*. One was *underzaggerate*. Someone with more classical training might opt for *subaggerate*. But nearly every native speaker of English would reject that for the simple reason that there is no English root *aggerate*. Rather, an anglophile might prefer *subzaggerate* or the more Englishy *underzaggerate* since the English root is *zaggerate*. Why? Because of the way *exaggerate* is pronounced, the *ex-* is readily segmented off, leaving *zaggerate*. This explains why, from the English point of view, *subzaggerate* or *underzaggerate* are preferable to the more Latinate *subaggerate*. There is in fact no reason *underzaggerate* should not be a perfectly good English word. All it would take to catch on is for enough people to hear it and repeat it.

Creation of *underzaggerate* has a certain parallel in *outro* [1967] 'concluding section (e.g. of a piece of music)', modeled after *intro* [1923], clipped from *introduction* (§11.2), ultimately from L *intrōductiō* [*intrō* 'inside' + *ductiō* 'a leading'] 'introduction'. By contrast, *outro* is purely English, taking *out* as the opposite of *in* in E *intro*.

Although *uncouth* has traditionally had no paired affirmative, *couth* is frequent. The *OED* online lists only five attestations from 1896 to 1968, but *couth* gets several hundred thousand hits on Google, including derivatives like *couthiness*, which originally meant 'familiarity' [1808]. In fact, the expected derivative might be *couthness* [1982] on the model of *uncouthness* [1435] but *couthy/ie* [1719] has provided another derivational base.

Another gap is (*)*lukecool* in the face of *lukewarm*, a very old word in English, first used by John of Trevisa in 1398. Nothing but tradition makes *luke* acceptable as a qualifier of warmth but not coolness. The older meaning of *luke*, in Laȝamon [?*a.*1200], was '(luke)warm'. Since only tradition stands in the way of *lukecool*, there is no reason it could not become generally accepted if a number of people started using it. In fact, *lukecool* is common on Google, and the *Urban Dictionary* quotes: "I went in for a cold shower. Unfortunately, that was too cold, so I had a lukecool one instead."

The Roman grammarian Varro [116–27 BCE], in his treatise 'On the Latin Language' [*c.*44 BCE], provided an interesting critique of both existing and nonexisting forms. Taking the label for a thing or concept to be arbitrary,[1] he criticized the 'name-givers' (8.7) for according *aquila* 'eagle' only one form when it can be male or female. In other words, he expected **aquilus* (m.), *aquila* (f.). He also realized (9.55f.) that this is pragmatic, that *columba* 'dove' was originally generic, but the need to distinguish males and females for breeding prompted the innovation between *columbus* (m.) and *columba* (f.). After Varro's time, some generics that he predicted could have separate male and female forms in fact developed them, e.g. early Latin *porcus* 'swine' in Classical Latin contrasts *porcus* 'swine; male swine' and *porca* 'female swine'.

Varro recognized (non-)gradable adjectives (Fortin 2011: §4.3, w. lit) and explained (9.72) that Latin had no comparative **luscior* 'more one-eyed' for the simple reason that no one can be more one-eyed than someone else!

Contraction of *am not* to *ain't*, followed by generalization through the paradigm (*you ain't, s/he ain't,* etc.), resulted in a prohibition against using *ain't* that left a gap in the system: *isn't, aren't,* ??. That gap is frequently filled by *amn't* (*pace* Hudson 2000: 298; *pace* Ackema and Neeleman 2005: 299f.; *pace* Embick and Marantz 2008: 32, 34f.), which is regular in some varieties of English and gets many hits on Google.

---

[1] Varro anticipated de Saussure's arbitrariness of the sign (1916: 100f., 106; 1966), dogmatically assumed by many, as emphasized by Bolinger (1946), Jakobson (1960), Anderson (1998), and others. De Cuypere (2008) considers de Saussure's view a maxim rather than a dogma. Piaget (1973: 83) noticed that children up to about the age of 11 uniformly perceive a natural link between word and meaning (cf. Allott 1995). Piaget of course accepted de Saussure's maxim and found it curious that it takes children so long to realize that words are arbitrary but conventional, which misses the point. In reality, even de Saussure (1916: 180ff.) recognized partial motivation, e.g. *twenty-one, twenty-two* vs. *twenty*, or "secondary iconicity", as De Cuypere calls it. The many aspects of iconicity discussed throughout the current work show that numerous labels and structures are not arbitrary. Still, the rarity of true iconicity, like *U-turn* [1937], *S-curve(d)* [1940], with a meaning iconic to the form of the letter, suggest that *(non-)arbitrary* is a more accurate label. See Haiman (1980), Anderson (1998), Nänny and Fischer (1999), Fischer and Nänny (2001), Croft (2003), De Cuypere (2008: ch. 5), who argues that much of what has been claimed to be iconicity falls short, Croft (2008), and Haiman (2008). The linguistic use of *iconicity*, incidentally, is usually attributed to Jakobson (1965), but it was first so employed by Morris (1946: 191).

Not all concepts for which there is need of a label have one. Even important cultural concepts sometimes lack lexical expression. Aristotle mentioned that Greek had no word for the 'union of a woman and a man', i.e. no word for marriage.[2] Benveniste makes the more general point that Proto-Indo-European had no word for marriage. That is a long time for such a major lexical gap to persist. Words sometimes translated as 'marriage' involve the ritual ceremony rather than the result state. English *marry* [a1325] derives from L *marītāre* which in turn derives from *marītus* 'husband', the underlying idea apparently being something like 'do what a husband does', i.e. 'provide (a woman) with a husband', perhaps an extension of the Roman custom in which the man took the marital initiative by literally LEADING (*dūcere*) the woman into the legal status of motherhood (*mātrimōnium*) (Benveniste 1969: 1.239–44; *LSDE* 46).

In contemporary American English, there is a major lexical gap in connection with a good word for either of the parties of a couple living together who are not legally married. *Significant other* [1977] (but only more recently productive) is ludicrously cumbersome. Even more absurd were the terms tried out in the counterculture of the 1960s—*old man, old lady*. In the 1970s and 1980s, *mate* and *partner* were experimented with but found too sterile and unemotive.[3] Then came *friend*, which was too ambiguous and insufficiently descriptive. All of these attempts illustrate American dissatisfaction with the terms people have come up with, but simultaneously reveal that no one has yet devised a term that adequately represents our mental image or schema of the nature of the relationship.

The flipside of the coin involves vacuous synonyms, words which duplicate the meaning of other words. Many have argued that "true synonymy is so rare as to be almost non-existent" (Goddard 1998: 17; cf. Allan 2008: 114). In the creative language of slang, however, AVOID SYNONYMY (§2.5.4) appears not to apply; cf. *cocaine, coke, snow, freebase, crack; heroin, smack, horse*... (Mattiello 2008: 160ff.), but expressive meanings are in fact distinct. Of course these are also codewords among the ingroup, a kind of secret language.

New coinages or borrowings are expressive in ways that conventional words are not. In short, there are many reasons for neologisms. Labeling concepts to facilitate communication is but one. Since at least 85% of all communication is non-verbal, one must not ignore the evolutionary role of language in thinking (Chomsky 1986a). Tournier (e.g. 1988; 1991) also signals the playful impulse, novelty, attention, expressiveness.

---

[2] Aristotle, *Politics* 1.3.2: *anṓnumos hē gunaikòs kaì andròs súzeuxis* 'nameless is the union of a woman and a man' (Benveniste 1969: i. 239).
[3] An anonymous referee points out that in British English "*partner* is now absolutely normal in this use".

5.3 Analogical creations

Analogy is the backbone of creativity, i.e. the native speaker's ability to extend the language system in a motivated but unpredictable (non-rule governed) way which may or may not subsequently become rule-governed, predictable and productive. (Klégr and Čermák 2010: 235)

Miller (2010: 2.121) argues that all morphological formatives, no matter how rule-governed, productive, or even automatic, as in the case of English number inflection, spread initially by lexical diffusion.[4] Regarding the spread of the *-en* suffix (§2.2), *whiten* [a.1300], *blacken* [a.1300], *darken* [a.1300], *lighten*[2] [a.1300] mutually reinforced one another, especially given *brighten* [c.10]; *harden* [c.1180] paved the way for *soften* [1375], *fatten* [1552] for *plumpen* [1787], *slacken* [1580] for *tighten* [1727], *widen* [1569] for *deepen* [a1605], etc. With *deaden* [1665], cf. *enliven* [1633] and *liven* [1884]. "Roughly synonymous and antonymical pairs were created around the same time or slightly later" (Miller 2010: 2.112).

Lexical diffusion is evidently called LOCAL ANALOGY by Klégr and Čermák because it behaves the same: it "yields formations closely linked to the trigger word (and together) within a lexical field by formal and functional similarities" (2010: 237). The reality is that *local analogy* is meaningless because all analogy is local (Miller 2010: vol. 1, ch. 4).

Analogy, then, is not a separate type of word formation but is rather the means by which word creation originates and spreads. The motivation for lexicogenesis can be morphological, phonological, semantic, or a combination of these and extralinguistic factors. For English *-en*, the Norse-derived models imposed certain formal constraints: monosyllabic base, trochaic foot structure, and root-final obstruent (stop or fricative).

Klégr and Čermák (2010: 231) cite a number of examples which they conceptualize as different categories, e.g. *implode* [1881] after *explode* [1794] (in the relevant sense), *introjection* [1866] (*projection* [1477]), *oldster* [1818] (*youngster* [1589]), *cacography* [1580] (*orthography* [a1460]), *hands-on* [1969] (*hands-off* [a.1593]), *ascent* [1600] (from *ascend*) after *descent* [Ch.] (from *descend*), *walkathon* [1930] (*marathon* [1896]), etc. *Sordor* [1823] was created beside *sordid* on the model of *squalor* [1621] beside *squalid*.

One of the case studies in Klégr and Čermák (2010: 233) involves the creation of *anklet* after *bracelet* [1438] by Percy Bysshe Shelley in 1819. They describe the creative process in terms of the item (a piece of jewelry) and the formation: diminutive *-et* was supplanted by *-let* because of alternations between *bracel* and *brace* that permitted the resegmentation of *bracel-et* as *brace-let*, hence application of *-let* to *ankle*:

---

[4] *Lexical diffusion* refers to a change that begins in a few words and gradually spreads through the lexicon by abrupt substitution of a phoneme or morpheme, affecting one word, cluster, or class at a time (Miller 2010: 1.68–71, w. lit).

ank<le>let, but probably by the haplological constraint rather than Klégr and Čermák's proportional analogy *handle : hand = ankle :* × (→ *ank*). The main problem with their account is that there is only one attestation of *bracel*, in an introductory French text [?1533]. In fact, Koziol (1972: 249f.) shows that *-let* was borrowed in many words from Old French and applied by c16 to native bases, e.g. *streamlet* [a.1552], *townlet* [a.1552], *ringlet* [1555]. More likely, then, *anklet* was modeled on *bracelet* [1438], *frontlet* [1478], *armlet* [1535], *earlet* [1610], *winglet* [1611], *hornlet* [a1794], *liplet* [1815]. These constructs were voguish at the time. Note especially *leglet* [1821], *wristlet* [1847], items of jewelry. For additional details, see Schneider and Strubel-Burgdorf (2011).

Million served as the model for *billion*, *trillion*, which prompted the popular *jillion* [1942], *squillion* [1943], *zillion* [1944] by reanalysis (Klégr and Čermák 2010: 231, 236).

Warmth has given rise to *coolth* [1547] (Durkin 2011: 105f., 198). *Intro* spawned *outro* (§5.2). *Software* [1960] was modeled on (systems) *hardware* [1947] (cf. Yaguello 1998: 41). *Mentee* [1965] was created to *mentor* [1750] on the model of *tutor/tutee* (Ayto 1990: 214).

Diehard [1844] is not a productive type of formation (Padrosa-Trias 2010: 171), yet it served as the model for *cryhard, tryhard, workhard* [1922].

Despite the novel suffix *-terous*, *ambimouseterous* 'able to use a mouse with either hand' was modeled on *ambidextrous* (Fodil, forthcoming). For playful application of standard suffixes, see §15.1.

5.4 Puns

Puns are a major part of language play, e.g. ROTC/*Rotsy*, mock fraternities $AX\Omega$ 'Alcoholomega', *TKB* 'Tappa-Kega-Beer'. They are also a frequent source of neologisms. *Gofer* [1967] 'an assistant employed to do menial duties' consists of *go + for*, suggested by *gopher* (Ayto 1989: 172).

Because of Napoleon's *Waterloo*, the incident at the Watergate Hotel readily became (as a pun) Nixon's *Watergate* [1972], from which could be extracted a formative *-gate* [1973] 'political scandal involving corruption (and causing the downfall of a prominent person)'. The process is described by Kemmer (2003: 91) as "a substitution blend giving rise to a new family of words." But this is only part of the story. From *Watergate* were derived *Volgagate* [1973], *Hollywoodgate* [1978], *Contragate*, *Irangate* [1986], and some clear puns: Oliver North's *Gategate* [1987], Oral Robert's *Gospelgate*, *Pearlygate* [1987] (Ayto 1989: 162f.), and, more recently, Clinton's *Whitewatergate* [1993], *travelgate* [1993], *filegate* [1996], *Monicagate* [1998], etc. (Baldi and Dawar 2000: 968). Chris Smith (p.c.) signals *DSKgate* [2011] from the exploits of Dominique Strauss-Kahn. When Beyoncé mimed the words of the US national anthem at the inauguration of President Barack Obama on January 21, 2013, the controversy quickly became known as *Beyoncégate* or *lipgate*. Hundreds of *-gate* scandals are listed at http://wiki/List_of_scandals_with_"-gate"_suffix.

The following examples are recorded by Cannon (1987): *monokini* [1964] was created as a pun on the *bi-* of *bikini* [1948] (assuming by folk etymology that *bi-* is the prefix *bi*); *safari* [1859] has generated *snowfari* [n.d.]; *girlcott* [1884] was modeled on *boycott* [1880]; and *edifice complex* is manifestly generated on *Oedipus complex*. *Ambisextrous* [1929] is a pun on *ambidextrous* [1646]. From *flashback* [1716] was made *flashforward* [1980]. *Softcore* [1966] is modeled on *hardcore* [1959]. Kastovsky (1986a: 419) cites *chaindrink* [n.d.], modeled on *chainsmoke* [1934] (cf. *chainsmoker* [1890], a calque on Germ. *Kettenraucher*). With *earwitness* [1597], cf. *eyewitness* [1539] (Szymanek 2005: 431). *Whitelist* [1900] was created as an antonym to *blacklist* [1624] (Adams 2001: 84).

Blends like *glitterati* [1956] are modeled on *lit(t)erati* [1620], as are the more recent *digerati* [1992], *jazzerati* [2000] (coined by Ken Burns), *numerati* [n.d.], *soccerati* [n.d.], etc. (cf. Klégr and Čermák 2010: 231).

A clear pun is *outercourse* [1986] 'sexual stimulation not involving penetration' (cf. Ayto 1990: 234).

Herstory [1970] was modeled on a sexist perception of history [a.1393] by misanalysis. *Palimony* [1927] is more of a pun on *alimony* [1656] than a haplological derivative of *pal[al]imony*; cf. *dallymony* [a.1987] (Ayto 1989: 100).

On the analogy of the *Black Panthers* [1966], an activist group of senior citizens calls themselves the *Gray Panthers* [1972].

A *pharm* [1990] is 'a place where genetically modified plants or animals are grown or reared in order to produce pharmaceutical products' (*ODNW* 235). *Pharm* follows the rules of blends (Chapter 12), but since a *pharmaceutical farm* does not exist to be clip-blended, a pun is more likely.

Phishing 'computer fraud' was first described in 1987 but the first recorded use was in 1995 (*OED* 1996). It is blended of *phreaking* [1971] [*phone* × *freak*] '(commit) phone fraud' × *fishing*, and bears the nuance of 'fishing' for information, hence the pun.

ScumOS is cited by Fodil (2010) as a pun on the Sun Operating Systems. One might also include here Fodil's example of *M$* for Microsoft and its notorious profits.

As in many of the other examples throughout this book, which are also produced by analogy, the boundaries among the various lexicogenic operations are not always clear. To be sure, even "the dividing line between analogical patterns and word-formation rules is hard to draw" (Plag 2003: 38).

5.5 Language play

Many forms of language play have been described in the literature, in particular by Farb (1973) and Bagemihl (1988+). All aspects of language are subject to play. Language play has no respect for morphological categories or boundaries (Chapter 15).

PUNNING, as mentioned in the previous section, is an important form of creative language play, especially among second-language learners and speakers. A particularly interesting example is reported by Kramsch (2009). An intermediate college French student wrote, *vous n'êtes pas des students mais des stupidents* 'you are not students but stupidents'. English *students* is inserted in place of Fr. *étudiants*, then punned with the created *stupidents* 'stupid ones' (cf. Bell 2012: 192).

TONGUE-TWISTERS involve sound sequences that are difficult to articulate rapidly, e.g. *The sixth sick sheik's sixth sheep's sick*; *She was a thistle sifter and sifted thistles through a thistle sieve* (Yaguello 1998: 53).[5] Tongue-twisters are a cacophonic variety of ONOMATOPOEIA (§10.2), and seldom if ever result in novel words. One reason is that tongue twisters are inherently phrasal. However, nothing precludes the invention of expressive compounds, e.g. *thistle-sifter*.

PIG LATIN presupposes a syllable structure with an onset and a rime, the latter consisting of a nucleus plus coda (§9.1).[6] In that structure, there is only one place to insert the onset in standard Pig Latin, e.g. *think* > [ɪŋk-þ-ey], *scram* > [æm-skr-ey]. By contrast, a flat structure with no inner constituents predicts two landing sites for the onset: *sick* → **[ɪ-s-k-ey] or [ɪk-s-ey], *rub* → **[ə-r-b-ey] or [ʌb-r-ey] (Miller 2010: 1.183). Some Pig Latin outputs are recognized as existing words. For instance, *amscray* 'scram' and *ixnay* [1929] (*OED*) 'nix' are well documented in the *Urban Dictionary* and on Google.

Simple blends, like *spoon* × *fork* → *spork*, delete the onset of the second word and the rime constituent of the first word (§12.5). In all cases, then, language play in English treats the nucleus and coda as a constituent (the rime).

Secret languages like Pig Latin are very common (Halle 1962). Applegate (1961) reports a secret language created by some children in which all but the first of identical consonants in a word is replaced by a glottal stop (*Bobby* → *Boʔy*), and all continuants are replaced by cognate stops (*does* → *doed*).

PALINDROMES involve letters that can be read the same from right to left and from left to right, e.g. *kayak, level, madam, Malayalam, racecar, rotator, testset*. Palindromes can ignore word boundaries, as in the following (Yaguello 1998: 50):

> LIVE NOT ON EVIL
> SEX AT NOON TAXES
> NEVER ODD OR EVEN

A potential objection is that palindromes never result in new words, but at least one good anthropological example is attested in the title *Nacirema* [1956] (for *American*).

---

[5] Nearly 550 examples can be found online at: http://www.uebersetzung.at/twister/en.htm
[6] In a survey of 442 speakers, Nevins and Vaux (2003a) identified four varieties of Pig Latin: (i) *truck* → *uck-tr-ay*, *struck* → *uck-str-ay* (74%); (ii) *truck* → *ruck-t-ay*, *struck* → *truck-s-ay* (10%); (iii) *truck* → *ruck-t-ay*, *struck* → *uck-str-ay* (4%); (iv) *truck* → *uck-tr-ay*, *struck* → *truck-s-ay* (2%).

The *Urban Dictionary*[7] quotes *aibohphobia* 'the irrational fear of palindromes', first attested in *The Devil's DP* [Data Processing] *Dictionary* (McGraw-Hill, 1981). Mattiello (2008: 68, 70) cites the backslang type *neves* [1851] (*seven*), *yob* [1859] (*boy*), derivatives *yobbish* [1972], *yobbishness* [1985], etc.

SPOONERISMS (§6.9) involve metathesis of the onset of the first syllable of adjacent (or near adjacent) major lexical items, e.g. *know your blows* for *blow your nose*, *hate of arts* for *eight of hearts*, *mad bunny* for *bad money*, *blushing crow* for *crushing blow*, *bass ackwards* for *ass backwards*, etc. Several music albums feature spoonerisms, e.g. *Punk in Drublic* for *drunk in public*, *The Shaming of the True* for *taming of the shrew*. There is a song title 'Don't Dink and Drance' and a band name *Com Truise* (Tom Cruise).

In a Cuna game, the first syllable is extracted and appended to the last (Sherzer 1970; 1976; Bagemihl 1989), e.g. *takke* 'to see' → *ketak*, *arkan* 'hand' → *kenar*, *ipya* 'eye' → *yaip*, /birga/ (> *bíriga*) 'year' → *gabir*.

The French game *verlan* (Sherzer 1976; Fradin, Montermini, and Plénat 2009) is metathetic, e.g. *l'envers* 'backwards' → *verlen*, plus a more complicated version which metathesizes the onset of consecutive syllables, e.g. *parler* 'to speak' → *larper*, *l'école* 'the school' → *qu'élole*.

A Peruvian Spanish game prefixes *cha-* to every syllable of the source word, e.g. *pájaro* 'bird' → *chapàchajàcharó* (Yu 2007: 195, w. lit).

In a Río de la Plata Spanish game called *jeringozo* (a variant of *jerigonza*) 'nonsense', an open syllable with a *p*-onset and a copy of the preceding vowel is suffixed to each syllable, e.g. *camiseta* 'T-shirt' → *capa-mipi-sepe-tapa*. A word like *agnóstico* 'agnostic' is treated syllabically as /a(g).no(s).ti.co/ to give *a-pag—no-pos—ti-pi—co-po* rather than **ag-pa(g)-nos-po(s)-* and other such formations with phonotactically illicit clusters, in this case *-gp-* (Irene Moyna, p.c.). This can be accounted for by a template that has no closed syllables followed by a structure *-pVX-* in which V is a copy of the preceding vowel and X is C (a consonant) or null.

A Zande game metathesizes the first two syllables: *degude* 'girl' → *gudede* (Bagemihl 1989).

Several infixation games are well known. In Homer Simpson's type, *-ma-* is inserted after a trochaic foot which may be 'ternary' (§9.2): *edumacate*, *saxomaphone*, *viomalin*, *Michamalangelo*, *syndimacated*, *hippomapotamus*, *sophistimacated*, *multiplimacation* (*multimaplication), *Meditermaranean* (*Medimaterranean). Forms are extended to comply with the trochaic foot requirement, e.g. *caremaful* /kɛɪrəmɑfəl/, and the infixation structure, e.g. *oboemaboe* for *oboe*, *tubamaba* for *tuba*, etc. (Yu 2007: 182–90). Yu (pp. 174–7) traces the origin of *-ma-* back to *thingamajig*,

---

[7] www.urbandictionary.com/define.php?term=aibohphobia

thingamabob, and the like (§8.1), ultimately via reanalysis of *ma(y)* in *whatchamacallum* 'what you may call him' beside *whatchacallum* 'what you call him'.

Hip-hop infixation inserts *-iz-* after the onset of the initial syllable: *hi̱zouse* (house), *bi̱zitch* (bitch), *si̱zoldiers* (soldiers), etc. (Yu 2007: 1).

The expressive verb *guaran-damn-tee* gets many hits on Google. The most productive infixation game involves the expletive *fuckin'*, which must be inserted at a foot boundary, preferentially at the left edge of a trochaic foot (§9.2), hence *fàn-fuckin'-tástic* but not **fàntást-fuckin'-ic*, **phý-fuckin'-sical* [*physical*].[8] Names like *Tatamagouchee* have two possible foot boundaries and two expletive insertion patterns: *Tata-fuckin'-magouchee* ~ *Tatama-fuckin'-gouchee* (McCarthy 1982: 580; Yu 2007: 120; Miller 2010: 1.260). Contrast illformed **Ta-fuckin'-tamagouchee* and **Tatamagou-fuckin'-chee*. Another condition is duple timing (two, four... beats, as in music), as shown by **To-fuckin'-ledo* [*Toledo*] vs. an output in which the vowel of the first syllable is lengthened and the form is acceptable. In *Tṑ-fuckin'-lédo* each foot has two beats and the stress pattern is 2-3-1 (Miller 2010: 1.265; cf. McCarthy 1982: 585 ftn. 9).

In Nootka, ancient imitative games (e.g. in myth Deer says *Ɫímiɫ* for *tcímis* 'black bear') have become grammaticalized to the extent that there are evaluative affixes for people considered abnormal (Sapir 1915): fat people, those with eye defects (cross-eyed, squinting, etc., plus deer and mink!), abnormally small people, hunchbacks, lame people, lefthanded people, circumcised males, greedy people, and ravens all get different affixes and affix combinations, some with phonological alterations. To concretize, compare *qwíɫʔiɫma'* 'he does so in afflicted eye fashion', *qwiçʔiçma* 'he—hunchback—does so', etc., all built on *qwísma'* 'he does so'.

5.6 Figures of speech and rhetorical devices

The standard rhetorical devices of antiquity are matched in language play by extension from words to higher units of speech. A recent discussion of these terms applied to literature in English can be found in Nänny and Fischer (2006). Their relevance is not in word creation *per se* but in an application to the creative arrangement and use of words.

---

[8] For discussion, see McCawley (1978), McMillan (1980), McCarthy (1982), Zonneveld (1984), Yu (2007). Zonneveld (1984: 56) plausibly suggests that expletive insertion is analogous to "middle name [i.e. epithet—DGM] formation", like *Johnny 'Guitar' Watson, Eric 'Slowhand' Clapton, Ray 'Boom-Boom' Mancini*. Different dialects are ignored here, since only syllable structure and morpheme boundaries are affected, e.g. *tonsi-fuckin'-lectomy* ~ *tonsil-fuckin'-ectomy* ~ *tonsil-fuckin'-lectomy* (McCawley 1978). Metrical structure is stable except that *aqua-fuckin'-marine* alternates with *aquama-fuckin'-rine* (with long /ī/), and there is occasional internal reduplication, e.g. *thermo-fuckin'-mometer* beside expected *ther-fuckin'-mometer* ~ *thermo-fuckin'-(o)meter* (ibid.).

ASYNDETON (coordination without a conjunction) can be used iconically to express simultaneity, as in *Women shrieked, cattle bellowed, dogs howled, men ran to and fro...* (Sir Walter Scott, *Old Mortality*, 1893: 185). Nänny and Fischer also illustrate the opposite, POLYSYNDETON (pleonastic conjunctions), with *Macbeth's* (V.v.19–20) *To-morrow, and to-morrow, and to-morrow.*

For inexplicable reasons, Nänny and Fischer do not mention APOSIOPESIS, which is a break in syntax iconic to the break in thought. An example is King Lear's *I will have such revenges on you both,/That all the world shall—I will do such things....* (II.iv.305–7). It differs from ANACOLUTHON, a change in syntax from one construction to another, as in *A plank that was dry was not disturbing the smell of burning and altogether there was the best kind of sitting there could never be all the edging that the largest chair was having* (Gertrude Stein, *A Portrait of Mabel Dodge*, 1912).

ZEUGMA (Greek for 'a yoking') involves conjoined objects, one idiomatic the other an ordinary complement, as in *Kill the boys and the luggage!* (Fluellen in *Henry V*, IV.VII).

EPANORTHOSIS is a correction or partial retraction, as in Simon's *Maybe there is a beast.... What I mean is... maybe it's only us* in William Golding's *Lord of the Flies* (1954).

CHIASMUS is a quasi-palindrome involving word linearization. Words are arranged in mirror-image symmetry X-Y-Y-X. Nänny and Fischer (2006: §3.4) cite many examples, including a simple one from *Macbeth* (I.i.11): The witches' *Fair is foul and foul is fair.*

The very term is iconic to the structure, being named after the form of the Greek letter *chi* X. This major rhetorical device was regularly employed by the ancients. One type involved a chiastic arrangement of lexical category items, e.g. A-N-N-A, or N-V-V-N. An example of V-NP-NP-V follows:

augēscunt	*aliae*	*gentēs,*	*aliae*	*minuuntur*	(Lucretius 2.77)
increase.3PL	some	nations	others	diminish.3PL.MEDP	

'some nations increase, others diminish'

On another interpretation, chiasmus can involve annular (ring) composition which returns to the point of departure: X-Y-Z-Y-X (cf. Nänny and Fischer 2006). This device was frequent in Homer, where some complex rings extend over entire books or sequences of books. In the *Odyssey*, for instance, the entire journey of Odysseus is laid out in a complex ring (Miller 1982: 81, w. lit). When he enters the twilight zone, he visits first the Ciconians and last the Phaeacians, who escort him back to Ithaca. The Underworld adventure, representing Odysseus' ritual death, constitutes the center of the ring.

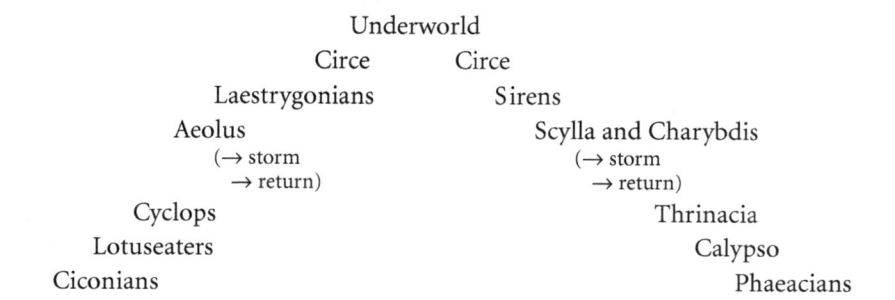

                            Underworld
                    Circe   Circe
             Laestrygonians   Sirens
             Aeolus   Scylla and Charybdis
             (→ storm   (→ storm
              → return)   → return)
          Cyclops   Thrinacia
          Lotuseaters   Calypso
          Ciconians   Phaeacians

The Underworld is conspicuously the seventh adventure. Because of the weekly cycle, the number 7 in Mesopotamia, the Near East, and Greece had an ambiguous position as both 'end' and 'beginning', whence its frequent associations with the life–death–rebirth cycle in ancient literature.

5.7 Verbal art

Poetic language is language made extraordinary (Perloff and Dworkin 2009b). Poets have traditionally played with the language in ways that prose writers seldom do. Yet, even within the poetic genre, some poets excel in the craft. Lewis Carroll is one of those, perhaps best known for Jabberwocky (1871: ch. ['rank'] 6), of which the first verse is reproduced here:

> 'Twas brillig, and the slithy toves
> Did gyre and gimble in the wabe:
> All mimsy were the borogoves,
> And the mome raths outgrabe.

The syntax is transparent even if the meaning is opaque. As Alice explains, the words are clear except for their meaning. From the total poem she gleans that "*somebody* killed *something*" (118). Indeed, the Jabberwocky is "an adventure in word recognition" (Goldfarb 1999: 86).

The paramount difficulties of translating Jabberwocky into any language must not be underestimated. Poetry in general is next to impossible to translate (Waldrop 2009), but Jabberwocky heads the list in difficulties. Imholtz (1987) evaluates a number of Latin (and other) translations for their creativity or lack thereof. Most fall flat for being painfully verbatim renderings and failing to capture the imaginative nature of the original. Some come across as parodies. And so on.

The most remarkable of the Latin translations is that of Augustus Arthur Vansittart (Trinity College, Cambridge, March 10, 1872). It is cited here because it illustrates the flexibility of even a dead language when it comes to poetic art.

> Coesper erat: tunc lūbricilēs ultrāvia circum
> Urgēbant gȳrōs gimbiculōsque tophī;
> Moestenuī vīsae borogōvides īre meātū;
> Et profugī gemitūs exgrabuēre rathae.

(Collingwood 2007 [1898]: 64; Imholtz 1987: 216)

The translation is brilliant in respecting Latin grammar and poetic style, all the while capturing the essence of Lewis Carroll's imaginative art, partly by Latinizing some of his coinages (*outgrabe* → *exgrab-*), partly by crafting equivalent Latin calques. Vansittart explains that *coesper* is a blend of *coena* (CL *cēna*) 'dinner' and *vesper* 'evening', fully in character with Humpty Dumpty's explanation that *brillig* is four o'clock in the afternoon, the time when things are broiled for dinner. *Lūbricilēs* conflates *lūbricus* 'slippery; greasy' and *gracilis* 'slender, slim', a perfect echo of E *slimy* and *lithe*, the ingredients of Lewis Carroll's *slithy*. *Ultrāvia* (*ultrā* 'beyond' + *via* 'way' or *āvia* 'pathless region' itself composed of *ā* + *via* 'off the path') is a clever calque on *wabe* which, according to one of Lewis Carroll's explanations, is "a long way before it, and a long way behind it... And a long way beyond it". *Mimsy* is a blend of *flimsy* and *miserable*, and *moestenuī* similarly conflates *maestus* 'sad, mournful, gloomy' and *tenuis* 'slender, thin; meagre; slight, faint'. *Mome* means 'from home', hence *profugī* (NOM PL) 'exiled from home; fugitive'.

In part, Vansittart's poem features a creative use of Latin words and in part coining new ones in the same manner as did Lewis Carroll. While blends were not frequent in Latin, they did exist (§12.1), and prior to Carroll they were not that frequent in English. Compounds were not plentiful in native Latin but there were many Greek calques (Bader 1962; see also Fruyt 2002; 2005), and the very type created by Vansittart, e.g. *ultrāvia* 'beyond the way', has a model in *ultrāmundus* 'beyond the world', implied in Apuleius' *ultrāmundānus* 'transcendent'. Latinization of foreign words was very frequent. In light of the hundreds of Latinized Greek words (Biville 1990, 1995), *exgrab-* and the like fit a long tradition of lexicogenesis by adaptation. In short, Vansittart's Latin formations, like their English counterparts, rely on ordinary processes of blending, calquing, adaptation, compounding, and general creativity. As will be emphasized in the next section, use of ordinary processes does not make the result any less artistic.

5.8 Art from the ordinary: P-stacking

Not all poetic art involves the creation of novel lexical items. A truly clever poet can take the everyday language and use it in unusual ways. One twist would be the use of an ambiposition, e.g. *the entire day through* for *through the entire day* (Libert 2006). Another is the stacking of prepositions, as in Morris Bishop's witty poem, "The

Naughty Preposition" (*The New Yorker* 9/27/1947), written in response to the nonsensical dictum against ending a sentence with a preposition:

> I lately lost a preposition;
> It hid, I thought, beneath my chair
> And angrily I cried, "Perdition!
> Up from out of in under there!"
>
> Correctness is my vade mecum,
> And straggling phrases I abhor,
> And yet I wondered, "What should he come
> Up from out of in under for?"

Everyday English features more limited P-stacking, as in *out from, off of, from under*. Morris Bishop has extended that but not in a way that violates English grammar, although some speakers may initially have difficulty processing the unusual number of stacked prepositions. That is the creativity that makes art of the ordinary.[9]

As to analysis, languages do not randomly iterate prepositions (Libert 1993: §4.3.1.1). English *into* [OE] has *to* adjoined to *in* (see below), so one cannot say, e.g. **I went to in the city*. Svenonius (2010) cites examples like *drifted out from over behind the hill* (with particles *out* and *over*). Ancient Greek allowed combinations like *hup'éks* (*hupó* 'under' + *eks* 'out of') 'out from under'. One way or another, languages express directionality in complex spatial relationships. In some languages an adposition can be case-inflected, e.g. Basque *arte-tik* [between-ABL] 'from between' (Lestrade 2010: 113), Evenki *xergi-duk* 'from under', *xergi-le* 'to under', etc. (ibid., p. 123). Some languages stack cases, e.g. Estonian *jala-l-le* [foot-LOC-GOAL] 'onto the foot' (ibid., p. 98).

The following examples are more complex:

dfiuŋ-phyaraŋ-mar-gəmsə [Chantyal]
tree-SUPER-CIRCUM-ABL
'from around the top of the tree' (Noonan 2005)

ganč'i-t':-an [Avar]
rock-SUB-GOAL & SOURCE
'to under the rock and out again' (Alice Harris, p.c., attributed to Togo Gudava)

Stacked cases may belong to separate inflectional category systems (Comrie and Polinsky 1998), but the examples mentioned here represent complex spatial relations.

---

[9] Thanks to Elly van Gelderen, Alice Harris, Alan Libert, and Peter Svenonius—all p.c.—for discussion of this section. The type *in front of* will not be discussed here; see Roy and Svenonius (2009), Svenonius (2010). For the history of the type *beside* from *by (the) side (of)*, see van Gelderen (2011: 182–7).

Crosslinguistically, ablative is the outermost case and locative the innermost, conforming to the spatial case hierarchy Ablative > Allative > Locative (Caha 2009). Additionally, there is evidence for the following parallel hierarchy of adpositions (Pantcheva 2011), concretized with an English example.[10]

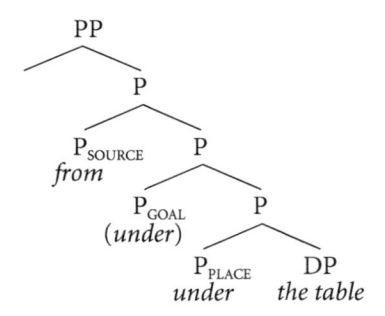

```
            PP
           /  \
          P
         / \
   P_SOURCE  P
    from    / \
         P_GOAL  P
         (under) / \
              P_PLACE  DP
              under   the table
```

Since *under* can be directional or locational in English, in principle it can merge at least abstractly in the Goal and the Place positions, both necessary for semantic interpretation, but they will conflate into one exponent by the identity sequencing constraint (§2.2). Since Goal precedes Place, the English order *into, onto* (for *to in, to on*) is even stranger. But only pairs of monosyllabic Ps exhibit this reverse order, suggesting that *into*, for instance, would originate syntactically as *to* (P_{GOAL}) and *in* (P_{PLACE}) followed by (left-)adjunction (§4.4) of *in* to *to*, yielding *into*. Historically *in* and *on* were adverbial.

The hierarchical structure is confirmed by languages like Polish where the higher P has scope over the lower one in terms of case assignment; cf. *z pod stołu* 'from under the table' with (ablatival) genitive *-u* in contrast to *pod stołem* 'under the table' with instrumental *-em* (Kuryłowicz 1964: 177).

In light of P-stacking in other Indo-European and non-Indo-European languages, such combinations can come about at any time. Following is a short list of English complex source Ps with the date of their first occurrence with a DP complement:

from beyond [c.1000]   *from beneath* [1638]   *from on* [1790]
from out of [1535]   *from within* [1644]   *from around* [1806]
from among [1594]   *from over* [1655]   *from amidst* [1835]
from below [1594]   *from behind* [1667]   *from inside* [1885]
from between [1601]   *from under* [1671]

Many of these occurred earlier in adverbial uses (without a complement), e.g. *from under* [1535]. The date for *from on* ignores the fixed phrases *from on high* [1380]

---

[10] Other languages and particular types of complex P may require more elaborate structures, as is clear from the discussion in Cinque (2010), the papers in Cinque and Rizzi (2010), and Pantcheva (2011).

(cf. *on high* [c.1200] 'heaven') and *from on board* [1666] (cf. *on board* [1508]), but the latter may be more compositional.

Several other complex Ps with complement were earlier. For example, *out of* was reanalyzed already in Old English from structures like [[Verb *out*] [*of* Place]], in which *out* was a directional particle or adverb and *of* the source P 'from', to a complex P with functional *of* (Peter Svenonius, p.c.), opposed to *into*. As with all reanalyses, this was contextual, and the older construction continued to exist beside the new one into the Modern English period.

The complex P *in under* may have existed in Old English, although in this instance the evidence is shakier; cf. *sīð ālȳfed* | *inn under eorðweall* [*Beowulf* 3089f.] 'a journey (was) allowed in under the earthwork'.[11]

What emerges from the above discussion is that Morris Bishop in fact used traditional combinations—*from out of* and *in under*. What is different is that he combined them. In the poem at hand, *up* in the second stanza is a directional particle in the phrasal verb *come up*. It is probably the same in the first stanza, where *come* is supplied contextually. Beyond that, *from out of* has locational *in under* as its complement. *There* is in turn the complement of *in under* but is omitted in the second stanza for metrical reasons or, rather, is displaced by *for* in the expression *what...for*, i.e. 'for what reason, why'. In short, the main P stacks are the traditional *from out of* and *in under*. The structure, then, is [up [[from [out of [in under [there]]]]]].

The transition has been demonstrated from P-stacking to new complex prepositions like *from out of* and *in under*. That this involves word creation is clear from the fact that the order is fixed. There is no **under in*, **out from of*, **out of from*, etc. They also cannot be separated or internally modified, e.g. **in very under*. While they are subject to limited derivation, e.g. *the inunderness of it all*, internal derivation is impossible: **inness under*. These are generally regarded among the atomic properties of complex words as opposed to freely occurring syntactic heads.

5.9 Summary

Lexicogenesis is about the creation of new words. This includes everything from new lexical items to new meanings of old words. The core motivations of these changes

---

[11] The scholarly tradition interprets *inn* as an adverb 'in(side)', which is usually *innan*, as in *burgum in innan* [*Beowulf* 1968] [in the castle inside] 'in the inside (of) the castle'. The passage in question seems to mean 'to the inside part beneath the earthwork/mound', in which case contemporary 'in under' may carry the right nuance. In any event, even if *inn* is an adverb here, a language acquirer might well analyze *in(n) under* as a complex P. Alan Libert (p.c.) points out that most speakers have a generalized constraint against adjacent locational Ps, e.g. **at behind*, but that *in under* is acceptable in an intensive or directional sense. In light of the configuration Source > Goal > Place, in which *under* would merge in P_{PLACE} and *in* in P_{GOAL}, that could be what makes the combination grammatical. But Peter Svenonius (p.c.) suggests that *in* is a PLACE-MODIFYING PARTICLE in *in under*, analogous to *up* in *up on the hill*.

have been briefly reviewed in §5.1. Perhaps the main motivation, however, is the following:

> [N]eologisms serve a perlocutionary intent, that of slowing down the reader's response with the use of a clever or puzzling new word, given that new words generally require greater processing effort. Thus a novel formation demands greater attention, in addition to providing pleasure, amusement and entertainment. (Munat 2007b: 179)

The main means by which novel words are created is analogy to existing words of a given form, meaning, or combination of the two.

Various types of language play have been described. These range from puns to specific games, like Pig Latin, spoonerisms, Homer Simpson's *-ma-* infixation, and expletive insertion. The domain for all of these involves the prosodic properties of output words. Most of these games are at least potentially lexicogenic (cf. §15.3), as illustrated by *ixnay, Nacirema, yob(bishness), thistle-sifter*, the band name *Com Truise*, and *fanfuckintastic*, listed by the *Urban Dictionary*[12] as "the superlative of *fantastic*". In fact, *fanfuckintastic* gets many hits on Google, as does *absofuckinlutely* for which the main three glosses in the *Urban Dictionary*[13] are (1) 'Confirming that a factual chunk of information is undeniably, and indisputably true', (2) 'A variation of *absolutely*, typically expressing extreme excitement or disgust', and (3) 'A without a doubt affirmative'. There is also the emphatic verb *guarandamntee* which is well attested on Google, also as a noun glossed 'the ultimate guarantee' in the *Urban Dictionary*.[14]

Many figures of speech and rhetorical devices involve the arrangement of output syntactic structures (phrases or sentences) in a manner that is iconic to the meaning, some form, or a break in thought. Although these are technically not examples of lexicogenesis, they involve an extension of the motivated properties of individual words to larger units of speech.

Our final examples derive from verbal art. One aspect is the creation of novel lexical items by various means, including compounding, blending, and borrowing. A second aspect involves use of the everyday language in unusual ways. This is, again, technically peripheral to the domain of our inquiry, except that lexicogenesis certainly includes innovations in complex prepositions, like *from out of* and *in under*. P-words, as noted in §1.9, cannot be created by language play unless an entire language is being created.

---

[12] www.urbandictionary.com/define.%20php?term=fan-fuckin-tastic
[13] www.urbandictionary.com/define.php?term=absofuckinlutely
[14] www.urbandictionary.com/define.php?term=guarandamntee

6

Metaphor and metonymy

Since the physical senses are our source of mental knowledge and understanding, much of semantic motivation is extralinguistic, grounded in personal experience, perception, and cognition. Metaphor and metonymy are the most basic types of neologistic assignment of word meaning. Body parts, animal names, and sensory (synesthetic) metaphors are ubiquitous. Metonymy involves transfer of labels by reanalysis mediated by associated contexts, e.g. from part to whole, from person to associated item. The earlier acquisition of concrete and lexical categories reflects the natural evolution from concrete to abstract. Simultaneously, all languages have affixes or other mechanisms to derive concrete nouns from abstract.

6.1 Metaphor

In its simplest form, the essence of metaphor is that X resembles Y. For instance, *labyrinth* [1533] has been applied since 1615 to any complicated building with an intricate maze of hallways. More formally, "[m]etaphor is the cognitive mechanism whereby one experiential domain is partially 'mapped', i.e. projected, onto a different experiential domain, so that the second domain is partially understood in terms of the first one" (Barcelona 2000b: 3). More simply, "one concept (the *target*) is structured (understood) in terms of the other (the *source*)" (Feyaerts 2000: 60). The mapping of one domain onto another can be illustrated with the conceptual metaphor THEORIES ARE BUILDINGS: they are *constructed* by *laying foundations* and *building* on other theories, but ultimately get *demolished* (Kövecses 2002: 108, 130f.). The idea of conceptual domains presupposes that knowledge is stored in groups of related concepts (Allan 2008: 11; cf. §15.2 below).

In recent years, there has been a focus on language-independent motivation, e.g. experiential, perceptual, cognitive (Allan 2008: 3, w. lit): "although animal metaphors are found in many (if not all) languages, the same animal can represent different human characteristics in different societies... [which] shows that in reality cultural and cognitive factors in motivation often interact." It must also be noted that "metaphor can create similarity, rather than simply reflect it" (Allan 2008: 143).

Hyperbolic metaphors, such as *splitting hairs* for detailed subdivisions, *paradise* [OE] for any pleasant place [?*a*.1300], and *iceberg* [1774] for an unemotional person [1840], are very frequent (Stern 1931: 310ff.). The last is the conceptual opposite of the EMOTION IS HEAT (OF FIRE) metaphor (Kövecses 2002: 113): *fiery* people have *hot* tempers and *burn* with emotion. Both love and anger share the fire metaphor (Kövecses, pp. 203ff.): an angry person is *fuming, burned up, smoking* from the ears, *red* in the face, and erupts like a *volcano*; *ardent* lovers carry a *torch* and *burn* with passion until the *flames* die down and the *fire* is out.

Sensory (synesthetic) metaphors include the following: *piercing* (sounds), *loud* (colors), *sweet* (personality, voices, perfume), *warm* (colors, scent), *hot* (music, mustard, people), *hard* (liquor, rock), *soft* (drink) (cf. Ullmann 1957: 233, 266–89; 1962: 216; Tournier 1985: 243ff.). Sweetser (1990: 29) explains the metaphor of *bitter* anger as follows: "the anger is unpleasant to our emotions in a way analogous to that in which a bitter taste displeases our tastebuds." She goes on (p. 30) to note that "bodily experience is a source of vocabulary for our psychological states, but not the other way around."

Body parts are basic and universally subject to polysemy (Wierzbicka 2007), especially metaphorical extension (Nyrop 1913: 229ff.; Guiraud 1980: ch. 3; Kopecka 2009), e.g. *head* of cabbage, column, committee, etc., *mouth* of a river, *face* of a watch, *eye* of a needle, *nose* of an airplane, *teeth* of a saw, *hand* of destiny, *arm* of justice, *foot* of a mountain (*Piedmont* = F *pied du mont* 'foot of the mountain'), *hearts* of celery, *arms, legs, back* of a chair, *back* of a book, *neck* of a bottle (*bottleneck*), electronic *brain*, OF/ME *dent-de-lion* 'lion's tooth' > DANDELION (from its sharply indented leaves). THE STRUCTURE OF AN ABSTRACT COMPLEX SYSTEM IS THE PHYSICAL STRUCTURE OF THE HUMAN BODY (Kövecses 2002: 129f.): the *head* of state may not be able to *cure* an *ailing* economy, which is *symptomatic* of deeper *illnesses* that can penetrate to the *heart* of society and destroy its very *backbone*, rendering it impossible for any governing *body* to put it back on its *feet*.

Social forces share the same metaphors as mechanical forces: *attraction, impulse, inertia, momentum, propulsion, resistance*, etc. (Stern 1931: 294).

Since "particular animals are perceived to be similar to humans in terms of specific characteristics or behaviours" (Allan 2008: 181), personal attributes and insults are frequently animal metaphors (Kiełtyka 2008; 2009; Górecka-Smolińska 2009; Kleparski 1990; 2013). Many instantiate the conceptual metaphors HUMANS ARE ANIMALS (Martsa 1999), OBJECTIONABLE BEHAVIOR IS ANIMAL BEHAVIOR, OBJECTIONABLE PEOPLE ARE ANIMALS (Kövecses 2002: 125ff.), e.g. *ass, bitch, chameleon, chicken, crab, dodo, dog, fox, gnat, grub, hawk, hog, jellyfish, louse, maggot, nag, ox, pig, rat, shark, sheep, skunk, slug, snail, snake, stag, swine, tiger, turkey, turtle, vermin, vixen, vulture, wolf, worm*. Mostly positive are *dove, lion*. The traits associated with some 140 animals are listed in Tournier (1985: 238–43). Palmatier (1995) and Allan (2008: 124–79) provide commentary. Kiełtyka (2008) examines animal words in terms of physical appearance, behavior (*ass, whelp, filly* . . .), morality (*bitch, nag, minx*...), and contempt (*puss(y), pup(pet), bob-tail*...). Note also *animal* and *beast* themselves applied to humans (Allan 2008: 138f.).

Animal metaphors can be qualified: *(jack)ass, (old) bat, (teddy) bear, (fat) cat, (fat) cow, (real) dog, (silly) goose* (Palmatier 1995: 347), *(big) horse, snake (in the grass), (bunch of) sheep*. For the idea of 'stupid', one finds early *goosish* [*c*.1374], *sheepish* [*c*.1380], *mule* [*c*.1470], etc., and more recent *bird-brain* [1943] etc. (Allan 2008: 172–9). Animals take adjectival suffixes (*bearish, catty, foxy, hawkish, loony, mousy, sheepish, squirrely*), and convert to verbs: *ape, carp, bitch, bug, dog, fish, hog, hound, nag, parrot, worm*. Animal verbs can acquire a particle: *ferret out* [1577], *wolf down* [1880], *monkey around* [1891], *clam up* [1920], *horse around* [1928], *chicken out* [1934], *rat out* [1957], *weasel out* [1962], *squirrel away* [1965], *pig out* [1978] (cf. Martsa 2012: 118–28).

In connection with sound effects (Chapter 10), Magnus (2001: 71f.) observes that /b/ is the initial segment for many animals that are large (*bear, behemoth, boa, boar, bovine, bull, buck, buffalo*, etc.) or annoying (*bee, beetle, bitch, bug*). Note also *beast*.

Parts of animal bodies are frequently transferred disparagingly to human parts: *beak, bill, paw, proboscis*, etc. Small animals, such as *lamb, kitten*, can be terms of endearment.

Animal names can be equally applied to instruments. An old metaphor involves the *crane*, with its long neck, applied to a lifting machine. Ancient Greek *géranos* 'crane' was also used thus (Hecht 1888: 52). Its diminutive *geránion* ['little crane'] was applied to a plant whose fruit resembles a crane's bill. The Romans borrowed the word as *geranium* GERANIUM. The bone at the base of the spine resembles the beak of a cuckoo and bears its name COCCYX (G *kókkūx* 'cuckoo; coccyx') (Skoda 1988: 224f.). From G *polúpous* 'many footed; octopus' is derived POLYP (Skoda, p. 232).

Metaphors are a frequent source of compounds for new concepts: *Milky Way, railroad, skyscraper* (Ullmann 1957: 183). Many compound metaphors are (neo) classical, e.g. *astronaut* [1929] ('star-sailor'), *psychedelic* [1956] ('mind-reveal').

By metaphorical application to new situations, modern computer scientists have recycled many older words, including *circuit* [a.1382], *digital* [?c.1425], *hardware* [?1518], *network* [1530], *compute* [1579], *program* [1633], *system* [a.1638], *algorithm* [1699] (Ahmad 2000: 714). *Program* is perhaps the most distant from the oldest meaning. The following changes are attested: 'public notice' [1633], 'introduction, commentary' [1671], 'advance notice or booklet of information' [1799], 'plan, scheme, outline' [1837], 'sequence of events, theme' [1854], 'broadcast presentation' [1922], 'signal' [1935], 'sequence of operations for a machine to perform automatically' [1942].

6.2 Metaphorical change

To figure out a given change, the comparison may require a little imagination and even extralinguistic (real world) knowledge, but remains essentially a comparison.

Examples:

(a) *window* [a.1250] < Old Danish *wind-ughæ* 'wind-eye' (cf. Brink 2002: 765);
(b) *butter* [OE] < G *boú-tūron* 'cow-cheese' (cf. G *tūrós* 'cheese', *EIE* 68f.);
(c) *galaxy* [Ch.] (< G *galaxías* (*kúklos*) 'milky (circle)') is slightly more complicated in that the comparison to milk is a metaphor, but the transfer of 'circle' involves metonymy (see below);
(d) *dactyl* [c.1420] (< G *dáktulos* 'finger') as a metrical foot type has a long constituent followed by two short, analogous to the joints of a finger;
(e) *electricity* [1646] (< G *ḗlektron* 'amber') requires the extralinguistic information that amber produces sparks when rubbed together, but it remains a simple comparison (metaphor). To figure out the link, one need only know what amber is/does, and what electricity is/does (cf. §13.6).

Color words frequently evolve from items which are prototypically that color (Fritz 1998: 140), e.g. *violet* (L *viola* 'violet plant; violet color'), *rose* (L *rosa* 'a rose'), *orange* (< Arab. *nāranj* < Pers. *nārang* < Skt. *nāranga-* 'orange (tree)'), *aubergine* (< Catalan *alberginia* < Arab. *al-bāḏinjān* < Pers. *bādingān* < Skt. *vatin-ganah-*).

Unrelated words can coalesce through phonological change or historical accident, such as borrowing (Bloomfield 1933: 436; cf. Ullmann 1957: 128ff.; Meier 1989: 64f.). *Ear* of corn (OE *ēar*) is etymologically not the same word as the body part *ear* (OE *ēare*), but fits the pattern of the metaphorical use of body parts, this time by folk etymology (Chapter 7). This type of metaphorical reinterpretation due to homophony is sometimes called FUSION. Other examples include *corn* 'hornlike hardening of skin' and *corn* 'grain', or *fuse* 'electric circuit protector' (Ital. *fuso* < L *fūsus* 'spindle') and *fuse* 'detonator of an explosive' (cf. *fuse* 'melt' < L *fūsus*, PPP to *fundere* 'to pour; melt'). In these cases, unrelated words merged. It can also happen that related words diverge. Only etymologists would relate *sole* 'bottom of a shoe' to the name of the fish, the adjective *long* to the verb *to long* (Ullmann 1962: 178), or *staff* 'stick; rod; wand' to *staff* 'workers assisting a manager'.

6.3 Concrete > abstract

Abstract concepts frequently arise cognitively from bodily experiences (Goddard 1998: 78ff.). "The physical senses are our key means of access to information about the world, and because of this we think and talk about mental perception in terms of physical perception, in other words mapping a concrete process onto an abstract one" (Allan 2008: 180). Nevertheless, Allan disputes the idea that abstract meanings evolve from concrete by metaphor, and insists that "the meanings of these lexemes do not show the kind of clear mapping from an earlier physical sense to a later mental sense" but rather "children learn a conflated sense that covers both physical and mental perception" (p. 180). In fact, despite her alleged evidence from language acquisition (p. 62), lexical and concrete categories are acquired before functional and abstract by as much as a year (Miller 2010: 1.25, 2.93, w. lit). Allan is right from the E-language point of view, that both meanings can be synchronically present as part of the acquirer's PLD (primary linguistic data), but the earlier acquisition of concrete and lexical categories reflects the natural evolution.

Where the history is clear, the development is predominantly from concrete to abstract. For instance, inherited *field* in Early Old English designated 'open country' and 'battlefield' then 'pasture land' and 'arable land'. Apart from one isolated occurrence in Old English (in a translation), *field* only comes to include 'sphere of interest' in 1340. The more abstract 'branch of study' (*field of math* etc.) does not occur until 1825.

Scale [1412] meant '(scaling) ladder' (< L *scāla(e)* 'stairs; ladder'). It was not until 1597 that the word was generalized to the musical octave by the similarity of shape.

Eliminate in Latin had only its concrete meaning: put (someone) 'out of' (*ē/ex*) the 'house' (*līmen* 'threshold'). It was initially borrowed as 'thrust out of doors' [1568]. The more abstract meaning 'get rid of' does not occur until 1714.

Understanding is frequently conceptualized as a metaphor of grasping or seizing (cf. Bloomfield 1933: 429f.; Ullmann 1962: 225; Sweetser 1990: 28): L *comprehendere* 'press together; get hold of; COMPREHEND'; cf. *grasp* 'clutch with the hand' [*a*.1382], 'understand' [1680]; *get* 'obtain possession' [?*a*.1200], 'understand' [1907]. That is, physical grasping leads to cognitive grasping (Williams 1986: 181; Sweetser 1990: 38). The metaphor underlying *understand* involves standing under; cf. the expression *get to the bottom of (something)*.

Normally in the sensory domain, concrete > abstract (perceptive/cognitive) > metalinguistic (expressive) > subjective, as in the evolution of *wit* (Koivisto-Alanko 2000a; 2000b). In 1350, *wit* meant 'five senses' (perception) and 'mind; seat of consciousness' (cognition). By Early Modern English, the perception meaning disappeared, replaced by *sense*. Also, *wit* acquired expressive new meanings, such as 'superior intelligence'. In Tillotson [*a*.1694], *wit* has the modern expressive sense. In Burnet [*a*.1715], it is personified (subjectified) by metonymy (see below).

The change from perception to cognition is also exemplified by the PHYSICAL VISION ⇒ MENTAL "VISION" metaphor (Sweetser 1990: 33), as in "I *see*" = 'I know', and several examples adduced by György László (*apud* Kövecses 2002: 219): *fantasy* (< G *phantasía* 'appearing; appearance; imagination; representation'); *idea* (< L *idea* 'archetype; idea' < G *idéā* 'form; semblance; archetype; idea'); *intuition* (< L *intuērī* 'to look at; observe; contemplate'); etc.: "vision is connected with intellection because it is our primary source of objective data about the world" (Sweetser 1990: 39). More generally,

From very early experience, humans have access to knowledge and understanding through the physical senses, and as a result the process (gaining knowledge/understanding) and the end result (being knowledgeable/having understanding) are inextricably linked, to the extent that one affects the way the other is perceived. Put simply, the way in which we are able to access knowledge affects our perception of what it is to be intelligent. (Allan 2008: 44)

The most exhaustive study of words involving the senses is by Allan (2008: 37–87). She argues (p. 58) that vision is unique, being the only sense that can include the others (hearing, touch, taste/smell). In non-Indo-European languages as well, 'see' and 'know' are often linked as meanings of one and the same verb (ibid., pp. 60f., 67). Allan (p. 62) disagrees that the usual evolution is from concrete to abstract, claiming that a conflated concept splits historically into two separate meanings. As will be shown below, changes from abstract to concrete are also well attested, but this does not presuppose conflated meanings. Allan's conflated meanings are after the fact, based on attested polysemy.[1] Her own account, like Sweetser's, explains the frequent polysemy: the physical senses are our source of mental knowledge and understanding. Finally, Allan (p. 52) mentions the Indo-European root *weid- 'see' but fails to appreciate the implication: 'know' is attested in a secondary o-grade form *woid- (see Indo-European Appendix), iconic to its DERIVED meaning.

Spatial notions are generalized to temporal by metaphor. For instance, *second* (unit of time) derives from the idea of following sequentially in space.

One of the ways in which concrete terms can evolve into abstract is by construal with abstractions. For instance, very concrete affective verbs can be used figuratively of abstractions (Nyrop 1913: 231f.): *wound* the soul, *break* the silence, *underscore* a question. From such contexts, abstract figurative meanings can be generalized, entailing that a wounding need not involve physical assault, an underscoring need not involve an actual line, and so on.

The evolution comes full circle when the original concrete meaning is lost entirely. For instance, L *errāre* originally meant 'to wander, stray, roam' in the concrete sense, but already in Early Latin could mean 'go astray; be mistaken'. Both sets of meanings were continued in OF *errer* and E ERR from Robert Mannyng [1303] to Dryden [1697], the last writer to use the concrete meaning (cf. Copley 1961: 64f.). English *insult* [1576] goes back to L *īnsultāre* 'to leap upon; assail' then 'insult' (Copley, p. 92); *offend* [a.1382] is from L *offendere* 'to knock against; strike' then 'offend' (Copley, p. 112). These and many similar examples (*debate, contend, convince*, etc.) illustrate the **speech is combat** metaphor (Sweetser 1987: 454).

It is of course not the case that abstract nouns derive only from concrete by metaphor. It is well known (cf. Nyrop 1913: §328) that there is no language in which

---

[1] "POLYSEMY designates a situation in which a single word has a set of related meanings" (Goddard 1998: 19). He illustrates with *chip*, as in chip of wood/glass, potato chip, computer chip, etc., all of which "contain the component 'small piece'" (ibid.). The tricky part is establishing what meanings are 'related'. As noted in §6.1, the bird *crane* was metaphorically applied to a lifting instrument since Ancient Greek, but for speakers who do not know what kind of bird a *crane* is, or, even if they do and fail to make the link, the building-site *crane* is merely a homonym (Traugott and Dasher 2002: 15; cf. Durkin 2011: 76). See the end of §6.2. Conversely, it is clear from folk etymology (§7.1) that speakers relate words that are not related.

abstract nouns cannot be derived directly by means of some morphological or syntactic operation.²

Finally, the change is not unidirectional. Changes from abstract to concrete are also attested. OE ʒeogoð YOUTH was derivationally an abstract noun 'youngness' with the IE suffix *-ti- > Gmc. *-þi- (cf. Krahe and Meid 1967: 156; see *yeu- in Watkins 2000: 103), but already in *Beowulf* the concrete collective meaning 'young persons; warriors' is also found (cf. Stern 1931: 351f.). This involves metonymy (below). Other examples of abstract > concrete include *beauty, failure, help, horror, curiosity, celebrity*, etc. (cf. Nyrop 1913: 224f.; Stern 1931: 370ff.). Abstract activity/event nouns in *-ing* frequently evolve into concrete/entity nouns: *crossing, writing, painting, covering, dripping(s), clipping(s), cutting(s), holding(s), earning(s), shaving(s)*, etc. (Miller 2002: 316, w. lit).

6.4 Metonymy

One of the leading ideas of metonymy is that "A stands for B" (Feyaerts 2000: 62). More specifically, X is associated to a conceptually proximous Y (cf. Feyaerts 2000). Although contiguity per se is too ambiguous to be of use (Allan 2008: 13), Allan's own idea (p. 182) of a CONTINUUM between metaphor and metonymy is descriptively less satisfying. It is reasonable to interpret metonymy as SEMANTIC REANALYSIS, reinterpretation of a word with meaning X as meaning Y (or X + Y) from an associated context (cf. Bain 1893: 186–95). Extralinguistic information is required to make the necessary link(s). All metonymy involves transfer of meaning in some way, either from one word to another closely associated word, or, more generally, by means of an associated social/cultural context. Following is the classic definition of metonymy, as stated by Stern (1931: 298):

Metonymy... is founded on contiguity, and consists of naming a thing by some accompaniment. The accompaniment may be (1) the Sign or Symbol, or any significant adjunct, (2) the Instrument for the Agent, (3) the Container for the thing contained, (4) an Effect for a Cause, (5) a Maker for his Works, (6) the name of a Passion for the name of its Object. Closely related to these forms of metonymy are the forms of synecdoche founded on contiguity: (1) Naming a thing by some Part, (2) the reverse operation of using the Whole for the Part.

The following sections represent several of the taxonomic types of metonymy that are recognized in the literature.³

---

² Curiously, only 70.91% of the languages in the sample of Štekauer, Valera, and Körtvélyessy (2012: 297–303) have recorded examples of abstract noun formation. It is difficult to imagine that the rest either have no abstract nouns or have no way to create or derive them.

³ Some scholars define metonymy more narrowly, others restrict it to synecdoche. For our purposes, it does not matter whether one includes all of what follows under the heading *metonymy* or creates separate categories. There have even been attempts to analyze metaphor in terms of metonymy (see Traugott and Dasher 2002: 27ff.). Other hypotheses are reviewed in Grygiel and Kleparski (2007: 99–111), Allan (2008), and, less directly, Allan and Robinson (2011).

6.5 Transferred epithet

An epithet (G *epítheton* 'added; assumed') is a name or label acquired by virtue of some trait or accomplishment. It is an associated modifier, as in *Richard the Lionhearted*. As a form of metonymy, the meaning of the head is transferred to an associated contiguous modifier. Stern (1931: 248) illustrates with a standard elliptical expression "sweet or dry?". If this were generalized to non-restaurant contexts, so that in standard English, *sweet* meant 'sweet wine', that would be an example of transferred epithet; cf. *private* = private soldier, *shrapnel* = Shrapnel shell, both generalized from a military context (Stern 1931: 274f.).

Examples of metonymic change by transferred epithet include:[4]

(a) *Flour* began as the same word as *flower*, specified as *flower of wheat, flower of barley*, etc. In 1691, there is a reference to *Milk, Water, and Flower, seasoned with Salt*. Already *Genesis and Exodus* 1013 [c.1250] reads: *Kalues fleis and flures bred And buttere* 'calf's flesh (meat) and bread of flour and butter' (cf. Stern 1931: 272; Durkin 2011: 84).

(b) G *galaxías* (*kúklos*) 'milky (circle)' → GALAXY [Ch.] by transfer of 'circle' to the 'milk' word.

(c) L *sermō religiōsus* 'religious speech' > LL *sermōn(e)- (religiōso-)* → SERMON [c.1250], in which the word for 'speech' also bears the sense of 'religious'.

(d) L *nātālem [diem (Jēsūs Christī)]* 'birth [day (of Jesus Christ)]' > F *Noël* → NOWELL [1390]/NOEL [1435].

(e) L *via strāta* 'roadway spread over (with stones or the like)' → LL *strāta* [c4] 'paved road' → STREET [OE] (Miller 2012: 63).

(f) L (**movimentum* >) *mōmentum temporis* 'movement of time', then '(brief) space of time', and the notion of time was transferred to *mōmentum* → MOMENT [Ch., Wyclif] (*LSDE* 82).

(g) L *Cyprium (aes)* '(copper) of Cyprus' → LL *cuprum* [= *cu* on the Periodic Chart] (→ COPPER [OE]), in which the original word for Cyprus bears the meaning of its export (*LSDE* 163; Miller 2012: 65). Copper was associated with Cyprus, and it is that (non-material) association that makes the change an example of metonymy. It is not a metaphor because copper does not resemble Cyprus!

---

[4] Given such examples as *ten-speed [bicycle]*, the question has rightly been asked whether these indeed involve a transferred epithet or simple clipping. Clips such as *penult, decaf* (Chapter 11) at least initially preserve the meaning of all components. If there is any distinction, it might be that clipping destroys some part of the remaining constituent. By that criterion, one of the classic examples of metonymy, *roasted meat* → *roast*, would actually be an example of clipping because the *-ed* of *roasted* is also deleted. Having asserted that it is not clear that there is any substantive difference, I will nevertheless follow the criterion that in standard metonymy by transferred epithet no part of the remaining component is clipped, and specific knowledge is required. Fritz (1998: 51) subsumes all examples like F *voiture automobile* [a.1876] 'self-moving vehicle' → *automobile* [1876] 'id.' under "Elliptical Uses" (cf. Geeraerts 1997: 101).

There are many examples of toponyms imparting their name to an associated product (Nyrop 1913: 391–5). Edible products include fruits (*cantaloup*), cheeses (*brie, camembert, gruyère, neufchâtel, parmesan, roquefort*), coffee (*java*), liquors (*armagnac, bourbon* [from Bourbon County, Kentucky], *tequila*, etc.),[5] and wines, e.g. (wine of) Bordeaux, Chablis, Champagne, etc. *Sherry* [1608] is backformed from *sherris* [1600] '(wine) of Xeres', a city in Spain (Mod. *Jerez*), where it was produced. (*Xeres* in turn goes back to L *Caesaris* [*urbs*] 'Caesar's [city]'.) A good example of the interchange between proper and common nouns is *madeira* (Nyrop 1913: §489). L *māteria* (for *māteriēs*) 'building material; timber' became *madeira* in Portuguese, which continued to mean 'material (timber) for construction', hence MADEIRA [1663] 'Cuban mahogany'. The word was applied to a small island whose forests furnished building material, resulting in the name *Madeira*. Wine from there, *Madeira* (wine) [1584], in turn gave rise to the common noun MADEIRA [c.1595] as a name of the wine.

Non-edibles include a variety of diverse products. *China*(-*ware*) [1634] remains transparent. From India come *cashmere* [1822] (Kashmīr), *calico* [1540] (Calicut), *madras* [1897] (Madras), *dungaree* [1696] (as a type of trousers [1891]). *Cologne* (water) [1814] was first made in Cologne, on the Rhine. *Jerseys* [1837] were originally woolen sweaters, made from Jersey worsted [1583], peculiar to fishermen on the Channel Island of Jersey. *Suede* [1923] is extracted from *suede gloves* [1859], a partial translation of F *gants de suède* 'gloves of Sweden' (*Suède* 'Sweden'). *Denim* [1864] is clipped from *Serge Denims* [1695], reanalyzed from F *serge de Nîmes* 'twilled cloth of worsted (for suits) from Nîmes, France'. *Worsted* [1293] (in Latin; first in English in Chaucer) 'firm-textured woolen yarn or fabric made from it' is itself a metonymy, going back to AL *pannus de Worthstede* [1296] 'cloth from Worthstede', a product of *Worthstede* (now *Worstead*), a village in Norfolk, England.

6.6 Pure metonymy

So-called "pure" metonymy involves the transfer from one property to another by one or more associated social contexts. It is perhaps better referred to as SEMANTIC REANALYSIS (so Eckardt 2006, who does not include it as a form of metonymy).

Social change can entail semantic reanalysis. *Purchase* [c.1300] (< AN/OF *po(u)r-chacier* 'to take, capture, procure' < VL *prō* + **captiāre* ⇐ L *captāre* 'to strive to capture': Miller 2012: 177) originally involved chasing and capturing. When the same items came to be obtained in a more civilized manner, *purchase* was reanalyzed as effected by money rather than capture (cf. Copley 1961: 131).

---

[5] *Gin* [1723] is often cited in this context as deriving from Geneva. But gin is produced by distilling rye or other grains with juniper berries, and is clipped from *geneva* [1689] < Du. *jenever* < MDu *genuuere* < OF *gene(i)vre* < L *jūniperus* JUNIPER [a.1400] (*HFW* 178).

L *persōna* 'player's mask; stage character' was reanalyzed (already in Latin) as the PERSON [1200] behind the character (Copley 1961: 120f.; *LSDE* 133).

VL **dom(i)niārium* 'authority' (cf. L *dominium* 'sovereignty') > OF *dang(i)er* > ME *da(u)nger* 'power; damage' > DANGER [1200], reanalyzed from contexts in which people are endangered by those in their power (Stern 1931: 369).

Sabot-eur [1921] (F 'one who [deals in] shoes') and *sabot-age*, literally an act of 'shoeing', came to be associated with the throwing of a *sabot* [1607] 'wooden shoe' into a machine and breaking it. From there, the meaning was generalized to describe any willfully destructive act, hence SABOTAGE [1910].

Premises 'real estate' [1610] originally meant 'the aforesaid, previously mentioned' [1429]. In announcements and sales documents the details were initially enumerated, viz. "house, with garden, land, tenements, etc." Later in the document, *the premises* was substituted for the description. From this context, in which the referent was identical, *the premises* was reanalyzed to designate the property itself (Stern 1931: 358ff.; Eckardt 2006).

Arrant was originally a variant of *errant* (L *errāns/errant-*) 'wandering, itinerant; vagrant' [1550]. In contexts such as *arrant thief* 'roving robber' (*thef errauntt* [Ch.]), *arrant* was reanalyzed as an intensive 'notorious/manifest/unmitigated' [1393] and extended to *traitor, rebel, coward*, etc. After 1575 it was "widely used as an opprobrious intensive, with *fool, dunce, ass, idiot...*" (Stern 1931: 394f.).

Rubric goes back ultimately to L *rubrīca* 'red ochre (esp. as a pigment)' continued in AN, MF, F *rubrique* [1372] (cf. L *ruber* 'red'). In post-Augustan Latin *rubrīca* was applied to the chapter headings in red letters in books of law, hence *rubric* in this sense [c.1425]. The heading function came to predominate, "and the word could then be extended [1575] to denote other headings, not printed in red" (Stern 1931: 405). From there, *rubric* came to designate a descriptive heading or category [1816].

Comedian and entertainer Arthur Roberts (1852–1933) invented a game called *Spouf* (first referred to in 1884) which involved trickery. It had no winners but the loser had to buy the next round of drinks in the pub. From the context of the swindle, evolved the word *spoof* [1889] 'hoax'. It seems to be unknown why Roberts called his game *Spouf*.

6.7 Part–whole transfer (synecdoche)

A part is substituted for the whole, i.e. the meaning of the whole is transferred to a word that originally designated only a part of the whole.[6] At issue here is perception in terms of Gestalts: one perceives the whole as an inseparable extension of the part. These substitutions can be characterized as "context-independent conceptual associations" (Eckardt 2006).

---

[6] The inverse (whole for a part) belongs with transferred epithet, e.g. *wearing a* mink [*coat*].

Examples include *blade* [Ch.] 'sword', *head* [1513] '(number of) people' (cf. *headcount* [1924]), *hands* [1644] 'laborers, workers', *brain* [1914] 'intelligent person', *threads* [1926] 'clothes', *prick* [1598] 'despicable person', *wheels* [1959] 'car'.

There are several subclasses of part–whole substitutions. One involves characterization by a garment or equipment, e.g. *ensign* [1579], *redcoat* [c.1605], *Green Beret* [1949], *skirt* [1899] 'woman', *jock* [1963] 'versatile young athlete' (probably earlier; note *surfing jock* [1961]). More generally, this subclass has been termed CONTAINER FOR CONTAINED, e.g. the *city* for its inhabitants, the *purse* for money, the *bottle* for alcoholic beverage, *dish, paperback*, etc. (cf. Bain 1893: 188f.).

The endless taxonomies (cf. Stern 1931: 319–82; Kövecses 2002: 152–6; 2005) can be avoided by mentioning several frequent types of substitution: material for object (*box* for an item made of boxwood; *horn, iron, glass, rubber*, etc.), object for person (*hunk, sponge, mouth-piece*), and producer for product: a [painting by] *Rembrandt, Picasso*, etc.; a [work by] *Molière, Shakespeare* (cf. Nyrop 1913: §297; Stern 1931: 373; Kövecses 2002: 143ff.; Benczes 2006: 170f.). These might also be considered elliptical and/or more like transferred epithet (Ullmann 1957: 243f.), illustrating the problem of subclassifying metonymy.[7]

Many toponyms derive from something notable about the place, e.g. *Hedges, Townsend, Newcastle*.

The part–whole relationship extends to entire situations, in which the effect can be substituted for the cause, as in a reference to a tedious activity as a *yawn* [1889], or to a stingy person as *tight(-fisted)* [1843].

So-called PROPRIETARY TERMS evolve by another type of synecdoche, involving genericization, or promotion of one member of a class to designate the class as a whole. Typical examples involve *kleenex* [1925] (at the expense of *tissue* and other companies that make tissues), *coke* [1940] (earlier examples may refer to Coca-Cola [1887]) as a generic for *cola* (the leading representative of the class becomes the name for the class), *xerox* [1952] for *photocopy*. Other proprietary terms are *bandaid* [1948] (*Band-Aid* [1920]), *jello* [1936] (*Jell-o* [1934]), etc.

This process is not unidirectional. There is also degenericization, as in the case of E *man*, the original generic, which supplanted OE *wer* (*werewolf, wergeld*, etc.) as the male of the species. In this case the male and the species itself were identified as coterminous.

The boundary between metaphor and metonymy is not always clear. Emotion metaphors, for instance, generally "have a metonymic basis" (Niemeier 2000: 198). Thus, *heart* is metonymic for the whole person, as shown by expressions such as *big-hearted, soft/tender-hearted, hard-hearted, heavy-hearted, heartless*, etc. (ibid.,

---

[7] With reference to the frequently discussed example from a restaurant context, "*The ham sandwich* wants a side dish of salad", Kövecses (2002: 156) makes the following comment: "The conceptual relationship might be specified as one of possession, part–whole, or control, but none of them seems to fully capture the 'essence' of the kind of 'contiguity' that we feel holds between a customer and his or her dish."

p. 199ff.); cf. *gutless, gutsy*. In expressions like *heart of stone*, *steel*, etc., the materials are "metaphorically mapped onto the domain of the heart" (ibid., p. 201). These metaphors are in turn used metonymically: a personal trait "stands for the whole moral outfit of that person" (Niemeier, p. 202).

Interaction between metaphor and metonymy has been referred to as METAPHTO-NYMY (Goossens 1990). For the overlap, see the contributions to Dirven and Pörings (2002), and compare the notion of a continuum in Allan (2008).

Examples like *egghead* [1907] involve complex interactions. First, there is the metaphoric comparison of the head to an egg. Then, transferred epithet imparts the meaning of 'individual/person' to the construct. The further metonymic association of baldness (more directly similar to an egg) with intellect (Tournier 1985: 294) is no longer present in the meaning of *egghead*, which can apply to someone with very thick hair. Similarly, *redneck* [1830] can apply to anyone with a comparable belief system, *bigwigs* [1703] no longer wear wigs at all, but *skinhead*, which originally designated the haircut of U.S. marines [1943], now often refers to neo-Nazis with shaved heads [1969].

In *acidhead* [1966] ('LSD user'), the modifier is metaphor-based and the profile determinant is metonymy-based (Benczes 2006: 179).

Hammerhead has several different metaphorical and metonymic uses. In the most literal 'head of a hammer' [1562], *head* is a simple metaphor: the striking part resembles a head. In the sense of a stubborn or blockheaded individual [1532], *head* is supposedly metaphorical with reference to *hammer* but metonymically in a part–whole relation with reference to the person (Benczes 2006: 171). In contemporary English, this analysis works better for the species of shark [1861]. The application to a person metaphorically identifies someone as having the traits of a hammerhead shark. Originally, however, the comparison was of a human head to that of a hammer, subsequently generalized by part–whole metonymy to the individual.

Via synecdoche of *head* for person, people are frequently compared to substances of density, e.g. *bone-headed* [1903], whence the exocentric metonym *bonehead* [1908]. This derivational pattern is not unidirectional; cf. *blockhead* [1549] but *blockheaded* [1606] as a reference to a 'stupid person'. Sometimes the density of the head itself is the element of comparison, as in *thick-headed* [1801] (literal sense [1707]) and *thickhead* [1824]. A food substance can be conceptualized as a dense item, as in *mutton-headed* [1768]/*mutton-head* [1803], *meathead* [1945]/*meatheaded* [1949], etc. Discussion of these and other examples can be found in Allan (2008: 88–123). For slang terms see Mattiello (2008: 78).

6.8 Transfer of characteristic (antonomasia, eponymy)

The transfer is from a proper noun to a common object or concept.[8]

---

[8] Eponyms from personal names can be separated from those based on geographical, literary, mythic, and commercial names (Stockwell and Minkova 2001: 15–18). Our heuristic separates English

Procrustes, in Greek legend, forced overnight travelers to fit his iron bed by stretching them or cutting them down to size, whence *procrustean* [1647], of the use of violence to force uniformity or conformity.

Tantalus, mythical king of Phrygia, abused the privilege of dining with the gods either by sharing ambrosia with mortals or by serving his son Pelops to the gods for dinner. As a punishment, he was doomed to be forever in sight of fruit and water that receded whenever he reached for it, hence *tantalize* [1597].

Pandarus, an archer who wounded Menelaus in Homer's *Iliad*, served in Chaucer's *Troilus & Criseyde* as the intermediary between the two lovers, Priam's son Troilus, and Cressida, daughter of a priest who fled Troy leaving her there, whence *pander* 'liaison in sexual intrigues; pimp; procurer' [c.1450]. The verb dates to a.1616.

Stentor, a Greek herald in the Trojan War known for his voice of fifty men (*Iliad* 5.785), is the source of a *stentorian* (very loud) voice [1606].

Epicurus [c.341–c.270] started a school (way of life) in Athens [306 BCE], advocating atheism, high living, and sensual gratification, and forbidding marriage, children, and participation in public life. From the associations with his name is derived *epicure* [1545]/*epicurean* [a.1572], one who cultivates refined tastes, especially in food and wine.

Pyrrhus [319/8–272] lost so many men in his defeat of the Romans at Asculum [279 BCE] that his name gave rise to the *pyrrhic* [1675] victory.

Philippic [c.1550] denotes a bitter invective as used by Cicero in his harangues against Marc Antony, modeled after Demosthenes' denouncement of Philip II of Macedon, the father of Alexander the Great.

Quintus Roscius [c1 BCE], a friend of Cicero's, was such a brilliant comic actor that *roscian* [1607] denotes eminence in the performing arts.

Caesar, a name acquired by Julius' grandnephew Octavian (known today by his honorary title *Augustus* conferred in 27 BCE) after his adoption by Julius Caesar. Since Octavian/Augustus was the first Roman emperor, the title *Caesar* was adopted by subsequent emperors, and came by association to be synonymous with *imperātor* 'emperor', giving rise to Germ. *Kaiser*, Slavic *czar, tsar*, etc.

L *Monēta*, a cult title of Juno, was used of her temple at Rome where money was coined, then of any mint, then 'coinage, money' [first in Ovid], yielding OF, AN *moneie* (many spellings), F *monnaie*, E *money* [1300] (Miller 2012: 56, w. lit).

John Duns Scotus [?1265–1308], born in Duns, Scotland, was a scholastic philosopher and theological archconservative. His followers, *Duns men* or *Dunses* [1527], because of their hair-splitting, were viewed contemptuously by opponents and later philosophers, whence *dunce* [1577] 'hair-splitting reasoner; cavilling sophist', [1587] 'dullard, dolt, blockhead'.

from non-English eponyms. Most of the examples cited here (plus others) are found in Boycott (1982) and Freeman (1997).

German *Taler* 'valleyer', Early Modern High German *thaler* [1540], clipped from *Joachimstaler* 'one from Joachimsthal' (Joachim's Dale), a place in Bohemia where silver was minted in 1519, corresponds to Low German *da(l)ler*, Early Modern Dutch *daler*, whence E *dollar* [1553].

Béchamel sauce is named after its inventor, the Marquis Louis de Béchamel, steward of Louis XIV [1643–1715], but is first recorded in English in a cookbook from 1789.

Chauvinism [1870] is eponymous for the (probably fictitious) overzealous French patriot Nicolas Chauvin who continually sang Napoleon's praises during the First Republic and Empire.

Paparazzo (pl. *paparazzi*) [1961], a freelance photographer who pursues celebrities, is Italian *paparazzo* [1961], derived from *Paparazzo*, a society photographer in Fellini's *La Dolce Vita* [1960]. Fellini reportedly took the name from an opera libretto because it suggested "a buzzing insect, hovering, darting, stinging" (*OED* online).

Ethnic names tend to evolve into pejoratives, perhaps the best known of which are *Viking* [OE]/*viking* [1807] but not nativized until 1840 (Miller 2012: 5, w. lit) and *Vandal* [1555]/*vandal* [1663] (cf. Nyrop 1913: 386f.).

The sciences have many well-known eponyms, e.g. *ampere* [1881] (André-Marie Ampère [1775–1836]), *(deci)bel* [1928] (Alexander Graham Bell [1847–1922]), *hertz* [1928] (Heinrich Rudolf Hertz [1857–94]), *ohm* [1861] (Georg Simon Ohm [1787–1854]), *volt* [1873] / *voltaic* [1812] (Alessandro Volta [1745–1827]), *watt* [1882] (James Watt [1736–1819]).

6.9 English-specific eponymy

The English language is fond of remembering people eponymically. Many common objects bear noble names. The *cardigan* [1868] sweater is named after James Thomas Brudenell [1797–1868], who became the 7th Earl of Cardigan. He so frequently wore the colorless sweater with buttons down the front that it came to be associated with him.

Dr. Thomas Bowdler [1754–1825] published a ten-volume edition of *The Family Shakespeare* (Bath, 1818) with all passages excised "which cannot with propriety be read aloud in a family." The word *bowdlerize* was coined in 1836 for this type of censorship.

The 4th Earl of Sandwich (John Montagu) [1718–92] was a passionate gambler. To avoid leaving the gambling table, he ordered that slices of toast with cold roast beef between them be brought to him, inventing the *sandwich* [1762].

Commoners so immortalized include John Loudon McAdam [1756–1836], a Scottish surveyor who developed *macadam* [1824], whence *tarmacadam* [1882], *tarmac* [1903], and Charles Macintosh [1766–1843], a Scottish chemist who invented the *mac(k)intosh* [1836] rubberized cloth raincoat.

Thomas Crapper [1836–1910], Chelsea Sanitary Engineer, in 1884 improved on the flush toilet with Crapper's Valveless Water Waste Preventer and Crapper's Seat Action Automatic Flush.[9] Thanks to the Thomas Crapper Company label on his toilets, Crapper has contributed to the sources of *crap*.[10]

Yahoo [1764] 'crude, uncultivated person; boor; violent person' derives from *Yahoo* [1726], invented by Jonathan Swift in *Gulliver's Travels* as the name for a fictional race of brutes in human form.

Malapropism [1830] (and *malaprop* [1814]) 'the ludicrous misuse of words' (*OED*) derives from Mrs Malaprop, a character in Richard Brinsley Sheridan's play *The Rivals* (1775), notorious for confusing similar-sounding words, as in her description of someone as "headstrong as an allegory [for *alligator*!] on the banks of the Nile" (*NDE* 155). Other examples are *fire distinguisher*, *pigment of the imagination*. Sheridan created the name after the French loan *malapropos* [1630] 'inappropriate(ly)'. A more recent version involves BUSHISMS, e.g. *preserving executive powers...for predecessors, weapons of mass production, time to restore chaos and order*.

Spoonerism [1900] received its name from the Reverend William Archibald Spooner [1844–1930], Dean and Warden of New College, Oxford, who was particularly prone to such extreme metatheses as *fighting a liar* for 'lighting a fire', *you hissed my mystery lecture* for 'you missed my history lecture', *our queer old Dean* for 'our dear old Queen', and many more. For spoonerisms as a form of language play, see §5.5.

Shyster [1844] may be from *Scheuster*, an unscrupulous New York attorney of the 1840s.[11]

Blurb [1907] is named for a fictional character, Blinda Blurb, used as an advertising gimmick on the dust jacket of 500 copies of Gelett Burgess' *Are You a Bromide?* [1906].

Bikini [1948] received its name from the type of swimsuit worn by women on the Bikini atoll of the Marshall Islands.

Clipping (Chapter 11) frequently obscures metonyms from proper names, e.g. *Saint Audrey* (pronounced /sẽ(n).tɒ.dri/ in British) > *tawdry* [1676] 'cheap and flashy; vulgar', from the cheap, gaudy lace neckties (*tawdries* [1612]) sold at fairs in honor of St Audrey [†679].

---

[9] Crapper made minor improvements on patent #4990 by Albert Giblin in 1898, itself modeled on the flush toilet patented by Alexander Cummings in 1775, based on the 1596 prototype by Sir John Harrington.

[10] *Crap* has had several contributors through its long history. The first occurrences in the *Promptorium Parvulorum* [c.1440] and the *Catholicon Anglicum* [1483] mean 'husk of grain, chaff' and go back to AF *crappe* 'chaff; husk' (Rothwell 1996: 47f.), but it also means 'dregs, scraps' (from melting fat); cf. OF *crappe* 'siftings; waste' and earlier Dutch *krappe* 'something plucked off; scrap', probably related to OIce *krap* 'slush', Ice, Norw. *krap* 'small clumps of ice or snow' (de Vries 1977: 328f.). Since 1898, *crap* means 'excrement' by analogy with *Crapper/crapper*.

[11] *Collins English Dictionary*: http://dictionary.reference.com/browse/shyster

St Mary of Bethlehem, a London insane asylum founded as a priory in 1247 > ME, EMnE *Bethlem/Bedlem* [1528] 'the Bethlehem asylum' > *bedlam* [a.1667] 'uproar, total confusion'.

6.10 Summary

Since the physical senses are our source of mental knowledge and understanding, much of semantic motivation is extralinguistic, grounded in personal experience, perception, and cognition. Vision is unique, being the only sense that can include the others (hearing, touch, taste/smell). Spatial notions are generalized to temporal by metaphor.

Body parts are ubiquitously applied to items in nature. Since animals are perceived to resemble humans, personal attributes and insults are freely derived from animal names and applied to different human traits in different cultures. Animal names are also applied to instruments that they resemble in shape or function, e.g. *crane*.

Sensory (synesthetic) metaphors are all pervasive. For example, *sweet* can be generalized from taste to personality, voice, perfume, and other items. *Warm* is extended from a moderate temperature to colors, scents, etc.

Popular attempts to classify and make sense of the universe place value judgments on objective labels. These subjective (e)valuations differ sometimes greatly from one person to another and as the conception of the referents evolves over time. Part of (e)valuation involves comparisons or utilization of a label from an item conceptualized as similar. Metaphors at least initially bear evaluative nuance. Metonymy involves transfer of labels by reanalysis mediated by associated contexts, e.g. from part to whole, from person to associated item. Attempting to itemize all forms of metonymy is no more feasible than taxonomizing mental interconnections.

The earlier acquisition of concrete and lexical categories reflects the natural evolution from concrete to abstract. Of course, this is not unidirectional because, among other reasons, all languages have affixes or other mechanisms to derive concrete nouns from abstract.

7

Folk etymology and tabu

The rationale for treating folk etymology and tabu together is twofold. First, both involve analogical creations. Second, both involve either a substitution for a prior form or an alteration of that form. They differ in that tabu involves conscious avoidance of a word that is negatively valued culturally while folk etymology involves an attempt to make sense of a synchronically isolated or obscure form.

7.1 Folk etymology

The essence of folk etymology is that some X is reanalyzed as the nearest Y it "sounds like" and that also in some manner accounts for the meaning. Examples include *pickaxe* [1428] for older *picas* [1256] from AN *pikeis*, OF *picois* 'id.', *chaise-lounge* [1807] for F *chaise longue* 'long chair' [1800], *old-timer's disease* [1983] for Alzheimer's disease.

Words are stored and processed according to sound and meaning (§15.2), and the relationship of the terms in folk etymology is always one of analogy (Coates 1987).[1] In the words of Meier (1989: 71), "'wrong' etymologies must be considered as a systematic expression of linguistic psychology, because the kind of equation involved is a creative activity endeavouring to make a word significant again—even where the new significance is only apparent" (cf. Rundblad and Kronenfeld 2000). For De Cuypere (2008: 210), folk etymology "crucially involves the replacement of an (allegedly) opaque form by means of a more transparent form-meaning pair." Similarly, Kursova (2013) argues that folk etymologies increase 'naturalness'. De Cuypere emphasizes that folk etymologies are especially frequent in vernacular varieties and the language of children.

Folk etymology is frequent in the adaptation of foreign expressions (Ullmann 1957: 91), e.g. *mayday* [1923] for F *m'aider* (or *m'aidez*) 'help me'. The most extensive study of folk etymologies from borrowings is by Kursova (2013).

---

[1] On one account, folk etymology involves hyponymy. In hyponymy, the meaning of one word is included in another, e.g. *affirm*, *deny*, and *narrate* include the meaning of *say* (cf. Goddard 1998: 16). According to McMahon (1994: 184), "the affecting form designates a superordinate term, and the affected one comes to resemble the superordinate term formally and denote a subtype semantically." In many cases, however, hyponymy is irrelevant.

As known since Palmer (1883), folk-etymologizing also applies to well-known words, often in surprising ways: "A folk etymology like *sparrow-grass* for *asparagus*... borders on the lunatic" (Sihler 2000: 87). The main attested forms are *sparagi* [c. 1000], *sparagus* [1543] (ML *sparagus*, *sparagi*), *asparagus* [1548] (L *asparagus*), *sperage(s)* [1548] (MF *esperage*), *sparrowgrass* [1652]. Durkin (2011: 203) tries to motivate the deformation by way of *sparagrass*, which is first recorded in the *OED* in 1664, but all of the forms are attested in Wallis (1653: 55): "*Asparagus, sparagus, sperage,* quod vulgus dequortet in [which the common people twist into] *sparagrass, sparrowgrass.*" In 1711 James Greenwood translates Wallis' passage with a slight variant in his own grammar: "*Sperage* which the Vulgar wrest to *Sparograss* or *Sparrowgrass.*" Growing asparagus resembles grass, hence that part of the folk etymology. The rest is due in part to the phonetic similarity of *spara-* to *sparrow*, and in part to the resemblance to a bird's nest.

Popular attempts at etymologizing frequently leave a portion of the word unanalyzed. For instance, the *cray* part of *crayfish* [1555] (< ME *creuess/krevys* [c.1400/1430] < F *écrévisse*) remains unmotivated. The twisting of F *femelle* 'little woman' into E *female* (already in Wyclif [a.1382] *maal and femaal*) fit the cultural notion of the extraction of the female from the *male*, and was paralleled in *woman*, even though both formations leave an unexplained residue (*fe-*, *wo-*), which have prompted recent popular attempts to resolve, e.g. *weeman* (see Rundblad and Kronenfeld 2000: 26f.).

Examples of folk etymology include:[2]

(a) *hurricane* 'tropical cyclone' < Sp. *huracán* (cf. Port. *furacão*) < Carib *huracán, furacan,* West Indian (Taino) *hurakan* 'an evil spirit of the sea; hurricane'. The borrowed form was altered to match *hurry* (cf. Shipley 1984: 185), an existing word with a meaning consistent with the storm's velocity. In fact, the word was borrowed into English in several forms, e.g. *furacan-* [1555], *haurachan-* [1555], *uracan-* [1588]. The first was folk etymologized with *fury* as *furican-* [1587]. Other adaptations include *hurlecan* [1617], *hero-cane* [1634], and the first unambiguous attestation of modern *hurricane* is in 1665.

(b) *miniature* [a.1586] is from Ital. *miniatura* '(the painting of) a small bright image' (esp. to decorate the initial letters of manuscript chapters or the illuminations in Medieval manuscripts), a derivative of *miniare* 'to illuminate' (L *miniāre* 'to color red with cinnabar [*minium* MINIUM]'). Under the influence of *minus, minuscule,* etc., and since the illuminations were generally small, *miniature* was reanalyzed as 'small picture or decorative letter', then 'on a small or greatly reduced scale' (cf. Nyrop 1913: 327f.).

---

[2] For additional examples see Koziol (1972: 317–20), Tournier (1985: 333ff., 421f.), Coates (1987), Meier (1989), Rundblad and Kronenfeld (2000), Knappe (2004), Fill (2004), Konieczna (2009), Klégr and Čermák (2010).

(c) *sacri-leg-ious* [1582] / *sacrilege* [a.1300] 'desecration', from L *sacri-leg-us* 'one who steals sacred things' (*leg-* 'gather; pluck; steal'), tends to be reanalyzed as if *sac-relig-ious* by analogy with *religion, religious*, in the same semantic field. *Religion* itself in the Christian sense may result from a folk etymology. Cicero (*On the Nature of the Gods* 2.28.72) derived L *religiō* from *re-legere* 're-collect' and understood it as a scruple that hinders (a subjective restraint). The Christian writers Lactantius and Tertullian derived it from *religāre* 'tie back' and understood it as a binding obligation, an objective tie that 'binds' us to the deity. Benveniste (1969: 2.267–73) argues for the former etymology. Hoad (*CDEE* 397) and the OED online leave it open, but *ligāre* [*$*leig$-^{1} 'bind' = LIV *$*leiǵ$-] is the most likely source (*AHDR* 47; *LSDE* 76; *EDL* 341).

(d) *hero* (sandwich) [1955], another term for a sub(marine) sandwich or hoagie, derives ultimately from G *gūros* 'circle', *gūrós* 'round' (cf. *gyro* [1971], *gyro-* [1817]). In Modern Greek, it is used of a sandwich made from meat grilled on a turning spit and pronounced /χiro/ which, of course, sounds like Eng. *hero*. The meaning is somewhat remote but possibly rationalized as a reference to the size/stalwartness of both the sandwich and its consumer.

(e) *cutlass* [1594] (spelled *coute-lace*) is etymologically from OF *coutelas*, a derivative of *couteau* (*coutel*) 'knife' (< L *cultellus*, diminutive of *culter* 'knife'). The word thus had nothing to do with E *cut* etymologically but, functionally, modification of the borrowing to conform to the spelling of *cut* is hardly unexpected. Further adaptations to English occur in *cuttleaxe* [1630], *cutlash* [1704], and modern *cutlass* [1678].

(f) *Aphrodite* (G *Aphrodítē*), despite the defense by Janda (2006: 7) of the traditional etymology from G *aphrós* 'foam' ('who flashes up in the foam of the sea'), is most likely from a pre-Greek source (*DELG* 148; *EDG* 179), and the connection with *aphrós* a folk etymology (cf. Nyrop 1913: 331).

(g) *andiron* [a.1300] was borrowed from OF *andier* 'firedog' (modern *landier* by metanalysis from *l'andier* 'the andiron'). The ending was early identified with ME *yre, yren* 'iron', whence the modern spelling *andiron* (Stern 1931: 234). Another folk etymology appears in *handiron* [?a.1500].

(h) *carnival* [1549] goes back to Ital. *carnevale* from OItal. *carnelevare* from ML *carnelevārium* [c11/12] 'the removal of meat', reshaped by folk etymology after ML *carne valē* 'flesh, farewell!' (*LSDE* 127).

(i) *miscellany* [1601] 'medley', [1615] 'literary collection', is from L *miscellus* 'inferior' (of grapes and wine) < *min(u)scellus*, diminutive of *minusculus* 'rather small, short, less' MINUSCULE [1701], later folk etymologized with L *miscēre* 'to mix', whence the meaning 'mixed' and the modern sense (*LSDE* 68).

(j) *catercornered* [1878] was analogized with *cat* (based on the sound of the two words), hence spellings like *cattycornered* [1838], *cat-a-cornered* [1902], *cattycorner* [1945], and even *kittycorner* [n.d.] (Szabóné Habók 2009: 33).

A word of caution. One must be careful not to confuse real etymologies (X derives from Y) with folk etymologies, according to which X is transformed into or reshaped/ relabeled after Y, where at least part of Y is a previously existing word that somehow resembles X in form and/or meaning.[3]

7.2 Religious tabu

A Polynesian (Tongan) word brought back by Capt. Cook in 1777, *taboo* (in technical writings generally spelled *tabu*) originally pertained to the sacred and prohibited, the *profane* [c.1450], in the etymological sense of L *profānus* (*prō* 'before' + *fānum* 'temple') 'contemptuous of sacred things; sacrilegious; secular'. All of the word formation and semantic processes discussed throughout this book are used to construct euphemisms (cf. Warren 1992; Linfoot 2001; 2005).

In most societies it is inappropriate to utter words of religious import with contempt. In the language of swearing, it is therefore not surprising to find many phonological modifications (Warren 1992) of *God*, e.g. *gog* [1390], *cod* [1569], *gad* [1608], *gadzooks* (= *God's hooks*) [1694], *egad* [1673], *gosh* [1757], *golly* [1775], *drat* (*God rot*) [1815], *doggone* (= *God-damn*) [1819], *dagnab* [1916], *Godfrey* [1853], *golda/urn(ed)* [1856], *good grief* [1900], etc. (cf. Hughes 2000: 47).[4] Similarly, for *Christ*, one finds such deformations as *cripes* [1910] (< *by Christ's stripes*), and for *Jesus*: *gee* [1895], *jeez(e)/Geez* [1923], *jeepers* [1929]. The devil gets at least twenty-five euphemisms. For *hell*, there are such circumlocutions as *Sam Hill* [1839], but the main tabu form is *heck* [1887]. *Damn(ed)* gets deformed into *deuced(ly)* [1779], *darn* [1781], *tarnation* [1784], *dang* [1793], *darnation* [1798], *dashed* [1881], *danged* [1886], etc.

One of the semantic devices of tabu replacement is ANTIPHRASIS (G *antiphrasis* 'opposite phrasing'), the use of words of good sense in place of those with negative connotations. The Greeks replaced *Erīnúes* [Myc.+] 'Erinyes; the Furies', the avenging deities (goddesses who fulfil curses and avenge crimes), with *Eumenídes* [c6/5 BCE] ['well-minded (ones)'] 'Eumenides (the gracious goddesses)'. Another group of goddesses, the *Moîrai* (pl. of G *moîra* 'portion, share; lot; fate; destiny'; i.e. 'Destiny'

---

[3] Often cited as folk etymology is the problematic *dormouse* (pl. *-mice*), a squirrel-like Old World rodent of the family *Gliridae*. Because it is nocturnal and a hibernator, often found sleeping, the animal's name was supposedly derived from L **dorm-ōsus* 'full of sleep', which yielded ME *dormowse* [c.1425]. From the similarity to *mouse*, another rodent, the subsequent history was influenced by forms of *mouse*, including the irregular plural *dormice* [c.1575], although *dormouses* [1570] is also known. Another suggested etymology is F *dormeuse* (fem.) 'sleeper' but that is unknown before c17. Also suggested is English dialectal *dorm* 'sleep' (< F *dormir* 'to sleep') + *mowse* 'mouse' (cf. Partridge 1983: 164). Sixteenth-century Dutch *slaep-muys* 'sleep-mouse' and *slaep-ratte* 'sleep-rat' may be calques with no bearing on the original etymology.

[4] Some French tabu forms for *Dieu* 'God' are known in English: *Ventre Dieu* 'God's belly' → *ventrebleu*; *Chair Dieu* 'God's flesh' → *Charbieu* (Villon), *Corps Dieu* 'God's body' → *Corbieu* (Rabelais), etc. (Nyrop 1913: 271f.).

personified) = L *Fāta* 'Fates', were identified in Latin with the *Parcae*, birth spirits, goddesses of birth. The identification was enhanced by the Roman folk etymology which connected *Parcae* with the verb *parcere* 'to spare', but, beginning with Horace, the Roman tradition loantranslated the Greek antiphrasis *Khárites* as *Grātiae* 'Graces', the goddesses who confer all grace, including the favor of victory in the games.

Whether or not the Samnian town *Mal(e)ventum* was derived from G *Malóenta* (ACC) 'apple orchard', the Romans interpreted it as 'ill-come' and changed the name to *Beneventum* 'well-come' (cf. Löfstedt 1959: 185.).

Certain animals are subject to religious tabu (Emeneau 1948). The Indo-European word for 'bear' *$h_2ṛtḱ$-o-* (G *árktos*, L *ursus*, Hittite *ḥartaggaš*) is preserved only in areas where there were no bears (Meillet 1906). Elsewhere, it was replaced, like E *bear* (= Lithuanian *běras* 'brown'), OIr *milchobur* ['honey-desiring'] (Watkins 1962: 114ff.; Uhlich 2002: 418f.), Old Slavic *medvědī* (cf. Sanskrit *madh(u)v-ád-* 'honey-eater'). In Celtic, the Indo-European word is preserved only in names, e.g. *Art*, *Hart*, OIr *ó h-art* 'son of bear' (*EDPC* 42f.). The bear is an animal to dread, to hunt, something mystical. It is dangerous to say its name unless it is associated with a person, hence the preservation in names, where the original meaning is readily forgotten.[5] Each language of the northern zones, where bears are prevalent, has replaced the original word with a euphemism.

7.3 Secular tabu

Not all tabu words are religious, even though it is not always easy to draw the line. What is religious in one culture may be secular in another, both being a reflection of cultural ideology (Linfoot 2001). Tabus surrounding natural life functions (birth, death, menstruation, evacuation, sex(uality), pregnancy, procreation) have been particularly rampant. Sickness is also prone to tabu substitution. For L *aeger* 'sick', the Romans frequently substituted *infirmus* INFIRM [c.1374], *gravis* GRAVE [1541], *languidus* LANGUID [1595], and Vulgar Latin negated *habitus* 'in good shape or condition' as *male habitus* [C1: Sabinus], whence F *malade* 'sick'; cf. MALADY (Nyrop 1913: 278f.). This use of LITOTES (negation of the positive term as a euphemism for the negative) is very common. Nyrop (1913: §443) cites *maladroit* [1685], *dishonest* [c.1386], *disagreeable* [c.1400], *inactive* [1725], *incapable* [1597], *inclement* [1621], *incompetent* [1597], *incontinent* [c.1380], *indecent* [1570], *indelicate* [1741], *indiscreet* [1413], *unjust* [a.1382], etc.[6]

---

[5] Names have a special property of being easily dissociated from their original meaning because their referent is to a particular person or place that bears the name (Coates 2006; Anderson 2007; Durkin 2011: 266–9).

[6] Copious examples of euphemisms in all categories can be found in Nyrop (1913: 257–321), Löfstedt (1959: 181–94), Tournier (1975; 1985: 261–87), Enright (1985), Allen and Burridge (1991), Warren (1992), Hughes (2000: 43–9), Linfoot (2001; 2005), Merlan (2006), Burridge (2006; 2012), Halmari (2011), Smith (2012b). The entire issue of *Lexis* 7 (2012) is devoted to "Euphemism as a Word-Formation Process."

An anonymous referee mentions the example of *bloody*, discussed by Vachek (1975), "which came to be banned in good society":

As Vachek notes, the impulse to the present-day state of things was given by the adjective *curse*. This form was tabooed and replaced with its semantic antonym *blessed* used in a quasi-ironical manner. This word soon became unacceptable and was replaced with another euphemism *bloody* reminding of the former word by the initial phonemic group *bl-*. Obviously, its fate was inevitably the same and was later replaced with some other *bl-* adjectives, like *bleeding*, *blooming, blinking*, etc. As a result, adjectives starting with *bl-* came to be stylistically suspicious.

Burridge (2012) discusses the numerous functions of euphemisms. One (p. 68f.) is misrepresentation, which one might also call disinformation. A recent example is *job creators* for the rich who dislike fair taxation.

Drunkenness is subject to humorous euphemisms, e.g. *tipsy* [1577], *lit up* [1914] (§10.7). Mental retardation has been the source of frequent mockery and euphemism: *imbecile* [c.1550] (L *imbēcillus* 'physically weak; feeble; fragile'), *idiot* [c.1384] (G *idiốtēs* 'private person; common person; unskilled or ignorant person') (Nyrop 1913: §§180, 184, 397), *cretin* [1779] (F *crétin* 'idiot' < Swiss F *crestin* 'Christian' < L *Christiānus*), the idea being that such an individual is deformed but still human (Nyrop 1913: 284f.).

Political correctness (§§5.1, 8.2) often takes the form of euphemism. Halmari (2011) discusses the PEOPLE FIRST criterion (*disabled person* ⇒ *person with a disability*; *deaf (and dumb)* ⇒ *people who are hearing impaired*; *paranoid, psycho* ⇒ *person with symptoms of mental illness*; *cripples* ⇒ *people who are mobility impaired*; etc.). She finds that politically correct (PC) language is generally obeyed in the media in connection with children and non-criminal adults but not with prisoners, fictional characters, or (paradoxically) victims. Also, headlines use non-PC language for sensationalism, shock value, and brevity. Finally, Halmari addresses the issue of artificial attempts to legislate language and thought, and "the continuous need for new circumlocutions" (p. 839).

Some humorous euphemisms involve "the most absurd, exaggerated and deliberately comical expressive forms that appear on the internet and which, consequently, have been humorously ridiculed there: *internal movement and information coordinator* (porter), *logistics and document distribution specialist* (messenger), *visual therapy expert* (stripper)," etc. (Casas Gómez 2012: 56).

The various tabu deformations, blends, truncations, replacements, and embellishments are all aspects of expressive creativity. Specifically, they are "cognitive processes of conceptualization of a certain forbidden reality" (Casas Gómez 2012: 60).

Certain body parts are subject to tabu replacement; cf. *butt(ocks)* [a.1300], *rear (end)* [1851], *posterior* [1605], *derrière* [1774], *gluteus maximus* [n.d.]. Among bodily functions, there are such euphemistic deformations as *shucks* [1843], *shoot* [1934] for *shit*, and even *dipstick* [1968] for 'penis' and for *dipshit* [1963].

In many cultures sex is especially prone to euphemism (Epstein 1985; Linfoot 2001; 2005). For *fucking* [1528], one finds *frigging* [c.1560], *flipping* [1911], *blinking* [1914], *mucking* [1929] (but *muck around* [1856] antedates *fuck around* [1931]), *fricking* [1937], *effing* [1945], and, two that were popular among my friends in the 1950s, *freakin'*, *frappin'*, and, still more recently, *shtup* [1969], *bonk* [1975] (cf. §10.7). Finally, there is the *f-word* [1973] (cf. Ayto 1990: 147). Another word widely adapted in the 1950s by folk etymology and phonological similarity to *fuck around* was *futz around*, which originally meant simply 'mess around' [1932], probably as an adaptation of Yiddish *arumfartzen* 'fart around'. The reanalysis is consistent with a blend of *fuck* × *putz*.

In all, English has some 800 words for copulation, 1,200 for vagina, 1,000 for penis, and 2,000 for whore (Allen and Burridge 1991: 96). Linfoot (2001: §5) argues that sex has become a great *secret*, "necessitating its constant discussion and the subsequent creation of new euphemisms" (ibid., §2.1). Writers through history have been concerned with politeness "either by adhering to the historical and cultural expectations, or by deliberately shattering them" (Linfoot 2001: §5.1; 2005).

Euphemistic adjectives suggest more colorful terms, e.g. *blasted* [1682], *blooming* [1882], *blankety-blank* [1900], and more recently, ideograms (!*#&*%!). Linfoot (2001: §5.2) also mentions graphological deletion (****), ellipsis (Did you —?" for "Did you have sexual intercourse?"), and aural deletion (radio and TV "bleeps").

Smith (2005; 2012b) explains why *unspeakables, unmentionables, unprintables* are ideal euphemisms. Among other things, *un-* contributes understatement, and adjective–noun conversion draws attention to these formations which simultaneously circumvent and underscore the tabu topic.

Even the facilities associated with bodily functions are prone to euphemistic replacement in so-called polite circles, e.g. *the john* [c.1650], *closet of ease* [1662], *water closet* [1775] (> W.C. [1815]), *lavatory* [1845] (earlier as 'bath' [a.1375] and 'bathing room' [1656]), *commode* [1851], *toilet* [1885] ([a.1684] as 'toiletry'), *bathroom* [1888], *lav* [1913], *loo* [1940], *potty* [1956], etc. (cf. Williams 1986: 186f.). Many of these are borrowed, as is frequent with euphemisms (Warren 1992), a tradition that began in antiquity on the evidence of Cicero's many Greek euphemisms (Nyrop 1913: 265).

Another euphemistic strategy to avoid a tabu word or phrase is truncation (Chapter 11), as studied in detail by Lefilliâtre (2012), who discusses such examples as *bi(sexual)*, *bull(shit)*, *homo(sexual)*, *mother (fucker)*, *(cock)roach*. He also argues that *flu (influenza)*, *detox (detoxification)*, and many more are euphemistic clips. *Wussy* must be clipped from *pussy-wussy* (§§12.5, 14.2.2) which, as Russ Nekorchuk reminds me, was widely used in the 1950s, long before *wussy* [1977] and backformed *wuss* [1976].

A word homophonous to a tabu word can be replaced. Since *gay* has replaced *homosexual*, it is avoided as a synonym for 'happy' (§8.2; Linfoot 2001: §2.0). The strongest motivation is avoidance of pernicious homophony. In contemporary

American English, for instance, *pussy* is no longer used of kittens,[7] *ass* for a donkey is restricted to Biblical contexts, and *cock* has ceased to mean 'rooster' (cf. de la Cruz Cabanillas and Tejedor Martinez 2002: 338ff.). As discussed by Miller (2010: 1.188f.) and Kaplan (2011), the inevitability of polysemy and homophony does not entail that accounts based on avoidance of a less optimal state are ad hoc. Lass (1997) cites examples of enduring homophony, such as *dike, come, boob, crap, clap, cream, shaft, screw, suck*, but most of these are not used in the same contexts. On this criterion, see Ullmann (1957: 132ff.; Malkiel 1979). Also, *horny*, cited by Lass, is becoming rare in American English in the sense of 'consisting of or resembling horn' [1398] since the sexual sense 'aroused' [1889] has come to predominate. In all parts of the country, Americans substitute *(made of) horn* or *hornlike*, and react with amusement to *horny* in a nonsexual context.

In the final analysis, as noted in §2.2.3, the maintenance (or establishment) of formal contrasts is important for successful communication.

7.4 Summary

Folk etymology is an important expression of popular psychology in which isolated forms perceived to be opaque are reformed in such a way as to make apparent sense of them. At least part of the rebuilt word appears to be transparent, even if an unexplained residue remains, which subsequent folk etymologizations may strive to resolve.

Tabu is conveniently, if not somewhat artificially, divided into religious and secular. Both involve conscious avoidance of words perceived to be negative, whether for reasons of fear, (in)sensitivity, offensiveness, or to observe what is considered to be 'good taste' on a culture specific basis. The result is often an alteration of a negatively valued word to remove the shock value while simultaneously suggesting it in a way that does not inhibit communication of the concept or the word itself. To this end, the prosodic structure (number of syllables) is generally maintained while one or more phonemes are changed, e.g. *gad* for *God*. Alternatively, the word can be replaced with another that is conventionally agreed on by a given speech community.

Both folk etymology and tabu typically involve substitution or alteration of a received form by analogy with a word that is similar in form and/or meaning.

---

[7] This is to some extent generational. My mother, for instance, would never have used *pussy* in a sexual context, so to her the word was normal for a kitten. Younger people around her reacted with extreme amusement.

8

The cycle of expressivity

This chapter describes the loss and subsequent renewal of expressivity by means of degree doubling (e.g. *mostest*), adjectival intensifiers (*filthy rich*), reinforcing adjectives (*totally*), fanciful coinages (*humongous*), hyperbole (*a real scorcher*), semantic change, calquing, borrowing, and semantic transfer. As an example of structured semantic change *filthy* in *filthy rich* has (i) lost semantic features relating to 'dirt' and (ii) acquired functional degree features. Simultaneously, semantic change is not constrained by the structure of links in the human mind/brain, which permit the meaning of a word to encroach on that of other words which in turn can shrink their meanings. One reason for this is that changes in the environment and interaction with subcultures constitute independent variables that shape the outcome of semantic change.

8.1 Loss and renewal of expressivity

Semantics is the study of meaning (Goddard 1998: 1). Semantic change, like all other change, begins with expressive usage in a given context, i.e. assignment of new meanings to old words.[1] In 1825, *cram* began to be used as expressive university slang for intensive study, the literal image being one of forcing knowledge into oneself by a stuffing process. The creative use of *hairy* to convey contorted difficulty dates to 1848. Since 1963, *jock* has been an expressive term for a versatile young athlete. And so on.

Emphatic language is one typical variety of expressivity. It is responsible for double superlatives of the type *bestest* [1868], *mostest* [1882] (Miller 2010: 1.193). Double comparatives like *more better* go back to Old English, peaked in Middle English between 1350 and 1450 (Włodarczyk 2007), and are on the rise today according to Zwicky's blog (2/4/2010).[2]

---

[1] Approaches to historical semantics are discussed in Allan and Robinson (2011). This includes problems with all approaches, not least of which involve use of the *OED* (Allan 2011).

[2] arnoldzwicky.wordpress.com/category/syntax/comparison/

A form that is seldom discussed is *goodest* [1602], which is in part a collateral form for expected *best*, and in part has a more specific meaning. An actress recently described her husband as the *goodest* man she's ever known, implying moral qualities of goodness. As such, it is a different word from *best*.

Adjectival intensifiers include *plumb* (crazy) [1587], *dead* (right) [1589], *filthy* (rich) [1616], *dreadfully* (bad) [1697], *awful* (good) [1818], *real* (sturdy) [1827], *totally* (awesome) [1972], etc. (§1.9; ODS 335ff.). *Awesome* only recently [1979] came to mean 'mind-boggling' (cf. *ODNW* 24).

A related category involves reinforcing adjectives (Paradis 2000): *absolute bliss, utter nonsense, total crap*, etc. Generally speaking, reinforcing adjectives have a long history in English: *utter* [c.1430], *extreme* [c.1460], *horrible* [a.1464], *absolute* [1531], *complete* [1645], *total* [1702], *awful* [1809].

For Stern (1931: 394), loss of expressivity is evident when an intensifier accompanies a word of contrary meaning, as *mighty little, pretty dirty*. In reality, in *mighty little* and the like, one set of meanings has been lost and another acquired. This is not the same as simple semantic BLEACHING, variously defined (and disputed) in the literature. I will take it to designate the reduction or loss of a distinctive property. In expressions like *the larger half* or *it broke into three halves*, a precise mathematical bipartization into identical portions loses the identity and/or bipartite requirement (cf. Stern 1931: 406). *Unique* [1601] shifted from non-quantifiable to quantifiable in *thoroughly unique* [1809], *totally unique* [1871], *very unique* [1908], *uniquest* [1885], and *most unique* [1939].

Expressivity leads to fanciful coinages, e.g. *discombobberate* [1838], *discombobulate* [1916] (but *discombombulation* [1839]); descriptions of speed: *lickitie* [1817], *licketty cut* [1831], *lickety-click* [1843], *lickety-split* [1859]; *skedaddle* [1861]; words for 'large' or 'great': *splendiferous* [1475] 'abounding in splendor', [1843] 'magnificent',[3] *bodacious* [1845] 'total(ly)', *hellacious* [1847] 'remarkable' (but 'dreadful' [1977]), *ginormous* [1948], *fantabulous* [1959], *humongous* [1970]; 'contorted verbiage': *ragman* [?1507], *rigmarole* [c.1736]; 'pretentious verbiage': *gobbledygook* [1944]; 'nothingness': *doodly-squat* [1934], *diddly-squat* [1963]; *zilch* [1966] (but 1931 as a name), *zip(po)* [n.d.] (cf. (?) *Zippo* lighter [1934]); 'unnamed or forgotten lexical item': *thingumbob* [1751], *thingumebob* [1832], *thingamabob* [1987], *thingamajig* [1824]; *contraption* [1825], *doohick(e)y* [1914], *gadget* [1886], *hoot(e/a)nanny* [1929], *widget* [1931], *gizmo* [1943], *razzmatazz* [1946] (in this sense; see §14.9); 'squalid, vile': *lousy* [Ch.], *slimy* [1575], *shabby* [1679], *crappy* [1846], *sleezy* [1941] ('flimsy' [1648]), *skuzzy* [n.d.]. Finally, any malfunction can be described as a *glitch* [1962] (of unknown etymology).

---

[3] An earlier, very fanciful coinage, with the meaning 'fantastic' was *supercalifragilisticexpialidocious* [1964] (a song in *Mary Poppins*) plus a variant in an earlier song [1949]. Although the word enjoyed some popular use from 1964 to 1982, its length was a major violation of economy that rendered it impractical. The more recent terms do not exceed one metrical foot (§9.2).

According to the *OED*, *bumpe/ity* (§14.2.3) is "a childish form" but it seems also to express iconicity with the rhythm of small bumps on a washboard-type of road. Similar is *raggedy* [1844] 'frayed; having a ragged appearance', which means more than *ragged* in expressing diminutivity and/or iconicity with multiple tears.

The woolly mammoth *Snuffleupagus*[4] is creative on many planes. *Sn-* is suggestive of the large nose (§§10.7, 12.7), *snuffle up* rhymes with *snuggle up*, and the Latinate ending suggests a classy character.

Creative exaggeration/hyperbole is responsible for countless descriptive terms, e.g. for very hot weather *roasting(ly)* [1830], *scorcher* [1874], *sizzler* [1901], and their opposites (*freezing* etc.) for very cold weather.

With loss of expressivity, a once expressive variant can become the standard. For instance, *moonlight* [1957] 'hold an additional evening job' (extended from 'conduct a night raid' [1887]) has become the usual verb for holding more than one job. With the loss of expressivity, there is a concomitant change in the direction of prototypicality, e.g. L *caballus* 'pack-horse, nag' in Vulgar Latin was used expressively for 'horse', and in Romance became the standard word for 'horse' (F *cheval*, Sp. *caballo*, etc.). L *bucca* '(puffed out) cheek' replaced *ōs* 'mouth' (cf. F *bouche* 'mouth', etc.); L *pellis* 'hide; leather' replaced *cutis* 'skin' (cf. F *peau* 'skin; hide'); and so on (Meillet 1965 [1905–6]: 264). Diminutives deprived of expressivity can replace the base noun, e.g. ML *sōliculus* 'little sun (*sōl*)' > F *soleil* 'sun' (e.g. Fruyt 1989: 129, w. lit).

8.2 Extralinguistic input

To trace the etymology of a word, it is not enough to know just its formal properties. Sociocultural history is part of a word's etymology. Specifically, it is the part that determines the semantic changes a word can undergo. For instance, German *Kopf* and E *cup* can be related formally, but *Kopf* means 'head' and *cup* is a drinking vessel. The link is provided by medieval battles, in which the smashing of heads was compared to the smashing of (clay/ceramic) cups. Since OE *cuppe* derives from LL *cuppa* 'drinking vessel', Germ. *Kopf* as 'head' was originally a metaphor based on the approximate shape and smashability (cf. Bloomfield 1933: 440; Fritz 1998: 108f., both w. lit).

Cultural change can be illustrated by the different uses of *dinner* and *supper* over time (Stern 1931: 196f., w. lit). *Dinner* was originally eaten around 9:00 a.m. It was etymologically 'breakfast': VL **disjējūnāre* (cf. ML *dējējūnāre*) 'break the fast' (L *jējūnium* 'fast(ing)') > OF *disner* [c12^b] (cf. ML *disnāre*) > F *dîner* DINE [1297]. Dinner gradually got later, closer to noon by c17 (cf. F *déjeuner* 'lunch'; the older meaning 'breakfast' is now generally subsumed under *petit déjeuner* 'little lunch').

---

[4] en.wikipedia.org/wiki/Mr._Snuffleupagus

Supper (OF *soper* [1175]) was the late-afternoon meal. By 1782 dinner was eaten around 3 p.m., and then became the evening meal, relegating supper to a light meal after the theater. Regional variation in these terms continues today.

Another culturally induced change involved the addition in early Roman times of the months January and February at the beginning of the year, which originally began with *Mārtius* 'of Mars' (> *March*), *Aprīlis* (? **ap(e)rīlis* 'next' EDL 48), *Maius* 'of (the goddess) Maia', *Jūnius* 'of Juno' (cf. Varro, *De lingua latina* 6.33; Ovid, *Fastae* 1.39; etc.). This entailed the shift of *Quīn(c)tīlis, Sextīlis, September, Octōber, November, December,* from the seventh through tenth months respectively (cf. *quīnque* 'five', *sex* 'six', *septem* 'seven', *octō* 'eight', *novem* 'nine', *decem* 'ten') to the ninth through twelfth months. *Quīn(c)tīlis* was renamed *Jūlius* JULY in 44 BCE to honor Julius Caesar, and *Sextīlis* was changed to *Augustus* AUGUST by the emperor himself in 8 BCE. Why the first two months (*Jānuārius* 'of Janus', *Februārius* 'of *februa*' [festival of purification]) were added to the Roman calendar is a complete mystery. It is also unclear when this innovation occurred. Based on the fact that the Roman consuls entered office on January 1 for the first time in 153 BCE, it is speculated that the two additional months were added in that year; but this is not conclusive and many unknowns remain (Miller 2010: 1.12ff.).

Political correctness, a special kind of psychosocial force, drove the replacement of *homosexual* (in English since 1892) by *gay* (§7.3). Initially, *gay* acquired the meaning 'homosexual' as an expressive variant with positive connotations around 1938 (earlier examples with this precise meaning are difficult to confirm). Given the negative and condemnatory connotations of *homosexual, queer* (since 1894 in this sense), and many other terms (Mattiello 2008: 172ff.), the non-judgmental term *gay* was preferred in some circles. Subsequently, political correctness elevated its status to standard usage.

8.3 The cognitive dimension

Cognition plays a role in the semantic organization of morphological categories as well as in semantic change. One aspect involves the mental links between actors, instruments, patients, activities, and locations (discussion in Miller 1993: 68ff.; Bauer 2002; Panther and Thornburg 2002; Rainer 2005b; Martsa 2012: 149–68; Štekauer et al. 2012: 239–60).

The English suffix *-er* is multiply polysemic, encompassing several thematic roles: agent (*gambler*), instrument (*blender, propeller, skewer, stapler*), location (*planter, diner*), source (*fertilizer* = the source of fertilization), theme/patient (*roaster* = a chicken for roasting), benefactor (*hearer, learner, inheritor*), and so on (Sproat 1985: 183–7). One and the same word can have multiple functions. A *planter*, for instance, can be a person who plants (actor), an object that plants (instrument), or a place for plants (location).⁵

Many constructs exhibit this polysemy (Štekauer et al. 2012; cf. Serbat 1975: 360-75). Hungarian *-ó / -ő* encodes the same thematic relations (Comrie and Thompson 1985: 355):

(1) Hungarian thematic role nominals
    (a) Agentive: *ir-ó* 'writer' (cf. *ir* 'to write')
    (b) Instrumental: *hegyez-ő* '(pencil) sharpener' (*hegyez* 'to sharpen')
    (c) Locational: *társalg-ó* 'place of conversing (parlor)' (*társalog* 'to converse')

Since activities presuppose places, action nouns frequently evolve into locationals. L *pr(eh)ēnsiō* 'act of apprehending' came to mean 'captivity', then 'place of captivity', as in F *prison* PRISON [OE] (Nyrop 1913: 223). Since practices presuppose places L *augurātus* is both 'augury' and 'the office of the augur' (*LSDE* 51). Words that remain ambiguous between the activity and location senses are *study, passage* (ibid., p. 216). Since agent, instrument, and means constitute the intermediary through which a process can be realized, activities can evolve into agents or instruments. *Trap* and *press*, which began as activities, today are instruments. Changes along the thematic relations hierarchy of agent–instrument–location–result–activity/event–state/entity can be seen as regular but, crucially, they are not unidirectional. Compare the evolution of event nouns into entities: *writing, painting, cutting(s), earning(s)*, etc. (§6.3, end). Mattiello (2008: 191) cites *-er* forms named for one function: *kisser* 'mouth', *sniffer* 'nose', *bender* 'knee'.

8.4 Polysemic extension, limitation, and semantic features

Traditional widening and narrowing of meaning (e.g. Grygiel and Kleparski 2007: 94-7) are examined from several different perspectives in this section.

A word will typically acquire an expressive meaning in a particular subculture, whence it may re-emerge with this new meaning in the speech community at large. Fritz (1998: 31) calls this "Meillet's Generalization". For instance, *arrive* (from French) goes back to Late Latin **ad rīp-ā-re* (*arrīpāre* [c9]) 'to reach the shore' (*ad* 'to, at', *rīpa* 'bank, shore'). In sailor's jargon the meaning was extended to mean 'reach (any

---

⁵ As to probabilities, *drinker* is most often agentive (only animate agents normally drink), *binder* is mostly instrumental (things normally bind), and *killer* can be agentive or instrumental since people (agents) and things (instruments) can kill (cf. Bauer 1983: 285-91). The locational use is also encountered in *diner* (restaurant), *sleeper* (coach on a train), *smoker* (a stag party), *mixer* (a coed party or dance), *freighter*, etc. Instrumentals in *-er* on intransitive bases generally lack the [+causative] feature: *rider* (on an insurance policy), *slider, speaker, racer*, but note *sleeper* [+caus], a martial arts hold that puts the victim to sleep.

place)' because when sailors reached shore, that was, broadly speaking, their prototypical destination (Meillet 1965 [1905–6]: 259; see also Nyrop 1913: 249ff.). English borrowed *arrive* [c.1200] from French with the generic meaning (cf. Görlach 2000: 106).

Many Greek examples are documented in which a word develops a specialized meaning in a subculture, and that meaning emerges as (at least one) standard use (Hecht 1888: 52–61). For instance, *sullogismós* originally meant 'computation; reasoning', but in the language of the philosophers developed the specialized meaning SYLLOGISM [1398]. G *krãsis* 'mixing, blending' in the language of the grammarians came to designate a special kind of contraction: CRASIS [1933]. G *ónux* 'hoof; claw; nail' in earth language meant ONYX [1300]. G *krústallos* in Homer meant 'ice'; in the language of earth science it came to mean '(rock-)crystal'. In English, CRYSTAL has also had the meaning 'ice' [OE–1610].

Salary [1377] goes back to AN *salarie*, from L *salārium* '(money) to buy salt (*sāl*)' (*LSDE* 141). Roman soldiers were paid a *salārium* to buy salt, which was expensive. In Anglo-French, the word for payment to a soldier or an employee was *salarie*, which came into use in Late Middle English, the restriction to salt (the original meaning) having been lost. For the value once attributed to salt, compare the expression *(not) worth one's salt*.

In Medieval Latin, different kinds of 'doctor' were recognized, e.g. university teachers, jurists (*Lēgis Doctor* LD 'doctor of law'), Church Doctors, doctors of medicine (*Medicīnae Doctor* MD). All of these meanings, including Latin 'teacher', are continued in the history of English. The specialization as 'practitioner of medicine' is recent. Chaucer, for instance, had to spell out *Doctour of Phisyk* 'Doctor of Medicine' (*Canterbury Tales*, Prologue 411) (Miller 2006: 95).

Extension/widening can be formalized as loss of a semantic feature. *Bird* originally meant a young or small fowl, and lost the feature [+young] (Williams 1986: 175f.). *Holidays* are no longer 'holy days', but include Labor Day, days off from school, etc., and have apparently lost the feature [religious], optionally at least (ibid. p. 175). British English then loses the 24-hour restriction and *holiday* becomes the equivalent of *vacation*. For additional details of these changes, see Lipka (1985: 342–6; 2002: 114).

More complicated changes are more difficult to describe/formalize as simple loss of a feature. *Apéritif* began as a medical term for a substance to open the pores and got generalized to a drink that "opens" the appetite (Nyrop 1913: §127). In an analysis that accounts for both types, "the range of application of the new meaning is a subset of the range of the old meaning" (Geeraerts 1997: 895; cf. Ullmann 1957: 117).

Narrowing/restriction has been analyzed as addition of a semantic feature, e.g. *liquor* [–solid, +fluid] → [–solid, +fluid, +alcoholic] (Williams 1986: 171). E *fowl* originally meant 'bird' (like Germ. *Vogel*), but became a specific kind of bird (Ullmann 1962: 229). L *doctrīna* 'instruction' > DOCTRINE 'lesson; teaching' [c14–c17^e], then came to be restricted to 'religious dogma' (Copley 1961: 59), formalizable by a feature [+religious]. Metaphoric uses of *nut* embody the features round, small, hard (Mattiello 2008: 208).

OE *dēor* designated a 'fourfooted animal as object of the chase' and thus excluded domestic animals and birds. Probably among hunters, *dēor* came to be specialized as *Cervidae*, the animal of the chase *par excellence*. The specialization occurred in Old English, but the more general meaning persisted into Middle English, where it was gradually supplanted by the loanwords *beast* and then *animal*, rendering the more general meaning of DEER obsolete (Stern 1931: 416). A formalization *dēor* [+quadruped, +hunted] → *deer* [+quadruped, +hunted, +Cervidae] is supposedly not insightful because, at every stage, "the new range includes the old one" (Geeraerts 1997: 95), but that can be built into the formalization.

Many examples can be formalized as a change from an underspecified feature to specified. For instance, *corpse* derives from F *corps* 'body', which can be alive or dead, i.e. underspecified for the feature [living] (viz. [*u*living]). The restriction to [–living] can be formalized as [*u*living] → [–living].

Another problem involves the conception of the feature-composition of a given word. What are the relevant features for *desert* (L *dēsertum* 'deserted; abandoned')? The following discussion is from Miller (2010: 1.12):

> There was supposedly a change in c19 from 'uninhabited/uncultivated region' to 'barren, sandy waste'. Now, anyone who has seen the deserts in the southwestern United States knows that 'barren, sandy waste' does not come remotely close to an accurate description. Yet, most of us have a prototypical schema (mental image) featuring an Arabian kind of desert, which can be so described. Was there a restriction in meaning for the word *desert*, or just for our desert schema? And if we cannot agree today on what a desert is, how can we be sure of how deserts were conceptualized in the past? Since Middle English, *desert* has designated a wasteland, but also in some texts included forests (for their lack of order), retreats, and some other things. Apart from that, even the idea of a wasteland is not clear. Maybe the word has not changed meaning. Perhaps it has always designated whatever one's conception of a barren wasteland might look like, and that may have changed over time.

What is the feature composition for a barren wasteland? A potential problem with componential analyses is that the infinite array of possible words may require an equal number of features. Attempts have been made since antiquity to devise semantic primitives. Plato in *The Statesman* defined the human being as a 'featherless biped' [+BIPED –FEATHERS]. This is humorous but mostly because of the choice of features. In reality the idea is no different from ±ANIMAL, ±DOMESTICATED, ±QUADRUPED, ±HERBIVORE, and other recent features (Goddard 1998: 46).

Although a componential analysis offers an appealingly explicit account, Goddard claims that it could never "achieve comprehensive analysis of the entire vocabulary, because it is doubtful that all lexical meanings could be assigned to clearly delimited semantic fields" (1998: 50). As suggested by people's ideas of the differences between what is considered a *cup, mug*, etc., a mental schema of the prototypical exemplar is more generally accepted.[6]

This discussion superficially appears to conflict with the universal inventory of formal features (§1.9), but those involve the formal properties of phonology, syntax, and semantics, which include ±human and functional features like volition, expectation, degree. Semantic features have not been investigated to anywhere near the same extent as syntactic and phonological features. Semantics will probably require prototype and modification features. The latter would articulate differences from a given prototype.

8.5 Semantic shifts

Specialization (or restriction) and generalization (or extension) can work together and produce the effect of a shift. Consider (2), from Bloomfield (1933: 430ff.).

(2)
STAGES	'nourishment'	'edible thing'	'edible part of animal'	'muscular part of animal'
I	food	meat	flesh	flesh
II	food	meat	meat	flesh
III	food	food	meat	flesh
IV	nourishment	food	meat	flesh

Stage I occurs in Old English. In Middle English [1250] (II) the meaning of *meat* was generalized to partly overlap with that of *flesh*, whose meaning was then restricted. Later, *food* encroached on *meat*, and eventually replaced it in its original meaning, except regionally. As late as 1575, *meat* still had the generic 'food' meaning. Around 1500 *nourishment*, an Anglo-French construct that meant 'act of nourishing; nurture' [1300], encroached on *food* but never completely ousted it from its original sense.

---

[6] On prototype semantics, see Rosch (1973), Geeraerts (1997; 2010), and several contributions in Geeraerts and Cuyckens (2007). For a prototype discussion of *cups, mugs, glasses, jars, jugs, carafes, bottles*, and related items, see Wierzbicka (1985: ch. 1); Goddard (1998: 230–37). A pre-prototype theory experiment was designed by Labov (1972) with drawings of cups and cuplike objects of different dimensions and functions. As an illustration of the role of function, the item was called a *vase* only in the context of flowers, but even there *cup* prevailed for an item with a high width-to-depth ratio.

The problems with feature accounts notwithstanding, robotic models have been based on such systems. For instance, Steels and Vogt (1997) describe an experiment with robots in which one assumes the role of speaker, the other of listener. In one scenario, the speaker does not have a word for a feature set, and may create one but as a low-probability strategy, since a word may already exist in the population for that feature set. In another scenario, the hearer lacks a word used by the speaker. The hearer can infer possible feature sets designated by the word, or attempt to reconstruct the meaning. Other scenarios involve some or all of the feature sets decoded by the hearer not matching some or any of the expected distinctive feature sets. All of these are predicated on the assumption that there can exist for every object in the universe a small and finite number of distinctive features, and that is challenged by scholars in different theoretical frameworks.

What emerges from this brief discussion is that Bloomfield's alleged stages are not discrete. The overlap in meaning from one 'stage' to another can last indefinitely. This complication does not render the example invalid because, ultimately, there was a shift in meaning involving several words. The means by which this occurred is more complex than (2) implies.

Consider the fate of L *testa* 'pot', *caput* 'head', and *crānium* 'skull' in French (cf. Benveniste 1966 [1954]: 295f.). *Crānium* survives as F *crâne* in the same meaning. *Caput* in Latin had the literal and many figurative meanings of 'head' (Moussy 1989), but survives as F *chef* only with figurative meanings. The literal meaning was taken over by *testa*: EL 'tile; brick; earthen pot' → CL 'sherd; shell; brick' → LL 'skull, cranium; sherd' [*a*.395 Ausonius] → 'skull; head; sherd' [c5 Caelius Aurelianus] → OF *teste* [1080] 'head; sherd' → F *tête* 'head' (cf. Fritz 1998: 109).

As in the case of *nourishment*, borrowing is a frequent source of semantic restriction. The range of *red* and *yellow* decreased with the borrowing of *orange* (Görlach 2000: 102). As to why orange affected red and yellow, the answer lies in an observation by Berlin and Kay (1969) and Kay, Berlin, and Merrifield (1991) that red shades into yellow, which shades into green. Yellow is the pivotal color. It can be grouped either with red or with green, but not both. English groups yellow with red, hence the red-orange-yellow continuum. In Basque, as reported by Trask (1996: 46), *urdin* originally covered the range of blue, green, and grey, which is typical in languages/cultures where green shades into blue and eventually into black (Kay et al. 1991). The green-blue identity is so frequent (e.g. Welsh *glas*) that the color literature devised the blend GRUE (not in the *OED*). In Basque, *urdin* came to be restricted to 'blue' with the borrowing of *berde* 'green' and *gris* 'grey' from Spanish (*verde, gris*). More examples are discussed in Fritz (1998: 139f.).

8.6 Melioration and pejoration

As a special kind of restriction, a word may acquire a positive value (*melioration*) or a negative connotation (*pejoration*).[7] *Accident* was originally neutral ('any happening'), but became negative, as did *casualty* and *fate*. By contrast, the originally neutral *fortune, luck*, and *success* acquired a positive valuation (cf. Nyrop 1913: 144–8; Tournier 1985: 290f.). *Drug* tends to have negative connotations unless qualified by *prescription*. *Cunning* originally meant 'knowledgeable; skillful' and was a positive term. Around the end of c16, it became more negative ('crafty; sly; devious'), and today it is mostly pejorative (Copley 1961: 47; Ullmann 1962: 174). Other examples follow.

---

[7] Restriction, generalization, melioration, pejoration, etc. are not even taxonomically useful, being non-discrete categories that are often difficult to distinguish (Traugott and Dasher 2002: 51–104).

Degeneration/Pejoration:

(a) *despot* [1781] < G *des-pót-ēs* 'head (lord) of the household' who had absolute power and control over his family;
(b) *villain* [1303] < ME/AN/OF *vilein* 'feudal serf' < ML *vīllānus* 'one who works at a villa/farm' became disposed to depraved criminal acts (Nyrop 1913: §180);
(c) *cheat*$_V$ [1597] < *(es)cheat*$_N$ [1377] 'property reverting to the state by *escheat* (< VL **ex-cadēre* 'fall out (to a person's share)');
(d) OE *hūswīf* 'woman of the house' > *hussy* [1647] (also 'mistress of a household' [1530–1800]) (Miller 2010: 1.146ff.);
(e) OE *cwene* 'woman' > *quean* 'whore' [*c*.1300];
(f) *grotesque* [1561] 'decorative painting', spelled *crotescque* after its French source, from Ital. *grottesca* (*grotta* 'cave') 'painting appropriate to grottoes (ancient chambers revealed by excavations)', hence the later meaning 'distorted, bizarre' [1643] with the later French spelling.

Elevation/Melioration (cf. Ullmann 1962: 234f.):

(a) OE *cniht* 'boy, knave, servant' > *knight* [*a*.1100];
(b) OE *hlāf* 'loaf' + *weard* 'keeper' [i.e. 'bread-provider'] > OE *hlāfweard/hlāford/ laford* 'master (of the house); lord of the manor; the Lord' > ME *laferd/loverd/ lord* 'lord' (Miller 2010: i. 146ff.);
(c) L *minister* (< *minus* 'less') 'attendant; servant' was elevated first in Christian contexts, then especially when ministers became counselors and representatives of the prince (Nyrop 1913: §§81, 192f.; *LSDE* 48);
(d) LL *cancellārius* [c4] 'door-keeper; secretary', properly 'one connected with the lattice grating or bars' (L *cancellī* > OF *chancel* [1160] CHANCEL [1303]) which separated the public from the judges in a lawcourt, yields OF *c(h)anceler* [1080]. In England, the *Anglo-Saxon Chronicle* attests *canceler(e)* [1093+] 'Chancellor (of England)' and the *Kyng Alisaunder* text [?*a*.1300] introduces the variant *chauncelere* (MS Laud Misc. 622: 1809) CHANCELLOR (Miller 2012: 153).

The etymology of *boy* is disputed, but at least some elevation/melioration is involved; cf. the proposed lexical entry by Liberman (2000: 224):

BOY, 1260. Original meanings 'churl, servant', 'devil' (rare); regularly used as a derogatory word. The meaning 'male child' does not occur before 1400. Apparently, a blend of an onomatopoeic word for a noisy evil spirit (**boi*) and a baby word for 'little brother' (**bo*). The latter can be extant in the proper name *Boia* (OE). Both words have numerous counterparts in and outside English and Germanic.

Consider the changes in *churl/carl* (Rinelli 2001). OE *ceorl* 'peasant; (free)man' (by contrast to *eorl* 'nobleman' and *þēow* 'slave') in Early Middle English was demoted to 'serf; bondman' [1200]. Also, the technical reference to the social class became an evaluative term 'one of rude manners; rustic, boor', then [c.1300] 'base fellow; villain'. The first change was prompted by the blurring of the lower classes, due to social advancement of the slaves: "ME *cherl* came to be applied also to former slaves, placed now on the same level as churls" (Rinelli, p. 269). Because the former slaves "still retained rude manners" (ibid.), there was a further decline of *churl*. In northern texts, Nordic *carl* was generally a term of address ('fellow') because peasants there had higher status, while *churl* was a mostly contemptuous term for 'slave; thrall'. In the London area, the opposite valuation occurred, and *carl* is the more contemptuous term.

The changes in this section are based on the tendency for objective labels to become subjective and/or evaluative (cf. Traugott 1989: 34f.). Traugott treats the subjectivization of modals from deontic (denoting obligation, permission) to epistemic, involving the speaker's knowledge or belief. For instance, she cites the change from *you must do that*, where deontic *must* signals an obligation, to *politicians must be living on the moon*, where epistemic *must* expresses a subjective judgment (cf. Sweetser 1990: ch. 3; Kövecses 2002: 216ff.). Fritz (1998: 55f.) relates the change from wishes to commands.

8.7 Borrowing and semantic transfer

On the mechanism of borrowing words for a new item or concept, Geeraerts (2002: 33) defines the following two mechanisms:

Logically speaking, two situations may occur: either the changes work in parallel, or they take place serially. The first situation occurs when members of a speech community are confronted with the same communicative, expressive problem, and independently choose the same solution. The introduction of *computer* as a loan from English into German (and many other languages) may at least to some extent have proceeded in this way. More or less simultaneously, a number of people face the problem of giving a name to the new thing in their native language; independently of each other, they then adopt the original name that comes with the newly introduced object.

The second type occurs when the members of a speech community imitate each other. For instance, when one person introduces a loan word, a few others may imitate him, and they in turn may be imitated by others, and so on.

For naming new scientific discoveries classical words were often used metaphorically especially with reference to the shape, e.g. LL *bacillus* [Isidore] 'little rod' BACILLUS [1883], G *baktḗrion* 'little rod' BACTERIUM [1847–9].[8] Words are frequently borrowed with a cultural item or concept, e.g. Icelandic *geyser* [1780], German *sauerkraut* [1617], *gestalt* [1909], French *liqueur* [1742], *cuisine* [1786].

---

[8] All of the examples in this and the next two paragraphs are discussed in Miller (2012).

Words can be borrowed back and forth. ME *bī god* 'by God', an insulting address to overly religious Normans, found its way back to English in the form of *bigot* [1598].

Some words are borrowed several times. L *discus* 'quoit; dish' gives *dish* [OE] (Miller 2012: 55). Later, VL **desku-* > Ital. *desco* 'desk, table', ML *desca* [c.1250] 'desk', ME DESK [Ch.]. More recently, *disk* [1664] (spelled *disc* first c.1727) and L *discus* [1656] have been borrowed.

The final stage of borrowing is total assimilation. Picone (1996: 291) cites as words of French origin *biology* [1799] (F *biologie* [1802]),[9] *sociology* [1842] (F *sociologie* [1839]), and *automobile* [1876] (F *automobile* [1860]). What is crucial is that nothing in their form betrays these words as borrowings (cf. Ahmad 2000: 713).

Writers use borrowings for a variety of reasons: characterization, eloquence, high culture and sophistication, eruditeness, authority, and association of the term with a foreign culture (Pons-Sanz 2012).

Simple semantic transfer is another possibility: a pre-existing word, affix, or phrase shifts in meaning due to contact (cf. Picone 1996: 4). Picone gives an example from French, where *réaliser* 'bring about; concretize' was influenced by E *realize* and acquired its meaning 'become aware of'.

Exposition 'expounding, explanation' [a.1340] and 'expulsion' [1530] is used in the sense of 'exhibition' [1851] under French influence (Stern 1931: 222).

Novel was borrowed from French as 'something new; novelty' [a.1450] and 'news, tidings' [c.1450]. Around 1500, it acquired the sense of 'short story' under the influence of Ital. *novella*, used of the stories in Boccaccio's *Decameron* [1350–53] (Stern 1931: 223).

L *conclūsiō* 'the enclosing (of an area)' was extended to CONCLUSION [Ch., Wyclif] under the influence of G *sumpérasma* 'conclusion of a syllogism' (Coleman 1989: 83).

Hebrew *ml'k* 'messenger' also meant 'angel'. Since Greek had no equivalent, the Bible redactors loantranslated *ml'k* as *ángelos* 'messenger' with the extended sense of 'angel' (Meillet 1951 [1925]: 40f.; cf. Geeraerts 1997: 89, 101).

G *ptōsis* 'a fall(ing)' was also used for '(grammatical) case'. Varro loantranslated the term as L *cāsus* 'a fall(ing); chance' CASE [a.1225] 'chance happening', thereby extending the meaning to 'grammatical case' [1393] (cf. Ullmann 1962: 167). The names of the cases were also modeled on the Greek (Coleman 1989: 83f.; *LSDE* 211f.).

OE *eorl* 'free man; noble; warrior', during the reign of Cnut [?994–1035], acquired the sense of the Nordic cognate *jarl* 'viceroy; provincial governor' (Pons-Sanz 2004). In the Anglo-Norman period, *earl* was used for AF *cunte* COUNT [1561] (*LSDE* 52), continued in MnE *earl* (Meillet 1965 [1905–6]: 249).

---

[9] In fact, E *biology* antedates the French word, but note NL *biologia* [1766].

8.8 Calquing, or loan translation

In calquing, a native equivalent is substituted for each constituent of a semantically transparent foreign word. *Superman* [1903] is a calque on Germ. *Übermensch* (*über* 'over' plus *Mensch* 'human being'). Other German calques: *world-famous* [1832] (*weltberühmt*), *antibody* [1901] (*Antikörper*), *standpoint* [1854] (*Standpunkt*) (Tournier 1985: 317).

Middle English had numerous Anglo-French calques, e.g. *cornerstone* [*a*.1300] (= *pierre angulaire*), *armed to the teeth* [*c*.1380] (= *armé jusqu'aux dents*), *a snail's pace* [*a*.1400] (= *à pas de tortue*) (Miller 2012: 172f.).

Rather than borrow L *ēvangelium* (G *eu-* 'good' + *angel-* 'message'), Old English loantranslated it as *gōdspell* [good-message] (→ OE *godspell* 'God-message' GOSPEL). Likewise, L *omnipotēns* OMNIPOTENT [1300] was loantranslated into Old English as *ealmihtig* ALMIGHTY, and OE *hēþendōm* HEATHENDOM is a calque on L *pāgānismus* PAGANISM [*c*.1425]. For discussion of these and other examples see Miller (2012: 45f.).

The Homeric nymph *Calypso* (G *Kalupsṓ*) is derived from G *kalúpt-ein* 'to hide' (*DELG* 488; Sihler 1995: §322; *EDG* 628f.), meaning something like 'the Concealer; she who conceals'. Since antiquity, she was associated with the island of Malta (Phoenician *Malet(h)* 'shelter, haven; hiding place'), implying a connection via loan translation.

CALQUE COINAGE involves the novel creation of a word from native constituents as a calque on the composition of a foreign word. Cicero (*Academica* 1.6.24ff.) coined L *quālitās* 'characteristic; QUALITY' [*c*.1300] from L *quālis/quāli-* 'of what sort' plus *-(i)tās* '-ness' on the model of G *poiótēs* 'quality' from *poîos/poio-* 'of what sort' + *-tēs* '-ness' (*LSDE* 32, w. lit).

From the possible but non-existing participle *essent-* 'being' (cf. *esse* 'to be') plus suffix *-ia*, L *essentia* ESSENCE [1398] was coined after G *ousíā* 'essence' (built on the participle *ont-* 'being' + abstract *-íā*). Seneca attributes *essentia* to Cicero, but Quintilian attributes it to the rhetorician Verginius Flavus or the philosopher Sergius Plautus (Coleman 1989: 80f.; *LSDE* 39).

CALQUE REMODELING, as the name implies, involves the rebuilding of a native word or constituent on the model of that in the donor language. Under the influence of OF *bien venu* (lit. 'well come'), OE *wilcuma* 'guest' (lit. 'pleasing-comer' with *wil(l)* 'pleasure') was reshaped to *welcome* with *well* plus the past participle of *come* (cf. Stern 1931: 234).

Indonesian *asbut* 'smog' is a blend calqued on the constituents of E *smog* (Chapter 12): *asap* 'smoke' × *kabut* 'fog' (Sihler 2000: 130). Hebrew has a similar constituent calque: *'arpi(y)ax* from *'arafel* 'fog' × *pi(y)ax* 'smoke/soot' (Štekauer et al. 2012: 133).

Interlingual blends, while not calques, can be mentioned here because they are similar to calques in their expressivity and use of foreign material in word formation by bilingual speakers. An example is Arabic *mumtastic*, which consists of Arab. *mumtaaz* 'excellent' and English *fantastic* (Youssef Haddad, p.c.; §12.3).

8.9 On the phonological form of loanwords

Since speakers punctuate their discourse with borrowed words for a variety of reasons, including expressivity, and the effect is sometimes enhanced by the presence of foreign sounds, a brief mention of the formal properties of borrowings is in order. Essentially, a foreign sound can be approximated or borrowed. Adaptations can be made according to spelling and/or for segments or sequences that violate the language's phonotactics (§9.1).

Studies of loan phonology reveal that with initial contacts, sounds are approximated, but with bilingualism, genuine phonological contrasts are captured (cf. Ito, Kang, and Kenstowicz 2006). In Early Latin, for example, the Greek aspirates were borrowed with *p, t, c*. After the middle of the 2nd century BCE, with increased knowledge of Greek and bilingualism, several strategies were introduced to capture the distinctive contrast, e.g. (i) borrowing the special Greek letter, (ii) representing the aspiration with *h*. Both strategies occur in *Theoφilus* 'Theophile' (Purnell 1989: 357).

A phoneme can be borrowed. After Latin represented distinctive aspiration in Greek words, e.g. *philosophia* 'philosophy', it began spreading to Latin words, e.g. *triump(h)us* 'triumphal procession', *Kart(h)āgō* 'Carthage' (Cicero, *Orator* 160).[10] Native English had /č/, /ǰ/, and /š/, but no /ž/. The latter was borrowed from French after 1500, e.g. *bourgeois* [1564], *cortège* [1679], *protégé* [1778], *régime* [1789], *beige* [1858] (Miller 2012: 158). In general, a phoneme is easier to borrow if the language has a counterpart, in this case the voiceless /š/.

Spelling pronunciation is frequent. It is evident in words provided with etymological spellings, like *describe* for ME *descrive*, *perfect* for ME *parfit*, and so on (Miller 2012: 212). For borrowings, compare the /ɔ/ of *sauna* with the /au/ of *sauerkraut*. The latter is from German, which is known by many more speakers of English than is Finnish, the source of the former word. While those familiar with Finnish may pronounce the word [sauna], the usual pronunciation matches words with *au* of Greek or Latin origin, like *glaucoma, audition*.

Speakers of Yiddish or Pennsylvania German ('Penn Dutch') have no difficulty with the /χ/ sound in words like *chutzpa(h)* 'audacity', which they will deliberately emphasize for greater expressivity; but when such words diffuse to the population at

---

[10] The lexical diffusion of new phonemes is discussed in Miller (2010: 1.214–18).

large, they are generally pronounced with initial /h/. Similarly, speakers who know German pronounce the initial /pᶠ/ of *Pfalzgraf, Pfeffernuss, Pfennig* (an old monetary unit), etc., while those unfamiliar with German generally drop the [p].

Sounds of greater phonetic complexity or 'too different' from the usual segmental inventory are seldom borrowed. No Dutch word with /γ/, e.g. *gas*, is ever pronounced that way in English.

When a borrowed form violates the phonotactics of a language, it can be pronounced with a close approximation or adapted.

English has no words beginning with a cluster [ts] or a unit phoneme /tˢ/, and some speakers will pronounce *tsar*, General *Tso*'s Chicken, or Germ. *Zeitgeist* with [ts], but most speakers have /z/ in *tsar* and *Zeitgeist*, and General Tso gets all manner of variants. Word-initial [ps] is a little different, given that many words have been nativized (see §8.7 for the concept of total assimilation). Thus, [ps] was an acceptable onset in Greek (cf. *psalmós, psūkhología*), and remains so in French *psaume, psychologie*, but English *psalm, psychology*, and the like lose the [p].

Similarly, English has no initial [pt], and words of Greek origin with this cluster simply drop the [p], e.g. *pterygium, pterodactyl*. Phonotactics thus impose at least a psychological constraint, since most speakers have no difficulty articulating [ptérə] or [ptʰeyDo] for *potato* in casual (informal) speech (Miller 2010: 1.266, w. lit).

Because of the rarity and skewed distribution of /ŋ/ in English, the initial /ŋ/ of *Ngoko, Nguni*, and the like is usually rendered [əŋ(g)-], and the name *Nguyen* is frequently pronounced /nwɛn/.

8.10 Dating borrowings and neologisms

For older periods, there is no scientific way of determining how and when a new construct, native or transferred, entered the language and by what precise source, or how institutionalized it was before it first appeared in written sources (cf. Käsmann 1958). Käsmann goes on to illustrate the difficulties of ascertaining which occurrences are evidence of borrowing as opposed to foreign forms utilized by multilingual poets for rhyme, etc. Moreover, Käsmann notes, earliest attestations can be meaningless if the next occurrence is several hundred years later. He introduces a criterion that if texts from different areas independently continue to use the native word, the foreign word has not yet been accepted into the language (cf. Käsmann 1961: 25). Still, colloquial terms could *ipso facto* be excluded from literature. In short, what is true of the dating of neologisms in general is equally true of borrowings.

One way of dating loanwords was mentioned in the previous section. English borrowed /ž/ from French after 1500. Even if no dates were available for some French loans with that sound, the borrowings would likely postdate the French change of /ǰ/ to /ž/ around 1500 (Miller 2012: 158). This can be skewed by modernization. For instance, French changed /č/ to /š/ around the same time, and an early loanword like *chivalry* [1297] was initially borrowed with /č/ but underwent more recent modernization.

In the modern era, it is easier to track when a word was first borrowed and even, in some cases, especially for technical terms, who coined it. As noted in §5.1, *onomasiology* was first coined in German by Zauner (1902). In fact, at the end of the 1800s, in the period 1875–99, German was the second most important source of loanwords: Latin 40.5%, German 18% (mostly scientific words), then French 15.5%, etc. (Durkin 2006: 29). Not surprising, French was the highest source in the period 1775–99, with 33% of the total borrowings, and (mostly scientific) Latin a close second with 30%. More recently (1975–99), Latin and French have been restored to the highest percentage of loans: Latin 20%, French 16.5%, etc. (ibid.).

In general, Durkin finds a decline in especially technical borrowings in the late 20th century sample, where a number of technical terms are coined in English, but in all three periods analyzed, relatively few general vocabulary items were borrowed. "Words borrowed together with a newly encountered item remain a feature of all periods, as is unsurprising" (Durkin 2006: 40).

8.11 Summary

After examining some of the most important issues in semantic change, it can be affirmed that various formulations and quasi-formalizations in the literature are premature for the simple reason that semantic change is determined in part by links in the human mind/brain, in part by phonological (phonosemantic) factors (Chapter 10; Magnus 2001: 34), and in part by extralinguistic factors.

Links in the mind/brain permit the meaning of a word to encroach on that of other words whose meaning(s) can in turn shrink. As to motivation for the change(s), mental schemata subsume an array of affiliated conceptions that change in response to stimuli, as reflected in meaning differences from speaker to speaker and over time.

The link-motivated structures can be derailed by extralinguistic factors. These include changes in the environment and interaction with various subcultures, which constitute independent variables that shape the outcome of semantic change.

The cycle of expressivity can be described as follows: with use over time, words lose their expressivity by a process often called SEMANTIC BLEACHING, e.g. 'larger' *half*. When this occurs, expressivity is renewed by various lexicogenic processes. These include degree doubling (e.g. *more better, mostest*), adjectival intensifiers (*filthy rich*), reinforcing adjectives (*totally*), fanciful coinages (*humongous*), hyperbole (*a real scorcher* §2.5.1), identical constituent compounding, e.g. LIKE-HIM *like him*. i.e. 'really like him' (§14.1), semantic change, calquing, borrowing, and semantic transfer. Finally, there is the novel type of quasi-superlatives produced by playful language and language play (word games), e.g. *gooo(-)ooood, bæææd* 'very good' (§10.4), JEALOUS *jealous* (§14.1), *fanfuckintastic* (§5.9). These are further discussed in §15.3.

9

Phonological form and abridgments

This chapter outlines the essential phonological structure of words that will be of crucial importance in subsequent chapters, and begins a discussion of word abridgments.

The prosodic hierarchy is presented. Words consist of feet, which are optimally binary trochaic in English. Feet consist of syllables, and syllables consist of segments which are arranged according to sonority. Support is offered for the leading idea that the sonority hierarchy constrains basic word form.

Abridgments are a form of economy. It is discussed how alphabetisms and acronyms become new words in their own right, capable of undergoing affixation and conversion in ways that are impossible for their source phrases. Because of high-tech communication, modern abridgments are argued to be getting more abstract.

9.1 Syllable structure and the sonority hierarchy

This section argues that (i) the syllable consists of an onset and rime (which includes the nucleus and coda), (ii) English word structure depends on syllable structure coupled with the sonority hierarchy (SH), and (iii) the SH determines the arrangement of segments in the syllable.[1] In subsequent chapters it will be demonstrated that syllable structure and the SH are crucial constraints on language play.

Sonority involves the ability of segments to bear tone (Shih 2013) and occur as syllable nuclei (Sylak-Glassman 2012). It is based on intrinsic prominence with phonetic and psychological reality (Parker 2002; B. Miller 2012). Somewhat more concretely, vowels with a high first formant frequency, i.e. low vowels, are the most sonorous. Vowels of lower frequency are less sonorous, high vowels being the lowest

---

[1] Syllables consist of segments. Segments are individual sounds which can be represented in several ways. Language-particular spellings appear in italics, e.g. *poof*, for which the distinctive (contrastive, phonemic) segments are *p*, *u*, and *f*, represented in slashes: /puf/. More phonetic detail is implied by brackets, viz. [pʰuf], with predictable initial aspiration indicated. In Ancient Greek, aspirated stops were phonemic, i.e. distinguished words; cf. *póros* 'ford' vs. *phóros* /pʰoros/ 'tribute'.

in sonority of the vowels. Next come consonantal segments that are most vowel-like (glides, liquids, and nasals), then voiced obstruents, and finally the least sonorous voiceless obstruents. The SH thus involves the arrangement of segments in the syllable outward from a nucleus of higher sonority to an onset and/or coda of preferentially lower sonority. The SH has had a long history, documented in Miller (1994) and Blevins (2004: 159ff.). This section reviews some of the predictions of the SH for the form of basic words.

Evidence from language play (§5.5), change (Miller 2010: 1.184–8), experimental data (Kapatsinski 2009), and neurolinguistic research (Buckingham and Christman 2006; 2008) supports a hierarchical structure in which the nucleus and coda constitute an inner constituent, called the rime/rhyme from its metrical function, as distinct from the onset.

Optimally, a syllable consists of a nucleus with an onset but no coda (Prince and Smolensky 2004 [1993]: 105, 111). The onset (which is absent in some languages) and coda (if present) may or may not be complex (Hansson 2008) (and if complex may or may not count as syllable 'weight': Ryan 2011), as in the elaborated illustration in (1).

(1) Syllable structure

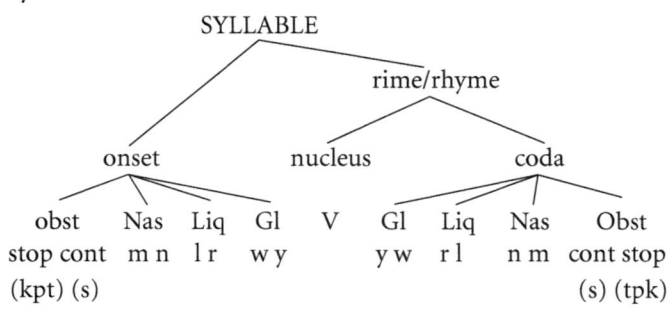

```
                    SYLLABLE
                   /        \
                  /       rime/rhyme
                 /          /    \
              onset      nucleus  coda
              /|\         /|\     /|\
           obst Nas Liq Gl  V  Gl Liq Nas Obst
        stop cont m n  l r  w y y w r l  n m cont stop
        (kpt) (s)                            (s) (tpk)
```

V (vowel) must be subdivided into low vowels, mid vowels, and high vowels, i.e. from highest to lower sonority (see Gordon 2002; Blevins 2004: 159; Kiparsky 2008: 49ff.). Additionally, some phonologists add *trills* to stops or fricatives, and/or include *flaps* with glides or between laterals and glides (see Harris 2002: 88).

As shown in (2), the SH (or whatever underlies it) has consequences for unmarked word formation, or PHONOTACTICS (permissible output sequences) of the basic word. The reason for emphasizing *basic* words is that affixation can create output exceptions to the SH (which are then subject to repair in change). Since the most frequent systematic violation of the SH is /s/, possible words in English include *strup, splim, stalms,* and *blarks* in addition to the word forms predicted by the SH in (2).

(2) English monosyllabic words and the SH

	OBST		NAS	LIQ	GL	V	GL	LIQ	NAS	OBST	
	Stop	Cont.								Cont.	Stop
knight											
OE:	k		n			i				χ	t
MnE:			n			a	y				t
brand	b			r		æ			n		d
trash	t	(š)		r		æ				š	
irons						a	y	r	n	z	

Permutations not licensed by the SH, e.g. *lg-, *rt-, *lf-, *rn-, are unattested as onsets (*nbik etc.). Since these are good coda sequences, *burn* is wellformed, *bunr, *taml are not (cf. Goldsmith 1990: 140–50; Kenstowicz 1994: 250–61; Hayes and Wilson 2008; Hayes 2009). This does not mean that such sequences cannot exist. Germanic had them but they were unstable and changed everywhere, e.g. OE *setl* > *seld* 'seat', *botl* > *bold* 'dwelling'; pre-OE *akr (Goth. *akrs*, OIce *akr* 'field') > *[ak̩r̩] > OE *æcer* 'field' ACRE.

The suffix *-th* added complexity to the coda, as in *sixth, hundredth*; it is highly restricted today and tends to result in cluster simplification, e.g. *thousan(d)th*.

According to the SH, *irons* [ayrnz] is a possible monosyllabic English word, but there can be no *[arynz], *[arnyz], *[ayrzn], etc. In a syllabifying environment, not adjacent to a vowel, the most sonorous segment in a string syllabifies. For the heavy coda of *irons*, the SH predicts that of the liquid and nasal, both of which are in an environment to syllabify, the liquid will syllabify first, giving disyllabic [ayr̩nz].

Onset consonants in English, and indeed most of Germanic, must occupy different places of articulation. This constraint on SONORITY DISTANCE (Steriade 1982) excludes initial *dl, *tl, *dn, *tn, *bw, *fw (cf. Harbert 2007: 69), and *ts.[2] This of course accounts for syllable divisions like At.lan.tic vs. a.tro.cious, etc. (Kenstowicz 1994: 251f., 257f.).

An alleged problem for the SH is the presence of initial *wr-, wl-* in early Germanic (Harbert 2007: 68), as in Goth. *wrikan* 'persecute', OE *wrecan* WREAK, or Goth. *wlits* 'face; appearance; form', OE *wlite* 'beauty, splendor'. Since all of the older Indo-European languages have *wr-* (and not **rw-*) onsets, this a problem for phonological theory involving the features of /w/, /r/, and /l/ (Miller 1994: 22ff.). Suffice it to say that /w/ behaves more like an obstruent both before /l/, /r/ and in forms like Goth. *snaiws* 'snow'. Nevertheless, the onset sequences were unstable. In English, which alone kept [w], those sequences disappeared. A word like *wrong* has a labialized

---

[2] "A serving of General Tso's Chicken does not entail that /ts/ is a valid onset consonant cluster for English" (Yang 2005: 266). Borrowed segments/clusters can increase in frequency and become nativized. For additional discussion, see §8.9.

(lip-rounded) /r/, viz. /rʷɔŋ/. All Old English words with *wl-* in the *OED* online are obsolete or extinct.

To conclude this section, the SH constrains basic word form and motivates changes to correct violations. Neologisms produced by aphasics rarely violate the SH (Buckingham and Christman 2006; 2008). Kiparsky (2008: 49–53) argues that the SH is universal, which is expected if the constraints are grounded in sensory/motor physiology but "represented in some multi-level, distributed fashion in the nervous system since they are impervious to even severe forms of brain damage" (Buckingham and Christman 2008: 130).

9.2 Prosodic structures

PROSODIC MORPHOLOGY (e.g. McCarthy and Prince 1986; 1990; 1993; 1998; Lappe 2007) is a theory of the interaction between morphological and phonological determinants of linguistic form. The leading idea is that the output of form-affecting operations crucially refers to prosodic categories. The PROSODIC HIERARCHY consists of prosodic word > foot > syllable > mora. Among other things, these prosodic categories determine the size and structure of templates for reduplication and truncation. Based on the monosyllabic structure of truncated names, McCarthy and Prince (1986) claim that the MINIMAL WORD delineates the structure of a template (word, foot, syllable).[3] Prosodic markedness constraints, like the ranking of the minimal word with respect to the binary metrical foot (below), affect the output structure of morphemes.

To relate this to the section above, syllables are organized into metrical feet. The simplest way to recognize a metrical foot in English is by stress. Words like *table* have one stress and one foot. A word like *ultimatum* has two stresses and two feet.

---

[3] In fact, minimal word and foot optimality do not predict the large number of monosyllabic forms (§12.5). Many aspects of the prosodic hierarchy are not universal (Schiering, Bickel, and Hildebrandt 2010). In fact, even the prosodic word has been decomposed into different types (Hyman 2008: 335f.): (a) the demarcative word (a property marks the beginning and/or end of the word); (b) the culminative word (a feature occurs only once per word); (c) the harmonic word (a feature is realized throughout the word); (d) the metrical word (a word consists of hierarchically arrayed moras or syllables); (e) the minimal word (a word must consist of a minimum of moras or syllables); (f) the maximal word (a word can consist of a maximum of moras or syllables); (g) the phonotactic word (a word permits only certain output segments/sequences); (h) the morphosyntactic word (a word permits only certain input segments/sequences). In light of the finer-grained distinctions suggested by Schiering et al. (2010), e.g. the Vietnamese tonal dissimilation word, they suggest that prosodic words are language-specific. Apart from that, "[s]tress-defined domains tend to be significantly larger than other domains" (p. 702). The authors argue that the absence of absolute universals does not mean that the distribution of structure is random, but rather that a prosodic word is emergent: "The prosodic word can thus be redefined as a language-particular category which emerges through frequent reference within the prosodic system" (p. 703).

9.2.1 The binary trochaic foot

Feet are optimally binary trochaic, like E *table* (cf. Broselow 2009: 216f.). Processes that yield disyllabic trochaic feet are the most frequent in acquisition and change (Miller 2010: vol. 1, ch. 9). In a language with prosody based on moras (time units), like Latin or Ancient Greek, a trochee has a heavy syllable (short vowel + coda, or long vowel) followed by a light syllable (short vowel and no coda), e.g. L *cēna* 'dinner' with a structure that splits the first syllable into two moras, i.e. long *ē* has two beats, as if two short *e* vowels.

The structure in (3a) is a classic binary trochaic foot in which the S (strong) syllable bears the stress, and the W (weak) syllable is unstressed. So-called 'ternary' feet have two binary cuts, as in the structure of a dactylic word like Ital. *femmina*, L *fēmina* 'woman' in (3b).

(3) Binary and dactylic foot structure (F = foot, σ = syllable, μ = mora)

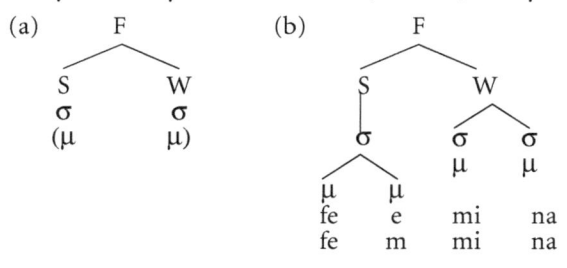

```
    (a)      F                (b)         F
           /   \                        /    \
          S     W                      S      W
          σ     σ                      |     / \
         (μ)   (μ)                     σ    σ   σ
                                      / \   μ   μ
                                     μ   μ
                                     fe  e  mi  na
                                     fe  m  mi  na
```

The long *ē* in L *fēmina* counts as two moras, represented artificially in (3b) by splitting the long *ē* of the first syllable into two short vowels. The Italian form is similar but with a closed syllable (nucleus plus coda). That is, a dactyl in a mora-counting language is actually quadramoraic but still ternary: a bimoraic strong branch (counting two beats) balanced by two monomoraic weak branches counting one beat each.

In languages like Spanish and Portuguese, the optimal foot structure is binary trochaic as in (3a) without the moraic realization (Wohlmuth 2008). English also prefers the binary trochaic foot and counts heavy syllables (moras) for stress placement (Kager 1999; Prince and Smolensky 2004 [1993]; Lappe 2007). In Latin and Italian the optimal foot has either two syllables with one mora each (3a), or two syllables with two moras each (a word like L *crēdō* 'I believe' CREDO), or three syllables with a total mora count of four, as in (3b). In short, "[f]eet must be binary at either the mora or syllable level" (McCrary 2004: 191); cf. Prince and Smolensky (2004: 70f.) for Latin. That is, a one-syllable foot with one mora is defective and tends to evolve into two moras or two syllables. A ternary foot (one with two binary cuts) is not inherently unstable unless it contains three moras (like L *patina*, which later syncopates to *panna* PAN) or otherwise involves non-duple timing. Duple timing is defined as in music: two beats, four beats, and multiples thereof. Triple timing (three beats) is unstable and subject to change to a word form with two or four beats (Miller 2010: vol. 1, ch. 9).

9.2.2 Templates and predictions

This section provides an illustration of the role that will be played by prosodic structures in subsequent chapters. Specifically, in anticipation of the structure of clips (§11.8), the interaction of prosody and phonological constraints is demonstrated.

In monosyllabic clips the sonority hierarchy (§9.1) is obeyed with respect to how many and which segments are tolerated on the right edge. In a word like *prof*[*essor*], the onset of the second syllable is segmented off and adjoined as the coda of the first syllable, as shown in (4).

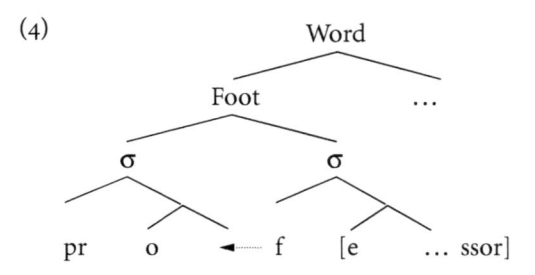

(4)
```
               Word
              /    \
           Foot     ...
          /    \
         σ      σ
        / \    / \
       pr  o ← f [e  ... ssor]
```

Since the only part of a syllable that can stand on its own is the nucleus, with truncation of the rime of the second syllable its onset is mapped onto the empty coda position of the preceding syllable—if and only if the template provides for a complex rime.

The truncation template for this clip-structure requires a complex rime. This means that the portion after the nucleus can be made up by a cluster that obeys the SH or by a sole consonant, both of which involve pirating from the onset of the second syllable, as in (4) above and *tarp*[*aulin*], *vamp*[*ire*], *pant*[*aloon*]*s*, etc. Truncation must not create a violation of the SH: *gym*[*nasium*] (not **gymn*), *mic*[*rophone*] (*mike* not **micr*). If the second syllable has a complex onset, it is maximized by the MAXIMIZE ONSET PRINCIPLE before truncation at the expense of a complex coda, e.g. *con*[*tra*], not **cont*[*ra*]. *Spec(k)*[*tacle*]*s* shows that sonority distance (Steriade 1982) is obeyed, since [kt] can be a possible syllable onset (e.g. in Ancient Greek, which also allows *pt-*, *ps-*, *tl-*, etc.), but not in English, which requires greater sonority distance between adjacent segments. In the case of *brother*, no English word with a short vowel ends in /ð/ (except the letter name *edh*), hence *bro* rather than */brʌð/.

9.3 Abbreviations and alphabetisms[4]

Technically, ALPHABETISMS or INITIALISMS like *ECG* [1952] differ from ABBREVIATIONS like *Mon.*, *Jan.*, but there are ambiguous cases, such as *c/o* [1889], *e.g.* [1682], *Au* [1814] etc. (López Rúa 2002: 48).

Initialisms and abbreviations are both as old as written records. Well-known Roman examples are *Imp(erator)* 'emperor' and *SPQR* for *Senātus Populusque Rōmānus* 'the senate and people of Rome' (cf. Biville 1989: 17). English has examples from Latin phrases, e.g. *MD* [1425] = *medicinae doctor* 'doctor of medicine'; *MA* [1678] = *magister artium* 'master of arts'; *p.m.* [1666] = *post merīdiem* 'after noon'; *a.m.* [1763] = *ante merīdiem* 'before noon'.

Alphabetisms are normally pronounced with the letter name and final stress: *IOU* [1618 1×; 1795] (I owe you), *NRA* [1860] (National Rifle Association), *PDQ* [*c.*1875] (pretty damn quick), *DUI* [1916] (driving under the influence [of alcohol]), *VIP* [1933] (very important person), *c.p.s.* [1940] (cycles per second), *TS* [1944] (tough shit), *LSD* [1950] (lysergic acid diethylamide), *DIY* [1955] (do it yourself), *TLC* [1960] (tender loving care), *R&D* [*a.*1965] (research and development), *ATF* [1969] (Alcohol, Tobacco, and Firearms [Bureau]), *CFO* [1971] (chief financial officer), *HMO* [1971] (Health Maintenance Organization), *CEO* [1972] (chief executive officer), *ATM* [1975] (automated teller machine), *ADD* [1979] (attention deficit disorder), *CD* [1979] (compact disc), *MRI* [1983] (magnetic resonance imaging), *G(-)7* [1986] (Group of Seven [leading industrial nations]), *SUV* [1987] (sports utility vehicle), *CSA* [1990] (Child Support Agency), *WMD* [1991] (Weapons of Mass Destruction), *WWW* [1992] (World Wide Web), *WTO* [1995] (World Trade Organization), *TGIF* [2001] ("Thank God it's Friday!"), Rachael Ray's *EVOO* [*a.*2005] 'extra virgin olive oil', etc.

Some alphabetisms are multivalent, e.g. *CCU* [1966] coronary care unit, [1974] cardiac care unit, [1979] critical care unit.

Because of the final stress, it is not surprising that alphabetisms undergo the American English "thirteen dog" rule (*thirtéen* but *thírteen dógs*): *US͑*, but *US̀ invólvement*, *US̀ Ópen*; *PM͑*, but *PM̀Mágazine*; *OK͑*, but *Ò.K. Corrál*.

An extreme example is the pronuciation of a letter or numeral representing a word it sounds like, as is frequent on license plates, e.g. DOIOU2 [do I owe you too] 'habitual debtor', 10SNE1 [tennis anyone?] 'tennis buff', YRUILL [why are you ill?] 'doctor' (Crystal 2001: 6). Once included under the rubric REBUS PUZZLES, this is the same 'vernacular orthography' that features prominently in the language of texting (Shortis 2007; Thurlow 2012).

---

[4] Copious examples of alphabetisms, abbreviations, and acronyms can be found in Koziol (1972: 309–13), Tournier (1985: 308–12), Cannon (1987; 1989), Rodriguez and Cannon (1994), Kreidler (1979, 2000), López Rúa (2002), Mattiello (2008: 135ff., w. lit).

Alphabetisms take inflections (cf. Fandrych 2008: 112, w. lit), e.g. *MVPs* = plural of *MVP* [1930] (most valuable player), *O.D.ed* [1965] = *overdosed*. Alphabetized verbs can take inflections which are impossible on the unaltered forms: *P.O.(e)d* [1945] (pissed off); the literal equivalent would be **pissoff-ed*. From *KO/ko/kayo* [1922] (knock out) or *TKO* [1942], the past tense is *(T)KO(e)d*, for which the unaltered equivalent is totally deviant: **technical-knock-out-ed*, **technical-knocked-out*, etc. The unshortened form is only a noun, but the alphabetism can undergo conversion to a verb and receive all verbal inflections. *RSVP* [1834] begins as a verb phrase (F *répondez s'il vous plaît* 'please reply') but can be a noun in English since 1850, as in the question, *How many RSVPs did you receive?* Finally, note prefixation in *un-PC*, as if 'un-politically correct'.

From *UFO* [1953] (unidentified flying object) have been derived *ufology* [1959], *ufologist* [1963], etc., but these are acronyms (see below).

Abbreviations and alphabetisms are important because they become separate words and undergo their own history. As abbreviation status is forgotten (or overridden), the form becomes a new word, and the stress is determined by the category (noun, verb, etc.): *OK* [1839] > *okay* [1895] (both adjectives) > verb *OK/okay* [1882].[5]

9.4 Acronyms

An acronym (from Greek 'top/extreme end (of a) name') is essentially an alphabetism that is pronounceable by ordinary rules of word structure (cf. Tournier 1991). This is not all there is to it, however, since not all pronounceable alphabetisms become acronyms. *COD* [1859] (cash/collect on delivery) is never /kad/, like the fish name.

The contextually ambiguous *IRA* (Irish Republican Army [1921]; individual retirement account [1974]) is pronounced [ayrə] only in the latter sense and only when a name occurs with it.

HIV [1986] (human immunodeficiency virus) is never [hɪv] or [hayv], even though *AIDS* [1982] (acquired immune deficiency syndrome) is an acronym.

LOL [1989] (laughing out loud) is rarely pronounced as an acronym except when hypocoristic *-s* (§11.7) is attached, viz. *lolz, lawlz, lulz* (Starr 2010; Baclawski 2012a).

Many acronyms are deliberately coined by REVERSE ACRONYMY (Stockwell and Minkova 2001: 91), starting from a word whose meaning is to be emphasized, e.g. *WASP* [1962] (White Anglo-Saxon Protestant), *MADD* [1981] (Mothers Against

---

[5] The abbreviation appeared in 1839, perhaps a slogan of the *O.K. Club*, the Democratic Party's political club [1840] for Old Kinderhook (Martin Van Buren, of Kinderhook, NY, president from 1837 to 1841), who may have quick-signed documents "O.K.", whence the reanalysis: *I "OK(e)d" it*. The potential problem is that the verb is not attested before 1882. Other speculations are recorded in the *OED*, which favors the derivation from a jocular alteration of 'all correct' as *oll/orl korrekt*.

Drunk Driving), *DAMM* [n.d.] (Drunks Against Mad Mothers), *GIFT* [1984] (gamete intra-fallopian transfer), *GASP* [n.d.] (Group Against Smoke and Pollution; Greater-Washington Alliance to Stop Pollution), *SANE* [n.d.] 'scientists against nuclear weapons'. Finally, that universal bane to women, the *SNAG* (sensitive new age guy) has been around since the mid-1960s, and is well attested on Google, but is not in the *OED*.

The major factors that distinguish an acronym from an alphabetism, then, are intent and creativity (Fandrych 2008: 110f.).

By contrast, neither baseball's *ERA* [1949] (earned run average) nor the *ERÁ* [1973] (Equal Rights Amendment) has ever been pronounced as the word *era*, which the latter might suggest. The flipside is that some unprounceable sequences are forced into acronyms. Such is *SCSI* [1982] 'small computer system interface', pronounced like *skuzzy*. Similarly, *wysiwyg* [1982] 'what you see is what you get' is pronounced as if *wizziwig*, and *posslq* [1978] 'person of the opposite sex sharing living quarters' is pronounced /pasəlkyū/. Another example is *twtwytt* [n.d.] 'that's what they want you to think'.[6]

An ancient acronym is *IXΘYΣ* (G *ikhthūs* 'fish'), a Christian symbol based on the initials of <u>Ἰ</u>ησοῦς <u>Χ</u>ριστὸς <u>Θ</u>εοῦ <u>Υ</u>ἱὸς <u>Σ</u>ωτήρ (*Iēsoūs Khristòs Theoū Huiòs Sōtḗr*) 'Jesus Christ/annointed God's son savior'. Acronyms are rare before c20. The word ACRONYM first appeared in print in 1940 when it designated an initialism. The modern sense first appears in 1943 but may have been used of the proliferation of alphabetic agencies during World War I [1914–18] (cf. German *Akronym* [1921]) and again in the 1930s during FDR's first term. It has many derivatives, including *acronymize* [1955] (Cassidy 1993: 400). The study by Rodriguez and Cannon (1994: 266ff.) reveals that acronyms mushroomed after World War II from about 1,200 dictionary entries to over half a million.

A few of the better-known examples include *gestapo* [1934] (Germ. *Gestapo* [1933] = GEheime STAatsPOlizei 'secret state-police'), *snafu* [1941] 'situation normal: all fouled/fucked up', *sonar* [1946] 'SOund NAvigation (and) Ranging', *scuba* [1952] 'self-contained underwater breathing apparatus', *deejay* [1955] 'disk jockey', *laser* [1960] 'light amplification by the stimulated emission of radiation', *ANWR* /ǽnwar/ [*c*.1960] 'Arctic National Wildlife Refuge', *SIDS* [1970] 'sudden infant death syndrome', *Epcot* [1982] 'Experimental Prototype Community of Tomorrow', *yuppie* [1984] (young urban professional + -ie of *Hippie* [1953] 'a hipster', *Yippie* [1968] 'Young International Party' + -ie, etc.), *WIMP* [1985] 'weakly interacting massive particle', *scaf* [1986] 'self-centered-altruism fad', *Raids* [1987] 'recently acquired income deficiency syndrome', *SIV* [1987] 'simian immunodeficiency virus', *Erops* [1988] 'extended range operations', *zift* [1988] 'zygote intra-fallopian transfer',

---

[6] *Urban Dictionary*: http://www.urbandictionary.com/define.php?term=twtwytt

NAFTA 'North Atlantic Free Trade Area' [1967] and 'North American Free Trade Agreement' [1990], *MILF* [1995] (but possibly as early as 1991) 'mothers I'd like to fuck', *SARS* /sarz/ [2003] 'severe acute respiratory syndrome'.

NCAR (National Center for Atmospheric Research) is half an acronym (N + *car*). Even though N is itself pronounced (*en*), it remains perceptually half an acronym, and children are aware of that. As is customary, children write thank-you notes after a fieldtrip, and those thank-you notes are displayed. One note to NCAR begins, "Dear NARC". Since this is the only metathesis in the note, it is reasonable to interpret it as a desire on the child's part to make the name a full acronym (or an otherwise recognizable word?).

A split acronym is AASMNEWS [n.d.] 'Anglo American School of Moscow NEWS', a gossip webpage (*Urban Dictionary*).

The link between the acronym and the full form can be at least partially severed, as in *PIN* (personal identification number) number (Fandrych 2008: 112).

Like alphabetisms, acronyms can undergo derivation and other word formation processes; cf. *WASPdom* [1969] 'the state of having the traits, beliefs, etc. of a White Anglo-Saxon Protestant'.

A more complicated combination is found in *lasing* [1963], *lasable* [n.d.], etc. The acronym *laser* is first backformed to *lase*, then suffixed to make further related forms.

Fodil (2010) applies the label COMPONYM to an acronym with additional complexity or morphosyntactic detail. One of his examples is *grep* [1973] 'global (search for the) regular expression (and) print [the lines containing matches to it]'. Fodil emphasizes that this is not a simple acronym because it consists of combinations of letters and words, many understood from the context.

The componym is thus an extension of standard acronymy in that more information must be gleaned from the context. Sadek Fodil (p.c.) adds: "The cyber era encourages the sort of devices that produce novel coinages because they are perfectly in tune with the spirit of the new era: they do more (say more) with less means (words), thus reducing both cost and speed of expression." Similar points about mass media have been made by Shortis (2007), Thurlow (2012), and others. It is certainly true that, prior to the era of mass media and high technology, there were very few acronyms for which much of the meaning remained understood. One of the few is *Oxfam* [1947] '**Ox**ford Committee for **Fam**ine Relief', and that is arguably a blend. As usual, the boundary between various lexicogenic operations is slippery.

9.5 Suffixes as full words

Another kind of non-clipped shortening involves the promotion of a suffix to the status of a full word.

In the process of GRAMMATICALIZATION, lexical material becomes grammatical, as in the evolution of *have* from 'possess' to an auxiliary of perfect aspect (*I have done that*).

Nevertheless, there are examples in the opposite direction documented by Miller (2010: vol. 2, ch. 3, w. lit). One easy illustration of a change from grammatical content to lexical is the functional Degree head *so* (OE *swā* 'id.'), as in *so high*, reanalyzed as a lexical adjective 'true' in examples like *this is no longer so*.

By all accounts suffixes are grammatical (functional), in which case the elevation of one to a full lexical word should exemplify a change in the opposite direction, i.e. from functional or grammatical to lexical. Two standard examples widely discussed in the literature are the following: (1) because it was the only person/number inflection in some paradigms, Irish 1pl. *-m(u)id* was reanalyzed as a pronoun *muid*; (2) the Modern Greek prefix *ksana-* 'again' was reanalyzed as a free adverb *ksana* 'id.'.

Our concern here is with suffixes and a specific route by which they become full words. This is different from clips promoted to full words, like *Tron* (§13.1).

The Middle English placename formative *-thwait* 'clearing' is from Scandinavian (Miller 2012: 105, w. lit). The earliest examples occur in a charter signed by Henry II [1154–89], designating land in Ireby, Cumberland, as *Langethweit et Stalethweit et aliōs Thweiter* 'Langethweit and Stalethweit and the other Thweits'. In Scandinavian, *þveit* is a full word, but from the English point of view, it was a toponym formative. In this charter, it is segmented off as an elliptical expression for 'places whose names end in *-thwait*'.

Although *ology, emic, etic* are often listed in this connection (Bauer 1983; Padrosa-Trias 2010: 110), the most important example in Modern English is *ism*. According to the OED online, *ism* is "A form of doctrine, theory, or practice having, or claiming to have, a distinctive character or relation...." The earliest example is 1680: "He was the great Hieroglyphick of Jesuitism, Puritanism, Quaquerism, and of all Isms...." The next example is 1756: "Arianism, Socinianism, Arminianism, or any other ism."

So far, *ism* is simply elliptical for 'word ending in *-ism*' (many examples in Urdang et al. 1986), on a par with *-thwait* above. But *ism* exists outside of this elliptical context. The first example in the *OED* is 1840: "All the untidy isms of the day shall be dissipated." The equivalent "all the untidy thwaits..." would be incomprehensible.

In terms of analysis, this means that at some point *ism* was able to be extracted from the elliptical context and reanalyzed as a noun. The elliptical context became so frequent, with numerous *OED* citations in the 1800s, that *ism* was readily recognizable as a noun outside of the elliptical context (Miller 2010: 2.74).

Another such suffix cited is *-ish*, as in "A: *Was it expensive?* B: *ish*" (Szymanek 2005: 436). Still, this seems prompted by the context. Can one as yet talk about "all the ishes" in a meaningful way? Spencer (2005: 83) remarks that "for some speakers *ish* has become a free morpheme with roughly the meaning 'approximately'."

Another potential example is *oid-y*, cited by Hohenhaus (2005: 363):

It's an oid-y world out there. Tabloids run factoids about humanoids on steroids. In a world gone synthetic, why should movies offer something as organic as a hero? Welcome, then, to the age of the heroid. (*Time* Magazine 8/10/1990, p. 90)

The relevant question for our purposes is whether *oid* has the status of *ism*. It is not yet listed as a separate word in the *OED*, which lags behind on many neologisms. The construct is contextually explained in the quote above, but there may be enough *-oid* forms in standard English that one might understand a statement like "All the oids in this culture are disturbing" in the absence of a prompting context. As to the specific construct *oid-y*, adjectival *-oidal* already exists, and *oidy* is the same kind of derivative with a different adjectival formative.

Lavrova (2010) cites Cole Paulson on *ness* 'aura, personality': "I don't like his ness" meaning 'I don't like him as a person'.

Examples of this kind have been adduced from other languages as well. Dutch *tig* 'quite a lot' was segmented off *twintig* 'twenty', *dertig* 'thirty', etc. (Hamans 2013: 313).

9.6 Summary

In the prosodic hierarchy, words consist of feet, feet consist of syllables, syllables consist of segments which may be associated with timing units, or moras.

Evidence from language play (§5.5) supports a hierarchical structure of the syllable in which the nucleus and coda constitute an inner constituent, called the rime/rhyme from its metrical function, as distinct from the onset.

Segments are arranged in the syllable according to sonority. Low vowels are the most sonorous, high vowels the least. Next come consonantal segments that are most vowel-like (glides, liquids, and nasals), and so on. The sonority hierarchy (SH) thus involves the arrangement of segments outward from a nucleus of higher sonority to an onset and/or coda of preferentially lower sonority.

The SH crosslinguistically constrains basic word form and motivates numerous changes to correct violations produced by affixation and phonological reductions.

Syllables are arranged into feet, which are optimally binary trochaic, in which the S (strong) syllable bears the stress, and the W (weak) syllable is unstressed, like E *table*. So-called 'ternary' feet have two binary cuts, as in the structure of a dactylic word such as E *cinema*.

Abridgments are a form of economy. "[S]hortenings mainly lack morphological motivation and, as a consequence, transparency, the phonological and graphic motivations gain in importance" (Fischer 1998: 179).

Abbreviations are mostly for economy in writing. People do not typically pronounce *Feb* for *February*. By contrast, alphabetisms and acronyms provide economy for speech as well as writing. Alphabetisms prototypically take the first letter (rarely, more than one) of each main lexical item in a phrase. The same holds in acronyms, in which the letters are pronounced as a word. Many acronyms are deliberate coinages to evoke another existing word, e.g. *MADD* 'Mothers Against Drunk Driving'.

Both alphabetisms and acronyms become new words in their own right, capable of undergoing affixation and conversion in ways that are impossible for the phrases from which they are abridged, e.g. *TKO'ed* '*technical knock-out-ed'. Needless to say, the hierarchical structure of words like this and *ufology* is very different from that of the phrase or compound from which they are derived.

With the dawn of the era of high tech, abridgments have become more radical and therefore more abstract, leaving considerably more to be ascertained from the context, e.g. *grep* 'global (search for the) regular expression (and) print [the lines containing matches to it]'.

Another form of abridgment involves the promotion of an affix to full word status. *Ism* was originally a shorthand way of referring to doctrines and the like that typically end in *-ism*, and is now the standard word for those doctrines and practices.

10

Sound symbolism

Various kinds of acoustic and perceptual motivation of word forms are treated, including (i) the motivation of words by our perception of sounds in nature or the environment, (ii) the inverse correlation between object size and formant frequency (the frequency code), and (iii) conventionalized links between sound and meaning (phonesthesia), perpetuated by analogical word creation that spawns classes of words with the same conventionalized iconic link(s). Crosscutting this are the inherent properties of segments, such as the flow of liquids and the stridency of certain fricatives.[1]

10.1 Types of sound-symbolic motivation

The basis for sound symbolism has been elusive. The study of symbolism in English word formation by Marchand (1959) failed to reach any conclusion about its basis. Jakobson and Waugh (1987) posit a natural similarity association between sound and meaning, founded on association between the different sensory modalities, especially vision and hearing. In other words, interaction among the sensory modalities allows for connections between phonetics, semantics, and the grammar as a whole.

The main problem has been the attempt to reduce sound symbolism to a single cause. Phoneticians typically reduce it to acoustic properties. Motor theorists like Allott (1995) reduce it to motor control. And so on. The result of such oversimplification has been vagueness almost to the point of vacuity.

---

[1] Thanks to Alan Bell and Chris Smith for discussion of this chapter. Literature includes Stoddart (1858), Jespersen (1922: ch. 20), Sauvageot (1964), Marchand (1959; 1969: 397–428), Genette (1976) (a historical study), Ultan (1978), Tournier (1985: 139–67), Pharies (1986), Joseph (1987), Meier (1989), Käsmann (1992), Bolinger (1992), Hinton, Nichols, and Ohala (1994a), Danchev (1995a; 1995b), Wynecoop and Levin (1996), Coleman (1997), Ohala (1997), Shisler (1997), Anderson (1998), Abelin (1999), Hamano (1994; 1998; 2000), Baldi and Dawar (2000), Waugh (2000), Magnus (1999; 2001) and her detailed website: www.trismegistos.com/MagicalLetterPage/, Cornish (2003), Hinton and Bolinger (2003), Bergen (2004), Lawler (2006), Tsur (2006), Bottineau (2008), Akita (2009), Kleparski and Skóra (2009), Szabóné Habók (2009), Shinohara and Kawahara (2010), Johansson (2011), Körtvélyessy (2011a; 2011b), Dingemanse (2012), Baclawski (2012b).

[S]ound symbolism is part of a complex event, comprising meanings, articulatory gestures, sound waves, etc. Each one of these components has an indefinite number of features, which give rise to a multiplicity of sometimes conflicting combinational potentials. Strong intuitions concerning sound symbolism are generated by selecting a subset of available features on the semantic, acoustic, and articulatory levels. When conflicting intuitions are reported, attention is shifted from one subset to another. (Tsur 2006: 920)

Sound symbolism is misleading in implying that sounds have some intrinsic semantic value. In reality, what is usually intended is (i) an inverse correlation between object size and acoustic frequency, (ii) conventionalized iconic links between sound and meaning, and (iii) the idea that many words are motivated by sounds in nature or the environment. Iconicity contradicts de Saussure's maxim that the sign is arbitrary and unmotivated, and that onomatopoeia is a numerically insignificant and inorganic part of linguistic systems (1916: 100ff.; cf. Ultan 1978: 551). No reference was made to Stoddart (1858: 231–74) who cited hundreds of examples from Western and non-Indo-European languages.

Jespersen (1922: 397–411) and Grammont (1933: 377–424) replied to de Saussure, the former arguing that languages grow richer in symbolic words, echoism, and motivated lexical items. On this point, one must distinguish between imitative roots (onomatopoeia) and conventionalized associations between sound and meaning.

As illustrated throughout this book, words are motivated in many different ways. The one relevant to this chapter is association of sound and meaning.[2] Brown (1958) reports on experiments on sound symbolism in many languages, and concludes that speakers of a given language realize the semantic implications of at least some phonetic sequences.

Several kinds of relationships between sound and meaning are customarily recognized. Ignoring symbolic signs (like $ for 'dollar') which are purely conventional, two supercategories of iconicity must be distinguished: (i) INDEXICAL ICONICITY, (ii) ICONIC or PRIMARY ICONICITY (Johansson 2011: 10).

Indexical iconicity subdivides into (i) SYN(A)ESTHESIA or RELATIONAL ICONICITY, based on oppositions like /i/ for small, slim, or close, /a/ for large or more distant, /o/ for large and round, etc.; (ii) PHON(A)ESTHESIA, SOUND SYMBOLISM, or COMPLEX ICONICITY, the network-like association between words sharing partial form and meaning (cf. De Cuypere 2008: 113), e.g. *gleam, glitter, glow* (Bergen 2004).

Primary iconicity subdivides into (i) IDEOPHONES, or PARAVERBAL MIMOLOGIES, which often involve sounds or sequences that violate the phonotactics of a language, e.g. *brrr, hmm, hmpf, ppff, psst, sshh, tsk tsk, zzzzz* (Anderson 1998: 124ff.; Ahlner and Zlatev 2010: 306–9, w. lit), and (ii) ONOMATOPOEIA, consisting of entire imitative

---

[2] A type to be excluded here is lexicalization and institutionalization of hypocoristics like *mama, papa,* which involve sounds associated with infant sucking (Jakobson 1959).

words with a simple relation between form and meaning, e.g. *splash, meow*, or bird names like *cuckoo*.

Ideophones will not be discussed here because they are peripheral in English except for spawning some derivatives, e.g. *hush* [1546]/*shush* [1924] (*s(h)sh* [1847]), *yucky* [1970] (*yuck* [1966]). In Japanese, ideophones preserve segments from older stages of the language (Hamano 1994; 1998; 2000). Ideophones have many cross-linguistic functions, ranging from hiccupping and coughing (Hinton, Nichols, and Ohala 1994b), to sensory imagery and, in discourse, reported speech and evidentiality (Dingemanse 2012).

This chapter will begin with onomatopoeia and then move on to indexical iconicity, which is very important in English, and close with an application to poetic art.

10.2 Onomatopoeia

Of the various kinds of echoic words, perhaps the best known is ONOMATOPOEIA: a word is coined and conventionalized in imitation of our conceptualization of sounds in nature or the environment (cf. Waugh 2000: 28). It derives from G *onomatopoiíā* 'the coining of a word in imitation of a sound', in turn from the verb *onomatopoieîn* 'to coin names', compounded of *ónoma* 'name' and *poieîn* 'to make, do, produce'.

Many of the following examples have been known since Stoddart (1858): *groan* [OE], *puff* [OE], *cackle* [1200] (Sw. *kackla*, Du. *kakelen*), *chatter* [1200], *cuckoo* [c.1240] (G *kókkūx*, L *cucūlus*, F *coucou*), *rattle* [1300], *twitter* [c.1374], *murmur* [Ch.] (L *murmur*), *growl* [a.1382], *hiss* [c.1400], *gag* [c.1400], *gargle* [1527], *giggle* [1509] (Du. *giggelen*), *thwack* [1533], *thump* [c.1537], *twang* [1542], *gurgle* [1562] (L *gurguliō* 'gullet'), *pow* [c.1580], *grumble* [a.1586], *sputter* [1598] (Du. *sputteren*), *sizzle* [1603], *slam* [1622], *splutter* [1677], *whack* [1719], *guffaw* [1720], *swish* [1756], *splatter* [1786], *whoosh* [1856], *splat* [1897], *bam* [1922], *wham* [1923], *zap* [1929], *boing* [1952], *thunk* [1952].

From [bababa], one of the most basic syllables of later infant babbling (MacNeilage 1999), conventionalized as /ba(r)-ba(r)-ba(r)/ (Stoddart 1858: §304; Létoublon 1988, w. lit), are derived the imitative words G *bárbaros* 'barbarian' (the Greek term for a non-Greek or speaker of a foreign language), *Barbara, babble, blab(ber)* (cf. *bla-bla*), *babe, baby*, etc. Some of these are opaquely imitative while others border on sound-symbolic.

Apart from borrowed forms, such as *Barbara, murmur* (from Latin), or monosyllabics (*roar* [OE], *lull* [Ch.]), English echoic words generally observe the dissimilatory constraint (§2.2) against identical liquids; cf. *grumble* (**grumber, *glumble*); *rattle* (**ratter, *lattle*); etc. (Raffelsiefen 1999: 237).

Onomatopoeic motivation can be obscured or lost by phonological change, e.g. LL *pīpiō/pīpiōn-* [c4] 'squab' (cf. *pīpīre* 'to peep') > AN *pig(e)on* PIGEON [1375] (de Saussure 1916: 102; Ullmann 1962: 94).

The main problem with attempts to generalize onomatopoeia across languages is that perceptions differ in part because phonological systems differ (Anderson 1998: 131, w. lit). For instance, while an anglophone might say that a large dog barks 'woofwoof' and a small dog barks 'yipyip' or 'yapyap', it is difficult to imagine a dog that would bark 'carcar', yet that is exactly one of the imitations of a barking dog in Latin. De Saussure (1916: 102) and Jespersen (1922) observe that since humans are incapable of precisely hearing or imitating non-human sounds, our impressionistic perceptions are somewhat accidental but become conventionalized in different ways in different languages.

No matter how similar an imitation is, it remains an imprecise approximation. Does a frog really CROAK [*a*.1500], or does it go RIBBIT [*c*.1968]? In Danish a frog is imitated *kvæk kvæk*,[3] resembling the sound of a duck in English. A Hungarian frog goes *brekeke, brekk brekk*; cf. Aristophanes' Greek imitation in the *Frogs* (209+), *brekekekèx koàx koáx*. The Onondaga word for 'frog' is *squárak*, which looks enough like *croak* and *koáx* to suggest an imitative origin. Compare also Tok Pisin *rokrok* 'frog', Indonesian *kodok* 'id.'. Frogs in Finnish are imitated *kurr kurr*, not so different from Japanese *kero kero*. Nevertheless, to illustrate the arbitrariness of even onomatopoeically motivated words, Mongolian frogs go *vaag vaag*, and Korean frogs *gaegool gaegool*.

From the point of view of language acquisition, a frog goes *croak* in English not because it really does but because that's what children learn it does. This is why nearly all English speakers reject *pipe* as a valid frog noise, even though the *OED* attests examples from around 1333 to 2002.

Finally, it is worth mentioning that similar phonetic sequences may or may not be perceived as onomatopoeic, depending on meaning and context. Hebrew *mataktek* 'ticktocking' is onomatopoeic but *mataktak* 'sweetish' is not. It is derived from *matok* 'sweet' by means of a productive pattern; cf. *yarakrak* 'greenish' from *yarok* 'green' (Tsur 2006: 906). "In the Hebrew word for 'ticktocking' the meaning directs attention to the sensory information underlying the voiceless plosives; in the Hebrew word for 'sweetish' it directs attention away, to an abstract lexical model" (p. 907).

10.3 Synesthesia

The first type of indexical iconicity is SYNESTHESIA, also called PHONETIC ICONICITY and various other things: a sound sequence is associated with an act, item, or intensity.[4]

---

[3] Hittite *akuwakuwa-* was originally thought to mean 'frog', and may designate a small amphibian (Hoffner and Melchert 2008: 49, 62), despite Puhvel's 'tarantula' based on an apparent variant *auwauwa-* with something to do with a spider (*HED* A 26), but there is no decisive evidence (Craig Melchert, p.c.).

[4] *Synesthesia* (Neo-Latin *synaesthēsia*) is derived from the Greek verb *sunaisthánomai* [Aristotle] 'I perceive simultaneously, share in a perception or sense'. It was first used in English in 1891 of a sensation in

Synesthetic sound symbolism is the process whereby certain vowels, consonants, and suprasegmentals are chosen to consistently represent visual, tactile, or proprioceptive properties of objects, such as size or shape. For example, segments such as palatal consonants and high vowels are frequently used for diminutive forms and other words representing small objects.

(Hinton, Nichols, and Ohala 1994b: 4)

The first subsection looks at synesthesia acoustically, and the second subsection applies this information to English word formation.

10.3.1 *The frequency code and cross-modal iconicity*

Ohala's FREQUENCY CODE (e.g. 1994) establishes a correlation between low-frequency voices of large creatures and typical concomitant traits (large size, power, agression, etc.) and between high-frequency voices of small creatures and typical concomitant traits (small size, deference, submission, familiarity, etc.).

Studies of cross-modal iconicity (e.g. Abelin 1999; Ahlner and Zlatev 2010; Johansson 2011) generalize the frequency code to links between high frequency and small form or size, light color or transparency, light weight, swift movement, thin consistency, bright sound, close spatial position, and proximal deixis ('here, this'), on the one hand, and between low frequency and round, heavy forms, large size, dark color, heavy weight, thick consistency, deep, noisy sounds, and distal deixis ('there, that'), on the other.

Sapir (1929) performed an experiment with two invented words, *mil* and *mal*. Of the 500 English-speaking subjects, over 80% associated *mil* with 'small table' and *mal* with 'large table'. Compare also the difference between G *mīkrós* 'small' and *makrós* 'long, tall' (Ohala 1997: tables 1, 2).

When confronted with the made-up words *bouba* and *kiki*, 95% of children and adults identify *bouba* with a roundish amoeboid figure and *kiki* with a pointy star figure (e.g. Ramachandran and Hubbard 2001; 2003). In an experiment by Ahlner and Zlatev (2010: 328ff.), 90% of the respondents associated /i/ with the star and /u/ with the amoeba form. Children as young as 2.5 show the *bouba/kiki* phenomenon (Maurer, Pathman, and Mondloch 2006).

There is a continuum of relative motivation of segments expressing the range from small size, proximal deixis, etc., to large size, distal deixis, etc. Of the voiced segments, high front vowels and palatal consonants have the highest second formant frequencies, then front mid vowels and dental consonants, then non-high central vowels and velar then labial consonants, and, with the lowest frequencies, back non-round vowels, and finally, back round vowels (Ahlner and Zlatev 2010; Johansson 2011).

---

a different place from the location of the stimulus. The modern linguistic sense seems to have first occurred in Whatmough (1956: 191).

Voiceless consonants and high front vowels are thus optimal for expressing small size, proximal deixis, etc., while back round vowels and voiced labial consonants are optimal for large size, distal deixis, etc. (Ultan 1978; Croft 2008; Johansson 2011); cf. Hungarian *itt* 'here', *ott* 'there'; *ez* 'this', *az* 'that' (Tsur 2006: 917); Pipil proximal *ini*, distal *uni*; Panjabi prox. *é*, dist. *ó*; Comanche prox. *i-*, mediodist. *o-*, invisible (remote) dist. *u-*; Tümpisa Shoshone prox. *i-*, mediodist. *e-*, dist. *a-*, invisible (remote) dist. *u-*; etc. (Diessel 2005; Baclawski 2012b). Examples this iconic are rare crosslinguistically. In Baclawski's (2012b) survey of over 200 languages, 125 have a front vowel (preferably /i/) for proximal deixis (and 55 for distal), 146 have a back vowel (preferably /a/) for distal deixis (and 84 for proximal). The exceptions are due to a variety of factors, not least of which are (i) language change (e.g. OL *olle* 'that' > CL *ille* 'id.' with the vowel of *hic* 'this' and *is/id* neutral deixis) and (ii) the fact that iconicity is an optimality consideration in varying degrees, never deterministic (Miller 2010: 1.195).

Based on 136 languages, Ultan (1978) observed that high front vowels are typically perceived as small or denoting small things, and low back vowels are typically perceived as big or denoting large things. More technically, small size correlates with high frequency and large size with low frequency (Ultan 1978: 545; Shinohara and Kawahara 2010; cf. Tsur 2006: 917). While acknowledging many crosslinguistic exceptions (see Körtvélyessy 2011b), a diminutive suffix in numerous languages contains the vowel /i/. More generally, Ultan found that diminutive sound symbolism is associated with high or front vowels, high tone, and/or consonant gradation, including palatal and fronted consonants. Štekauer et al. (2012: 270–73) agree with Bauer (1996) that iconicity is not a strong factor in the development of evaluative markers, but suggest that it may be areal.

The Lao expressives in (1) are based on different vowel gradations ranging from small to big as follows: [ī] > [ɔ̄] > [ō] (Wayland 1995).

(1) Lao expressives
    [cīŋ^4 pīŋ^4]   appearance of small hole
    [cɔ̄ŋ^4 pɔ̄ŋ^4]   appearance of (round) medium-size hole
    [cōŋ^4 pōŋ^4]   appearance of (round) big hole
    [cāŋ^4 pāŋ^4]   appearance of wide, open space (no dimension)

Wayland accounts for the gradations by means of the size of the resonance chamber, which for [ī] is much smaller than for [ɔ̄], while [ō] has the largest anterior resonance chamber because of the lip rounding. She also notes that this correlates inversely with frequency of the second formant acoustically: [ī] 2749 Hz : [ɔ̄] 1245 Hz : [ō] 977 Hz.

In Jamaican Creole, likewise, /o/ represents something large and heavy, /e/ something small and light, and /a/ is neutral (DeCamp 1974: 49–53; Miller 2010: 2.282):

(2) Apophonic degree expressions (Jamaican Creole)
  (a) *tug* > *togo-togo* 'pull/drag sthg. heavy'
          taga-taga 'drag sthg. (not heavy or light)'
          tege-tege 'drag sthg. light'
  (b) *lug* > *logo-logo* 'carry/lift sthg. heavy'
          laga-laga 'carry/lift (sthg.)'
          lege-lege 'carry/lift sthg. light'
  (c) *mucky* > *moko-moko* 'very deep thick mud'
            maka-maka 'muddy, mucky'
            meke-meke 'thin watery layer of mud over hard clay'

In Batak Mandailing (Malayo-Polynesian) 'creep' is *djirir* for small beings, *djurur* for large beings, and *djarar* for beings of neutral size (cf. Carnoy 1917: 266).

Ohala (1997) states: "The phonetic generalization that can be made is that the expression of size utilizes speech sounds whose characteristic acoustic frequencies vary inversely with size of the thing designated." Ohala links this frequency code to biological evolution. Perceptually, small size correlates with high acoustic frequency and large size with low frequency. In visual terms, there is also an iconic relation between the size of the object and the size of the resonance chamber.

10.3.2 Synesthesia and English apophony

In the examples in (3), different degrees of intensity are iconically associated with mostly vowel gradations (cf. Marchand 1959; 1969: 426f.; Koziol 1972: 38f.).

(3)
ping	[1835]	*trip*	[c.1380]	*tink(le)*	[a.1382]	*crinkle*	[1807]
bing	[1922]	*drip*	[c.1000]	*ting*	[1495]	*crimp*	[1834]
bang	[?c.1550]	*dribble*	[1567]	*tang*	[1556]	*crumple*	[?c.1450]
bong	[1924]	*drop*	[c.1000]	*tonk*	[1910]	*crunch*	[1801]
clink	[c.1386]	*click*	[1581]	*clip*	[c.1440]	*splish*	[1735]
clank	[a.1614]	*clack*	[a.1250]	*clap*	[?c.1225]	*splash*	[1699]
clunk	[a.1796]	*cluck*	[1481]	*clop*	[1901]	*splosh*	[1857]

Note also in (3) CONSONANT GRADATION: *ping/bing, trip/drip* (cf. *slutch* [1669]/*sludge* [1649], *smutch* [1530]/*smudge* [1768], *snicker* [1694]/*snigger* [1706]). This is sporadic in English but grammaticalized in some languages. For instance, in Japanese, a small/light balloon pops p̲an-to, while a heavy/large balloon pops b̲an-to. A light door clatters k̲atat-to; a heavy door, g̲atat-to (Hamano 2000). Palatalization is also used: *patya-patya* 'hitting the water with a big splash' vs. *pata-pata* 'hitting a flat surface' (Hamano 1994: 148). Zulu features such alternations as *kete* 'chatter' : *khethe* 'babble' : *gede* 'chatter loudly' (Childs 1994: 192).

Most conspicuous in (3) are the apophonic alternations.[5] "Forms with -*i*- signify high-pitched and/or low-amplitude sounds. Generally they have a diminutive sense" (Rhodes 1994: 284). This includes hypocoristics in -*ie* (cf. Waugh 2000: 29ff.). Forms with low vowel and nasal (*clunk* [*a*.1796], *plunk* [1822], *thump* [*c*.1537], etc.) "signify distinctively low-pitched sounds" (Rhodes, p. 284). Forms like *pop* [*c*.1390], *plop* [1821], *bong* [1924] represent non-high-pitched sounds. Moreover, initial *p*- signals an abrupt onset, while *b*- represents an abrupt, loud onset (pp. 277, 280).

In several of the examples in (3), a degree word was formed after one or more of the others, as if to complete the set. For instance, *bong* [1924] was added shortly after *bing* [1922], *click* [1581] postdates both *clack* [*a*.1250] and *cluck* [1481]. EME *clap* [?*c*.1225] antedates *clip* [*c*.1440], and *snap* [1495] antedates *snip* [1587]. Conversely, *splosh* [1857] completes the set after the creation of *splash* [1699] and *splish* [1735]. Note also *bling blang* introduced together in 1974.

Another such alternation is *creak–crack–croak*. The oldest form was *crack* [*c*.1000] 'make a sharp noise'. *Creak* [1606] 'strident noise' occurred first as a verb [*c*.1325] 'utter a harsh cry', but was displaced in this sense by *croak* [1460], fixing *creak* in a meaning that is denominal to the noun *creak*.

English *ding* [*a*.1340] 'knock, dash' today is the sound of a small bell in contrast to *dong* [1587] 'to sound as a large bell'.

There are also expressions of motion and (in)stability which got assimilated to the apophonic pattern as examples of cross-modal iconicity: *totter* [*c*.1200], *titter* [*a*.1618], *teeter* [1843]; *didder* [*c*.1420], *dadder* [1483], *dodder* [*c*.1600].

10.4 Stretch

"Speech communities have various ways of realizing emphasis, emotion, hypocoristics, chants, song, etc. Lengthening, repetition, and reorganization are obvious strategies" (Alan Bell, p.c.). Lengthening is the one focused on in this section, specifically the variety labeled STRETCH by Bell (1975). Several kinds of stretch occur in English as "more or less codified expressive variants" (Alan Bell, p.c.). It is included as a potential type of synesthesia because, as in the case of reduplication, length of the word(s) relates to the meaning expressed: a stretched sound (sequence) is associated with intensity.

Alternations between -*oing* and -*wang* represent various degrees of "resonance, vibration, oscillation, undulation, pulsation, elasticity, recoil, spring, bounce"

---

[5] Formally, the examples in (3) are not so different from *sing–sang–sung–song*, which raises the question of what makes the words in (3) expressive. One thing is the link to an extralinguistic as opposed to a grammatical referent. Another factor is the use of a standard derivational mechanism for a nonstandard purpose. For similar examples in Vulgar Latin and Romance, see Carnoy (1917).

(Ostwalt 1994: 304): *boing–boioioing–bawáng–bwang; toing–tawáng–twang; bloing–blang; doing; sproing*.

Another kind of stretch is illustrated by *strike* in the lingo of baseball umpires: *steeeee-riiiiiike*. Of interest is both the fact that the vowel *i* is stretched and also that the word is resyllabified. The stretched form has two syllables of great duration, as if the word were actually disyllabic (*)*sterike*. Of the two processes at issue, stretch and resyllabification, the former is more variable. I once heard an imitator stretch the /r/, viz. *stərrrr-riiiiiike*. In both cases, the word is assigned two syllables, divided at the same point (between /t/ and /r/), but stretch behaves differently. In the second syllable, the nucleus is stretched, in the first, the sonorous coda.

Interjections like *yikes* are often articulated as *eeee-yiiikes*, *shit* as *sheeeee-iit*, *Christ* as *kərr-riiiiiist/keee-riiiiiist*, or *splash* as *spəəəə-laaaaash*.

Another well-known example occurs in song, where a syllable can be stretched over any number of beats. An example is the four-syllable *hallelujah*, which in one well-known song is stretched over ten notes and twelve beats: *ha-a-a-a-āl-le-e-lū-u-jah*.

Bell (1975) tested what happens to short sentences 2 to 3 seconds in duration when speakers stretch them out to progressively longer durations—0.6 seconds, 0.9 seconds, 1.2 seconds, etc., up to four times the 'normal' duration. Not all speakers stretched syllable nuclei. One stretched *this rule's* into [ði-ʂ-ru-]-ʐ], in effect five syllables with three syllabic consonants. This differs from what speakers of English normally do in expressive speech. According to Alan Bell (p.c.), his experimental conditions were designed to focus attention away from the usual English variants and the speech situations for which they are appropriate.

Speakers of English frequently stretch monosyllabic words or the stressed syllable(s) of a polysyllabic as a discourse emphatic, e.g. *very easy* → *vaaaar-ry eeeeee-zy*, *unbelievable* → *uuunn-be-leeeeeee-va-ble*. For 'excellent, super-good', one frequently hears either *goooood* or disyllabic *goooo-ooood*, the former often in *sooooo gooood* (well attested on Google). The main reason for thinking in terms of codification is that /ay/ is resyllabified as *iiii-aaay*, /ɪ/ as *iiii-ɪɪɪ*, /æ/ as *əəəə-æææ*, etc., where other combinations would be at least as plausible phonetically. Moreover, the idiosyncratic variants produced by some individuals confirm the conventionalization of certain patterns. So long as stretch remains a discourse emphatic, it is unlikely to be used as a lexicogenic process to coin new words, although two examples are increasing in frequency. One is the quasi-superlative *gooo(-)ooood*, the other is *bææææd* 'really good', an antonym of *bad* with a non-stretched vowel. Within the speech communities where these forms prevail, they constitute neologisms (cf. §§8.11, 15.3).

10.5 Movable *s-*/*s*-mobile

Lexicogenic *s-* is synesthetic in that a sound is associated with intensity. It can be applied if word structure is not violated. It attaches to some sonorants, e.g. *lather* [c.950] : *slather* [1866], *melt* [OE] : *smelt* [1543], *mush* [1781] : *smush* [1825], *nick* [?1440] : *snick* [c.1700] 'cut', *pernickety* [1808] : *persnickety* [1892], but not to fricatives (**sflutter*, **sthrash*). Initial stops must agree in voicelessness (cf. Raffelsiefen 1999: 257f.). See (4).

(4) | *cratch* | [c.1320] | : | *scratch* | [1474] | but | *gash* | [1548] | : | **sgash* |
     | *plunge* | [c.1380] | : | *splunge* | [1839] | but | *bash* | [a.1642] | : | **sbash* |
     | *tramp* | [a.1425] | : | *stramp* | [c.1423] | but | *dash* | [c.1290] | : | **sdash* |
     | *trample* | [a.1382] | : | *strample* | [a.1610] | | | | | |
     | *quench* | [OE] | : | *squench* | [1535] | | | | | |

The *s-* can be traced to degemination in Indo-European phrasal syntax. Its subsequent expressivity can be related to onset salience and its instability in this position in language acquisition (Southern 1992: 177f.; 1999: 175ff., 262–78). Additional doublets arose in English by blending (§2.2), e.g. *smash* [1699] (beside *mash* [c.1275]) if from *smite/smack* × *mash*; and possibly *scrunch* [1825] (beside *crunch* [1801]) if from *squeeze* × *crunch* (cf. Southern 1992: 175; 1999: 170). Note also *cranch* [1632]/*scranch* [1658] and *craunch* [1726]/*scraunch* [1620], all variants of *(s)crunch*. Other such pairs are *creak* [c.1325]/*screak* [?a.1500], *crumple* [?c.1450]/*scrumple* [c.1575], etc.

The process is shared with other Germanic languages, e.g. Germ. *strampeln* 'kick' beside *trampeln* 'trample'; *trudeln* 'roll' : *strudeln* 'whirl'; *prasseln* 'crackle; clatter' : *sprasseln* 'spray; splash' (Southern 1999: ch. 4). Such pairs, which arose after Grimm's Law (see Appendix II, p. 251), are paralleled by cross-dialectal doublets antedating Grimm's Law, e.g. *throat* vs. Du. *strot* (**(s)treud-*). Unlike English, German has alternations like *dumm* 'stupid' : *stumm* 'mute' (Southern 1999: 229). These are unproductive and lexicalized. In Germanic overall, *s*-mobile is well entrenched. Southern records over 200 doublets.[6] This former productivity is shared with Germanic's Baltic neighbor; cf. Lith. *mùkti* 'escape; slip away' : *smùkti* 'slide away' (Southern 1999: ch. 5).

To conclude this section, intensive *s-* has at least two sources: (i) inherited, (ii) blends. Unfortunately, it is not easy to untangle the two because the second reinforced the first quite early in the history of English.

10.6 Prefixation of *ka-/ker-*

Another type of synesthesia involves the sound sequence *ka-/ker-* which is associated with intensity. At least American English has this intensive formation, which the *OED* online labels as "U.S. vulgar". The "meaning [is] (approximately) 'extra loud and/or acoustically complex'" (Rhodes 1994: 290).

---

[6] Cohen (2002) adds two more doublets: *hop* (Gmc. **hupp-* < **kup-*) beside *skip* (WGmc. **s-kup-*) and *mole* (**mōl-*) beside *small* (**smal-* < **smə₁l-o-* [**(s)meh₁l-o-* 'small animal']).

(5) ka-/ker-prefixation
   (a) *pow*   *ka-pow*   (b) *splash*   *ker-splash*
       bang   *ka-bang*   *smack*   *ker-smack*
       thump *ka-thump*   *plop*   *ker-plop*

Early attestations of *ka-* include *chewallop* [1836] (= *co-wallop* [1844]), *ca-smash* [1844], *ke-souse* [1850], *ca-blam* [1924]. Apart from *ker-woosh* [1908], *ker-* (rarely *ka-*) frequently enters into vowel and consonant gradation patterns in (6).

(6) Prefixed intensive gradation
   kerslash [1843]   *kerslosh* [1843]   *co-slush* [1854]
   ker-slap [1858]   *ker-slam* [1899]   *ker-blam* [1884]
   ker-splash [1897]   *ker-splosh* [1935]
   ker-plunk [1903]   *ker-plonked* [1963]
   ker-flip ker-flop [1939]

Especially interesting is the reduplicated type *ker-blam-er-lam-er-lam* [1942], in which each repetition of *ker-* and *blam-* deletes the first or only onset consonant. As to currency, a made-up *kerbonk* was checked on Google where many uses are found. In the *Urban Dictionary*, *kerplonk* is glossed "A plonker whose actions are especially idiotic, eliciting surprise from any witnesses to their actions." This implies that *ker-* is beginning to be used as an ordinary lexicogenic prefix with some loss of expressivity (cf. §15.3).

10.7 Phonesthesia

Phonesthesia "is the analogical association of certain phonemes and clusters with certain meanings" (Hinton, Nichols, and Ohala 1994b: 5).[7] These "submorphemic meaning-carrying entities are sometimes called phonesthemes" (p. 5) but represent a type of lexical/morphological (De Cuypere 2008: 110) or multilevel (Smith 2012a) iconicity.

Many of the examples in this section are known at least since John Wallis [1616–1703]. His section on Etymology (e.g. 1653: 40–57; 1765: 143–64) contains a subsection on *Derivata remotiora* 'more remote derivatives' in which Wallis treats these analogical interrelations.[8] The most extensive modern discussions are in Magnus (1999; 2001).

---

[7] *Phonesthesia* [1950] (but *phonaestheme* first occurs in an article by Firth in 1930) is an English creation from *phone* (G *phōnḗ* 'sound; voice') plus *(a)esthesia*; cf. G *aisthēsíē/aísthēsis/-aisthēsíā* 'sense perception; impression of sense'.

[8] *Praeter ea quae analogice formata diximus vocabula, sunt et apud nos (ut in aliis linguis) copiosae vocum affinium seu cognatarum familiae, ab eodem quasi communi themate varie flexae* (Wallis 1653: 45; 1765: 143) 'beyond those which we have called analogically formed words, there are also among us (as in

In the meaning of 'intoxicated', a number of low-register words (DYSPHEMISMS) begin with /s/: *stewed* [1737], *slewed* [1801], *swizzled* [1843], *sozzled* [1886], *sotted* [1898?], *soused* [a.1625?; 1902], *sloshed* [1946], *schnockered* [1955], *snockered* [1961], *smashed* [1962], *slammed* [n.d.], *slashed* [n.d.], *sauced* [n.d.] (cf. §7.3 and Hughes 1988: 20).

Sn- is associated with the nose: *snite* [a.1100] 'wipe the nose', *snout* [c.1220], *snivel* [c.1325], *snore* [c.1330], *sniff* [c.1340], *snort* [a.1366], *snot* [c.1425], *sneeze* [1493], *snuff* [1527], *sneer* [1553], *snuffle* [1583], *snarl* [1590], *snicker* [1694], *snigger* [1706], *snooze* [1789], *snook* [1791], *sniggle* [1815], *sniffle* [1819], *snub* [1830] 'snub nose', *snoot* [1861], etc. (Wallis 1653: 46; 1765: 146; Tournier 1985: 140; Joseph 1987: 2; Bergen 2004: 293). *Snarf* [1958] (created after *scarf* [1960] 'devour') according to *American Speech* 38: 176 (1963) means 'the act of eating like an animal' (*OED* online).

Sn- is also used for personal derogation (Wallis 1765: 146f.; Käsmann 1992: 339): *snub* [a.1340], *snudge* [1545], *snidge* [1548], *snake* [1590], *snipe* [a.1616], *snig* [1629], *sneak* [a.1643], *snitch* [1785], *snot* [1607 as a name; 1809], *snob* [1848].

In general, /s/ plus a nasal has several associations (Wallis 1653: 49; 1765: 158), e.g. parting of lips in kissing: *smick smack* [?1550], *smack* [1570], *smick* [1572], *smacker* [1611], *smooch* [1932], etc. (Coleman 1997: 6). Words containing /š/ or /č/ can be suggestive of lip smacking: *delicious* [c.1300], *voluptuous* [Ch.], *luscious* [c.1420], *salacious* [1661], *voracious* [1693], *scrumptious* [1894]; cf. *ravish* [1300], *relish* [1566].

Some insulting neologisms end in /b/: *shab* [1637] 'low fellow', *grub* [1653] 'slovenly person', *bub* [1839], *slob* [1861], *rube* [1891] 'yokel or rustic simpleton', *boob* [1909], *zob* [1911] 'worthless person', *feeb* [1914] 'feeble-minded individual', *blob* [1916], *droob* [1933] 'dull person', *schlub/zhlub* [1964] 'dull, unpolished person; jerk; oaf', *dweeb* [1968] 'meganerd', *gweeb* [n.d.] 'stupid, dull person', *goob* [2004] 'stupid, unsophisticated person', etc. (Danchev 1995a: 136f.; Lawler 2006).

Many words beginning with a fricative or glide and ending with a stop mean 'defeat decisively' (by pummeling): *swack* [c.1425], *whap* [c.1440], *whop* [c.1440], *thwack* [1533], *thump* [c.1537], *thwick-thwack* [1575], *whack* [1719], *whump* [1897], *whomp* [1952], *thwock* [n.d.], etc. (cf. Ostwalt 1994: 303).

Sexual violence is associated especially with words beginning with a labial, ending in a velar and containing a low/back vowel: *buck* [1530], *bag* [1600 (passive)], *poke* [1602], *pump* [1730], *bang* [1937], *prong* [1942], *pork* [1968], *bonk* [1975], *boink* [1986], *block* [n.d.], *peg* [n.d.], *pluck* [n.d.], *bone* [n.d.], *pound* [n.d.], *prick* [n.d.] (Ostwalt 1994: 305; Coleman 1997: 7). The words marked 'no date' represent meanings not recognized by the *OED*, most of which are known to nearly any (at least) American male. These are perhaps an extension of the *p-/b-*words that refer to "paths with respect to one end-point" (Rhodes 1994: 292 n.12), but in §7.3 it is suggested that some of these are substitutions for *fuck*. As often with lexicogenic processes, the boundary

---

other languages) copious families of closely related forms or cognates, variously modified by the same, as it were, common thematic element' [translation my own—D.G.M.].

between them is not clearly delineated. Most likely, some of these are tabu substitutions of *fuck* by means of words that metaphorically represent similar actions, shapes, insertion of a pointed object, etc.

In the psycholinguistic study of Markel and Hamp (1960–61), *fl-* was assigned a preferred cultural connotation of 'quite dirty'. But *fl-* can also signal (a) light and fire: *flint* [EOE], *flame* [1377], *flash* [c.1540], *flare* [1633], *flicker* [1608], *fluorescence* [1852], *flimmer* [1880]; (b) non-terrestrial motion: *flutter, flap, fly, flit, flitter, float, flow, flush, flurry, fluid* (Liberman 1990; Shisler 1997). Smith (2013) discusses the recent literature and documents the entire history of *fl-*, which has been most associated with the semantic features of (i) move through air (*flicker* originally meant 'flutter, move the wings' [c.1000], (ii) move through liquid (*flush, float*), (iii) sudden violent (*flit, flick*), (iv) fail struggle confuse (*flop, floonder*), (v) strike blow throw (*flog, flail*).

Similarly, *sl-* has several mental associations (Wallis 1653: 49; Käsmann 1992: 328–36): (a) fluid (to some extent unintentional) motion: *slide* [OE *slīdan*], *slidder* [OE], *slither* [c.1200], *slick* [a.1225], *slip* [a.1340], *slive* [a.1425], *sleek* [c.1440], *slike* [c.1400], *slather* [1809] (cf. Shisler 1997); (b) messy liquid (cf. Rhodes 1994: 287; Durkin 2011: 128f.): *slime* [OE *slīm*], *sleet* [c.1300], *slaver* [c.1325], *slotter* [c.1340], *slobber* [c.1400], *slike* [c.1425] 'slime', *slitch* [1425], *slag* [c.1440], *slubber* [1530], *slabber* [1573], *sleech* [1587] 'mud', *slush* [a.1642], *sludge* [1649], *slew* [1708], *slosh* [1808], *slather* [1809]; (c) (act) improper (lazy, slovenly, sluttish, deceitful, etc.): OE *slāw* 'obtuse; SLOW', *slǣwþ* 'sloth; SLEUTH', *slæc* 'lazy, idle, SLACK'; *sloth* [c.1175], *sly* [a.1200], *slick* [a.1225], *slut* [1402], *slug* [c.1425], *sloven* [c.1450], *slouch* [?1518], *slattern* [1639], *slink* [1792], *sloppy* [1825], *slob* [1861], *slop* [1866], *slick* [1921], *sleazy* [1941]; and (d) violence: *slay* [OE], *sling* [a.1225], *slit* [c.1275], *slaughter* [a.1300], *slash* [1382], *slap* [1632], *slam* [1691]. Some words, of course, belong in several categories.

The sequences /sl/ and /fl/ can be associated with prostitution and promiscuity: *slut* [1402], *slattern* [1639], *slag* [1958], *slagger* [n.d.], *slapper* [1988], *sloop* [n.d.], *slock* [n.d.]; *flagger, fleecer, fling, flit, flop, flounce, floozie, flutter,* etc. (Coleman 1997: 7), of which only *floozie* [1911] appears in the OED in the relevant sense.

Abelin (1999) has collected the various associations of many Swedish clusters, one being *sl-* (p. 118f.): pejorative (*slampa* 'slut'), wetness (*slipprig* 'slippery'), long, thin form (*slank* 'slender'), slackness (*sla(c)k* 'slack'), degrees of movement (*slinka, slinta* 'slip', *slutta* 'slant', *släntra* 'saunter'), talking (*sladdra* 'chatter', *slidder* 'gossip'), beating (*slag* 'slug, stroke'), smooth surface (*slipa* 'polish').

Words ending in *-ash* represent (a) 'bodily harm' (Marchand 1969: 420) or 'violent impact' (Wallis 1653: 49; 1688: 137; 1765: 160; Tournier 1985: 148; Lawler 2006): *quash* [c.1275], *dash* [c.1290], *lash* [c.1330], *slash* [1382], *crash* [?a.1400], *gnash* [1496], *clash* [?1518], *gash* [1548], *squash* [1565], *bash* [a.1642], *smash* [1725], etc.; (b) 'ostentation': *dash* [1715], *flash* [1785], *splash* [1804], *panache* [1898]; (c) 'haphazard': *slapdash* [1680], *hash* [1733], *dash* [1809], *trash* [n.d.] (Lord 1996: 243f.).

Anderson (1998: 128) discusses words in -*izzle* that "connote the sound of liquid on a surface": *pizzle* [1486] 'animal penis', *mizzle* [1490] 'fine misty rain', *drizzle* [1543], *sizzle* [1603], *swizzle* [1813], *frizzle* [1839] 'sputter while frying', *fizzle* [1859] 'sputter'.

Similarly, -*am* is mentally linked to several different semantic features: (a) 'crowd': *cram* [c.1000], *jam* [1706], *gam* [1850], etc.; (b) 'block, stop up': *cram* [c.1000?], *clam* [1399], *dam* [1553], *clamp* [1678], *jam* [1805]; (c) 'foodstuff': *clam* [1508], *cram* [1614], *lamb* [1620], *ham* [1650], *gram* [1702], *jam* [1736] (Lord 1996: 293ff.; Lawler 2006).

Advertisers use the subliminal effects of sound associations. They avoid vowels with negative associations, like the *u* of *ugh*, *yuck*; back vowel sounds are preferred for smooth and rich (e.g. *ice cream*), front vowels for cold, clean, crisp items; and so on. Pleasing, exotic-sounding sequences are used in made-up names like *Exxon*, *Lexus*, *Kodak* (Lowrey and Shrum 2007). Szabóné Habók (2009: 45f.) cites *Prozac*, *Zoloft*, *Viagra* (rhymes with *Niagara*), and Russ. *zima* 'winter' used for a brand of vodka.

The psychological salience of phonesthetic sequences is clear (Joseph 1987: 5; Bergen 2004), even if their linguistic status is unclear (Hopper 1990: 157; Bottineau 2008; Argout 2010). Some are blends, but "show radiation beyond their original spheres of acoustic, optic, and kinetic expression" (Meier 1989: 61).

10.8 Initial *gl*- in Germanic and English

English has many *gl*- words for 'shine' (cf. Bolinger 1950; 1992; Pharies 1986) and other meanings (Sadowsky 2001; Bergen 2004), analogous to the semantic fields of *gl*- in Swedish (Abelin 1999: 134ff.) and Norwegian (Magnus 2001: 38–44). Most important are (i) (INDIRECT) LIGHT / BRIGHTNESS / TRANSPARENCY, (ii) LOOKING, (iii) SWIFTNESS, (iv) JOY, (v) SMOOTHNESS. The major expansions of this phonestheme are traced in Table 10.1. The first column is the semantic field ((i) = LIGHT, etc.), the second column is the English word, the third column Old English. The fourth column is the Old Norse cognate or some other Germanic (or other) equivalent, and the fifth column is a Germanic reconstruction (most are West Germanic), following Orel (2003: 135ff.), with **g* for his **ʒ*. Glosses are provided only for forms that do not mean the same as the English word.

The fifth semantic field, SMOOTHNESS or REFLECTING SURFACE (Magnus 2001: 38), expanded more recently and independently in the various Germanic languages; cf. *glossy* [1556], *glib* [1594] 'smooth and slippery' (cf. *glibbery* [1601] 'shifty', Du. *glibberig* 'id.'), *glabrous* [1640] (L *glaber* 'hairless'), *glacé* [1847] (F *glacé* 'iced, glossed'), etc.

In the semantic field of NOISE, Eng. *glam* [a.1400] 'noise' was borrowed from Old Nordic *glam(m)* 'noise, din'. An inherited word OE *glēam* 'joyous noise', cognate with OIce *glaumr* 'merry noise' (Gmc. **glaumaz*), probably vanished because of competition with *gleam* in the more productive LIGHT/BRIGHTNESS field.

Most of the words in Table 10.1 derive from the IE root **ǵhel-* 'bright-colored (yellow); shine'. The most productive of the semantic fields in West Germanic (and

168   English Lexicogenesis

TABLE 10.1 Expansion of the *gl-* phonestheme

	English	OE	ON (unspecified)	Germanic
(i)	†*glad* 'bright, shining'	*glæd* 'shining'	*glaðr* 'bright'	**glaðaz*
	glass	*glæs*	*gler*	**glas/zan*
	gleam	*glǣm* 'bright light'	cf. OS *glîmo* 'brightness'	**glaimiz*
	gleed 'red hot embers'	*glǣd*	*glóð*	**glōðiz*
	glise 'glitter, shine'	*glisian*	MLG *glisen* 'shine'	**glisōjan-*
	glisten	*glisnian* [*c*.1000]		
	glow	*glōwan* [*c*.1000]	*glóa*	**glō(w)an-*
	gloaming 'twilight'	*glōmung* [*c*.1000]		**glōm-*
	glare [*c*.1250]		MLG *glaren* 'gleam'	[< **glaz-*]
	glore [*c*.1300] 'shine, glitter'		Ice. *glóra* 'gleam'	[< **glō(w)-*]
	glaze [*c*.1369]	(see §12.2)		
	glister [*c*.1380] 'sparkle, glitter'		MLG *glisteren*	[< **glis+t+r-*]
	glitter [*a*.1400]		*glitra*	**glit(a)rōjan-*
	glimmer [*c*.1400]		Sw. *glimma* 'shine'	**glimmōjan-*
	glim [*c*.1400] 'brightness'	[< *gleam, glimmer*]		
	glimpse [*c*.1400] 'glimmer'		MHG *glimsen*	**glimmisōjan-*
	gloom [*c*.1420] 'glow'	[cf. *glōm-*]		
	glint [*c*.1440] 'shine, flash'	[cf. *glent*]		
	gloss [1538]		MDu. †*gloos*	[cf. **glas/z-*]
	gloze [1820] 'shine brightly'	[cf. *gloss*]	'a gleaming'	
	glitzy [1966]		cf. OHG *glīzan* 'shine'	**glītan-*
(ii)	*gleg* [1325] 'clear-sighted'	(*glēaw* †GLEW)	*glǫgg-r* 'clear-sighted'	**glawwaz*
	glee/y [1325] 'look asquint'		[etym. obscure]	
	gloom [1380] 'look sullen'		MDu. *gloom* 'foggy'	
	glimpse [*c*.1386] 'look quickly'		MHG *glimsen*	**glimmisōjan-*
	glent [1390] 'glance'		Norw. *gletta* 'look'	**glentēn-*
	glore [?*a*.1400] 'gaze intently'		Ice. *glóra* 'glare, stare'	**glōrōjan-*
	glum [1460] = *gloom* (above)	[< *gloom*]		
	glim [*c*.1620] 'glimpse'	[cf. *glim* above]		
	glower [1535]	[cf. *glow, glore*]		
	glaik [*c*.1560] 'gaze idly'		[etym. obscure]	
	glance [1570]		[etym. obscure]	
	gloat [1575]		*glotta* 'smile scornfully'	
(iii)	*glide*	*glīdan*	MSw. *gliidha*	**glīðan-*
	glent [*c*.1330] 'move quickly'		Sw. dial. *glänta* 'slide'	**glentēn-*
	glace [*a*.1400] 'glance, glide'		[OF *glacer* 'glide, slip']	
	glint [*c*.1440] 'move quickly'	[a variant of *glent*]		
(iv)	*glad*	*glæd* 'cheerful'	*glaðr*	**glaðaz*
	glee	*glīu* 'play, sport'	*glý* 'joy, gladness'	**glīwan*

to some extent Proto-Germanic) was LIGHT/BRIGHTNESS/TRANSPARENCY. Cognates in Slavic are cited by Magnus (2001: 41). Even in that field, only about a third of the entries have a clear Germanic heritage. The expansions from Early Middle English onward are either derived from earlier words (*glisnian* GLISTEN is a morphological replacement of *glisian* GLISE: Miller 2010: 2.110) or are borrowings, mostly from Scandinavian, e.g. *glitter* (cf. OIce *glitra*); with *glore* [*c*.1300] 'shine, glitter', [?*a*.1400] 'gaze intently' cf. Swedish dialectal *glora* 'glow, stare' and Ice. *glóra* 'gleam, glare' (not attested in Old Icelandic). *Glent* is Nordic; cf. Swedish dial. *glänta, glätta* 'slip, slide; shine, gleam'. *Glister* diffused from Middle Low German or Dutch *glisteren*. *Gloss* [1538] corresponds to obsolete Dutch *gloos* 'a glowing, gleaming', but note Ice. *glossi* 'a blaze', etc. One of the most recent words, *glitzy*, probably entered English via Yiddish.

In the semantic field of LOOKING, likewise, about a third of the words are inherited from Germanic. The rest are borrowings (e.g. *gleg, glent, glore, gloat*), derivatives, or of unknown origin.

The sections on phonesthesia support Magnus's main principle of phonosemantic association: "When semantic domain S is associated disproportionately frequently with phoneme X, then people will be inclined to associate semantic domain S with phoneme X productively" (Magnus 2001: 34).

To summarize, this discussion by no means exhausts the semantic fields of *gl-*, but the diachronic trajectory indicates a spread both within several specific semantic fields and from one semantic field to others. The spread was from (indirect) light and bright to other psychologically bright states of joy and glee, and their setting, the festivals that yielded *glutton* [1200] and *glut* [*c*.1315] (both from French), hence also a generalization from the noise arising from merriment to noise more generally. Another implication of light and bright was transparent, hence glossy, glassy, and other smooth or reflective surfaces. Smooth surfaces can be slick, hence the notions of sliding and gliding. And so on.

10.9 Sound and meaning in poetry

Poetry inherently involves the structuring of sound (Perloff and Dworkin 2009b). Poets have always been attuned to the interplay of sound and meaning. The introduction of Nestor in the *Iliad* contains an instructive example of iconicity between phonetic and semantic structure:

hēduepès	*anórouse*	*ligùs*	*Pulíōn*	*agorētḗs*	
sweet-speaking	leaped up	clear-toned	Pylian.GEN.PL	assembly-convenor	
toū kaì apò	*glṓssēs*	*mélitos*	*glukíōn rhéen*	*audḗ*	(*Iliad* 1.248f.)
his and from	tongue	honey.GEN	sweeter flowed	speech	

'sweet-speaking (Nestor) leaped up, the Pylians' clear-toned assembly-convenor even from whose tongue speech flowed sweeter than honey'

The iconicity of the high number of light-tripping liquids (/l/ and /r/) to the meaning of these lines has been known since antiquity. In Plato's *Cratylus*, there is a dialogue between Socrates and Cratylus (433d1–435d1) in which Socrates asks whether /r/ expresses rapidity, motion,[9] and hardness, and /l/ smoothness and softness. Cratylus agrees that they do. Socrates presses the issue, interjecting dialectal derivatives of *sklērós* 'hard' and asserting that, despite both soft /l/ and hard /r/, the word indicates hardness.[10]

In his rendition of *Il.* 1.249, Cicero (*Cato Minor* 10.31) imitated Homer:

ex	eius	linguā	me_ll_e		dulcior	fluēbat	ōrātiō
from	his	tongue	honey.ABL		sweeter	flowed	Speech

'from whose tongue speech flowed sweeter than honey'

In Cicero's version, as in Homer's line, a series of words containing /l/ are followed by a word with /r/, the last containing a dental stop (*t/d*). Even the voiced dental has high second formant frequency compared to voiced velar and labial stops. Generally speaking, high-frequency segments outnumber lower-frequency segments in this line. Despite the scepticism of Waldrop (2009), who argues that the sound in poetry cannot be translated because the sound/sense interconnection differs from one language to another, Cicero in fact captured the essence of Homer's sound/sense.

Sapir (1921: 160) comments that a poet composing a rapid line would use lightly tripping syllables with liquids rather than words like *dreamed, hummed, buzz* which yield a clumsy retardation. In the words of Alexander Pope [1688–1744], "the sound must seem an echo to the sense" (2006: 'Essay' 29). For Grammont (1933: 408), /l/ can give the impression of gliding, flowing, fluency, softness. For Magnus (e.g. 1998), /l/ can denote flight/flying, sliding, leaking, speech, calming, but also some unrelated meanings.

Miall (2001) argues that sounds have no "fixed quality that can be translated into literary meaning" (p. 69) but that phoneme distributions contextually embody contrasts of meaning (cf. Tsur 2006), as in the positive effect of the liquids in Coleridge's "Frost at Midnight", line 35: *Lulled me to sleep, and sleep prolonged my dreams* (Miall 2001: 66). Galt (1973: 91) similarly reports on the positive effects of /l/ in

---

[9] Compare the NON-VEHICULAR MOTION (with a human agent and no source or path) of Magnus (2001: 56, 115, 117, 123): *race, raid, range, reach, rip, roam, romp, rove, run, rush*; source or path is implied after an obstruent and *tr-* suggests an implicit goal: *break, crawl, creep, cross, cruise, drag, drift, drop(by), frisk, prance, press, prowl, thread, trace, track, trail, tramp, tread, trek, tromp, troop, trot, trudge*.

[10] Commentators do not agree on the meaning of the passage because Socrates, after arguing the naturalist position that names of entities are based on imitation, appears to contradict himself in concluding that convention is more important. In fact, all he says is that convention must contribute *something* because, even if mimesis is an ideal, names and numerals can never be perfect icons of their referent or they would be infinite (Crema 2010). Convention is necessary for understanding all words including those that are iconically motivated (cf. Genette 1976: 36; Magnus 2001: 12f.). The *Cratylus* was probably written in the middle of Plato's career and slightly revised later in his life (Sedley 2003).

love poems and in tender and musical poems but different effects elsewhere (cf. Perloff and Dworkin 2009b).

Poets make extensive use of onomatopoeia and the various kinds of sound symbolism and auditory imagery discussed throughout this chapter in conjunction with alliteration, rhyme, meter, and other devices. Consider, for instance, Shakespeare's *a tale told by an idiot, full of sound and fury, signifying nothing* (*Macbeth* V. v.25–7). The staccato of the dentals and the alternating strident fricatives suggest a certain shrillness that accompanies the vacuity of the discourse under discussion. This can be subsumed under INDIRECT SUPPORT OF THE ARGUMENT BY RELATED ECHOES (Holcombe 2007–12).

The sounds can serve as "musical" background for the message conveyed, or echo the action or imagery of a poetic line. For the interaction of sound, meaning, and feeling, Holcombe cites *The way the shy stars go stuttering on... Slurs its soft wax, flatters* (Carol Ann Duffy, *The Grammar of Light*). Holcombe documents (w. lit) some fifty samples of the uses of sounds in English poetry. To this, one can add the expressive effects of binomials like *pitter patter* (Chapter 14), blends like *snark* (Chapter 12), and so on.

In summary, it is true that segments have no inherent meaning, but poets exploit the acoustic effects that issue from the occlusivity of voiceless stops, the flow of liquids, the soft, appeasing perception of nasals (Tsur 2006: 914), the retardation of clustering nasals and voiced obstruents, and the stridency of certain fricatives.[11]

10.10 Summary

There can be no doubt that sound symbolism is a reality. Many experiments are discussed by Brown (1958), Allott (1995), Magnus (2001), Szabóné Habók (2009), Ahlner and Zlatev (2010), and Körtvélyessy (2011a). The findings are essentially that sound symbolism is unequivocal within languages, and that there is limited carryover to non-cognate languages. Ultan (1978) argued that it can be areal (cf. Körtvélyessy 2011a: 141, w. lit). Some properties are general but not universal. Tone languages have been claimed to be exceptions in that sound symbolism may be based on different principles, but Lao in (1) above is a tone language, and its synesthesia is quite canonical. Chinese is often mentioned in this connection, but that myth should have been dispelled by Chan (1996), who documents a rich array of sound symbolic phenomena in Mandarin and other dialects.

---

[11] Tangentially, it is of some interest that female names contain significantly more glides, liquids, nasals, and front vowels than male names, which contain more voiced fricatives, aspirates, and medium back vowels (Miall 2001: 63, w. lit).

Five different but interacting parameters have been established:

(1) The frequency code, or association of small size with high frequency and of large size with low frequency (cf. Körtvélyessy 2011a: 141, w. lit). In visual terms, there is an iconic relation between the size of the object and the size of the resonance chamber.
(2) Generalization of the frequency code to links between high frequency and light color, light weight, swiftness, proximality, etc., and between low frequency and round, heavy forms, dark color, heavy weight, distality, etc.
(3) Inherent properties of segments, such as the occlusivity of voiceless stops, the flow of liquids, the soft, mellow, appeasing perception of nasals, the retardation of clustering nasals and voiced consonants, and the stridency of certain fricatives.
(4) Perception of sounds in nature and the environment, which is conditioned partly by culture, partly by acoustic properties (the frequency code), and partly by our sensory cortical areas.
(5) The role of analogy in the creation of words similar to other words because of the perceptual effect, the result being classes of words with the same conventionalized iconic link(s) between sound/form and meaning.

At least some types of synesthetic sound symbolism seem to be a special type of derivational morphology (Rhodes 1994; cf. Waugh 2000). They differ in their link to an extralinguistic as opposed to a grammatical referent and use of a derivational mechanism for extragrammatical purposes. Perhaps more to the point, derivational alternations are part of a more generalized apophony (§14.4) which must, itself, be due to the same acoustic properties of high-frequency vowels before low that play a role in sound symbolism.

Most forms of sound symbolism (phonesthesia etc.) are independent of the grammar in the sense that they can affect any part of the word or its constituent morphemes. Moreover, since core morphological operations and expressive processes affect sound symbolic words no differently than they affect ordinary words, there is no evidence for any separate treatment in the lexicon (§15.2).

In conclusion, de Saussure's principle that the sign is arbitrary holds to the extent that it is not contravened by formations of varying degrees of motivation. Even among words with one or more kinds of sound symbolic motivation, only a portion is actually motivated (in varying degrees) and the rest is arbitrary. In other words, convention is necessary to interpret even the parts of words that are motivated. It has also been argued that most of the so-called motivated forms are in reality conventionalized.

11

Clipping

Clipping derives new words by truncating a portion of a word. This type of truncation excises far more contentful material in playful than in core morphology (§15.1). Whether a word is clipped on the left or right edge (the most frequent type) is argued to depend on the stress pattern, the length of the word, and its status as a common or proper noun. Long forms (especially first names) with non-initial stress favor clipping on the left. The relative predictability of first names enables more drastic clipping that would eradicate too much informational content in ordinary words. English is relatively anomalous in preferring monosyllabic clips. The more usual output is a binary trochaic foot. Truncation draws attention to the form, and monosyllabics are high in expressivity, as evidenced by 'four-letter' words. Hypocoristics and clipped female names are often disyllabic, which softens the rhetorical impact. Clips can become institutionalized and replace their source word(s).

11.1 Clipping as a process

Clipping is an expressive shortening of words by truncation of some part, most frequently at the right edge, as determined by stress and output prosodic factors. Apart from occasional semantic differentiation, and with names a register difference, the clipped word substantially remains the same as its base. In any event, the syntactic category (noun, etc.) is never altered.[1]

Clipping can eliminate the right edge of the word (*lab*[*oratory*] [1895]), the left edge ([*air*]*plane* [1908]), or both (*fridge* [1926] for *refrigerator*). Compounds and fixed phrases can also be clipped, e.g. *zoo*[*logical garden*] [c.1847]. Ultimately, the retained portion of the truncated word and its structure are more significant than the means by which the clip is produced. In terms of prosodic morphology (§9.2), varying degrees of prosodic optimality should predict the output form, but it is not that simple and the descriptive operations remain a useful starting point.

---

[1] Many examples of clips and analyses can be found in Sundén (1904), Marchand (1969: 441–50), Koziol (1972: 302–8), Kreidler (1979), Tournier (1985: 297–308), Ronneberger-Sibold (1995), Hamans (1997), Fischer (1998: 39–43), Davy (2000), Lappe (2003; 2007), Mattiello (2008: §3.2), Berg (2011).

Clipping has many functions, one of which is euphemism (§7.3). With the dawn of the high-tech era, the main function is economy.

11.2 Right-edge English clips

The most frequent English type is the monosyllabic remaining from a right-edge clip: *butt* [c.1450] (*buttock* [a.1300]), *coz* [1563] (*cousin* [c.1290]), *con*[*tra*] [1572], *chap* [1577] (*chapman* [OE]), *fizz* [1665] (*fizzle* [?1533]), *miss*[*tress*] [1606], *bro*[*ther*] [c.1660], *fan*[*atic*] [1682], *sub*[*ordinate*] [1696], *rep*[*utation*] [a.1705], *gin* [1723] (< *gen*[*eva*] §6.5), *brig*[*antine*] [1720], *mag*[*azine*] [1742], *bod*[*y*] [1788], *ad*[*vertisement*] [1799], *spec(k)*[*tacle*]*s* [1807], *pant*[*aloon*]*s* [1835], *prof*[*essor*] [1838], *prep*[*aratory*] [1839], *vet*[*eran*] [1848], *doc*[*tor*] [?1850], *mod*[*ulo*] [1854], *pro*[*fessional*] [1856], *biz* [1862] (*bus*[*iness*]), *pop*[*ular*] [1862], *vet*[*erinarian*] [1862], *beaut*[*y*] [1866], *perk* [1869] (*perquisite* [1567]), *grad*[*uate*] [1871], *gym*[*nasium*] [1871], *chimp*[*anzee*] [1877], *sec*[*ond*] [1878], *chaps* [1884] (Sp. *chaparreras* [1861]), *croc*[*odile*] [1884], *pic*[*ture*] [1884], *max*[*imum*] [1886], *ref*[*eree*] [1890], *lab*[*oratory*] [1895], *dorm*[*itory*] [1900], *vamp*[*ire*] [1904], *tarp*[*aulin*] [1906], *chem*[*istry*] [1910], *ump*[*ire*] [1915], *perk* [1920] (*percolate* [1626]), *pix* [1924] (*pictures*), *mike* [1926] (*microphone*), *hood*[*lum*] [1930], *rep*[*etition*]*s* [1936], *pot* [1938] (if from *potiguaya* [1936] 'marijuana leaves'), *vib*[*raphon*]*es* [1940], *ed*[*ucation*] [1955], *spec*[*ification*] [1956], *clit*[*oris*] [1958], *teach*[*er*] [1958], *hash*[*ish*] [1959], *kook* [1960] (*cuckoo*), *porn*[*ography*] [1962], *bi*[*sexual*] [1966], *vibes* [1967] (*vibrations* [1899]), *perp*[*etrator*] [1968], *arb* [1983] (for *arbitrageur* [1875]), *app*[*lication*]*s* [1985].

Rats [n.d.] (*rations*) is well known in the military but has not made it to the *OED*.

Stat [1875] for L *statim* 'immediately' (on prescriptions) is sometimes listed here, but that was an abbreviation, not a clipping, again illustrating the overlap of these categories.

Sig for *signature* at the end of an email message is a recent clipping, but as a printer's abbreviation *sig.* has been around since 1866.

Rad occurs since 1820 as a clipping of *radical*, but the modern sense 'awesome; cool' [1982] derives from *radical* 'excellent' in the sense of a difficult manoeuvre in surfing [1968] (*ODNW* 254; Fischer 1998: 113).

Mod began as an abbreviation, e.g. *Mod. Fr.* 'Modern French' [1882], rather than as a clipping. At least since 1965 it has been used as a clip for *modern*, but note *Mod girls* [1964], and *Teds and Mods, Beatniks and Ravers* [1960].

Dis [1980] 'reject or dismiss contemptuously; put down' is ultimately from *disrespect* in African-American Rap Culture (Ayto 1989: 114), but the meaning suggests that *dismiss* might have played a role too. *Gank* (from *gangster*) can mean the same as *dis*, but *gank* more commonly implies a forceful crime, such as theft.

Disyllabic forms clipped on the right edge are the second most frequent type: *brandy*[*wine*] [a.1640], *memo*[*randum*] [1705], *curio*[*sity*] [1851], *photo*[*graph*] [1860], rhino[ceros] [1870], hippo[potamus] [1872], exam[ination] [1877], prelim[inary] [1877], Cosmo[politan] [1879],[2] congrat[ulation]s [1884], legit[imate] [1908] (earlier as a noun), psycho[path] [1919], intro[duction] [1923], homo[sexual] [1929], nympho[maniac] [1934], rehab[ilitation] [1935], demo[nstration] [1936], postdoc[toral] [1942], schizo[phrenic] [1945], porno[graphy] [1952], deli[catessen] [1954], klepto[maniac] [1958], condo[minium] [1964], disco[thèque] [1964], mono[nucleosis] [1964], limo[usine] [1968], detox[ify] [1970], pyro[maniac] [1971], impro[visation] and improv[isation] [1979], camo[uflage] [1994].

A right-edge truncation plus -y suffixation is loony [1872] from lunatic [c.1290]. Another is telly [1940] for television.

Right-edge truncations rarely yield trisyllabic remnants, as in intercom[munication] [1940].

11.3 Left-edge clips

Initial clipping, leaving a right-edge monosyllabic, is less frequent in English: gin [?a.1200] (< engine [1250] < AN, OF engin 'inborn talent; wit; tool; ruse'), sport [a.1425$_N$, ?a.1425$_V$] (< AN/ME disport [1303] 'pastime' < OF desport 'amusement'). In fact, the largest number of examples are borrowings from French and will be ignored in our tally for the simple reason that most of the truncated forms are not derivable synchronically. These include [es]cheat, [e]strange, [e]spy, [e]squire, [at]tend, [de]fend, [de]spite, [di]splay (Koziol 1972: 302f.). Historically, fence [c.1330] was a clipping of OF/ME defens(e) DEFENSE [a.1300] but, since it is obsolete in the sense of 'defense' it is no longer analyzable as a clip.

Bezzle originally meant 'plunder, spoil' [c.1430] and derived from OF besiler, besillier, itself clipped from embesillier, the source (via AN enbesiler) of EMBEZZLE [1469], which has more recently engendered the clip bezzle [1987] 'overall (temporary) benefit conferred by undetected embezzlement' (Ayto 1989: 34).

It is not surprising that initial clips were most common in words of French origin because of the end-stress in French. Since English featured initial stress, clips of the first syllable are not to be expected. In fact, the earliest examples involve words with non-initial stress because the first syllable was not the root word, e.g. [a]lone [1377] (ME al ōn 'all one'), [a]live [1531] (OE on līfe 'on/in life'). Clipping of prepositional be- was early, as in [be]tween [1300], [be]cause [a.1513].

Other examples (several from compounds) are [rac]coon [1742], [turn]pike [1812], [cock]roach [1822], [cara]van [1829], [omni]bus [1832], [tele]phone [1880], [air]plane [1908], [para]chute [1920], [car]toon [1932], [tele]fax [1946] (telefax [1943] is itself clipped from telefacsimile or facsimile telegraphy), [neighbor]hood [1969], [Quaa]lude

---

[2] The first attestation of Cosmo in the OED is 1989, but Sundén (1904: 126) finds it as a name in 1879.

[c.1970], [a]fro [1970], [su]burb [1977], [inter]net [1983], [ta]bloids [n.d.], blog [1999] (for weblog [1993]).

For semantic reasons the noun *quake* [1325] may be segmented from *earthquake* [c.1325] even though *quake* had a prior existence as a verb 'shake, tremble' in Old English.

Disyllabics with the left edge clipped are rare: [hi]story [1200], [ad]venture [a.1430], ticket [1528]—all from French. The last is from obsolete F *etiquet* 'little note, bill', but cf. F *étiquette* 'label; tag; ticket; ETIQUETTE'. All of these have completely severed the link with the (original) full form.

Examples that are not of French origin include [violon]cello [1848] (prob. from Germ. *Cello* [1813]), [ham]burger [1939] (see §13.3), [alli]gator [1844].

Trisyllabics with a left clip are the rarest: *varsity* [1846] (from *university*).

11.4 Clips of compounds and fixed phrases

Compounds and fixed phrases yield mono- or disyllabic forms. Although modern research focuses on what part of the base is retained in the truncated form (cf. Lappe 2007: 37), it is heuristically useful to separate them according to the ways in which truncated remnants are produced:

(1) Right-edge monosyllabic clip: L *mōbile vulgus* 'unstable crowd' [c.1599] → *mobile* [1676] → *mob* [1688]; *zoo[logical gardens]* [c.1847]; *graph[ic (formula)]* [1878]; *con[fidence man]* [1889]; *perm[anent wave]* [1927]; *fed[eral officer]* [1916]; *temp[orary employee]* [1932], *nuclear weapon* → *nuke* [1955] (freq. a verb [1962] by conversion); *narc[otics agent]* [1966]; *meg[abyte]* [1983].

(2) Right-edge disyllabic clip: *penult[imate]* [1490] (of syllables [c.1620]), *Canterbury trot* → *canter* [1706], *pro tem* [1777] (*pro tempore* [1468]), *prefab[ricated building]* [1937], *showbiz* [1945] (*show bus[iness]*), *kidvid[eo]* [1955], *decaf[feinated coffee]* [1956], *low-cal[orie]* [c.1985], *prenup[tial agreement]* [1983].

(3) Left-edge monosyllabic clip: [motor]car [1896], but since *car(re)* was in use since Wyclif [a.1382] for various forms of wheeled transport, this form is insecure and will not figure in our tally (§11.8).

(4) Monosyllabic right-edge truncations of both words: *phys[ical] ed[ucation]* [1926], *cyb[ernetic] org[anism]* [1960], *lit[erature] crit[ic]* [1963], *pop[ular] psych[ology]* [a.1965], *situation comedy* [1953] → *sitcom* [1964], *flexible [market] specialization* → *flec spec* [1988] (Ayto 1990: 136), etc., frequent in campus slang: *British Literature* → *BritLit*, *GenEd*, etc. Since *sitcom* is almost universally counted as a blend (§12.4), the rest of these might be as well. These will therefore not be counted.

(5) Monosyllabic beginning of the first word plus the last or only syllable of the second: *quas[i-stell]ar* [1964], *sat[urated]fat* [a.1975], *e[lectronic-]mail* [1979], *cu[mulative]sum* [1989] (Ayto 1990: 87). Again, these are more likely blends.

(6) Monosyllabic clip on both edges ([*sub*]*scrip*[*tion receipt*] [1762]; [*head*]*shrink*[*er*] [1966]).

Compounds and phrases rarely yield trisyllabic clips: *internet[work]* [1974], *bio-tech[nology]* [1980] (earlier [1970] as the name of a project); *para[chute]sail* [1964], *Poli[tical]-Sci[ence]* [1930].

Alky is ambiguous. It exists as a clip + hypocoristic for *alcohol* as early as 1844, and in 1944 is used of an alcohol addict, but is it a clip for the phrase *alcohol addict* (as sometimes claimed) or just for *alcoholic*? Similarly, is *benny* [1955] truncated + suffixed from *benzedrine* or from *benzedrine tablet*?

NL (*musculus*) *lātissimus dorsī* 'the broadest (muscle) of the back' yields a monosyllabic form clipped on the right, often with plural -*s*: *lats* [1939].

11.5 Truncated names

Clipping in names has been frequent since Middle English. McClure (1998: 108f.) mentions *Col* for *Nicol*, *Naud* for *Reynaud*, *Maret* for *Margaret*, *Phip* for *Philip*, *Bet* for *Be(a)trice*, *Gef* for *Geoffrey*, *Teb* for *Tebald*, *Mal* for *Mald*, *Til* for *Matilde*, *Ib* for *Isabel*, *Heb* for *Herbert*. Many of these are from French, where initial clips prevailed (§11.3).

The entire book by Karl Sundén (1904) is devoted to a thorough analysis of over 500 truncated names and suffixed truncated hypocoristics, complete with dates of attestation in a novel, play, or other (mostly fictional) work.

A large number of older names have left-edge clips (Sundén, pp. 129–38), e.g. *Belle* (Isabel), *Bertie* (Albert, Herbert, Hubert), *Bess*, *Bet*, *Betty*, *Betsy* (Elizabeth), *Drew* (Andrew, but already an independent name in 1400 [p. 186]), *Duke* (Marmaduke), *Fina* (Josephine), *Lottie* (Charlotte), *Milly* (Emily, Amelia), *Netty* (Annette), *Sander*, *Sandy* (Alexander), *Stacie* (Eustace), *Tavia* (Octavia), *Tina* (Geraldine), *Tony* (Anthony), *Becky* (Rebecca), *Gus* (Augustus), *Liz(zie)* (Elizabeth), *Tilly* (Mat(h)ilda), *Tish* (Letitia), *Zeke* (Ezekiel).

As correctly analyzed by Sundén (pp. 176–86), position of the stress is a major factor in determining what part of the name gets truncated. Truncated names most frequently preserve material from the initial or the stressed syllable, and the result is a disyllabic or preferentially a monosyllabic construct (p. 195). Minority patterns are accounted for by analogy with existing forms of similar phonological content (p. 146).

On pp. 77–128, Sundén (1904) records hundreds of attested hypocoristic names with right-edge clip, e.g. *Abb(e)y* (Abigail; also Arabella [p. 147] by phonological similarity), *Addy* (Adelaide), *Aggie* (Agatha, Agnes), *Ally/ie* (Alice, Alison), *Alf(y)* (Alfred), *Althy* (Althea), *Amy* (Amelia; originally [c13] an adaptation of F *Aimée* [p. 148]), *Andy* (Andrew), *Angie* (Angela), *Archie* (Archibald), *Artie* (Arthur), *Barbie* (Barbara), *Barney* (Barnard), *Ben(ny)* (Benjamin), *Bill(y)* (William), *Bob(by/ie)* (Robert), *Caddy*, *Carrie* (Carolyn), *Cassie*, *Cathy*, *Cattie* (Catharine), *Charley* (Charlotte), *Charlie* (Charles), *Chrissy* (Christina), *Christy* (Christopher), *Cindy* (Cinderella), *Connie* (Constance) (cf. Mattiello 2008: 105). These were especially prevalent in Scottish English from 1400 to c16 (see *-y/-ie*, suffix[6] in the *OED* online).

What is interesting about the hypocoristic names above is that, regardless of where they are truncated, the *-y/-ie* formations are invariably a binary trochaic foot.

The hypocoristics differ in register, closeness, diminutiveness, affection, etc. from the standard 'adult' monosyllabic truncated names (Schneider 2003; Lappe 2007: 23ff.).

In contemporary English, names are standardly truncated on the right edge, and the result is invariably monosyllabic (barring addition of *-y/-ie*). In order of frequency the most common type ends in a consonant, e.g. *Frederick* → *Fred*, *David* → *Dave*, *Timothy* → *Tim*. Next comes the type *Abraham* → *Abe*, then the vowel-final type *Diana* → *Di*, *Susan* → *Sue* (Lappe 2003: 139). Note that *Suz(e)* is also a possible clipping of *Susan*. That is, most truncated names are monosyllabic with a preference for a single (non-clustering) final consonant. Clusters must consist of consonants of higher sonority, as in *Bart*, *Barb*, *Alf*. In other words, truncated names prototypically have one heavy syllable. A single vowel is lengthened/diphthongized, as in *Sue* [suu̯], *Joe* [jou̯], etc.

More names end in a consonant today than formerly. While *Jude* /jud/ is the truncated form of *Judith* in contemporary English, as recently as 1904 and earlier, there were numerous attestations of *Ju* (Sundén 1904: 95).

More technically, the most frequent name clips result in a monosyllabic with a single final consonant. This is the output of clipping from the nucleus of the second syllable to the end, mapping the previous second-syllable onset to the coda of the first syllable.

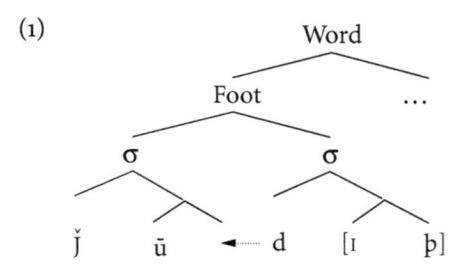

(1)

```
                    Word
                   /    \
                Foot     ...
               /    \
              σ      σ
             / \    / \
            ǰ   ū ◄--d [ɪ  þ]
```

Since the only part of a syllable that can stand on its own is the nucleus, with deletion of the rime of the second syllable its onset is mapped onto the empty coda position of the preceding syllable (cf. McCarthy and Prince 1986; 1998). To insist on maintenance of the input quantity of the /ū/, the name is spelled <Jude>.

Even with the suffixed type, the consonant(s) remaining must be syllabifiable as a coda, hence *Barbie, Andy*, not **Andry*. Only *Andy* is a possible suffixed truncation of *Andrew* because the hypothetical truncated form *And* is a possible syllable, **Andr* is not (§9.1; Lappe 2007: 38). Hence also *Ed(die)/*Edwie, Doug(ie)/*Dougly*, etc. This implies that *-y/-ie* is suffixed to a truncated base (Sundén 1904; Lappe 2007: 39, w. lit). Phonotactics may also play a role, as noted by Lappe (2007: 39), following McCarthy and Prince (1998: 304): *Amby* (for *Ambrose*) cannot be derived from a monosyllabic because **Amb* is not a possible word in English. This is questionable. In addition to the /b/ at the end of *iamb*, it is presupposed by the derivatives *iambic, iambify*, etc., and formations like *bombard* presuppose a final /b/ in *bomb*. More simply, complex onsets are avoided in the second syllable of a truncated suffixed name (cf. Plag 2003: 120).

Some truncated names (and hypocoristics) are variable in syllable structure, e.g. *Tom/Tommy, Liz/Lizzie*, and some are invariably disyllabic: *Wally* (Wallace), *Terry* (Terrance). Tessier (2010) asterisks *Terr*, but as kids many in my circle used it but only as a form of direct address, never in the third person.[3] Perhaps most important, she finds a sociolinguistic condition, that monosyllabic truncations ending in a less sonorous consonant are most preferred in male names.

In an analysis of 955 clips, Berg (2011) finds that whether a word is clipped on the left or right edge depends on the stress pattern, length of the word, and whether it is a common or proper noun. Specifically, long forms (especially first names) with non-initial stress favor clipping on the left. A productive constraint favors left-edge clipping and a perceptual constraint favors right-edge clipping. The restricted context and high degree of predictability of first names enables more drastic clipping that could not occur in common nouns without straining communication. Alber and Arndt-Lappe (2012) also find that names and common nouns typically truncate differently but predictably.

11.6 Special formations

Apart from the virtually anomalous *flu* [1827] for *influénza*, clipping preferentially eliminates accentually non-prominent syllables; cf. *triff* for *terrífic, Liz* for *Elízabeth, pram* [1884] for *perámbulator* [1853].

Clipping is less predictable in scientific terminology (Bauer 1983: 233f.): *paraxylene* → *parylene* [1965], *phosphorodithioate* → *phorate* [1959]. But given the stresses on

---

[3] Normally, however, truncated names do not end in /r/, which can change to /l/, as in *Hal* (Harry) (but in some varieties *Harr* /hær/ is perfectly good as a vocative), *Sal* (Sarah) (cf. Plag 2003: 120). Similarly, the older language nomally substituted /t/ for /þ/, e.g. *Art(ie)* for *Arthur, Bart* for *Bartholomew, Bet(ty)* for *Elizabeth*, but *Beth* is frequent today.

prèimprégnated, the expected clipping is *prepreg* [1954] 'the reinforcing or molding material already impregnated with a synthetic resin'.

This raises the issue of truncation in LANGUAGES FOR SPECIFIC PURPOSES. Indeed a complete taxonomy would have to take into account how clips work in technical and other language. In German, likewise, scientific terminology also has special shortening processes, e.g. *Diethylenglykol* > *Diglykol* > *Digol* (cf. Steinhauer 2000: 147ff.). A more general typology is developed by Michel (2006).

Haplological syllable reduction is a frequent witticism in compounds and phrases, e.g. *slang[lang]uage* [1879], *alco[hol]holidays* [1913], *sex[ex]pert* [1924], *sex[ex]ploitation* [1924], *Japan[an]imation* [1985]. Since these do not obey the syllable limits of canonical clips, but bear a closer resemblance to blends (§12.4), they will not be counted in this chapter.

Clips may carry a derogatory nuance, e.g. *shrink* [1966], *teach[er]* [1958], reminiscent of *cheat, tease, flirt, bore, spy, sponge*, etc., on whose "attitudinal" status see Kornexl (2002). Of course, *head-shrinker* [1950] was derogatory to begin with.

Another form of derogatory formation was applied to females seeking the right to vote. They applied the word *suffragist* [1822] to themselves around the 1880s, but in 1906 the *Daily Mail* clipped *suffragist* and applied the feminine deprecative -*ette* (Miller 1977) to create *suffragette*. *The Athenaeum* picked up the word in 1907, and it quickly caught on. More recently, the even more demeaning blend *fluffragette* [1997] has made the scene.

Sometimes the clipped forms displace the original (in a certain meaning, at least): *tarp[aulin]* [1906], *[omni]bus* [1832]. Note the splits: *fanatic* [c.1525] ≠ (sports) *fan* [1682]; *caravan* [1596] ≠ *van* [1829]; *vampire* [1734] ≠ *vamp* [1904]; *cuckoo* even in the sense of 'looney person' [1889$_N$, 1918$_A$]) is not entirely the same as *kook* [1960] (cf. *kooky* [1959]).

A word may engender multiple clippings, especially with names, e.g. *Patricia* → *Pat* and *Trish, Elizabeth* → *Liz* and *Beth, Alexander* → *Alex* and *Sander, Christina* → *Chris* and *Tina*.

Taxicab was clipped from *taxi[meter]* [1907] and *cab[riolet]* [1766], unless *taxicab* was compounded of clipped *taxi* and the prior existing clip *cab* [1826]. *Cabriolet* was a two-wheeled one-horse vehicle for hire, diminutive of Ital. *cabriole* 'caper' (a reference to the bounding motion of L *caper* 'goat', *capreolus* 'wild goat'). From the native French word for 'goat', *chèvre*, was created *Chevrolet*, etymologically equivalent to *cabriolet*.

A monosyllabic clip can acquire a particle: *confess* → *fess (up)* [1930]; *smog up* [1966], *psych (out)* [1973], *max (out)* [1977], *vegetate* → *veg (out)* [1980], *spastic/spasm* → *spazz (out)* [1984], etc., parallel to the backformed *lase (off)*. This is certainly rhythmic and not related to the many monosyllabic verbs in English that require a particle for semantic/thematic reasons: *I set it down* (*I set it); *I laid it down* (*I laid it); *I put it down* (*I put it), etc. That rhythm is involved in the clips and backformed monosyllabics is clear from the contrast between *boot up* [1980] 'start a computer' (with particle) but *reboot* [1971] (without).

Different words may be clipped in such a way as to yield homonyms. *Sub* is the clip for *subordinate* [1696], *substitute* [1830], *subsist(ence)* [1866], *submarine* [1917], *submarine sandwich* [c.1950], etc. (Koziol 1972: 306).

Rep stands for *reputation* [a.1705], *representative* [a.1850], and *repetition* [1864]. *Mag* is for *magazine* [1742], *magnitude* [1840], *magneto* [1918], *magnesium* [1952].

Con is the clip for *contra* [1362] in *pros and cons* [1572], *con[fidence man]* [1889], *con[vict]* [1893], plus a verb *to con* [1896] by conversion. *Condominium* [1962] (also 'joint rule or sovereignty [a.1715]) yields *condo* [1964] rather than **con*, plus *-minium*, whence *dockominium* [1981] 'boat mooring which can be bought outright' (Ayto 1989: 115), recent *barndominium* (Bill Bridges, p.c.), etc. Although *con* is overloaded, the explanation of why *confess* yields *fess (up)* rather than **con (up)* involves the locus of stress on *conféss*.

11.7 Suffixed formations

A class of clips ends in *-o*, e.g. *memo* [1705], *curio* [1851], *psycho* [1919], *homo* [1929], *nympho* [1934] (§11.2). These plus the types *calico* [1540], *lingo* [1660], and interjection *(h)o* in *righto* [1893] etc. motivated suffixed *kiddo* [1896], *wino* [1915], *pinko* [1925], *daddy-o* [1949], *neato* [1951], *weirdo* [1955], *dumbo* [1960] (but *Dumbo* [1941]), *cheapo* [1967], *nutso* [1973], *wacko* [1977], *sicko* [1977], *creepo* [1977], etc. (*OED* s.v. *-o*; Mattiello 2008: 113ff.; cf. Hamans 1997: 1735).

A variety of genuine clip takes hypocoristic *-y/-ie*: *hubby* [1682] (= *husband*), *comf[ortable]y* [1829], *panties* [1845] ('boy's shorts'; [1908] 'female underpants'), *Philly* [1869] (= *Philadelphia*), *book[maker]ie* [1885], *und[erware]ies* [1906], *falsies* [1943], *druggie* [1966], *techie* [1969], *[Star] Trek(k)ie* [1976], etc. These triggered deprecative *hottie/y* [?1913], *biggie/y* [1926], *groupie/y* [1967], etc. (cf. Mattiello 2008: 105–8).

A new variety of clip that is popular among young people ends in *-s* (Starr 2010; Baclawski 2012a):[4] *adorbs* (*adorable*), *awks* (*awkward*), *inappropes* (*inappropriate*), *lates* (*late(r)*), *obvs* /ɑbvz/ (*obviously*), *probs* (*probably*), *tomorrs* (*tomorrow*), *totes* (*totally*) (possibly built on *tote* [a.1772], a shortened form of *total*), *whatevs* (*whatever* as a dismissive). Baclawski traces *-s* back in part to adverbial *-s* (*always, anyways*, hence *lates, probs, tomorrs, totes*), in part to interjection *-s* (*gadzooks* [1694], *oops* [1922], *whoops* [1937], hence *awks, whatevs*) (cf. interjectional plurals *rats* [1816], *congrats* [1884]), and in part to diminutive *-s*. Starr (2010) relates the "abbrevs" (a standard abbreviation since 1883) to irony. For instance, *lulz* (from LOL: §9.4) can be used derisively when the speaker is not laughing. Ropert (2009: §3.5) cites *auds* for

---

[4] Thanks to Kenny Baclawski for discussion of this section and for the Starr (2010) reference.

audience, and Mattiello (2008: 68f.) adds the slang *nuts* [1908], *bananas* [1957], *bonkers* [1945] 'mad, crazy', and *preggers* [1942] 'pregnant'.

The OED online claims that diminutive *-s* is clipped from hypocoristic *-sy/-sie*, as in *palsy* [c.1250]. Despite the absence of **pals*, there are supposedly some alternating forms, like *toots* [1936], a familiar form of address to a female, beside *tootsie/tootsey* [1895] 'woman, girl, sweetheart', earlier *tootsy* [1854] 'endearing term for a child's or woman's small foot'; cf. *footsy* [1944], jocular and amorous diminutive of 'foot'. Still, *footsy* has no clipped **foots*, and the oldest forms on names and kinship terms do not alternate, e.g. *Tibs* [1615] (*Isabel(la)*) (Sundén 1904: 139), *Babs* [1900] (*Barbara*) (p. 81), *Bobs* [1900] (*Roberts*) (p. 116).

Last names like *Roberts* yielding *Bobs*, and clips like *Dex* for *Dexter* (Sundén, p. 87), provide additional possible sources of *-s*. Affectionate forms of address especially to females seem to have originally favored names ending in /b/; cf. *Tibs, Babs, Bobs* above. Lappe (2007: 4) cites *Gabs* (*Gabriele*), *Pabs* (*Pablo*), and there is also *Abbs* (for *Abigail/Abby* [Pauley Perrette]) beside *Gibbs* [Mark Harmon] on NCIS. Consistent with favoring labial-final stems, *-s* seems to have been generalized from names to *pops* [1893] 'father', *moms* [1925] 'mother', then to other affectionate forms of address like *ducks* [1936], *toots* [1936], then to other names like *Cuts* for *Cutler* (Lappe 2007: 4), *Wills* for *William* (Baclawski 2012a). There are also hypocoristic diminutive plurals like *veggies* [1907], *panties* [1845], *undies* [1906], *falsies* [1943] that may have contributed to the modern productivity of *-s*, especially in the diminutive plurals cited by Starr (2010): *realsies* (*real*), *neatsies* (*neat*), *whatevskies, unfortchskies* (*unfortunate*), etc. Lefilliâtre (2012) cites *hols* for *holidays*.

There are few constraints on *-s* affixation. Kenny Baclawski (p.c.) notes that *obvs* violates English phonotactics, but that the identity-sequencing prohibition (§2.2) seems to apply: *natch* not **natches* 'naturally', *dees/dece* not **deces* 'decent'.

11.8 Essential properties of English clips

Excluding scientific clips, names, the haplological type *alcoholidays*, the 12 ambiguous examples that are usually considered blends (*sitcom, quasar, cyborg, satfat*, etc.), the non-clips with added *-o* (*sicko, creepo*), the modern *-s* type (*probs, adorbs*) about which too many unknowns remain, and the early words of French origin with initial clips (*fence, cheat, sport*), this section tabulates the 168 clips discussed to this point that are independently documented in the OED.

Right-edge monosyllabic clips of single words are the most frequent, with 76 tokens in our list.[5] If one adds the rare types *fridge, triff, pram, flu, scrip, shrink,*

---

[5] This includes 2 *vibes*, 2 *vet*, 4 *mag*, 4 *sub*, 3 *rep*, and 3 *con*. These are counted as tokens rather than types because different words are represented at different times and places in history.

and the 11 right-edge monosyllabic clips of phrases (*mob, zoo, graph, con, perm, fed, temp, nuke, narc, meg, lats*), the 93 monosyllabic clips outnumber the second most frequent 30 disyllabic right-edge clips by over three to one. Adding the 9 disyllabic phrasal clips (*penult, canter, pro tem, prefab, showbiz, kidvid, decaf, low-cal, prenup*) yields a total of 38 disyllabic clips, still way under half of the 93 monosyllabic clips.

The 21 left-edge monosyllabic clips come in third. It is not always clear why those are clipped on the left edge. At least the following should have been accented on the first syllable: *airplane, caravan, cockroach, neighborhood, omnibus, quaalude, suburb, telephone, tabloids, turnpike, weblog*. In all cases, the final-syllable remnant constitutes a metrical foot, but that *per se* does not explain why the first foot of the word should be truncated. Pragmatic considerations (e.g. Berg 2011) play a role for some of these. For instance, *web* and *car* were already in use in a context that would have created ambiguity. Similarly, *omni, tele*, and *air/aero*. *Lude* and *hood* are more optimal clips than *quaa* and *neigh* because they end in a voiced stop. *Cock* had become too negative to refer felicitiously to a rooster. Why *pike* was selected over *turn* and *bloids* over *tabs* requires more speculation. The latter contains *-oid*, making it not as good as the 'real' newspapers with larger sheets and less sensationalistic news, and is therefore inherently more disparaging than *tabs* would be.

Thirteen clips take the hypocoristic suffix, yielding a disyllabic output: *alky, benny, bookie, comfy, druggie, falsies, hubby, loony, panties, Philly, techie, telly, Trek(k)ie, undies*.

Finally, a small number of clips yield trisyllabic outputs: *biotech, intercom, internet, parasail, Poli-Sci, telefax, varsity*—some of which may be blends.

Clipping is predominantly a right-edge phenomenon in English, as is expected since most English words are stressed near the left edge. Since English prefers the trochaic foot, the surprise is the predilection for monosyllabic clips. Even though they have a heavy (mostly closed) single syllable, the trochaic foot predicts a higher proportion of disyllabic (and trisyllabic) forms.

As emphasized by Lappe (2007), it is necessary to account for why English prefers monosyllabic truncated forms when the optimal foot structure is the binary trochee. A heavy monosyllable, even assuming quantity sensitivity for English (e.g. Kager 1999; Prince and Smolensky 2004 [1993]; Lappe 2007), is not inherently optimal. This implies that clips target something other than the ideal metrical foot.

In fact, monosyllabic clips are based on the syllable rather than the foot, as is clear because the Sonority Hierarchy (§9.1) is obeyed with respect to how many and which segments are tolerated on the right edge. In *prof*[*essor*], the onset of the second syllable is clipped off and adjoined as the coda of the first, as in (2).

(2)

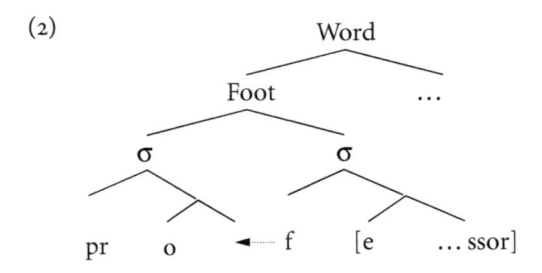

```
                    Word
                   /    \
               Foot      ...
              /    \
            σ        σ
           /|\      /|\
         pr o  ◄--f [e  ...ssor]
```

Since the only part of a syllable that can stand on its own is the nucleus, with deletion of the rime of the second syllable its onset is mapped onto the empty coda position of the preceding syllable (cf. (1) above).

What is most interesting is the conflict resolution. Since the truncation template requires a complex rime, the portion after the nucleus can be made up by a cluster that obeys the sonority hierarchy (SH) or by a sole consonant, both of which involve pirating a consonant from the onset of the second syllable, as in (2) above and *tarp[aulin]*, *vamp[ire]*, *pant[aloon]s*, *perq[uisite]* (*perk*). Truncation must not create a violation of the SH: *gym[nasium]* (not **gymn*), *mic[rophone]* (*mike* not **micr*), *ad[vertisement]* (not **adv*). If the second syllable has a complex onset, it is maximized before truncation at the expense of a complex coda, hence *miss[tress]*, *con[tra]*. *Spec(k)[tacle]s* shows that sonority distance (Steriade 1982) is obeyed, since [kt] is a possible syllable onset (e.g. in Ancient Greek, which also allows *pt-*, *ps-*, *tl-*, etc.) but not in English, which requires greater sonority distance between adjacent segments. In the case of *brother*, no English word with a short vowel ends in /ð/ (except the letter name *edh*), hence *bro* rather than */brʌð/. These examples constitute the norm.

Left-edge clips are simpler. The clip begins with the onset of the first accented syllable (usually the second syllable). Onsets are maximized, as in *weblog*, resyllabified as *we.blog*, hence *blog*.

Truncation draws attention to the form, and in English typically yields monosyllabics which are high in expressivity, as evidenced by 'four-letter' words (§7.3). Significantly, hypocoristics and clipped female names are frequently a trochaic foot, which softens the rhetorical impact.

11.9 Clips in other languages

French prefers dissyllabic clips of the type *kilo[gramme]* [1863] and *typo[graphe]* [1865] (Hamans 1997: 1738), but there are many clips with closed final syllable, such as *manif[estation]* 'public demonstration' (Ronneberger-Sibold 1995: 425).

In Spanish clips, gender morphology plays an important role: *Agustín* : *Tín* ~ *Tíno*, *Ramón* : *Món* ~ *Móncho*; *Isabél* : *Bél* ~ *Béla*, *Concepción* : *Chón* ~ *Chón(ch)a* (Roca and Felíu 2003: 196). Note also the type *Matílde* : *Tíla*, *Silvéstre* : *Véto* (p. 206). Beside these, there is the type with persistent base: *Cleménte* : *Ménte*, *Silvéstre* : *Véche*, *Arancéli* : *Céli*, etc. (p. 209). Another pattern is the following: *Yolánda* : *Yóli*, *Amélia* : *Méli*, *Milágros* : *Míli*, etc. (p. 212). Barring one minor type, then, the preference is for clips that leave a binary trochaic foot (§9.2).

The majority of German clips are dissyllabic, e.g. *Schoko*[*lade*] 'chocolate', *Limo*[*nade*] 'carbonated soft drink', but about a third are either monosyllabic (e.g. *Klo*[*sett*] 'WC') or trisyllabic, e.g. *Eduscho* = *Edu*[*ard*] *Scho*[*pf*], a coffee brand-name (Ronneberger-Sibold 1995: 422f.). German clips are inflected (plural *die Limo-s*). Apart from that, they differ in optimality from the normal lexicon in preferring open syllables (p. 424): of the disyllabic clips, 89.5% have two open syllables, e.g. *Alu* /á.lu/ 'aluminum', *Nazi* (*Nationalsozialist*). In the normal lexicon only 12.6% of the disyllabics have this structure, and most end in -ə (e.g. *bitte* /bí.tə/ 'please') which is strongly avoided in clips: *Ami* /á.mi:/ 'American', *Kino* /kí:no:/ for *Kinematograph* 'cinema' (Ronneberger-Sibold 1995: 427). The rare trisyllabic English clip *varsity* [1846] (from *university*) stands in marked contrast to the German clip *Uni*. The pattern of disyllabicity reflects the optimality of the binary trochaic foot (Wiese 2001). So-called -*i*-derivations like *Studi* for *Student* 'student' (Wiese 2006) contribute a hypocoristic meaning (Meibauer 2014).

The German type *Rudi* (*Rudolf*), *Bini* (*Sabine*) is possibly analogous to the disyllabic English hypocoristics in -*y*, like *Lizzy* (*Elizabeth*), *Timmy* (*Timothy*), but Lappe (2003: 170–8; 2007: 38ff.) argues that they are different. Note that *Annie*, *Sammy* seem to be suffixed to *Ann*, *Sam*. Since the English hypocoristics seem to have the binary trochaic foot as their output target, as do the German forms, it is not clear that they are structurally different.

11.10 Summary

Whether a word is clipped on the left or right edge depends on the stress pattern, length of the word, and its status as a common or proper noun. Long forms (especially first names) with non-initial stress favor clipping on the left. In our data, right-edge monosyllabic clips of single words are the most frequent, outnumbering the second most frequent disyllabic right-edge clips. Left-edge monosyllabic clips come in third, and it is not always clear why those are clipped on the left edge.

The relative predictability of first names enables more drastic clipping that would eradicate too much informational content in ordinary words. "Nicknames and hypocoristic terms of endearment are (typically) purely expressive" (Fortin 2011: 184).

Blocking is irrelevant in the sense that clipped forms do not block unclipped or vice versa, possibly because a hypocoristic meaning is added (Meibauer 2014).

English is relatively anomalous in preferring monosyllabic clips (Lappe 2003). The usual result is a binary trochaic foot (Wiese 2001), as in Spanish, e.g. *Agustín* > *Tíno*, *Isabél* > *Béla*, *Cleménte* > *Ménte*, *Aracéli* > *Céli*, etc. (Roca and Felíu 2003). But these languages have inflections that are typically monosyllabic in their own right. In a language like English, truncation draws attention to the form, and monosyllabics are high in expressivity, as evidenced by 'four-letter' words (§7.3). Significantly, hypocoristics and clipped female names are frequently a binary trochaic foot, which softens the impact.

12

Blending

Blending is typically the fusion of two clipped words. Input constituents of blends are selected and sequenced for extralinguistic, pragmatic, and in some cases sound-symbolic reasons, all with a view to compositional transparency of the prosodically constrained output. The majority of blends can be derived by several templates. For monosyllabic and disyllabic inputs, the output is normally a word of one metrical foot. For longer input words, choices exist among several two-foot types. This is one reason for the creation of different blends from the same input words. Outputs are conditioned but not determined by several preferred output prosodic structures.[1]

12.1 Blending as a process

Blending is a type of compounding of clipped words, but the clipped base can differ from a standard clip (Fradin, Montermini, and Plénat 2009, w. lit). Although a playful process, it differs less in substance than on the types of bases on which it operates (cf. §15.1). In contrast to compounds which combine whole words (but see Chapter 14), blends combine parts of lexical source words (Kemmer 2003: 75) into standard-type compounds (Smith 2012a).

Most frequently, the first part of one word is combined with the last part of another, e.g. *tragico-* × *cōmoedia* → *tragicōmoedia* (Plautus, *Amphitruo* 59) TRAGI-COMEDY [c.1580] (Biville 1989: 16). Blends in fourteen languages are reported in Štekauer et al. (2012: 131–4), but the importance of blending has only recently come to be appreciated. For this reason, in older languages they have largely gone unnoticed, as emphasized by Biville (1989). The *OED* online remains hesitant about applying the label "blend" to words in older English. For instance, on Wyclif's *austerne* [a.1382] (*austere* × *stern*), cited by Wood (1911: 174), there is no mention of a blend. On *argle* [1589] 'argue disputatiously, haggle', which Wood (ibid.) derives from *argue* × *haggle*, the *OED* states: "probably a popular perversion of *argue*, or confusion of that word with haggle"—as if a blend were a priori absurd. On *glimmer*

---

[1] Thanks to Chris Smith and the audiences at the University of Florida (3/14/13) and Sam Houston State University (3/26/13) for discussion of the issues and data in this chapter.

[1390], derived by Sturtevant (1947: 112) from *gleam* × *shimmer*, the *OED* refers to an alleged Old English frequentative **glimorian*, but in this instance the earliest occurrences are in northern texts and the word is Nordic-derived (cf. Dan. *glimre*, Sw. *glimra* §10.8). The *OED* declares *squiggle* [1816] imitative rather than a blend of *squirm* [1791] and *wiggle* [1200] or *wriggle* [1495]. Likewise, *sniggle* [1815] is supposedly imitative rather than a blend of *snicker* [1694]/*snigger* [1706] and *giggle* [1509]. Even recent words like *prissy* [1894] the *OED* will not unequivocally label a blend of *prim* and *sissy*.

The clearest blends in older stages of a language are those signalled by the writer (which is rare). Lewis Carroll invented several well-known blends in *Through the Looking-Glass* (1871),[2] and adapted PORTMANTEAU (originally a travelbag [1584]) for such creations: "*slithy* means 'lithe and slimy' .... You see it's like a portmanteau— there are two meanings packed up into one word" (Carroll 1871: 6.127). Carroll also invented *chortle* (*chuckle* × *snort*), *galumph* (*gallop* × *triumph*), and others (§5.7).

The intentional blends by Wallace Irwin in his 'Letters of a Japanese Schoolboy' [1907+] are reported by Wood (1911: 174f.) but do not appear in the *OED*. These include *fidgitated* 'uneasy, agitated' (*fidgety* × *agitated*) and *flimsical* (*flighty* × *whimsical*).

Sir Thomas Chaloner in 1549 sarcastically labeled those who sprinkle their English with foreign words as *fooleosophers* (*fool* × *philosopher*) (Pound 1914: 11, 32). In 1849 Herman Melville coined *snivelization* (*snivel* × *civilization*). In connection with Arnold Schwarzenegger, *governator* is a blend of *governor* and *terminator* (§2.3). Other humorous blends are *futilitarian* [1827] and *beautilitarian* [1911].[3] Lehrer (2003; 2007) notes that blends are witty, involve puns or allusions, and afford the puzzle of novelty. *Brunch* [1896] (*breakfast* × *lunch*) originated as Oxford University slang (Wood 1911: 174; Pound 1914: 29). Language Log[4] (1/18/2012) on *snowmanteaux* records *blizzle* (*blizzard* × *fizzle*) for a non-materializing snowstorm, and *snowmageddon* [2008], its conceptual opposite (§13.3). Compare *snizzard* 'snowy blizzard' (many hits on Google).

Comedian Ken Dodd's *plumptuous* (*plump* × *sumptuous*) is now the name of a lipgloss and a regular word in the *Urban Dictionary*: 'extremely enlarged; maximally filled'.

Concoctions by Rachael Ray on the Food Network include *entréetizer* (*entrée-sized appetizer*) and *choup* [2007] (*chowder* × *soup*) 'thicker than soup but thinner than chowder'. She also popularized *stoup* [c.1964] (*stew* × *soup*).

---

[2] In fact, Lewis Carroll's *slithy* (6.127) and *mimsy* (vi.129) first appeared in an earlier version of the Jabberwocky in his *Rectory Umbrella & Mischmasch* (1855), where *slithy* was spelled *slythy*.

[3] *Beautilitarian* is mentioned by Wood (1911: 174), citing the word from *Good Housekeeping Magazine* (March 1911: 281). It is not in the *OED*.

[4] http://languagelog.ldc.upenn.edu/nll/?p=3711

To express the frequent *green–blue* identity, the color literature devised the blend *grue* (§8.5; not in the *OED*).

Blends are supposedly paralleled in slips of the tongue, such as *evoid* (*evade* × *avoid*), *upcry* (*uproar* × *outcry*), *sleatest* (*slightest* × *least*), *searlier* (*sooner* × *earlier*), etc. (cf. Sturtevant 1947: 37ff., 110ff.; Butterworth 1981; Pharies 1983: 209).[5] However, (i) speech errors tend to be recognized and corrected immediately (Bragdon 2008), (ii) blends of the *brunch* type are rare in speech errors (Dressler 1978: 147), and (iii) intentional blends and speech errors have different properties (Gries 2012). On balance, studies of aphasic speech production provide insights into blending by demonstrating that syllable nuclei and rime segments are more stable than onsets, trochaic feet are preferred, and so on (Buckingham and Christman 2004; Brown 2004; Ziegler 2005).

Spontaneous creations by children indicate an innate capacity. Jespersen (1922: 132) reports that one girl (age 1.8–2) made *backet* from *bat* × *racquet*. Another (age 2.0) devised *breakolate* from *breakfast chocolate*, and coined *Chally* as a child's name from *Charity* × *Sally*. On *snangle* (*snarl* × *tangle*), Wood (1911: 176) comments: "This word was used by a girl of eleven, who... would frequently make such blends." Once again, I-language (§1.8) and individual creativity are crucial.

12.2 Typical lexical blends

In the following chronological list of blends, Bragdon's (2008) discussion of the earliest examples is revised and updated, with additions from the appendix in Smith (2012a); only words that do not survive today are glossed.[6]

---

[5] Speech errors include what was traditionally referred to as LEXICAL CONTAMINATION (cf. Sturtevant 1947: 110ff.). A recent example occurred in a recycling news streamer on MSNBC (January 17, 2013), reporting that Michelle Obama *unvealed* a new hairstyle. Since there was no evidence of an intentional blend, it had to be a simple error for *unveiled* × *revealed*.

[6] The list excludes the manifestly literary blends like Lewis Carroll's *snark* [1876], a fictitious animal half snake and half shark. Many examples can be found in Wood (1911; 1912), Pound (1914), Koziol (1972: 42–7), Algeo (1977), Soudek (1978), Bauer (1983: 234–7), Tournier (1985: 130–38), Thurner (1993) [some 2,500 entries], Cannon (1986; 2000), Quinion (1996), Fischer (1998: 34–9), Kelly (1998), Davy (2000), López Rúa (2002; 2004), Kemmer (2003), Hong (2004), Bat-El (2006), Lehrer (2007), Fandrych (2008), Bragdon (2008), Cook (2010), Gries (2004; 2012), papers in Renner, Maniez, and Arnaud (2012), and Smith (2010; 2012a). For French, see Fradin et al. (2009), and for Spanish, Trommer and Zimmermann (2010). As Bragdon emphasizes, blends can have a short life in the history of a language. Many of the examples in Pound (1914) and Thurner (1993) no longer exist. Of the 60 English blends in Wood (1911: 174ff.; 1912), e.g. *fruice* 'a fruit-juice drink', very few appear in the *OED*. This testifies to the fact that blend formation, more than regular core morphology, is influenced by style, register, and I-language creativity (§1.8). For the productivity of blends, see Zwicky <http://arnoldzwicky.wordpress.com/2008/12/27/manecdotes-and-brobituaries/> and <http://arnoldzwicky.wordpress.com/category/morphology/portmanteaus/page/2/>. The advantage of a historical list is that the words can be verified and glosses minimized. Forms from modern corpora are unverifiable and often ephemeral, but are included for comparison in the discussion section.

clasp [1307]: *clip/close* (?) × *hasp*
drubly [a.1340] 'turbid': *drof* 'turbid, disturbed' × *troubly* 'turbid, muddy, murky'
wlappe [c.1380] 'wrap': *wrap* × *lappe* 'coil, fold, wrap'
prance [c.1380]: *proud* × *dance* (Wallis 1653: 57; OED lists as etymology unknown)
crash [?a.1400]: *crack* × *dash*
scroll [c.1400]: *scrow* × *roll*
clash [?1500]: *clap* × *crash, smash, splash*
blatterature [1512] 'bad literature': *blatter* 'babble, prate' × *literature*
twiddle [a.1547]: *twirl/twist* × *fiddle/piddle*
trudge [1547]: derived by Wallis (1653: 57; 1765: 190) from *tread/trot* × *drudge* (cf. Sundby 1995); the OED merely lists as origin obscure
flare [c.1550]: perhaps *flame* × *glare* (OED: etymology unknown)
flaunt [1566]: *fly* × *flout* × *vaunt* (see §12.3; OED "Of unknown origin.")
grumble [a.1586]: cf. F *grommeler* 'mutter' × *mumble* (Wallis 1653: 57 *grutch* × *mumble*)
twirl [1598]: *tirl* 'rotate' × *whirl*
glaze [a.1616] 'stare': perhaps *glare* × *gaze* (unless derived from *glass*)
bash [a.1642]: *beat/bat* × *dash*
dumbfound [1653] *dumb* × *confound*
flurry [1698]: *flaw/flurr* 'throw, fly' (?) × *hurry*
smash [1699]: *smite/smack* × *mash* (but see §10.5)
flabbergast [1772]: *flabby/flap* (?) × *aghast*
squiggle [1804]: *squirm* × *wiggle* (OED lists as imitative)
adaptitude [1806]: *adapt* × *attitude*
scrunch [1825]: *squeeze* × *crunch* (but see §10.5)
Eurasian [1844]: *European* × *Asian*
recomember [1852]: *recollect* × *remember*
Republicrat [1872]: *Republican* × *Democrat*
slanguage [1879]: *slang* × *language*
penultimatum [1882]: *penultimate* × *ultimatum*
smog [1884; OED 1905]: *smoke* × *fog*
contraception [1886]: *contra* × *conception*
banjolin [1889]: *banjo* × *mandolin*
cat(t)alo [1889]: *cattle* × *buffalo*
electrocution [1889]: *electric/electro-* × *execution*
brunch [1896]: *breakfast* × *lunch*
happenstance [1897] *happening* × *circumstance*
Amerindian [1899]: *American* × *Indian*
travelogue [1903]: *travel* × *monologue*
tangelo [1904]: *tangerine* × *pomelo*

dramedy [1905]: *drama* × *comedy*
moonscape [1907]: *moon* × *landscape*
spork [1909 1×; 1970]: *spoon* × *fork*
advertorial [1914]: *advertisement* × *editorial*
chunnel [1914]: *channel* × *tunnel*
um(p)teen [1918]: *umpty* indefinite number × *-teen*
cultivar [1923] 'a horticulturally derived variety of plant': *cultivated* × *variety*
sexploitation [1924]: *sex* × *exploitation*
motel [1925]: *motor* × *hotel*
palimony [1927] (modern sense 1977): *pal* × *alimony*
positron [1933]: *positive* × *electron*
gues(s)timate [1936]: *gu[ess]* × *estimate*
meld [1936]: *melt* × *weld*
celebutante [1939]: *celebrity* × *débutante*
icecapade [1941]: *ice* × *escapade*
imagineer [1942]: *imagine* × *engineer*
sexercise [1942]: *sex* × *[ex]ercise*
radome [1944] 'radar-protecting structure on a ship or aircraft': *radar* × *dome*
zillion [1944]: *z* = last in a sequence × *million*
hydramatic [1951]: *hydraulic* × *automatic*
skort [1951]: *skirt* × *shorts* (not in OED but pictures are readily available online, e.g.
 <http://www.zappos.com/skorts?gclid=CKizm52Zj7ACFTSytgodmHGipw)>.
medicare [1953]: *medical* × *care*
priviligentsia [1953]: *privilege* × *intelligentsia*
smaze [1953]: *smoke* × *haze*
cafetorium [a.1955]: *cafeteria* × *auditorium* (not in OED)
sci-fi [1955]: *science* × *fiction*
glitterati [1956]: *glitter* × *lit(t)erati*
modem [1958]: *modulator* × *demodulator*
fantabulous [1959]: *fantastic* × *fabulous*
muppet [1959]: *marionette* (?) × *puppet*
breathalyzer [1960]: *breath* × *analyzer*
docudrama [1961]: *documentary* × *drama*
sitcom [1964]: *situation* × *comedy*
mockumentary [1965]: *mock* × *documentary*
stagflation [1965]: *stagnation* × *inflation*
dancerciz/se [1967]: *dance* × *-ercise* (after *(sex)-ercise*)
pulsar [1968]: *pulsating* × *star* (cf. *quasar* [1964] = *quasi-stellar*)
shoat [1969]: *sheep* × *goat*
geep [1971]: *goat* × *sheep* (see under *shoat* in OED)

animatronics [1971]: *animated* × *(audio-)electronics*
televangelist [1973]: *television* × *evangelist*
beefalo [1974]: *beef* × *buffalo*
jazzercise [1976]: *jazz* × *-ercise* (cf. *danc-ercise* [1967])
wog [n.d.]: *walk* × *jog* (not in *OED*)
limon [n.d.]: *lime* × *lemon* (not in *OED*)
brangus [n.d.]: *brahma* × *(black) angus* (not in *OED*)
Snausage [n.d.]: *snack sausage* (not in *OED*)
cineplex [1978]: *cinema* × *complex*
affluenza [1979] 'psychological disturbance arising from an excess of wealth':
   affluent × *influenza* (Ayto 1989: 6)
hazmat [1980]: *hazardous* × *material*
broasted [1980s]: *broiled* × *roasted* (*COED*; not in *OED*)
infomercial [1981]: *information* × *commercial*
netiquette [1982]: *(inter)net* × *etiquette*
dallymony [1987]: *dalliance* × *palimony* (not in *OED*)
guppie [1984]: *gay* × *yuppie*
Buppie [1984]: *Black* × *yuppie*; *buppie* [1988]: *black* × *guppie* (not in *OED*)
Pictionary [1985]: *picture* × *dictionary* <http://en.wikipedia.org/wiki/Pictionary>
emoticon [1990]: *emotion* × *icon*
carjack(ing) [1991]: *car* × *hijack(ing)*[7]
metrosexual [1994]: *metropolitan* × *hetero/homosexual*
hacktivist [1995]: *hack(er)* × *activist*
adultescent [1996]: *adult* × *adolescent*
Demopublican [n.d.]: *Democrat* × *Republican* (cf. *Republicrat* [1872])

12.3 Special formations

Animal blends are particularly interesting. A *geep* [1971] is 'a cross between a sheep and a goat produced by genetic engineering' (Ayto 1989: 164). Linguistically, *geep* is from *goat* × *sheep*; *shoat* [1969] is the same thing (Bauer 1983: 234) but blended of *sheep* × *goat*. *Brangus* [n.d.] (not in *OED*) is slightly more complicated, consisting of *brahma (bull)* × *(black) angus*.

A blend may be composed of more than two words: *flaunt* [1566] is apparently from *fly* × *flout* × *vaunt* (Pound 1914: 54). Fandrych (2008) mentions *Clinterngate*

---

[7] The *OED* lists *carjack* as a backformation from *carjacking* but *carjack* is attested 16 days (!) later (Sept. 14, 1991) than *carjacking* (Aug. 29, 1991), which is no evidence at all. Since *hijack* has been an independent verb since 1929, there is no reason to deny that *carjack* was directly derived by blending *car* × *hijack*. The *OED* also lists *carjacker* as a backformation, but from what? Since *carjacker* [1991] occurs first in the same newspaper article as *carjacking*, the obvious conclusion is that *carjack* underlies both.

from *Clinton* × *intern* × *-gate* and *burbulence* from *burp* × *burble* × *turbulence*. Neither is in the OED.

A blend can spawn related blends: *motor hotel* → *motel* [1925], whence *boatel* [1956] (*boat* × *hotel*) 'waterfront hotel', *floatel* [1959] 'chalet on a moored barge', etc. (Ayto 1989: 151). Nuclear examples generate families (López Rúa 2002: 41; 2004).

Most complicated of all are the scientific blends, for which the wildest license reigns. *Pixel* [1969] is composed of *pix* × *el*[*ement*]; cf. *pic* [1884], *pix* [1924], established truncations of *picture(s)*. The more recent the scientific term, the less predictable its formation. Examples include *Quaalude* [1966] for *methaqualone* × *sleep interlude*; *amoxycillin* [1971] for *amino* × *hydroxyphenyl* × *penicillin*; and *ethambutol* [1961] for *ethylene* × *amine* × *butanol*.

Some seem more like abbreviations: *aphoxide* [n.d.] for *aziridinyl* × *phosphine* × *oxide*; *DNase* [1949] for *deoxyribonuclease*; *rubisco* [1980] for RuBisCO: *ribulose 1,5-bisphosphate carboxylase*, a plant enzyme that catalyzes the fixing of atmospheric carbon dioxide in photosynthesis (*ODNW* 268).

Some scholars include as blends *hi-fi* [1950] for *high fidelity*, *slo-mo* [1978] for *slow motion* (Hughes 1988: 21), but these are treated here as clippings. Once again, the boundary between lexicogenic processes is not discrete.

Interlingual blends are frequent among bilinguals. Youssef Haddad (p.c.) cites Arabic *mumtastic* (Arab. *mumtaaz* 'excellent' × *fantastic*).

12.4 Attempts at classification

The simplest type of blend is produced by haplology, e.g. *gues(s)timate* [1936] (*gu*[*ess*] × *estimate*), *mocktail* [1936] (*m*[*ock*] × [*cock*]*tail*), Chef Emeril Lagasse's *smellevision* [c.2000], *swelegant* [n.d.] (*sw*[*ell*] × *elegant*), *s*[*lang*]*language*, *swaption* [a.1988] (*swap* × [*op*]*tion*), *alco*[*hol*]*holiday* [n.d.], *sexclusive* (*sex* × [*ex*]*clusive*) [n.d.], *Whackademia*,[8] etc. Smith (2012a) also cites *sexcapade* [1951] and *sext(ing)* [2005][9] (*sex* × *text*).

Two recent formations that get many hits on Google are *slopportunity* (*slop* × *opportunity*) and *shopportunity* (*shop* × *opportunity*). This type is crosslinguistically widespread; cf. F *Républicoquin* 'Republic-rogue; opportunistic Republican' (*républicain* 'Republican' × *coquin* 'knave, rogue') (Wood 1911: 177). Another French type is *Homactu*, a website for largely gay men, consisting of *homme* 'man' + *actuel* 'current', cited by Arnold Zwicky in his blog (2/16/2012).[10]

From German and its dialects Wood cites 90 examples, e.g. (p. 182) *Kramatz* 'threadbare waste, useless junk' from *Kramm* 'junk' × *kratz-* 'scratch/scraping',

---

[8] books.google.com/books/about/Whackademia.html?id=6MYLsqqaApIC
[9] en.wikipedia.org/wiki/Sexting
[10] arnoldzwicky.wordpress.com/category/truncation/clipping/

(p. 183) *Latüchte* 'lantern' from *Laterne* 'lantern' × *Leuchte* 'lamp, lantern'.[11] Note also Ancient Greek *amphoreús* 'two-handled jar' for *amphi-phoreús* '(jar) having a handle on both sides' (cf. Wood 1911: 177).

In a related type, the two source-words share one or more segments or sounds, e.g. *rurban* [1915] (*rur*[*al*] × *urban*), *medicare* (*medi*[*cal*] × *care*), *televangelist* (*telev*[*ision*] × [*ev*]*angelist*), *rockumentary* (*ro*[*ck*] × [*do*]*cumentary*) (cf. Ayto 1989: 323; 1990: 218; Fischer 1998: 163ff.), *Motown* [1959] (*Motor* × *town*), *himbo* [1988] (*him* × *bimbo*), *Californication* [1997] (*California* × *fornication*), *cultivar* (*culti*[*vated*] × *var*[*iety*]), *radome* (*ra*[*dar*] × *dome*), *gaydar* [1988] (*gay* × *radar*), *fuzzword* [1983] (*fuzzy* × *buzzword*), *staycation* [2005] (*stay*[*at home*] × *vacation*) (Cook 2010: 51; *COED*). Two-hundred and thirty of the blends in Kelly (1998) have overlapping segments.

Algeo (1977), Soudek (1978), and Gries (2004) classify blends primarily according to degree of overlap, as in the above and *motor hotel* (*motel*), *austere-stern* (*austern*), *clandestiny* (*clandestine* × *destiny*), etc. The SWITCH POINT at the shared segments determines the order of the input constituents (Bat-El 2006: 69).

The term SPLINTER (clipped fragment) was introduced by Berman (1961: 279) to define blends. Subsequently, Soudek (1978) distinguished initial from final splinters, also applied to -*gate* (*Watergate* etc.); cf. also López Rúa (2002; 2004). Lehrer (2003; 2007) classifies blends according to composition by whole words or splinters. For instance, *narcoma* consists of a splinter of *narcotic* plus a full word *coma*. *Sitcom* consists of two splinters (*situation* and *comedy*) at the beginning of each word, but the splinter can be at the beginning of one word and the end of the other, e.g. *psychergy* (*psychic* × *energy*). And so on.

The type with discontinuous, or intercalative (Kemmer 2003), constituents, e.g. *entreporneur* (*entre*{*pre*}*neur* × *porn*[*ography*]) and Lewis Carroll's *chortle* (*ch*{*uck*}*le* × [*sn*]*ort*), is less frequent.

Lehrer also describes *frankfurter*, *turkeyfurter*, etc. the same way: "Once a blend is created, the splinter can be reused" (Lehrer 2007: 120). She goes on (p. 121ff.) to describe combining forms (§13.4), like -*gate* (§5.4), -*(a)holic* (§13.3), -*(a)thon* (§13.2), etc., as splinters that have become bound morphemes. At the same time, many have pointed out differences between generalizable affixes like -*(a/o)holic* and the unique constituents of a blend, like the -*og* of *smog* (Tournier 1985: 87). Extracted formatives like -*(a/o)holic* impart a semantic role to the lefthand constituent, e.g. *chocoholic* 'addicted to chocolate' (§13.3), which the -*og* of *smog* does not (Fradin et al. 2009: §4.5). And so on.

For some researchers, the splinter has unfortunately become the main classifier of blends (cf. Fandrych 2008: 115):[12]

---

[11] Thanks to Jules Gliesche (p.c.) for discussion of these words.
[12] Most of the entries are discussed in this chapter. Of those that are not, several are not immediately transparent, e.g. *AIM* is *AOL* (America Online) × *IM* (Instant Messenger). *WAPathy* is for *WAP* × *apathy*,

Initial and final splinter with overlap	*affluenza, burbulence, celebutante, pong*
Two initial splinters with overlap	*modem*
Two final splinters with overlap	*Kongfrontation*
Overlap of full words ('telescope')	*thinspirations, WAPathy*
Initial splinter + full word with overlap	*AIM, Coca-Colonization, emoticon*
Final splinter + full word with overlap	*netiquette*
Full word + final splinter with overlap	*adultescent, gundamentalist, himbo*
Insertion of one word into the other with overlap	*Clinterngate*
More than two constituents	*burbulence, Clinterngate, SMART*
Graphic blends	*Inglish, Lo-CALL, WAPathy*

Although the attempt to bring together acronyms, clips, blends, graphic play (*Lo-CALL*), etc., under one umbrella is admirable, what disadvantages such taxonomies is the absence of any analysis as to what predicts the form of the splinter(s) or the form of the output construct.

12.5 Analysis of blends

Since every analyst uses a different database, precise statistical counts are impossible. What is important is that the 100 (counting *buppie* 1×) historical blends in §12.2 illustrate the canonical blend types in English. As to distribution, there are 24 disyllabics, 23 monosyllabics, and 21 trisyllabics beside 32 of every other type. More significant is that all of the examples have one or two metrical feet.

That stresses and metrical feet play a role is clear from *cíne[ma cóm]plèx* and *dòcu[méntary] dráma* (Hong 2004). For Trommer and Zimmermann (2010), blends are a templatic effect of integrating segmental material under a prosodic word node. Lappe (2007) rejects the idea of templates in favor of optimality and constraint interaction because foot optimality does not predict the large number of monosyllabic forms. In fact, since most analyses are based on prosodic structures and the metrical foot, that is the overriding generalization.

in which *WAP* [1997] is 'wireless access/application protocol'. SMART is 'Swatch, Mercedes & Art', *Inglish* = Indian English, and *Lo-CALL* is *local* × *low [cost]* × *[phone] call*. Finally, *pong* is a most infelicitous blend of *poetry* and *song* because it is entirely opaque and in no way suggestive of the meaning. Fandrych does not mention her source for this construct which I have not located elsewhere.

All 22 of the monosyllabics in §12.2 are of course single-footed with a heavy syllable (two moras). The 25 disyllabics are split into one trochaic foot (15 tokens), and two monosyllabic feet:[13] 7 όὸ (*dumbfound, moonscape, radome, sitcom, pulsar, hazmat, carjack*) and 3 òό (*umpteen, motel, sci-fi*).

The 21 trisyllabics are also split between 1 dactylic foot όσσ (*catalo, dramedy, tangelo, beefalo, netiquette*[14]), 2 feet όσὸ (*flabbergast, banjolin, cultivar, happenstance, travelogue, positron, icecapade, medicare, cineplex, hacktivist*), four variable examples depending on the category N or V (*jazzercise, dancercize, sexercise* (Kolin 1985), *gues(s)timate*), correlating with conversion (§1.5.4), another way to derive the same output structures, and two examples with the main stress on the second syllable: òóσ (*Eurasian, stagflation*).

Barring some potential blends longer than six syllables, all 32 of the words longer than three syllables are two-footed. The preferred patterns are òσόσ (*contraception, sexploitation, hydramatic, recomember, docudrama, affluenza, adultescent, glitterati*) and òσόσσ (*Amerindian, advertorial, cafetorium, mockumentary* (cf. *rockumentary* [1969]), *televangelist, metrosexual, Demopublican*). Another common pattern is όσσσ (*palimony, breathalizer, infomercial, dallymony, Pictionary*). Note also *gerrymander* [1812] from *Elbridge Gerry* × *salamander*.

The remaining two-footed patterns are variations: σόσὸ (*adaptitude, Republicrat, celebutante, fantabulous, emoticon*), σòσό (*imagineer*), σòσόσ (*penultimatum, electrocution*), òσσόσ (*animatronics*), òσσόσσ (*priviligentsia*), όσσὸ (*blatterature*).

Factoring out the differing positions of the main stress, the main types are όσόσ (14 tokens), όσόσσ (8 tokens), and σόσό (5 tokens).

Given that the number of feet in words of two or three syllables is contingent on the weight of e.g. the final syllable (*dúmbfoùnd* vs. *búppie, flábbergàst* vs. *tángelo*), all of these types admit the same kind of analysis.

The simplest monosyllabic blends in §12.2, like *spoon* × *fork* → *spork*, or *smoke* × *fog* → *smog*, literary *snake* × *shark* → *snark*, and popular *moobs* [1990] (*man* × *boobs*) (COED) delete the onset of the second word and the nucleus and coda of the first, as illustrated in (1), for the structure of which see §9.1 (cf. Plag 2003: 124).

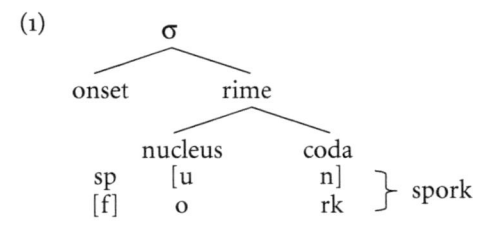

(1)
```
              σ
           ／＼
        onset   rime
               ／＼
           nucleus  coda
        sp   [u     n]  ⎫
        [f]   o     rk  ⎬ spork
                        ⎭
```

---

[13] In what follows, σ = syllable; ό = syllable with main stress; ὸ = syllable with secondary stress.

[14] There is regional and other variation in some of these. For Smith (2012a), *netiquette* is stressed òσό. In the OED, *banjolin* is a dactyl like *netiquette, ecotage* [1971] (*ecological* × *sabotage*), όσὸ in American.

If the first word is disyllabic, it can truncate the rime of the first syllable and everything after that, as in br[eakfast] × [l]unch → brunch (cf. Hong 2004). If the second word is a trochaic foot, it can remain, with the onset replaced by that of the first which behaves as in (1), yielding the type *twiddle* [a.1547], *grumble* [a.1586], *squiggle* [1804], *mimsy* [1855], *mingy* [1911] (*mean* × *stingy*), *sheeple* [1945] (*sheep* × *people*), *pleather* [1982] (*plastic* × *leather*), *Snausage* [n.d.] (*snack* × *sausage*). Smith (2012a) cites *snuba* [1989] (*snorkel* × *scuba*), *Groupon* (*group* × *coupon*), *bromance* (*bro(ther)* × *romance*), and *flustrate* (*fluster* × *frustrate*) http://www.urbandictionary.com/define.php?term=flustrated, a separate word (?) from the *OED*'s *flustrate* [1712], listed as an *-ate* extension of *fluster*. *Wussy* [1977] is supposedly from *wimp* × *pussy*, but Russ Nekorchuk reminds me that it must be clipped from *pussy-wussy*, widely used in the 1950s (§§7.3, 12.5).

The common *sitcom* type preferentially clips from the nucleus of the second syllable to the end of both words, mapping the previous second-syllable onset to the coda of the first syllable, as in the case of many clips (§11.5):

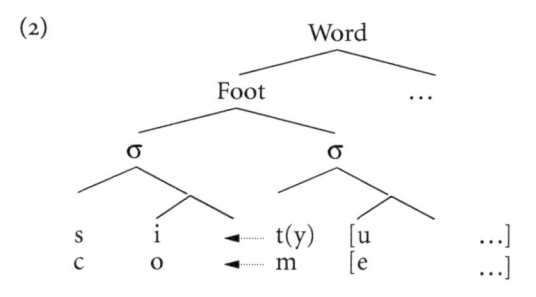

(2)
```
              Word
             /    \
           Foot    ...
          /    \
         σ      σ
        /\     /\
       s  i ◄─ t(y) [u    ...]
       c  o ◄─ m    [e    ...]
```

Since the only part of a syllable that can stand on its own is the nucleus, with deletion of the rime of the second syllable its onset is mapped onto the empty coda position of the preceding syllable (cf. McCarthy and Prince 1986; 1998).

Of the four-syllable blends, the optimal rhythm is two trochaic feet (§9.2): όσόσ (13 examples out of 18), e.g. *docudrama, recomember*. The most frequent five-syllable pattern (8 examples out of 11) is όσόσσ, i.e. one binary foot followed by a 'ternary' foot, e.g. *advertorial, televangelist*. The όσόσ and όσόσσ types are the same given the difference in input words. *Docudrama* has a second input word *dráma*, and *recomember* has [rè]*mémber*, both trochaic feet. In *advertorial, televangelist*, the input of the second word is [èdi]*tórial*, [è]*vángelist*, dactylic feet. In both types, the last or only foot of the second word remains and the first word is truncated from the second foot to the end:

(3)

```
                    Word
         ┌───────────┴───────────┐
         F                       F
       ┌─┴─┐                   ┌─┴─┐
       σ   σ                   σ   σ
      ╱╲  ╱╲                  ╱╲  ╱╲
     r e  k o               [l e  kt]
          [r e]              m e  m  b e  r
```

(4)

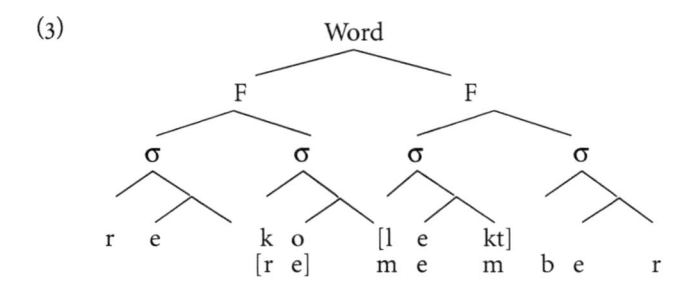

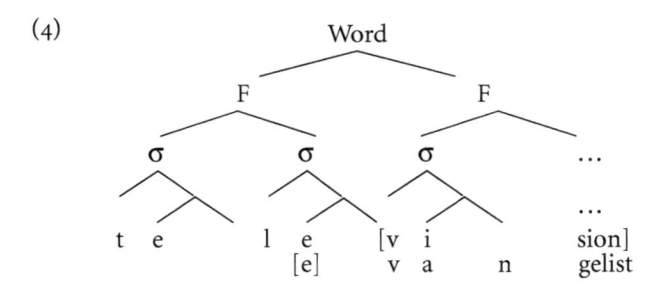

```
                    Word
         ┌───────────┴───────────┐
         F                       F
       ┌─┴─┐                   ┌─┴─┐
       σ   σ   σ                ...
      ╱╲  ╱╲  ╱╲                 ...
     t e  l e  [v i           sion]
          [e]  v  a   n        gelist
```

For an input string *situation comedy*, there seems to be no way to predict whether pattern (2) or (4) will prevail. Institutionalized *sitcom* is more economical than *situcomedy*, which should also be a valid blend by (4). When the first input word is polysyllabic, the (3/4) pattern can apply, as in *cíne[ma cóm]plèx*, where the first word is truncated after the initial trochee, and the last foot of the second word remains. In *theocon* [n.d.] (*theological* × *conservative*), cited by Cook (2010: 52), only the first syllable of the second word remains. Again, there are several ways to arrive at the same output structure, this time óσὸ.

These variations imply that the templates themselves can be blended. In *camcorder* [1982], *cam[era]* behaves like the first foot of (2), and *[re]corder* the second foot of (3):

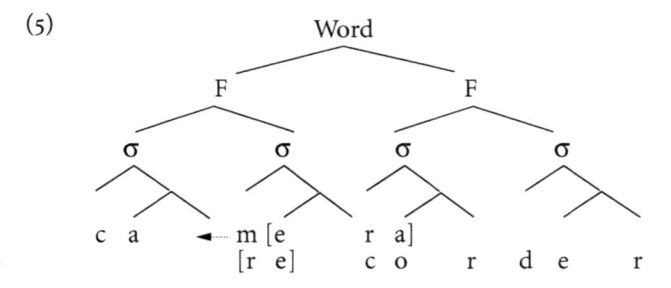

(5)

```
                    Word
         ┌───────────┴───────────┐
         F                       F
       ┌─┴─┐                   ┌─┴─┐
       σ   σ                   σ   σ
      ╱╲  ╱╲                  ╱╲  ╱╲
     c a  m [e              r a]
          [r e]              c o   r d e  r
```

Transistor [1948] (*tran(s)[fer]* × *[re]sistor*) is the same except that the stress is different because *camera* is stressed on *cam-*. Exactly like *transistor* are *Eurasian* [1844] (*European* × *Asian* [which is a binary trochee and needs no clipping]), *ginormous* [1948] (*gi[gantic]* × *[e]normous*), *stagflation* [1965] (*stag[nation]* × *[in]flation*), and *funtastic* (*fun* × *[fan]tastic*), which is not in the *OED* but gets many hits on Google, e.g. *funtastic* entertainment, toys, photos, times, getaways, etc.,[15] and even a softcore adult site *Funtasticus* <http://www.funtasticus.com/>.

The availability of more than one template for blend formation is responsible for different formations being produced by different people for the same input words, as reported by Bragdon (2008) in connection with psycholinguistic tests.

Finally, if a member of a blend lacks an onset, the first rime plus second onset is substituted: <u>in</u>formation x <u>commercial</u> → infomercial, <u>af</u>fluent x in<u>fluenza</u> → affluenza; cf. *edutainment* [1983], *advertainment* [2001]. In case of a complex cluster, the onset of the second syllable is also deleted, as in *Oxbridge* [1849] from <u>Ox</u>ford x <u>Cambridge</u>.

When both words have the same onset (<u>l</u>ime × <u>l</u>emon) and the normal template would yield an output identical to one of the input words (*lemon*), the rime of the first member is substituted for the onset, yielding *limon* [n.d.].

12.6 Selection and sequencing of input constituents

Bauer (1983: 235) inquires why Lewis Carroll's form is *mimsy* (*miserable* × *flimsy*) rather than **fli(m)(s)erable*, **mimera(m)sy*, **miserlimsy*, **misimsy*, etc. *Geep* and *shoat* invite the hypothesis that *mimsy* has *flimsy* as its second element, and that, as in most of the examples above, blends prototypically pluck out the onset of the first element and replace the onset of the second element with it. Forty-one of the blends in Kelly (1998) align an onset from the first component with a rime from the second. Thus, *brunch* has the *br-* of *breakfast* superimposed on the *l-* onset of *lunch*. Likewise, *mimsy* has the first onset *m-* of *miserable* in place of the onset *fl-* of *flimsy*; the rest of [*fl*]*imsy* remains the same. If the order had been reversed, the output of *flimsy* × *miserable* should have been **fliserable*, but blends require an output of one or two metrical feet, and its óσσσ form does not comply with that constraint. It is of some interest that with syncope or secondary final footing, the output *flisrable* óσσ or *flíserablè* óσσὸ seems slightly better.

Several input conditions are discussed by Kelly (1998: 580f.), Cook (2010: 47ff.), and Gries (2004; 2006; 2012): the first component of the blend (a) has fewer syllables than the second, and / or (b) denotes a more prototypical object, and / or (c) is more frequent. Also, the shorter word tends to contribute more phonological content than the longer, and blend constituents often have partial segmental and/or semantic overlap or other similarity. *Tangelo* consists of *tangerine* × *pomelo*. Since *tangerine* and *pomelo* are equisyllabic, *tangerine* is the first constituent by conditions (b) and (c). Apart from that, since *tangelo* would be rhythmically similar to **pongerine*, the input conditions are supposedly accorded higher priority. However, *tángelo* is a

---

[15] The earliest reference known to me is the company name *J & S Funtastic* <http://www.jsfuntastic.com/> which dates to 1972.

single dactylic foot, and *pòngeríne* (*pomelo* × *tangerine*) a two-foot word in the least optimal configuration of stresses, which is not attested in any of the blends in §12.2.

To return to *mimsy* and **fliserable*, *mimsy* violates at least one of the input conditions (longer *miserable* precedes shorter *flimsy*), but is selected because the output rhythm of **fliserable* is anomalous (cf. Bat-El and Cohen 2012).

In short, outputs are conditioned but not determined (*pace* Lappe 2007) by several preferred output prosodic structures.

Finally, there is the element of human creativity that defies formalization. *Affluenza* is transparently appealing in a way that *pong* is not. Although it is as wellformed as *brunch* or any other monosyllabic blend, *pong* is too opaque for anyone to figure out the meaning. It is therefore unlikely that any native speaker of American English would accept *pong* as a suitable blend of *poetry* and *song*, and Chris Smith points out (p.c.) that in British English it is even more unacceptable because it means 'stink'. For Americans, *pong* would make better sense as a blend of *poorman's bong*, or the like.[16] Even *affluenza* is not as straightforward as it appears. Since for most speakers *influenza* has been clipped to *flu* since 1827 (§11.6), the obvious question is why the full form [*in*]*fluenza* was selected over *flu*. *Afflu* would have been a perfectly good blend, and more economical, but *fluenza* carries with it a humorous insistence that affluence is a disease, and this is not really present in *afflu*.

In sharp contrast to *pong*, the misogynistic *feminazi* [1989] is completely transparent (*feminist* × *Nazi*) and has an optimal όσόσ rhythm. It is a variant of pattern (3) in that the second word is an optimal trochaic foot and no part needs to be clipped. The longer input constituent precedes the shorter to enforce the transparency of both.

Gries (2012) suggests that *foolosopher* may have been favored over *moronosopher*, *idio(to)sopher*, and the like, in order to exploit the phonological similarity of *fool* and *phil-*, which permits easy recognition of the constituents and the referent. At the same time, *moronosopher* has a certain appeal too, although the second constituent and the output construct are more opaque.

Op art [1964] is blended of *optical* × *art*. An input sequence *art* × *optical* would have yielded a totally nondescript **artical*.

Especially instructive is the minimal pair *cyborg* (*cyber* × *organism*) and *cyborgasm* (*cyber* × *orgasm*) (§13.2). The latter is due in part to the fact that *cyborg* was already preempted and in part to insist on the sexuality involved. Then there is the *boregasm*

---

[16] This implies that the frequency condition for recognizability of the input constituents of a blend is not as significant a factor as claimed by Lehrer (2003; 2007), Cook (2010: 45ff.), and Gries (2004; 2006; 2012). Compositional transparency of the output is at least as important. For *banalysis, banal* × *analysis* is more transparent than *banal* × *electrolysis* (discussion in Cook 2010: 63). At least one of the constituents must be recognizable (Fischer 1998: 176f.), even if in varying degrees.

[n.d.], 'the result of or act of reaching the apex or climax of boredom' (*Urban Dictionary*[17]).

Several blends have reversible input constituents, e.g. *absotively* [1914] (*absolutely × positively*) beside *posilutely* [1920] (*positively × absolutely*); *tigon* [1927] (*tiger × lion*) beside *liger* [1938] (*lion × tiger*) (Bat-El 2006: 66).

12.7 Sound-symbolic motivation

Snausage, a dog treat (http://snausages.com/), is a canonical blend of *snack* and *sausage*, except that one might logically expect it to have been a blend of *sausage snack*, as in their ad. In that case, however, the output would not have the initial *sn-* which, for a canine treat, yields the appropriate subliminal suggestion of *snout, snarf, snarl, snoot, snort,* etc. (§10.7).

According to Smith (2010; 2012a), some blends are motivated phonesthetically, and some non-blends were reanalyzed by folk etymology as phonesthetically motivated blends. She writes (p.c.): "My claim is that some shorter blends tap into the sound symbolic atoms of the English language giving them extra resonance (secondary motivation) and thereby giving them the appearance of a simplex word (no longer a blend)." Following are some of her examples (with phonesthetic values after Tournier):

Smog (*smoke × fog*) is preferable to *foke (*fog × smoke*) because *sm-* denotes taintedness. Likewise motivated is *smaze* (*smoke × haze*) as opposed to *hoke.

Glaze, if not derived from *glass*, is a blend of *glare × gaze*, consistent with the light, bright value of *gl-* (§10.8), as also in *glitterati* (*glitter × lit(t)erati*).

Flare is perhaps from *flame × glare*, but with *fl-* in the sense of light and fire (§10.7) rather than Tournier's surface or flow.

Twirl [1598] (*tirl* 'rotate' *× whirl*) has *tw-* denoting slight torque/torsion. Additional evidence for this meaning of *tw-* is that *twist* originally meant 'divide, separate' but by the mid-1500s assimilated to the torsion meaning 'unite by twining', which provides strong evidence for the torque/torsion meaning of *tw-*.

Squiggle [1804] (*squirm × wiggle*) contains *sk-* denoting some form of movement.

Crash (*crack × dash*), *clash* (*clap × crash, smash, splash*), *bash* (*beat/bat × dash*),[18] *smash* (*smite/smack × mash* or intensive of *mash* §10.5) are all consistent with diffusion of *-ash* in the sense of Wallis's and Tournier's 'violent harsh impact' (§10.7). Additional evidence for the violent harsh impact meaning of *-ash* is provided by *blash* [1725] (*blashy*) 'a b̲i̲g̲ (s)pl̲a̲s̲h̲ of liquid', which in 1861 assimilated to the

---

[17] http://www.urbandictionary.com/define.php?term=boregasm
[18] As one possibility, the *OED* speculates that *bash* could be from Scandinavian, which is at odds with everything that is known about words originating in primarily northern texts, where /š/ was converted to [sk] even in the absence of a corresponding Nordic word (Miller 2012: 125ff.).

harsh impact meaning 'gash, smash, bash'. Another input order, *splash* × *clap*, would yield **splap*, which would mean something akin to *splat* but in a messier sort of way, and would not have the 'violent harsh impact' sense.

Examples based on the blends in this chapter include the following:

Scrunch [1825] (*squeeze* × *crunch* or intensive of *crunch* §10.5) has *sk(r)-* which suggests (violent) compression (Wallis 1653: 49; 1688: 137; 1765: 160).

Spork [1970] (*spoon* × *fork*) has *sp-* denoting pointedness, sharpness. The reverse order *fork* × *spoon* would yield **foon*, an object more round and not as pronged as a *spork*. For the sound symbolism of round vowels and voiceless fricatives, see §10.3.

Blatterature [1512] 'bad literature' consists of *blatter* 'babble, prate' and *literature*. Of the many possible ways to coin a blend for the intended meaning, e.g. **biterature/ *blit* (*bad* × *literature*), **craplit* (*crappy* × *literature*), etc., *blatter* was selected as initial input because of the sound symbolic suggestion of *bla-bla-bla* (§10.2); cf. the *OED*: "the use of the word is probably largely influenced by its phonetic suggestiveness of forcible and repeated noise...." For *bl-* (*blab, bleat, blare*, etc.), cf. Argout (2010: §3.3f.).

Grumble [a.1586] is probably from a word akin to F *grommeler* 'mutter' plus *mumble* because low (especially non-front) vowels plus a nasal consonant represent low-pitched sounds (§10.3).

Bonk [1931] (*bang* × *conk*) is more expressive than either *bang* or *conk* because /ɔ/ has a frequency that represents items bigger and heavier than /æ/, and /b/ is more abrupt and louder than /k/ (§10.3). The alternative input order would yield the rather bland **cang*.

Snark (*snake* × *shark*) is preferable to the nondescript ⁽*⁾*shake* (*shark* × *snake*) not only because *shake* would not be distinctive but also because *snark* has *sn-* suggestive of the animal's large nose/mouth. *Sn-* also suggests derogation (§10.7), as in my made-up *snizzle* (*snow* × *fizzle*), and has both implications in *snivelization* (*snivel* × *civilization*).[19]

Prissy [1894] (*prim* × *sissy*) has all high-frequency voiceless consonants and front vowels characteristic of small size, light weight, deference, submission (§10.3).

Skort [1951] (*skirt* × *shorts*) contains *sk-* in the sense of 'cover' (Argout 2010), and the high-frequency voiceless consonants indicate small size and light weight (§10.3).

As noted in §9.4, styles changed in the high-tech era. Longer units of speech are truncated in such a way that more must be ascertained from the context. As Sadek Fodil puts it (p.c.), more is done/said with less. Chris Smith (2012a, and p.c.) observes that the constructs between 1300 and 1900 considered blends by the *OED* have some sort of sound symbolic motivation. This differs markedly from those in her sample from 1900 to present that rarely have sound symbolic motivation. This is entirely expected as a result of the streamlining of speech in the high-tech era. Modern blends

---

[19] According to the *Urban Dictionary* http://www.urbandictionary.com/define.php?term=snizzle *snizzle* exists as 7 different blends, one of which is *snow* × *drizzle* and denotes a mixture of the two.

are more functional/economical, like *docudrama, infomercial, Pictionary, Demopublican*. There is little room for sound symbolism in these. Words made up to be synesthetically suggestive or sound symbolic in some manner are currently most frequent in syndicated columns, brand names, and the language of advertising (Bragdon 2008, w. lit), e.g. *Craisin*s are dried cranberries that look like raisins. Older blends, like Lewis Carroll's *snark*, were created as much for their sound and sound-meaning as for their economy, while the reverse is true today. There is always room for creative individuals to coin words for their sound and sound-meaning as well as their economy, but it is becoming more rare.

12.8 Summary

The majority of blends can be derived by several templates, but the preferred output structures (one or two feet, with initial and/or alternating stress) are more important than the templates in that there is more than one way to arrive at the same output structures. English has a predilection for blends that begin with a stress and maintain alternating stresses:

Preferred types

όσ	*broasted, buppie, chunnel, flurry, guppie, himbo, liger, mingy, mimsy, modem, muppet, pleather, prissy, rurban, sheeple, slanguage, Snausage, snuba, squiggle, swaption, tigon, twiddle*
όὀ	*carjack, cyborg, dumbfound, hazmat, moonscape, Oxbridge, pulsar, radome, sitcom*
όσὀ	*banjolin, cineplex, cultivar, flabbergast, hacktivist, happenstance, icecapade, medicare, positron, theocon, travelogue*
όσσ	*camcorder, catalo, dramedy, tangelo, beefalo, netiquette*
όσὀ ~ όσσ	(V/N pairs): *dancercize, gues(s)timate, jazzercise, sexercise*
ό	*bash, brunch, crash, flare, geep, meld, moobs, prance, scroll, sext, shoat, skort, smash, smaze, smog, snark, spork, twirl*
ὀσόσ	*absotively, adultescent, affluenza, contraception, docudrama, edutainment, glitterati, hydramatic, positutely, recomember, sexploitation*
όσὀσ	*breathalizer, dallymony, feminazi, gerrymander, infomercial, palimony, Pictionary*
ὀσόσσ	*Amerindian, advertorial, cafetorium, Demopublican, metrosexual, mockumentary, televangelist*

Minor types

ὀόσ	*Eurasian, funtastic, ginormous, stagflation, transistor*
σόσὀ	*adaptitude, Republicrat, celebutante, fantabulous, emoticon*

σὸσό   imagineer
ὸσ́   austern, motel, sci-fi, umpteen
σὸσόσ   penultimatum, electrocution
ὸσσόσ   animatronics
ὸσσόσσ   priviligentsia
όσσὸ   blatterature

Trochaic structures are preferred for the first foot. If a dactylic foot is present, it is ideally at the end of the blend. An initial dactyl is the least preferred structure unless it is the entire word, i.e. consists of three syllables with a weak ultima.

For monosyllabic and disyllabic inputs the output is normally a one-foot word, i.e. pattern (1) above. For longer input words, choices are available among patterns (2) through (5). This is one reason why different people asked to create blends from the same words will produce different outputs, based on varying degrees of optimal foot structure. In all cases, syllable onsets and rimes behave as separate constituents in blending. Outputs are conditioned but not determined by prosodic wellformedness, specifically the preferred structures above.

Input constituents are selected and sequenced for a variety of reasons, some extralinguistic or phonesthetic, all with a view to compositional transparency of the output, given that the outputs are prosodically constrained.

Appendix: Alphabetical list of blends

absotively [1914]: *absolutely* × *positively*
adaptitude [1806]: *adapt* × *attitude*
adultescent [1996]: *adult* × *adolescent*
advertorial [1914]: *advertisement* × *editorial*
affluenza [1979]: *affluent* × *influenza*
Amerindian [1899]: *American* × *Indian*
animatronics [1971]: *animated* × *electronics*
austerne [a.1382]; *austere* × *stern*
banjolin [1889]: *banjo* × *mandolin*
bash [a.1642]: *beat/bat* × *dash*
beefalo [1974]: *beef* × *buffalo*
blatterature [1512]: *blatter* 'babble' × *literature*
bonk [1931]: *bang* × *conk*
breathalyzer [1960]: *breath* × *analyzer*
broasted [1980s]: *broiled* × *roasted*
brunch [1896]: *breakfast* × *lunch*
Buppie [1984]: *Black* × *yuppie*
buppie [1988]: *black* × *guppie*

cafetorium [a.1955]: *cafeteria* × *auditorium*
Californication [1997]: *California* × *fornication*
camcorder [1982]: *camera* × *recorder*
carjack(ing) [1991]: *car* × *hijack(ing)*
cat(t)alo [1889]: *cattle* × *buffalo*
celebutante [1939]: *celebrity* × *débutante*
chunnel [1914]: *channel* × *tunnel*
cineplex [1978]: *cinema* × *complex*
clash [?1500]: *clap* × *crash, smash, splash*
contraception [1886]: *contra* × *conception*
crash [?a.1400]: *crack* × *dash*
cultivar [1923]: *cultivated* × *variety*
cyborg [1960]: *cyber(netic)* × *organism*
dallymony [1987]: *dalliance* × *palimony*
dancercise [1967]: *dance* × *exercise*
Demopublican [n.d.]: *Democrat* × *Republican*
docudrama [1961]: *documentary* × *drama*
dramedy [1905]: *drama* × *comedy*

dumbfound [1653]: *dumb* × *confound*
edutainment [1983]: *education* × *entertainment*
electrocution [1889]: *electric* × *execution*
emoticon [1990]: *emotion* × *icon*
Eurasian [1844]: *European* × *Asian*
fantabulous [1959]: *fantastic* × *fabulous*
feminazi [1989]: *feminist* × *Nazi*
fidgitated [c.1907] 'uneasy': *fidgety* × *agitated*
flare [c.1550]: *flame* × *glare* (?)
flimsical [c.1907]: *flighty* × *whimsical*
flurry [1698]: *flurr* 'throw, fly' (?) × *hurry*
fooleosophers [1549]: *fool* × *philosopher*
funtastic [c.1972]: *fun* × *fantastic*
futilitarian [1827]: *futile* × *utilitarian*
gaydar [1988]: *gay* × *radar*
geep [1971]: *goat* × *sheep*
gerrymander [1812]: *Gerry* × *salamander*
ginormous [1948]: *gigantic* × *enormous*
glitterati [1956]: *glitter* × *lit(t)erati*
governator [c.2002]: *governor* × *terminator*
gues(s)timate [1936]: *guess* × *estimate*
guppie [1984]: *gay* × *yuppie*
hacktivist [1995]: *hack(er)* × *activist*
happenstance [1897]: *happening* × *circumstance*
hazmat [1980]: *hazardous* × *material*
himbo [1988]: *him* × *bimbo*
hydramatic [1951]: *hydraulic* × *automatic*
icecapade [1941]: *ice* × *escapade*
imagineer [1942]: *imagine* × *engineer*
infomercial [1981]: *information* × *commercial*
liger [1938]: *lion* × *tiger*
medicare [1953]: *medical* × *care*
meld [1936]: *melt* × *weld*
metrosexual [1994]: *metropolitan* × *hetero/homosexual*
mimsy [1855]: *miserable* × *flimsy*
mingy [1911]: *mean* × *stingy*
mocktail [1936]: *mock* × *cocktail*
mockumentary [1965]: *mock* × *documentary*
modem [1958]: *modulator* × *demodulator*
moobs [1990]: *man* × *boobs*
moonscape [1907]: *moon* × *landscape*

motel [1925]: *motor* × *hotel*
Motown [1959]: *Motor* × *town*
muppet [1959]: *marionette* (?) × *puppet*
netiquette [1982]: *(inter)net* × *etiquette*
Oxbridge [1849]: *Oxford* × *Cambridge*
palimony [1927]: *pal* × *alimony*
penultimatum [1882]: *penultimate* × *ultimatum*
Pictionary [1985]: *picture* × *dictionary*
pleather [1982]: *plastic* × *leather*
posilutely [1920]: *positively* × *absolutely*
positron [1933]: *positive* × *electron*
prance [c.1380]: *proud* × *dance*
prissy [1894]: *prim* × *sissy*
priviligentsia [1953]: *privilege* × *intelligentsia*
pulsar [1968]: *pulsating* × *star*
quasar [1964]: *quasi* × *stellar*
radome [1944]: *radar* × *dome*
recomember [1852]: *recollect* × *remember*
Republicrat [1872]: *Republican* × *Democrat*
rockumentary [1969]: *rock* × *documentary*
rurban [1915]: *rural* × *urban*
sci-fi [1955]: *science* × *fiction*
scroll [c.1400]: *scrow* × *roll*
sexcapade [1951]: *sex* × *escapade*
sexercise [1942]: *sex* × *exercise*
sexploitation [1924]: *sex* × *exploitation*
sext(ing) [2005]: *sex* × *text(ing)*
sheeple [1945]: *sheep* × *people*
shoat [1969]: *sheep* × *goat*
shopportunity [n.d.]: *shop* × *opportunity*
sitcom [1964]: *situation* × *comedy*
skort(s) [1951]: *skirt* × *shorts*
slanguage [1879]: *slang* × *language*
smash [1699]: *smite/smack* × *mash*
smaze [1953]: *smoke* × *haze*
smog [1884]: *smoke* × *fog*
snark [1876]: *snake* × *shark*
Snausage [n.d.]: *snack* × *sausage*
snivelization [1849]: *snivel* × *civilization*
snuba [1989]: *snorkel* × *scuba*
spork [1909 1×; 1970]: *spoon* × *fork*
squiggle [1804]: *squirm* × *wiggle*
stagflation [1965]: *stagnation* × *inflation*

staycation [2005] *stay [at home]* × *vacation*
swaption [a.1988]: *swap* × *option*
tangelo [1904]: *tangerine* × *pomelo*
televangelist [1973]: *television* × *evangelist*
theocon [n.d.]: *theological* × *conservative*
tigon [1927]: *tiger* × *lion*

transistor [1948]: *transfer* × *resistor*
travelogue [1903]: *travel* × *monologue*
twiddle [a.1547]: *twirl/twist* × *fiddle/piddle*
twirl [1598]: *tirl* 'rotate' × *whirl*
zillion [1944]: *z* = last in a sequence × *million*

13

Formative extraction, combining forms, and neoclassical compounding

This chapter discusses the extraction of new formatives, like *-(a)thon, -(a/o)holic*, which behave parallel to neoclassical combining forms (e.g. *-phobia, -(o)logist*) in the creation of neoclassical-type compounds (*talkathon, cosmologist*). Neoclassical compounding is argued to have begun with combining forms borrowed from Ancient Greek, some via Latin and especially Medieval Latin. In scientific language, these were augmented by freely combining Greek roots. More recently, truncated forms of Greek, Latin, and English words have provided additional input to neoclassical compounding. Neoclassical compounds with Latin and especially Greek roots continue to figure prominently in scientific and medical lexis. Both classical roots and modern truncated forms are frequent in playful language (cf. §15.1). Structurally, neoclassical roots are freely combinable, like the constituents of native English compounds.[1]

13.1 Formative extraction/secretion

New formatives can be *extracted* by clipping and blending. Various labels, including *secretion*, have been given to this process, which Rundblad and Kronenfeld (2000)

---

[1] Literature: Jespersen (1922: 384ff.), Marchand (1969: 211); Bareš (1974), Stein (1977), Bauer (1983: 213–16, 236f., 255–78), Tournier (1985: 86–102), Warren (1990), Baldi and Dawar (2000: 968), Plag (2003: 155–9), Baeskow (2004: ch. 3), Szymanek (2005: 435f.), Petropoulou (2009), Bauer, Díaz-Negrillo, and Valera (2009).

Haspelmath (1995) incorrectly takes secretion to be a subclass of affix reanalysis, whereby a portion of the root is reanalyzed as part of an affix. Consider extensions of Latin adjectival *-li-*: *animā-li-s* 'characterized by breath' → *-āli-*: *anim-ālis* ANIMAL, hence *carn-ālis* CARNAL, *jūdici-ālis* 'relating to the law courts' → *-iāli-*: *jūdic-iālis* JUDICIAL, hence ML *cord-iālis* cordial (*LSDE* 127f.). Neither of Haspelmath's conditions (affix syllabicity and syllable onset maximization) is relevant. True secreted suffixes like *-burger* and *-thon* also violate these conditions. Nor is type frequency a prerequisite (Enger 2007: 58). Haspelmath's morphotactic opacity is potentially the most relevant condition. Both affix generalization and formative extraction affect only word formation and the lexicon. Neither is a simplification or optimization of any sort (Maiden 2005; Enger 2007: 61ff.). In fact, the result is a complication of the available allomorphs of a given suffix (*LSDE* 11f.).

subsume under folk etymology (§7.1). New formations are created by analogy, e.g. *turkey burger* after *hamburger* (Klégr and Čermák 2010: 229f., w. lit).

A simple illustrative example is *e-*, extracted from *electronic* [1902], as in *e-mail* [1979], *e-text* [1990], *e-journal* [1991], *e-bill/payment* [1993], *e-commerce* [1993], *e-zine* [1994] 'e-magazine' (cf. *fanzine* [1949] 'fan magazine'), *e-currency* [1995], *e-dollar* [1995], *e-money* [1995], *e-credit* [1998], *e-ticket* [1998], *e-dissertation* [1999], *e-document* [2000], *e-flirting* [2000], *e-banking* [2001]. Also well attested on the internet are *e-reader, e-shopping*, and so on.

Prequel [1958], because of its meaning, is not a blend of *pre* + *sequel*. Rather, *-quel* '(film) story' is syphoned off (*film*) *sequel*, hence *prequel* is the '(story) before the story'.

13.2 Extractions from Ancient Greek words

The formative *-(a)thon* derives from Greek *Marathṓn* 'place overgrown with *márathon* (fennel)' (B. Olsen 2004: 230, 232). When the Persians led by Darius invaded Greece in 490 BCE, Pheidippides ran 150 miles to Sparta in two days for help. At the fennel field of Marathon, the Athenians, under Miltiades, defeated ten times their number of Persians (or so the Greeks tell the story). Pheidippides ran from Marathon to Athens with news of the victory, cried it out, and fell dead. In his memory, the *marathon* race of 26 miles 385 yards was added to the Olympic Games. From *marathon* [1896] 'the Marathon Race', [1908] 'long-distance run', [1915] 'event or extraordinary feat of long duration', comes clipped *-(a)thon* and numerous derivatives: *walkathon* [1930], *talkathon* [1934], *readathon* [1936], *telethon* [1949], *skatathon* [1970], *sellathon* [1976], *bike-a-thon* [n.d.], *danceathon* [n.d.], *singathon* [n.d.], *jumpropeathon* [n.d.]. *Megathon* [1987] 'event of impressive size or length' may be directly coined on *marathon* rather than compounded of *mega* 'large' plus clipped *-(a)thon* (Ayto 1989: 245f.).

Panorama was coined by Robert Barker in 1787 from G *pān* 'all' plus *hórāma* 'sight; spectacle', whence *diorama* [1823], *cyclorama* [1840], *motorama* [1947], *cinerama* [1951], *liquorama* [1954], *launderama* [1962], etc.

From Greek *neutron* [1899], *electron* [1891], derives *positron* [1937] 'the antiparticle of the electron', clipped from *posi*[*tive elec*]*tron*, whence *negatron* [1934], *cyclotron* [1935], *mesotron* [1938], *phantastron* [1943], *levitron* [1960], *teletron* [n.d.], the video games *Maze-a-Tron, Robotron*, and a free form *Tron*, plus facetious formations like *orgasmatron* [1973] 'device for inducing orgasm' (Ayto 1989: 278; 1990: 118f.).

13.3 Modern extractions

The formative *-burger* was extracted from *Hamburger steak*, a variety of steak served in Hamburg, Germany (= Salisbury steak), and bearing the German actor suffix *-er*

(Germ. *Burg* is 'castle, fort', *Bürger* 'citizen'); cf. *Hamburger* [1617] 'native or inhabitant of Hamburg'. For the suffix, cf. *Wien* 'Vienna' : *Wiener* 'Viennese', the latter in *Wienerwurst* 'Vienna sausage' (!), whence, by clipping, *wiener* [1889]. From 1884 the term *hamburg(er) steak* was applied to a kind of ground beef in America, where it was clipped to *hamburger* [1908]. The word was readily segmentable because of *ham*, even though *burger* did not exist as an independent word. Compare *cranberry* (< *crane + berry*), which was segmentable despite the absence of *cran*. Thanks to *cranapple*, etc., *cran* has been reinstated as a fully segmentable word.[2] Since *ham* existed, *burger* [1939] was accorded an interpretation, involving the chopped character of the meat. The fact that it was beef and not ham was evidently ascribed to idiosyncrasy, although some speakers noticed the discrepancy, hence *beefburger* [1940]. When applied consistently to a product containing cooked hamburger in a bun, various *burger* embellishments could be created. The *Observer* [28 Feb. 1960] writes: "Recently the Hamburger has become just a 'burger', and there are 'beefburgers', 'chefburgers', 'cheeseburgers', 'eggburgers' and even 'kingburgers'." Regionally, other kinds of (nonbeef-)burgers have made the menu: *deerburger, buffaloburger, kangarooburger, turkeyburger,"Smorgasburger"* (a brand of dogfood) (cf. Klégr and Čermák 2010: 229f., w. lit). Once the original meaning was lost, one could have a *steakburger* [1960].

One could theoretically distinguish a (chopped) *fishburger* [1976] from a (filleted) *fishwich*, with -*wich* clipped from *sandwich*, itself from a placename via a person from that place (§6.9). *Cheeseburger* was originally [1938] a ham and cheese sandwich, but by 1959 it had become a hamburger with cheese. In *eggburger* [1959], *chiliburger* [c.1975], and the like, -*burger* is merely an ABBREVIATED COMBINING FORM since these are (beef)burgers with egg, chili, etc. In *porkburger* [1939], *vegeburger* [1945] (~ *veggie burger* [1978]), *fishburger* [1976], etc., -*burger* is a genuine extracted element. *Fishburger* is not 'hamburger with fish' but 'fried patty made of fish served in a bun' (Warren 1990: 119). In abbreviation, all of the semantic elements are kept, while in formative extraction some elements of meaning are discarded.

The formative -*(a/o)holic*, denoting 'a person obsessed with or addicted to' (Ayto 1989: 7f.), derives initially from *alcoholic* (Kolin 1979; Bauer 1983: 236). There is no necessary reason *alcoholic* should mean 'person *addicted to* alcohol'; it could just as well have meant 'person producing (selling, etc.) alcohol'. But 'addicted to' became institutionalized as an integral part of the meaning. As observed by Warren (1990: 112), at the first encounter of words like *foodaholic* [1965], *workaholic* [1968], one must associate with -*(a)holic* the semantic elements 'person' and 'addicted to', which crucially presupposes knowledge of the meaning of *alcoholic*. The most frequent construct is *chocoholic* [1972]. Other examples include *sugarholic* [1965], *golfaholic*

---

[2] *The Herb Companion* (Dec./Jan. 1994/1995), p. 48: "Huckleberries are my first choice for the fruity sauce, but you could substitute any tart berry, including the traditional cran."

[1971], *carboholic* [1973], *footballaholic* [1974], *computerholic* [1977], *newsaholic* [1979], *spendaholic* [1982], *bookaholic* [1985], *milkaholic* [1986], *clothesaholic* [1987], *jadeaholic* [1987], *gasaholic* (car) [n.d.], *speedaholic* [n.d.], *runaholic* [n.d.], etc.

Recently *-mageddon* (from *Armageddon* [1811]) has become a productive combining form; cf. *snowmageddon* (§12.1). Arnold Zwicky in his blog for 6/7/2012 cites *foodmageddon*, weather *-mageddons*, traffic *-mageddons*, political *-mageddons*, and links to many more.[3]

Pyles (1952: 197, 199) discusses the new suffix *-eroo* 'conveying playfulness and jocularity' (Mattiello 2008: 69), segmented off *bucke/aroo* [1907], an adaptation of Sp. *vaquero* 'cowboy', first in English in the form *bakhara* [1852]. Documented words include *flopperoo* [1936] 'flop, failure', *pipperoo* [1939] 'pleasing person or thing', *brusheroo* [1941] 'brush-off', *boozeroo* [1943] 'drinking spree', *jerkeroo* [1964], *chickeroo* [n.d.] 'attractive female' and the more deprecative *chickeroonie*, both frequent in California slang in the 1970s, if not earlier.

From *pianola* [1898], an automated player-piano, and *granola* [1970], trademarked in 1886 and 1928, were made other commercial products, e.g. *Shinola* [1902], a brand of shoe polish, *Victrola* [1905], *moviola* [1923], etc. In slang *-ola* became a derogative, e.g. *payola* [1937], *shinola* [1944] 'shit', which spawned *crap(p)ola* [n.d.], etc.

Lavrova (2010) mentions *-dar* segmented off *radar*, hence *gaydar* [1988] (alone in the OED), *nerdar*, *jerkdar*, *geekdar*, *redneckdar*, etc., and *-licious* (segmented off *delicious*), e.g. *applelicious*, *babelicious*, *conjugalicious*, *crispalicious*, *crunchalicious*, *sodalicious*, etc. Hamans (2013: 315) mentions *-cade* 'parade', *-istan*, and others.

Extracted formatives differ from similar-appearing items in imparting a semantic role to their lefthand member, e.g. *gaydar* 'attuned to gays; able to spot a gay', *chocoholic* 'addicted to chocolate', and so on. This is not present with the constituents of a blend, e.g. the *-og* of *smog* (§12.4).

13.4 Combining forms

Combining forms are the constituent roots of compounds, initially of the neoclassical variety. They are often created by various forms of truncation (Chapter 11), including formative extraction.

Three groups of combining forms have been discussed by Warren (1990: 116).[4] See Table 13.1, where initial combining forms are modifiers and final combining forms are heads, which is normal for Greek and neoclassical compounds. The final elements in Group II involve formative extraction.

---

[3] arnoldzwicky.wordpress.com/2012/06/
[4] Combining forms are discussed by Stein (1977), Bauer (1983: 213–16, 255–78), Tournier (1985: 86–102), Warren (1990), Plag (2003: 155–9). Useful lists of neoclassical combining forms can be found in Borror (1960) and Partridge (1983: 867–970).

TABLE 13.1 **Functions of combining forms**

		Initial	Final
I	Non-truncated variant forms of model words (G *ástron* 'star', G *drómos* 'course; race'	*astro-*: *astrodome* 'stadium with translucent domed roof'	*-drome*: *alpinodrome* 'place for climbing contests'
II	Truncated forms of model words (here, *cybernetics, alcoholic, muzak*)	*cyber-*: *cyberphobia* 'fear of computers'	*-aholic*: *spendaholic* 'compulsive spender'
			-zak: *newzak* 'repeated news coverage of the same event'
III	Parts of model words which happen to be existing words		*-gate*: *Yuppiegate* 'scandal involving five Yuppies'

Cybernetic [1948] (cf. G *kubernḗtēs* 'steersman') was clipped to *cyber-* which became a combining form for 'machine, computer', as in the following *cyber-*words (cf. *ODNW* 79f.).:

cyborg [1960]	*cybercrime* [1991]	*cybermall* [1993]
cybertron [1961]	*cyberlife* [1991]	*cyberpet* [1993]
cybernate [1962]	*cybersex* [1991]	*cyberschool* [1993]
cyberculture [1963]	*cyberspeak* [1991]	*cybershop* [1993]
cybernaut [1965]	*cyberstore* [1991]	*cyberslacker* [1993]
cyberkid [1966]	*cyberworld* [1991]	*cybersmut* [1993]
cyberman [1966]	*cybrarian* [1991]	*cybersurf(er)* [1993]
cyberart [1971]	*cyberage* [1992]	*cyberterrorist* [1993]
cyberland [1975]	*cyberbabe* [1992]	*cyborgasm* [1993]
cybersphere [1978]	*cybercrook* [1992]	*cyber affair* [1994]
cyberphobia [1981]	*cyberfeminism* [1992]	*cyberbully* [1994]
cyberphobic [1981]	*cybergeek* [1992]	*cybercafé* [1994]
cyberspace [1982]	*cyberlaw* [1992]	*cyberjournalist* [1994]
cyberpunk [1983]	*cyber romance* [1992]	*cybersnob* [1994]
cyberfriend [1986]	*cyberthriller* [1992]	*cyberstalker* [1994]
cybercop [1989]	*cyberwar* [1992]	*cybersquatter* [1995]
Cyberia [1989]	*cybercash* [1993]	*cyberattack* [1996]
cyberporn [1989]	*cyberchondriac* [1993]	*cyberathlete* [2005]
cybersecurity [1989]	*cybercommunity* [1993]	*cyberlover* [2007]

Especially noteworthy are the blends *cybrary* [*cyber* × *library*], *cyborg* [*cyber* × *organism*], *cyborgasm* [*cyber* × *orgasm*] (§12.6), and the pun *Cyberia* (after *Siberia*). Generally speaking, nonce creations with *cyber-* increased after 1994 (Fischer 1998: 144), and *cyber-* became more productive than *techno-* in the period 1990–96 (p. 165), but it is also a fact that cyberisms have been to some extent displaced by the more productive *e-* formations.

From G *nánnos/nānos* 'dwarf' comes the combining form *nano-* [1947] 'a billionth', then 'relating to molecular proportions' (*ODNW* 203); then 'extremely small':

nanofarad [1951]	*nanokelvin* [1981]	*nanoparticle* [1989]
nanosecond [1958]	*nanolithography* [1981]	*nanoscopic* [1989]
nanoampere [1962]	*nanofabrication* [1983]	*nanowire* [1990]
nanometer [1963]	*nanocrystal* [1984]	*nanodevice* [1991]
nanoliter [1964]	*nanocomposite* [1986]	*nanotask* [1991]
nanowatt [1965]	*nanomachine* [1986]	*nanotube* [1992]
nanoskirt [1966]	*nanoscale* [1986]	*nanocellular* [1993]
nanoequivalent [1967]	*nanotech* [1987]	*nanomouse* [1994]
nanotesla [1970]	*nanophase* [1988]	*nanopause* [1994]
nanoelectronics [1972]	*nanorobot* [1988]	
nanotechnology [1974]	*nanobot* [1989]	
nanocomputer [1977]	*nanomaterial* [1989]	
nanoinstruction [1977]	*nanomechanical* [1989]	

Note in particular *nanobot* [1989] with the combining form *-bot* extracted from *robot*, whence also *mobot* [1959], *microbot* [1989], etc. (*ODNW* 46). To illustrate individual creativity, Zwicky (3/7/2012) cites *bro-bot* (*bro*[*ther*]) for men and *ho-bot* ([w]*ho*[*re*]) for women,[5] and Bill Maher ("Real Time with Bill Maher", TV, 3/23/2012) coined *Mitt-bot 3000* as a description of Mitt Romney.

The combining form *-nik* is extracted from (i) *sputnik* [1957] lit. 'fellow traveler' (Russ. *s* 'with, together' + *put'* 'path, way') and (ii) (Russian-) Yiddish *-nik*. The former include *Flopnik* [1957], *Kaputnik* [1957], *Muttnik* [1958], *Mousenik* [n.d.], *hoaxnik* [n.d.], and *spoofnik* [n.d.] (Koziol 1972: 251; Bauer 1983: 255–66; Szymanek 2005: 437). To the latter belong *realestatenick* [1905], *alrightnick* [1919], *nudn:i(c)k* [1925] 'tedious person', *nogoodnik* [1936], *stuck-upnick* [1945], *kibbutznik* [1949], *beatnik* [1958], *folknik* [1958], *beachnik* [n.d.], *boatnik* [n.d.], *draftnik* [n.d.], *jazznik* [n.d.], *neatnik* [1959], *peacenik* [1962], *protestnik* [1965], *computernik* [1973], *refusenik* [1973], *conferencenik* [1989], *thriftnik* [1989], *waitnik* [1989], *sportnik* [n.d.], etc. (cf. Bauer 1983: 259ff.; Ayto 1990: 322f., 341).

From *ecology* [1876], a combining form *eco-* was extracted, as in the following:

ecogeographical [1939]	*eco-activist* [1969]	*eco-art* [1970]
ecocultural [1949]	*ecocatastrophe* [1969]	*ecoconscious* [1970]
ecomorph [1954]	*ecocide* [1969]	*ecocrisis* [1970]
econiche [1958]	*ecofreak* [1969]	*ecodisaster* [1971]
ecomanagement [1968]	*ecospace* [1969]	*ecogift* [1971]

[5] arnoldzwicky.wordpress.com/category/truncation/clipping/

econut [1971]   eco-justice [1973]   econightmare [1989]
ecotage [1971] (§12.5) eco-audit [1980]   ecotourism [1989]
ecotraveler [1971]   ecoterrorism [1980]   eco-philosophy [1990]
ecodoom [1972]   ecominded [1985]   eco-efficiency [1992]
ecohouse [1972]   ecosabotage [1985]   eco-footprint [2002]

A combining form can begin as a clip (Chapter 11). *Information* was clipped to *info*, whence many compounds and blends, e.g. *infocenter* [1942], *infosphere* [1970], *infostructure* [1974], *infomania* [1975], *infographic* [1979], *infotainment* [1980], *infomercial* [1981], *infotech* [1981], *infoline* [1982], *infoglut* [1984], *infopreneur* [1985], *infowar* [1985], *infonaut* [1986], *info-poor* [1990], *info-rich* [1990]. (cf. *ODNW* 156f.). Fischer (1998: §4.3) predicts that *info-* will follow the path of *cyber-*. Recent examples on Google include *infobank*, *infoblog*, *infogroup*, *infolab*, *infolinks*, *infomart*, *infomine*, *infonet*, *infopass*, *infoplease*, *infoQ*, *infospace*, *infotopia*, *infovision*, *infovista*, and many others.

To conclude this section, combining forms are morphologically and semantically motivated. Their diffusion via existing words with the same element leads to productivity and promotes institutionalization (Fischer 1998: 178f., 181).

13.5 Combining forms of Ancient Greek origin

Greek was rich in compounds, and many combining forms in English originated as combining forms in Ancient Greek. Neoclassical compounds in English began with these. A short list is repeated from Miller (2012: 218f.):

acro- 'high; of the extremities'
agath(o)- 'good'
all(o)- 'other, alternate, distinct'
arch- 'chief; original'
argyr(o)- 'silver'
aut(o)- 'self(-induced); spontaneous'
bary-/bar(o)- 'heavy; low; internal'
brachy- 'short'
brady- 'slow'
cac(o)- 'bad'
chlor(o)- 'green; chlorine'
chrys(o)- 'gold; golden-yellow'
cry(o)- 'freezing; low-temperature'
crypt(o)- 'secret; concealed'
cyan(o)- 'blue'
dipl(o)- 'twofold, double'

dolich(o)- 'long'
erythr(o)- 'red'
eu- 'good, well'
glauc(o)- 'bluish-green, grey'
gluc(o)- 'glucose'
glyc(o)- 'sugar; glycerol'
glycy- 'sweet'
gymn(o)- 'naked, bare'
heter(o)- 'other, different'
hol(o)- 'whole, entire'
homeo- 'similar; equal'
hom(o)- 'same'
leuc/k(o)- 'white'
macro- '(abnormally) large'
mega- 'huge; very large'
megal(o)- 'large; grandiose'

-megaly 'abnormal enlargement'
melan(o)- 'black; dark-; pigmented'
mes(o)- 'middle'
micr(o)- '(very) small'
nano- 'thousand-millionth; very small'
necr(o)- 'dead; death'
ne(o)- 'new; modified; follower'
olig(o)- 'few; diminished; retardation'
orth(o)- 'upright; straight; correct'
oxy- 'sharp, pointed; keen'
pachy- 'thick'
pan(to)- 'all'
picr(o)- 'bitter'
platy- 'broad, flat'

poikil(o)- 'variegated; variable'
poly- 'much, many'
proto- 'first'
pseud(o)- 'false'
scler(o)- 'hard'
soph(o)- 'skilled; wise'
-sophy 'skilled; wise'
tachy- 'swift'
techno- [craft] 'technical; of technology'
tel(e)- '(operating) at a distance'
tele(o)- 'complete; totally developed'
therm(o)- 'warm, hot'
trachy- 'rough'

Some of these have become very productive in English. Under *mega-*, the *OED* online lists 25 technical words and 24 non-technical, with additional examples available in cross-reference. Among the oldest in the technical category are *megacosm* [1617], *megameter* [1768], *megascope* [1831], *megabacteria* [1883], *megacocci* [1883]. Non-technical examples include *megabuck(s)* [1946], *megaton* [1952], *megastructure* [1965], *megacity* [1967], *megavitamin* [1968], *megastar* [1969], *megafestival* [1970], *megabusiness* [1973], *megadeal* [1978], *megabank* [1979], *megamall* [1980], *megaseller* [1983], *megabid* [1985], *megabitch* [1985]. Since, as the last word shows, *mega-* is completely productive in English (cf. *ODNW* 188f.), no further examples are necessary.

Another generalization from the technical type (*megacephalous* [1857], *megaphonic* [1881]) involves prefixing *mega-* to adjectives, e.g. *megarich* [1980] (cf. *superrich* [1969], *ultrarich* [n.d.]). Although documentation is scarce in technical sources, most speakers can freely create constructs like *megaspacious* which occurs in many online descriptions of living quarters. Also attested on Google are *megadelicious*, *megalovely*, *megapsychotic*, *megasmall*(!), *megaspecific*, *megatired*, etc. *Megafast*, *Megasoft*, and *Megaspeedy* are brand names.

Techno- has also enjoyed recent proliferation (*ODNW* 310f.), but mostly in nonce words, especially in the period 1990–96, even if they are compositionally transparent (Fischer 1998: §4.2). As with some other neoclassical formations, the older examples are more scholarly; cf. *technological* [1627], *technography* [1840], *technonomy* [1882], *technocracy* [1895], *technoeconomic* [1917], *technocrat* [1932], *technoculture* [1946]. *Technophobia* [1947], *technomania* [1948], *technophile* [1955], and the like mark the transition to more colloquial:

technorock [1971]   technobabble [1981]   techno-shaman [1989]
technojargon [1972] technojunkie [1981]   techno-catch-up [2000]
technofreak [1973]   technostress [1982]   technoblunder [2007]
techno-aids [1975]   technonerd [1984]
technospeak [1976]   technothriller [1986]

Despite its use in telecommunications, *tele-* is of limited productivity (*ODNW* 311f.), e.g. *teleteaching* [1953], *telecommute* [1974], *teleshopper* [1978], *telemarketing* [1980], *telebanking* [1981]. In the *OED*, the older use of *tele-* in its Greek sense of 'at a distance' (*telekinetic* [1890], *telepsychic* [1914], etc.) in fact outnumbers the modern uses, which have been partly displaced by *cyber-* and especially *e-*.

13.6 Neoclassical compounds

Many learned English words are compounds derived from Greek (or, more rarely, Latin) but not necessarily used as compounds in Greek.[6] These are referred to as neoclassical compounds. *Astronaut* [1929] consists of G *astḗr* 'star' + *naútēs* 'sailor', but *astronaútēs* is not attested as a compound in Ancient Greek. There were many *astro-* compounds, and formations like *Argonaútēs* 'sailor on the ship Argo' ARGONAUT [1596], *mesonaut* [1623] 'galley slave', and Horace Walpole's nonce *airgonaut* [1784], on which *astronaut* could be modeled. Similarly, *cosmonaut* [1959], with G *kósmos* 'universe', was first coined and used in Russian, but readily borrowed into English because it fits established patterns, earliest in the hybrid *aquanaut* [1881] (for expected *hydronaut* [n.d.]). As a result of these words in English, *-naut* has become a combining form (see below), hence *oceanaut* [1962], *lunarnaut* [1965], *cybernaut* [1965], etc. (Bauer 1983: 270ff.).

---

[6] From the English point of view these are supposedly not compounds because they are formed with stems rather than whole words. This Anglocentric view, however, is irrelevant to Greek, where inflectional affixes must be at the right edge of the word, entailing that all modifying words in a compound be bare roots or derivational stems. Bauer (1983: 213f.), Plag (2003: 155ff.), Kastovsky (2009: 326), and others rightly treat neoclassical compounds together with native English compounds because of the formers' increasing frequency in Western languages and semantic and structural parallels with the latter. The real problem is that some behave like compounding stems and some like affixes (Kastovsky 2013).

Since many combining forms in neoclassical compounds have nothing to do with classical bases, Picone (1996) calls the process PSEUDO-CLASSICAL NEOLOGY. Still, the model was Greek compounding, and *neo-* can imply departure from the established, leaving *neoclassical* as a reasonable term.

Neoclassical compounds are discussed in Hatcher (1951), Nybakken (1959), Ayers (1972), Stiles (1993). The last three treat medical terminology. More general studies are Baeskow (2004: ch. 3) and Petropoulou (2009). Many righthand constituents were bound stems (combining forms) already in Ancient Greek (Petropoulou, pp. 46, 48, w. lit), as were lefthand constituents (§13.5). As will be shown in the main text below, neoclassical compounds have the recursive character of standard English compounds (Bauer et al. 2009).

The combinatory properties of combining forms vs. other compound types are summarized by Plag (2003: 156) as follows:

[A] bound root can take an affix (...*bapt-ism, prob-able*), but cannot combine exclusively with another bound root (e.g. **bapt-prob*). Combining forms, however, can combine either with bound roots (e.g. *glaciology, scientology*), with words (*lazyitis, hydro-electric, morpho-syntax*), or with another combining form (*hydrology, morphology*) to make up a new word.

Like the type *horserace/racehorse*, combining forms in neoclassical compounds are freely sequenced (given interpretability), e.g. *metrology* [1801] / *logometric* [1813], *cosmonaut/nautocosm*—nonexistent but possible, e.g. in the sense of 'sailor world'; cf. *autocosm, nanocosm* attested on Google but not in the *OED*. There are also exocentric compounds like *polyglot* [1650] (lit. 'many-tongue'), and deverbal compounds like *gastroscope* [1888] ('stomach-observ(ing)') (Petropoulou 2009: 51f.). Blends also behave as canonical compounds: endocentric *bacne* [2003] (*back acne*) identificational *tottle* [*top* × *bottle*], dvandva *Brangelina* [*Brad* × *Angelina*], etc. (Smith 2012a). The principles of compounding can thus apply to underlying, derived, or output forms.

Neoclassical compounds tend to insert a juncture vowel *-o-* between constituents. This was becoming productive but far from obligatory in Greek. The Romans took it to be a characteristic feature and abused it in borrowings and their own creations (Biville 1995: 83–9). For instance, Ecclesiastical Greek *pseud-apóstolos* 'false apostle' was adapted directly by Tertullian [*c*.150/60–220] as *pseud-apostolus*, but Cyprian [*c*.200–58] and Jerome [*c*.340–420] write *pseud-o-apostolus* PSEUDOAPOSTLE [*c*.1449] with juncture *-o-* even before a vowel.

Juncture *-o-* has become so productive in neoclassical compounding that it appears in creations like *sadomasochism* [1919], with *sad-o-* extracted from *sadism* [1818], *sadist* [1892], etc., all derived from the Marquis de Sade [1740–1814]. Additional examples can be found in Baeskow (2004: 87) and Petropoulou (2009: 44).

The more technical the word, the more likely it is to be a neoclassical compound. Consider *electro/en/cephalo/graph* (slashes mark individual word-stem boundaries), lit. 'electric/in/head/record(er)', in which 'in-head' was G *enképhalos* 'brain'. The *electric* root goes back to G *élektron* 'amber', which produced sparks when rubbed—a relatively minor adaptation of an old word to the modern world of *electronics* (§6.2e).

Apart from that, the compound is linguistically illformed, as are numerous neoclassical compounds, for the formation of which linguists are seldom consulted. In a compound in Greek or English, the verb's complement is adjacent to the verb; cf. *tree-pasta-eating* (Selkirk 1982: 36f.) 'eating pasta in a tree' (or 'eating tree-pasta'); **pasta-tree-eating* would be more difficult to interpret, viz. 'eating trees with pasta' or 'eating pasta trees'! Therefore, *electro-encephalo-graph* [1935] should mean '(instrument) recording the brain with electric current'; the intended '(instrument that) records electric current within the brain' should be **encephal(o)-electro-graph*.

Despite the illformedness, however, since compounds freely enter into derivation, it is no surprise to find constructs like *electroencephalograph-y* [1935].

Neoclassical compounds are recursive (Bauer et al. 2009). One of the longest words in English is the neoclassical spoof *necro/bio/neo/palaeont/hydro/chthon/anthropo/pitheko/logy* [dead/alive-young/old-water/earth-man/ape-study], a satire of medical jargon by Charles Kingsley in *The Water-Babies* (cf. Grove 1950: 56). Another is *pneumon/o[ultra/micro/scop/ic][silic/o/volcan/o]coni/osis*, a lung disease caused by inhalation of extremely fine particles of siliceous dust.[7] The literal composition is 'lung-ultramicroscopic-silica-volcanic-dust-condition'. For the sake of comparison, observe the actual lung disease *pneumo/coni/osis* [lung-dust-condition] [1881] 'lung disease caused by prolonged inhalation of metallic dusts', and *silicosis* [1881] '(lung) fibrosis caused by prolonged inhalation of silica dust'. A more descriptively accurate formation for the latter would be *pneumo(no)/silico/coni/osis* but, as always, economy enters the picture.

Neoclassical compounds made with Greek and Neolatin roots figure most prominently in scientific and medical terminology.

Finally, it must be emphasized that classical combining forms are frequent in language play. Examples cited in this chapter include *econut*, *infoglut*, *megabitch*, *technobabble*. Arnold Zwicky cites *hungerectomy* and *truthectomy*,[8] both of which are readily processable.

13.7 Derivation from neoclassical compounds

Constraints on derivation from neoclassical compounds can be illustrated by actor and instrument nouns. The affix *-ian* is used on nominal bases, and *-ist* primarily on nominal bases, while *-er* appears on all kinds of bases. It is on nominal bases where complications arise. Different formatives favor one or the other affix, as shown in Table 13.2.

Two frequent words have mixed patterns: *astrologer* [a.1382] / *astrologian* [Ch.] / *astrologist* [1681], *astronomien* [1300] / *astronomer* [a.1382] / *astronomist* [1663]. Despite recent attestations of all three of the latter, only *astronomer* is current, in

---

[7] The word is usually attributed to Frank Scully, who popularized it in his *Bedside Manna* (1936) (cf. Hughes 2000: 43), but Scully repeated it (incorrectly) from the opening session of the National Puzzlers' League (1935), for which it was probably coined by the League's president Everett M. Smith "in imitation of polysyllabic medical terms" (*OED* online).

The suffix *-osis* itself is from Greek. Of the 5645 Greek feminine abstract nouns in *-si-*, 156 occur first in Hippocrates. Not surprisingly, then, of the 315 Latin borrowings, 109 are medical (André 1971: 45, 50f.), e.g. *sclerosis* [1398], *necrosis* [1583], *anadiplosis* [1589], *enarthrosis* [1634], *diagnosis* [1681], *hematosis* [1684], *glaucosis* [1706], *cyanosis* [1834]. The use of *-osis* in the sense of 'medical condition' has become productive in English via borrowings, neoclassical formations like *psychosis* [1847] (1846 in German), *trichinosis* [1866], *halitosis* [1874], *psittacosis* [1896], and English coinages like *hallucinosis* [1905].

[8] itre.cis.upenn.edu/~myl/languagelog/archives/003514

TABLE 13.2 Actor suffixes on neoclassical compounds

-o-graph- favors -er	(never allows -ian)	
ge-o-graph-er	*ge-o-graph-ist	*ge-o-graph-ian
cart-o-graph-er	*cart-o-graph-ist	*cart-o-graph-ian
sten-o-graph-er	*sten-o-graph-ist	*sten-o-graph-ian
chore-o-graph-er	*chore-o-graph-ist	*chore-o-graph-ian
-o-log- favors -ist	(occasionally allows -ian)	
*ec-o-log-er	ec-o-log-ist	*ec-o-log-ian
?ge-o-log-er	ge-o-log-ist	*ge-o-log-ian
*anthrop-o-log-er	anthrop-o-log-ist	*anthrop-o-log-ian
*the-o-log-er	the-o-log-ist	the-o-log-ian
-o-nom- favors -ist	(never allows -ian)	
*ec-o-nom-er	ec-o-nom-ist	*ec-o-nom-ian
?agr-o-nom-er	agr-o-nom-ist	*agr-o-nom-ian
*tax-o-nom-er	tax-o-nom-ist	*tax-o-nom-ian

reverse of the normal pattern for *-nom-*. Evidently these common examples are regarded as exceptional, which implies that the selection of *-er*, *-ist*, and *-ian* is determined by feature matching, choices being contingent on the combining form.

Historically, institutionalization of *geologist* was far from immediate. English had *geologist* [1778], *geologer* [1797–1993], *geologue* [1799–1876], *geologian* [1813–1931], and *geologician* [1818–55]. *Anthropologist* [1798] was contemporaneous with the *geolog-* set but had no alternate forms. For more recent words, like *ecologist* [1893], *-ist* on *-log-* bases is the norm.

Theologer [1588–1876] was a collateral form to *theologist* [a.1638] (ML *theologista*) and *theologian* [1483] (from French), but the authority of Medieval Latin and French prevailed.

Although *taxonomer* once existed [1885, 1897], *taxonomist* [1877] follows the pattern of the *-nom-* class, which, like *-log-* (Urdang et al. 1986), had paired verbs in *-ize* (*-nom-ize*, *-log-ize*), which on the Ancient Greek model made nouns in *-ist*; cf. *chronologize* [c.1616]/*chronologist* [1611] (from French), *etymologize* [c.1530]/*etymologist* [1625], *apologize* [1597]/*apologist* [1640], *economize* [1649]/*economist* [1586], *homologize* [1716]/*homologist* [1849], etc. (Miller 2012: 216f.). Recent words like *agronomist* [1818] follow the Greek-derived pattern.

Geographer was early [1534], but LL *geōgraphus* [c4] also came into English [1547], and would have been adapted as **geograph*, to which productive *-er* was added. An attested example is agentive *choreograph* [1876] (from French), to which *-er* was applied, hence *choreographer* [1886]. There were also words like *chirographer* [1400] from F *chirographaire* 'id.' adapted with *-er*. These various types institutionalized *-er* with *-graph-* but not without some variation, like *cosmographer* [a.1527] ~ *cosmographist*

[1656–1812], *stenographer* [1809] ~ *stenographist* [1839–1905]. Recent words like *cartographer* [1863] comply with the established derivational pattern.

13.8 Summary

Neoclassical compounding began with combining forms borrowed from Ancient Greek, some via Latin and especially Medieval Latin (Miller 2012: ch. 7). In scientific language, these were augmented by combining Greek roots freely. More recently, truncated forms of Greek, Latin, and English words have provided additional input to neoclassical compounding. Neoclassical compounds with Latin and especially Greek roots continue to figure prominently in scientific and medical lexis. Structurally, neoclassical roots are freely combinable, like the constituents of native English compounds. Both classical roots and modern truncated forms are frequent in language play. This is one of the few cases in which core and playful morphology differ very little (§15.1).

14

Reduplicative and conjunctive formations

This chapter discusses the principles that underlie the formation and ordering of the constituents in reduplicative and conjunctive formations, some with rhyme or near-rhyme, others with vowel gradation in a generalized apophonic pattern, numbering around 1800 lexical items (Thun 1963: ix). The conjunctive formations follow several different patterns. The most basic for non-equisyllabic constituents is Pāṇini's rule of shorter before longer. Beyond that, pragmatic, cultural, and formal factors determine the order, e.g. iconic sequencing, perceptual and formal markedness, power/importance, and vowel position. Also discussed are the properties of echoic dismissive *shm-*, phrases with linking prepositions, including *-cum-*, and *-a-* of different sources and function.

14.1 Total reduplication

Reduplication can be partial or full (Moravcsik 1978; Rubino 2005). Partial reduplication can be a morphological copy (Inkelas and Zoll 2005) or a phonological copy (Inkelas 2008). The former can be affix-like or compound-like (McCarthy and Prince 1998; Urbanczyk 2011). With full (or total) reduplication, words can be doubled in such a way that the second constituent is related to the first by alliteration and/or assonance.

Although reduplication has many different functions, it is the simplest way to express inherent repetition or an increase (or decrease) in quantity or degree. Reduplication is often used for intensification, iterativity, plurality, distributivity, progressivity, degree, etc. (Moravcsik 1978; Haiman 1980: 530f.; Rubino 2005; Urbanczyk 2011; Štekauer et al. 2012: 101–31), e.g. *very very big, long long ago* (Moravcsik 1978: 306–10). In these functions, reduplication abounds in creole syntax and morphology (Miller 2010: 2.280–83). In language play the primary function of reduplication is contrastive. It is thus similar to one of the uses of stress in standard English, as in *I said applic*ATION, *not applic*ATIVE.

The most productive reduplicative pattern involves identical constituent compounding (Hohenhaus 2004; Ghomeshi et al. 2004) and is accompanied by contrastive stress, e.g. *Do you LIKE-HIM like him?*; *It's not tuna salad, it's SALAD-salad*; *I meant LATIN-Latin, not British Latin*; *HOT hot, not spicy hot*, etc. The emphatic copied item contrasts with related items. Hohenhaus stresses that this process is lexicogenic in that it modifies the meaning: a *JOB job* is a prototypical job, and *JEALOUS jealous* is a quasi-superlative (cf. §§8.11, 15.3). With verbs, reduplication expresses intensification ('really'), e.g. *LIKE-HIM like him*. The type *HOT hot* clarifies the divergent meanings of *hot*. Since whole phrases (such as *like him*) or idioms can be copied, the construction is a combination of phonological, morphosyntactic, syntactic, and lexical properties, and therefore relies on packaged (sometimes called right-hemispherical) information.

Exact reduplication is ignored here, e.g. *glug glug* [1768], *swish-swish* [1833], *goody-goody* [1871] (1745 as a sweet), *din-din* [1905] 'dinner', *dum(b)-dum(b)* [1928], *boo-boo* [1938], *bling-bling* [1999] 'jewelry', *yackety-yackety* [1953] (67 examples in Dienhart 1999: 14ff.; cf. Mattiello 2008: 134f.).

The reduplicative patterns in this chapter do not serve the phonological purposes in Inkelas (2008) but they unequivocally have a metrical function. Most are expressive, and their motivation "is not morphological, but phonological and semantic-pragmatic" (Minkova 2002: 137; cf. §15.2). Some originate in child language. At least three subclasses of partial reduplication occur: (1) rhyming; (2) apophonic (vowel gradation); (3) conjunctive.

14.2 Rhyming pairs

14.2.1 Monosyllabic constituents

hotchpotch [c.1410], *hodgepodge* [c.1426], *humdrum* [1553], *deadhead* [1576] (modern sense [1942]), *habnab* [1580] (have-not have) 'hit or miss', *tagrag* [1582], *hotshot* [1593] (modern sense [1927]), *hobnob* [a.1616] (modern sense [1866]), *tidbit* [a.1641], *bigwig* [1703], *ragtag* [1725], *claptrap* [1727], *picnic* [1748] (< F *pique-nique*), *rag-bag* [1789], *nitwit* [1914], *wingding* [1927], *fat cat* [1928], *gang bang* [c.1945], *jet set* [1949], *braindrain* [1960], *rock jock* [1961] 'disc jockey', [1980] 'rock climber', *boob tube* [1966], *chill pill* [1981], *toy boy* [1981], *boy toy* [1982],[1] *snail mail* [1982], *bunch punch* [n.d.] 'group sex' (not in *OED*), *love dove* [1986] 'cocaine; Ecstasy', *fake-bake* [n.d.] 'tanning machine suntan' (not in *OED*), etc. (cf. Mattiello 2008: 133).

---

[1] Unlike Minkova (2002), I mention formations like *boy toy* (Chris Smith informs me that *toy boy* is more frequent in British English) because of the rhyming intentionality with which they were coined. It is true that genuine compounds like these have a different status from the reduplicated constructs in this chapter, but many of the rhyming formations in this section are canonical compounds of various kinds.

Near-rhyme: *flapjack* [1620], *humbug* [1751], *hopscotch* [1801], *hock shop* [1871]; *lame-brain* [1945], *wise guy* [1896] 'wiseacre', [1956] 'gangster'.

14.2.2 *Disyllabic constituents*

handy-dandy [1362]	*rumble-tumble* [1777]	*funny money* [1938]
hurly-burly [c.1440]	*lovey-dovey* [1781]	*walkie talkie* [1939]
†*hudder-mudder* [1461]	*teeny-weeny* [1825]	*itty-bitty* [1940]
'secrecy'	*trigger finger* [1829]	*nitty-gritty* [1940]
hugger-mugger [a.1529]	*hanky-panky* [1841]	*super-duper* [1940]
'secretly'	*tootsy-wootsy* [1854]	*culture vulture* [1945]
helter-skelter [1593]	*even-steven* [1866]	*arty-farty* [1946]
roly-poly [1602]	*razzle-dazzle* [1885]	*pussy-wussy* (§7.3, 12.5)
willy-nilly [1608]	*fuzzy-wuzzy* [1892]	*pooper-scooper* [1956]
hocus pocus [1624]	*teeny-weeny* [1894]	*wheeler-dealer* [1960]
hoity-toity [1668]	*jelly-belly* [1896]	*artsy-fartsy* [1962]
harum-scarum [1674]	*fuddy-duddy* [1904]	*loosey-goosey* [c.1965]
humpty-dumpty [1698]	*teensy-weensy* [1906]	*fender-bender* [1966]
namby-pamby [1726]	*heebie-jeebies* [1923]	*gender bender* [1975]
hurry-scurry [1732]	*hotsy-totsy* [1924]	*happy-clappy* [1990]
mumbo-jumbo [1738]	*snuggly wuggly* [1928]	*herky-jerky* [1994]
hurdy-gurdy [1749]	*jeepers-creepers* [1937]	*thriller chiller* [n.d.]
piggy-wiggy [1766]	*itsy-bitsy* [1938]	*chiller killer* [n.d.]

Roly-poly originally meant 'worthless person' [1602], then 'plump person' [1808], then 'a millipede' [1960]. *Hocus pocus* [1624] may be a corruption of the Eucharist formula *hoc est corpus* 'this is the body', as conjectured by John Tillotson [a.1694]. *Namby Pamby* [1726] was the title of a parody of the sentimental verses of Ambrose Phillips; cf. adj. 'insipid, sentimental, childish' [1745], then 'affectedly dainty' [1774]. *Happy-clappy* [1990] is a disparaging name for enthusiastic Christians (*ODNW* 137).

Like the equivalent Spanish formation, *tírotíro* 'a shooting' (cf. *tíro* 'a shot'), *tíquis míquis* 'unwarranted scruples', etc., the English rhyming pairs violate the same quasi-universal prosodic constraint as dvandvas (§3.5) in allowing two main stresses on a word (Wiltshire and Moyna 2002: 317ff.).

There is also the type with optional clip: *rinky-dink* [1895], *rinky-dinky* [1913], *okey-dokey* [1932], *okey-doke* [1934], *ricky-tick(y)* [1937], and with obligatory clip: *honky-tonk* [1924] (*honk-a-tonk* [1894]), *stumble-bum* [1932].

Eager beaver [1947] represents a near-rhyming type.

14.2.3 *Trisyllabic constituents*

Higgledy-piggledy [1598], (*nimini-primini*...) *niminy-piminy* [1786], *flibberty-gibberty* [1879] (~ *flybbergyb(e)* [1549], *Fliberdigibbet* [1603], *Flibber de'Jibb* [1640], etc.: see *flibbertigibbet* in the *OED*).

With clip: *lickety-click* [1843], *lickety-split* [1859], *bumpe/ity-bump* [1874], *blankety-blank* [1900], *clickety-click* [1913], *clinkety-clink* [1927], *muckety-muck* [1928], *yackety-ya(c)k* [1958].

14.3 Yiddish-English echoic dismissive *shm-*

Echoic dismissive *shm* applies to words of all categories (§15.1). It has been traditionally claimed to be inserted into the onset of the initial syllable of the copied word (cf. Steriade 1988: 78): *gelt shmelt (money shmoney)* 'money–who cares?', *moon shmoon, fancy shmancy, cancer shmancer, value shmalue, spoiled shmoiled, linguistics shminguistics, gadgets shmadgets*, etc. (cf. Spitzer 1952); note the identity constraint: **shmuck shmuck*. But this analysis leaves unexplained cases where *shm-* does not replace the entire onset, e.g. *breakfast shmreakfast ~ shmeakfast*, overwrites a medial onset, as in *obscene obschmene*, causes stress shift, like *árcade shmárcade* (Nevins and Vaux 2003b), or clips an unstressed initial syllable: *incredible shmedible* (Spitzer 1952).

Shm- echoes have several properties (Southern 2000b: 257): they are (1) "stripped-down topic/comment mini-utterances"; (2) "highly affective"; and (3) "verbless and elliptical". Southern (2002) traces the history of this process. Originally a single-word tabu-deformation pattern, Yiddish derogatory and affectionate echoes entered Eastern Yiddish from contact with East Slavic expressive patterns and began to be productive around the end of the 19th century. The Slavic patterns in turn derive from Turkic; cf. Turkish *para mara* 'money and suchlike', with the same identity constraint: **masa masa (masa* 'table').[2] In the 20th century, playful/deprecative *shm-* doublets were borrowed into Israeli Hebrew and (especially American) English, first in 1929, where they became productive in the 1950s.

As to analysis, Nevins and Vaux (2003b) note that many hypotheses are available to a learner hearing *bagel shmagel*: overwrite the first consonant, overwrite the first nucleus, overwrite up to the nucleus, overwrite in the stressed syllable, etc. These different hypotheses allow for variation, as exhibited among the 190 respondents to their survey. For instance, words that begin with a glide may or may not keep the glide, e.g. *union shmoonion* (75%) ~ *shmyoonion* (19%), *wig shmig* (92%) ~ *shmwig* (5%). Additionally, they discovered speakers with strident consonant dissimilation and some who reduplicate internally with optional initial clipping: *obscene shmobscene* (33%) ~ *(ob)shmene* (31%), *massage s(h)massage* (36%) ~ *(ma)s(h)mage* (11%), *arcade shmarcade* (87%) ~ *arshmade* (3%) ~ *shmade* (1×). They also cite *understandable undershmandable*, and other examples of interior *shm*-reduplication, as well as doubled *shm-* in *forbidden shmorshmidden* (rare because *sh-...sh-* is normally

---

[2] For additional examples of echoic reduplication (or echo copy) from other languages, see Rubino (2005), Urbanczyk (2005), Stolz (2008).

dissimilated), and metathetic variation: *Donald Shmumsfeld* (26.5%) ~ *Shmonald Rumsfeld* (18.5%).

As to lexicogenic potential, *fancy s(c)hmancy* gets a surprising number of hits on Google, is defined by the Urban Dictionary as (i) 'insulting high class', (ii) 'a high brow word for a common item', and by the Online Slang Dictionary as 'overly fancy'.[3]

14.4 Gradation

Apophonic gradation accounts for 490 (27%) of the 1,800 reduplicative constructs in Thun (1963: 220). Of those, 63.9% have the [ɪ-æ] pattern, 23.2% have [ɪ-ɔ/ɒ], and the remaining 12.9% exhibit nine other patterns (Minkova 2002: 157). Apophonic gradation is no longer productive (Dienhart 1999: 33), but this is true only of the E-language. Many individuals continue to coin formations of this type.

14.4.1 *Monosyllabic constituents*

mishmash [c.1475] (cf. Germ. *Mischmasch* [c16]), *riffraff* [c.1475] (cf. AN, OF *rifraf*, or shortened from *riff and raff* [1338], AN, OF *rif et raf* 'everyone, everything'), *trimtram* [1523], *whimwham* [a.1529], *flipflap* [1529], *pitpat* [a.1535], *flimflam* [c.1538], *jimjam* [c.1540], *mizmaze* [1547] 'maze', *tick-tack/tictac* [c.1550], *smick smack* [?1550], *riprap* [1557] 'undersea shoal', *thwick thwack* [1575], *dingdong* [1577], *wigwag* [1582], *snipsnap* [1597], *crisscross* [1602] (< *Christ-cross* [c.1430]), *singsong* [1609], *knickknack/nicnac* [a.1625], *chip-chop* [1630], *see-saw* [1640], *flipflop* [1661] (modern sense [1890]), *kit-cat* [1664] 'game of tip-cat', *hip-hop* [1672] 'with hopping movement', *slipslop* [1675], *tiptop* [1702], *swing swang* [a.1703] (and *swing swong* [1773]), *chitchat* [1710], *zigzag* [1712], *click-clack* [1782], *ticktock* [1847], *jim-jams* [1881], *clipclop* [1884], *pingpong* [1900], *King Kong* [1946], *hip-hop* [1982] 'rap music and culture'.

14.4.2 *Polysyllabic constituents*

Disyllabic (cf. Sp. *zípizópo* 'vain, stupid', to *zópo* 'malformed' etc.: Wiltshire and Moyna 2002: 317ff.): *pitter patter* [a.1450], *ribble-rabble* [1475], *busybody* [1526], *tittle tattle* [a.1529], *titter totter* [1530], *mingle mangle* [1549], *fiddle faddle* [1577], *dilly dally* [1592], *snipper snapper* [a.1593], *skimble-skamble* [1598] 'confused, nonsensical', *dingle dangle* [1598], *gibble gabble* [1600] 'senseless chatter', *jingle jangle* [1640], *fingle fangle* [a.1652] 'trifle', *wishy washy* [1693] 'feeble, trifling, trashy', *shilly shally* [1700] (< Shall I? Shall I?), *wiggle waggle* [1778], *mixty-maxty* [1786] 'jumbled, muddled', *higgle haggle* [1841], *didder dodder* [1878], *jibber jabber* [1922], *teeter totter* [1888], *wienie waggler* [n.d.] 'flasher' (not in *OED*), *hopey-changey* (Eugene Robinson, "Morning Joe" (MSNBC), 5/11/2012).

---

[3] onlineslangdictionary.com/meaning-definition-of/fancy-schmancy

With optional clip: *ticky-tacky* [1962] ~ *ticky-tack* [n.d.] (not in OED).
Trisyllabic: *hippety-hoppety* [1825], *rickety-rackety* [1840], *plinkity plunkity* [1924].
Trisyllabic with clip: *clickety-clack* [1877], *hippety-hop* [1888], *plinkety-plank* ~ *plinkety-plunk* [1891], *clinkety-clank* [1901].

14.4.3 *Phonological configurations*
In all of the above reduplicatives, a high front lax vowel occurs in the first constituent and a low vowel in the second. This configuration is irreversible; cf. **raff-riff*, **washy-wishy*, etc. (Minkova 2002: 139), just as *tic-tac* 'pendulum noise' is in French, where **tac-tic* is impossible, as noted by Grammont (1933: 379f.) and Sauvageot (1964), citing other examples, e.g. *pif-paf, pif-paf-pouf, bim-bam-boum, flic-flac, cric-crac, clic-clac*. Hilmer (1914), Paul (1920: 181), Grammont (1933: 379f.), Ségéral and Scheer (1998) cite such German examples as *bimbam(bum)* 'ding-dong', *fickfack, Flickflack* 'backflip', *Gickgack* 'clock' (child language), *kliffklaff* 'dog's bark', *klimperklamper, klingklang* 'cling-clang', *Klippklapp* 'clip-clop' (of hooves), *klitschklatsch* 'slipslop', *kribbeskrabbes, Krimskrams* 'odds and ends, bits and pieces', *mickmack, Mischmasch* 'hodgepodge, jumble', *pinkepanke, pitsch-patsch* 'pitter patter', *plitsch-platsch, Rips-raps* 'rip rap (rubble) retaining wall', *ritschratsch* 'rip!', *schwippschwapp* 'splish-splash', *Singsang* 'singsong; monotonous singing', *Schnickschnack* 'paraphernalia; balderdash!', *schwippschwapp* 'splish-splash', *stripstrap, ticktack* 'tick-tock', *wigenwagen, Wirrwarr* 'muss, tangle, clutter', *Zickzack* 'zigzag'.

English exceptions, such as *topsy-turvy* [1528], are rare (cf. Cooper and Ross 1975; Dienhart 1999: 30; Bauer 2001: 12f.). Still, there is a type with a central vowel in the first syllable: *upsy-daisy* [1862], *hunky-dory* [1866], *touchy-feely* [1968], etc. Minkova (2002: 150) cites six forms that conform to other properties, e.g. *flum-flam* [1546], *crush-crash* [1583], *flush-flash* [1583].

Prosodically, the reduplicatives are all two-footed with primary stress on the first or only syllable of the first constituent, and secondary stress on the first or only syllable of the second constituent (Minkova 2002). This is also true of playful reduplicatives in Spanish (Wiltshire and Moyna 2002). Minkova further relates this template to the metrical dipod in poetry. That is, *wishy-washy* is a trochaic dimeter. As to the vowel sequencing, the least marked vowel, lowest in sonority, and shortest phonetically precedes the more marked vowel of higher sonority and greater phonetic length, a variation on shorter before longer.[4]

Minkova disputes sound symbolic accounts, but the question is whether her account (apart from the Optimality Theory formalization) is truly different: high-

---

[4] On the final syllable *ritardo*, see also the discussion in Miller (2010: 1.239ff.). It is not a simple matter of markedness, as Minkova formulates it, but is rather contingent on a number of factors, especially position of the word in the utterance, adjacency to lower order constituents, and so on. In other words, markedness, if one insists on that term, must be defined contextually.

frequency vowels are iconically linked to light weight and rapidity while low-frequency vowels are linked to heavier weight and retardation (§10.3). It is also a fact that apophonic patterns like *sing–sang–sung* were a major part of the language long before the ablauting reduplicatives emerged in the 15th century. Ségéral and Scheer (1998) relate the reduplicative and grammatical pattern to a more generalized theory of apophony. Additionally, it must ultimately be explained how and why this type emerged in Anglo-French and the languages of Europe around the same time. It is misleading to say, with Minkova (2002: 155), that the type was borrowed from French when it has no more of a known ancestry in French than it does in English. Finally, the apophonic pattern $i > a > u$ is widespread crosslinguistically and the rule in Afroasiatic as well (Guerssel and Lowenstamm 1996; Ségéral 1995). This must be due to the same acoustic properties of high-frequency vowels before low that play a role in sound symbolism.

14.5 Conjunctive binomials

Binomials appear phrasal but, unlike phrasal idioms, have a generalizable phonological structure and other wordlike properties. They share with proverbs "preference for abbreviation; internal and/or initial phonetic figures such as assonance and alliteration; semantic / referential metonymy; ellipsis and marked word order" (Southern 2000b: 260). Structurally, there are three core types, all of which have good Indo-European antecedents (p. 261): (i) argument + negation [p + ~p] (or antithetical argument, e.g. *wax and wane*); (ii) argument + synonym [p + Δp] (type *safe and sound*); (iii) merism (a whole constructed of parts: [p + q = whole]), as in *flesh and blood* = physical life. From the point of view of content, the similarity to dvandvas (§3.5) is noteworthy.

These bipartite formulas rely fundamentally on harmonic complementarity between their two members: their close-woven formal structure is iconic of their ability to express unitary meaning, and a whole referent, with intensified force. Their formulaic power depends on specific expressive properties at this "holistic" phrasal-syntactic level.... Much of their capacities for popular endurance and survival can be ascribed directly to these artfully playful aesthetics of near-identity.   (Southern 2000b: 260)

As in the case of blends (§12.6), the first constituent of conjoined elements of equal length tends to be more prototypical or frequent than the second (Kelly, Bock, and Keil 1986; Kelly 1998), which tends to be informationally richer (Fenk-Oczlon 1989).

That many of the early conjoined words alliterate may be a retention from the Old English and Germanic alliterative poetic tradition (Jespersen 1938: 53f.).

14.5.1 Symmetrical and/or rhyming

one and one [OE], *thither and thither* [OE], *more and more* [?a.1200], *out and out* [c.1300], *by and by* [1300], *through and through* [1490], *(by) hook or crook* [1566], *so and so* [1596], *fair and square* [1604], *again and again* [a.1600], *on and on* [1631], *long and strong* [1650], *wear and tear* [1666], *neck and neck* [1672], *hot and hot* [1771], *high and dry* [1822], *highways and byways* [1839], *town and gown* [1854], *up-and-up* [1863], *slice and dice* [1941], *huff and puff* [1959], *surf and turf* [1961], *wheel and deal* [1961], *wine and dine* [1965], *sea and ski* [n.d.] (not in *OED*).

Rhyming pairs are a frequent source of unofficial university course titles: *Maps and Naps* (Introduction to Physical Geography), *Stones and Bones* (Anthropology: World Pre-History), *Bag'em and Tag'em* (Field Zoology), *Socks and Jocks* (General Physical Education). See Eschholz and Rosa (1970).

Near-rhyming: *kith and kin* [1377], *thick and thin* [Ch.], *neat and clean* [1693], *push and pull* [1881$_N$, 1886$_A$], *down and out* [1889], *blood and guts* [1894], *day and age* [1910], *S & M* [1965].

14.5.2 Non-rhyming

night and day [EOE]	*hip and thigh* [1560]	*give and take* [1769]
~ *day(s) and night(s)* [c.1000]	*spic and span* [a.1580]	*cut and paste* [1772]
	hot and dry [1580]	(adj. [1937])
south and north [EOE]	*horse and cart* [1596]	*bride and groom* [1789]
~ *north and south* [LOE]	*rank and file* [1598]	*heart and soul* [1798]
far and wide [OE]	*back and forth* [1613]	*still and all* [1829]
out and in [OE]	*wet and cold* [1614]	*front and back* [1838]
might and main [OE]	~ *cold and wet* [1617]	*open and shut* [1841]
meek and mild [?a.1200]	*fore and aft* [a.1618]	*nip and tuck* [1845]
up and down [?a.1200]	*full and by* [1627]	*pots and pans* [1850]
high and low [c.1200]	*aid and abet* [1636]	*hard and fast* [1867]
dumb and deaf [1200]	*cats and dogs* [1651]	*fish and chips* [1876]
in and out [a.1240]	*null and void* [1653]	*cat and mouse* [1887]
right and left [1325]	*touch and go* [1655]	*hit and run* [1899]
born and bred [a.1340]	*rant and rave* [1657]	*coal and steel* [1901]
to and fro [a.1340]	*ups and downs* [1659]	*stop and go* [1926]
here and there [a.1375]	*dogs and cats* [1661]	*cut and paste* [1937]
safe and sound [a.1375]	*by and large* [1669]	*hunt and peck* [c.1940]
hot and cold [1390]	*ins and outs* [a.1670]	*rock and roll* [1941]
black and white [1395]	*hide and seek* [1673]	*nuts and bolts* [1947]
deaf and dumb [1400]	*food and drink* [1683]	*show and tell* [1950]
wax and wane [c.1440]	*dry and hot* [1688]	*tried and true* [1954]
skin and bone [c.1450]	*cut and dried* [1710]	*steel and coal* [1957]
free and frank [1481]	*wait and see* [1719]	*wash and wear* [1959]
tooth and nail [1534]	*kiss and tell* [1726]	*grunt and groan* [n.d.]
rich and poor [1539]	*cut and dry* [1730]	*plug and play* [1970]
fast and loose [1557]	*odds and ends* [?1746]	(adj. [1984])

Safe and sound [a.1375] is a remodeling of *whole and sound* (OE *hāl ond ʒesund*) after F *sain et sauf* (Koskenniemi 1968: 89, 108, 114). *Wax and wane* [c.1440] dates to the end of Middle English, but Ælfric [c.1000] already set the two in contrast. With *null and void* [1653] cf. *null or void* [1646] and *void and null* [1× 1651].

Click and Clack [1977], the Tappet brothers on Car Talk.[5]

Examples with a conjunction *(n)or* include: *sink or swim* [c.1410], *win or lose* [1555], *friend or foe* [1580], *hit or miss* [1609], *do or die* [a.1625], *heads or tails* [1684], *make or break* [1784] (adj. [1961]), *life or death* [1842], *hide nor hair* [1857], *all or none* [1900], *trick or treat* [1947].

The polysyllabic type includes: *genus and species* [1565], *before and after* [1578], *above and below* [1624], *tweedledum and tweedledee* [1725] ~ *tweedledee and tweedledum* [1769], *trial and error* [1806], *inner and outer* [1825], *flotsam and jetsam* [1840], *dirty and greasy* [1857], *nature and nurture* [1874], *bigger and better* [1920], *teachers and parents* [1921] ~ *parents and teachers* [1930], *forgive and forget* [1974], *marriage and divorce* [1997].

14.5.3 On predicting the order

The order of binomial constitutents can be predicted by a number of factors discussed by Benor and Levy (2006) and Mollin (2012).[6] The most important of those factors are cited here along with examples (A refers to the first constituent, B to the second).

(1) Iconic sequencing (A precedes B temporally or logically): *born and bred* [a.1340], *hide and seek* [1673], *kiss and tell* [1726], *cut and dried* [1710], *trial and error* [1806], *hit and run* [1899], *wash and wear* [1959].

(2) Perceptual markedness (A is perceptually less marked or more animate, positive, concrete, or proximal than B): *up and down* [?a.1200], *high and low* [c.1200], *in and out* [a.1240], *right and left* [1325], *to and fro* [1340], *here and there* [a.1375], *win or lose* [1555], *before and after* [1578], *horse and cart* [1596], *above and below* [1624], *bride and groom* [1789], *front and back* [1838], *open and shut* [1841].

(3) Formal markedness (A is structurally simpler or has a more general meaning or wider distribution than B): *might and main* [OE], *genus and species* [1565], *food and drink* [1683], *dirty and greasy* [1857].

---

[5] www.cartalk.com/

[6] Power accounts for a large number of examples in Mollin (2012) because she includes things like *food and drink*, which in this account are classified as formal markedness because food has a wider distribution than drink. This raises a more general problem with all of the statistical studies: it is not entirely evident which phrases belong in which categories. Some of the classificatory criteria are quite subjective.

(4) Power (A is more powerful or important than B): *rich and poor* [1539], *town and gown* [1854], *cat and mouse* [1887].
(5) Vowel position (the stressed vowel of A is higher and/or more front than B's): *meek and mild* [?a.1200], *skin and bone* [c.1450], *free and frank* [1481], *hip and thigh* [1560], *spic and span* [a.1580], *inner and outer* [1825], *still and all* [1829].

When more than one factor applies, as in *in and out* or *inner and outer*, satisfying (2) and (5), the phrase is more fixed. *Rich and poor* [1539] satisfies (4), (5), and (2) (rich is more positive than poor). *Poor and rich* is contrastive, not formulaic.

In some instances the factors themselves can be in conflict. Mollin (2012) notes that *mom(my)* and *dad(dy)* should have the reverse order because of power, but perceptual markedness puts mothers first, as also with *bride and groom* [1789] "because the bride is more salient in a wedding" (p. 95).

Competition is predicted when there is a conflict as to which factor applies, e.g. *cats and dogs* [1651] (front vowel first) vs. *dogs and cats* [1661] (power). In both cases, of course, closeness (perceptual markedness) can set one order or the other.

Wet and cold [1614] obeys (5); *cold and wet* [1617] obeys temperature before humidity, i.e. perceptual markedness (Benor and Levy 2006: 239); cf. *hot and dry* [1580], which is more frequent than *dry and hot* [1688].

Values and beliefs [1974] is predicted by power or perceptual markedness, but Mollin (2012: 84) finds it completely reversible, probably because *beliefs and values* follows (5).

Teachers and parents [1921] could be predicted by power and/or vowel position, while *parents and teachers* [1930] is probably due to perceptual markedness, which would also be a factor in favor of the former in a teacher's lounge. This underscores the crucial importance of CONTEXT (a.k.a. perceptual markedness). Similarly, *town and gown* is the norm but in an Oxford context, it is *gown and town* [1911–12].

Iconic sequencing trumps all other factors, and the markedness conditions are next. In the absence of decisive ordering factors, the binomial is predicted to be reversible, e.g. *tweedledum and tweedledee* [1725] ~ *tweedledee and tweedledum* [1769]. In the case of *night and day* [EOE] ~ *day(s) and night(s)* [c.1000], the latter is favored by perspective (perceptual markedness) and front vowel before back. In (pre-)Old English, when *night and day* was created, the vowels were reversed: /nɪχt/ and /daɪ̯/.

14.6 Pāṇini's rule

The general principle that shorter constituents precede longer in the unmarked case was first articulated by the ancient Indian grammarian Pāṇini (2.3.34). It is also called

BEHAGHEL'S FOURTH LAW after Behaghel (1909; 1928); cf. Krause (1922). It is the main condition for Cooper and Ross (1975: 78f.). Despite recent work that ignores the studies of the past, some 70% of all relevant tokens obey Pāṇini's rule. The first subsection illustrates the principle, and the second discusses the rationale for exceptions.

14.6.1 *Illustrations of Pāṇini's rule*

gold and silver [a.1123]
high and mighty [a.1200]
fire and brimstone [a.1300]
good and evil [ME]
first and foremost [1377]
part and parcel [1463]
fire and water [1489]
rules and statutes [1558]
words and phrases [1565]
direct and indirect [1584]
head and shoulders [a.1586]
nook and cranny [1592]
free and easy [1594]
law and order [1598]
skill and knowledge [1598]
rack and ruin [1599]
bread and butter [a.1625]
past and present [1629]
first and only [1660]
each and every [1663]
for and against [1667]
intents and purposes [1709]
pins and needles [1710]
faint and feeble [1727]
rough-and-ready [1730]
time and money [1786]
checks and balances [1787]
rough-and-tumble [a.1798]
trial and error [1806]
sick and tired [1812]

hot and heavy [1822]
time and energy [1837]
mental and physical [1839]
cloak-and-dagger [1841]
far and away [1852]
rich and famous [1854]
prim and proper [1855]
judge and jury [1874]
out and about [1881]
wild and woolly [1884]
kit and caboodle [1888]
up-and-coming [1889]
vim and vigor [?c20]
horse and carriage [1909]
salt and pepper [1915]
cash and carry [1917]
books and articles [1922]
slap and tickle [1928]
bits and pieces [1931]
gin and tonic [1935]
front and center [a.1955]
rules and regulations [1955]
design and development [1958]
down and dirty [1959]
feast and famine [1970]
tried and tested [1978]
assets and liabilities [1978]
smoke and mirrors [1980]
health and fitness [1986]

Skill and knowledge [1598] exists beside two attestations of *knowledge and skill* [1581, 1893]. *Words and phrases* [1565] coexists with *phrases and words* [1864]. *Vim and vigor* [?c20] is a replacement of Chaucer's *might and vigor* or Fowler's *force and vigor*.

And *books and articles* [1922] coexists with *articles and books* [1947]. Beside *time and money* [1786] is *money and time* [1791].

Examples from advertising abound, e.g. *Nut 'n Honey, Fruit & Fiber*. Exceptions, such as *Kibbles and Bits*, are less frequent.

With conjunction *or*: *for or against* [1647], *dead or alive* [1685], *rhyme or reason* [1729], *plus or minus* [1747], *all-or-nothing* [1765], *now or never* [1856], *feast or famine* [n.d.] (but note *feast and famine* [1970]).

Triads: *here, there, and everywhere* [a.1593]; *good, bad, and indifferent* [1638]; *ifs, ands, or buts* [a.1680] (cf. *ifs and ands* [a.1535]); *Tom, Dick, and Harry* [1734]; *hop, skip and a jump* [1760]; *good, bad, or indifferent* [1805]; *hook, line, and sinker* [1838]; *lock, stock, and barrel* [1842]; *signed, sealed, and delivered* [1847]; *cool, calm, and collected* [1992]; *judge, jury, and executioner* [n.d.], *way, shape, or form* [n.d.], etc. (Miller 1977: 3f.; Southern 2000b: 265).

Examples from pop culture include *Bed Bath and Beyond* (store name); *Sex, Lies and Videotape* (film title) (Southern 2000b: 265).

German obeys the same principle: *Leib und Leben* 'life and limb', *Blut und Boden* 'blood and soil', *Land und Leute* 'land and people', etc. (Behaghel 1928: §1051; Lambrecht 1984; Fenk-Oczlon 1989; Southern 2000b; 2002: ch. 11).

14.6.2 Derailments of Pāṇini's rule

Although modern scholarship (e.g. Mollin 2012) denies that the tradition considered exceptions or reversibility, Scott (1913) cites 276 phrases of which 42% have the reverse order. Genuine exceptions are, however, rare: *hither and yon* [OE], *silver and gold* [1340], *brightest and best* [1811], *nickel and dime* [1879]. Several of his examples (*crackers and cheese, pepper and salt, needles and pins*) occur more frequently in the expected order. Except for one example of *needles and pins* [1786], *pins and needles* is the only order recognized by the OED since 1710. *Pepper and salt* [1774] antedated *salt and pepper* [1915]. *Tonic and gin* (Billy Joel, "Piano Man") satisfies poetic rhyme.

No one ever claimed that shorter must categorically precede longer in English or any other language. Behaghel (1909: 110f.) specifically allowed for logical, chronological, and status factors to override prosodic.

The expected order is disrupted by a number of factors (cf. Malkiel 1959). Following are the most important of the relevant ones in Benor and Levy (2006) and Mollin (2012):[7]

---

[7] Some category conflations in Benor and Levy (2006) and Mollin (2012) make little sense and skew the results. As noted above, power is a huge category because many things are conflated with legitimate power.

(1) Iconic sequencing (A precedes B temporally or logically): *winter and spring* [1670], *summer and fall* [1792], *breakfast and lunch* [1843].
(2) Perceptual markedness (A is perceptually less marked or more animate, positive, concrete, or proximal than B): *hither and yon* [OE], *better or worse* [1484], *heaven and hell* [1509], *profit and loss* [1553], *pleasure and pain* [1690], *physical and mental* [1852].
(3) Formal markedness (A is structurally simpler or has a more general meaning or wider distribution than B): *flowers and pods* [1712], *singular and plural* [1783] (placed in the perceptual category by Benor and Levy).
(4) Power (A is more powerful or important than B): *Adam and Eve* [LOE], *husband and wife* [1399], *father and son* [1443], *shillings and pence* [1622], *chapter and verse* [1628], *paper and ink* [1656], *captain and crew* [1699], *fathers and sons* [1808], *mother and child* [1837], *dollars and cents* [1837], *bacon and eggs* [1862], *coffee and cream* [1863], *peaches and cream* [1893], *chicken and egg* [1959], *Tarzan and Jane* [n.d.], *Clinton and Gore, Obama and Biden*.
(5) Vowel position (the stressed vowel of A is higher and/or more front than that of B): *silver and gold* [1340], *brightest and best* [1811], *needle and thread* [1859], *nickel and dime* [1879].

The full hierarchy of factors (Mollin 2012: 96) is as follows (> marks hierarchy levels):

[sequential] iconicity, perceptual markedness, formal markedness > power > number of syllables, avoidance of lapse [unstressed syllable sequences], avoidance of ultimate stress, word frequency > syllable weight, vowel length, syllable openness, vowel backness, final consonants, initial consonants > vowel height, initial sonority, final sonority

Within hierarchy levels, there is little predictive value compared to that from one level to another. The so-called semantic constraints take priority over the metrical ones. Number of syllables (Pāṇini's rule) does not rank higher than avoidance of ultimate stress because most of the violations of Pāṇini's rule also violate Avoid Final Stress.

The following illustrate competition among the factors (PR = Pāṇini's rule):

PR and power predict *gold and silver* [a.1123]; front vowel before back and perceptual markedness (silver is the poor person's gold!) predict *silver and gold* [1340].

Profit and loss [1553] is the only order attested in the *OED*, as predicted by perceptual markedness, but Mollin (2012: 84) finds it completely reversible. Of course *loss and profit* (not in the *OED*) obeys PR.

Flowers and fruits [1690] obeys formal markedness while *fruits and flowers* [1626] satisfies PR.

Time and money [1786], predicted by PR, occurs 90.14% more frequently than *money and time* [1791] in the sample of Mollin (2012: 83), the latter presumably due to a correlation of money with power, but the correlation is evidently a weak one.

Past and present [1629] conforms to PR and iconic sequencing but *present and past* [1821] conforms to proximal before distal (perceptual markedness).

Local and regional [2004] fits PR but *regional and local* [1969] conforms to the subset categorization (markedness).

Girls and women [1704] conforms to PR and iconic (scalar) sequencing, but *women and girls* [1758] is power first.

PR predicts *mental and physical* [1839]; *physical and mental* [1852] is predicted by concrete before abstract (perceptual markedness).

Words and phrases [1565] is predicted by PR, *phrases and words* [1864] by the more general first (markedness).

Principal and interest [1663] is predicted by power (Benor and Levy 2006: 239), but with *interest* contracted to two syllables, *interest and principal* [1694] obeys PR.

Beginning and end [1644] is iconic sequencing; *end and beginning* [1×: 1605] satisfies PR but iconic sequencing normally trumps all other factors.

Binomials ordered by power are most likely to undergo freezing. Those ordered by iconic sequencing and formal markedness are next in irreversibility (Mollin 2012: 99).

A curiosity noted by Scott (1913), which is responsible for a high percentage of his counterexamples to PR, is that college colors regularly have the longer first: *crimson and gold/blue/white, orange and blue/black, scarlet and gray/brown, yellow and blue/white*, etc. College colors not only violate PR and Avoid Final Stress, but also more before less frequent, less before more marked. Obviously crimson, orange, and scarlet are not less marked than gold, blue, black, brown, etc. (§8.5, end). However, with crimson and scarlet the more exotic color comes first by power and/or perceptual markedness, with *orange and blue/black*, brighter precedes darker (perceptual markedness), and yellow is universally important (§§8.5, 10.8) (power) and satisfies brightness/perceptual markedness as well. Also, several of these combinations are arranged according to light syllable before heavy or front/high vowel before back/low vowel. Incidentally, in American English, *orange* is generally monosyllabic, which alters the rationale for the ordering.

In the final analysis, Pāṇini's rule accounts for about 70% of the data in its domain. Exceptions are motivated by semantic and cultural factors, which are naturally of greater importance in equisyllabic collocations.

14.7 Linking prepositions

14.7.1 *to*

day to day [1297], *face to face* [1340], *back to back* [c.1500], *hand to hand* [a.1533], *foot to foot* [1603] (cf. *feet to feet* [1553]), *head to head* [c.1728], *heart to heart* [1867], *toe to toe* [1942], *wall-to-wall* [1953], *peer-to-peer* [1979].

Asymmetrical: *top to toe* (many variants since EME, e.g. Juliana 59 [*a*.1225]: *from þe top to þe tan*), *hand to mouth* [1509], *face to foot* [1567], *top to bottom* [1624], *head to toe* [1676], *floor to ceiling* [1824], *dawn to dusk* [1938].

Generalized: *rags to riches* [1897], *nine to five* [1927], *down to earth* [1932] (literal sense [1930]), *out to lunch* [1955], *right to life* [1867] (adj. [1970]).

14.7.2 *by*

Word by word [OE], *side by side* [?*a*.1200], *day by day* [1362], *one by one* [1410], *piece by piece* [1425], *little by little* [1483], *step by step* [1565], *two by two* [1709], *bit by bit* [1849], *blow by blow* [1933].

Generalized: *fly-by-night* [1796].

14.7.3 *Other*

Word for word [1300], *sleight of hand* [*c*.1400], *hand in hand* [*c*.1500], *house of cards* [1645], *rule of thumb* [*a*.1658], *head over heels* [1771], *step for step* [1785], *all in all* [*a*.1824] (earlier examples seem to have the literal meaning 'all in all (things)'), *change of life* [1828], *hat in hand* [1853], *hill of beans* [1863], *case in point* [1875], *out of whack* [1885], *meals-on-wheels* [1926], *tongue-in-cheek* [1933], *one on one* [1939], *change of pace* [1940], *pay-per-view* [1950], etc.

14.8 Linking *-cum-*

Linking *-cum-* originated with Latin phrases like *cum grānō salis* 'with a grain of salt', then with early placenames from Latin documents, e.g. *Prestwich-cum-Oldham*, and Latin phrases borrowed into English, e.g. *cum div(idend)* 'with dividend'. In contemporary English it subordinates the second constituent to the first and typically means 'including; combined with; and also': *coffee cum chicory* [1871], *motor-bike-cum-sidecar trips* [1913], *philosophic-cum-economic tinge* [1939], *laboratory-cum-workshop* [1959], *dinner-cum-cocktail dresses* [1959], *pub-cum-hotel* [1986], *grammarian-cum-lexicographer* [1993], *bar-cum-café* [1995], *ladder-cum-mast* [1997], *reading-cum-book signing* [1998], etc. (cf. Stein 2000; Szymanek 2005: 433). Google attests *bookstore cum cafe-bar, bar-cum-bistro, attic-cum-studio, kitchen-cum-dining room, garage-cum-workshop, bus-cum-greenhouse, art gallery-cum-bar-cum-café*, and many others. Stein emphasizes that these combinations are ad hoc coinages and, like syntax, not necessarily subject to lexicalization. Productivity, however, insofar as the word is applicable at all, seems to be limited to literate and elite (or pretentious) circles.

14.9 Infixing reduplicatives

This type consists of apophonic and rhyming constructs with linking -a- of different sources and functions: *weilawei* (< *wā lā wā*) [OE] / *wel(l)awo* [?a.1200] / *wellaway* [1303] 'exclamation of lament', *welladay* [1570] (alteration of *wellaway*), *lullaby* [1577], *jig-a-jog* [1602], *pit-a-pat* [a.1625], *rub-a-dub* [a.1661], *(a)lackaday* [1703] (< *alack the day* [1599]), *rub-a-dub-dub* [1714], *hushaby* [1796], *rockabye* [1805], *thataway* [1839], *bricabrac* [1840] (< F *bric à brac*), *chockablock* [1840] 'jammed tackle; crammed', *scallywag/scalawag* [1848], *buckaroo* [1852] (< Sp. *vaquero* [1826]), *muck-a-muck* [1852], *outasight* (*out-of-sight*) [1893], *honk-a-tonk* [1894], *ding-a-ling* sound [1894], person [1935], *chugalug* [1903], *bangaram* [1935] 'rubbish', *bangarang* [1943] 'commotion', [n.d.] 'events boomeranging back from the banger the night before; rad, awesome' (*Urban Dictionary*), *portapak* [1951], etc. (38 examples in Thun 1963: 222ff.). Minkova (2002: 164f.) classifies the *clickety-clack* type (§14.4.2) here (cf. *click-clack* §4.4.1, *Click and Clack* §14.5.2), but in general the infixed reduplicatives are far more variable than the type(s) her paper targets. It is true that there is some overlap, like *muckety-muck/muck-a-muck*, *honky-tonk/honk-a-tonk*, but the apophonic reduplicatives are much more tightly constrained in form. *Razz(a)matazz* [1900] 'ostentatious, dazzling' may even belong here, assuming a relationship to *razzle-dazzle* (§14.2.2).

14.10 Summary

The reduplicatives and conjunctive formations, while superficially similar and sharing some overlap, are in fact quite different. The reduplicatives follow a relatively tight apophonic pattern not unlike the crosslinguistically widespread $i > a\ (> u)$ pattern. This in turn relates to the same acoustic properties of high-frequency vowels before low that play a role in sound symbolism.

The conjunctive formations follow several different patterns. The most basic for non-equisyllabic constituents is Pāṇini's rule of shorter before longer. Beyond that a number of pragmatic, cultural, and formal factors determine the order of the constituents. These include (1) iconic sequencing (A precedes B temporally or logically); (2) perceptual markedness (A is perceptually less marked or more animate, positive, concrete, or proximal than B); (3) formal markedness (A is structurally simpler or has a more general meaning or wider distribution than B); (4) power (A is more powerful or important than B); (5) vowel position (the stressed vowel of A is higher and/or more front than B's). These by no means exhaust the conditions, but are certainly among the most important. Iconic sequencing trumps all of the others, including (in most cases) Pāṇini's rule.

The less prevalent formations include echoic dismissive *shm-*, a number of phrases with linking preposition, and a final type linked by *-a-* of different sources and function. Most of the constructs with linking preposition began as ordinary phrases that became institutionalized and acquired new members analogically. Those with *-cum-* started off in Latin phrases, and *shm-* was borrowed from Yiddish.

15

Core and expressive morphology

Conclusion

This chapter summarizes the similarities and differences between core and expressive (or playful) morphology from English and theoretical perspectives, with notes on typology. The distinction between the processes based on implicit knowledge and those deployed with varying degrees of consciousness is upheld and reinforced. The structures of core morphology are distinguished from those that apply templatic or other prosodic structures to output representations. Finally, language play is separated from playful lexicogenesis.[1]

15.1 General properties

Not all word formation is equal in status. Derivation, inflection, compounding, and most backformations are governed by implicit knowledge (principles of grammar). By contrast, clipping, blending, formative extraction, acronyms, and the other playful processes are deliberate. Dressler (2000) classifies these as PARAMORPHOLOGY, distinct from METAMORPHOLOGY, the result of deliberate reflection and production. Hagège (1993) refers to the constructors of such formations as LANGUAGE BUILDERS because they manipulate the language with varying levels of consciousness.

Explicit knowledge is also assumed by Mattiello, who lists four hearer-oriented functions of expressive morphology (2008: 60, 211f.): (1) amusement, playfulness,

---

[1] Monolinguals are mostly relevant in this discussion. More explicit / conscious knowledge of core morphology is found among bilinguals and second language learners, as argued by several papers in Sanz and Leow (2011). Language play among children, e.g. punning, rhyming nonsense syllables, begins at a very young age and with limited L2 proficiency (Cekaite and Aronsson 2005). Monolingual children are also exposed to playful language and language play in children's verse, riddles, puns, inversions, parodies, and various other games (Cook 2000). Dressler (e.g. 1997: 1401) cites *papapia*, analogically modeled on *mamma mia* by a 22-month-old Austrian boy, as 'extragrammatical', subdivided into 'premorphology' in Dressler (2000). Such constructs provide an insight into the slightly later formations which are intentional forms of language play. Almost counterintuitively, children who do not have older siblings perform better with expressive morphology than those who do (Aronovitch 2012).

humor; (2) freshness, novelty, release from stylistic monotony; (3) the desire to impress someone with colorful terminology or bizarre expressions; and (4) impertinence, aggression, offensiveness.

While these functions are unequivocal, they can be motives for playful manipulation of core morphology as well as for expressive morphology. Our review of the differences between the two will begin with observations by Zwicky and Pullum (1987), for whom core and expressive morphology differ as follows:

1. The playful, poetic, or even ostentatious effects of expressive morphology are not present with core morphology.

While (1) is generally true, speakers can play with core morphology, and some core morphological operations can appear playful. Clausal modifiers of compounds, like "I have the *that-I-am-being-called-upon-every-five-minutes* headache" (§3.1), have been identified as peripheral or expressive morphology, but Meibauer (2007) argues that it is the fact that they are ad hoc creations and often witty that imparts this perception. However, this does not entail that in some languages the process is not part of playful morphology. In early Roman comedy, where compounds were not very productive, this was the case with mock Greek names (§3.1, end).

2. Core derivational morphology applies to specific inputs; expressive morphology can apply to inflected forms (*drygoodsteria*), compounds (*Madison goddamn Avenue*), and various other things. For instance, echoic *shm-* (§14.3) applies to output words of any lexical-syntactic category (Baldi and Dawar 2000: 965).

3. Expressive morphology belongs to varying levels of conscious knowledge, and, I would add, language play/word games are entirely conscious. Speakers vary greatly in their ability to control and manipulate that knowledge. Core morphology belongs to implicit language knowledge, and competence does not vary significantly among adult native speakers. Manipulation on a conscious level is not as frequent, but does occur.

Some recent examples of morphological manipulation can be cited from executive chef Sara Moulton's "Cooking Live" (Food Network, 1997–2003). These include *cookalong-ers* and *bake-along-ers*. One caller-inner described herself as "an oldtime *pressure cooker-er*" (i.e. one who prepares food with pressure cookers). Roeper (1999: 48) specifically declares **coffee-maker-er* ungrammatical (in contrast to *coffee-maker-maker*) and has no possible way to derive it. If that is correct, then the expressive effect of *pressure cooker-er* could derive from the violation of core derivational morphology. But what is the violation? The correct analysis is [[[pressure [[cook]er] er], in which the innermost *-er* is the instrument suffix on (*pressure*) *cook-* and the outer *-er* is the actor suffix attached to a noun, like *jeweler, artificer* (*LSDE* 142). While English has always allowed suffix recursion (§2.7), until recently it obeyed the identity constraint (§2.2.1). That is, examples like *-less-ness-less* and the like were perfectly wellformed, but *-esque-esque* and other identity types (*-ness-ness, -er-er,* etc.) were avoided. For most older speakers these sequences still sound somewhat odd. For younger speakers, they are near normal. Consider *strongerer* 'even stronger than someone claiming to be stronger' cited from child language, and the yogurt ad *Grow Strongerer* (Fortin 2011: 35f.).

4. Alternative outputs in one and the same speaker are frequent with expressive morphology (*drygoodseteria ~ drygoodsteria*), but not with core morphology, where variation even from one speaker to another is less pronounced than the individual differences with expressive morphology.

Another example of the playful application of a standard suffix is *ambimouseterous* with unique *-terous* (§5.3), perhaps for metrical reasons to maintain duple timing after the heavy base *mouse*. This contrasts with *ambisextrous* [1929] 'bisexual' cited by Mattiello (2008: 63), among others (§5.4).

5. The processes involved in expressive morphology are unconventional or atypical with respect to core morphological operations.

This is questionable, at least regarding atypicality (cf. Bat-El 2000). It is true that total reduplication plays a greater role in expressive than in core morphology in English (§14.1), but reduplication is extremely widespread in core morphology (Štekauer et al. 2012: 101–31). Also, apophonic patterns are fairly general in both (§§1.5.3, 10.3.2, 14.4).

Infixation is inconsequential in English morphology (§1.5.1) but features prominently in several types of language play (§5.5). The full-word insertion types are indeed outside the bounds of ordinary core morphology (cf. Mattiello 2008: 68). A humorous example of iconic insertion in early Latin is *saxō cere-comminuit-brum* 'split the skull (*cerebrum*) with a stone', traditionally attributed to Ennius.

Truncation (Chapters 9, 11–13) excises far more contentful material in playful than in core morphology. Playful morphology truncates essential parts of roots, which almost never happens in core morphology.[2]

Formative extraction (Chapter 13) is paralleled by suffix generalization except that a larger unit is segmented off in contrast to suffix generalization which rarely eliminates parts of roots. As combining forms in compounds of the neoclassical variety, both classical roots and modern truncated forms are frequent in expressive morphology and language play. At the same time, neoclassical roots are freely combinable, like the constituents of native English compounds, and in that sense take part in core morphological operations.

---

[2] The major exception in core morphology is the removal of reanalyzed vacuous material, as in the future tense formation in Modern Serbian (Miller 2010: 2.85, w. lit, where *pisati* is inadvertently glossed 'read'):

pisati = hć – u ~ písa–ć–u 'I will write'
write.INF-FUT-1SG ~ write-FUT-1SG

The part that gets eliminated (*-ti h*) is a relic of older *pisa-ti hoć–u* [write-inf want-1SG] 'I want to write'. When the construct was reanalyzed as a future, indicated by *-(h)ć-*, infinitival *-ti* became vacuous, and was eliminated, leaving a simple future suffix *-ć-* attached to the verbal base *pisa-*.

Blending (Chapter 12) is a variety of compounding and therefore differs less in substance than on the types of bases on which it operates. Blending applies not to morphological roots or bases but to prosodic formations, which ignore morphological boundaries. Core compounding is not subject to the prosodic constraints of blends.

15.2 Specific properties

Kilani-Schoch and Dressler (2005) propose a model in which grammatical morphology can be prototypical or non-prototypical/marginal (e.g. hypocoristics); extragrammatical (outside of Dressler's morphological component) consists of a variety of heterogeneous phenomena. Grammatical morphology is regular and predictable (given domains and classes), and based on implicit knowledge. Adult extragrammatical productions can be unsophisticated manipulations (abbreviation, simple and echoic reduplication), or sophisticated and totally conscious manipulations (blends, language games, secret languages, etc.). This implies that blends and the like cannot be prototypical, which is problematic.

Fradin, Montermini, and Plénat (2009) propose four criteria for extragrammatical morphology: (1) conscious creation, (2) extensive use of infrequent processes, like truncation or infixation, (3) unproductivity, (4) interaction of different components of the grammar.

All of these criteria are verified by the present study except for unproductivity. If productivity were any criterion, half of core morphology would be excluded from "morphology". Apart from that, depending on the meaning of *productive*, it is difficult to imagine anything more productive (defined by I-language potential) than clipping, blending, diminutive application, and the other processes that Dressler (e.g. 2000: 7) considers marginal.

The prosodic templates for clips and blends are unequivocally productive (cf. Lappe 2007; Alber and Arndt-Lappe 2012). Even the fact of competing templates is not probative, because core morphology can have competing rules and competing outputs. If there is any difference, it is in the number of competing templates and possible outputs, to the extent that it is difficult to ascertain which are the "most regular" beyond the requirement of one or two metrical feet. The maximum unpredictability, however, is in language play (word games), like echoic *shm-* (§14.3), the infixation games, and "dialects" of Pig Latin (§5.5). It seems, then, that language play must be separated from clipping, blending, and other types of playful lexicogenesis.

As noted by Bat-El (2000), there do not seem to be affixes that attach only to "extragrammatical" forms, which could support the idea that they are extragrammatical. However, the converse is also true. Affixes produced by "extragrammatical" processes can occur on core morphological derivations. Bat-El rightly considers the only true "extragrammatical" (or "non-grammatical") phenomena to be language games, which

manipulate grammatical structures, employ morphological operations which do not exist in natural languages (e.g. shifting a word final syllable to the beginning of the word, or inserting a phonological unit after every syllable in a word. (Bat-El 2000: §1.3)

Bat-El goes on to demonstrate that acronyms and blends are full words in every sense. This implies that the processes that override the outputs of core morphology create new structures with their own boundaries and inflections.

It has been suggested that playful lexicogenesis involves a subsystem of the lexicon (Itô and Mester 1995) "which provides the potential for creating new forms along the same lines in playful contexts" (Wiltshire and Moyna 2002: 318). But what sort of subsystem could be at issue when playful forms make use of the entire lexicon (or lexicons: §1.10)?

Phonesthesia (§10.7f.) might be considered a subset of the lexicon, but that seems like a stretch when all that is necessary is a link to other words with the same phonological sequences and related meanings. Moreover, since prosodic templates and other expressive processes affect words with phonesthetic value no differently from those without, there is no evidence for separate lexical subsystems. Additionally, phonesthetic roots undergo the same core morphological operations as non-phonesthetic roots.

Lexical links are pervasive. Metaphor presupposes that knowledge is stored in groups of related concepts (§6.1). Folk etymology crucially relies on the storage of words by sound and meaning (§7.1), as does the typical prosodic structure of tabu (de)formations (§7.4). More generally, Slobin (1974: 82ff.) and Mattiello (2008: 159f.) discuss antonymy contrast (*back/front, wet/dry, rich/poor*, etc.), associative grouping (*summer/sunshine/garden/flower/blossom, dog/eat, wing/bird/fly*), hyponymy (*daffodil > flower*), collocation linkage (*forward/forward-march*), and formal groups, e.g. phonological/rhyming patterns (*pack/tack, bread/red*), and syllable structure. People frequently recall the number of syllables but not the word.[3] And so on (discussion in Miller 2010: 1.98ff.).

For Dressler (e.g. 2000), paramorphology does not belong to a separate module because it represents an interface phenomenon. But *interface* has a technical meaning in generative grammar, and making use of information from different parts of the grammar is not the same thing. What is needed is recognition of the array of interconnections in the lexicon together with information from different components of the grammar.

---

[3] I have personally witnessed the following isosyllabic lapses: *Catanni* for *Minelli*, *Heffenträger* for *Zettelmoyer*, *Monty E. Python* for *Milton E. Proby*, and *Juanita* for *Geneva*.

Consider the following statement about blends:

Morphological structure is not particularly relevant to blends. Source lexemes are combined without regard to their morphological boundaries, and the internal structure of the resultant blend is not necessarily morphologically analyzable concatenatively. It is usual to find morphological overlap, residue, and/or clipped forms, rather than exhaustive divisibility of the blend into sequential, whole morphemes. (Kemmer 2003: 75f.)

What Kemmer says about morphological structure being irrelevant to blends is equally true of clips, acronyms, Pig Latin, and all forms of expressive language and speech play, in which it is the prosodic domain (syllable and foot) that is most significant. Like the reduplicative and conjunctive formations in Chapter 14, the motivation is semantic-pragmatic and phonological-prosodic rather than morphological.

Core morphology is restricted to certain regular positions within the word, as defined by apophony, consonant gradation, and the loci of affixation. Much of language play is unrestricted. For instance, sound symbolism can affect any part of a word (cf. Szabóné Habók 2009: 31).

Hypocoristic *-ie/y* is indiscriminately applied to nouns (*druggie*), adjectives (*biggie*), verbs (*clippie*), and adverbs (*downie*) (Mattiello 2008: 238). This is typical of evaluative morphology in many languages (Prieto 2005; Fortin 2011).

Numerous formations are constructed on deviant lexical bases, e.g. *hotsy-totsy* (§14.2.2), *yob(bishness)* (§5.5); cf. Mattiello (2008: 238).

Playful language habitually violates constraints, is immune to morphological and lexical boundaries, freely combines parts of words in accord with phonological and prosodic templates, and generally involves the packaging of information from different parts of the grammar. For this reason, there is a fundamental difference between principle-governed morphology which yields hierarchical structures and the expressive or playful phenomena that are better described in terms of schemata. This is the fundamental point missed by Bybee (2001), Kemmer (2003), and other cognitivists who analyze all linguistic data in terms of schemata. The preferred metrical outputs of blends, for instance, are best described in terms of PRODUCT-ORIENTED SCHEMAS (e.g. Kapatsinski 2013) rather than as SOURCE-ORIENTED (rule- or constraint-based) generalizations.

The parallel architecture of Ghomeshi et al. (2004) is also unnecessary. They contrast a model of grammar knowledge, which is supposedly not equipped for handling all lexicogenic processes, but do not discuss why a parallel architecture should fare any better at accomplishing this task. Architecture is not at issue. As noted above, what is relevant is the packaged use of information from different components, e.g. phonology/prosody and the lexicon. Moreover, truncation operations range over an entire word or collocation, clipping from an edge or other subsection.

Additional factors have been mentioned throughout this work. In §10.3, it was pointed out that the pattern in *bing–bang–bong* (etc.) is not formally different from *sing–sang–sung–song*, which raises the question of what makes the former expressive. Two factors were noted: (i) the link to an extralinguistic as opposed to a grammatical referent, and (ii) the use of a standard derivational mechanism for nonstandard purposes. Generally speaking, many aspects of expressive or playful morphology rely on the use of standard grammatical patterns for nonstandard functions, often with an extralinguistic referent. It was also noted that both grammatical and expressive/reduplicative apophony are widespread crosslinguistically, especially the type $i > a > u$, which is likely rooted in the same acoustic properties of high-frequency vowels before low that play a role in sound symbolism (§14.4.3).

Another general property of playful language is that the relationship between base and playful form is a relationship between two (or more) output forms (Wiltshire and Moyna 2002). The only exception known to me is the Cuna game in which the output *gabir* is based, not on the non-playful output *bíriga* 'year', but on its input form /birga/ (§5.5). Why this exception exists (or if it exists, depending on analysis) is not clear,[4] but in all other instances investigated here, the mapping of playful speech is from one output to another output.

15.3 Summary and conclusions

This work has examined the similarities and differences between core morphology and expressive or playful lexicogenesis from the point of view of the history of English and linguistic theory. Typologically, expressive morphology and language play make greater use of total reduplication, infixation, and radical truncation. Formative extraction is paralleled by suffix generalization, but the latter seldom affects roots. Apophonic patterns are general in both. Blending is a variety of compounding, and differs less in substance than in the bases on which it operates, and core compounding is not subject to the prosodic constraints of blends.

In theoretical terms, core morphology is hierarchical, determined by grammatical principles, recursive, and able to be manipulated to a limited extent. By contrast, playful language operates on output forms, violates grammatical constraints, is immune to morphological and lexical boundaries, combines parts of words in accord with phonological and prosodic templates, yields partly non-hierarchical constructs and partly new hierarchical structures, and generally involves packaging of information from different parts of the grammar. Crucially, the output forms to which expressive processes apply need not be fully inflected. They can be from the stage of the derivation prior to spellout where inflection is adjoined.

---

[4] Speakers of Cuna seem to have options of applying the game to underlying or surface forms. For *aili* 'mangrove', the game form can be *liak* from underlying /akli/ or *liai* from surface *aili* (Sherzer 1976: 33).

The main differences can be summarized as follows:

(1) Core morphology creates words by merging roots and formatives; playful lexicogenesis creates words from output formations, often prior to spellout.
(2) Core morphology driven by grammatical principles yields a hierarchical structure; expressive lexicogenesis based on prosodic templates typically does not. If anything, hierarchical constituent structure is overridden by expressive processes. In some cases, a new hierarchical structure is formed, as for instance when an abridged form enters derivation (*ufologist*) or is inflected (*TKO(e)d*) (§§9.3, 9.6).
(3) Core morphology is restricted to regular positions within the word; various forms of expressive lexicogenesis (e.g. sound symbolism, truncation, metathesis) can affect any part of the word.
(4) Core morphology is irrelevant to blends, clips, acronyms, Pig Latin, and all forms of speech play, which make use of the prosodic domain (syllable and foot).
(5) Playful lexicogenesis presupposes information from different parts of the grammar and lexicon, especially metrical phonology and semantics-pragmatics.
(6) Derivation by core morphology yields morphological and lexical boundaries, which playful language partly ignores and partly creates new ones. Boundaries are necessarily included in the schemas to prevent an infinite number of additions: "while schemas can straddle morpheme boundaries, they must have SOME specified alignment with them" (Kapatsinski 2013: 126).
(7) Apophonic processes are widespread crosslinguistically but may have either a grammatical (core morphological) or extralinguistic (e.g. sound-symbolic) referent. In English, the morphological function is no longer productive in E- or I-language, but the sound symbolic use remains available on an I-language basis.
(8) Infixation is rare crosslinguistically, but language play can insert entire words, which is not part of core morphology in any natural language. Extreme metathesis and the insertion of some unit before or after each syllable is also found in language play (§5.5) but not in core morphology.
(9) Even among exceptionally creative individuals, core morphology is less subject to conscious manipulation than is deliberate playful lexicogenesis.
(10) Core morphology is recursive; playful lexicogenesis is not, except in the trivial sense of multiple imitative reduplications (*bam bam bam*).

Finally, despite the differences, there are crucial points of overlap between core and expressive morphology:

(1) New formatives are readily created by clipping and other expressive processes, e.g. *-gate* 'scandal' (§5.4), *-(a/o)holic* 'addicted to', *-licious* 'appealing', *-dar* 'attuned to' (§13.3), hypocoristic *-s/z* in *obvs, lulz*, etc. (§11.7), *ker-* in *kerplonk* 'idiotic plonker' (§10.6). Clipping differs primarily in degree from the perceptual reanalysis that yields formatives in language change (Chapter 13, ftn. 1; Miller 2010: vol. 2, ch. 3). The major difference is that expressive lexicogenesis cannot create functional elements (§1.9) apart from degree words (§8.1), which also have lexical meaning, not unlike evaluative prefixes, e.g. *mega-* (§13.5), *nano-* (§13.4).

(2) Discourse emphatic processes like STRETCH have not traditionally been lexicogenic, but that seems to be changing on the evidence of the quasi-superlatives *gooo(-)ooood, bæææd* 'very good' (§10.4; cf. §8.11). What is most interesting about *bæææd* is that the extra-long vowel is distinctive, creating a different word from *bad*. This is consistent with what is known about the phonology of expressive formations: that they can make use of segments that are not a normal part of a language's inventory (§10.1) or are marginal in the grammar and lexicon (Stonham 1994).

(3) Identical constituent compounding is producing a new kind of degree modifier, e.g. JEALOUS *jealous* 'very jealous', LIKE-HIM *like him* 'really like him' (§14.1; cf. §8.11).

(4) Straight speech play (word games) can be lexicogenic, as shown by *ixnay, thistle-sifter, Com Truise, Nacirema*, the backslang type *yob(bishness)* (§5.5), *fancy shmancy* (§14.3), *guarandamntee*, and the quasi-superlatives *fanfuckintastic* and *absofuckinlutely* (§§5.5, 5.9).

(5) AVOID SYNONYMY (§2.5.4) motivates distinctions among competing words or morphological derivatives such that *thief* and *stealer*, for instance, prefer different contexts (§2.1). Superficially, it appears irrelevant to expressive morphology, including slang (§5.2), but an expressive or hypocoristic meaning is in fact distinct, as suggested throughout this work (esp. Chapters 8, 11). When expressive meaning is lost, as in *phone*, for instance, the non-clipped form, *telephone*, is gradually displaced or relegated to a more formal or monitored register. Slang also has ingroup significance. These considerations provide contextual domains for apparent synonyms.

Playful lexicogenesis and core morphology are independent in the sense that both can exist without the other. Core morphology could happily thrive without any of the playful or expressive processes, or word games. On the flipside, certain playful processes like sound symbolism minimally require a lexical root, no core morphological operations. At the same time, the two are mutually interdependent. A fully derived and inflected form is subject to playful processes, and playful constructs can undergo further derivation and must inflect like any other word.

Finally, language play (word games) can feature the most severe departures from core morphology, and thus comprise the most extravagant examples of something approaching extragrammaticality. The entire-word infixations and total metatheses are constrained only by prosodic properties of the metrical foot. Expressive lexicogenic processes like clipping and blending are similarly constrained, but at most feature radical truncation and do not permit the extreme violations of core morphological typology that characterize language play.

Since productivity can be evaluated for individuals (§1.8), there is no reason to exclude poetic art, clever advertisers, idiosyncratic constructs, and the products of speech play. Every type of conscious creativity and implicit word formation potentially contributes to lexicogenesis.

Appendix I
Special phonetic symbols

The phonetic symbols employed here are frequent on this side of the Atlantic because they are more systematic than IPA. For instance, a back vowel with an 'umlaut' is always front and rounded. IPA *y* lacks informativity and is too easily confused with consonantal *y*, for which IPA uses *j*, easily confused with /ǰ/. And so on. Unless otherwise indicated, the symbols are exemplified from English to clarify the sound values.[1]

Vowels

		front		*central*	*back*
		UNROUND	ROUND		
high	tense	i	ü	ɨ	u
	lax	ɪ	ü̇	ɪ̵	ʊ
mid	tense	e	ö	ʌ	o
	lax	ɛ	œ	ə	ɔ
low		æ		a	ɑ

Examples

/i/	marine, mean, me, serene, sleep, Caesar /sízr̩/ (= /sízɚ/)
/ɪ/	bit, sit, fit, Cyprian /síprɪ(y)ən/
/e/	sane, explain, vein, grey /gre(y)/, say /se(y)/
/ɛ/	set, treasure /trɛžr̩/, thread /þrɛd/, said /sɛd/, Aeschylus /ɛ́sk(y)ələs/
/æ/	bat, fat, that /ðæt/
/ɨ/, /ɪ̵/	American party /parr̃ɨ/ ~ /parr̃ɪ̵/ vs. British /pāti/
/ʌ/	but, putt /pʌt/, rough /rʌf/
/ə/	the sofa [ðəsóu̯fə], edible, telegraph /télərgræf/, telegraphy /təlégrəfì/
/ɚ/	the sound of *-er* in non-rhotic varieties of English
/u/	tube, boot, group, tooth /tuþ/, impugn /ɪmpyún/
/ʊ/	pull, put, good /gʊd/
/o/	cone, boat, moan, home /hom/, toe /to(w)/, tow /to(w)/
/ɔ/	American pronunciation of *bought, caught* /kɔt/, *cause* /kɔz/ [kʰɔ̯ǝz], *law* [lɔ̯ǝ]

[1] The symbols elucidated here are those needed for the main languages cited in this work. A more comprehensive and technical discussion can be found in any standard textbook, e.g. Kenstowicz (1994). Spellings appear in italics, e.g. *poof*, the phonemic (contrastive) representation of which is given in slashes: /puf/; more phonetic detail is implied by braces, viz. [pʰuf], with predictable aspiration indicated.

/a/   bomb /bam/, conical /kanɪk(ə)l/, pot /pat/ in most American varieties
/ɑ/   father, balm /bɑm/ (in some varieties)
/ɒ/   (low back round) British pronunciation of cot; contrast /ɔ̄/ in bought, caught, etc.
/ü/   French rue /ʁü/ 'street'; German Bücher /büçɚ/ 'books'
/ö/   Fr. bleu /blö/ 'blue', Germ. böse /bözə/ 'bad' (cf. Scandinavian /ø/)
/œ/   Fr. chartreuse /šaʁtʁœz/ 'chartreuse'

Diphthongs[2]

/ay/   aisle, wife /wayf/, align /əláyn/, right /rayt/, Cyprus /sáyprɪs/
/aw/   house /haws/ (also /hæws/, həws/, etc.), plow /plaw/, bough /baw/
/aə/   ah! (etc.)

Special diacritics

A long vowel can be indicated with a macron, e.g. /ō/ or (especially if length is optional) with a colon-like diacritic, e.g. [o(:)] (= optionally or partially long). In English, a vowel is lengthened phonetically and diphthongized before a voiced segment. Contrast *mate* [met] : *made* [mēd] / [me(:)yd]. There is a technical difference between a glide [i̯, u̯] and a consonant [y, w]. For simplicity, the consonant is used here in most places, reserving the glide for technical notation, e.g. the Ancient Greek diphthongs αι *ai*, αυ *au* were technically /ai̯/, /au̯/ in contrast to the English diphthongs with lower glide /ae̯/, /ao̯/. A word like Eng. *tow* ends with a slight phonetic lip-rounding, which can be represented [tʰoʷ], phonemically /to/, since the initial aspiration and final lengthening / offgliding are predictable. *Law* is phonemically /lɔ/, phonetically [lɔ̄ə]. Anticipatory vowels are represented by raising, e.g. Old Irish *cóic* /kōⁱg/ 'five' (raised *i* is a slight offglide anticipating palatalization). An acute accent mark indicates length in some scripts, e.g. Old Irish, Icelandic, Old English manuscripts. Otherwise, accent diacritics will be understood to indicate some sort of accent (stress or pitch).

Nasal(ized) vowels are represented in some systems as ę, ǫ, ą, and in others as ẽ, õ, ã. The former are common in Slavic and some other orthographies, and will be used here to represent nasal(ized) vowels. The latter are used here primarily as accent marks, e.g. for falling pitch in Ancient Greek.

Some languages have extra short vowels, the so-called *yers* in Slavic, namely ь and ъ, typically transcribed ĭ, ŭ, respectively. For Russian, they are transcribed ' and " respectively. Reduced vowels are otherwise represented by raising, e.g. /sᵊpóz/ *suppose*.

So-called SYLLABIC consonants are represented here as [r̩, l̩, m̩, n̩], e.g. *simple* [símpl̩], *circus* [sŕ̩kɪs]. Since these are environmentally predictable, phonemically they are /simpl/, /srkəs/. By convention, [m̥, n̥] in Welsh mutations are voiceless, and the circle beneath a vowel designates voicelessness.

---

[2] Diphthongs are essentially of two types, offgliding (vowel plus glide) and ongliding (glide plus vowel), in which the glide and the vowel pattern together as part of the rime of the syllable and in some languages contribute to its weight (see Gordon 2002; Miller 2010: 1.182, 252; Ryan 2011).

Consonants

Classification of consonants

Part of the problem involved in the classification of the consonants is that nearly any of the columns can be horizontal or vertical. For instance, that continuants can be treated as a category in a vertical column is evident from the fact that they can be aspirated [s^h], glottalized [s'], palatalized [s^y], and labialized [s^w]. Labiovelar as a category is somewhat artificial, since the true labiovelars are /k^p/, /g^b/, etc. They are given category (as opposed to feature) status here simply because they can be palatalized, aspirated, etc. Pharyngeal could be subdivided into uvular and pharyngeal. Glottals could be collapsed with pharyngeals since all EXTREME BACK sounds are produced in the pharyngeal cavity. The division here is purely heuristic. The continuants and nasals have a bilabial [ɸ, β], labiodental [f, v], and interdental [þ, ð] place of articulation. In the following chart, PAL is palatal, VEL velar, PALA palato-alveolar, AFFRIC affricate, and RTFLX retroflex.

Consonants

	LAB	DENT	RTFLX	AFFRIC		PAL	VEL	LABVEL	PHRYNG	GLO
				DENT	PALA					
STOP										
[−VOICE]	p	t	ṭ	c	č	ḱ	k	(k^w)	q	ʔ
[+VOICE]	b	d	ḍ	j	ǰ	ǵ	g	(g^w)	G	
[PALATALIZED]										
[−VOICE]	p^y	t^y	ṭ^y	c^y	č^y	ḱ^y	k^y	k^{wy}	q^y	
[+VOICE]	b^y	d^y	ḍ^y	j^y	ǰ^y	ǵ^y	g^y	g^{wy}	G^y	
[LABIALIZED]										
[−VOICE]	p^w	t^w	ṭ^w	c^w	č^w	ḱ^w	k^w		q^w	
[+VOICE]	b^w	d^w	ḍ^w	j^w	ǰ^w	ǵ^w	g^w		G^w	
[ASPIRATED]										
[−VOICE]	p^h	t^h	ṭ^h	c^h	č^h	ḱ^h	k^h	k^{wh}	q^h	
[+VOICE]	b^h	d^h	ḍ^h	j^h	ǰ^h	ǵ^h	g^h	g^{wh}	G^h	
[AFFRICATED]										
[−VOICE]	p^f	t^s	ṭ^s			t^š	k^x		q^h	
[+VOICE]	b^v	d^z	ḍ^z			d^ž	g^γ		G^ʕ	
[PHARYNG]	ṗ	ṭ		ċ	c̣		k̇		q̇	
[GLOTTALIZED]	p'	t'		c'	č'	ḱ'	k'		q'	
CONTINUANT										
[−VOICE]	ɸ f	þ s	ṣ		š	s^y	χ	χ^w	ḥ χ	h
[+VOICE]	ƀ v	ð z	ẓ		ž	z^y	γ	γ^w	ʕ	ɡ
SONORANT										
[NASAL]	m ɯ	n	ṇ			ń n^y	ŋ	n^w		
[LIQUID]			ṛ			ŕ r^y		r^w	ʁ	
[LATERAL]		l	ḷ			l' l^y	ɫ	l^w		
[GLIDE]	ω					y		w		

Of course /š, ž/ are palato-alveolar continuants, not affricates, but the only place for palato-alveolars in this chart is under the affricates, emphasizing my point that nearly all of the columns must be both horizontal and vertical.

Some languages have (distinctive) voiceless sonorants, transcribed here with four different notations: (i) small capitals L R M N, e.g. /ple/ [pʰLēy] *play* with phonetically voiceless /l/ after voiceless consonants in English; (ii) [λ], sometimes a palatal lateral, here represents a voiceless lateral fricative, as in many Amerindian languages; (iii) a circle beneath, e.g. [m̥, n̥] in Welsh mutations; and (iv) voiceless /r/ is here transcribed [ɹ̥], as in *freak* /frik/ [fɹ̥ii̯k], *treasure* [čɹ̥ēžɹ̥], etc. This is not to be confused with approximant [ɹ], which is used only in the section on loss of coda /r/.

One final caution involves potential confusion between individual scripts and transcription symbols. Although [c, j] are here equivalent to dental affricates [tˢ, dᶻ] (as in some Slavic scripts), in the customary transliteration of Sanskrit, for instance, *c, j,* represent the palato-alveolar affricates [č, ǰ], i.e. [tš, dž]. *Dental* is also used as a generic category, encompassing true dentals as well as alveolars, which were not contrasted in any of the older Indo-European languages. Retroflexes (produced with the tip of the tongue touching the central palate) are encountered in the older Indo-European languages only in the Indic branch.

Examples[3]

/k̂/	*keel* /kil/, phonetically [k̂ʰi(ː)ył], vs. *cod* [kʰád], *caught* [qʰɒ̄t] (British)
/kʷ/	*quick* /kʷɪk/
/rʷ/	lip-rounded /r/ (initial position in English): *rat* [rʷæt]
/ń/	*knee* /ni/ [ńīʸ]
/nʸ/	or /ñ/ *mignon, onion,* Sp. *mañana*/manʸana/ 'later; tomorrow'
/ŋ/	*tank* [tʰæŋk], *sing* /sɪŋ/
/þ/	(runic *thorn*) *thin, thing* /þɪŋ/ (usually transcribed with θ from Modern Greek, but I have opted for þ because of its extensive use in Germanic scripts)
/ð/	(runic *edh*) *then, they* (also transcribed with δ from Modern Greek)
/γ/	(Greek *gamma,* with its modern pronunciation): voiced velar spirant
/š/	*shock* /šak/, *sugar*
/ž/	*pleasure* [pʰLɛ(ː)žɹ̥], *seizure*
/x/	German *ach* 'ach!'
/ç/	the German "*ich*-Laut", e.g. Germ. *Bücher* /büçɚ/ 'books'
/č/	or /tš/ *change* (more technically, /tš/ can indicate the transition from /tš/ to /č/)
/ǰ/	or /dž/ *ginger, change* [čę̆ⁱ(ń)ǰ] /čenǰ/ (or /tšendž/)
/ʔ/	(glottal stop), as in the break between the two *oh*'s of "oh oh!"
/ɾ/	(flap) as in Am. Eng. *latter* [læɾɹ̥], *ladder* [læ(ː)ɾɹ̥]
/ʁ/	uvular /r/, as in French *rue* /ʁü/ 'street'

---

[3] Only the less transparent symbols will be clarified. Those that resemble English letters can be taken (roughly) at face value.

Appendix II
The Indo-European phonological system

The main catalogue of information about the traditionally reconstructed Proto-Indo-European (PIE) phonological system is Mayrhofer (1986). Recent synopses in English are available in Meier-Brügger (2003), Ringe (2006), and Fortson (2010).

The inventory of traditional contrasting segments is laid out in (1).

(1) PIE phonological segments
   (a) Obstruents

Labial	Coronal	Palatal	Velar	Labiovelar
p	t	$\acute{k}$	k	k^w
b	d	$\acute{g}$	g	g^w
b^h	d^h	$\acute{g}^h$	g^h	$g^w h$
s	h_1	h_2	h_3	

   (b) Sonorants

Non-syllabic	Syllabic
m	m̥
n	n̥
r	r̥
l	l̥
y	i
w	u
	e o a
	ē ō ā

The voiced aspirates were kept only in Indic, where they remain to this day. They are typically described as breathy voiced but they are in fact voiced and aspirated, as demonstrated instrumentally by Dixit (1975).

The palatal series merged with the velars in all the geographically Western IE languages (including Ancient Greek). For instance, PIE *$\acute{k}$onk-, as in Vedic śaṅk-ate 'worries, hesitates', yields pre-Gmc. *kank-, whence Goth. hāhan* 'to hang', etc. Though easternmost of the Indo-European languages, Tocharian patterns in part with Western Indo-European in having a velar stop (e.g. TochA känt, B kante 'hundred' = L centum [kéntum], G he-katón, etc.) where the (other) eastern dialects have a palato-alveolar continuant, e.g. Skt. śatám, Lith. šim̃tas 'hundred' < PIE *(d)$\acute{k}$m̥t-ó-m 'id.'.

In Germanic, the dialectal IE stop system shifted by Grimm's Law.

(2) Grimm's Law

Dialectal IE					Proto-Germanic			
p	t	k	kʷ		f	þ	χ/h	χʷ/hʷ
b	d	g	gʷ	→	p	t	k	kʷ
bʰ	dʰ	gʰ	gʷh		b/b	ð/d	γ/g	*gʷ (> b/g/w)

Grimm's Law is responsible for such correspondences as G *pod-* / L *ped-* and E *foot* (< *pōd-*) or L *quod* 'what' < *kʷod* > Gmc. *hʷat* (OE *hwæt*, E *what*). For a recent discussion, see Miller (2010: 1.83–93).

The non-vocalic syllabic sonorants (also called resonants) subdivide into three categories. The glides */y, w/ alternate with vowels */i, u/. The syllabic nasals remained intact nowhere. In Greek and Sanskrit, they became *a*, in Latin *en/in, em/im*, and in Germanic *un, um*. So, for instance the PIE negating particle *ṇ yields G *a(n)-*, as in *a-theist* or *an-archist*, L *in-*, as in *insecure*, and Gmc. *un-*, as in *un-likely*.

The syllabic liquids remained intact only in Indo-Iranian. In Germanic, they developed like the syllabic nasals, i.e. *-uR-* (R = any resonant), e.g. PIE *wl̥kʷ-o-s* > Skt. *vŕ̥kaḥ*, PGmc. *wulf-az ~ *wolf-az* > *wolf*.

One of the archaic features of Anatolian is preservation of at least some of the Proto-Indo-European so-called laryngeals, usually transcribed *ḫ* in Hittite. The number and phonetic nature of these sounds is disputed (most scholars assume three), and they are variously transcribed. Watkins (2000), for instance, writes *ə₁, ə₂, ə₃*; others *h₁, h₂, h₃*. There is also a convention that writes *h₁* etc. when consonantal, *ə₁* etc. when syllabic (e.g. *pə₂tér* 'father' > Skt. *pitā́* / *pitár-*, G *patḗr*, L *pater*),[1] and *H* (or *X*) when the precise laryngeal is indeterminate or irrelevant. Some core reflexes follow.

(3) Core laryngeal reflexes
   h₁e > /e/   *eh₁* > /ē/
   h₂e > /a/   *eh₂* > /ā/
   h₃e > /o/   *eh₃* > /ō/
   Ho > /o/   *oH* > /ō/

At least some long vowels result from contraction of a vowel plus laryngeal, and */o/ was not colored by any laryngeal. Note that *h₁* is not written in any of the Anatolian scripts and had no vowel-coloring effects. With the possible exception of *h₁*, the laryngeals were all fricatives (Byrd 2010: 4).

(4) Examples of laryngeal developments
   h₁es-ti 'is': Hitt. *ēš-zi*, G *es-tí*, L *est*, PGmc. *isti* > Goth. *ist*, E *is*
   séh₁-mṇ 'seed' (L *sēmen* 'seed; SEMEN') / collective *séh₁-mō* > PGmc. *sēmō̃* > OS, OHG *sāmo* 'seed' (Ringe 2006: 74)

---

[1] The reason for the reconstruction of */ə₂/ in *pə₂tér- is that (i) since the root vowel shows up as /a/ in Greek, Latin, and Germanic, but as /i/ in Sanskrit *pitár-*, it cannot be simply */a/, which would yield /a/ also in Sanskrit; cf. *ǵhans-* 'goose' (OHG *gans*) > Vedic *haṃsá-* 'id.' (IEL 82), and (ii) the specific choice of */ə₂/ (as opposed to, e.g., */ə₃/) is that Greek has the /a/ reflex, not e.g. the /o/ reflex of */ə₃/ (see below).

*$h_2ént$-i 'in front' > *$h_2ánti$ > Hitt. ḫānza 'in front' / ḫanti 'opposite; against; facing; apart' (see Miller 2010: 1.255), G antí 'against; ANTI-', L ante 'in front; ANTE-', PGmc. *andi 'in addition; and' > OE and AND

*$méǵh_2$ 'great' > Hitt. mēg by laryngeal deletion, but the rest of Indo-European had epenthesis: *$méǵh_2ə$ > Skt. máhi, G méga (Byrd 2010: 85)

*peh_2- 'protect; feed' (Skt. pá-ti 'protects'): *peh_2-trom / *peh_2-dhlom > *pah_2-trom / *pah_2-dhlom > Gmc. *fōðra- FODDER / L pābulum 'food; fodder; nourishment' PAB(U)-LUM; enlarged *peh_2-s- > *pah_2-s- > Hitt. paḫš- 'protect', L pāstor 'shepherd' PASTOR

*-$éh_2$ (factitive suffix) > *-ah_2, e.g. *new-eh_2- 'make new' > Hitt. nēw-aḫḫ- 'renew; recopy', L (re)nov-ā-re 'to renew' RENOVATE (LSDE 240ff.)

*peh_2wr 'fire' > *pah_2wr > Hitt. pāḫḫur; zero-grade *ph_2ur- > *puh_2r- (by metathesis) > G pûr (PYRE); Gmc. *fūr-i- > OE fȳr FIRE

*$h_2ów$-i- 'sheep' > Hitt. ḫāwi-, Lycian χawa-, L ovis (cf. OVINE), PGmc. *awiz > OS ewi 'lamb' (cf. *awjō > OE ēowu EWE)

*h_2ost- 'bone' > L os / oss- (OSS-ify); cf. *h_2ost-ei-o- > G ostéon OSTE(O)-; collective *$h_2ést$-ōi > Hitt. ḫaštāi 'bone(s)'

*h_3ep-en-e/ont- > *h_3op-en-e/ont- 'rich' > Hitt. ḫappenant-, L opulent-us OPULENT (same root [*op-¹] as Lat. opera 'works' etc. LSDE 173f.)

*$peh_3(i)$- > *$poh_3(i)$- > *pō(i)- 'drink' > L pō-tiō 'a drink' POTION, POISON; zero-grade *ph_3-tí- > *$pə_3$-ti- > G *poti- > posi- in sumpósion 'a drinking together; drinking party' SYMPOSIUM; cf. enlarged *peh_3-s- > Hitt. pāš- 'take a swallow' (Hittite lost *h_3 in many environments)

Some of these examples, e.g. the last, raise the issue of PIE apophony. The most frequent alternations are between */e/, */o/, and Ø (zero-grade). While many details of these alternations are disputed, the three hypotheses in (5) seem generally accepted.

(5) Hypotheses of Indo-European apophony
  (a) e-grade (or full grade) is the basic vocalism of most primary verbal roots, e.g. *$leik^w$- > G leípō 'I leave'; *leǵ- 'collect' (LIV 397) > G légō 'I gather, count, tell, say'
  (b) o-grade is conditioned by certain morphological categories; cf. the Greek perfect léloip-a 'I have left' (< *le-lóik^w-h_2e), or deverbal nouns like lógos 'account; reason(ing); speech; word' (< *lóǵ-o-s).
  (c) zero-grade originally occurred when the root was unaccented; cf. the Greek aorist é-lip-on 'I left' (< *(é-)lik^w-óm), Latin past passive participle (re)lic-tus '(having been) left' (< *lik^w-tó-).

This brief synopsis of PIE phonology is intended solely as background to the historical discussions in this work. For more details, the reader is referred to the basic handbooks.

One final caution: IE (or Indo-European) is frequently used as a non-technical shorthand, especially in reconstructions, as the equivalent of PIE (or Proto-Indo-European).

References

Abelin, Åsa (1999). Studies in sound symbolism. Ph.D. University of Gothenburg.
Abney, Steven P. (1987). The English noun phrase in its sentential aspect. Ph.D. MIT.
Ackema, Peter (1999). *Issues in Morphosyntax*. Amsterdam: Benjamins.
Ackema, Peter (2005). Word-formation in Optimality Theory. In Štekauer and Lieber (2005: 285–313).
Ackema, Peter, and Ad Neeleman (2004). *Beyond Morphology: Interface Conditions on Word Formation*. Oxford: Oxford University Press.
Adams, Valerie (1973). *An Introduction to Modern English Word-Formation*. London: Longman.
Adams, Valerie (2001). *Complex Words in English*. Harlow: Longman.
Agel, Vilmos, Andreas Gardt, Ulrike Hass-Zumkehr, and Thorsten Roelcke (eds) (2002). *Das Wort: seine strukturelle und kulturelle Dimension. Festschrift für Oskar Reichmann zum 65. Geburtstag*. Tübingen: Niemeyer.
Ahlner, Felix, and Jordan Zlatev (2010). Cross-modal iconicity: a cognitive semiotic approach to sound symbolism. *Sign Systems Studies* 38: 298–348.
Ahmad, Khurshid (2000). Neologisms, nonces and word formation. In Heid et al. (2000: 2.711-30).
Aitchison, Jean (2003). Psycholinguistic perspectives on language change. In Joseph and Janda (2003: 736–43).
Akita, Kimi (2009). A grammar of sound-symbolic words in Japanese: theoretical approaches to iconic and lexical properties of mimetics. Ph.D. Kobe University.
Alber, birgit, and Sabine Arndt-Lappe (2012). Templatic and subtractive truncation. In Trommer (2012: 289–325).
Alexiadou, Artemis (2001). *Functional Structure in Nominals: Nominalization and Ergativity*. Amsterdam: Benjamins.
Alexiadou, Artemis, Elena Anagnostopolou, and Martin Everaert (eds) (2004). *The Unaccusativity Puzzle: Explorations of the Syntax–Lexicon Interface*. Oxford: Oxford University Press.
Algeo, John (1977). Blends: a structural and systemic view. *American Speech* 52: 47–66.
Algeo, John (1978). The taxonomy of word making. *Word* 29: 122–31.
Algeo, John (1980). Where do all the new words come from? *American Speech* 55: 264–77.
Algeo, John (1991). *A Dictionary of Neologisms, 1941-1991*. Cambridge: Cambridge University Press.
Allan, Kathryn (2008). *Metaphor and Metonymy: A Diachronic Approach*. Malden, Mass.: Wiley-Blackwell.
Allan, Kathryn (2011). Using OED data as evidence. In Allan and Robinson (2011: 17–40).
Allan, Kathryn, and Justyna A. Robinson (eds) (2011). *Current Methods in Historical Semantics*. Berlin: de Gruyter.

Allen, Keith, and Kate Burridge (1991). *Euphemism and Dysphemism: Language Used as Shield and Weapon*. Oxford: Oxford University Press.
Allott, Robin (1995). Sound symbolism. In Figge (1995: 15–38).
Alsina, Alex, and Boban Arsenijević (2012a). The two faces of agreement. *Language* 88: 369–79.
Alsina, Alex, and Boban Arsenijević (2012b). There is no third face of agreement. *Language* 88: 388–9.
Alsina, Alex, Joan Bresnan, and Peter Sells (eds) (1997). *Complex Predicates*. Stanford: CSLI.
Andersen, Henning (ed.) (1995). *Historical Linguistics 1993: Selected Papers from the 11th International Conference on Historical Linguistics, Los Angeles, 16–20 August 1993*. Amsterdam: Benjamins.
Andersen, Henning, and Konrad Koerner (eds) (1990). *Historical Linguistics 1987: Papers from the 8th International Conference on Historical Linguistics*. Amsterdam: Benjamins.
Anderson, Earl R. (1998). *A Grammar of Iconism*. Cranbury, NJ: Associated University Presses.
Anderson, John M. (2007). *The Grammar of Names*. Oxford: Oxford University Press.
Anderson, Stephen (1985a). Typological distinctions in word formation. In Shopen (1985: 3–56).
Anderson, Stephen (1985b). Inflectional morphology. In Shopen (1985: 150–201).
André, Jacques (1971). *Emprunts et suffixes nominaux en latin*. Paris: Minard.
Anshen, Frank, and Mark Aronoff (1988). Producing morphologically complex words. *Linguistics* 26: 641–55.
Applegate, Joseph Roy (1961). Phonological rules of a subdialect of English. *Word* 17: 186–93.
Arad, Maya (2003). Locality constraints on the interpretation of roots: the case of Hebrew denominal verbs. *Natural Language & Linguistic Theory* 21: 737–78.
Arad, Maya (2005). *Roots and Patterns: Hebrew Morpho-syntax*. Dordrecht: Springer.
Arcodia, Giorgio Francesco (2010). Coordinating compounds. *Language and Linguistics Compass* 4/9: 863–73.
Arcodia, Giorgio Francesco, Nicola Grandi, and Bernhard Wälchli (2010). Coordination in compounding. In Scalise and Vogel (2010: 177–98).
Argout, Line (2010). Réalité des idéophones anglais (phonesthèmes): propositions dans le cadre d'une approche de linguistique cognitive. *E-rea: Revue électronique d'études sur le monde anglophone* 8.1. file://localhost/<http://www.erea.revues.org:1301>.
Arndt-Lappe, Sabine (2011). Towards an exemplar-based model of stress in English noun-noun compounds. *Journal of Linguistics* 47: 549–85.
Aronoff, Mark (1976). *Word Formation in Generative Grammar*. Cambridge, Mass.: MIT Press.
Aronoff, Mark (1983). Potential words, actual words, productivity and frequency. *Preprints of the Plenary Session Papers of the XIIIth International Congress of Linguists*. Tokyo, 163–70.
Aronoff, Mark (1988). Review of Di Sciullo and Williams (1987). *Language* 64: 766–70.
Aronoff, Mark (2001). The semantics of *-ship* suffixation. *Linguistic Inquiry* 32: 167–73.
Aronoff, Mark (2011). Morphology. Oxford Bibliographies Online http://www.oxfordbibliographiesonline.com/view/document/obo-9780199772810/obo-9780199772810-0001.xml?rskey=dL5yWa&result=43&q=

Aronoff, Mark, and Kristen Fuderman (2005). *What is Morphology?* Oxford: Blackwell.
Aronoff, Mark, and Shikaripur N. Sridhar (1988). Prefixation in Kannada. In Hammond and Noonan (1988: 179–91).
Aronovitch, Paula (2012). The relationship between older siblings and child language. M.Sc. thesis, William Paterson University of New Jersey.
Ayers, Donald M. (1972). *Bioscientific Terminology: Words from Latin and Greek SteMS.* Tucson: University of Arizona Press.
Ayers, Donald M. (1986). *English Words from Latin and Greek Elements.* 2nd edn, rev. by Thomas D. Worthen. Tucson: University of Arizona Press.
Aygen, Nigar Gülşat (2002). Finiteness, Case and clausal architecture. Ph.D. Harvard University.
Ayto, John (1989, 1990). *The Longman Register of New Words.* 2 vols. Harlow: Longman.
Ayto, John (1998). *The Oxford Dictionary of Slang.* Oxford: Oxford University Press.
Baayen, R. Harald (2006). *Corpus Linguistics in Morphology: Morphological Productivity.* Online at: http://www.ualberta.ca/~baayen/publications/BaayenCorpus Linguistics2006.pdf
Bacchielli, Rolando (2010). Our worries about 'nonce': something more than a terminological problem. *Linguae: Rivista di lingue e culture moderne* 1: 83–90. Online at: http://www.ledonline.it/linguae/
Baclawski, Kenneth (2012a). A frequency-based analysis of the modern *s* register-marking suffix. Poster presentation at the Annual Meeting of the Linguistic Society of America.
Baclawski, Kenneth (2012b). Demonstratives and primate loud call frequency variation. MS, Dartmouth College.
Bader, Françoise (1962). *La formation des composés nominaux du latin.* Paris: Les Belles Lettres.
Baerman, Matthew (2011). Defectiveness and homophony avoidance. *Journal of Linguistics* 47: 1–29.
Baerman, Matthew, Dunstan Brown, and Greville G. Corbett (2005). *The Syntax–Morphology Interface.* Cambridge: Cambridge University Press.
Baeskow, Heike (2004). *Lexical Properties of Selected Non-Native Morphemes of English.* Tübingen: Narr.
Baeskow, Heike (2012). -*Ness* and -*ity*: phonological exponents of *n* or meaningful nominalizers of different adjectival domains. *Journal of English Linguistics* 40: 6–40.
Bagemihl, Bruce (1988). Alternate phonologies and morphologies. Ph.D. University of British Columbia, Vancouver.
Bagemihl, Bruce (1989). The Crossing Constraint and backwards languages. *Natural Language & Linguistic Theory* 7: 481–549.
Bagemihl, Bruce (1995). Language games and related areas. In Goldsmith (1995: 697–712).
Bailey, Charles-James N., and Roger W. Shuy (eds) (1972). *New Ways of Analyzing Variation in English.* Washington, DC: Georgetown University Press.
Bain, Alexander (1893). *English Composition and Rhetoric.* Enlarged edn. Part I: *Intellectual Elements of Style.* London: Longmans, Green.
Baker, Mark C. (1988). *Incorporation: A Theory of Grammatical Function Changing.* Chicago: University of Chicago Press.

Baker, Mark C. (2003). *Lexical Categories: Verbs, Nouns, and Adjectives.* Cambridge: Cambridge University Press.
Baker, Mark C. (2008). *The Syntax of Agreement and Concord.* Cambridge: Cambridge University Press.
Baker, Mark C. (2009). Is Head movement still needed for noun incorporations? *Lingua* 119: 148–65.
Baldi, Philip, and Chantal Dawar (2000). Creative processes. In Booij et al. (2000: 963–72).
Balteiro, Isabel (2007a). *A Contribution to the Study of Conversion in English.* New York: Waxmann.
Balteiro, Isabel (2007b). *The Directionality of Conversion in English: A Dia-Synchronic Study.* Frankfurt am Main: Lang.
Bandle, Oskar, with Kurt Braunmüller, Ernst Håkon Jahr, Allan Karker, Hans-Peter Naumann, and Ulf Teleman (eds) (2002). *The Nordic Languages: An International Handbook of the History of the North Germanic Languages*, vol. 1. [Vol. 2 appeared in 2005.] Berlin: de Gruyter.
Barcelona, Antonio (ed.) (2000a). *Metaphor and Metonymy at the Crossroads: A Cognitive Perspective.* Berlin: Mouton de Gruyter.
Barcelona, Antonio (2000b). Introduction: the cognitive theory of metaphor and metonymy. In Barcelona (2000a: 1–28).
Bareš, Karel (1974). Unconventional word-forming patterns in present-day English. *Philologica Pragensia* 17: 173–86.
Barker, Chris (1998). Episodic *-ee* in English: a thematic role constraint on new word formation. *Language* 74: 695–727.
Barrie, Michael Jonathan Mathew (2006). Dynamic antisymmetry and the syntax of noun incorporation. Ph.D. University of Toronto.
Basilico, David (2008). The syntactic representation of perfectivity. *Lingua* 118: 1716–39.
Basilico, David (forthcoming). *Transitivity and Theticity.* Cambridge, Mass.: MIT Press.
Bat-El, Outi (1996). Selecting the best of the worse: the grammar of Hebrew blends. *Phonology* 13: 283–328.
Bat-El, Outi (2000). The grammaticality of 'extragrammatical' morphology. In Doleschal and Thornton (2000: 61–84).
Bat-El, Outi (2006). Blend. In Brown (2006: 2.66–70).
Bat-El, Outi, and Evan-Gary Cohen (2012). Stress in English blends: a constraint-based approach. In Renner et al. (2012: 193–212).
Bauer, Laurie (1983). *English Word-Formation.* Cambridge: Cambridge University Press.
Bauer, Laurie (1996). No phonetic iconicity in evaluative morphology. *Studia Linguistica* 50: 189–206.
Bauer, Laurie (1998). Is there a class of neoclassical compounds, and if so is it productive? *Linguistics* 36.3: 403–22.
Bauer, Laurie (2000). Word. In Booij et al. (2000: 247–57).
Bauer, Laurie (2001). *Morphological Productivity.* Cambridge: Cambridge University Press.
Bauer, Laurie (2002). What you can do with derivational morphology. In Bendjaballah et al. (2002: 37–48).

Bauer, Laurie (2003). *Introducing Linguistic Morphology*, 2nd edn. Washington, DC: Georgetown University Press.
Bauer, Laurie (2004). Adjectives, compounds, and words. *Nordic Journal of English Studies* 3: 7–22.
Bauer, Laurie (2005). Productivity: theories. In Štekauer and Lieber (2005: 315–34).
Bauer, Laurie (2006). Competition in English word formation. In van Kemenade et al. (2006: 177–98).
Bauer, Laurie (2008). Dvandva. *Word Structure* 1: 1–20.
Bauer, Laurie (2009). Typology of compounds. In Lieber and Štekauer (2009: 343–56).
Bauer, Laurie (2010a). Co-compounds in Germanic. *Journal of Germanic Linguistics* 22: 201–19.
Bauer, Laurie (2010b). An overview of morphological universals. *Word Structure* 3: 131–40.
Bauer, Laurie, Ana Díaz Negrillo, and Salvador Valera (2009). Recursiveness in neoclassical compounds. Paper presented at the SLE 42nd Annual Meeting, 9–12 September, Lisbon.
Bauer, Laurie, Rochelle Lieber, and Ingo Plag (2013). *The Oxford Reference Guide to English Morphology*. Oxford: Oxford University Press.
Bauer, Laurie, and Antoinette Renouf (2001). A corpus-based study of compounding in English. *Journal of English Linguistics* 29: 101–23.
Bauer, Laurie, and Salvador Valera (eds) (2005). *Approaches to Conversion/Zero Derivation*. Münster: Waxmann.
Bauer, Laurie, Salvador Valera, and Ana Díaz Negrillo (2009). Affixation vs. conversion: the resolution of conflicting patterns. To appear in the Proceedings of the 13th International Morphology Meeting, Vienna.
Beckman, Jill, Laura Walsh-Dickey, and Suzanne Urbanczyk (eds) (1995). *Papers in Optimality Theory: University of Massachusetts Occasional Papers (UMOP)* 18. Amherst, Mass.: Graduate Linguistic Student Association.
Beekes, Robert (2009). *Etymological Dictionary of Greek*. 2 vols. Leiden: Brill.
Behaghel, Otto (1909). Beziehungen zwischen Umfang und Reihenfolge von Satzgliedern. *Indogermanische Forschungen* 25: 110–42.
Behaghel, Otto (1928). *Deutsche Syntax: eine geschichtliche Darstellung*, vol. 3: *Die Satzgebilde*. Heidelberg: Winter.
Bell, Alan (1975). If speakers can't count syllables, what can they do? Indiana University Linguistics Club, October 1975.
Bell, Alan, and Joan Bybee Hooper (eds) (1978). *Syllables and Segments*. Amsterdam: North-Holland.
Bell, Alan, and Mohamad M. Saka (1983). Reversed sonority in Pashto initial clusters. *Journal of Phonetics* 11: 259–75.
Bell, Nancy (2012). Formulaic language, creativity, and language play in a second language. *Annual Review of Applied Linguistics* 32: 189–205.
Belletti, Adriana (ed.) (2004). *Structures and Beyond: The Cartography of Syntactic Structures*, vol. 3. Oxford: Oxford University Press.
Benczes, Réka (2006). *Creative Compounding in English: The Semantics of Metaphorical and Metonymical Noun–Noun Combinations*. Amsterdam: Benjamins.

Benczes, Réka (2010). Setting limits in the production and use of metaphorical and metonymical compounds. In Onysko and Michel (2010: 219–42).
Bendjaballah, Sabrina, Wolfgang U. Dressler, Oskar E. Pfeiffer, and Maria D. Voeikova (eds) (2002). *Morphology 2000: Selected Papers from the 9th Morphology Meeting, Vienna, 24–28 February 2000.* Amsterdam: Benjamins.
Benor, Sarah Bunin, and Roger Levy (2006). The chicken or the egg? A probabilistic analysis of English binomials. *Language* 82: 223–78.
Benveniste, Émile (1949). Euphémismes anciens et modernes. *Die Sprache* 1: 116–22. [Repr. in Benveniste 1966: 308–14.].
Benveniste, Émile (1966). *Problèmes de linguistique générale.* Paris: Gallimard.
Benveniste, Émile (1969). *Le vocabulaire des institutions indo-européennes.* 2 vols. Paris: Minuit.
Benveniste, Émile (1973). *Indo-European Language and Society.* [= Benveniste (1969), translated by Elizabeth Palmer.] Coral Gables, Fla.: University of Miami.
Berg, Thomas (1998). The (in)compatibility of morpheme orders and lexical categories and its historical implications. *English Language and Linguistics* 2: 245–62.
Berg, Thomas (2011). The clipping of common and proper nouns. *Word Structure* 4.1: 1–19.
Bergen, Benjamin K. (2004). The psychological reality of phonaesthemes. *Language* 80: 290–311.
Berlin, Brent, and Paul Kay (1969). *Basic Color Terms: Their Universality and Evolution.* Berkeley: University of California Press.
Berman, J. M. (1961). Contribution on blending. *Zeitschrift für Anglistik und Amerikanistik* 9: 278–81.
Bermúdez-Otero, Ricardo (2012). The architecture of grammar and the division of labour in exponence. In Trommer (2012: 8–83).
Bermúdez-Otero, Ricardo, David Denison, Richard M. Hogg, and C. B. McCully (eds) (2000). *Generative Theory and Corpus Studies: A Dialogue from 10 ICEHL.* Berlin: Mouton de Gruyter.
Biłynsky, Michael (2013). Unanalysable verb-related coinages as reflected in the *OED*-textual prototypes. In Fisiak and Bator (2013: 139–93).
Birdsong, David P. (1979). Psycholinguistic perspectives on the phonology of frozen word order. Ph.D. Harvard University, Cambridge, Mass.
Birdsong, David P., and Jean-Pierre Montreuil (eds) (1988). *Advances in Romance Linguistics.* Dordrecht: Foris.
Biville, Frédérique (1989) Un processus dérivationnel méconnu du latin: la dérivation par troncation. *L'Information grammaticale* 42 (June): 15–22.
Biville, Frédérique (1990, 1995). *Les emprunts du latin au grec: approche phonétique.* 2 vols. Louvain: Peeters. Vol. 1: *Introduction et consonantisme* (1990); vol. 2: *Vocabulaire et conclusions* (1995).
Blevins, Juliette (2004). *Evolutionary Phonology: The Emergence of Sound Patterns.* Cambridge: Cambridge University Press.
Bloomfield, Leonard (1933). *Language.* New York: Holt, Rinehart & Winston.

Bode, Christoph, Sebastian Domsch, and Hans Sauer (eds) (2004). *Anglistentag 2003 München: Proceedings of the Conference of the German Association of University Teachers of English* 25. Trier: Wissenschaftlicher Verlag.

Bolinger, Dwight L. (1946). The sign is not arbitrary. *Boletín del Instituto Caruso y Caro* 5: 52–62.

Bolinger, Dwight L. (1950). Rime, assonance, and morpheme analysis. *Word* 6: 117–36.

Bolinger, Dwight L. (1975). *Aspects of Language*, 2nd edn. New York: Harcourt Brace Jovanovich.

Bolinger, Dwight L. (1980). *Language: The Loaded Weapon*. New York: Longman.

Bolinger, Dwight L. (1992). Sound symbolism. In Bright (1992: iv.28–30). See Hinton and Bolinger (2003).

Booij, Geert (1996). Inherent versus contextual inflection and the Split Morphology Hypothesis. *Yearbook of Morphology 1995*: 1–16.

Booij, Geert (2009). Lexical storage and phonological change. In Hanson and Inkelas (2009: 487–505).

Booij, Geert (2010). *Construction Morphology*. Oxford: Oxford University Press.

Booij, Geert, Emiliano Guevara, Angela Ralli, Salvatore Sgroi, and Sergio Scalise (eds) (2005). *Morphology and Linguistic Typology. On-line Proceedings of the Fourth Mediterranean Morphology Meeting (MMM4) Catania, 21–23 September 2003*. University of Bologna: http://www.morbo.lingue.unibo.it/mmm/

Booij, Geert, Christian Lehmann, and Joachim Mugdan (eds) (with Wolfgang Kesselheim and Stavros Skopetas) (2000, 2004). *Morphologie/Morphology: Ein internationales Handbuch zur Flexion und Wortbuildung/An International Handbook on Inflection and Word Formation*. 2 vols. Berlin: de Gruyter.

Booij, Geert, and Jaap van Marle (eds) (1988). *Yearbook of Morphology*. Dordrecht: Foris.

Bork, Hans Dieter (1990). *Die lateinisch-romanischen Zusammensetzungen Nomen + Verb und der Ursprung der romanischen Verb-Ergänzung-Komposita*. Bonn: Romanistischer Verlag.

Borror, Donald J. (1960). *Dictionary of Word Roots and Combining Forms: Compiled from the Greek, Latin, and Other Languages, With Special Reference to Biological Terms and Scientific Names*. Palo Alto, Calif.: National Press Books.

Botha, Rudolf P. (1984). *Morphological Mechanisms: Lexicalist Analyses of Synthetic Compounding*. Oxford: Pergamon.

Bottineau, Didier (2008). The submorphemic conjecture in English: towards a distributed model of the cognitive dynamics of submorphemes. *Lexis* 2: http://screcherche.univ-lyon3.fr/lexis/spip.php?article90

Bouchard, Denis (1984). *On the Content of Empty Categories*. Dordrecht: Foris.

Bouchard, Denis, and Katherine Leffel (eds) (1988). *FOCAL: Florida Occasional Contributions to the Advancement of Linguistics* 1. University of Florida, Gainesville, Department of Linguistics.

Boycott, Rosie (1982). *Batty, Bloomers and Boycott: A Little Etymology of Eponymous Words*. London: Hutchinson (1983).

Bragdon, Janice F. (2006). Verb–particle nominals in English. MA University of Florida, Gainesville.

Bragdon, Janice F. (2008). Blends. MS, University of Florida, Gainesville.
Bright, William (ed.) (1992). *International Encyclopedia of Linguistics and Language*. 4 vols. Oxford: Oxford University Press.
Brink, Stefan (2002). Sociolinguistic perspectives in the transitional period between Proto-Nordic and Old Nordic. In Bandle et al. (2002: 761–8).
Broselow, Ellen (2009). Review of Kager et al. (2004). *Language* 85: 214–20.
Brown, Dunstan, Greville G. Corbett, and Carole Tiberius (eds) (2003). *Agreement: A Typological Perspective*. (= *Transactions of the Philological Society* 101.) Oxford: Blackwell.
Brown, E. Keith (ed.) (2006). *Encyclopedia of Language and Linguistics*, 2nd edn. 14 vols. Amsterdam: Elsevier.
Brown, J. C. (2004). Eliminating the segmental tier: evidence from speech errors. *Journal of Psycholinguistic Research* 33: 97–101.
Brown, Roger W. (1958). *Words and Things*. New York: Free Press.
Buckingham, Hugh W., and Sarah S. Christman (2004). Phonemic carryover perseveration: word blends. *Seminars in Speech and Language* 25: 363–73.
Buckingham, Hugh W., and Sarah S. Christman (2006). Phonological impairments: sublexical. In Brown (2006: 509–18).
Buckingham, Hugh W., and Sarah S. Christman (2008). Disorders of phonetics and phonology. In Stemmer and Whitaker (2008: 127–36).
Burridge, Kate (2006). Taboo, euphemism, and political correctness. In Brown (2006: 12.455–62).
Burridge, Kate (2012). Euphemism and language change: the sixth and seventh ages. *Lexis* 7: 65–92.
Butt, Miriam, and Wilhelm Geuder (eds) (1998). *The Projection of Arguments: Lexical and Compositional Factors*. Stanford, Calif.: CSLI.
Butterworth, Brian (1981). Speech errors: old data in search of new theories. *Linguistics* 19: 627–62.
Bybee, Joan L. (1985). *Morphology: A Study of the Relation Between Meaning and Form*. Amsterdam: Benjamins.
Bybee, Joan L. (2001). *Phonology and Language Use*. Cambridge: Cambridge University Press.
Bye, Patrik, and Peter Svenonius (2010). Exponence, phonology, and non-concatenative morphology. MS, University of Tromsø. Available online at: http://www.hum.uit.no/a/svenonius/paperspage.html
Bye, Patrik, and Peter Svenonius (2012). Non-concatenative morphology as epiphenomenon. In Trommer (2012: 427–95).
Byrd, Andrew Miles (2010). Reconstructing Indo-European syllabification. Ph.D. University of California, Los Angeles.
Caha, Pavel (2009). The nanosyntax of Case. Ph.D. University of Tromsø.
Cannon, Garland (1986). Blends in English word formation. *Linguistics* 24: 724–53.
Cannon, Garland (1987). *Historical Change and English Word-Formation: Recent Vocabulary*. Bern: Lang.
Cannon, Garland (1989). Abbreviations and acronyms in English word-formation. *American Speech* 64: 99–127.
Cannon, Garland (2000). Blending. In Booij et al. (2000: 952–6).

Cappelle, Bert (2003). Meervoudig -er bij Engelse partikelwerkwoorden [Multiple -er on English particle verbs]. Paper presented at 'Morfologiedagen 2003', University of Ghent, December.
Cappelle, Bert (2005). Particle patterns in English: a comprehensive coverage. Doctoral dissertation, Katholieke Universiteit Leuven.
Cappelle, Bert (2010). Doubler-upper nouns: a challenge for usage-based models of language? In Onysko and Michel (2010: 335–74).
Carnoy, Albert J. (1917). Apophony and rhyme words in Vulgar Latin onomatopoeias. *American Journal of Philology* 38: 265–84.
Carr, Charles T. (1939). *Nominal Compounds in Germanic*. London: Oxford University Press.
Carroll, Lewis (1871). *Through the Looking-Glass and What Alice Found There*. London: Macmillan.
Carstairs-McCarthy, Andrew (1992). *Current Morphology*. London: Routledge.
Carstairs-McCarthy, Andrew (1998). Phonological constraints on morphological rules. In Spencer and Zwicky (1998: 144–8).
Carstairs-McCarthy, Andrew (2005). Basic terminology. In Štekauer and Lieber (2005: 5–23).
Carstairs-McCarthy, Andrew (2010). Review of Lieber and Štekauer (2009). *Word Structure* 3: 252–82.
Carter, Ronald (2004). *Language and Creativity: The Art of Common Talk*. London: Routledge.
Casagrande, Jean (ed.) (1983). *The Linguistic Connection*. Lanham, Md.: University Press of America.
Casas Gómez, Miguel (2012). The expressive creativity of euphemism and dysphemism. *Lexis* 7: 43–64.
Cassidy, Frederic G. (1993). Review of Algeo (1991). *Language* 69: 397–400.
Cavoto, Fabrice (ed.) (2002). *The Linguist's Linguist: A Collection of Papers in Honour of Alexis Manaster Ramer*. 2 vols (continuous pagination). Munich: Lincom Europa.
Cekaite, Asta, and Karin Aronsson (2005). Language play: a collaborative resource in children's L2 learning. *Applied Linguistics* 26: 169–91.
Chan, Marjorie K. M. (1996). Sound symbolism and the Chinese language. In Cheng et al. (1996: 2.17–34).
Chapman, Don (2008). *Fixer-uppers* and *passers-by*: nominalization of verb–particle constructions. In Fitzmaurice and Minkova (2008: 265–99).
Cheng, Tsai Fa, Yafei Li, and Hongming Zhang (eds) (1996). *Proceedings of the 7th North American Conference on Chinese Linguistics* [NACCL] *and the 4th International Conference on Chinese Linguistics* [ICCL]. 2 vols. Los Angeles: GSIL, UCLA.
Childs, G. Tucker (1994). African ideophones. In Hinton et al. (1994a: 178–204).
Cho, Young-mee Yu (2009). A historical perspective on nonderived environment blocking: the case of Korean palatalization. In Hanson and Inkelas (2009: 461–86).
Choe, Sook Hee, et al. (eds) (2007). *Phases in the Theory of Grammar*. Seoul: Dong-In.
Chomsky, Noam (1981). *Lectures on Government and Binding*. Dordrecht: Foris.
Chomsky, Noam (1986a). *Knowledge of Language*. New York: Praeger.

Chomsky, Noam (1986b). *Barriers.* Cambridge, Mass.: MIT Press.
Chomsky, Noam (1995). *The Minimalist Program.* Cambridge, Mass.: MIT Press.
Chomsky, Noam (2001). Derivation by phase. In Kenstowicz (2001: 1–52).
Chomsky, Noam (2004). Beyond explanatory adequacy. In Belletti (2004: 104–31).
Chomsky, Noam (2005). Three factors in language design. *Linguistic Inquiry* 36: 1–22.
Chomsky, Noam (2007). Approaching UG from below. In Sauerland et al. (2007: 1–29).
Chomsky, Noam (2008). On phases. In Freidin et al. (2008: 133–66).
Chomsky, Noam, and Morris Halle (1968). *The Sound Pattern of English.* New York: Harper & Row.
Cinque, Guglielmo (1999). *Adverbs and Functional Heads: A Cross-Linguistic Perspective.* Oxford: Oxford University Press.
Cinque, Guglielmo (2010). Mapping spatial PPs: an introduction. In Cinque and Rizzi (2010: 3–25).
Cinque, Guglielmo, and Richard Kayne (eds) (2005). *The Oxford Handbook of Comparative Syntax.* Oxford: Oxford University Press.
Cinque, Guglielmo, and Luigi Rizzi (eds) (2010). *Mapping Spatial PPs: The Cartography of Syntactic Structures 6.* Oxford: Oxford University Press.
Cinque, Guglielmo, and Giampaolo Salvi (eds) (2001). *Current Studies in Italian Syntax: Essays Offered to Lorenzo Renzi.* Amsterdam: Elsevier.
Clackson, James, and Birgit A. Olsen (eds) (2004). *Indo-European Word Formation: Proceedings of the Conference held at the University of Copenhagen, October 20th–22nd 2000.* Copenhagen: Museum Tusculanum Press.
Clark, Eve V., and Herbert H. Clark (1979). When nouns surface as verbs. *Language* 55: 767–811.
Coates, Richard (1987). Pragmatic sources of analogical reformation. *Journal of Linguistics* 23: 319–40.
Coates, Richard (2006). Properhood. *Language* 82: 356–82.
Cohen, Paul S. (2002). Two new *s*-movable etymologies in English. In Cavoto (2002: 109–16).
Coleman, Julie (1995). The chronology of French and Latin loan words in English. *Transactions of the Philological Society* 93: 95–124.
Coleman, Julie (1997). Phonaesthesia and other forms of word play. In Hickey and Puppel (1997: 1.3–12).
Coleman, Julie, and Christian J. Kay (eds) (2000). *Lexicology, Semantics and Lexicography: Selected Papers from the Fourth G. L. Brook Symposium, Manchester, 1998.* Amsterdam: Benjamins.
Coleman, Robert (1989). The formation of specialized vocabularies in philosophy, grammar and rhetoric: winners and losers. In Lavency and Longrée (1989: 77–89).
Collingwood, Stuart Dodgson (1898). *The Life and Letters of Lewis Carroll.* London: Fisher Unwin. [Repr. Teddington, Middx: Echo Library, 2007.]
Comrie, Bernard, and Maria Polinsky (1998). The Great Daghestanian Case Hoax. In Siewierska and Song (1998: 95–114).
Comrie, Bernard, and Sandra Thompson (1985). Lexical nominalization. In Shopen (1985: 349–98).

Conklin, Kathy, and Norbert Schmitt (2012). The processing of formulaic language. *Annual Review of Applied Linguistics* 32: 45–61.
Cook, C. Paul (2010). Exploiting linguistic knowledge to infer properties of neologisms. Ph.D. University of Toronto. Available on the author's website: http://www.cs.toronto.edu/~pcook/
Cook, Guy (2000). *Language Play, Language Learning*. Oxford: Oxford University Press.
Cooper, William E., and John R. Ross (1975). World order. *Papers from the Parasession on Functionalism* (CLS 11), 63–111. Chicago: Chicago Linguistic Society.
Copley, James (1961). *Shift of Meaning*. London: Oxford University Press.
Corbett, Greville G. (2007). Canonical typology, suppletion, and possible words. *Language* 83: 8–42.
Corbett, Greville G. (2009). Canonical inflectional classes. In Montermini et al. (2009: 1–11).
Corbett, Greville G. (2010). Canonical derivational morphology. *Word Structure* 3: 141–55.
Corbin, Danielle (1987). *Morphologie dérivationnelle et structuration du lexique*. Tübingen: Niemeyer.
Cornish, Jennifer L. (2003). A historical and psycholinguistic investigation of phonaesthesia. MS, SUNY.
Cowgill, Warren, and Manfred Mayrhofer (1986). *Indogermanische Grammatik*. 2 vols. Heidelberg: Winter.
Cowie, Claire (2000). The discourse motivations for neologising: action nominalization in the history of English. In Coleman and Kay (2000: 179–207).
Cowie, Claire, and Christiane Dalton-Puffer (2002). Diachronic word-formation and studying changes in productivity over time: theoretical and methodological considerations. In Díaz Vera (2002: 410–37).
Crema, Michael (2010). What is the purpose of the '*sklerotes* argument' in Plato's *Cratylus* (433d1–435d1)? MS, University of Chicago.
Croft, William A. (1991). *Syntactic Categories and Grammatical Relations: The Cognitive Organization of Information*. Chicago: University of Chicago Press.
Croft, William A. (1998). Event structure in argument linking. In Butt and Geuder (1998: 1–43).
Croft, William A. (2003). *Typology and Universals*. Cambridge: Cambridge University Press.
Croft, William A. (2008). On iconicity of distance. *Cognitive Linguistics* 19: 49–58.
Croft, William A., Keith Denning, and Suzanne Kemmer (eds) (1990). *Studies in Typology and Diachrony: Papers Presented to Joseph H. Greenberg on his 75th Birthday*. Amsterdam: Benjamins.
Crystal, David (2001). *Language Play*. Chicago: University of Chicago Press.
Csirmaz, Aniko, Zhiqiang Li, Andrew Nevins, Olga Vaysman, and Michael Wagner (eds) (2002). *Phonological Answers (and Their Corresponding Questions)*. MITWPL 42.
Cuyckens, Hubert, Thomas Berg, René Dirven, and Klaus-Uwe Panther (eds) (2003). *Motivation in Language*. Amsterdam: Benjamins.
Dalton-Puffer, Christiane (1994). Productive or not productive? The Romance element in Middle English derivation. In Fernández et al. (1994: 247–60).
Dalton-Puffer, Christiane (1996). *The French Influence on Middle English Morphology: A Corpus-Based Study of Derivation*. Berlin: Mouton de Gruyter.

Dalton-Puffer, Christiane, and Elke Mettinger-Schartmann (1993). Frenglish? Sur la productivité de la morphologie française dans le moyen anglais. *Travaux de linguistique et de philologie* 31: 183–93.

Dalton-Puffer, Christiane, and Nikolaus Ritt (eds) (2000). *Words: Structure, Meaning, Function. A Festschrift for Dieter Kastovsky*. Berlin: Mouton de Gruyter.

Danchev, Andrei (1995a). The development of word-final /b/ in English. In Andersen (1995: 133–42).

Danchev, Andrei (1995b). Notes on the history of word-final /g/ in English. In Fisiak (1995a: 55–79).

Davis, Stuart, and Michael Hammond (1995). Onglides in American English. *Phonology* 12: 159–82.

Davy, Dennis (2000). Shortening phenomena in modern English word formation: an analysis of clipping and blending. *Franco-British Studies* 29: 59–76.

DeCamp, David (1974). Neutralizations, iteratives, and ideophones: the locus of language in Jamaica. In DeCamp and Hancock (1974: 46–60).

DeCamp, David, and Ian F. Hancock (eds) (1974). *Pidgins and Creoles: Current Trends and Prospects*. Washington, DC: Georgetown University Press.

De Cuypere, Ludovic (2008). *Limiting the Iconic: From the Metatheoretical Foundations to the Creative Possibilities of Iconicity in Language*. Amsterdam: Benjamins.

Dehé, Nicole, Ray Jackendoff, Andrew McIntyre, and Silke Urban (eds) (2002). *Verb–Particle Explorations*. Berlin: Mouton de Gruyter.

de la Cruz Cabanillas, Isabel, and Cristina Tejedor Martínez (2002). Chicken or Hen? Domestic Fowl Metaphors Denoting Human Beings. *Studia Anglica Posnaniensia* 42: 337–54.

den Dikken, Marcel (1995). *Particles: On the Syntax of Verb–Particle, Triadic, and Causative Constructions*. Oxford: Oxford University Press.

den Dikken, Marcel (2003). When particles won't part. MS, CUNY.

den Dikken, Marcel (2005). Comparative correlatives comparatively. *Linguistic Inquiry* 36: 497–532.

Denison, David (2008). Patterns and productivity. In Fitzmaurice and Minkova (2008: 207–30).

de Saussure, Ferdinand (1916). *Cours de linguistique générale*. Lausanne and Paris: Payot. [Trans. Wade Baskin, New York: Philosophical Library, 1959.]

de Saussure, Ferdinand (1966 [1959]). *Course in General Linguistics*, trans. Wade Baskin. New York: McGraw-Hill.

de Vaan, Michiel (2008). *Etymological Dictionary of Latin and the Other Italic Languages*. Leiden: Brill.

de Vries, Jan (1977). *Altnordisches etymologisches Wörterbuch*, 2nd edn. Leiden: Brill.

Díaz Vera, Javier E. (ed.) (2002). *A Changing World of Words: Studies in English Historical Lexicography, Lexicology and Semantics*. Amsterdam: Rodopi.

Dickson, P. (1985). *Words: A Connoisseur's Collection of Old and New, Weird and Wonderful, Useful and Outlandish Words*. New York: Delacorte.

Dienhart, John M. (1999). Stress in reduplicative compounds: mish-mash or hocus-pocus? *American Speech* 74: 3–37.

Diessel, Holger (2005). Distance contrasts in demonstratives. WALS 170–3. Available online at: http://wals.info/example/41A/all

Dingemanse, Mark (2012). Advances in the cross-linguistic study of ideophones. *Language and Linguistics Compass* 6: 654–72.

Dirk, Lynn (2006). Synonymy blocking: a non-phenomenon? MS, Dept of Linguistics, University of Florida.

Dirven, René, and Ralf Pörings (eds) (2002). *Metaphor and Metonymy in Comparison and Contrast*. Berlin: Mouton de Gruyter.

Di Sciullo, Anna Maria (ed.) (2003). *Asymmetry in Grammar*. 2 vols. Amsterdam: Benjamins.

Di Sciullo, Anna Maria (2005). *Asymmetry in Morphology*. Cambridge, Mass.: MIT Press.

Di Sciullo, Anna Maria, and Edwin Williams (1987). *On the Definition of Word*. Cambridge, Mass.: MIT Press.

Dixit, R. Prakash (1975). Neuromuscular aspects of laryngeal control, with special reference to Hindi. Ph.D. University of Texas, Austin.

Dixon, R. M. W., and Alexandra Y. Aikhenvald (eds) (2003). *Word: A Cross-Linguistic Typology*. Cambridge: Cambridge University Press.

Doleschal, Ursula, and Anna M. Thornton (eds) (2000). *Extragrammatical and Marginal Morphology*. Munich: Lincom Europa.

Don, Jan (2004). Categories in the lexicon. *Linguistics* 42: 931–56.

Don, Jan (2005a). On conversion, relisting and zero-derivation. *SKASE: Journal of Theoretical Linguistics* 2: 2–16.

Don, Jan (2005b). Roots, deverbal nouns and denominal verbs. In Booij et al. (2005: 91–103).

Don, Jan, Mieke Trommelen, and Wim Zonneveld (2000). Conversion and category indeterminacy. In Booij et al. (2000: 943–52).

Dressler, Wolfgang U. (1977). Phono-morphological dissimilation. In Dressler and Pfeiffer (1977: 41–8).

Dressler, Wolfgang U. (1978). How much does performance contribute to phonological change? In Fisiak (1978: 145–58).

Dressler, Wolfgang U. (1985). *Morphonology: The Dynamics of Derivation*. Ann Arbor, Mich.: Karoma.

Dressler, Wolfgang U. (1987a). Word formation (WF) as part of natural morphology. In Dressler (1987b: 99–126).

Dressler, Wolfgang U. (ed.) (1987b). *Leitmotifs in Natural Morphology*. Amsterdam: Benjamins.

Dressler, Wolfgang U. (1997). Universals, typology, and modularity in natural morphology. In Hickey and Puppel (1997: 1399–1422).

Dressler, Wolfgang U. (2000). Extragrammatical vs. marginal morphology. In Doleschal and Thornton (2000: 1–10).

Dressler, Wolfgang U. (2005). Compound types. In Libben and Jarema (2005: 38–62).

Dressler, Wolfgang U., Hans C. Luschützky, Oskar E. Pfeiffer, and John R. Rennison (eds) (1990). *Contemporary Morphology*. Berlin: Mouton de Gruyter.

Dressler, Wolfgang U., and Wolfgang Meid (eds) (1978). *Proceedings of the Twelfth International Congress of Linguists (Vienna, August 28 to September 2, 1977)*. Institut für Sprachwissenschaft, University of Innsbruck.

Dressler, Wolfgang U., and Oskar E. Pfeiffer (eds) (1977). *Phonologica 1976*. Institut für Sprachwissenschaft, University of Innsbruck.
Durkin, Philip (2006). Lexical borrowing in present-day English. *Oxford University Working Papers in Linguistics, Philology and Phonetics* 11: 26–42.
Durkin, Philip (2011). *The Oxford Guide to Etymology*, paperback edn. [Original, 2009.] Oxford: Oxford University Press.
Eckardt, Regine (2006). *Meaning Change in Grammaticalization: An Enquiry into Semantic Analysis*. Oxford: Oxford University Press.
Elenbaas, Marion B. (2007). The synchronic and diachronic syntax of the English verb–particle combination. Ph.D. LOT, Utrecht.
Elsen, Hilke (2010). Between phonology and morphology. In Onysko and Michel (2010: 127–46).
Embick, David (2004a). Unaccusative syntax and verbal alternations. In Alexiadou et al. (2004: 137–58).
Embick, David (2004b). On the structure of resultative participles in English. *Linguistic Inquiry* 35: 355–92.
Embick, David (2007). Blocking effects and analytic/synthetic alternations. *Natural Language & Linguistic Theory* 25: 1–37.
Embick, David (2010). *Localism versus Globalism in Morphology and Phonology*. Cambridge, Mass.: MIT Press.
Embick, David, and Alec Marantz (2008). Architecture and blocking. *Linguistic Inquiry* 39: 1–53.
Embick, David, and Rolf Noyer (2007). Distributed morphology and the syntax–morphology interface. In Ramchand and Reiss (2007: 289–324).
Emeneau, Murray B. (1948). Taboos on animal names. *Language* 24: 56–63.
Enger, Hans-Olav (2007). Grammaticalisation due to homonymy avoidance in Gudbrandsdalen/æprede/? *Transactions of the Philological Society* 105: 42–65.
Enright, Dennis Joseph (ed.) (1985). *Fair of Speech: The Uses of Euphemism*. Oxford: Oxford University Press.
Epstein, Joseph (1985). Sex and euphemism. In Enright (1985: 56–71).
Erteschik-Shir, Nomi, and Tova Rapoport (eds.) (2005). *The Syntax of Aspect: Deriving Thematic and Aspectual Interpretation*. Oxford: Oxford University Press.
Eschholz, Paul A., and Alfred R. Rosa (1970). Course names: another aspect of college slang. *American Speech* 45: 85–90.
Fábregas, Antonio, and Sergio Scalise (2012). *Morphology: From Data to Theories*. Edinburgh: Edinburgh University Press.
Fabri, Ray, Albert Ortmann, and Teresa Parodi (eds) (1998). *Models of Inflection*. Tübingen: Niemeyer.
Fandrych, Ingrid (2008). Submorphemic elements in the formation of acronyms, blends and clippings. *Lexis* 2: 105–23; available online at: http://screcherche.univ-lyon3.fr/lexis/spip.php?article93
Fanego, Teresa, María José López-Couso, and Javier Pérez-Guerra (eds) (2002). *English Historical Syntax and Morphology: Selected Papers from 11 ICEHL, Santiago de Compostela, 7–11 September 2000*. Amsterdam: Benjamins.

Fanego, Teresa, Belén Méndez-Naya, and Elena Seoane (eds) (2002). *Sounds, Words, Texts and Change: Selected Papers from 11 ICEHL, Santiago de Compostela, 7–11 September 2000*. Amsterdam: Benjamins.

Fanselow, Gisbert (1988). 'Word syntax' and semantic principles. *Yearbook of Morphology 1988*: 95–122.

Farb, Peter (1973). *Word Play: What Happens When People Talk?* New York: Bantam.

Farrell, Patrick (2001). Functional shift as category underspecification. *English Language and Linguistics* 5: 109–30.

Farrell, Patrick (2005). English verb–preposition constructions: constituency and order. *Language* 81: 96–137.

Fenk-Oczlon, Gertraud (1989). Word-frequency and word order in freezes. *Linguistics* 27: 517–56.

Fernández, Francisco, Miguel Fuster and Juan José Calvo (eds) (1994). *English Historical Linguistics 1992: Papers from the 7th International Conference on English Historical Linguistics, Valencia, 22–26 September 1992*. Amsterdam: Benjamins.

Feyaerts, Kurt (2000). Refining the Inheritance Hypothesis: interaction between metaphoric and metonymic hierarchies. In Barcelona (2000a: 59–78).

Figge, Udo L. (ed.) (1995). *Language in the Würm Glaciation*. Bochum: Brockmeyer.

Fill, Alwin (2004). Remotivation and reinterpretation. In Booij et al. (2004: 1615–25).

Finkenstaedt, T., E. Leisi, and D. Wolff (eds) (1970). *A Chronological English Dictionary*. Heidelberg: Carl Winter.

Fischer, Andreas (ed.) (1989a). *The History and the Dialects of English: Festschrift for Eduard Kolb*. Heidelberg: Winter.

Fischer, Andreas (1989b). Lexical change in late Old English: from *Æ* to *Lagu*. In Fischer (1989a: 103–14).

Fischer, Olga, and Max Nänny (1999). Introduction: iconicity as a creative force in language use. In Nänny and Fischer (1999: xv–xxxvi).

Fischer, Olga, and Max Nänny (eds) (2001). *The Motivated Sign: Iconicity in Language and Literature 2*. Amsterdam: Benjamins.

Fischer, Roswitha (1998). *Lexical Change in Present-Day English: A Corpus-Based Study of the Motivation, Institutionalization, and Productivity of Creative Neologisms*. Tübingen: Narr.

Fisiak, Jacek (ed.) (1978). *Recent Developments in Historical Phonology*. The Hague: Mouton.

Fisiak, Jacek (ed.) (1985). *Historical Semantics and Historical Word-Formation*. Berlin: Mouton.

Fisiak, Jacek (ed.) (1995a). *Linguistic Change Under Contact Conditions*. Berlin: Mouton de Gruyter.

Fisiak, Jacek (1995b). *An Outline History of English*, vol. 1: *External History*. Poznań: Kantor Wydawniczy Saww.

Fisiak, Jacek, and Magdalena Bator (eds) (2013). *Historical English Word Formation and Semantics*. Frankfurt am Main: Lang.

Fitzmaurice, Susan M., and Donka Minkova (eds) (2008). *Studies in the History of the English Language IV: Empirical and Analytical Advances in the Study of English Language Change*. Berlin: Mouton de Gruyter.

Fodil, Mohammed Sadek (2010). MICUs: componyms and the triple articulation of cyber language. *Revue El Khitab, Laboratoire d'analyse de discours*, June, 66–83. Mouloud Mammeri University of Tizi-ouzou.

Fodil, Mohammed Sadek (2011). Saussure and the new lexicogenic processes. *Comunicacion social en il siglo XXI*, vol. 1. Centro de linguistica aplicada, Ministerio de ciencia, tecnología y medio ambiente, Santiago de Cuba (ISBN 978-959-7174-13-4).

Fodil, Mohammed Sadek (forthcoming). The jargon dictionary of the hackers in the light of Tournier's lexicogenic processes. MS, Dept of English, Mouloud Mammeri University of Tizi-ouzou.

Folli, Raffaella, and Heidi Harley (2007). Causation, obligation, and argument structure: on the nature of little v. *Linguistic Inquiry* 38: 197–238.

Fortson, Benjamin W., IV (2010). *Indo-European Language and Culture: An Introduction*, 2nd edn. Malden, Mass.: Blackwell.

Fortin, Antonio (2011). The morphology and semantics of expressive affixes. D.Phil., University of Oxford.

Fradin, Bernard (2009). IE, Romance, French. In Lieber and Štekauer (2009: 417–35).

Fradin, Bernard, Françoise Kerleroux, and Marc Plénat (eds) (2009). *Aperçus de morphologie du français*. Saint-Denis: Presses universitaires de Vincennes.

Fradin, Bernard, Fabio Montermini, and Marc Plénat (2009). Morphologie grammaticale et morphologie extragrammaticale. In Fradin, Kerleroux, and Plénat (2009: 21–45).

François, Jacques, Éric Gilbert, Claude Guimier, and Maxi Krause (eds) (2009). *Autour de la préposition*. Caen: University of Caen Press.

Frawley, William J. (ed.) (2003). *International Encyclopedia of Linguistics*, 2nd edn. 4 vols. Oxford: Oxford University Press.

Freeman, Morton S. (1997). *A New Dictionary of Eponyms*. Oxford: Oxford University Press.

Freidin, Robert, Carlos Peregrín Otero, and Maria Luisa Zubizarreta (eds) (2008). *Foundational Issues in Linguistic Theory: Essays in Honor of Jean-Roger Vergnaud*. Cambridge, Mass.: MIT Press.

Fritz, Gerd (1998). *Historische Semantik*. Stuttgart: Metzler.

Fruyt, Michèle (1989). Étude sémantique des 'diminutifs' latins: les suffixes *-ulus, -culus, -ellus, -illus* ... dé-substantivaux et dé-adjectivaux. In Lavency and Longrée (1989: 127–38).

Fruyt, Michèle (2002). Constraints and productivity in Latin nominal compounding. *Transactions of the Philological Society* 100.3: 259–87.

Fruyt, Michèle (2005). Le statut des composés nominaux dans le lexique latin. In Moussy (2005: 11–28).

Fu, Jingqi, Thomas Roeper, and Hagit Borer (2001). The VP within process nominals: evidence from adverbs and the VP anaphor *do-so*. *Natural Language & Linguistic Theory* 19: 41–88.

Galt, Alan (1973). *Sound and Sense in the Poetry of Theodor Storm: A Phonological-Statistical Study*. Frankfurt am Main: Lang.

García Velasco, Daniel (2009). Conversion in English and its implications for Functional Discourse Grammar. *Lingua* 119: 1164–85.

Gąsiorowski, Piotr (2006). A shibboleth upon their tongues: Early English /r/ revisited. *Studia Anglica Posnaniensia* 42: 63–76.

Geeraerts, Dirk (1997). *Diachronic Prototype Semantics: A Contribution to Historical Lexicology*. Oxford: Clarendon Press.
Geeraerts, Dirk (2002). The scope of diachronic onomasiology. In Agel et al. (2002: 29–44).
Geeraerts, Dirk (2010). *Theories of Lexical Semantics*. Oxford: Oxford University Press.
Geeraerts, Dirk, and Hubert Cuyckens (eds) (2007). *The Oxford Handbook of Cognitive Linguistics*. Oxford: Oxford University Press.
Genette, Gérard (1976). *Mimologiques. Voyages en Cratylie*. Paris: Seuil.
Gess, Randall (2003). Constraint re-ranking and explanatory adequacy in a constraint-based theory of phonological change. In Holt (2003: 67–90).
Ghomeshi, Jila, Ray Jackendoff, Nicole Rosen, and Kevin Russell (2004). Contrastive focus reduplication in English (The salad-salad paper). *Natural Language & Linguistic Theory* 22: 307–57.
Giegerich, Heinz J. (2001). Synonymy blocking and the Elsewhere Condition: lexical morphology and the speaker. *Transactions of the Philological Society* 99: 65–98.
Giegerich, Heinz J. (2004). Compound or phrase? English noun-plus-noun constructions and the stress criterion. *English Language and Linguistics* 8: 1–24.
Giegerich, Heinz J. (2009). The English compound stress myth. *Word Structure* 2.2: 1–17.
Goddard, Cliff (1998). *Semantic Analysis: A Practical Introduction*. Oxford: Oxford University Press.
Goldfarb, Nancy (1999). Carroll's Jabberwocky. *The Explicator* 57.2: 86–9.
Goldsmith, John A. (1990). *Autosegmental and Metrical Phonology*. Oxford: Blackwell.
Goldsmith, John A. (ed.) (1995). *Handbook of Phonological Theory*. Cambridge: Cambridge University Press.
Good, Jeff (ed.) (2008). *Linguistic Universals and Language Change*. Oxford: Oxford University Press.
Goossens, Louis (1990). Metaphtonymy: the interaction of metaphor and metonymy in expressions for linguistic action. *Cognitive Linguistics* 1: 323–40.
Gordon, Matthew (2002). A phonetically driven account of syllable weight. *Language* 78: 51–80.
Gordon, Matthew (2007). Typology in Optimality Theory. *Language and Linguistics Compass* 1.6: 750–69.
Gordon, Peter (1985). Level-ordering in lexical development. *Cognition* 21: 73–93.
Górecka-Smolińska, Małgorzata (2009). On how people, animals and birds of feather flock together: the scope of zoosemy in Polish and Russian. In Górecka-Smolińska et al. (2009: 17–24).
Górecka-Smolińska, Małgorzata, Grzegorz A. Kleparski, and Anna Włodarczyk-Stachurska (eds) (2009). *Galicia Studies in Language Literature and Culture: English Historical Semantics Brought to the Fore*. Chełm: TAWA.
Görlach, Manfred (2000). Conceptual and semantic change in the history of English. In Dalton-Puffer and Ritt (2000: 95–109).
Grammont, Maurice (1933). *Traité de phonétique*, 8th edn. Paris: Librairie Delagrave. [Repr. 1965.]
Greenberg, Joseph H. (ed.) (1978). *Universals of Human Language*. 4 vols. Stanford, Calif.: Stanford University Press.

Gries, Stefan Th. (2004). Shouldn't it be breakfunch? A quantitative analysis of blend structure in English. *Linguistics* 42: 639–67.

Gries, Stefan Th. (2006). Cognitive determinants of subtractive word-formation processes: a corpus-based perspective. *Cognitive Linguistics* 17.4: 535–58.

Gries, Stefan Th. (2012). Quantitative corpus data on blend formation: psycho- and cognitive-linguistic perspectives. In Renner et al. (2012).

Grimshaw, Jane (1990). *Argument Structure*. Cambridge, Mass.: MIT Press.

Grove, Victor (1950). *The Language Bar*. New York: Philosophical Library.

Grygiel, Marcin, and Grzegorz Andrzej Kleparski (2007). *Main Trends in Historical Semantics*. Rzeszów: Wydawn.

Grzega, Joachim, and Marion Schöner (2007). *English and General Historical Lexicology: Materials for Onomasiology Seminars*. Katholische Universität Eichstätt–Ingolstadt.

Guerssel, Mohand, and Jean Lowenstamm (1996). Ablaut in classical Arabic, measure I: active verbal forms. In Lecarme et al. (1996: 62–76).

Guiraud, Pierre (1980). *Le langage du corps*. Paris: Presses Universitaires de France.

Haegeman, Liliane (ed.) (1997). *Elements of Grammar*. Dordrecht: Kluwer.

Hagège, Claude (1993). *The Language Builder: An Essay on the Human Signature in Linguistic Morphogenesis*. Amsterdam: Benjamins.

Haiman, John (1980). The iconicity of grammar: isomorphism and motivation. *Language* 56.3: 515–40.

Haiman, John (2008). In defense of iconicity. *Cognitive Linguistics* 19: 59–66.

Hale, Ken, and Samuel Jay Keyser (eds) (1993a). *The View From Building 20: Essays in Linguistics in Honor of Sylvain Bromberger*. Cambridge, Mass.: MIT Press.

Hale, Ken, and Samuel Jay Keyser (1993b). On argument structure and the lexical expression of syntactic relations. In Hale and Keyser (1993a: 53–109).

Hale, Ken, and Samuel Jay Keyser (1997). On the complex nature of simple predicators. In Alsina et al. (1997: 29–65).

Hale, Ken, and Samuel Jay Keyser (1998). The basic elements of argument structure. MITWPL 32: 73–118.

Hale, Ken, and Samuel Jay Keyser (1999a). A response to Fodor and Lepore: 'impossible words?' *Linguistic Inquiry* 30: 453–66.

Hale, Ken, and Samuel Jay Keyser (1999b). Bound features, Merge, and transitivity alternations. MITWPL 35: 49–72.

Hale, Ken, and Samuel Jay Keyser (2002). *Prolegomenon to a Theory of Argument Structure*. Cambridge, Mass.: MIT Press.

Hale, Ken, and Samuel Jay Keyser (2005). Aspect and the syntax of argument structure. In Erteschik-Shir and Rapoport (2005: 11–41).

Halle, Morris (1962). Phonology in generative grammar. *Word* 18: 54–72.

Halle, Morris (1973). Prolegomena to a theory of word formation. *Linguistic Inquiry* 4: 3–16.

Halle, Morris (1997). Distributed morphology: impoverishment and fission. MITWPL 30: 425–49.

Halle, Morris, and Alec Marantz (1993). Distributed morphology and the pieces of inflection. In Hale and Keyser (1993a: 111–76).

Halle, Morris, and Alec Marantz (1994). Some key features of distributed morphology. MITWPL 21: 275-88.
Halle, Morris, and Bert Vaux (1998). Theoretical aspects of Indo-European nominal morphology: the nominal declensions of Latin and Armenian. In Jasanoff et al. (1998: 223-40).
Halmari, Helena (2011). Political correctness, euphemism, and language change: the case of 'people first'. *Journal of Pragmatics* 43: 828-40.
Halpert, Claire, Jeremy Hartman, and David Hill (eds) (2009). *Proceedings of the 2007 Workshop on Greek Syntax and Semantics at MIT*. Cambridge, Mass.: MITWPL 57.
Hamano, Shoko (1994). Palatalization in Japanese sound symbolism. In Hinton et al. (1994a: 148-57).
Hamano, Shoko (1998). *The Sound-Symbolic System of Japanese*. Cambridge: Cambridge University Press.
Hamano, Shoko (2000). Voicing of obstruents in Old Japanese: evidence from the sound-symbolic stratum. *Journal of East Asian Linguistics* 9: 207-25.
Hamans, Camiel (1997). Clippings in Modern French, English, German and Dutch. In Hickey and Puppel (1997: 2.1733-41).
Hamans, Camiel (2013). Historical word-formation caught in the present: changes in modern usage. In Fisiak and Bator (2013: 299-324).
Hammond, Michael, and Michael Noonan (eds) (1988). *Theoretical Morphology: Approaches to Modern Linguistics*. New York: Academic Press.
Hanson, Kristin, and Sharon Inkelas (eds) (2009). *The Nature of the Word: Studies in Honor of Paul Kiparsky*. Cambridge, Mass.: MIT Press.
Hansson, Gunnar Ólafur (2008). Diachronic explanations of sound patterns. *Language and Linguistics Compass* 2.5: 859-93.
Harbert, Wayne (2007). *The Germanic Languages*. Cambridge: Cambridge University Press.
Hardcastle, William J., and John Laver (eds) (1999). *The Handbook of Phonetic Sciences*. Oxford: Blackwell.
Harley, Heidi Britton (1995). Subjects, events and licensing. Ph.D. MIT.
Harley, Heidi Britton (2005). How do verbs get their names? Denominal verbs, manner incorporation, and the ontology of verb roots in English. In Erteschik-Shir and Rapoport (2005: 42-64).
Harley, Heidi Britton (2006). *English Words*. Malden, Mass.: Blackwell.
Harley, Heidi Britton (2009). Compounding in distributed morphology. In Lieber and Štekauer (2009: 129-44).
Harley, Heidi Britton, and Colin Phillips (eds) (1994). *The Morphology-Syntax Connection*. MITWPL 22.
Harris, James (2002). Flaps, trills, and syllable structure in Spanish. In Csirmaz et al. (2002: 81-108).
Hartmann, Jutta M., and László Molnárfi (eds) (2006). *Comparative Studies in Germanic Syntax: From Afrikaans to Zurich German*. Amsterdam: Benjamins.
Haspelmath, Martin (1995). The growth of affixes in morphological reanalysis. *Yearbook of Morphology 1994*: 1-29.
Haspelmath, Martin (2002). *Understanding Morphology*. London: Arnold.

Haspelmath, Martin, Matthew S. Dryer, David Gil, and Bernard Comrie (eds), with Hans-Jörg Bibiko, Hagen Jung, and Claudia Schmidt (2005). *The World Atlas of Language Structures*. Oxford: Oxford University Press. Also online at: http://www.wals.info/index

Hatcher, Anna Granville (1951). *Modern English Word-Formation and Neo-Latin: A Study of the Origins of English (French, Italian, German) Copulative Compounds*. Baltimore: Johns Hopkins University Press.

Hauser, Marc D., Noam Chomsky, and W. Tecumseh Fitch (2002). The faculty of language: what is it, who has it, and how did it evolve? *Science* 298: 1569-79.

Hay, Jennifer B. (2001). Lexical frequency in morphology: is everything relative? *Linguistics* 39: 1041-70.

Hay, Jennifer B. (2002). From speech perception to morphology: affix-ordering revisited. *Language* 78: 527-55.

Hay, Jennifer B., and R. Harald Baayen (2005). Shifting paradigms: gradient structure in morphology. *Trends in Cognitive Sciences* 9.7: 342-8.

Hay, Jennifer B., and Ingo Plag (2004). What constrains possible suffix combinations? On the interaction of grammatical and processing restrictions in derivational morphology. *Natural Language & Linguistic Theory* 22: 565-96.

Hayes, Bruce (2009). *Introductory Phonology*. Malden, Mass.: Wiley-Blackwell.

Hayes, Bruce, and Colin Wilson (2008). A maximum entropy model of phonotactics and phonotactic learning. *Linguistic Inquiry* 39: 379-440.

Hecht, Max (1888). *Die griechische Bedeutungslehre: eine Aufgabe der klassischen Philologie*. Leipzig: Teubner.

Heid, U., S. Evert, E. Lehmann, and C. Rohrer (eds) (2000). *Proceedings of the Ninth EURALEX International Congress (8-12 August 2000)*. 2 vols. Stuttgart: University of Stuttgart.

Hickey, Raymond, and Stanisław Puppel (eds) (1997). *Language History and Linguistic Modelling: A Festschrift for Jacek Fisiak on his 60th Birthday*. 2 vols. Berlin: Mouton de Gruyter.

Hilmer, Hermann (1914). *Schallnachahmung/Wortschöpfung und Bedeutungswandel*. Halle: Niemeyer.

Hinton, Leanne, and Dwight Bolinger (2003). Sound symbolism. In Frawley (2003: 4.110-15).

Hinton, Leanne, Johanna Nichols, and John J. Ohala (eds) (1994a). *Sound Symbolism*. Cambridge: Cambridge University Press. [Repr. in paperback, 2006.]

Hinton, Leanne, Johanna Nichols, and John J. Ohala (1994b). Introduction: sound-symbolic processes. In Hinton et al. (1994a: 1-12).

Hoad, Terry F. (ed.) (1996 [1986]). *The Concise Oxford Dictonary of English Etymology*. Oxford: Oxford University Press.

Hoffner, Harry A., Jr., and H. Craig Melchert (2008). *A Grammar of the Hittite Language*, pt 1: *Reference Grammar*. Winona Lake, Ind.: Eisenbrauns.

Hogg, Richard M. (1992a). *A Grammar of Old English*, vol. 1: *Phonology*. Oxford: Blackwell.

Hogg, Richard M. (1992b). Introduction. *CHEL* 1.1-25.

Hogg, Richard M. (gen. ed.) (1992-). *The Cambridge History of the English Language* [*CHEL*]. 5 vols. Cambridge: Cambridge University Press. Vol. 1: *The Beginnings to 1066*, ed. Richard

M. Hogg (1992); vol. 2: *1066–1476*, ed. Norman Blake (1992); vol. 5: *English in Britain and Overseas: Origins and Development*, ed. Robert Burchfield (1994).

Hogg, Richard M., and Linda van Bergen (eds) (1998). *Historical Linguistics 1995: Selected Papers from the 12th International Conference on Historical Linguistics, Manchester, August 1995*, vol. 2: *Germanic Linguistics*. Amsterdam: Benjamins.

Hohenhaus, Peter (2004). Identical constituent compounding: a corpus-based study. *Folia Linguistica* 38.3–4: 297–332.

Hohenhaus, Peter (2005). Lexicalization and institutionalization. In Štekauer and Lieber (2005: 353–73).

Holcombe, C. John (2007–12). *Sound in Poetry*. Available online at: http://www.textetc.com/traditional/sound.html

Holt, Eric D. (ed.) (2003). *Optimality Theory and Language Change*. Dordrecht: Kluwer.

Hong, Sung-Hoon (2004). Properties of English word-blends: structural description and statistical distribution. *English Language and Linguistics* 18: 117–40.

Hopper, Paul J. (ed.) (1977). *Studies in Descriptive and Historical Linguistics: Festschrift for Winfred P. Lehmann*. Amsterdam: Benjamins.

Hopper, Paul J. (1990). Where do words come from? In Croft et al. (1990: 151–60).

Hsieh, Feng-fan, and Michael Kenstowicz (eds) (2006). *Studies in Loanword Phonology*. MITWPL 52.

Huddleston, Rodney D., and Geoffrey K. Pullum (2002). *The Cambridge Grammar of the English Language*. Cambridge: Cambridge University Press.

Hudson, Richard (2000). *I amn't. Language 76: 297–323.

Hughes, Geoffrey (1988). *Words in Time: A Social History of the English Vocabulary*. Oxford: Blackwell.

Hughes, Geoffrey (2000). *A History of English Words*. Oxford: Blackwell.

Hurch, Bernhard (ed.) (2005). *Studies on Reduplication*. Berlin: Mouton de Gruyter.

Hyman, Larry M. (2008). Directional asymmetries in the morphology and phonology of words, with special reference to Bantu. *Linguistics* 46: 309–50.

Imholtz, August A., Jr. (1987). Latin and Greek versions of 'Jabberwocky': exercises in laughing and crying. *Rocky Mountain Review of Language and Literature* 41: 211–28.

Inkelas, Sharon (2008). The dual theory of reduplication. *Linguistics* 46: 351–401.

Inkelas, Sharon, and Cheryl Zoll (2005). *Reduplication: Doubling in Morphology*. Cambridge: Cambridge University Press.

Ito, Chiyuki, Yoonjung Kang, and Michael Kenstowicz (2006). The adoption of Japanese loanwords into Korean. In Hsieh and Kenstowicz (2006: 65–104).

Itô, Junko, and Armin Mester (1995). The core–periphery structure of the lexicon and constraints on reranking. In Beckman et al. (1995: 181–210).

Iwata, Seizi (2004). *Over*-prefixation: a lexical constructional approach. *English Language and Linguistics* 8: 239–92.

Jacobsen, William H., Jr. (1982). Basque copulative compounds: a problem in irreversible binomials. In *Proceedings of the Eighth Annual Meeting of the Berkeley Linguistics Society*, ed. Monica Macaulay, Orin D. Gensler, et al., 384–97.

Jakobson, Roman (1959). Why 'Mama' and 'Papa'? In Jakobson (1962: 538–45).

Jakobson, Roman (1960). Closing statement: linguistics and poetics. In Sebeok (1960: 350–77).
Jakobson, Roman (1962). *Selected Writings*, vol. 1: *Phonological Studies*. The Hague: Mouton.
Jakobson, Roman (1965). Quest for the essence of language. In Jakobson (1971: 345–59).
Jakobson, Roman (1971). *Selected Writings*, vol. 2: *Word and Language*. Berlin: de Gruyter.
Jakobson, Roman, and Linda R. Waugh (1987). *The Sound Shape of Language*, 2nd edn. [3rd augmented edn, 2002.] Berlin: Mouton de Gruyter.
Janda, Michael (2006). The religion of the Indo-Europeans. In Jones-Bley et al. (2006: 1–29).
Jasanoff, Jay, H. Craig Melchert, and Lisi Oliver (eds) (1998). *Mír Curad: Studies in Honor of Calvert Watkins*. Institut für Sprachwissenschaft der Universität Innsbruck.
Jespersen, Otto (1909–49). *A Modern English Grammar on Historical Principles*, vols 1 (1909), 2 (1914), 3 (1927), 4 (1931), 5 (1940), 6 (1942), 7 (1949). Copenhagen: Munksgaard. [Repr. London: Allen & Unwin, 1970.]
Jespersen, Otto (1922). *Language: Its Nature, Development and Origin*. London: Allen & Unwin. [Repr. 1950.]
Jespersen, Otto (1924). *The Philosophy of Grammar*. London: Allen & Unwin. [Repr. New York: Norton, 1965.]
Jespersen, Otto (1935). A few back-formations. *Englische Studien* 70: 117–22.
Jespersen, Otto (1938). *Growth and Structure of the English Language*, 9th edn. [Repr. with foreword by Randolph Quirk, 1982.] Chicago: University of Chicago Press.
Johansson, Niklas (2011). Motivations for sound symbolism in spatial deixis: a study of 101 languages. BA, Lund University.
Jones, Rodney H. (ed.) (2012). *Discourse and Creativity*. Harlow, UK: Pearson Education.
Jones-Bley, Karlene, Martin E. Huld, Angela Della Volpe, and Miriam Robbins Dexter (eds) (2006). *Proceedings of the Seventeenth Annual UCLA Indo-European Conference, Los Angeles, October 27–28, 2005*. Washington, DC: Institute for the Study of Man.
Joseph, Brian D. (1987). On the use of iconic elements in etymological investigation: some case studies from Greek. *Diachronica* 4: 1–26.
Joseph, Brian D. (1998). Diachronic morphology. In Spencer and Zwicky (1998: 351–73).
Joseph, Brian D., and Richard D. Janda (eds) (2003). *The Handbook of Historical Linguistics*. Oxford: Blackwell.
Julien, Marit (2002). *Syntactic Heads and Word Formation*. Oxford: Oxford University Press.
Julien, Marit (2007). On the relation between morphology and syntax. In Ramchand and Reiss (2007: 209–38).
Kager, René (1999). *Optimality Theory*. Cambridge: Cambridge University Press.
Kager, René, Joe Pater, and Wim Zonneveld (eds) (2004). *Constraints in Phonological Acquisition*. Cambridge: Cambridge University Press.
Kaisse, Ellen M. (2005). Word-formation and phonology. In Štekauer and Lieber (2005: 25–47).
Kalpakidis, Haralampos, and William Salmon (eds) (2006). *Poetry and Candy Colored Syntax: Language Presented to Háj Ross*. Style 40.1&2.
Kapatsinski, Vsevolod (2009). Testing theories of linguistic constituency with configural learning: the case of the English syllable. *Language* 85: 248–77.

Kapatsinski, Vsevolod (2013). Conspiring to mean: experimental and computational evidence for a usage-based harmonic approach to morphology. *Language* 89: 110–48.

Kaplan, Abby (2011). How much homophony is normal? *Journal of Linguistics* 47: 631–71.

Karius, Ilse (1985). *Die Ableitung der denominalen Verben mit Nullsuffigierung im Englischen*. Tübingen: Niemeyer.

Käsmann, Hans (1958). Zur Rezeption französischer Lehnwörter im Mittelenglischen. *Anglia* 76: 85–298.

Käsmann, Hans (1961). *Studien zum kirchlichen Wortschatz des Mittelenglischen 1100–1350: ein Beitrag zum Problem der Sprachmischung*. Tübingen: Niemeyer.

Käsmann, Hans (1992). Das englische Phonästhem *sl-*. *Anglia* 110: 307–46.

Kastovsky, Dieter (1969). Wortbildung und Nullmorphem. *Linguistische Berichte* 2: 1–13.

Kastovsky, Dieter (1986a). Diachronic word formation in a functional perspective. In Kastovsky and Szwedek (1986: 409–21).

Kastovsky, Dieter (1986b). The problem of productivity in word formation. *Linguistics* 24: 585–600.

Kastovsky, Dieter (2002). The derivation of ornative, locative, ablative, privative and reversative verbs in English: a historical sketch. In Fanego, López-Couso, and Pérez-Guerra (2002: 99–109).

Kastovsky, Dieter (2005). Conversion and/or zero: word-formation theory, historical linguistics, and typology. In Bauer and Valera (2005: 31–50).

Kastovsky, Dieter (2009). Diachronic perspectives. In Lieber and Štekauer (2009: 323–40).

Kastovsky, Dieter (2013). English prefixation: a historical sketch. In Fisiak and Bator (2013: 9–30).

Kastovsky, Dieter, and Arthur Mettinger (eds) (2001). *Language Contact in the History of English*. Frankfurt am Main: Lang.

Kastovsky, Dieter, and Aleksander Szwedek (eds) (1986). *Linguistics Across Historical and Geographical Boundaries: In Honour of Jacek Fisiak on the Occasion of His Fiftieth Birthday*. 2 vols. Berlin: Mouton de Gruyter.

Katamba, Francis, and John T. Stonham (2006). *Morphology*, 2nd edn. London: Macmillan.

Kay, Christian, and Irené Wotherspoon (2002). Wreak, wrack, rack, and (w)ruin: the history of some confused spellings. In Fanego, Méndez-Naya, and Seoane (2002: 129–43).

Kay, Paul, Brent Berlin, and William Merrifield (1991). Biocultural implications of systems of color naming. *Journal of Linguistic Anthropology* 1: 12–25.

Kaylor, Noel Harold, Jr., and Richard Scott Nokes (eds) (2007). *Global Perspectives on Medieval English Literature and Culture*. Kalamazoo, Mich.: University of Kalamazoo Press.

Kelly, Michael H. (1998). To 'brunch' or to 'brench': some aspects of blend structure. *Linguistics* 36: 579–90.

Kelly, Michael H., J. Kathryn Bock, and Frank C. Keil (1986). Prototypicality in a linguistic context: effects on sentence structure. *Journal of Memory and Language* 25: 59–74.

Kemmer, Suzanne (2003). Schemas and lexical blends. In Cuyckens et al. (2003: 69–97).

Kenstowicz, Michael (1994). *Phonology in Generative Grammar*. Oxford: Blackwell.

Kenstowicz, Michael (ed.) (2001). *Ken Hale: A Life in Language*. Cambridge, Mass.: MIT Press.

Kiełtyka, Robert (2008). *On Zoosemy: The Study of Middle English and Early Modern English Domesticated Animals*. Rzeszów: University of Rzeszów Press.
Kiełtyka, Robert (2009). A panchronic account of canine verbal zoosemy. In Górecka-Smolińska et al. (2009: 25–36).
Kilani-Schoch, Marianne, and Wolfgang U. Dressler (2005). *Morphologie naturelle et flexion du verbe français*. Tübingen: Narr.
Kiparsky, Paul (1982a). Lexical phonology and morphology. In Yang (1982: 3–91).
Kiparsky, Paul (1982b). From cyclic phonology to lexical phonology. In van der Hulst and Smith (1982: 1.131–75).
Kiparsky, Paul (1983). Word-formation and the lexicon. In *Proceedings of the Mid-American Linguistics Conference*, ed. Frances A. Ingeman, 3–29. Lawrence: University of Kansas Press.
Kiparsky, Paul (1997). Remarks on denominal verbs. In Alsina et al. (1997: 473–99).
Kiparsky, Paul (2008). Universals constrain change; change results in typological generalizations. In Good (2008: 23–53).
Kiparsky, Paul (2010). Dvandvas, blocking, and the associative: the bumpy road from phrase to word. *Language* 86: 302–31.
Kirshenblatt-Gimblett, Barbara (ed.) (1976). *Speech Play*. Philadelphia: University of Pennsylvania Press.
Klégr, Aleš, and Jan Čermák (2010). Neologisms of the 'on-the-pattern-of' type: analogy as a word-formation process? In Procházka et al. (2010: 229–41).
Klein, Ernest (1966–7). *A Comprehensive Etymological Dictionary of the English Language: Dealing with the Origin of Words and thus Illustrating the History of Civilization and Culture*. 2 vols. Amsterdam: Elsevier. [Repr. 1971.]
Kleparski, Grzegorz Andrzej (1990). *Semantic Change in English: A Study of Evaluative Developments in the Domain of Humans*. Lublin: Catholic University of Lublin Press.
Kleparski, Grzegorz Andrzej (1997). *Theory and Practice of Historical Semantics: The Case of Middle English and Early Modern English Synonyms of Girl/Young Woman*. Lublin: Catholic University of Lublin Press.
Kleparski, Grzegorz Andrzej (2007). Despotic mares, dirty sows, and angry bitches: on Middle English zoosemy and beyond. In Kaylor and Nokes (2007: 93–116).
Kleparski, Grzegorz Andrzej (2009). On language-internal causes of diachronic changes of word meaning. In Górecka-Smolińska et al. (2009: 37–44).
Kleparski, Grzegorz Andrzej (2013). Historical semantics: a sketch on new categories and types of semantic change. In Fisiak and Bator (2013: 59–87).
Kleparski, Grzegorz Andrzej, and Szymon Skóra (2009). On sound symbolism: a pilot study of pejorative load of selected English phoneme-clusters. In Górecka-Smolińska et al. (2009: 57–64).
Kleparski, Grzegorz Andrzej, and Agnieszka Uberman (eds) (2008). *Galicia Studies in English with Special Reference to English and Diachronic Semantics*. Chełm: TAWA.
Knappe, Gabriele (2004). Greyhounds are not grey: on folk-etymological change and its role in the history of English. In Bode et al. (2004: 491–505).
Knowles, Elizabeth, with Julia Elliott (eds) (1997). *The Oxford Dictionary of New Words*. Oxford: Oxford University Press.

Koivisto-Alanko, Päivi (2000a). Mechanisms of semantic change in nouns of cognition: a general model? In Coleman and Kay (2000: 35-52).

Koivisto-Alanko, Päivi (2000b). *Abstract Words in Abstract Worlds: Directionality and Prototypical Structure in the Semantic Change in English Nouns of Cognition.* Helsinki: Société Néophilologique.

Kolin, Philip C. (1979). The pseudo-suffix *-oholic. American Speech* 54: 74-6.

Kolin, Philip C. (1985). The pseudo-suffix *-(er)cise. American Speech* 60: 91-2.

Konieczna, Ewa (2009). De-obscuring the language: folk etymology in Modern English and Polish. In Górecka-Smolińska et al. (2009: 71-8).

Konkol, Evelyn (1960). Die Konversion im Frühneuenglischen in der Zeit von etwa 1580 bis 1600. Doctoral dissertation, University of Cologne.

Kopecka, Beata (2009). On the interlocking nature of metaphor and metonymy: a case study of body parts and proper names. In Górecka-Smolińska et al. (2009: 79-90).

Kornexl, Lucia (2002). From *gold-gifa* to *chimney sweep*? Morphological (un)markedness of modern English agent nouns in a diachronic perspective. In Fanego, López-Couso, and Pérez-Guerra (2002: 111-29).

Körtvélyessy, Lívia (2009). Productivity and creativity in word-formation: a sociolinguistics perspective. *Onomasiology Online* 10: 1-22.

Körtvélyessy, Lívia (2011a). Phonetic iconicity: lost in universality. *Bulletin of the Transilvania University of Braşov* 4.53: 137-44.

Körtvélyessy, Lívia (2011b). A cross-linguistic research into phonetic iconicity. *Lexis* 6 (*Diminutives and Augmentatives in the Languages of the World*): 27-39.

Koskenniemi, Inna (1968). *Repetitive Word Pairs in Old and Early Middle English Prose.* Turku: Turun Yliopisto (University of Turku).

Kövecses, Zoltán (2002). *Metaphor: A Practical Introduction.* Oxford: Oxford University Press.

Kövecses, Zoltán (2005). *Metaphor in Culture: Universality and Variation.* Cambridge: Cambridge University Press.

Koziol, Herbert (1972). *Handbuch der englischen Wortbildungslehre*, 2nd edn. Heidelberg: Winter.

Krahe, Hans, and Wolfgang Meid (1967). *Germanische Sprachwissenschaft*, vol. 3: *Wortbildungslehre.* Berlin: de Gruyter.

Kramsch, Claire (2009). *The Multilingual Subject.* Oxford: Oxford University Press.

Krause, Wolfgang (1922). Die Wortstellung in den zweigliedrigen Wort-Verbindungen. *KZ* 50: 74-129.

Kreidler, Charles W. (1979). Creating new words by shortening. *Journal of English Linguistics* 13: 24-36.

Kreidler, Charles W. (2000). Clipping and acronymy. In Booij et al. (2000: 956-63).

Kursova, Anya (2013). Folk-etymologies: on the way to improving naturalness. In Fisiak and Bator (2013: 369-434).

Kuryłowicz, Jerzy (1964). *The Inflectional Categories of Indo-European.* Heidelberg: Winter.

Labov, William (1972). The boundaries of words and their meanings. In Bailey and Shuy (1972: 340-73).

Lambrecht, Knud (1984). Formulaicity, frame semantics, and pragmatics in German binomial expressions. *Language* 60: 753–96.
Lapointe, Steven G., Diane K. Brentari, and Patrick M. Farrell (eds) (1998). *Morphology and its Relation to Phonology and Syntax*. Stanford, Calif.: CSLI.
Lappe, Sabine (2003). Monosyllabicity in prosodic morphology: the case of truncated personal names in English. *Yearbook of Morphology 2002*: 135–86.
Lappe, Sabine (2007). *English Prosodic Morphology*. Dordrecht: Springer.
Lass, Roger (1997). Arse longa, vita brevis: last words on 'harmful homophony'. *Studia Anglica Posnaniensia* 32: 21–31.
Lavency, Marius, and Dominique Longrée (eds) (1989). *Proceedings of the Vth Colloquium on Latin Linguistics* (= CILL 15: 1–4). Louvain-la-Neuve: Peeters.
Lavrova, Natalie (2010). Toward some innovative lexems in modern English. Short essay, available online at: http://www.grin.com/en/e-book/151438/toward-some-innovative-lexems-in-modern-english
Lawler, John (2006). The data fetishist's guide to rime coherence. In Kalpakidis and Salmon (2006): http://www.umich.edu/~jlawler/rimecoherence.pdf
Lecarme, Jacqueline, Jean Lowenstamm, and Ur Shlonsky (eds) (1996). *Studies in Afroasiatic Grammar*. The Hague: Holland Academic Graphics.
Lee, James F., Kimberly L. Geeslin, and J. Clancy Clements (eds) (2002). *Structure, Meaning, and Acquisition in Spanish: Proceedings of the 4th Annual Hispanic Linguistics Symposium*. Somerville, Mass.: Cascadilla Press.
Lefilliâtre, Boris (2012). *La troncation à stratégie euphémique*. Predoctoral (M2) thesis, University of Caen.
Lehrer, Adrienne (2003). Understanding trendy neologisms. *Italian Journal of Linguistics/ Rivista di linguistica* 15: 369–82.
Lehrer, Adrienne (2007). Blendalicious. In Munat (2007a: 115–33).
Leisi, Ernst (1974). *Das heutige Englisch: Wesenzüge und Probleme*. Heidelberg: Winter.
Lestrade, Sander (2010). The space of case. Ph.D. Radboud University, Nijmegen.
Létoublon, Françoise (1988). Dérivés d'onomatopées et délocutivité. In *Logopédies*, 137–54.
Levinson, Lisa (2007). The roots of verbs. Ph.D. New York University.
Levinson, Lisa (2010). Arguments for pseudo-resultative predicates. *Natural Language & Linguistic Theory* 28: 135–82.
Levinson, Stephen C. (2013). Recursion in pragmatics. *Language* 89: 149–62.
Libben, Gary, and Gonia Jarema (eds) (2005). *The Representation and Processing of Compound Words*. Oxford: Oxford University Press.
Liberman, Anatoly (1990). Etymological Studies 3. Some Germanic words beginning with fl-: language at play. *General Linguistics* 30: 81–107.
Liberman, Anatoly (2000). The etymology of English *boy*, *beacon*, and *buoy*. *American Journal of Germanic Linguistics & Literatures* 12: 201–34.
Liberman, Anatoly (2002). Origin unknown. In Minkova and Stockwell (2002: 109–23).
Liberman, Anatoly (2009). *Word Origins and How We Know Them: Etymology for Everyone*. Oxford: Oxford University Press.
Libert, Alan (1993). On the distinction between syntactic and semantic Case. Ph.D. McGill University.

Libert, Alan (2006). *Ambipositions*. Munich: Lincom Europa.
Lieber, Rochelle (1980). On the organization of the lexicon. Ph.D. MIT. [Published Bloomington: Indiana University Linguistics Club, 1981.]
Lieber, Rochelle (1981). Morphological conversion within a restrictive theory of the lexicon. In Moortgat et al. (1981: 161–200).
Lieber, Rochelle (1983). Argument linking and compounds in English. *Linguistic Inquiry* 14: 251–85.
Lieber, Rochelle (1992). *Deconstructing Morphology: Word Formation in Syntactic Theory*. Chicago: University of Chicago Press.
Lieber, Rochelle (2004). *Morphology and Lexical Semantics*. Cambridge University Press.
Lieber, Rochelle (2005). English word-formation processes: observations, issues, and thoughts on future research. In Štekauer and Lieber (2005: 375–427).
Lieber, Rochelle (2008). On the lexical semantics of English compounds. Paper presented at the CompoNet Congress on Compounding, 2008, University of Bologna.
Lieber, Rochelle (2009a). A lexical semantic approach to compounding. In Lieber and Štekauer (2009: 78–104).
Lieber, Rochelle (2009b). IE, Germanic: English. In Lieber and Štekauer (2009: 357–69).
Lieber, Rochelle, and Pavol Štekauer (eds) (2009). *The Oxford Handbook of Compounding*. Oxford: Oxford University Press.
Linfoot, Kerry (2001). The linguistics of euphemism: a diachronic study of euphemism use and formation. MA University of Surrey.
Linfoot, Kerry (2005). The linguistics of euphemism: a diachronic study of euphemism formation. *Journal of Language and Linguistics* 4: 227–63.
Lipka, Leonhard (1985). Inferential features in historical semantics. In Fisiak (1985: 339–54).
Lipka, Leonhard (2000). Word-formation and (proper) names: a neglected field. In Dalton-Puffer and Ritt (2000: 187–203).
Lipka, Leonhard (2002). *English Lexicology: Lexical Structure, Word Semantics and Word-Formation*. Tübingen: Narr.
Löfstedt, Einar (1959). *Late Latin*. Cambridge, Mass.: Harvard University Press.
Logopédies (1988). ἭΔΙΣΤΟΝ ΛΟΓΟΔΕΙΠΝΟΝ / *Logopédies: mélanges de philologie et de linguistique grecques offerts à Jean Taillardat*, ed. J. Hasenshor, M. Casevitz, O. Masson, J. L Perpillou, and F. Skoda. Paris: Peeters/Selaf.
López Rúa, Paula (2002). On the structure of acronyms and neighboring categories: a prototype-based account. *English Language and Linguistics* 6: 31–60.
López Rúa, Paula (2004). The categorical continuum of English blends. *English Studies* 85: 63–76.
Lord, Robert (1996). *Words: A Hermeneutical Approach to the Study of Language*. Lanham, Md.: University Press of America.
Lowrey, Tina M., and L. J. Shrum (2007). Phonetic symbolism and brand name preference. *Journal of Consumer Research* 34: 406–14.
MacNeilage, Peter F. (1999). Acquisition of speech. In Hardcastle and Laver (1999: 301–32).
Magnus, Margaret (1998). Effects of position on phonestheme semantics. Available on the author's website: http://www.trismegistos.com/MagicalLetterPage/

Magnus, Margaret (1999). *A Dictionary of English Sound*. Available on the author's website: http://www.trismegistos.com/MagicalLetterPage/

Magnus, Margaret (2001). What's in a word? Studies in phonosemantics. Ph.D. Norwegian University of Science and Technology, Trondheim. Available on the author's website: http://www.trismegistos.com/MagicalLetterPage/

Maiden, Martin (2005). Morphological autonomy and diachrony. *Yearbook of Morphology 2004*: 137–75.

Malkiel, Yakov (1959). Studies in irreversible binomials. *Lingua* 8: 113–60.

Malkiel, Yakov (1977). Why ap-*ish* but worm-*y*? In Hopper (1977: 341–64).

Malkiel, Yakov (1979). Problems in the diachronic differentiation of near-homophones. *Language* 55: 1–36.

Marantz, Alec (1995). 'Cat' as a phrasal idiom: consequences of late insertion in distributed morphology. MS, MIT.

Marantz, Alec (1997). No escape from syntax: don't try morphological analysis in the privacy of your own lexicon. *U. Penn Working Papers in Linguistics* 4: 201–25.

Marantz, Alec (2007). Phases and words. In Choe et al. (2007: 191–222).

Marchand, Hans (1959). Phonetic symbolism in word-formation. *Indogermanische Forschungen* 64: 146–68, 256–77.

Marchand, Hans (1960). *The Categories and Types of Present-Day English Word-Formation: A Synchronic-Diachronic Approach*. Wiesbaden: Harrassowitz.

Marchand, Hans (1963). On the question of contrary analysis with derivationally connected but morphologically uncharacterized words. *English Studies* 44.3: 176–87.

Marchand, Hans (1964). Die Ableitung desubstantivischer Verben mit Nullmorphem im Englischen, Französischen und Deutschen. *Die Neueren Sprachen* 10: 105–18.

Marchand, Hans (1969). *The Categories and Types of Present-Day English Word-Formation: A Synchronic-Diachronic Approach*, 2nd edn. Munich: Beck.

Markel, Norman N., and Eric P. Hamp (1960–61). Connotative meanings of certain phoneme sequences. *Studies in Linguistics* 15: 47–61.

Martsa, Sándor (1999). On exploring conceptual structure of folk knowledge: the case of animal terms. *Linguistica e filologia* 9: 73–88.

Martsa, Sándor (2012). Conversion in English: a cognitive semantic approach. Habilitation thesis, University of Pécs.

Matasović, Ranko (2009). *Etymological Dictionary of Proto-Celtic*. Leiden: Brill.

Matellán, Victor Acedo (2010). Argument structure and the syntax–morphology interface: a case study in Latin and other languages. Ph.D. University of Barcelona.

Mattiello, Elisa (2008). *An Introduction to English Slang: A Description of its Morphology, Semantics and Sociology*. Milan: Polimetrica.

Matushansky, Ora (2011). Review article of Roberts (2010). *Journal of Linguistics* 47: 538–45.

Maurer, Daphne, Thanujeni Pathman, and Catherine J. Mondloch (2006). The shape of boubas: sound–shape correspondences in toddlers and adults. *Developmental Science* 9.3: 316–22.

Mayhew, Anthony Lawson (ed.) (1908). *The Promptorium Parvulorum: The First English-Latin Dictionary, c.1440 A.D., Edited from the MS, in the Chapter Library at Winchester, with Introduction, Notes, and Glossaries*. London: Kegan Paul/Oxford: Oxford University Press.

Mayrhofer, Manfred (1986). *Indogermanische Grammatik*, Band i, ii. Halbband: *Lautlehre* [*Segmentale Phonologie der Indogermanischen*]. Vol. 2 of Cowgill and Mayrhofer (1986).
McCarthy, John J. (1982). Prosodic structures and expletive infixation. *Language* 58: 574–90.
McCarthy, John J., and Alan S. Prince (1986). *Prosodic Morphology*. [Final revision, 1996.] MS, University of Massachusetts, Amherst, and Rutgers University.
McCarthy, John J., and Alan S. Prince (1990). Foot and word in prosodic morphology: the Arabic broken plurals. *Natural Language & Linguistic Theory* 8: 209–82.
McCarthy, John J., and Alan S. Prince (1993). *Prosodic Morphology I: Constraint Interaction and Satisfaction*. MS, University of Massachusetts, Amherst, and Rutgers University.
McCarthy, John J., and Alan S. Prince (1998). Prosodic morphology. In Spencer and Zwicky (1998: 283–305).
McCawley, James D. (1978). Where you can shove infixes. In Bell and Hooper (1978: 213–21).
McClure, Peter (1998). The interpretation of hypocoristic forms of Middle English baptismal names. *Nomina* 21: 101–32.
McCrary, Kristie Marie (2004). Reassessing the role of the syllable in Italian phonology: an experimental study of consonant cluster syllabification, definite article allomorphy and segment duration. Ph.D. UCLA.
McGinnis, Martha Jo (2005). UTAH at Merge: evidence from multiple applicatives. In McGinnis and Richards (2005: 183–200).
McGinnis, Martha Jo, and Norvin Richards (eds) (2005). *Perspectives on Phases*. MITWPL 49.
McIntyre, Andrew (2001). Introduction to the verb–particle experience: semantics, argument structure and morphology. MS, University of Neuchâtel.
McIntyre, Andrew (2002). Idiosyncrasy in particle verbs. In Dehé et al. (2002: 95–118).
McIntyre, Andrew (2003). Preverbs, argument linking and verb semantics: Germanic prefixes and particles. *Yearbook of Morphology 2003*: 119–44.
McIntyre, Andrew (2004a). Event paths, conflation, argument structure, and VP shells. *Linguistics* 42: 523–71.
McIntyre, Andrew (2004b). Sum: English affix reduplication. *Linguist List* (27 June): http://www.linguistlist.org/issues/15/15-1929.html
McIntyre, Andrew (2007). Particle verbs and argument structure. *Language and Linguistics Compass* 1.4: 350–97.
McIntyre, Andrew (2009). Synthetic compounds and argument structure: messages from a *bandwagon-jumper-onner* and a *two-cents-worth-thrower-inner*. Paper presented at the Roots Workshop, University of Stuttgart.
McMahon, April M. S. (1994). *Understanding Language Change*. Cambridge: Cambridge University Press.
McMillan, James (1980). Infixing and interposing in English. *American Speech* 55: 163–83.
Meibauer, Jörg (2007). How marginal are phrasal compounds? Generalized insertion, expressivity, and I/Q-interaction. *Morphology 2007*: 17.233–59.
Meibauer, Jörg (2014). Word-formation and contextualism. *International Review of Pragmatics* 6.1.
Meier, Hans H. (1989). Etymological modes in Modern English. In Fischer (1989a: 59–76).

Meier-Brügger, Michael (with Matthias Fritz and Manfred Mayrhofer) (2003). *Indo-European Linguistics*, trans. Charles Gertmenian. Berlin: de Gruyter.
Meillet, Antoine (1905–6). Comment les mots changent de sens. In Meillet (1965: 230–71).
Meillet, Antoine (1906). Quelques hypothèses sur des interdictions de vocabulaire dans les langues indo-européennes. In Meillet (1965: 281–91).
Meillet, Antoine (n.d.). La religion indo-européenne. In Meillet (1965: 323–34).
Meillet, Antoine (1925). Les interférences entre vocabulaires. In Meillet (1951: 36–43).
Meillet, Antoine (1951–65). *Linguistique historique et linguistique générale*, vol. 2 (1951); vol. 1 (1965). Paris: Champion.
Meissner, Torsten, and Olga Tribulato (2002). Nominal composition in Mycenaean Greek. *Transactions of the Philological Society* 100: 289–330.
Merlan, Francesca (2006). Taboo: verbal practices. In Brown (2006: 12.462–6).
Miall, David S. (2001). Sounds of contrast: an empirical approach to phonemic iconicity. *Poetics* 29: 55–70.
Michel, Sascha (2006). Kurzwortgebrauch: Plädoyer für eine pragmatische Definition und Prototypologie von Kurzwörtern. *Germanistische Mitteilungen* 64: 69–83.
Millar, Neil (2011). The processing of malformed formulaic language. *Applied Linguistics* 32: 129–48.
Miller, Brett (2012). Sonority and the larynx. In Parker (2012: 266–88).
Miller, D. Gary (1975). Indo-European: VSO, SOV, SVO, or all three? *Lingua* 37: 31–52.
Miller, D. Gary (1977). Tripartization, sexism, and the rise of the feminine gender in Indo-European. *Florida Journal of Anthropology* 2: 3–16.
Miller, D. Gary (1982). *Improvisation, Typology, Culture, and 'The New Orthodoxy': How 'Oral' is Homer?* Washington, DC: University Press of America.
Miller, D. Gary (1983). English vs. woman. In Casagrande (1983: 171–206).
Miller, D. Gary (1987). Morphological theory and the structure of dvandva compounds. Paper presented at the Annual Meeting of the Linguistic Society of America.
Miller, D. Gary (1993). *Complex Verb Formation*. Amsterdam: Benjamins.
Miller, D. Gary (1994). *Ancient Scripts and Phonological Knowledge*. Amsterdam: Benjamins. Available online at: http://en.bookfi.org/book/1093690
Miller, D. Gary (2002). *Nonfinite Structures in Theory and Change*. Oxford: Oxford University Press.
Miller, D. Gary (2003). Semantic change. *English Language and Literature* 45: 135–82.
Miller, D. Gary (2006). *Latin Suffixal Derivatives in English and Their Indo-European Ancestry*. Oxford: Oxford University Press. [Repr., with corrections, 2012.]
Miller, D. Gary (2010). *Language Change and Linguistic Theory*. 2 vols. Oxford: Oxford University Press.
Miller, D. Gary (2012). *External Influences on English from its Beginnings to the Renaissance*. Oxford: Oxford University Press.
Miller, D. Gary (2013). On the history and derivation of V–P nouns. In Fisiak and Bator (2013: 31–58).
Minkova, Donka (2000). Middle English prosodic innovations and their testability in verse. In Taavitsainen et al. (2000: 431–59).

Minkova, Donka (2002). Ablaut reduplication in English: the criss-crossing of prosody and verbal art. *English Language and Linguistics* 6: 133–69.
Minkova, Donka, and Robert Stockwell (eds) (2002). *Studies in the History of the English Language: A Millennial Perspective*. Berlin: Mouton de Gruyter.
Mollin, Sandra (2012). Revisiting binomial order in English: ordering constraints and reversibility. *English Language and Linguistics* 16: 81–103.
Montermini, Fabio, Gilles Boyé, and Jesse Tseng (eds) (2009). *Selected Proceedings of the 6th Décembrettes: Morphology in Bordeaux*. Somerville, Mass.: Cascadilla Proceedings Project; available online at: http://www.lingref.com, document #2231
Moortgat, Michael, Harry van der Hulst, and Teun Hoekstra (eds) (1981). *The Scope of Lexical Rules*. Dordrecht: Foris.
Moravcsik, Edith (1978). Reduplicative constructions. In Greenberg (1978: 3.297–334).
Morris, Charles (1946). *Signs, Language and Behavior*. New York: Prentice-Hall.
Moussy, Claude (1989). Les métaphores lexicalisées et l'analyse sémique. In Lavency and Longrée (1989: 309–19).
Moussy, Claude (ed.) (2005). *La composition et la préverbation en latin*. Paris: University of Paris/Sorbonne Press.
Moyna, María Irene (2011). *Compound Words in Spanish: Theory and History*. Amsterdam: Benjamins.
Mukai, Makiko (2008). Recursive compounds. *Word Structure* 1: 178–98.
Müller, Peter O., Ingeborg Ohnheiser, Susan Olsen, and Franz Rainer (eds) (To appear). *Word-Formation: An International Handbook of the Languages of Europe*. Berlin: Mouton de Gruyter.
Munat, Judith Elaine (ed.) (2007a). *Lexical Creativity, Texts and Contexts*. Amsterdam: Benjamins.
Munat, Judith Elaine (2007b). Lexical creativity as a marker of style in science fiction and children's literature. In Munat (2007a: 163–82).
Muñoz, Carmen Portero (2003). Derived nominalizations in -ee: a role and reference grammar based semantic analysis. *English Language and Linguistics* 7: 129–59.
Nänny, Max, and Olga Fischer (eds) (1999). *Form Miming Meaning: Iconicity in Language and Literature 1*. Amsterdam: Benjamins.
Nänny, Max, and Olga Fischer (2006). Iconicity: literary texts. In *Encyclopedia of Language and Linguistics* 5, 2nd edn. Oxford: Elsevier, 462–72.
Naumann, Bernd, and Petra M. Vogel (2000). Derivation. In Booij et al. (2000: 929–43).
Nevins, Andrew, and Bert Vaux (2003a). Underdetermination in language games: survey analysis of Pig Latin dialects. Paper presented at the Annual Meeting of the Linguistic Society of America.
Nevins, Andrew, and Bert Vaux (2003b). Metalinguistic, shmetalinguistic: the phonology of shm- reduplication. In *Papers from the 39th Annual Meeting of the Chicago Linguistic Society*, ed. J. Cihlar, A. Franklin, D. Kaiser, and I. Kimbara, 702–22.
Nicholas, Nick, and Brian D. Joseph (2009). Verbal dvandvas in Modern Greek. In Halpert et al. (2009: 171–85).
Nielsen, Hans Frede, and Lene Schøsler (eds) (1996). *The Origins and Development of Emigrant Languages: Proceedings From the Second Rasmus Rask Colloquium, Odense University, November 1994*. Odense: Odense University Press.

Niemeier, Susanne (2000). Straight from the heart: metonymic and metaphorical explorations. In Barcelona (2000a: 195–213).

Noonan, Michael (2005). Spatial reference in Chantyal. In *Contemporary Issues in Nepalese Linguistics*, ed. Yogendra Yadava. Kathmandu: Linguistic Society of Nepal.

Nybakken, Oscar E. (1959). *Greek and Latin in Scientific Terminology*. Ames: Iowa State College Press.

Nyrop, Kristoffer (1913). *Grammaire historique de la langue française*, vol. 4: *Sémantique*. Leipzig: Harrassowitz/Paris: Picard/New York: Stechert.

Ohala, John J. (1994). The frequency code underlies the sound-symbolic use of voice pitch. In Hinton et al. (1994: 325–47).

Ohala, John J. (1997). Sound symbolism. *Seoul International Conference on Linguistics* (SICOL) 4: 98–103.

Olsen, Birgit Anette (2004). The complex of nasal stems in Indo-European. In Clackson and Olsen (2004: 215–48).

Olsen, Susan (2000a). Compounding and stress in English. *Linguistische Berichte* 181: 55–69.

Olsen, Susan (2000b). Composition. In Booij et al. (2000: 897–916).

Olsen, Susan (2001). Copulative compounds: a closer look at the interface between morphology and syntax. *Yearbook of Morphology 2000*: 279–320.

Olsen, Susan (2004). Coordination in morphology and syntax: the case of copulative compounds. In ter Meulen and Abraham (2004: 17–38).

Olsen, Susan (ed.) (2010). *New Impulses in Word-Formation*. Hamburg: Buske.

Onysko, Alexander, and Sascha Michel (eds) (2010). *Cognitive Perspectives on Word Formation*. Berlin: Mouton de Gruyter.

Orel, Vladimir (2003). *A Handbook of Germanic Etymology*. Leiden: Brill.

Ostwalt, Robert L. (1994). Inanimate imitatives in English. In Hinton et al. (1994a: 293–306).

Padrosa-Trias, Susanna (2010). Complex word-formation and the morphology–syntax interface. Ph.D. University of Barcelona.

Palmatier, Robert Allen (1995). *Speaking of Animals: A Dictionary of Animal Metaphors*. Westport, Conn.: Greenwood Press.

Palmer, Abram Smyther (1883). *Folk-Etymology: A Dictionary of Verbal Corruptions or Words Perverted in Form or Meaning, by False Derivation or Mistaken Analogy*. New York: Greenwood Press. [Repr. 1969.]

Palmer, Chris C. (2009). Borrowings, derivational morphology, and perceived productivity in English, 1300–1600. Ph.D. University of Michigan, Ann Arbor.

Pantcheva, Marina Blagoeva (2011). Decomposing path: the nanosyntax of directional expressions. Ph.D. University of Tromsø.

Panther, Klaus-Uwe, and Linda L. Thornburg (2002). The roles of metaphor and metonymy in English -*er* nominals. In Dirven and Pörings (2002: 279–319).

Paradis, Carita (2000). Reinforcing adjectives: a cognitive semantic perspective on grammaticalisation. In Bermúdez-Otero et al. (2000: 233–58).

Parker, Stephen (2002). Quantifying the sonority hierarchy. Ph.D. University of Massachusetts, Amherst.

Parker, Stephen (ed.) (2012). *The Sonority Controversy*. Berlin: Mouton de Gruyter.

Partridge, Eric (1983). *Origins: A Short Etymological Dictionary of Modern English*. New York: Greenwich House.
Paul, Hermann (1920). *Prinzipien der Sprachgeschichte*, 5th edn. Halle. [Repr. Tübingen: Niemeyer, 1975.]
Pennanen, Esko V. (1966). *Contributions to the Study of Back-Formation in English*. Tampere: Julkaisija Yhteiskunnallinen Korkeakolu.
Pennanen, Esko V. (1971). Conversion and zero-derivation in English. *Acta Universitatis Tamperensis* (ser. A), 40.
Pennanen, Esko V. (1975). What happens in back-formation? In E. Hovdhaugen (ed.), *Papers from the Second Scandinavian Conference on Linguistics*. Dept of Linguistics, University of Oslo, 216–29.
Perloff, Marjorie, and Craig Dworkin (eds) (2009a). *The Sound of Poetry/The Poetry of Sound*. Chicago: University of Chicago Press.
Perloff, Marjorie, and Craig Dworkin (2009b). The sound of poetry/The poetry of sound. In Perloff and Dworkin (2009a: 1–28).
Petropoulou, Evanthia (2009). On the parallel between neoclassical compounds in English and Modern Greek. *Patras Working Papers in Linguistics* 1: 40–58.
Pharies, David A. (1983). The role of speech play in word formation. In Casagrande (1983: 207–13).
Pharies, David A. (1986). *Structure and Analogy in the Playful Lexicon of Spanish*. Tübingen: Niemeyer.
Philps, Dennis (2008). Submorphemic iconicity in the lexicon: a diachronic approach to English 'gn' words. *Lexis* 2. Available online at: http://screcherche.univ-lyon3.fr/ lexis/spip.php?article95
Piaget, Jean (1955). *The Child's Construction of Reality*. London: Routledge & Kegan Paul.
Piaget, Jean (1973). *Memory and Intelligence*. New York: Basic Books.
Pickett, Joseph P. (gen. ed.) (2000). *The American Heritage Dictionary of the English Language*, 4th edn. Boston: Houghton Mifflin.
Picone, Michael D. (1994). Lexicogenesis and language vitality. *Word* 45.3: 261–85.
Picone, Michael D. (1996). *Anglicisms, Neologisms and Dynamic French*. Amsterdam: Benjamins.
Pinker, Steven, and David Birdsong (1979). Speakers' sensitivity to rules of frozen word order. *Journal of Verbal Learning and Verbal Behavior* 18: 497–508.
Pinker, Steven, and Alan Prince (1988). On language and connectionism: analysis of a parallel distributed processing model of language acquisition. *Cognition* 28: 73–193.
Plag, Ingo (1999). *Morphological Productivity: Structural Constraints in English Derivation*. Berlin: Mouton de Gruyter.
Plag, Ingo (2003). *Word-Formation in English*. Cambridge: Cambridge University Press.
Plag, Ingo (2005). The variability of compound stress in English: structural, semantic, and analogical factors. *English Language and Linguistics* 10: 143–72.
Polomé, Edgar C. (ed.) (1990). *Research Guide on Language Change*. Berlin: Mouton de Gruyter.
Pons-Sanz, Sara María (2004). The Norsified vocabulary in the works of Archbishop Wulfstan II of York. Ph.D. University of Cambridge.

Pons-Sanz, Sara María (2012). *The Lexical Effects of Anglo-Scandinavian Linguistic Contact on Old English*. Turnhout: Brepols.
Pope, Alexander (2006 [1688–1744]). *The Major Works*, ed. Pat Rogers. Oxford: Oxford University Press.
Poser, William J. (1992). Blocking of phrasal constructions by lexical items. In Sag and Szabolcsi (1992: 111–30).
Pound, Louise (1914). Blends: their relation to English word formation. *Anglistische Forschungen* 42: 1–58. [Repr. 2007.]
Preuss, Fritz (1960–62). Backformation oder Noun-incorporation. *Lebende Sprachen (LES)* 5: 110–12, 165–7; 6: 6–7, 39; 7: 37.
Prieto, Victor M. (2005). Spanish evaluative morphology: pragmatic, sociolinguistic, and semantic issues. Ph.D. University of Florida.
Prince, Alan, and Paul Smolensky (2004 [1993]). *Optimality Theory: Constraint Interaction in Generative Grammar*. Oxford: Blackwell.
Procházka, Martin, Markéta Malá, and Pavlína Šaldová (eds) (2010). *The Prague Structure and Theories of Structure*. Göttingen: Vandenhoeck & Ruprecht.
Purnelle, Gérald (1989). La transcription des noms grecs dans les inscriptions latines: le cas des aspirées. In Lavency and Longrée (1989: 355–66).
Pyles, Thomas (1952). *Words and Ways of American English*. New York: Random House.
Pylkkänen, Liina, Angeliek van Hout, and Heidi Harley (eds.) (1999). *Papers From the UPenn/MIT Roundtable on the Lexicon*. MITWPL 35.
Quinion, Michael (1996). Blends. Available online at: http://www.worldwidewords.org/articles/blend.htm
Radford, Andrew (2000). Children in search of perfection: towards a minimalist model of acquisition. *Essex Research Reports in Linguistics* 34. Available online at: http://www.privatewww.essex.ac.uk/~radford/PapersPublications/perfection.htm
Raffelsiefen, Renate (1999). Phonological constraints on English word formation. *Yearbook of Morphology 1998*: 225–87.
Raffelsiefen, Renate (2010). Idiosyncrasy, regularity, and synonymy in derivational morphology: evidence for default word interpretation strategies. In Olsen (2010: 173–232).
Rainer, Franz (2005a). Constraints on productivity. In Štekauer and Lieber (2005: 335–52).
Rainer, Franz (2005b). Typology, diachrony and universals of semantic change in word formation: a Romanist's look at the polysemy of agent nouns. In Booij et al. (2005: 21–34).
Ralli, Angela (2009). Modern Greek VV dvandva compounds: a linguistic innovation in the history of the Indo-European languages. *Word Structure* 2.2: 48–68.
Ralli, Angela, and Athanasios Karasimos (2009). The bare-stem constraint in Greek compound formation. *Gengo Kenkyu* 135.
Ramachandran, Vilayanur S., and Edward M. Hubbard (2001). Synaesthesia: a window into perception, thought and language. *Journal of Consciousness Studies* 8.12: 3–34.
Ramachandran, Vilayanur S., and Edward M. Hubbard (2003). The phenomenology of synaesthesia. *Journal of Consciousness Studies* 10.8: 49–57.
Ramchand, Gillian Catriona (2008). *Verb Meaning and the Lexicon: A First Phase Syntax*. Cambridge: Cambridge University Press.

Ramchand, Gillian Catriona, and Charles Reiss (eds) (2007). *The Oxford Handbook of Linguistic Interfaces*. Oxford: Oxford University Press.
Randall, Janet H. (1982). Morphological structure and language acquisition. Ph.D. University of Massachusetts, Amherst. [Published New York: Garland, 1985.]
Rappaport Hovav, Malka, and Beth Levin (1989). -*Er* nominals: implications for the theory of argument structure. In Wehrli and Stowell (1989).
Rappaport Hovav, Malka, and Beth Levin (1998). Building verb meanings. In Butt and Geuder (1998: 97–134).
Rappaport Hovav, Malka, and Beth Levin (2001). An event structure account of English resultatives. *Language* 77: 766–97.
Renner, Vincent (2008). On the semantics of English coordinate compounds. *English Studies* 89.5: 606–13.
Renner, Vincent, François Maniez, and Pierre Arnaud (eds) (2012). *Cross-Disciplinary Perspectives on Lexical Blending*. Berlin: Mouton de Gruyter.
Rhodes, Richard (1994). Aural images. In Hinton et al. (1994a: 276–92).
Richards, Marc (2009). Internal Pair-Merge: the missing mode of movement. *Catalan Journal of Linguistics* 8: 55–73.
Richardson, John F., M. Marks, and A. Chukerman (eds) (1983). *Papers from the Parasession of the Interplay of Phonology, Morphology and Syntax*. Chicago: Chicago Linguistic Society.
Rinelli, Gabriele (2001). Scandinavian and native social terms in Middle English: the case of *cherl/carl*. In Kastovsky and Mettinger (2001: 267–77).
Ringe, Don (2006). *From Proto-Indo-European to Proto-Germanic*. Oxford: Oxford University Press.
Rizzi, Luigi (1997). The fine structure of the left periphery. In Haegeman (1997: 281–37).
Rizzi, Luigi (2001). On the position 'Int(errogative)' in the left periphery of the clause. In Cinque and Salvi (2001: 287–96).
Rizzi, Luigi (ed.) (2004). *The Structure of CP and IP: The Cartography of Syntactic Structures*. 2 vols. Oxford: Oxford University Press.
Roberts, Ian (2010). *Agreement and Head Movement: Clitics, Incorporation, and Defective Goals*. Cambridge, Mass.: MIT Press.
Roca, Iggy, and Elena Felíu (2003). Morphology in truncation: the role of the Spanish desinence. *Yearbook of Morphology 2002*: 187–243.
Rodriguez, Féliz, and Garland Cannon (1994). Remarks on the origin and evolution of abbreviations and acronyms. In Fernández et al. (1994: 261–72).
Roeper, Thomas (1987). Implicit arguments and the head–complement relation. *Linguistic Inquiry* 18: 267–310.
Roeper, Thomas (1988a). Compound syntax and head movement. In Booij and van Marle (1988: 187–228).
Roeper, Thomas (1988b). Aspect and compounds: syntactically constrained semantics. *Lexicon Project Working Papers* 24: 59–72. Center for Cognitive Science, MIT.
Roeper, Thomas (1999). Leftward movement in morphology. *MITWPL* 34: 35–66.
Roeper, Thomas (2005). Chomsky's *Remarks* and the Transformationalist Hypothesis. In Štekauer and Lieber (2005: 125–46).

Roeper, Thomas (2007). *The Prism of Grammar: How Child Language Illuminates Humanism*. Cambridge, Mass.: MIT Press.

Roeper, Thomas (2011). The acquisition of recursion: how formalism articulates the child's path. *Biolinguistics* 5: 57–86.

Roeper, Thomas, and Muffy E. A. Siegel (1978). A lexical transformation for verbal compounds. *Linguistic Inquiry* 9: 197–260.

Roeper, Thomas, William Snyder, and Kazuko Hiramatsu (2003). Learnability in a Minimalist framework: root compounds, merger, and the syntax–morphology interface. MS, University of Massachusetts, Amherst.

Roeper, Thomas, and Angeliek van Hout (1999). The impact of nominalization on passive, *-able*, and middle: Burzio's Generalization and feature-movement in the lexicon. In Pylkkänen et al. (1999: 185–211).

Roeper, Thomas, and Angeliek van Hout (2001). The representation of movement in *-ability* nominalizations: evidence for covert category movement, edge phenomena, and local LF. In *Motivating Movement*, ed. Alison Henry. Oxford: Oxford University Press. Available on Roeper's website: http://www.umass.edu/linguist/people/faculty/roeper/roeper.html

Ronneberger-Sibold, Elke (1995). On different ways of optimizing the sound shape of words. In Andersen (1995: 421–32).

Ropert, François (2009). Distance et proximité entre plusieurs discours dans l'argot journalistique de la revue *Variety*. *La Revue du GERAS (ASp)* 55. Available online at: http://www.asp.revues.org/222?lang=en

Rosch, Eleonore (1973). Natural categories. *Cognitive Psychology* 4: 328–50.

Ross, John R. (1967). Constraints on variables in syntax. Ph.D. MIT.

Rothwell, William (1996). Adding insult to injury: the English who curse in borrowed French. In Nielsen and Schøsler (1996: 41–54).

Rousseau, André (ed.) (1995a). *Les préverbes dans les langues d'Europe: introduction à l'étude de la préverbation*. Lille: Université Charles-De-Gaulle (Presses Universitaires du Septentrion).

Rousseau, André (1995b). En guise de conclusion: identité et fonctions des préverbes. In Rousseau (1995a: 383–91).

Rovai, Francesco (2012). Between feminine singular and neuter plural: re-analysis patterns. *Transactions of the Philological Society* 110: 94–121.

Roy, Isabelle, and Peter Svenonius (2009). Complex prepositions. In François et al. (2009: 105–16).

Rubino, Carl (2005). Reduplication: form, function and distribution. In Hurch (2005: 11–30).

Rundblad, Gabriella, and David B. Kronenfeld (2000). Folk-etymology: haphazard perversion or shrewd analogy? In Coleman and Kay (2000: 19–34).

Ryan, Kevin M. (2011). Gradient syllable weight and weight universals in quantitative metrics. *Phonology* 28: 413–54.

Sadowsky, Piotr (2001). The sound as an echo to the sense: the iconicity of English *gl-* words. In Fischer and Nänny (2001: 69–88).

Safire, William (1995). Return of the retronyms. *New York Times Magazine*, 19 March, section 6.

Sag, Ivan, and Anna Szabolcsi (eds) (1992). *Lexical Matters*. Stanford, Calif.: CSLI.

Sanches, Mary, and Barbara Kirshenblatt-Gimblett (1976). Children's traditional speech play and child language. In Kirshenblatt-Gimblett (1976: 65–110).
Sanz, Cristina, and Ronald P. Leow (eds) (2011). *Implicit and Explicit Language Learning: Conditions, Processes, and Knowledge in SLA and Bilingualism*. Washington, DC: Georgetown University Press.
Sapir, Edward (1915). Abnormal types of speech in Nootka. In Sapir (1963: 179–96).
Sapir, Edward (1921). *Language: An Introduction to the Study of Speech*. New York: Harcourt, Brace & World.
Sapir, Edward (1929). A study in phonetic symbolism. *Journal of Experimental Psychology* 12: 225–39.
Sapir, Edward (1963). *Selected Writings of Edward Sapir in Language, Culture and Personality*, ed. David G. Mandelbaum. Berkeley: University of California Press.
Sauer, Hans (1992). *Nominalkomposita im Frühmittelenglischen. Mit Ausblicken auf die Geschichte der englischen Nominalkomposition*. Tübingen: Niemeyer.
Sauerland, Uli, and Hans-Martin Gärtner (eds) (2007). *Interfaces + Recursion = Language? Chomsky's Minimalism and the View from Syntax-Semantics*. Berlin: Mouton de Gruyter.
Sauvageot, Aurélien (1964). *Portrait du vocabulaire français*. Paris: Larousse.
Scalise, Sergio, and Antonietta Bisetto (2009). The classification of compounds. In Lieber and Štekauer (2009: 34–53).
Scalise, Sergio, Antonio Fábregas, and Francesca Forza (2009). Exocentricity in compounding. *Gengo Kenkyu* 135: 49–84.
Scalise, Sergio, and Irene Vogel (eds) (2010). *Cross-Disciplinary Issues in Compounding*. Amsterdam: Benjamins.
Schiering, René, Balthasar Bickel, and Kristine A. Hildebrandt (2010). The prosodic word is not universal, but emergent. *Journal of Linguistics* 46: 657–709.
Schneider, Klaus P. (2003). *Diminutives in English*. Tübingen: Niemeyer.
Schneider, Klaus P., and Susanne Strubel-Burgdorf (2011). Diminutive *-let* in English. *SKASE Journal of Theoretical Linguistics* 9: 15–32.
Schröder, Anne, and Susanne Mühleisen (2010). New ways of investigating morphological productivity. *Arbeiten aus Anglistik und Amerikanistik* 35: 43–59.
Schultz-Lorentzen, Christian Wilhelm (1967 [1927]). *Dictionary of the West Greenland Eskimo Language*. Copenhagen: Reitzel.
Schultz-Lorentzen, Christian Wilhelm (1967 [1945]). *A Grammar of the West Greenland Language*. Copenhagen: Reitzel.
Scott, Fred Newton (1913). The order of words in certain rhythm-groups. *Modern Language Notes* 28.8: 237–9.
Sebeok, Thomas (ed.) (1960). *Style in Language*. Cambridge, Mass.: MIT Press.
Sedley, David (2003). *Plato's Cratylus*. Cambridge: Cambridge University Press.
Ségéral, Philippe (1995). *Une théorie généralisée de l'apophonie*. Ph.D. University of Paris 7.
Ségéral, Philippe, and Tobias Scheer (1998). A generalized theory of Ablaut: the case of Modern German strong verbs. In Fabri et al. (1998: 28–59).
Selkirk, Elisabeth O. (1982). *The Syntax of Words*. Cambridge, Mass.: MIT Press.
Serbat, Guy (1975). *Les dérivés nominaux latins à suffixe médiatif*. Paris: Les Belles Lettres.

Sherzer, Joel (1970). Talking backwards in Cuna: the sociological reality of phonological descriptions. *Southwestern Journal of Anthropology* 26: 343–53.
Sherzer, Joel (1976). Play languages: implications for (socio)linguistics. In Kirshenblatt-Gimblett (1976: 19–36).
Shih, Stephanie S. (2013). The similarity basis for consonant–tone interaction in agreement by correspondence. Paper presented at the 87th Annual Meeting of the Linguistic Society of America, Boston.
Shimamura, Reiko (1983). Backformation of English compound verbs. In Richardson et al. (1983: 271–82).
Shinohara, Kazuko, and Shigeto Kawahara (2010). A cross-linguistic study of sound symbolism: the images of size. *Berkeley Linguistics Society* 36.
Shipley, Joseph T. (1982). *Dictionary of Word Origins*. New York: Philosophical Library.
Shipley, Joseph T. (1984). *The Origins of English Words: A Discursive Dictionary of Indo-European Roots*. Baltimore: Johns Hopkins University Press.
Shisler, Benjamin K. (1997). *Dictionary of English Phonesthemes*. Available online at: http://www.geocities.com/SoHo/Studios/9783/phond1.html
Shopen, Timothy (ed.) (1985). *Language Typology and Syntactic Description*. 3 vols. Cambridge: Cambridge University Press.
Shortis, Tim (2007). Gr8 Txtexpectations: the creativity of text spelling. *English, Drama, Media* 8. Available online at: http://www.nate.org.uk/ index.php?page=9&id=9
Siegel, Dorothy (1979). *Topics in English Morphology*. New York: Garland.
Siemund, Peter, and Noemi Kintana (eds) (2008). *Language Contact and Contact Languages*. Amsterdam: Benjamins.
Siewierska, Anna, and Jae Jung Song (eds) (1998). *Case, Typology and Grammar*. Amsterdam: Benjamins.
Sihler, Andrew L. (1995). *New Comparative Grammar of Greek and Latin*. Oxford: Oxford University Press.
Sihler, Andrew L. (2000). *Language History: An Introduction*. Amsterdam: Benjamins.
Simpson, John A. (ed.) (2000–). *The Oxford English Dictionary Online*, 3rd edn. (in progress). Oxford: Oxford University Press. http://oed.com/
Skoda, Françoise (1988). Les métaphores zoomorphiques dans le vocabulaire médical, en grec ancien. *Logopédies* 221–34.
Slobin, Dan I. (1974). *Psycholinguistics*. Glenview, Ill.: Scott, Foresman.
Smith, Christine Anne (2005). La substantivation des adjectifs en anglais contemporain. Doctoral thesis, University of Paris, Sorbonne.
Smith, Christine Anne (2010). The phonaesthetics of blend-words: the role of sound symbolism and metonymy in lexical blending in English. Paper presented at the International Conference on Lexical Blending, Lyon, France, 10–11 June.
Smith, Christine Anne (2012a). Phonesthetics of blends: the case for sound symbolic remotivation in English blends. MS, University of Caen.
Smith, Christine Anne (2012b). Double whammy! The dysphemistic euphemism implied in *unVables* such as *unmentionables, unprintables, undesirables*. *Lexis* 7: 121–43.
Smith, Christine Anne (2013). The semantics of *fl-* monomorphemes in the English lexicon: considering the evidence of phonesthetic attraction. MS, University of Caen.

Sneed, Elisa (2002). The acceptability of regular plurals in compounds. *Chicago Linguistic Society* 38: 617–31.
Soudek, Lev I. (1978). The relation of blending to English word-formation: theory, structure, and typological attempts. In Dressler and Meid (1978: 462–6).
Southern, Mark R. V. (1992). The wandering *s: the problem of the *s*-mobile in Indo-European and Germanic. *Penn Review of Linguistics* 16: 166–80.
Southern, Mark R. V. (1999). *Sub-Grammatical Survival: Indo-European s-Mobile and its Regeneration in Germanic*. Washington, DC: Institute for the Study of Man.
Southern, Mark R. V. (2000a). *Tabula rāsa*: the 'tablet' word in Italic, and its Indo-European relatives. *Münchener Studien zur Sprachwissenschaft* 60: 89–133.
Southern, Mark R. V. (2000b). Formulaic binomials, morphosymbolism, and Behagel's Law: the grammatical status of expressive iconicity. *American Journal of Germanic Linguistics & Literatures* 12: 251–79.
Southern, Mark R. V. (2002). *Contagious Couplings: Yiddish shm- and the Contact-Driven Transmission of Expressives*. Westport, Conn.: Greenwood.
Speake, Jennifer (ed.) (1997). *The Oxford Dictionary of Foreign Words and Phrases*. Oxford: Oxford University Press.
Spencer, Andrew (1991). *Morphological Theory: An Introduction to Word Structure in Generative Grammar*. Oxford: Blackwell.
Spencer, Andrew (2005). Word-formation and syntax. In Štekauer and Lieber (2005: 73–97).
Spencer, Andrew (2011). Review article of Lieber and Štekauer (2009). *Journal of Linguistics* 47: 481–507.
Spencer, Andrew, and Arnold M. Zwicky (eds) (1998). *The Handbook of Morphology*. Oxford: Blackwell.
Spitzer, Leo (1948). *Essays in Historical Semantics*. New York: Vanni.
Spitzer, Leo (1952). Confusion schmooshun. *Journal of English and Germanic Philology* 51: 226–33.
Sproat, Richard W. (1985). On deriving the lexicon. Ph.D. MIT.
Sridhar, Shikaripur N. (1990). *Kannada: Descriptive Grammar*. London: Routledge. [Repr. as *Modern Kannada Grammar*, Manohar, 2010.]
Starr, Rebecca (2010). 'Abbrevs is totes the lang of the fuche': variation and performance of abbreviation slang. Presented at the Annual Meeting of the American Dialect Society, Baltimore.
Steels, Luc, and Paul Vogt (1997). Grounding adaptive language games in robotic agents. In *Proceedings of the Fourth European Conference on Artificial Life*, ed. Phil Husbands and Inman Harvey, 474–82. Cambridge, Mass.: MIT Press.
Steels, Luc, and Vittorio Loreto (2010). Modeling the formation of language in embodied agents: conclusions and future research. In *Evolution of Communication and Language in Embodied Agents*, ed. Stefano Nolfi and Marco Mirolli, 283–8. Berlin: Springer.
Stein, Gabriele (1977). English combining-forms. *Linguistica* 9: 140–47.
Stein, Gabriele (1985). *The English Dictionary Before Cawdrey*. Tübingen: Niemeyer.
Stein, Gabriele (2000). The function of word-formation and the case of English -*cum*-. In Dalton-Puffer and Ritt (2000: 277–88).
Steinhauer, Anja (2000). *Sprachökonomie durch Kurzwörter: Bildung und Verwendung in der Fachkommunikation*. Tübingen: Narr.

Steinmetz, Sol, and Barbara Ann Kipfer (2006). *The Life of Language: The Fascinating Ways Words Are Born, Live & Die*. New York: Random House.
Štekauer, Pavol (1996). *A Theory of Conversion in English*. Frankfurt am Main: Lang.
Štekauer, Pavol (2005). Onomasiological approach to word-formation. In Štekauer and Lieber (2005: 207–32).
Štekauer, Pavol (to appear). The delimitation of derivation and inflection. In Müller et al. (to appear).
Štekauer, Pavol, Don Chapman, Slávka Tomaščíková, and Štefan Franko (2005). Word-formation as creativity within productivity constraints: sociolinguistic evidence. *Onomasiology Online* 6: 1–55. Available at: http://www.citeseerx.ist.psu.edu/viewdoc/download?doi=10.1.1.92.9286&rep=rep1&type=pdf
Štekauer, Pavol, and Rochelle Lieber (eds) (2005). *Handbook of Word-Formation*. Dordrecht: Springer.
Štekauer, Pavol, Salvador Valera, and Lívia Körtvélyessy (2012). *Word-Formation in the World's Languages: A Typological Survey*. Cambridge: Cambridge University Press.
Stemberger, Joseph Paul (1981). Morphological haplology. *Language* 57: 791–817.
Stemmer, Brigitte, and Harry Whitaker (eds) (2008). *Handbook of the Neuroscience of Language*. Amsterdam: Elsevier.
Steriade, Donca (1982). Greek prosodies and the nature of syllabification. Ph.D. MIT.
Steriade, Donca (1988). Reduplication and syllable transfer in Sanskrit and elsewhere. *Phonology* 5: 73–155.
Stern, Gustaf (1931). *Meaning and Change of Meaning: With Special Reference to the English Language*. Bloomington: Indiana University Press. [Repr. 1968.]
Stiles, Lewis (1993). *The Anatomy of Medical Terminology*. Saskatoon, Saskatchewan: Wordbooks.
Stockwell, Robert, and Donca Minkova (2001). *English Words: History and Structure*. Cambridge: Cambridge University Press.
Stoddart, Sir John (1858). *Glossology; Or the Historical Relations of Languages*. London: Richard Griffin.
Stolz, Thomas (2008). Total reduplication vs. echo-word formation in language contact situations. In Siemund and Kintana (2008: 107–32).
Stonham, John T. (1994). *Combinatorial Morphology*. Amsterdam: Benjamins.
Sturtevant, Edgar H. (1947). *An Introduction to Linguistic Science*. New Haven, Conn.: Yale University Press.
Sundby, Bertil (1995). *English Word-Formation as Described by the English Grammarians 1600–1800*. Oslo: Novus.
Sundén, Karl Fritiof (1904). *Contributions to the Study of Elliptical Words in Modern English*. Uppsala: Almqvist & Wiksell.
Svenonius, Peter (2010). Spatial P in English. In Cinque and Rizzi (2010: 127–60).
Sweetser, Eve E. (1987). Metaphorical models of thought and speech: a comparison of historical directions and metaphorical mappings in the two domains. *Berkeley Linguistics Society* 13: 446–59.
Sweetser, Eve E. (1990). *From Etymology to Pragmatics: Metaphorical and Cultural Aspects of Semantic Structure*. Cambridge: Cambridge University Press.

Sylak-Glassman, John (2012). *Audibility and Syllabic Nuclei*. MS, University of California, Berkeley.

Szabóné Habók, Marianna (2009). *Sound Symbolism in English and German: What Meanings Can Sounds Carry* [*sic*: no punctuation]. Saarbrücken: VDM (Verlag Dr Müller).

Szymanek, Bogdan (1988). *Categories and Categorization in Morphology*. Lublin: Catholic University of Lublin Press.

Szymanek, Bogdan (2005). The latest trends in English word-formation. In Štekauer and Lieber (2005: 429–48).

Taavitsainen, Irma (2000). Scientific language and spelling standardisation 1375–1550. In Wright (2000: 131–54).

Taavitsainen, Irma, Terttu Nevalainen, Päivi Pahta, and Matti Rissanen (eds) (2000). *Placing Middle English in Context*. Berlin: Mouton de Gruyter.

ter Meulen, A., and W. Abraham (eds) (2004). *The Composition of Meaning*. Amsterdam: Benjamins.

Tessier, Anne-Michelle (2010). Short, but not sweet: markedness preferences and reversals in English hypocoristics. Poster presented at the ACL–CLA.

Thun, Nils (1963). *Reduplicative Words in English: A Study of Formations of the Types 'Tick-Tock', 'Hurly-Burly', and 'Shilly-Shally'*. Lund: Bloms.

Thurlow, Crispin (2012). Determined creativity: language play in new media discourse. In Jones (2012: ch. 10).

Thurner, Dick (1993). *Portmanteau Dictionary: Blend Words in the English Language, Including Trademarks and Brand Names*. Jefferson, NC: McFarland & Co.

Tournier, Jean (1975). L'expression euphémique des tabous. *Recherches en linguistique étrangère* 2: 151–77.

Tournier, Jean (1985). *Introduction descriptive à la lexicogénétique de l'anglais contemporain*. Paris: Champion/Geneva: Slatkine. [Repr. 2007.]

Tournier, Jean (1988). *Précis de lexicologie anglaise*. Paris: Nathan. [3rd edn 1993.]

Tournier, Jean (1991). *Structures lexicales de l'anglais*. Paris: Nathan.

Trask, Robert L. (1996). *Historical Linguistics*. London: Arnold.

Traugott, Elizabeth Closs (1989). On the rise of epistemic meanings in English: an example of subjectification in semantic change. *Language* 65: 31–55.

Traugott, Elizabeth Closs (2004). A critique of Levinson's view of Q- and M-inferences in historical pragmatics. *Journal of Historical Pragmatics* 5: 1–25.

Traugott, Elizabeth Closs, and Richard B. Dasher (2002). *Regularity in Semantic Change*. Cambridge: Cambridge University Press.

Trips, Carola (2006). Syntactic sources of word-formation processes: evidence from Old English and Old High German. In Hartmann and Molnárfi (2006: 299–328).

Trommer, Jochen (ed.) (2012). *The Phonology and Morphology of Exponence*. Oxford: Oxford University Press.

Trommer, Jochen, and Eva Zimmermann (2010). Blends as word templates. Paper presented at the CUNY Conference on the Word.

Trousdale, Graeme, and Thomas Hoffmann (eds) (2013). *The Oxford Handbook of Construction Grammar*. Oxford: Oxford University Press.

Tsur, Reuven (2006). Size–sound symbolism revisited. *Journal of Pragmatics* 38: 905–24.

Tyler, Andrea (1988). Recursion in the lexicon. In Bouchard and Leffel (1988: 81–105).
Tyler, Leslie Jo (1999). The syntax and semantics of zero verbs: a Minimalist approach. Ph.D. University of Florida.
Uhlich, Jürgen (2002). Verbal governing compounds (synthetics) in Early Irish and other Celtic languages. *Transactions of the Philological Society* 100: 403–33.
Ullmann, Stephen (1957). *The Principles of Semantics*. Oxford: Blackwell. [2nd edn, 3rd impression, with updated bibliography, 1963; repr. 1967.]
Ullmann, Stephen (1962). *Semantics: An Introduction to the Science of Meaning*. Oxford: Blackwell.
Ultan, Russell (1978). Size–sound symbolism. In Greenberg (1978: 2.525–68).
Urbanczyk, Suzanne (2005). Enhancing contrast in reduplication. In Hurch (2005: 211–38).
Urbanczyk, Suzanne (2011). Reduplication. Oxford Bibliographies Online at: http://www.oxfordbibliographiesonline.com/view/document/obo-9780199772810/obo-9780199772810-0036.xml?rskey=n3uQYN&result=41&q=
Urdang, Laurence, Anne Ryle, Tanya H. Lee, and Frank R. Abate (1986). *-Ologies & -isms*. 3rd edn. Detroit: Gale Research Co.
Vachek, Josef (1975). *Linguistic Characterology of Modern English*. Bratislava: Comenius University Press.
van der Hulst, Harry, and Norval Smith (eds) (1982). *The Structure of Phonological Representations*, pt 1. Dordrecht: Foris.
van Gelderen, Elly (2011). *The Linguistic Cycle: Language Change and the Language Faculty*. Oxford: Oxford University Press.
van Gelderen, Elly (2012). Semantic and formal features in language change. Paper presented at the Deutsche Gesellschaft für Sprachwissenschaft, March. Available online at: file:http://www.//localhost/http/::www.public.asu.edu:~gelderen:DGfS-features-2012.ppt
Van Hout, Angeliek, and Thomas Roeper (1998). Events and aspectual structure in derivational morphology. MITWPL 32: 175–200.
van Kemenade, Ans, and Bettelou Los (2003). Particles and prefixes in Dutch and English. *Yearbook of Morphology 2003*: 79–117.
van Kemenade, Ans, and Bettelou Los (eds) (2006). *The Handbook of the History of English*. Oxford: Blackwell.
Varro, Marcus Terentius [116–27] (c.44 BCE). *De lingua latina* [LL: On the Latin Language], ed. and tr. Roland G. Kent. Cambridge, Mass.: Harvard University Press (1938, 1977, etc.).
Varro, Marcus Terentius [116–27] (c.44 BCE). *De re rustica* [RR: On Agriculture]: *M. Terenti Varronis Rerum Rusticarum libri tres*, ed. Henricius Keil and Georgius Goetz. Leipzig: Teubner, 1929.
Vendler, Zeno (1967). *Linguistics in Philosophy*. Ithaca, NY: Cornell University Press.
Violi, Patrizia (ed.) (2000). *Phonosymbolism and Poetic Language*. Turnhout: Brepols.
Wackernagel, Jacob (1926, 1928). *Vorlesungen über Syntax, mit besonderer Berücksichtigung von Griechisch, Lateinisch und Deutsch*. 2 vols. Basel: Birkhäuser.
Wälchli, Bernhard (2005). *Co-compounds and Natural Coordination*. Oxford: Oxford University Press.
Wald, Benji, and Lawrence Besserman (2002). The emergence of the verb–verb compound in twentieth century English and twentieth century linguistics. In Minkova and Stockwell (2002: 417–47).

Waldrop, Rosmarie (2009). Translating the sound in poetry: six propositions. In Perloff and Dworkin (2009a: 60–5).
Walinska de Hackbeil, Hanna (1983). X̄ categories in morphology. In Richardson et al. (1983: 301–13).
Walinska de Hackbeil, Hanna (1985). *En*-prefixation and the syntactic domain of zero derivation. *Berkeley Linguistics Society* 11: 337–57.
Walinska de Hackbeil, Hanna (1986). The roots of phrase structure: the syntactic basis of English morphology. Ph.D. University of Washington, Seattle.
Walker, Jim (2009). Double *-er* suffixation in English. *Lexis: E-Journal in English Lexicology* 1: 5–14.
Wallis, John (1653). *Grammatica linguae anglicanae, Cui praefigitur de loquela, sive sonorum omnium loquelarium formatione tractatus grammatico-physicus* [Grammar of the English language, to which is attached a grammatical-scientific treatise on speech, or on the organization of all speech sounds]. Hamburg: Gotfried Schultzen.
Wallis, John (1688). 3rd edn of Wallis (1653). Hamburg: Gotfried Schultzen.
Wallis, John (1765). 6th edn of Wallis (1653), with revisions by Thomas Beverley. London and Leipzig: Dodsley and Moser.
Warren, Beatrice (1978). *Semantic Patterns of Noun–Noun Compounds*. Gothenburg: Gothenburg University Press.
Warren, Beatrice (1984). *Classifying Adjectives*. Gothenburg: Acta Universitatis Gothoburgensis.
Warren, Beatrice (1990). The importance of combining forms. In Dressler et al. (1990: 111–32).
Warren, Beatrice (1992). What euphemisms tell us about the interpretation of words. *Studia Linguistica* 46: 128–72.
Warren, Beatrice (1998). What *is* metonymy? In Hogg and van Bergen (1998: 301–10).
Watkins, Calvert (1962). Varia ii.1: Irish *Milchobur*. *Ériu* 19: 114–6. [Repr. in Watkins 1994: i. 92–6 (#18).]
Watkins, Calvert (1994). *Selected Writings*, ed. Lisi Oliver. 2 vols. Institut für Sprachwissenschaft, University of Innsbruck.
Watkins, Calvert (ed.) (2000). *The American Heritage Dictionary of Indo-European Roots*. 2nd edn. Boston: Houghton Mifflin.
Waugh, Linda R. (2000). Against arbitrariness: imitation and motivation revived. In Violi (2000: 25–56).
Way, Albert (ed.) (1843–65). *Promptorium Parvulorum sive Clericorum, Lexicon Anglo-Latinum* [vol. 3: *Dictionarius Anglo-Latinus*] *Princeps, auctore fratre Galfrido Grammatico dicto, e predicatoribus Lenne Episcopi, Northfolciensi, circa A.D. M.CCCC.XL.* [Treasury/Promptor of Boys and/or Clerics: The first Anglo-Latin dictionary, authored by Friar Galfrid, called grammarian, from among the preachers at Lynn Episcopi, Norfolk, *c*.1440]. 3 vols (continuous pagination of the dictionary itself). [Vol. 1, 1843; vol. 2, 1853; vol. 3, 1865]. London: Camden Society.
Wayland, Ratree (1995). Lao expressives. *Mon-Khmer Studies* 26: 217–31.
Wechsler, Stephen, and Larisa Zlatić (2012). The wrong two faces. *Language* 88: 380–87.
Wehrli, Eric, and Timothy Stowell (eds) (1989). *Syntax and the Lexicon*. New York: Academic Press.

Whatmough, Joshua (1956). *Language: A Modern Synthesis*. New York: New American Library.
Whitney, Paul (1998). *The Psychology of Language*. Boston: Houghton Mifflin.
Wierzbicka, Anna (1985). *Lexicography and Conceptual Analysis*. Ann Arbor, Mich.: Karoma.
Wierzbicka, Anna (2007). Bodies and their parts: an NSM approach to semantic typology. *Language Sciences* 29: 14–65.
Wiese, Heike (2006). Partikeldiminuierung im Deutschen. *Sprachwissenschaft* 31.4: 457–89.
Wiese, Richard (2001). Regular morphology vs. prosodic morphology? The case of truncation in German. *Journal of Germanic Linguistics* 13: 131–78.
Williams, Edwin (1981). On the notions 'lexically related' and 'head of a word'. *Linguistic Inquiry* 12: 245–74.
Williams, Edwin (2007). Dumping lexicalism. In Ramchand and Reiss (2007: 353–82).
Williams, Joseph M. (1986 [1975]). *Origins of the English Language*. New York: Free Press.
Wiltshire, Caroline, and Joaquim Camps (eds) (2002). *Romance Phonology and Variation*. Amsterdam: Benjamins.
Wiltshire, Caroline, and Alec Marantz (2000). Reduplication. In Booij et al. (2000: 1.557–67).
Wiltshire, Caroline, and M. Irene Moyna (2002). Phonological idiosyncrasies of Spanish playful words. In Lee et al. (2002: 317–35).
Włodarczyk, Matylda (2007). '*More strenger and mightier*': some remarks on double comparison in Middle English. *Studia Anglica Posnaniensia* 43: 195–217.
Wohlmuth, Sonia Ramírez (2008). Persistence of the Latin accent in the nominal system of Castilian, Catalan and Portuguese. Ph.D. University of Florida, Gainesville.
Wood, Francis Asbury (1911). Iteratives, blends, and 'Streckformen'. *Modern Philology* 9: 157–94.
Wood, Francis Asbury (1912). Some English blends. *Modern Language Notes* 27: 179.
Wray, Alison (2002). *Formulaic Language and the Lexicon*. Cambridge: Cambridge University Press.
Wray, Alison (2008). *Formulaic Language: Pushing the Boundaries*. Oxford: Oxford University Press.
Wray, Alison (2012). What do we (think we) know about formulaic language? An evaluation of the current state of play. *Annual Review of Applied Linguistics* 32: 231–54.
Wulff, Stefanie (2013). Words and idioms. In Trousdale and Hoffmann (2013: 274–89).
Wynecoop, Shelly, and Golan Levin (1996). A bibliography of synesthesia and phonesthesia research. Available online at: http://www.flong.com/texts/lists/list_synesthesia_ bibliography/
Yaguello, Marina (1998). *Language Through the Looking Glass: Exploring Language and Linguistics*. Oxford: Oxford University Press.
Yang, Charles D. (2002). *Knowledge and Learning in Natural Language*. Oxford: Oxford University Press.
Yang, Charles D. (2005). On productivity. *Yearbook of Language Variation* 5: 265–302.
Yang, Charles D., Kyle Gorman, Jennifer Preys, and Margaret Borowczyk (2013). Productivity and paradigmatic gaps. Paper presented at the 87th Annual Meeting of the Linguistic Society of America, Boston.
Yang, In-Seok (ed.) (1982). *Linguistics in the Morning Calm*. Seoul: Hanshin.

Yip, Moira (1998). Identity avoidance in phonology and morphology. In Lapointe et al. (1998: 216–63).

Yoon, James (1996). Nominal gerund phrases in English as phrasal zero derivations. *Linguistics* 34: 329–56.

Yu, Alan C. L. (2007). *A Natural History of Infixation*. Oxford: Oxford University Press.

Zauner, Adolf (1902). Die romanischen Namen der Körperteile: eine onomasiologische Studie. Ph.D. University of Erlangen. [Published in *Romanische Forschungen* 14: 339–530 (1903).]

Zettler, Howard G. (1978). *-Ologies and -Isms: A Thematic Dictionary*. Detroit: Gale Research Co.

Zgusta, Ladislaw (1990). Onomasiological change. In Polomé (1990: 389–98).

Ziegler, Wolfram (2005). A nonlinear model of word length effects in apraxia of speech. *Cognitive Neuropsychology* 22: 1–21.

Zonneveld, Wim (1984). The game of the name: expletive insertion in English. *Linguistic Analysis* 13: 55–60.

Zwicky, Arnold M. (1985). Heads. *Journal of Linguistics* 21: 1–29.

Zwicky, Arnold M. (1988). Morphological rules, operations, and operation types. *ESCOL* 4: 318–34.

Zwicky, Arnold M., and Geoffrey Pullum (1987). Plain morphology and expressive morphology. *Berkeley Linguistics Society* 13: 330–40.

Index of affixes and affixed forms

Bold is used to indicate the main discussion of the term.

a- 16
-a- 235
-able 3, 15, 33, 64, **79ff.**, 216
-able...-able 64, 78
-age 17, 110
-al 32, 33f., 39
-(a/o)holic 194, 207, **209f.**, 211, 245
-ar 32
   Sp. -*ar* 9
-ate 8f., 15, 197
-(a)thon 88, 194, 207, **208**
-ation 15, 31, 33, 65
   (cf. -tion)
-tor/-ator 15, 16
bi- 90
-cade 210
-ce 27
-cum- 234, 236
cyber- 211, 213, 215
-damn- 8, 93, 100, 245
-dar 210, 245
dis- 9, 37
eco- 212f., 217
-ectomy 217
-ed 49, 54, 108, 148, 153
-ed...-ed 76
-ee 17, 37, 64, 74ff.
-eer 31
en- 4, 8f.
-en 18f., 32f., 42, 88
-en (participle) 9
-er (agent etc.) 14, 28, 36, 37, 45, 49, 61, 64, 74, 75–9, 128f., 217ff., 238
-er (degree) 29
-er-er 39f., 76, 238f.
-er...-ee 76

-er...-er 64, 75–9
-eroo 210
-esque-esque 39, 238
-ess 30
-est 125
-et 88f.
-ette 180
ex- 85, 134
-fuckin- 93, 100, 140, 245
-gate 89, 193, 194, 245
-graph- 216, 218
-hood 38
-ian 217f.
-id 33
-ie/-y 149, 161, 178f., 181, 183, 242
-ification 33
-ify 31, 33, 42, 65
in- (locational) 9, 53, 68, 70
in- (negating) 121, 252
-in 53
-iness 35
info- 213
-ing 49, 64, 65, 107
-ing...-ing 64
-ish 4, 8, 17, 34, 35, 151
-ism 35, 151, 153, 216
-ist 17, 35, 217ff.
-istic 35
-ity 17, 25, 28, 31, 33, 39
-iz- 93
-ize 17, 33, 65, 218
-izzle 167
ka-/ker- 163f., 245
-less 39, 42, 238
-let 88f.
-licious 210, 245

-log- 218
-ly 31
-ma- 92f., 100
-mageddon 210
mega- 213, 214, 217, 245
-ment 8, 16, 34, 39
-n- 8
nano- 212
-naut 215f.
-ness 8, 17, 28, 30, 33, 34f., 39, 42, 137, 238
-ness-ness 39, 238
-nik 17, 212
-nom- 218
non- 52, 612
-o 216, 218
-oid 152, 183
-oidy 15f.
-ola 210
-(o)logy 39, 148
-ology-ology 39
-or 14f.
-osis 217
-osity 30, 33
-ous 33
out- 64, 71
-out 71–4, 148
-out- 76
over- 17, 64, 67, 69f.
over-over- 41
-over 39

-over-over 39
pro-pro- 39
re- 40, 41, 43, 52, 61
re-re- 40
-ric 33
-s- (juncture) 47, 51
-s (3SG) 4, 5
-s (plural) 5
-s . . . -s 60, 76, 78
s- (movable) 162f.
-s/z (hypocoristic) 148, 181f., 245
sad-o- 216
-ship 38
shm- 223f., 236, 238, 240
techno- 211, 214f., 217
tele- 214, 215
-ter 33
-terous 89, 239
-th 39, 44, 143
-thwait 151
-tion 17, 27, 65
   (cf. -ation)
-tor 14, 16
-trous 89, 239
un- 3, 4, 79, 123, 148, 252
un-un- 39
under- 17, 64, 70, 85
-up/up- 39, 64, 71, 75f., 78, 79
-y (see -ie)

Index of selected names

Aronoff, Mark 3, 16, 22, 23, 25, 26, 27, 30, 33, 38, 48, 52, 58

Bat-El, Outi 189, 194, 200, 201, 239–41
Bauer, Laurie 3, 5, 10, 15, 16, 18, 33f., 45, 51, 55ff., 59, 128, 129, 151, 159, 179, 189, 192, 199, 207, 209, 210, 212, 215, 217, 225

Cannon, Garland 90, 147, 149, 189

De Cuypere, Ludovic 86, 117, 155, 164
Dressler, Wolfgang U. 31, 45, 47, 189, 237, 240, 241

Halle, Morris 3, 15, 22, 39, 63, 78, 91

Jespersen, Otto 32, 49, 75, 79, 154, 155, 157, 189, 207, 226

Kastovsky, Dieter 8, 9, 10, 45, 51, 90, 215
Kiparsky, Paul 10, 11, 12, 13, 23, 27, 29, 37, 47, 53, 55
Kleparski, Grzegorz A. 102, 107, 129, 154
Körtvélyessy, Lívia[1] 16, 17, 107, 154, 159, 171, 172
Koziol, Herbert 15, 45, 89, 118, 147, 160, 173, 175, 181, 189, 212

Lieber, Rochelle 3, 10, 36, 37, 45, 47, 48, 49, 53, 54, 56, 57, 59, 67, 69, 73

Marchand, Hans 10, 14, 33, 45, 54, 154, 160, 166, 173, 207

Mattiello, Elisa 46, 55, 87, 92, 112, 128, 129, 131, 147, 173, 178, 181, 182, 210, 221, 237, 239, 241, 242
McIntyre, Andrew 14, 39, 41, 63, 64, 69, 75, 76, 78, 79

Nyrop, Kristoffer 102, 106, 107, 109, 111, 114, 118, 119, 120, 121, 122, 123, 129, 130, 133, 134

Padrosa-Trias, Susanna 3, 45, 48, 49, 51, 53, 56, 57, 59, 89, 151
Plag, Ingo 10, 11, 14, 15, 16, 22, 27, 31, 33, 34, 39, 46, 90, 179, 196, 207, 210, 215, 216

Raffelsiefen, Renate 31, 33, 47, 156, 163
Roeper, Thomas 36, 39, 44, 45, 47, 48, 49, 63, 70, 74, 81, 238

Saussure, Ferdinand de 21, 86, 155, 156, 157, 172
Sproat, Richard W. 3, 7, 27, 28, 37, 48, 49, 51, 52, 53, 54, 55, 57, 128
Štekauer, Pavol 3, 5, 6, 7, 8, 9, 10, 13, 14, 16, 42, 43, 45, 46, 51, 52, 53, 55, 56, 107, 128, 129, 137, 159, 187, 220, 239
Szymanek, Bogdan 25, 48, 90, 151, 207, 212, 234

Tournier, Jean 45, 83, 84, 87, 102, 112, 118, 121, 133, 137, 147, 148, 154, 165, 166, 173, 189, 194, 201, 207, 210

Zwicky, Arnold M. 4, 33, 34, 35, 46, 52, 54, 60, 125, 189, 193, 210, 212, 217, 238

---

[1] Since most of the Štekauer references are to Štekauer, Valera, and Körtvélyessy (2012), those references should be consulted for Körtvélyessy and Valera as well.

Index of subjects

Bold is used to indicate the main discussion of the term.

abbreviation 147f., 152, 193, 209, 240
ablaut (*see* apophony)
abridgement 147–53
abstract noun 33, 50, 54, 61, 72f., 75, 106f., 217
accent 9f., 26, 57, 179f., 183, 248, 253
acceptance x, 85f.
acronym(y) 148ff., 152f., 195, 237, 241f., 244
    reverse 148f.
    split 150
actor suffix (*see* agentive formation)
adaptation 96, 117f., 119, 138, 177, 210, 216
adjective / adjectival
    adverbial 45, 53
    comparative 4, 6, 29, 86, 124
    conversion 10, 123
    euphemistic 122f.
    head 4, 69, 79
    intensifier 125f., 140
    (non)gradable 4, 44, 86
    Phrase 1, 68
    reinforcing 126, 140
    resultative 56
    result state 53
adjunction 2, 79, 81f.
    (left-)adjunction 54, 63, 67f., 72, 98
    (*see also* inflection)
adposition 38, 98
    hierarchy 98
adverbial 45, 53, 73, 80, 98, 181
affix(ation) 8f., 26
    locus (*see* specific affixes, morphosyntactic)
affix iteration: *see* recursion
affixal restrictions 33ff.
agent 11f., 35ff., 53, 74, 107, 128f., 170, 208, 217f., 238
    by-phrase 49, 79f.
agentive (formation) 14, 16, 36, 48f., 66ff., 70, 72, 77–82, 218

Agree 5ff., 26, 67
agreement/Agr 5ff., 20, 26, 59
alphabetism 147–53
ambiguity 183
    avoidance 38, 84
anacol(o)uthon 94
analogy 24, 88ff., 100, 115, 117, 119, 124, 177, 208
    in word creation 88ff., 172
animal names/terms 101ff., 116, 121, 192
antipassive 70
antiphrasis 120f.
antisymmetry 2, 49, 51, 61, 76
antonomasia (*see* eponymy)
antonym(y) 84, 85, 88, 90, 122, 162, 241
aphasic speech 144, 189
apophony 9, 26, 242f.
    English 160f.
    generalized 172, 226, 243
    grammatical 161
    Indo-European 253
Applicative (Phrase) 68, 72
arbitrariness 21, 23, 25, 86, 155, 157, 172
architecture 66f.
    parallel 242
argument (structure) 37, 45, 48f., 56, 72f., 77
Aspect Phrase/AspP 47, 79f.
asyndeton 94
attribute 53, 102, 116
automatic 5, 88
Avoid final stress 232f.
Avoid Synonymy 27, 30, 38, 87, 123, 245

backformation 14f., 26, 56, 83, 109, 123, 150, 180, 192, 237
backslang 92, 245
BECOME operator 66, 68, 70

Index of subjects

Behaghel's Fourth Law
   (*see* Pāṇini's rule)
bilingualism 18, 138, 193, 237
binomial 55, 171, 226–9, 233
   non-rhyming 227f.
   rhyming 227
   symmetrical 227
blend(ing) 83, 90, 91, 96, 123, 137, 138, 150,
      163, 180, **ch. 12**, 210, 211, 213, 216, 240ff.,
      243, 244
   component overlap 194
   discontinuous 194
   foot structure 196–9, 203f.
   French 193
   German 193f.
   graphic 195
   haplological 193
   input conditions 199ff.
   phonesthetic 201ff.
   splinter 194f.
blocking 23, 27–30
   partial 30
   Poser 29
   synonymy 28, 30
body parts 102, 104, 116, 122
borrowing 14, 83, 104, 117, 119, 133, 135–40
   assimilation 136
   dating of 139f.
bouba/kiki phenomenon 158
bound adjunct 49
boundary
   foot/prosodic 93
   lexical 242f., 244
   morphological 39, 90, 240, 242, 244
   new 241, 244
   word 91
   word-stem 216
bounded object 69

c-command 2, 6, 49–51, 61, 67, 74
calque 51, 90, 96, 120, **137f.**
   coinage 137
   remodeling 137
case stacking 97ff.

categorization 3, 8, 10, 13, 26, 51, 65, 68, 69,
      70, 72
category 2ff., 5, 10, 20, 25, 47, 65
   lexical-syntactic 51, 54, 55, 61, 105, 151
causative 12, 42f., 65, 66, 68, 70, 72, 74, 129
   analytic 42
   lexical 42
   synthetic 42
   Turkish 42f.
change
   cultural 84, 127f.
   lexical 84
   metaphorical 103–7
   metonymic 107–12
   of state 7, 21, 36
   real-world referent 84
   scientific knowledge 135
   world view 84
chiasmus 94f.
child language acquisition 20, 44, 104f., 117,
      157, 189, 221, 225, 237, 239
   L2 learners 18, 91, 237
   monolingual 237
circumfix 8f.
circumlocution 120, 122
classical (*see* neoclassical)
clausal modifier 48, 238
clip(ping) 54, 108, 146, **ch. 11**
   disyllabic 174f., 176, 179, 183, 185
   German 185
   Spanish 184–6
   trisyllabic 176, 177, 183, 185
clitic position 63, 70, 81
cluster
   illicit 92
   simplification 143
codeword 87
cognition 44, 101, 104f., 116, 128f.
cognitive schema(ta) 242
coinage 15–18, 33, 96
   ad hoc 234
   fanciful 125, 126, 140
   potential 15, 17f.
coindexation 75

collocation 22, 47, 233, 241, 242
colloquial 139, 214f.
color words 104, 133, 189
   college colors 233
combining form 194, **ch. 13**
   abbreviated 209
   compound constituent 210, 216
communication 32, 38, 87, 124, 179
comparative 4, 6, 29, 86
   double 125
   particle 64, 70
competition
   in blocking 27f.
   in change 167
   of linearization factors 229, 232f.
complex
   coda 142f., 146, 184, 199
   onset 139, 142f., 146, 179, 184
   P(reposition) 97f., 100
   rime 142, 146, 184
   spatial relation(ship) 97f.
component
   morphological (*see* constituent)
   of the grammar 19, 24f., 65,
      240, 242
componential analysis 22, 131f.
componym 150
compositional(ity) 21, 23, 26, 29, 37, 77, 99,
      200, 204, 214
compound
   [[A–N]*ed*] 53
   appositional/identificational 59f., 62
   appositive 59
   ATAP 59
   bahuvrihi 54
   coordinate 4, 55
   dvandva 45, 46, 55–9, 60, 61f., 78, 216,
      222, 226
   endocentric 3, 45f., **51ff.**, 52, 56, 57, 58, 60,
      61, 70, 216
   exocentric 45, **53ff.**, 61, 112, 216
   identical constituent 140, 221, 245
   neoclassical (*see* neoclassical)
   reversible 52, 56, 57f., 61

concrete
   early acquisition of 101, 105, 116
   > abstract 104–7, 116
conjunction 55f., 58f., 78
conjunctive 9, **ch. 14**, 242
conscious (*see* knowledge, motivation)
constraint
   arbitrary formal 32f.
   dissimilatory 32, 44
   haplological 31, 44, 76, 89, 182
   homophony 31f., 38, 44
   lexical 34f.
   locational 70
   metrical/prosodic 40, 144, 146, 195, 222,
      232, 240, 243
   no-phrase 48
   phonological 30–3
   processing 39–43, 44
   semantic 36ff.
   syntactic 35f.
contrast
   emphasis 69, 220f., 229
   lexical 32, 61, 86, 124, 161, 181, 228
   morphological 239
   phonological 32, 138, 141, 247f., 250, 251
   semantic 27, 28, 30, 76, 84, 161,
      170, 241
   syntactic 98, 181
conventional(ization) 21, 86, 87, 155ff., 162, 172
   conventionalized link 154, 155, 162
conversion 7, **10–13**, 15, 26, 32, **50f.**, 53, 57, 70f.,
   73f., 78, 81, 83, 123, 141, 148, 153, 176,
   181, 196
coordination 55, 59, 94
copy
   lexical 221
   morphological 220
   phonological 40ff., 76ff., 220
counterculture 87
creativity 16, 19, 20, 26ff., 30, 35, 38, 44, 83, 88,
      95ff., 122, 149, 189, 200, 212, 246
culture/cultural
   affixes 7, 21
   change 84, 127f.

concept/ideology 87, 118, 121, 123, 124, 133, 135, 172
factors 57f., 61, 101, 107, 116, 117, 172, 220, 233, 235
high 136
pop 231
salience 84
subculture 129f., 140
Cuna game 92, 243

default 5, 16
degree
  apophonic expressions 160
  doubling 29, 125, 140
  feature 4, 21, 125, 132
  head/word 7, 20, 21, 29, 69f., 151, 161
  phrase 68ff.
  scalar 40-4, 166, 220
deixis 158f.
deletion 32, 123, 178, 184, 197, 253
demographic(s) 84
deprecative 181, 210, 223
  -ette 180
derivation
  abstract 50, 54, 61, 73ff., 107
  deadjectival 17, 69
  denominal 7f., 10ff., 27f., 32, 69, 78, 161
  deradical 7f., 10, 12f.
  deverbal 7f., 27f., 34, 45, 48, 52, 61, 70, 79f., 216, 253
derogation/derogative 30, 134, 165, 180, 202, 210, 223
diminutive (affix) 44, 88f., 103, 119, 159, 180, 181f., 240
  hypocoristic 127, 161, 178, 182
  iterativity 40
  sound symbolism 159
disinformation 84, 122
dissimilation 32, 44, 144, 223, 224
Distributed Morphology 24f., 29, 63,
domain
  conceptual/experiential 101, 105, 112, 169
  contextual 245

of rule or constraint 16, 21, 26, 27, 31, 33, 34, 44, 83, 100, 233, 240
(*see also* prosodic)
double plural 76
duple timing 93, 145f., 239
dvandva (*see* compound)
dysphemism 165

E-language 18f., 26, 44, 105, 224, 244
economy 141, 152, 174, 198, 200, 203, 217
  communicative 84
  violation of 126
ellipsis/elliptical 10, 36, 83, 108, 111, 123, 151, 223, 226
emphatic (language) 27, 30, 40, 41, 43, 44, 80, 100, 125, 162, 221, 245
emulation 84
endocentric (*see* compound)
eponymy 112-16
EPP 66
euphemism (*see* tabu)
evaluative 7, 21, 40, 64, 69f., 80, 93, 116, 135, 159, 242, 245
  Nootka 93
event (feature) 26, 37, 41, 42, 50f., 54, 61, 66, 72-5, 79, 107, 129
existential closure 76f.
exocentric (*see* compound)
expletive infixation 93, 100
explicit knowledge 237f.
exponence/exponent 4, 5, 16, 25, 29, 78, 98
expressive/expressivity 9, 35, 87, 93, 105, 122, ch. 8, 128, 129, 135, 138, 140, 163, 171, 185, ch. 15
  loss of 125ff., 164
  patterns 43, 91, 161f., 172, 202, 223, 226
  shortening 173, 184, 186
expressives in Lao 159
external argument 35f., 49, 67, 72, 74
extragrammatical 237, 240f., 246
  purpose 161, 172
extralinguistic 16, 46, 88, 187
  input 101, 103, 104, 107, 116, **127f.**, 140, 204
  referent 5, 15, 161, 172, 243, 244

feature
  [AG/INDIVIDUAL] 54, 73
  [+cent(ral)] 68, 72, 74, 75, 77, 80, 81
  formal 19ff., 132
  functional 19ff., 25, 125, 132
  interpretable 6, 19ff., 22
  lexical 19, 27, 44, 65
  phi 6, 19ff.
  phonological 19, 25, 132
  semantic 29, 42, 53, 65, 71, 125, 129–32, 167
    addition of 130f.
    loss of 20f., 130
    underspecified 13, 131
  uninterpretable 6, 19ff.
fientive (projection) 66, 68ff., 72–5, 77, 80f.
fission(ing) 78f., 82
folk etymology 90, 104, 106, 117–20, 121
foot (structure) 144ff., 146
  boundary 93
  dactylic 104, 145f.
  defective 145
    metrical 104, 126, **144ff.**, 183f., 187, 195–8, 200, 204, 225, 242, 244, 246
    trochaic 32, 88, 92f., **145f.**, 173, 178, 185f.
foreign sound 138f.
form(ation)
  input 14, 24, 26, 29, 144, 178, 187, 194, 197–202, 204, 238, 243
  output 24ff., 29f., 40, 63, 69, 71ff., 81, 83, 91, 93, 100, 142, 144, 173, 178, 183, 185, 187, 195f., 198ff., 201, 203f., 216, 237–44
formal split 84
formant (frequency) 154
  first 141
  second 158, 159, 170
formative
  extraction ch. 13, 237, 239, 243
French game *verlan* 92
frequency
  acoustic *see* (formant)
  code 158ff., 172
  condition 200, 207
  type 16f., 207
  token 16f.

functional
  category 3, 5, 20f., 24, 61, 65f.
  element 20, 47, 54, 58f., 65, 245
  in compounds 47, 58f.
functional phrase 47, 65f.

generic (meaning) 69, 76f., 86, 111, 130, 132
genericization 111
  degenericization 111
gradation
  consonant 9, 159, 160, 164, 242
  vowel 159, 160f., 164, 220
  (*see also* apophony)
grammaticalization 150f.

head 1–5, 20, 25, 45, 51f., 61f., 69, 74, 76, 78, 79f., 210
  complex 29, 49
  conjoined 55, 61
  empty/null 10, 25, 26, 50, 53, 54, **72ff.**
  movement 11, 13, **67f.**, 69, 72ff., 80ff.
  syntactic 1ff., 21, 26, 46, 59, 99
high tech(nology) 140, 141, 150, 153, 174, 202f.
Hip-hop -*iz*- 93
history
  sociocultural 127
holistic storage 22, 226
Homer Simpson's -*ma*- 92f., 100
homonym 106, 181
homophony 31f., 38, 44
  pernicious 84, 123f.
hyperbole 84, 125, 127, 140
hyperonym 56
hypocoristic 155, 184, 185, 240, 245
  -*ie/y* 161, 177ff., 181, 183, 185, 242
  -*o* 181
  -*s/z* 148, 181f., 245
hyponym(y) 117, 241

I-language 18f., 26, 44, 189, 240
iconic 40, 86, 94, 100, 106, 159f., 170
  insertion 239
  sequencing 55, 58, 220, 228, 229, 232f., 235
iconicity 86, 127, 155, 159

Index of subjects 307

cross-modal 158, 161, 226
indexical 155, 157f.
lexical/morphological 164
multilevel 164
phonetic 157f.
primary 155f.
relational 155, 172
secondary 86
sound-meaning 169ff.
identity (sequencing) (*see* constraint haplological)
ideophone 155f.
imagery
  auditory 171
  sensory 156
implicit argument 49
incorporation 42, 51, 67
individual
  level predicate 38
infix(ation) 8, 235, 239, 240, 243, 244, 246
  expletive 93, 100
  games 8, 92f., 100, 239
inflected
  fully 243, 245
inflection 5ff.
  adjunction of 7, 26, 243
  double 76, 78
initialism 147ff.
inseparability 47, 48
institutionalization 17, 18, 21, 23, 26, 85, 139, 155, 173, 198, 209, 213, 218, 236
instrument
  verb 11f., 37f.
instrumental
  free 45, 48f.
intensity 157, 160–3
internal/theme role 12, 35ff., 45, 48f., 128f.

Jabberwocky 95f., 188

ka-/ker-prefixation 163f., 245
knowledge
  conscious/explicit 84, 117, 124, 237f., 240, 244, 246

grammar 84, 242
implicit/mental 116, 237f., 240
language 101, 238, 241
storage 22, 24f., 101, 117, 241

label
  need for 85ff., 108
  objective 116, 135
  value judgments on 116
  subjective 116, 135
language
  builders 237
  evolutionary role 87
  natural 23, 241
  play 8, 18, 20, 28, 33, 34, 35, 37, 39, 41, 44, 48, 74, 82, 83, 84, 87, 89, 90–3, 100, 140, 141, 142, 152, 173, 195, 207, 210, 217, 219, 220, 223, 225, ch. 15
  specific purposes 180
  tone 171
Latinate 9, 17, 33, 34, 65, 85, 127
left-headed 52
lexeme 3, 17, 24, 104, 242
lexical
  base 14, 242
  boundary 242f., 244
  bundle 22
  category 51, 54, 55, 61, 101, 105, 151
  change 83f., 99f.
  constraints 34f., 44
  contamination 189
  content 64, 71, 73, 74, 151
  diffusion 88, 138, 201, 213
  expression 83, 87
  field 88
  freezing 56
  gap 15, 28, 34, 36, 86f.
  listing 5, 21–6, 27f.
  meaning 20f., 25f., 27f., 131
  morpheme 3, 25, 151
  restructuring 24
  storage 22, 24f., 101, 117, 241
lexicalization 21–6, 47, 163, 234
  constraint 37

lexicon 21-6
  mental 22, 24, 26, 65
  open 85
  subsystem of 241
listedness 5, 21-6, 27f.
litotes 121
loan
  phonology 138f.
  translation (see calque)
  word (see borrowing)
location 11f., 128
locational 45, 48, 70, 98f., 129
locative 7, 98
locatum 11f.

malapropism 115
manner
  of motion verb 37f.
mapping
  output to output 243
  prosodic 178, 197
  semantic 101, 104
markedness
  contextual 225
  formal 228, 232f., 235
  Optimality Theoretical 29
  perceptual 58, 228f., 232f., 235
  prosodic 144
mass media 150
matching (feature) 6, 67, 218
Maximize Onset 146, 184
melioration 133ff.
mental
  lexicon (see lexicon)
  link 128, 140, 166f.
  schema 13, 87, 131, 132, 140
Merge/merge 2, 24, 35f., 42, 45, 49, 50-4, 65-8, 70, 72, 98
merism 226
metanalysis 119
metamorphology 237
metaphor 55, 83, 84, **ch. 6**, 127, 131, 135, 166, 241
  sensory/synaesthetic 102, 104, 116
metaphtonymy 112

metonymy 54, 55, 61, 104, 105, **107-16**
  pure 109f.
misanalysis 90
modal(ity) 2f., 79f.
  deontic 135
  epistemic 2, 80, 135
model (robotic) 132
modernization 139f.
modification (internal) 58f.
Mood as head of S 2f., 50, 79f.
mora 144f., 152, 196
morpheme 3, 6, 9, 18, 24f., 27, 31, 34f., 36, 43, 78, 88, 144, 151, 172, 194
  boundary 39, 93, 242, 244
morphology
  core 9, 41, 82, 172, 173, 189, 219, **ch. 15**
  expressive 9, 172, 173, **ch. 15**
  playful 173, 219, **ch. 15**
  prosodic 144f., 173, 240, 242
morphosyntactic locus 4, 60, 76, 78
morphotactic opacity 207
motivation
  acoustic 154f., 172
  lexicogenic 84f., 88, 99f.
  onomatopoeic 21, 156f.
    loss of 156
  partial 78f., 86
  perceptual 101, 140, 154
  phonological 152
  relative 158
  semantic-pragmatic 116, 221, 242
  sound symbolic 154ff., 172, 201ff.
movable s- 162f.

name-givers 86
names
  brand 167, 185, 203, 209, 214
  female/male 171, 173, 179, 180, 184, 186
  hypocoristic 177ff., 182, 185
  meaning dissociation 121
  mock Greek 48, 238
  truncated 144, 173, 177ff.
neoclassical
  compound ch. 13, 239

derivation from 217ff.
juncture vowel 216
recursion 215, 217
Greek root 208, 213ff.
Latin/Neolatin root 207, 217, 219
modern extraction 208ff.
neologism x, 21, 26, 83f., 87, 139f., 144, 152, 162
  insulting 165
  types 83
neurolinguistics 142
  aphasic evidence 144, 189
nominalization 28f., 33, 76
Nootka evaluatives 93
null head (*see* head)

obligatory argument 49
(oblique) semantic role 37f., 45, 50, 194, 210
onomasiology 3, 16, **83f.**
onomatopoeia 21, 83, 84, 91, 134, 155, **156f.**, 171
optimal(ity) 23, 124, 141f., 144, 145, 152, 159, 173, 183, 185, 195, 197, 200, 204
  Optimality Theory 24, 29, 78, 225
overgeneration 49, 61
over-prefixation 67, 69f.

P-stacking 96–9
P-word 75, 77, 100
p-word 4, 5
  full status 57, 150, 153
packaging of information 221, 242, 243
palindrome 91f., 94
Pāṇini's rule 58, 220, **229–33**, 235
parameter 4, **19**, 49, 172
paramorphology 237, 241
paraverbal mimology 155
particle
  adverbial 73
  comparative 64, 70
  directional 99
  functional 64, 70, 71, 81
  phrase 72
  scalar/evaluative 70
  typology 64
  with clip 180f.
pejoration 114, **133ff.**, 166

perception/perceptual 24, 39, 68, 90, 101, 104ff., 110, 116, 154, 157, 160, 164, 171, 172, 179, 238
  as onomatopoeic 157
  impressionistic 157
  of sounds in nature 154, 155f., 172
  perceptual markedness 58, 220, 228f., 232f., 235
  physical and mental 104ff.
phase (theory) 68, 77f., 82
phonaesthesia (*see* phonesthesia)
phoneme/phonemic 88, 122, 124, 141, 164, 169, 170, **247**
  borrowed 138f.
  lexical diffusion of 88
phonesthesia 154, 164–9, 172, 241
phonetic
  complexity 24, 139
  reality 141
  –semantic iconicity 155, 169ff.
phonological
  configuration 225f.
  contrast 32
  copy 40ff., 76ff., 220
  heaviness 78
  independence 77f.
phonosemantic
  association 169
phonotactic(s) 39, 138, 139, **142–4**, 155, 179, 182
phrase structure, bare 3
Pig Latin **91**, 100, 240, 242, 244
playful language (*see* expressive)
poetic art/poetry 18, 95f., 169–71
political correctness 84, 122, 128, 148
polysemic
  extension, limitation 129–32
polysemy 11, 12, 102, 106, 124, 128f.
polysyndeton 94
popular formation 34f., 89
portmanteau (*see* blend)
pragmatic 15, 34, 46, 57, 61, 86, 183, 187, 220, 221, 235, 242, 244
prefix(ation) 8, 37, 39f., 41f., 44, 52, 163f.
  iterativity (*see* recursion)
premorphology 237

preposition
  abstract 72
  complex 100
  incorporation 67f.
  in word formation 74f., 80f.
  linking 233f.
  -cum- 234
  stacking 96-9
principles of grammar 19, 237, 243, 244
processing 22, 97, 100
  constraints 39-43, 44
property concept 84
proprietary term 111
prosodic
  domain 83, 100, 144, 242, 244
  hierarchy 144
  markedness 144
  optimality 144, 173, 195
  template 92, 144, 146, 184, 195-9, 203, 240ff., 244
  wellformedness 204
  word 5, 26, 144, 152, 195, 240
  (see also morphology)
prototype 84, 132
prototypical(ity) 7, 35, 37, 61, 84, 104, 127, 132, 152, 178, 199, 221, 226, 240
psycholinguistic test 22, 166, 199
psychological
  association 169
    (see also analogy)
  constraint 139
  salience 141, 167
pun(ning) 18, 84, **89ff.**, 100, 188, 237

raising verb 37
reanalysis
  affix (see also formative extraction) 207
  by associated context 101, 116, 123, 148
  grammatical 15, 20, 56, 245
  lexical 89, 93
    (see also metanalysis)
  perceptual 245
  semantic 107, 109

rebus puzzle 147
recursivity/recursion 39-44, 243, 244
  compound 46
    neoclassical 215, 217
  prefix 40, 41f., 43f.
  suffix 39f., 42ff., 238f.
redundant/redundancy 25f., 76
reduplication 31, 43, 44, 161, 164, 239
  exact 221
  imitative 244
  internal 93, 223
  partial 220f.
  rhyming 221ff.
  suffixal 40, 76
  template 144
  total 220, 239, 243
reduplicative 9, 221-6
  French 225
  German 225
  infixing 235
  Spanish 224
referent
  extralinguistic 161, 172, 243, 244
  grammatical 161, 172, 243, 244
  real world 84
register 33, 173, 178, 189
  formal/monitored 245
  informal 178
  low 165
regular(ity)/irregular(ity) 22f., 27, 31, 47, 52, 68, 86, 120, 129, 240
regularization
  morphological 84
remnant 175, 176f., 183
result state 53, 66, 72, 73, 84
retronym 60f.
rhyming
  pair (see reduplication)
  pattern 221ff., 235, 241
root
  compound 45, 47, 48f., 52, 58
  eventive 34, 66, 69
  imitative 155f.

s-mobile (see movable s-)
salience
  anthropological 84
  cultural 84
  perceptual 24, 39, 163, 229
  psychological 167
  vs. frequency 22, 29
scientific
  blend 179f., 193
  borrowing 135, 140, 217
  clip 179f.
  and medical lexis 207, 217, 219
  terminology 179f., 217
secret language 87, 91, 240
secretion (see formative extraction)
segment
  inherent properties of 154, 172
  marginal 155, 245
semantic
  adjunct 48f.
  bleaching 126, 140
  change (see change)
  differentiation/split 23, 29f., 180
  feature (see feature)
  field 119, 131, 167, 169
  generalization 129–33
  primitive 12, 131
  restriction 129–33
  shift 10, 128, 132f., 136
  transfer 107, 109, 116
    by borrowing 125, 135f.
  value, intrinsic 155
semantics
  prototype 132
sensory
  cortex 172
  imagery 156
  modalities 154
sentential NP modifier
  (see clausal modifier)
sequencing
  factors 220, 228f., 232f., 235
    competition 229, 232f.
    hierarchy 232, 235
    iconic 55, 220, 228, 229, 232, 233, 235

power 58, 220, 228f., 231f., 233, 235
shorter before longer
  (see Pāṇini's rule)
slang 38, 46, 87, 112, 125, 176, 182, 188, 210, 224, 245
  backslang 92, 245
slip of the tongue 189
sonority 32, 141–4, 152, 178, 225, 232
  distance 143, 146, 184
  hierarchy 141–4, 146, 183f.
sound symbolism ch. 10, 201ff., 225f., 242ff.
  areal 159, 171
Spanish game 92
speech
  casual/informal 139
  community 16, 124, 129, 135
  error 189
spelling pronunciation 138
spellout 7, 26, 74, 77, 243, 244
spoonerism 92, 100, 115
stage level predicate 38
state
  result 53, 66, 72, 73, 84
  specific (of actors) 77
  variable generic 77
stress
  clash 31, 57, 78
  final 34, 147, 232, 233
  pattern 93, 173, 179, 185, 196, 198, 200
  shift 31, 47, 223
  two main per word 57, 60, 78, 222
  variable 47, 60, 196
stretch 161f., 245
structure
  hierarchical 26, 59, **65**, 98, 153, 242f.
  of the syllable 142, 152
subculture 125, 129, 130, 140
suffix
  full word from 150ff.
  generalization 207, 239, 243
suffixation 8f., 83, 175
superlative 6
  double 125
  quasi- 100, 140, 162, 221, 245
swearing 122

312   Index of subjects

syllable 91ff., 141-4, 170, 175, 179, 204, 223, 225, 232, 244
   affixation to 92f., 241
   closed 92, 145, 184, 184
   coda 141f., 145f., 178, 184, 197, 204
   division 143
   final 183, 184, 196, 225
   heavy 145, 178, 196
   inversion 92, 241
   light 145
   nonsense, rhyming 237
   nucleus 141f., 145f., 162, 178, 184, 189, 197
   onset 91, 141f., 146, 178, 184, 189, 197, 207
   open 92, 185
   reduction
      haplological 180
   rime/rhyme 91, 141f., 146, 184, 189, 204
   strong 145, 152
   structure 25, 141-4, 179
   weak 145, 152
   (*see also* complex)
symbolic sign 155
synaesthesia (*see* synesthesia)
synecdoche 107, 110ff.
synesthesia 9, 157-61, 163, 171
synonym
   (*see* Avoid Synonymy)
synthetic compound 45, 48-51, 52, 61
syntactic morphology 5, 24f., 29, 35f., 63-9

tabu 84, 120-4
   deformation 84, 120-4, 223, 241
   euphemism 84, 120-4, 174
   religious 120f.
   secular 121-4
   substitution/replacement 120-4, 166
template
   (*see* prosodic)
texting (language) 147
thematic/theta role 4, 11, 35, 37, 44, 45, 49ff., 67, 128f.
"thirteen dog" rule 147
tongue twister 91
toponym 109, 111, 151

transferred epithet 108f., 110, 111, 112
transitive shell 36
triplication 43
truncation 83, 122, 123, ch. 11, 210, 239, 242, 244
   radical 239, 243, 246
   template 144, 146, 184
   vacuous material 239

unaccusative 37, 44, 70, 73f.
underspecification
   of shape 13
unergative 37, 44
unexplained residue 118, 124
unpredictability 23f.

v[AG] 73
v[CAUS/AG] 66, 68, 72, 77
v[FIENT] 66, 68ff., 72-5, 77, 80f.
vP 36, 66, 68, 72-5, 77, 80, 81
   [pass(ive)] 80f.
verbal
   art 95ff., 100
   iteration 41-4
verbalization 55, ch. 4
verbalizing head 21, 55, 66, 70, 72, 75, 80

wit(ticism) 180
word
   basic 21, 141-4, 152
   echoic 156, 240
      shm- 220, **223f.**, 236, 238
   games (*see* language play)
   imitative 155ff., 188, 244
   maximal 144
   metrical 144
   minimal 144
   schema rule 36

X-bar theory 1f.

zero derivation
   (*see* conversion)
zeugma 94